Sociology for A2

Stephen Moore

Dave Aiken

Steve Chapman

Published by HarperCollins *Publishers*
77–85 Fulham Palace Road
Hammersmith
London W6 8JB

www.**Collins**Education.com
On-line Support for Schools and Colleges

First published 2002

10 9 8 7 6 5 4 3 2

British Library Cataloguing-in-Publication Data
A catalogue record for this publication
is available from the British Library.

ISBN 0 00 713465 7

Sociology for A2 is not an official publication of AQA or
OCR. All material is the sole responsibility of the publisher
and has not been provided or approved by AQA or OCR.

Commissioned by Thomas Allain-Chapman
Consultant editor Peter Langley
Project management and layout by Hart McLeod Ltd
Picture research by Susan Nicholas
Text design Patricia Briggs
Cover design by Blue Pig Design
Printed and bound in Thailand by Imago.

You might also like to visit:

www.**fire**and**water**.com
The book lover's website

Author dedications

Dave Aiken:
Initial thanks to students and colleagues at Hackney
Community College, to Steve and Pete for your guidance
and encouragement.

Thanks more than ever to Maggie and the kids, Amelia,
Laurie and Leo for getting me through it and for letting me
again put you through it.

Thanks to mum and dad for all your support over the
years and for making Christmas as normal as possible under
the circumstances.

Final thoughts go to Jean Wooldrage, a wonderful person and neighbour of ten years who died suddenly aged 76
on Dec 29 2001 and to whom I would like to dedicate my
efforts.

Steve Chapman:
To my sons Jake and Joe. Whatever you do, don't follow
your dad on to the sociology stage.

Contents

iii

Sociology for A2

Acknowledgements

The publishers would like to thank the following for permission to reproduce photographs in this book:

Unit 1 title page: © PA Photos; p.2: top left, © Trip/H. Rogers; top right, © David & Peter Turnley/Corbis; bottom left, © Trip/H. Rogers; bottom right, © Liz Gilbert/Corbis Sigma; p.3: © Trip/H. Rogers; p.4: top, © Tim Graham/Corbis; middle, © Trip/Joe Plimmer; bottom, © Homer Sykes/Impact Photos; p.8: © Greg Martin/Corbis Sygma; p.10: top left, © Trip/J.D. Dallet; top right, © Trip/H. Rogers; bottom left, © G. Robert Bishop/Getty Images; bottom right, © Trip/B. Turner; p.16: © Mirrorpix; p.24: © San Antonio Express News/Corbis Sygma; p.25: © Trip/J. Wender; top right, © Phil Schermeister/Corbis; bottom right, © Bettmann/Corbis; p.28: top, © Archivo Iconografico, S.A./Corbis; bottom, © Painting by Henry Coller/Trip/H. Rogers; p.32: © Trip/Trip; p.33: © Trip/H. Rogers; p.36: © PA Photos; p.42: top right, © Trip/H. Rogers; top left, © Trip/P. Kwan; bottom right, © Hulton-Deutsch Collection/Corbis; bottom left, © TH Photo/Alamy.com; p.44: top, © Trip/D. Butcher; middle, © Trip/Trip; bottom, © EPA/PA Photos; **Unit 2 title page**: © Patrick Zachmann/Magnum Photos; p.52: top and bottom, © Trip/Trip; p.62: top left, © Trip/D. Davis; top middle, © Trip/M. Beard; top right, © Trip/Eric Smith; middle left, © Trip/Trip; middle right, © Trip/Nissan; bottom left, © Trip/M. Jelliffe; bottom middle, © Trip/P. Treanor; bottom right, © Corbis; p.63: top and bottom, © Trip/H. Rogers; p.73: top left, © Brian Harris/Impact Photos; top right, © Trip/B. Turner; bottom left, © Trip/P. Musson; bottom right, © Trip/T. Bognar; p.78: top left, © Trip/H. Rogers; top right, © Trip/B. Turner; bottom, © Steve Raymer/Corbis; p.87: Alain Le Garsmeur/Corbis; p.94: top left, © Hartmut Schwarzbach/Still Pictures; top right, © Mark Edwards/Still Pictures; bottom left, © Trip/H. Rogers; bottom right, © Trip/Trip; p.98: © Mark Edwards/Still Pictures; p.100: left, © courtesy of Ronald Grant Archive; right, © Trip/J. Okwesa; **Unit 3 title page**: PA Photos; p.110: top left, © Robin Laurance/Impact Photo; top right, © Kennerly David Hume/Corbis Sygma; middle left, © Corbis Sygma; middle centre, © Cardinale Stephane/Corbis Sygma; middle right, © PA Photos; bottom, © Bagla Pallava/Corbis Sygma; p.112: © Topham Picturepoint; p.113: top, © Trip/Chris Parker; middle, © Trip/Th-Foto Werbung; bottom, © UPPA Ltd; p.114: left, © Trip/M. Stevenson; right, © Trip/J. Okwesa; p.120: top and middle, © Trip/H. Rogers; bottom, © Trip/Trip; p.124: top left, © Magnum Photos; top right, © Trip/B. Turner; middle left, © Ed Kashi/Corbis; bottom left, © Trip/H. Rogers; bottom right, Chris Salvo/Getty Images; p.132: © Mirrorpix; p.134 and p .135: left to right, © Hulton-Deutsch Collection/Corbis; © Hulton-Deutsch Collection/Corbis; © Corbis; © Hulton-Deutsch Collection/Corbis; © Bettman/Corbis; © Bettman/Corbis; © Hulton-Deutsch Collection/Corbis; © Owen Franklin/Corbis; © Najlah Feanny/Corbis SABA; © Beirne Brendan/Corbis Sygma; p.145: top left, PA Photos; top right, © EPA/PA Photos; middle left, courtesy of www.adbusters.org; middle right, © Stewart Weir/Impact Photos; © Greenpeace; p.150: top left, © Nick Cobbing/Alamy.com; top right, bottom left and bottom right, PA Photos; **Unit 4 title page**: © Lawrence Manning/Corbis; p.160: left, © Trip/M. Barlow; right, © Trip/S. Grant; p.168: top left, © Trip/Trip; top middle, top right and bottom, © Trip/H. Rogers; p.176: © Trip/Picturesque; p.182: top row, left to right, © Naijlah Feanny/Corbis SABA; © Trip H. Rogers; © David Katzenstein/Corbis; © Trip/Andrews; middle row, left to right, © Trip/H. Rogers; © Miki Kratsman/Corbis; © Trip/Trip; bottom left, © Roger Ressmeyer/Corbis; © R. W. Jones/Corbis; p.186: top left, © Trip/V. Pinto; top right, © Trip/H. Rogers bottom left, © Trip/Eric Smith; middle right and bottom right, © Trip/H. Rogers; p.188: top left, © Trip/H . Rogers; middle left, © Trip/Picturesque; bottom left, © Trip/H. Rogers; top right, EPA/PA photos; p.196: top left, © Misha Japaridze/Associated Press, AP; top right, © Katsumi Kasahara/Associated Press, AP; bottom left, © Associated Press, XINHUA;

p.201: © Dorothea Lange, Getty Images; p.202: top left and top right, © Steve Parry/Impact Photos; bottom left, PA Photos; bottom right, © Alex Macnaughton/Impact Photos; p.203: top left, © Red Herring/Alamy.com; top middle, © Trip/H. Rogers; top right, © Peter Arkell/Impact Photos; bottom right, EPA/PA Photos; **Unit 5 title page**: © PA Photos; p.210: unable to locate source; p.215: left, © Associated Press, AP; right, © James Nachtwey/Magnum Photos; p.216: top left, © Trip/H. Rogers; top middle, © Patrick Zachmann/Magnum Photos; top right, © Peter Marlow/Magnum Photos; bottom left, © Kelly/Mooney Photography/Corbis; bottom middle, © Kent Klich/Magnum Photos; bottom right, © Charles Milligan/Impact Photos; p.220: top left, © Rune Hellestad/Corbis; top middle, © Simon Shepheard/Impact Photos; top right, © Trip/H. Rogers; left upper middle, © Popperfoto/Popperfoto; left lower middle, © Shelley Gazin/Corbis; bottom left, © Trip/S. Grant; p.222: © Trip/G. Grieves; p.228: left, © Reuters/Popperfoto; right, © Daniel White/Impact Photos; p.232: © Trip/K. Cardwell; p.234: top left, © celebritymediagrou.comBob Carlos-Clarke; top middle, © Eve Arnold/Magnum Photos; top right, © Herbert List/Magnum Photos; bottom, © Trip/J. Garrett; p.239: top left, © Steve Parry/Impact Photos; top right, © PA Photos; middle left, © Trip/H. Rogers; bottom left, © John Cole/Impact Photos; p.240: top left, © Nigel Barklie/Impact Photos; top middle, © Peter Arkell/Impact Photos; top right, © Trip/H. Rogers; bottom left and right, © Trip/H. Rogers; p.248: top left, © Trip/B. Turner; top right, © Piers Cavendish/Impact Photos; middle right, © Richard T. Nowitz/Corbis; bottom right, © Nik Wheeler/Corbis; p.254: © Zach Gold/Corbis; p.258: © PA Photos; p.260: top right, © Trip/Chris Parker; middle left, © Gavin Milverton/Impact Photos; middle right, © Trip/P. Kaplan; bottom left, © Pintailpictures/ Alamy.com; p.266: © The Police Federation of England and Wales; p.271: left and right, © Bill Gentile/Corbis; p.272: left, © Trip/H. Rogers; middle, © Ana Gonzales/Impact Photos; right, © Peter Arkell/Impact Photos; p.281: top right, © Trip/M. Mackenzie; middle left, © Trip/A. Gigg; middle right, © Chase Swift/Corbis; bottom, © Bruce Stephens/Impact Photos; p. 281: © Carmen Taylor/Associated Press, KHBS KHOG; p.286: left, © Trip/H. Rogers; middle, © Getty Images; right, © Trip/J. Okwesa; p.291: top left, © Sherwin Crasto/Associated Press, PA; top right, © David & Peter Turnley/Corbis; bottom left to right, © Trip/H. Rogers; © Robrt F. Bukaty, Associated Press, PA; © Trip/H. Rogers; © David Montford/Photofusion/Alamy.com; p.292: top right, © Trip/H. Rogers; 2nd row top right, © Trip/R. Wilkins; 3rd row left to right, © Trip/H. Rogers; © Trip/H. Rogers; © Trip/B. Turner; © Trip/H. Rogers; bottom row left to right, © Trip/B. Turner; © Trip/H. Rogers; Getty Images; p.298: left, © Trip/S. Grant; right, © George Shelley/Corbis; p.300: top left, © Hulton-Deutsch Collection/Corbis; top right, © Getty Images; bottom left, © Michael Boys/Corbis; bottom right, © Trip/R. Ewing; p.313: © Trip/H. Rogers; p.314: top left, © Trip/H. Rogers; top right, © Trip/F. Torrance; middle left, Paul Stuart, Eye Ubiquitous/Corbis; middle right, © Trip/J. Okwesa; © Baverel Didier/Corbis Sygma; p.316: left, © Hulton-Deutsch Collection/Corbis; right, © Reuter Raymond/Corbis Sygma; p.320: from top to bottom, © Trip/H. Rogers; © Trip/J. Stanley; © Trip/H. Rogers; © Trip/H. Rogers; p.322: top left, © Trip/H. Rogers; middle and bottom left, © Trip/B. Turner; top right, © Trip/B. Turner; bottom right, © courtesy of Dave Aiken; p.330: all, © Trip/H. Rogers; p.336: © Commission for Racial Equality; p.338: left, © Trip/H. Rogers; middle, © Trip/J. Okwesa; right, © Trip/H. Rogers; p.344: right, Trapper Frank/Corbis Sygma; p.346: left, © Trip/M. Jelliffe; right, © Jon Mitchell/Alamy.com; p.348: right, © Janine Wiedel/Alamy.com; p.351: © Bill Bachmann/Alamy.com; **Preparing for the A2 exam title page**: PA Photos.

iv

Sociology for A2

The organisation of the book

Sociology for A2 covers the most common modular routes through the A2 specifications of both awarding bodies. A further Unit on Social Policy will be available on the Collins Educational web site in late 2002. The book can be used in conjunction with *Sociology for AS level* to make up a complete A-level course.

The book is divided into a series of Units, each linking into AQA and OCR A2 modules. Each Unit consists of a number of Topics which break it up into manageable parts. Each Topic starts by building on students' prior knowledge, then goes on to provide the knowledge required, before checking understanding and reinforcing key concepts. There are then opportunities to build wider skills, extend the material covered into research and web-based activities and practise exam questions in the style of both boards.

Features of each topic

Getting you thinking
The opening activity draws on students' existing knowledge and experiences to provide a 'way in' to some of the main issues in the topic. The questions are usually open and, although suitable for individual work, may be more effective discussed in pairs or small groups, where experiences and ideas can be shared.

Main text
This provides the necessary essential knowledge. Key concepts are highlighted and explained in *Key terms* (see below).

Links
These short questions punctuate the main text and encourage students to make the connections necessary for the synoptic elements of A2 assessment. They test students' ability to make links between the material they are learning and:

- core themes of the course, such as socialisation, culture and identity and social differentiation
- key concepts such as social control and ideology
- research methods
- the main perspectives such as Marxism, feminism and post-modernism.

Key terms
These are simple definitions of important terms and concepts used in the text. Definitions are linked to the context in which the word or phrase occurs. Most words or phrases are sociological but they also include some of the more difficult but essential vocabulary used.

Check your understanding
In this section there are a small number of basic comprehension questions, the answers to all of which are contained in the text.

Exploring…
These are data-response questions that aim to develop AO2 skills of analysis and evaluation. There may be one or two in each Topic.

Research ideas
These activities encourage students to use a range of methods in order to conduct their own investigations of issues raised in the Topic. The research ideas could form the basis of A2 coursework projects. The tasks are suitable for individual, small group or whole class work. Many are suitable for the collection of Key Skills evidence.

Webtask
There is a wealth of relevant material available on the worldwide web. However, much of it is unreliable and/or represents the views of particular groups. The activities here take this into account and give students specific tasks that involve a critical reading of information.

Exam practice
Examination questions, or extracts from questions, in the style of both awarding bodies are provided at the end of each Topic, along with appropriate mark allocations. These allow students to gain experience of relevant methods of assessment. In a small number of cases the Topic is not covered in one or other of the specifications. Where this is the case, no question is provided.

Matching the units in *Sociology for A2* to AQA and OCR specifications		
	AOA	**OCR**
Unit 1 Religion	A2 module 4: Religion	Option within Culture and Socialisation AS module Religion*
Unit 2 World Sociology	A2 module 4: World sociology	
Unit 3 Power, Politics and Protest	A2 module 4: Power and politics	Option within Power and Control A2 module: Protest and social movements
Unit 4 Theory and Methods	A2 module 5: Theory and methods	A2 module: Applied Sociological Research Skills
Unit 5 Crime and Deviance	A2 module 6 (synoptic): Crime and deviance	Option within Power and Control A2 module: Crime and deviance
Unit 6 Stratification and Social Difference	A2 module 6 (synoptic): Stratification and differentiation	A2 synoptic module: Social Inequality and Difference

* Note that Religion is part of the OCR AS specifications

Religion

Getting you thinking

A funeral

Soldiers praying before engaging in battle

Churches have much older congregations than society as a whole

Jewish 'settlers' are seen as illegitimate occupiers of Palestinian territory

1 What purpose does religion serve for the individuals in each picture?

2 What might happen to these individuals if religion suddenly ceased to exist?

3 What purpose does religious ceremony serve for the Trobriand Islanders?

4 How does religion help people in modern society to cope with death?

In the nineteenth and early twentieth centuries the founding fathers of Sociology were particularly interested by religion for the following reasons.

- Their quest to develop explanations relating to the impact of industrialisation and modernity on social life involved a consideration of pre-modern societies which were characterised by religious explanations of the world.
- They were interested in the continuing role that religion may or may not have once some of those explanations came to be replaced by more rational scientific explanations.

From your studies of other sociological topics, identify and briefly explain any two social changes.

Writers on religion tend to fall into one of two camps:

- those who see religion as a conservative force
- those who see religion as a force for social change.

Religion as a conservative force

In his famous work *The Elementary Forms of Religious Life* (1912/1961), Durkheim relates religion to the overall structure of society. He based his work on a study of **totemism** among Australian aborigines. (A totem is an object, usually an animal or plant which has deep symbolic significance.) He argued that totemism represents the most elementary form of religion.

- The totem is believed to have divine properties which separate it from those animals or plants that may be eaten or harvested.
- There are a number of ceremonies and rituals involved in worship of the totem which serve to bring the tribe together as a group and consequently re-affirm their group identity.

What other social institutions can be seen as bringing society together? How?

Durkheim defined religion in terms of a distinction between the **sacred** (holy or spiritual) and the **profane** (unspiritual, non-religious). Sacred objects and symbols are treated apart from the routine aspects of existence which are the realm of the profane.

Why is the totem so sacred?

Durkheim suggests that this is because it is symbolically representative of the group itself. It stands for the values of the community and by worshipping it they are effectively 'worshipping' their society.

Durkheim argues that religion is rarely a matter of individual belief. Most religions involve collective worship, ceremony and rituals during which group solidarity is affirmed or heightened. An individual is temporarily elevated from their normal profane existence to a higher level in which they can recognise divine influences or gods. These divine influences are attributed with providing the moral guidance for the particular social group concerned. However, gods for Durkheim are merely the expression of the influence of the

The untouchable caste endure their poverty and perform the worst social duties because they believe that this will assure them of a place in a higher caste in the next life

Trobriand Island fishermen

In Malinowski's study of the Trobriand Islanders he discovered that they preceded events over which they felt they had little control such as fishing in the open sea with religious ceremonies. These religious acts involved the islanders committing themselves to the protection of their gods. As a result death at sea whilst fishing was interpreted by the islanders as the will of the gods thus minimizing grief and therefore potential for disorder.

Source: A. Giddens (2001) *Sociology*, Cambridge: Polity Press

collective over the individual. The continual act of group worship and celebration through ritual and ceremony serves to forge group identity, and create cohesion and solidarity. God is actually a recognition that society is more important than the individual.

Durkheim used secondary data to study the role of religion in aboriginal tribes. What problems are associated with the use of secondary data?

The functions of religion in modern society

Socialisation

In modern societies the major function of religion is to socialise society's members into a value consensus by investing values with a sacred quality. These values become 'moral codes' – beliefs that society agrees to revere and socialise children into. Consequently such codes regulate our social behaviour – for example, the Ten Commandments are a good example of a set of moral codes that have influenced both formal controls such as the law (e.g. 'Thou shalt not kill/steal' etc.) as well as informal controls such as moral disapproval (e.g. 'Thou shalt not commit adultery').

What is the difference between formal and informal social control? Give examples from your studies in Sociology.

Social integration

Encouraging collective worship enables individuals to express their shared values and strengthens group unity. It fosters the development of a **collective conscience** or moral community so that deviant behaviour is restrained and social change restricted.

Civil religion

In modern societies ritual and ceremony is a common aspect of national loyalties. Street parades, swearing allegiance to Queen and country, and being part of a flag-waving crowd all remind us of our relationship to the nation.

This idea has been developed into the theory of '**civil religion**' by some functionalist thinkers. Civil religion refers to a situation where sacred qualities are attributed to aspects of the society itself. Hence religion in one form or another continues to be an essential feature of society. This is very evident in America where the concept of civil religion was first developed by Bellah (1970), himself American. America is effectively a nation of immigrants with a wide range of co-existing cultural and religious traditions. What does unite them, however, is their faith in 'Americanism'. Whilst traditional religion binds individuals to their various communities, civil religion in America unites the nation. Although civil religion need not involve a connection to supernatural beliefs, according to Bellah, God and Americanism appear to go hand in hand. American coins remind their users 'In God we trust' and the phrase 'God bless America' is a common concluding remark to an important speech. Even the phrase 'President of the United States of America' imbues the country's leader with an almost divine quality. The God that Americans are talking about, however, is not allied to a particular faith, He is in a Durkheimian sense the God of (or that is) America.

Bellah, however, suggests that even civil religion is in decline as people now rank personal gratification above

4

Sociology for A2

Exploring civil religion

Item A

A rock concert

Football supporters

1 Look at Item A and answer the following.

   a Identify some of the key characteristics of a religion.

   b In what ways do the situations shown:
- share the characteristics of a religion?
- not share the characteristics of a religion?

   c To what extent do you agree that the concept of civil religion is helpful in understanding religion today?

obligation to others and there is in his view a deepening cynicism about established social institutions. However, the events of September 11 and its aftermath have undoubtedly led to a re-affirmation of Americanism and its associated symbolism.

Preventing anomie

Durkheim's main fear for modern industrial society was that individuals would become less integrated and their behaviour less regulated. Should this become widespread, **anomie** (a state of normlessness) could occur whereby society could not function because its members would not know how they should behave relative to one another.

What social problems might be caused by a high level of anomie in society? Explain your answer.

Clearly religious and civil ceremony prevents this happening by encouraging an awareness of common membership of an entity greater than, and supportive of, the individual. Some religious movements seem to have grown when anomie may have been occurring in times of social upheaval. For example, the industrial revolution in Britain was marked by a series of **revivalist** movements such as Methodism and Presbyterianism.

Coming to terms with life-changing events

Functionalist thinkers such as Malinowski (1954) and Parsons (1965) see religion as functioning to relieve the stress and anxieties created by life crises such as birth, puberty, marriage and death. In other words, such events can undermine people's commitment to the wider society and therefore social order. Religion gives such events meaning, helping people come to terms with change. Most societies have evolved religious 'rites of passage' ceremonies in order to minimise this social disruption. For example, the death of a loved one can cause the bereaved to feel helpless and alone, unable to cope with life. However, the funeral ceremony allows people to adjust to their new situation. The group mourning also re-affirms the fact that the group outlives the passing of particular individuals and is there to support its members.

Criticisms of functionalism

- It is difficult to see how religion can be functioning to socialise the majority of society's members into morality and social integration if only a minority of people regularly attend church.
- Some have argued that Durkheim's analysis is based on flawed evidence: he misunderstood both totemism and the behaviour of the Aboriginal tribes themselves.
- It is difficult to see how Durkheim's analysis can be applied to societies which are culturally diverse.
- Religion often has dysfunctional consequences. Rather than binding people together, many of the world's conflicts have been caused by religion – for example, in Northern Ireland and the former Yugoslavia.

Marxism and religion

Like Durkheim, Marx also argued that religion was a conservative force in society. However, he did not agree that this force is essentially positive and beneficial to society. Rather, Marx argued that the primary function of religion is to reproduce, maintain and legitimate class inequality. In other words, religion is an **ideological apparatus**, which serves to reflect ruling class ideas and interests. Moreover, Marx described religion as the 'opium of the people' because in his view it lulls the working class into a state of false class-consciousness by making the true extent of their exploitation by the ruling class invisible.

Give examples of other 'ideological apparatuses'. How do they 'reflect ruling-class ideas'?

Religion is seen by Marx to be ideological in three ways (Marx and Engels, 1957).

1. *Legitimating social inequality*

Religion serves as a means of controlling the subject population by promoting the idea that the existing hierarchy is natural, god-given and therefore unchangeable. We can particularly see this during the **feudal period** when it was widely believed that kings had a divine right to rule. During the eighteenth and nineteenth centuries it was generally believed that God had created both rich and poor as reflected in the hymn 'All Things Bright and Beautiful'. This stated (in what is now an obscure verse):

> The rich man in his castle,
> The poor man at his gate,
> God made them, high or lowly,
> And order'd their estate.

2. *Disguising the true nature of exploitation*

Religion explains economic and social inequalities in supernatural terms. In other words, the real causes (exploitation by the ruling class) are obscured and distorted by religion's insistence that inequality is the product of sin or a sign that people have been chosen by God, etc.

What, according to Marxists, are the real causes of inequality in society?

3. *Keeping the working class passive and resigned to their fate*

Some religions present suffering and poverty as a virtue to be accepted, and even welcomed, as normal. It is suggested that those who do not question their situation will be rewarded by a place in heaven. Such ideas promote the idea that there is no point in changing society now. Instead, people should wait patiently for divine intervention. Religion thereby produces passive and fatalistic people who instead of trying to change the world for the better are simply content to accept spiritual alternatives.

Evidence to support Marxist views of religion

- Halevy (1927) argued that the Methodist religion played a key role in preventing working-class revolution in nineteenth century Britain. Most European nations experienced some type of proletarian attempt to bring about social change in this period except for Britain. Halevy argued that working-class dissatisfaction with the establishment was instead expressed by deserting the Church of England which was seen as the party of the **landed classes**. Methodism attracted significant numbers of working-class worshippers and Halevy claims Methodism distracted the proletariat from their class grievances by encouraging them to see enlightenment in spirituality rather than revolution. In this sense, religion inhibited major social upheaval and, therefore, social change.
- Leach (1988) is critical of the Church of England because it recruits from what is essentially an upper-class base (80% of bishops were educated at public school and Oxbridge). The Church is also extremely wealthy. Leach argues that consequently the Church has lost contact with ordinary people. He suggests it should be doing more to tackle inequality, especially that found in the inner cities.

What research methods would you use to investigate the hypothesis that the Church of England has 'lost contact with ordinary people'? Explain your answer.

- Religion is used to support dominant groups in America. It has been suggested that modern Protestant **fundamentalist** religions in the USA support right-wing, conservative and anti-communist values. Fundamentalists often suggest that wealth and prosperity are a sign of God's favour whilst poverty, illness and homosexuality are indicators of sin.
- Hook (1990) notes that the Pope has a very conservative stance on contraception, abortion, women priests and homosexuality. He points out that the Vatican's stance on contraception is causing problems in less developed areas of the world such as South America. Hook also suggests that the considerable wealth of the Church could be doing more to tackle world poverty.

Criticisms of Marxism

Like functionalism, the Marxist theory of religion fails to consider **secularisation**. Surely the ideological power of religion is undermined by the fact that less than 10% of people attend church?

There exist examples of religious movements which have brought about radical social change and consequently helped remove ruling elites, (as discussed later). They demonstrate that religion can legitimate radical revolutionary ideas as well as ideologically conservative ones. Marx failed to recognise this. Neo-Marxists have recognised the way in which religion is sometimes used as the only means to oppose the ruling class. Recently in Britain, for example, churches have often provided safe havens for immigrant groups facing deportation by the government, enabling such groups to further publicise their case and gain time and support.

Religion as a force for change

The problem of theodicy

Interactionists suggest that religion gives people's lives meaning. It answers fundamental questions for them. Weber suggests that religion deals with the problem of theodicy – how to make sense of and explain a world full of difficulties and contradictions, unfairness, inequality and danger. Religions answer questions such as 'why am I poor whilst he is rich?' and 'Why did my loved ones have to die?'. All religions see their God as being essentially good. How, though, can God allow such awful things to happen in the world? Berger (1967) uses the metaphor of a **sacred canopy** to refer to the different religious theodicies that enable people to make sense of, and come to terms with, the world. Where such ideas justify low socio-economic status they are referred to as a '**theodicy** of disprivilege'. Some sect members may believe that they are God's chosen people and the promise of salvation may be seen as compensation for their poverty. Such ideas promote the view that there is no point in trying to change the here and now.

In what other ways might people respond to poverty? Give examples from your studies.

Examples of religious theodicies
- In many Western religions, there is a belief that suffering in this life will bring rewards in the next.

- Hinduism suggests that living the 'right way' in this life will lead to a better future life on earth through **reincarnation**.
- Some religions emphasise constant conflict between the forces of good and evil in the world. Whilst good will ultimately triumph, we will have to put up with some evil in the meantime.
- Some theodicies include a belief in fate – that people's lives are predestined and there is nothing they can do to change them. They may, however, devise ways to counter the bleakness of this perception. One way might be to be as successful as possible in order to highlight God's favour and thus reassure themselves of their ultimate place in heaven.

Theodicy and social change
All of these ways of dealing with theodicy have social consequences. For example, Islamic fundamentalists may gain strength from the **trade sanctions** and other material deprivations they suffer. One aspect of Islamic theodicy is the belief that suffering plays a role in gaining entry to heaven. Western sanctions, therefore, are seen as a means to divine salvation and so provide greater resolve.

Max Weber, in his famous work *The Protestant Ethic and the Spirit of Capitalism* (1958) identified one particular theodicy which may have helped to facilitate social change.

The Protestant ethic and the spirit of capitalism

Calvinists were a Protestant group who emerged in the seventeenth century and believed in **pre-destination**. You were either damned or saved and there was nothing you or any religious figure could do to improve your chances of going to heaven. There was also no way of knowing your fate. However, it was believed that any form of social activity is of religious significance, and that material success which arose from hard work and an **ascetic** life would demonstrate God's favour and, therefore, one's ultimate destiny – a place in heaven.

Weber argued that these ideas helped initiate Western economic development through the industrial revolution and capitalism. Many of the early **entrepreneurs** were Calvinists and their obsessive work ethic and self-discipline, inspired by a desire to serve God, meant that they re-invested rather than spent their profits. Such attitudes were ideal for the development of industrial capitalism.

Criticisms of Weber
- Some countries with large Calvinist populations such as Norway and Sweden did not industrialise. However, Marshall (1982) points out that Weber did not claim that Calvinism caused capitalism, he only suggested that it was a major contributor to a climate of change. Calvinist beliefs had to be supplemented by a certain level of technology, a skilled and mobile workforce and rational modes of law and bureaucracy.
- Some commentators have suggested that slavery, colonialism and piracy were more important than Calvinist beliefs in accumulating the capital required for industrialisation.
- Marxists are also critical because, as Kautsky (1953) argues, capitalism predates Calvinism. He argues that early

capitalists were attracted to Calvinism because it made their interests appear legitimate.

Religion and radical change

Some revolutionary movements have deliberately used religion in an attempt to change society. In many Central and South American countries such as Guatemala, Chile and El Salvador where the police and military have been used to crush opposition, religion is the only remaining outlet for dissent. This fusion of Christianity and Marxism is known as **liberation theology**. Parkin (1972) argues that political leadership of the black population in the southern states of the USA was frequently taken on by clergymen and that churches provided an organisational focus for the civil rights movement. He also points out that in Eastern Europe the church was the major focus of opposition to communist governments.

Charisma

Another strand of Weberianism illustrates how religion, rather than being a conservative force, can initiate social change. This is connected to Weber's ideas regarding authority. Charismatic authority occurs where people are attracted by the ideas of a person who has a powerful personality and they then do what that person wants them to do.

There are many charismatic leaders who have caused social change. For example, Adolf Hitler (who was more an advocate of a form of civil religion), changed the world's political landscape. Religion has also had its share of charismatic leaders such as Jesus Christ and Mohammed. Many religious sects have been founded by charismatic individuals who have had the power of personality to influence others and in so doing cause significant social changes.

What makes religion conservative or radical?

MacGuire (1981) argues that there are a number of factors that determine whether religion promotes or prevents change.

- *Beliefs*
  Religions that emphasise strong moral codes are more likely to produce members who will be critical of and challenge social injustice. The Reverend Martin Luther King and the Southern Baptist Church were at the forefront of the black civil rights campaign in the 1960s. King's non-violent demonstrations were important in dismantling segregation and bringing about political and social rights for black people. Also, Christianity was a powerful opponent of apartheid in South Africa. Religious beliefs that focus on this world will have more potential to influence it than those that focus on spiritual and other-worldly matters. Christianity and Hinduism thus have more revolutionary potential than Buddhism, for example.

- *Culture*
  Where religion is central to the culture then anyone wishing to change the society is more likely to use religion. In India for example, Gandhi used the Hindu concept of

Sarvodaya (welfare for all) to attack British colonial rule and inspire rural peasants and the urban poor to turn against the British.

What is culture? Apart from religion, what is culture made up of?

- *Social location*
  Where a religious organisation plays a major role in political or economic life there is considerable scope for it to influence social change. Where the clergy come from and remain in close contact with their communities they are more able to mobilise them against negatively perceived outside influences. An Islamic revolution led by the Ayatollah Khomeini overthrew the Shah's pro-Western regime in Iran in 1979.

- *Internal organisation*
  Religions with a strong centralised source of authority have more chance of affecting events. The Roman Catholic church was instrumental in bringing about the collapse of communism in Poland through its support of the opposition 'Solidarity' movement. This same authority can, however, have the opposite effect by restraining the actions of some parts of its organisation. For example, the Pope has expelled some Latin American bishops for supporting Liberation theology.

One other aspect of the discussion involves the extent to which religion is conservative yet still committed to change by essentially turning back the clock in an attempt to counter the perceived immorality which characterises modern times. Christian and Muslim fundamentalist illustrate the position well. This will be further discussed in the next Topic.

Research idea

Interview a sample of people who participate in different religions. Find out their views on the relationship between religion and society. Do they believe that religion should get involved with politics and social change or is it purely a private matter?

KEY TERMS

Anomie – a state of confusion and normlessness.

Ascetic – self-denying.

Calvinists – A seventeenth century Protestant sect based on the thinking of John Calvin.

'Civil religion' – events or activities that involve ritualistic patterns and generate the collective sentiments usually associated with established religions.

Collective conscience – Beliefs, values and moral attitudes shared by members of a society which are essential to the social order.

Entrepreneurs – self-made, successful business people.

Feudal period – medieval period when wealth in society was based on the ownership of land.

Fundamentalist – belief in the need to subscribe or return to

Item A

The Number 11 Mysteriously Dominates the Events of the September 11, 2001 Terrorist Attacks in the USA

The incomprehensible events of September 11 have led some to suggest that it was the result of mysterious and influential forces associated with the number eleven demonstrable historically. The number 11 has been linked to mystery and power since ancient times. All forms of number research and study, including Numerology, the ancient science of Gematria, and the secret wisdom of Kabbalah, all give significant importance to 11, and 11 derivatives – 22, 33, 44, 55, 66, 77, 88, and 99.

The first Great War, World War 1, ended on the 11th hour, of the 11th day, of the 11th month. To this day, victims and veterans are remembered at that specific time. The USA skipped sequence numbers on the Apollo moon missions to ensure it was Apollo 11 that landed on the moon. In ancient Egypt King Tutankhamen's tomb had combinations of 11 in the jewelry he wore, and he had 11 oars placed on the floor surrounding his tomb. The number 11, and particularly the number 33, have significance to Freemasons, and other secretive groups.

The overwhelming quantity of elevens, surfacing from the events, people, and places related to the 11-9-2001 attacks, is remarkable. It is as if someone or something planned the events to occur around the number eleven. If it was not planned, then the coincidence of the numbers, seems even more mysterious and improbable.

The date of the attack: 9/11 – 9 + 1 + 1 = 11.
September 11 has 9 letters and 2 numbers: 9 + 2 = 11.
The number 911 is the international telephone number for emergencies.
September 11th is the 254th day of the year: 2 + 5 + 4 = 11.
After September 11th there are 111 days left to the end of the year.
New York City (11 Letters)
The first plane to hit the towers was American Airlines Flight 11.

Four of the hijackers on flight AA11 have the initials A. A. for their names: AA=11.
Flight AA11 had 92 people on board – 9 + 2 = 11.
Flight AA11 had 11 crew members – 2 pilots and 9 flight attendants.
The State of New York was the 11th State added to the Union.
The WTC Twin Towers – standing side by side, look like the number 11.
The 1st Fire Unit to arrive to the WTC towers was FDNY Unit 1. Unit 1 lost 11 firemen.
The WTC towers collapsed to a height of 11 storeys.

Source: September11.com- a web site dedicated to the events of September 11th 2001.

1 Use the term 'theodicy' to help explain the thinking behind Item A.

2 How might those who believe the extract above explain the events of September 11?

Item B

The Rev WA Criswell: an obituary

The curious tunnel vision of conservative America is once again evident with the death, at 92, of the Rev WA Criswell, former president of the Southern Baptist Convention. As the United States wages war on Taliban fundamentalism, its own Christian fundamentalists have heaped praise on a man who spent 50 highly influential years insisting that the Bible is the unerring word of God and that its historical accuracy is beyond question.

Though this may seem a fringe attitude on this side of the Atlantic, Criswell led a denomination of some 16m people, ran four radio stations and established a seminary which has turned out hundreds of young graduates to spread the same message. He paid lip service to the constitutional separation of church and state, yet he and his followers worked untiringly to ensure that their conservative social agenda dominated US political debate.

Based in Dallas, Texas, Criswell was part of the influential network surrounding the Bush family. The Rev Billy Graham, a White House adviser for 50 years, is a leading member of the First Baptist Church, which Criswell led; the elder George Bush regularly worshipped there, and his son made strenuous efforts to retain the backing of Criswell's adherents during his own presidential election campaign.

The relentless energy of this core conservative group – drawn from such disparate fields as the oil industry and the Christian right – led a Washington Post commentator to observe four weeks ago that "for the first time since religious conservatives became a modern political movement, the president of the United States has become the movement's de facto leader" – a development for which Wallie Amos Criswell could claim much credit.

But Criswell's message, often delivered at enormous length, went back uncompromisingly to Genesis, where God created the world in six days and made man in his image. That led, quite naturally, to a repeated effort to encourage the teaching of creationism (the Bible story of creation) in American schools. It also brought such church rulings as its 1998 declaration that a woman's duty was to submit graciously unto her husband's leadership.

Source: The *Guardian*, Jan 15 2002

3 In what ways can the Rev WA Criswell be described as a fundamentalist?

4 How have Christian fundamentalists such as the Rev WA Criswell attempted to ensure that their views have influenced American politics?

5 To what extent are Christian fundamentalist groups such as those described above an influence for social change or a conservative influence?

---

traditional values and practices, usually involving the literal translation and belief in a religious text.

Ideological apparatus – agencies (such as religion, education and the mass media) that transmit ruling-class ideology to persuade subordinate groups (e.g. the working-class that inequality is natural and normal, thereby ensuring their consent to it.

Landed Classes – wealthy, land-owning aristocracy.

Liberation theology – a fusion of Christianity and Marxism influential in Central and South America.

Predestination – belief that an individual's destiny is fixed before their birth.

Profane – ordinary, unreligious aspects of life.

Reincarnation – being re-born after death into another life.

Revivalist – movements that seek to revive religious commitment where it is perceived to have declined; often through organising revival meetings and inviting lapsed believers to attend.

Sacred – holy or spiritually significant.

Sacred canopy – an overarching set of religious ideas that serve to explain the meaning of life.

Secularisation – a process whereby religious beliefs and practices lose their social significance.

Theodicy – a set of ideas that explain fundamental question about the nature of existence.

Totemism – primitive religion which involves the worship of certain objects seen to have a widespread influence over tribal life.

Trade sanctions – international boycott of the trade in key goods imposed on a country for its perceived wrongdoing.

CHECK YOUR UNDERSTANDING

1 What is the distinction between the sacred and the profane?

2 Explain how Durkheim explains the true nature of the 'totem' and 'god'.

3 Identify and explain four functions of religion.

4 Explain, using examples, how civil religion performs similar functions.

5 How have functionalist ideas about religion been criticised?

6 How according to Marxists does religion benefit the capitalist class?

7 What evidence is there to support such views?

8 What purpose do religious theodicies serve?

9 Identify and explain three ways in which religion may contribute to social change.

10 What factors may determine whether religion has a conservative or radical influence?

- Go to the guardianunlimited website's special report on Religion at http://www.guardian.co.uk/religion/Story/0,2763,209804,00.html

  Use the A–Z index to find out the background details of one or more religions in Britain. Summarise them for other members of your class.

- Search the net for examples of liberation theology. Use a search engine such as Google and type in the following names: Archbishop Romero, Camilo Torres, Dom Helder Camara.

- Go to the archive search at http://www.guardianunlimited.co.uk and key in the words 'government' and 'church'. What evidence can you find for the continuing influence of the church on politics in modern society?

EXAM PRACTICE

Extract from AQA-style question

'Some theories see religion as a conservative force, others as a force for social change'.

Examine the evidence and arguments for each of these views. (40 marks)

OCR-style AS question

a Identify and explain two ways in which religion is an agency of social control. (15 marks)

b Outline and discuss the view that religion can be a force for social change. (30 marks)

Getting you thinking

HOROSCOPE

Gemini

Gemini has an instinct for choosing the right associates. You can switch the subject without missing a beat, and everything still gets finished on time. Both parties in a courtship feel that it's going to happen.
Curious Geminis can analyze a relationship and find out if it's worth their time.

1 In what ways might each of the items above represent religious belief?

2 Suggest two other actions or situations that could be seen as 'religious'.

3 What problems are there in measuring the extent of religious belief in Britain?

The activity above should have alerted you to the difficulties in attempting to judge the **religiosity** of an individual, group or society. Religiosity may be judged through assessing belief, practice, affiliation or membership. However, as Brierley (1999) points out, each of these presents us with problems.

Belonging: affiliation to a religion

According to Brierley, the religious community can be defined as 'all those who would positively identify with belonging to either a particular church i.e. place of worship or church category (e.g. Anglican, Roman Catholic, Muslim), even if they may only attend irregularly, or were just initiated (e.g. **baptised**) as a child'.

In *Religious Trends 2000* (see Brierley, 2000) the Christian percentage is given as 64% of the entire population and the total religious percentage as 71%. Though the percentages may have dropped from 85% and 86% respectively in 1910, a very high percentage of the population still claim to be affiliated to one religion or another, however loosely. The figure below provides a rough guide to changes in religious affiliation over the past quarter of a century.

Belonging: membership of a church

Membership refers to those who are recorded as being members of a religious organisation. In the Christian church most sub-groups define membership differently. In an Anglican (Church of England) church, members are often taken as those on the **Church Electoral Roll** whereas in some Pentecostal churches (see Topic 3), membership is confined to those who are **baptised**, born again, speak in tongues, and give evidence of living an active Christian life over at least six months.

The value of membership figures is that they are frequently collected over time, sometimes for many decades, and occasionally, even centuries. They have usually been collected using the same definition within a particular religion and therefore the trends in the figures can be judged as accurate.

In the United Kingdom, religious membership has been decreasing. In 1900 membership of all religions was 34%, but by 2000 it had dropped to 17%. From these figures, we can also see that relatively few people who say they belong to a religious community actually take it seriously enough to become formal members.

Practice: attendance

Another possible means by which religiosity can be measured is by seeing how often people attend religious services or meetings. Either people are there on a Sunday (for Christians) or Friday (for Muslims) or they are not!

Attendance figures, however, are not always collected by the different religious organisations, and even when regularly counted, will often be counted on different Sundays. The 1851 census of the Population of England and Wales included a count of religious worship, but the only non-Christian worshippers identified were the Jews. On the day of the census 24% of the population attended at least once. The 1998 English Church attendance Survey (see Brierley, 2000) put this figure at around 7.5%.

What is the census? Identify three areas of social policy that might be influenced by census data.

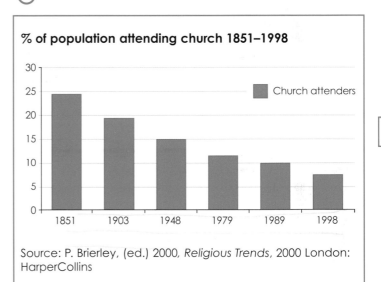

% of population attending church 1851–1998

■ Church attenders

Source: P. Brierley, (ed.) 2000, *Religious Trends*, 2000 London: HarperCollins

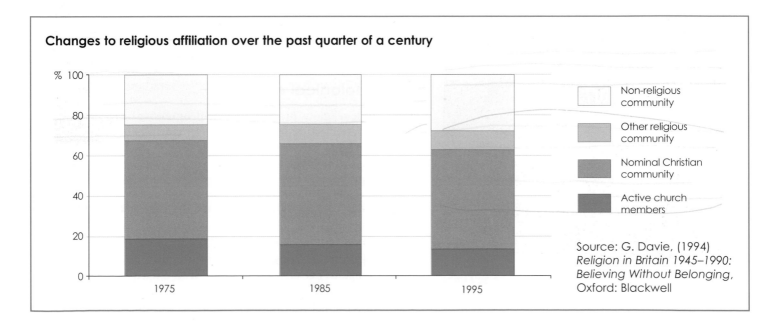

Changes to religious affiliation over the past quarter of a century

☐ Non-religious community

▨ Other religious community

▨ Nominal Christian community

▨ Active church members

Source: G. Davie, (1994) *Religion in Britain 1945–1990: Believing Without Belonging*, Oxford: Blackwell

The 1989 figure of 10% compares with 25% in Australia and 42% in the United States.

Whilst the attendance rates show a steady decline, it should be noted that the figures are based on Sunday attendance. The 1998 survey showed, however, that 11% of the population attend on other days of the week and that this proportion has increased. As intimated earlier, some people attend church more than once on Sundays and may also attend midweek. So, the snapshot of 'at least once on Sunday' being used as the general measure does not give us the full picture.

Are there other possible reasons why non-believers might attend a religious place of worship?

Practice: other forms

Religious practices can be conducted in many other ways beyond formal communal activities. How often people pray or think about their God and whether religious commitment affects the decisions they make in life, although difficult to measure, can be seen as indicators of religiosity. Does, for example, a young person delay having a sexual relationship because of their religious conviction or secular morality? Does a lapsed Catholic refuse to have an abortion because of the guilt derived from her religious roots regarding such issues or because of other moral influences?

Apart from religion, what other influences are there on our morals and values? Which do you think are most important and why?

Belief

Belief is the final and perhaps most controversial indicator. It has been regularly and frequently measured in numerous surveys, social and otherwise. Although what someone means when they say that they believe in God can be questioned, there are plenty of surveys that show that people have religious beliefs. Trends in answers to questions about belief are summarised by Gill (1999) below.

Traditional belief, 1940s–1990s

	1940/50s	1960s	1970s	1980s	1990s
Traditional Belief	%				
God	–	79	74	72	67
God as personal	43	39	32	32	31
God as spirit or life force	38	39	38	39	40
Jesus as Son of God	68	62	–	49	–
Heaven	–	–	52	55	52
Life after death	49	49	37	43	44
The devil	24	28	20	24	26
Hell	–	–	21	26	25

Source: R. Gill (1999) *Churchgoing and Christian Ethics*, Cambridge: Cambridge University Press

Variations in belief according to social position

Studies that measure religious belief tend to generalise about any particular population. However, there are variations between different groups.

- According to the British Social Attitudes Survey (1998), only one third of 18–24 year olds 'belong to a religion'. But the equivalent for those over 65 is just over three-quarters.
- 36% of men are frequent or regular church attenders compared with 64% of women (see Topic 4).
- 16% of the middle classes attend church compared with 12% of the working class, yet of the non-attenders, more members of the middle class are non-believers.
- Ethnic minority groups are generally more religious than 'whites' (see Topic 5).

Suggest reasons why these patterns exist.

What can we include as religious belief?

Any discussion regarding the extent of religiosity or its decline is affected by how we come to define religiosity. If we take a broad (sometimes referred to as 'inclusive') definition of religion then belief appears to be much more widespread than if we adopt a definition that requires affiliation to a recognised religious organisation. Is a belief in fate or luck a religious belief? What about witches, ghosts or flying saucers? If they are, then an awful lot of people share such beliefs and may be termed 'religious', as we shall see in the next topic.

Modes of religious expression

Different religious organisations demand varying degrees of commitment and religious intensity. Whilst many people may say they are religious, the effect of that commitment on their lives and the society that they live in may vary immensely. This is not only true of differences in intensity between religions but also within the same religion. There may be differences in:

- **theological** emphasis
- relationships with others.

Theological emphasis

Some religious practice may be **progressive or reforming**, attempting to re-fashion religious principles in line with changes in modern society. To be true to what made their religious heritage great, progressives say, they must convey in religious form the aspirations of people today, as saints and prophets did in earlier times. Progressives generally believe that individuals should be free to make up their own minds about what is religiously significant. Hence, some progressive factions call themselves **liberal**.

In contrast, **conservative religion** identifies the content of a religious heritage as revelation with a fixed subject matter which is not open to re-interpretation. They focus upon a conventional translation of religious teachings and try to keep

Exploring religious belief

Item A

Which, if any, of the things I'm going to read out do you believe in?

		Yes %	No %	Don't know %
Q1	God	64	26	10
Q2	Life after death	45	42	13
Q3	A soul	67	24	9
Q4	Heaven	54	37	9
Q5	Astrology	38	53	9
Q6	Ghosts	40	52	8
Q7	Telepathy	54	37	9
Q8	Guardian Angels	31	61	8
Q9	Premonitions/ESP	64	29	7
Q10	Fortune Telling/Tarot	18	75	7
Q11	Deja-vu*	66	30	4
Q12	Out of body experience	31	58	11
Q13	Reincarnation	24	64	12
Q14	Near-death experience	51	37	12
Q15	Psychics/Mediums#	28	63	9
Q16	Faith-healers	32	56	12
Q17	That dreams can predict the future	30	60	10

*a feeling that you have done something or been somewhere before
#people who can communicate with the dead

Source: MORI poll, Feb. 1998

1 Which of the list above would you count as indicating religious belief and which would you not count? Explain your answers.

2 How effective do you consider this interview question as a method of measuring religious belief?

Features of fundamentalist groups

● *Interpret 'infallible' sacred texts literally*
They do this in order to counter what they see as the diluting influence of excessive intellectualism among more liberal organisations. They often make use of selective retrieval of evidence from such scriptures.

● *Reject religious pluralism*
Tolerance of other religious ideas waters down personal faith and consequently fundamentalists have an 'us' and 'them' mentality.

● *Find a personal experience of God's presence*
They define all areas of life as sacred thus requiring a high level of engagement. e.g. Fundamentalist Christians are born again to live the rest of their lives in a special relationship with Jesus.

● *Oppose secularisation and modernity and are in favour of tradition*
They believe that accommodation to the changing world undermines religious conviction and leads to moral corruption.

● *Promote conservative beliefs including patriarchal ones*
They argue that God intends humans to live in heterosexual societies dominated by men. In particular, they condemn abortion and detest lesbian and gay relations.

● *Emerge in response to social inequality or a perceived social crisis*
They attract members by offering solutions to desperate, worried or dejected people.

● *Paradoxically, they tend to make maximum use of modern technology*
To compete on a level playing field with those that threaten their very existence, e.g. the Christian Right use television (in their view the prime cause of moral decay) to preach the 'word'. Use of the internet is now widespread by all fundamentalist groups.

Source: Adapted from Caplan (1987), Hunter (1987), and Davie (1995)

religious observance in line with the way it has traditionally been for centuries.

Fundamentalism

Perhaps the most extreme expression of religious belief concerns those who subscribe to a **fundamentalist** position. Examples include Zionist groups in Israel, Islamic fundamentalists in Iran, Afghanistan and elsewhere and the New Christian Right in the USA. In the past 30 years, Islamic and Christian fundamentalism have grown in strength, largely in response to **globalisation** shaping national and international politics as they confront the policies of modernising governments.

How might globalisation have encouraged the growth of fundamentalism in some countries?

Fundamentalism can sometimes lead to violence. This violence can result when fundamentalists value their beliefs above tolerance of those who do not share them. In some cases, the beliefs of fundamentalists can be so strong as to overcome any respect or compassion for others. These beliefs can sometimes even overcome the basic human values of the preservation of one's own life and the lives of others. The bombing of abortion clinics in the USA and the attacks on the Pentagon and World Trade Centre Towers on September 11, 2001 are specific examples.

Relationships with others

Members of many religions believe that their religion has a **monopoly of truth** such that it is their moral and religious duty to persuade others to become members of their faith. **Evangelism** involves preaching 'the word' in the non-believing community. **Televangelism** has increased in popularity in the USA as a means to achieve the same ends but on a much larger scale by using the medium of television. Many argue, however, that such evangelists are really only preaching to existing believers.

Conversionist religions require members to seek new converts. This usually involves door-to-door selling where well-groomed representatives, often accompanied by children, talk people round outside their own homes. Mormons, Jehovah's Witnesses and the Salvation Army all subscribe to conversionism in one form or another.

Many religious cults use the internet to communicate among their members and you need only type the name of a religious organisation into a search engine to find that religious people actively use the internet to practise their faith through discussion groups and other means.

Organisational types

Religious organisations can be broadly grouped into four main types:

- churches
- sects
- denominations
- cults.

Churches and sects

Weber (1920) and Troeltsch (1931) first distinguished between churches and sects. A church is a large well-established religious body such as the mainstream organisations that represent the major world religions – the Roman Catholic Church, Anglican and Eastern Orthodox churches, Judaism, Islam and Hinduism, and so on. A sect is a smaller, less highly organised grouping of committed believers usually setting itself up in protest at what a church has become – as Calvinists and Methodists did in preceding centuries (which would now be considered denominations). In terms of membership, churches are far more important than sects. The former tend to have hundreds of thousands or even millions of members whereas sect members usually number no more than a few hundred. Hence, the media attention they are given is somewhat disproportionate.

Explain why the media might give more attention to sects than to the established churches.

Denominations

According to Becker (1950) a denomination is a sect that has 'cooled down' to become an institutionalised body rather than an active protest group. Niebuhr (1929) argues that sects that survive over a period of time become denominations because a **bureaucratic**, non-hierarchical structure becomes necessary once the **charismatic leader** dies. Hence, they rarely survive as sects for more than a generation. Whilst they initially appear deviant, sects gradually evolve into denominations and are accepted as a mere offshoot of an established church. They no longer claim a monopoly of truth, and tend to be tolerant and

The differences between churches, denominations, sects and cults

FEATURE	CHURCH	DENOMINATION	SECT	CULT
Scope	National (or international); very large membership; inclusive	National (or international); large membership; inclusive	Local (or national); exclusive; small	Local; national or international; inclusive; varies in size
Internal organisation	Hierarchical; bureaucratic	Formal bureaucratic	Voluntary; tight-knit; informal	Voluntary; loose structure
Nature of leadership	Professional clergy with paid officials	Professional clergy; less bureaucratic; uses lay preachers	No professional clergy or bureaucratic structure; often charismatic leader	Individualistic; may be based on a common interest or provision of a service; inspirational leader
Life span	Over centuries	Often more than 100 years	Sometimes more than a generation, may evolve into a denomination	Often short-lived and dies with the leadership
Attitude to wider society	Recognises the state and accepts society's norms and values. Often seen as the establishment view	Generally accepted but not part of formal structure. Seen as a basis of non-conformist views	Critical of mainstream society; often reclusive with own norms and values	May be critical or accepting of society but has a unique approach which offers more
Claims to truth	**Monopoly view of the truth**. Strong use of ritual with little arousal of strong emotional response.	No monopoly on truth, less ritual but clear emphasis on emotional fervour	Monopoly view of truth; aim to re-establish fundamental truths	No monopoly; borrows from a range of sources
Type of membership	Little formal commitment required. Often by birth	Stronger commitment and rules, e.g. teetotalism or non-gambling	Exceptional commitment	Membership flexible
Examples	Anglicanism, Catholicism, Islam, Judaism, Hinduism, Sikhism	Baptists, Methodists Pentecostalists, Evangelical protestants	Mormons, Jehovah's Witnesses, Moonies, Branch-Davidian; Salvation Army, Quakers	Scientology; spiritualism Transcendental Meditation, New Age ideas

open, requiring a fairly low level of commitment. However, Brian Wilson (1966) rejects Niebuhr's view and suggests that some sects do survive for a long time without becoming denominations and continue to require a high level of commitment.

Cults

Whilst there is some disagreement among sociologists over how to classify a cult, most agree that it is the least coherent form of religious organisation. Cults' focus is on individual experience, bringing like-minded individuals together. People do not formally join cults, rather they subscribe to particular theories or forms of behaviour. Scientology, for example, is claimed to have eight million members worldwide.

The terms 'sect' and 'cult' are often used interchangeably by the media to describe new forms of religious organisation and there can be considerable **moral panic** about them, as we shall see in the next Topic. Recently, sociologists such as Wallis (1984) have developed the terms 'new religious movement (NRM)' and 'new age movement (NAM)' to describe these new forms of religion.

CHECK YOUR UNDERSTANDING

1 a) What percentage of the British population in 2000 claimed to belong to a particular religion?
   b) How has this figure changed since 1910?

2 How might membership figures be said to be 'reliable' rather than 'valid' measures of religiosity? Give examples.

3 Why in your view might mid-week attendance figures have increased whilst Sunday figures declined?

4 What are the limitations of using attendance figures as a measure of religiosity?

5 What is the relationship between social position and religiosity?

6 What is meant by theological emphasis? Give examples.

7 In your own words, outline the key features of fundamentalism.

8 Why do the members of conversionist groups frequently come into contact with non-believers?

9 Briefly define 'church', 'denomination', 'sect' and 'cult', giving examples of each.

Research ideas

1 Conduct a survey to discover the extent of belief in a range of supernatural and spiritual phenomena among students at your school or college. To what extent do your results indicate widespread 'religious belief'? Would your conclusions be different if you used different criteria for measuring 'religious belief'?

2 Conduct unstructured interviews with a small sample of people who belong to different religious groups and organisations. Compare their beliefs, practices and attitudes to other religions.

KEY TERMS

Baptised – initiated into the faith by a religious ceremony involving anointment or immersion in water whilst being blessed by a priest.

Bureaucratic – centralised form of organisation run by official representatives.

Charismatic leader – leader who has a magnetic and powerful personality.

Church Electoral Roll – a list of church members, usually over 16, which is regularly updated. Applicants generally have to have habitually attended public worship in the parish during a period (e.g. six months) prior to enrolment or need to reside in the parish. They must also have an affinity with the religious denomination in question.

Conservative religion – religion that wishes to conserve things as they are.

Conversionist – a faith that requires members to convert others to the faith.

Evangelism – a common strand in many religions involving using a range of methods to win over converts, e.g. door-to-door canvassing, leafleting, preaching.

Fundamentalist – see key terms in Topic 1.

Globalisation – a process whereby social and economic activity spans many nations with little regard for national borders.

Liberal – a concern with individual freedoms.

Monopoly of truth – a view that only the viewpoint of the holder can be accepted as true.

Moral panic – media-induced panic about the behaviour of particular groups.

Progressive – forward looking, modernising.

Reforming – re-interpreting in line with a new rationale.

Religiosity – the importance of religion in a person's life.

Televangelism – mainly Christians in the United States using television to convert viewers.

Theology – study of religious beliefs.

WWWebtask

There are many sites that represent and discuss churches, sects and cults. Many are the websites of the groups themselves. Search for the websites of churches, sects and cults and compare the organisations using some of the criteria on the previous page. What other differences and similarities can you identify?

EXAM PRACTICE

Extract from AQA-style question

a Distinguish between church and denomination. (8 marks)

b Examine reasons for the movement to religious fundamentalism. (12 marks)

OCR-style AS question

a Identify and explain two characteristics, of religious fundamentalism. (15 marks)

b Outline and discuss the view that there is no way of really knowing the extent of religiosity in society. (30 marks)

Item A

Shades of Islam

Islam, like Christianity, is a religion that has continually stimulated activism. The Qu'ran is full of instructions to believers to 'struggle in the way of God'. This struggle is against both unbelievers and those who introduce corruption in the Muslim community. Like Christianity, Islam is internally divided. Shi'ites are the most traditional faction and believe that Mohammed the prophet's rightful heir will one day be instituted, doing away with the tyrannies and injustices associated with existing regimes. Shi'ism is the official religion of Iran and there are large Shi'ite populations in other Middle Eastern countries including Iraq, Turkey and Saudi Arabia. Islamic leadership in these countries is, however, in the hands of the majority, the Sunni, who follow the 'Beaten Path', a series of traditions deriving from the Qu'ran which tolerate a considerable diversity of opinion, thus being more liberal than the rigidly defined views of the Shi'ites.

Adapted from: A. Giddens (2001) *Sociology* (4th edition) Cambridge: Polity Press

1 Read Item A and say which type of Islamic belief can be considered 'progressive' and which 'orthodox'? Explain your answer.

Item B

What caused the 'Islamic Revolution' in Iran in 1978–9?

In the late nineteenth century, the inability of the Muslim world to effectively resist the spread of Western culture led to reform movements seeking to restore Islam to its original purity and strength. A key idea was that Islam should respond to the Western challenge by affirming the identity of its own beliefs and practices. Such ideas sparked the revolution, which was initially fuelled by internal opposition to the modernising Shah of Iran who had tried to promote Western forms of modernisation such as land reform, extension of the vote to women, and the introduction of secular education. The movement that overthrew the Shah, (the Mojahadin) (some but not all of which was attached to Islamic fundamentalism), possessed a key figure, the Ayatollah Khomeini, who provided a radical re-interpretation of Shi-'ite ideas. Following the revolution, driven by the Islamic socialism of the Mojahadin, he established a government organised according to traditional Islamic law. Religion, as specified in the Qu'ran, became the direct basis of all political and economic life. Men and women are kept rigorously separated, women are obliged to cover their bodies and heads in public, practising homosexuals are sent to the firing squad and adulterers stoned to death.

The aim of the revolution was to Islamicise both the state and society such that Islamic teachings become dominant in all spheres of life.

There are differing factions within Iran who wish to push forward to complete this process and export it elsewhere, some who feel it has gone far enough, wishing to maintain the status quo and those who wish to open up the economy to foreign investment and trade and oppose the strict imposition of Islamic codes on women, the family and the legal system. The tensions are evident in Iran today and have gradually surfaced since the death of Khomeini in 1979.

Adapted from: A. Giddens (2001) *Sociology* (4th edition) Cambridge: Polity Press

2 Read Item B and identify what caused the Iranian revolution.

3 In what ways can those who came to power after the Iranian revolution be seen as fundamentalist?

4 How did their religious beliefs affect the behaviour of people in Iran?

Item C

From OM to Amen
(via Harvey Nicks)

Geri Halliwell's at it, and even disgraced Tory MP Jonathan Aitken swears it's changed him forever. It's the Alpha course, a free intensive and informal course in Christianity, with two million converts in the UK so far! Perhaps it's proof that, despite the popularity of Eastern mysticism, many still crave traditional, structured religion. New recruits attend study meetings and go on retreats in their search for God. Alpha sessions are held at Holy Trinity Brompton in London's Kensington – said to be the Church of England's answer to Harvey Nicks. Apparently, anyone who's anyone goes there darling. ■

Source: Zoe Seymour, *She* magazine, March 2002

A poll conducted by MORI in September 2000 revealed that over three and a half million adults in the UK – 6 per cent of the population – have now either done an 'Alpha' course, on-line or know someone in their circle who has.

Devised in the UK, the 'Alpha' course is supported by the Archbishops of Canterbury and York and by leaders of all the main denominations. The course is now running in over 18,000 churches in 122 countries around the world and the materials have been translated into 33 different languages from Shona, French, Croatian, Chinese and Russian.

Source: Alpha course website

5 How would you account for the appeal of the Alpha course?

6 To what extent would Durkheim have considered this form of religious activity functional or dysfunctional? Explain your answer.

Getting you thinking

The Celestine Prophecy

The Celestine Prophecy by James Redfield fast became one of the top commercial publishing events of the1990s, hovering at the top of the *New York Times* best-seller list for several months. Originally self-published in 1992, it grew through New Age bookstore popularity to an $850,000 purchase by Time Warner books and sales approaching a million copies. The fictional narrative centres around a search for ancient Mayan manuscripts known as the Nine Insights. These insights purport to contain information and ancient wisdom about ultimate reality and man's place in it. Essentially, according to the book, life's 'chance coincidences', strange occurrences that feel like they were meant to happen, are actually events, indicative of another plane of existence and following them will start you on your path to spiritual truth – a oneness of human spirit with the forces of the universe.

The author and publisher have not made a tremendous effort to explain that the book's story never actually happened. A recent New Age journal points out this oversight: 'A true story? Well, not exactly, though many Celestine devotees have apparently thought so. (Some reportedly walked out on readings after getting the facts.) And booksellers, too: At least one major chain had the novel prominently displayed in the non-fiction section.'

Source: *Body, Mind, & Spirit*, July/August 1994

1 Have you ever experienced strange coincidences? Do you think that there may be something more to them than mere coincidence?

2 Do you think there is something beyond the physical world that traditional religions are unable to explain?

3 Do you believe that human beings have a spiritual aspect to their nature? Explain the reasoning behind your answer.

4 Which of the following would you be more interested in and why:

a an alternative religion or movement that promised you greater spiritual fulfilment?

b an alternative movement or religion that offered you the opportunity to be more financially and romantically successful?

If you answered 'yes' to any of questions 1–3, you are not alone. A growing number of people are rejecting traditional religious explanations of spirituality as well as scientific accounts of the natural world. There seems to be increasing interest and activity around anything that promises to provide better explanations of the spiritual side to life. Some are even prepared to make life-changing commitments to realise their goal of spiritual fulfilment. This process of what some have called **re-sacrilisation** has been accelerating since the 1960s.

*Which perspective takes as one of its starting points the rejection of '**grand narratives**' such as religion and science?*

The emergence of new religious movements (NRMs)

As we saw in the previous Topic, membership of established 'mainstream' churches has dropped dramatically. However, affiliation with other religious organisations (including Pentecostal, Seventh-Day Adventists and Christian sects) has risen just as noticeably. It is estimated that there may now be as many as 25,000 new religious groups in Europe alone, over 12,000 of whose members reside in the UK (see the figure opposite).

Membership of new religious movements, UK 1980–1995			
	1980	1990	2000
The Aetherius Society	100	500	700
Brahma Kumaris	700	900	1,500
Chrisemma	–	5	50
Da free John	35	50	70
Crème	250	375	510
Eclankar	250	350	450
Elan Vital*	1,200	1,800	2,400
Fellowship of Isis	150	250	300
Lite training	–	250	350
Mahikari	–	220	280
Barry Long Foundation	–	400	–
Outlook seminar training	–	100	250
Pagan Federation	500	900	5,000
The Raelin movement	100	100	100
Shinnyean UK	10	30	60
Sahaja Yoga	220	280	365
Solara	–	140	180
3HO	60	60	60
Hare Krishna	300	425	670
Others	50	575	1,330
Total	**3,925**	**7,710**	**14,625**

* previously known as the Divine Light Mission

Compiled from: P. Brierley (ed.) (2000) *Religious Trends 2000*, London: HarperCollins

Difficulties in measuring affiliation to NRMs in Britain

- Many of the organisations above have a large number of followers who are not formally registered in any way. It is estimated that about 30,000 people have attended meditation courses run by Brahma Kumaris, for example.
- Some groups have disbanded their organisations but still have 'devotees'. For example the Divine Light Mission whose followers, once initiated with 'the Knowledge', continue to practise the techniques of meditation independently.
- Many organisations are based overseas and their supporters in the UK are not traceable.
- The commitment required varies enormously between organisations. Whilst those who devote themselves full time to their movement are generally quite visible (if only by their absence elsewhere), part-time commitment is more difficult to identify.

Affiliation through practice and belief is much higher than formal membership for both traditional and new religions.

Suggest an alternative method for finding out the extent of participation in new religious movements.

Classifying NRMs

Sociologists have attempted to classify such movements in terms of shared features. One way is to identify their affinities with traditional mainstream religions. For example, some may be linked to Hinduism (e.g. Hari Krishnas) and others to Buddhism (various Zen groups). Some NRMs such as the Unification Church (Moonies) mix up a number of different theologies, while others have links with the Human Potential Movement which advocates therapies such as Transcendental Meditation and Scientology to liberate human potential.

Wallis (1984) identifies three main kinds of NRM:

- World-affirming groups
- World-rejecting groups
- World-accommodating groups.

Using other topics you have studied, give one other example of sociologists' attempts to classify social phenomena. What problems do these categorisations face?

World-affirming groups

These are usually individualistic, life-positive and aim to release 'human potentials'. They tend to accept the world as it is, but involve techniques which enable the individual to participate more effectively and gain more from their worldly experience. They do not require a radical break with a conventional lifestyle, nor strongly restrict the behaviour of members. Research suggests that these are more common amongst middle-aged, middle-class groups – often disillusioned and disenchanted with material values and in search of new, more positive meanings. These groups generally lack a church, ritual worship or strong ethical systems. They are often more like 'therapy groups' than traditional religions. Two good examples of world affirming groups are:

- *The Church of Scientology* founded by L. Ron Hubbard. Hubbard developed the philosophy of dianetics, which stresses the importance of 'unblocking the mind' and leading it to becoming 'clear'. His church spread throughout the world (from a base in California). Its business income is estimated at over £200 million per year through the courses members pay for, as well as through the sale of books.
- *Transcendental Meditation* or TM was brought to the West by the Hindu Maharishi Mahesh Yogi in the early 1950s and further popularised through the interest shown in it by the Beatles in the 1960s. It focuses upon building a personal **mantra** which is then dwelt upon for periods each day. Again, the focus is upon a good world – not an evil one – and a way of 'finding oneself' through positive thinking.

New age movements

The term 'New Age' refers to a large number of religions and therapies that have become increasingly important since the

1970s. Bruce (1996) suggests that these groups tend to take one of two forms.

- *Audience cults* involve little face-to-face interaction. Members of the 'audience' are unlikely to know each other. Contacts are maintained mostly through the mass media and the internet as well as occasional conferences. Both astrology and belief in UFOs would be good examples. Audience cults feed a major market of 'self-help therapy' groups and books which regularly appear in best-seller lists.
- *Client cults* offer particular services to their followers. They have led to a proliferation of new 'therapists' (from astrological to colour therapists) establishing new relationships between a consumer and a seller. Amongst the practices involved are **tarot readings**, **crystals**, **reflexology**, **channelling** and **I Ching**. Many bookshops devote more to these sorts of books than to books on Christianity.

NAMs seem to appeal to all age groups, but more especially to women (see Topic 4). Bruce (1995) suggests that those affiliated, however, already subscribe to what Heelas (1996) calls the **cultic milieu** – a mish-mash of belief in the power of spirituality, ecology and personal growth and a concern that science does not have all the answers. An annual celebration of New Age beliefs – the Festival for the Mind, Body and Spirit – takes place annually in London and Manchester.

Suggest reasons why the New Age Movement might be more attractive to women than men.

World-rejecting groups

These organisations are similar to sects in so far as they are always highly critical of the outside world and demand significant commitment from their members. In some ways, they are quite like conventional religions in that they may require prayer and the study of key religious texts, and have strong ethical codes. They are exclusive, often share possessions and seek to relegate members' identities to that of the greater whole. They are often **millenarian** – expecting divine intervention to change the world. Examples include:

- The Unification Church (popularly known as the Moonies), founded in Korea by the Reverend Sun Myung Moon in 1954. The Unification Church rejects the mundane secular world as evil and has strong moral rules such as no smoking and drinking.
- Members of Hare Krishna (Children of God, or ISKCON International Society for Krishna Consciousness) are distinguished by their shaved heads, pigtails and flowing gowns. Hare Krishna devotees repeat a mantra 16 times a day.

World-rejecting sects are the movements that have come under most public scrutiny in recent years, largely because of the public horror at the indoctrination that has even led to mass suicide. There is a growing list of extreme examples – the mass suicide of Jim Jones's People's Temple in Jonestown, Guyana in 1987; the Aum Supreme Truth detonating poisonous gas canisters on a Tokyo underground train in 1995, (leaving 12 dead and 5,000 sick), and the suicidal death in 1997 of the 39 members of the Heaven's Gate cult in California.

The anti-cult movement

While most of these new religious forms have adopted strategies no different from those of other religions, they are commonly seen by the press and public as deviant – in particular, those that involve open sexuality (thus challenging conventional religious ethics). Some sects, for example, have recruited members by sending young female members into the community to promise sexual favours to encourage converts. Others promote very open relationships where members have many sexual partners within the group. Such sects are particular targets of the anti 'cult' movement. (Note that the term 'cult' is misused in this context, 'sect' being more accurate.)

Why do sociologists face problems in defining these religious movements as deviant?

A number of individuals and agencies have attempted to raise public concern about what they feel are serious emotional, spiritual and physical abuses by some new religious movements. Some parents of 'cult' members and disillusioned former members have become '**deprogrammers**'. For a fee (which in some cases in the US has exceeded $10,000), deprogrammers hold cult members against their will in order to make them abandon their religious faith. Sometimes techniques such as physical and mental abuse and sleep and food deprivation are used. It is ironic that deprogramming involves the use of the very same practices that the cults are accused of.

Cult apologists

Some writers (e.g. Haddon and Long, 1993), whilst not members themselves, both defend the right of such groups to exist and argue for more religious tolerance. They claim that:

- most cults are simply misunderstood minority 'religions'
- these movements only seem weird because people don't know enough about them and believe sensational media accounts
- anti-cult organisations and individuals misrepresent the beliefs and practices of such movements
- anti-cult organisations are intolerant of religious freedom.

World-accommodating groups

This final category of religious movement is more orthodox. They maintain some connections with mainstream religion, but place a high value on inner religious life. The Holy Spirit 'speaks' through the Neo-Pentecostalists, giving them the gift of 'speaking in tongues'. Such religions are usually dismayed at both the state of the world and the state of organised mainstream religions. They seek to establish older certainties and faith whilst giving them a new vitality.

New theologies

Apocalypticism

Apocalypticism is the belief in divinely revealed teachings about the final events of history. Apocalyptic movements regard certain events in the social world as signs that the end of the world is imminent. In recent decades, apocalyptic movements have grown in size and number with the

After carrying out research into the religious sect called the 'Moonies' in 1984, the UK government helped Eileen Barker set up an organisation called 'Inform' whose aim was to provide impartial information about new religious movements and to build bridges between them and the wider society.

Item A

Cult advisers in clash over clampdown

The Government has promised to take a closer look at religious sects following the recent hullabaloo over the Jesus Christians. But it may be hampered by bad advice, according to one cult watchdog.

Tom Sackville, the former Tory Home Office minister and anti-cult campaigner, abolished government funding for the Information Network Focus on Religious Movements (Inform) in 1997, only to see it reinstated this year.

'I cancelled Inform's grant and I think it's absurd that it's been brought back,' he said. Inform is the result of research carried out by Professor Eileen Barker at the London School of Economics. It has been criticised by other cult watchdogs, including Mr Sackville's own Family Action Information Resource (Fair), because she refuses to condemn all 'new religions' as cults.

'The Government is taking non-judgemental advice as an excuse for its non-action on cults,' says Sackville.

But Professor Barker is short with her critics. 'We are not **cult apologists**,' she says. 'People make a lot of noise without doing serious research - so much so that they can end up sounding as closed to reason as the cults they're attacking. Besides, I imagine Fair was disappointed not to get our funding.'

Source: The *Daily Telegraph*, July 7, 2000

Item B

Dealing with the end of the world time after time

Eileen Barker: Professor whose faith in people wins trust of the cults

No one has seen the end of the world come round more times than Eileen Barker. 'The last date the Jehovah's Witnesses set was 1975. I remember going to Wembley Stadium in 1973 and sitting next to a lady who told me that it was going to be 1975. She was fascinating, but she had this awful halitosis and it proved too much for me.'

Since then she has talked to more disappointed end-time believers than anyone except St Peter: as the professor of the sociology of religion at London School of Economics, she has an unrivalled reputation for being trusted by journalists as well as the people she writes about. The only people who really dislike her are the anti-cult zealots, who have never forgiven her research on the Moonies, which showed that most members, far from being brainwashed, simply grow up and grow out of it. The Moonies didn't much like it either.

Andrew Brown, the *Guardian*, Saturday January 8, 2000

Read Items A and B and answer the following questions.

1 Why was Inform's government grant removed?

2 How does Barker defend the organisation?

3 Suggest reasons why Barker's research on the Moonies was unpopular with both the Moonies *and* the anti-cult movement.

approach of the new millennium. According to Robbins and Palmer (1997), events such as the emergence of AIDS, the fall of communism, the Gulf War, the threat of ecological disaster, and the rise of information technology, all fuelled apocalyptic visions that the 'last days' were near.

Millennialism

Millennial belief (**Millennialism**) is connected to Apocalypticism in that it anticipates massive social upheaval through the involvement of outside supreme forces – for example divine intervention or even aliens. The widespread nature of such beliefs is evident in the popularity of programmes like 'The X files' and films like 'Independence Day' and 'Close Encounters of the Third Kind'.

What is the appeal of new religious and New Age movements?

For sociologists, one of the most interesting questions is *why* people join or support new religious movements.

Pragmatic motives

Motivations for affiliation with world-affirming groups can be very practical – financial success and a happier life, for example. These '**pragmatic motives**' are not the sort that many religious people would recognise and this is probably one of the main reasons why the religious nature of many NRMs is questioned.

Spiritual void

Since the decline in the importance of established religion, people seek alternative belief systems to explain the world and its difficulties. In addition, as postmodernists argue, there is also an increased cynicism about the ability of science to provide solutions to these problems. In the absence of either **grand narrative**, (religion or science), people seek to acquire a personal rationale for existence. This can involve a process of 'spiritual shopping', trying out the various alternatives until they find a belief system that makes sense to them.

Marginality

Weber pointed out how those marginalised by society may find status and/or a legitimising explanation for their situation through a theodicy of disprivilege (see Topic 1) which offers ultimate salvation. This could explain the appeal of world-rejecting sects to some members of ethnic minorities or young social 'drop outs'.

Relative deprivation

People may be attracted to an NRM because it offers something lacking in the social experience of the seeker – whether spiritual or emotional fulfilment. This could explain the appeal of NRMs to certain members of the middle class who feel their lives to be lacking spiritual meaning.

Using information from another topic you have studied, give a further example of sociologists' use of the idea of relative deprivation.

The appeal of world-rejecting movements to the young

Many young people are no longer children but lack adult commitments such as having their own children. Being unattached is an outcome of the increasing gap between childhood and adulthood which, as Wallis (1984) has argued, has been further extended by the gradual lengthening of education and wider accessibility of higher education. It is to these unattached groups that world-rejecting movements appeal. They try to provide some certainty to a community of people who face similar problems and difficulties. What seems to be particularly appealing is the offer of radical and immediate solutions to social and personal problems.

Barker, in her famous study *The Making of a Moonie* (1984), found that most members came from happy and secure middle-class homes with parents whose jobs involved some sort of commitment to public service such as doctors, social workers or teachers. She argued that the sect offered a **surrogate** family in which members could find support and comfort beyond the family, whilst fulfilling their desire to serve a community, in the same way as their parents did in the wider society. High patterns of drop-out from NRMs suggest that the need they fulfil is temporary.

The appeal of world-affirming movements

World-affirming sects appeal to those who are likely to have finished education, are married, have children and a mortgage. There are two issues in the modern world that add to the appeal of world-affirming movements. First, as Weber had suggested, the modern world is one in which rationality dominates – that is, one in which magical, unpredictable and ecstatic experiences are uncommon. Furthermore, there is tremendous pressure (for example, through advertising), to become materially, emotionally and sexually successful.

According to Bird (1999), world-affirming sects simultaneously do three things that address these issues.

- They provide a spiritual component in an increasingly rationalised world.
- They provide techniques and knowledge to help people become wealthy, powerful and successful.
- They provide techniques and knowledge which allow people to work on themselves to bring about personal growth.

In some ways, there are common issues which motivate both the young and old. They both live in societies where there is great pressure to succeed and therefore great fear of failure. Religious movements can provide both groups with a means to deal with the fear of failure by providing techniques that lead to personal success.

KEY TERMS

Apocalypticism – the belief in divinely revealed teachings about the final events of history.

Channelling – where a spiritually attuned person (or medium) can allegedly enable a spirit of the dead to communicate with the client through enabling it to enter their body.

Crystals – belief in the healing power of semi-precious stones.

Cult apologists – non-cult members who are religiously tolerant and challenge the misinterpretation of cult practice common in the wider society.

Cultic milieu – a prevailing spiritual predisposition whereby there is a sympathetic body of belief in supernatural rather than scientific explanations.

Deprogrammers – individuals or groups who remove people from sects and re-socialise them back into mainstream society.

Grand narrative – belief system such as religion or science which claims to explain the world.

I Ching – I Ching readings are a form of stichomancy (gaining insight through random readings). Three coins are cast, or the yarrow sticks are divided, and the result is referenced in the I Ching or 'Book of Changes', one of Confucianism's Five Classics. The selected passages convey information and philosophy that pertains to the life of the questioner.

Mantra – personal word or phrase given by a religious teacher (guru) which is used to free the mind of non-spiritual secular awareness and provide a focus for meditation.

Millenarian – belief in a saviour.

Millenialism – belief that human progress is destructively coming to a head and intervention by a supreme being or beings is imminent.

Pragmatic motives – desire to acquire personally beneficial practical outcomes.

Reflexology – a belief that pressure points on the foot relate to parts of the body such that ailments can be cured or a general sense of well-being induced through special techniques of applying pressure to the feet of the client.

Re-sacrilisation – renewed interest and belief in religion and therefore a religious revival.

Surrogate – replacement.

Tarot readings – an occult practice which claims to predict the future through analysis of specific cards which are alleged to relate to the fate of the client.

CHECK YOUR UNDERSTANDING ✓✓✓✓

1 Summarise the membership trends for NRMs shown in the figure earlier in the Topic.

2 Why are the numbers of those involved with NRMs probably much higher than membership figures suggest?

3 Briefly explain what Wallis means by the term 'world-affirming movements'. Give examples.

4 How does Bruce classify New Age movements?

5 What does Wallis mean by the term 'world-rejecting movements'? Give examples.

6 What is the response of mainstream society to world rejecting movements?

7 What are world-accommodating movements? Give examples.

8 Identify and explain two examples of beliefs that predict fundamental world change.

9 Give three reasons for the appeal of NRMs/NAMs.

10 What is the relationship between age, social attachment and the appeal of NRMs?

Research idea

Conduct a survey or interview a sample of other students to discover the extent of New Age beliefs such as re-incarnation among your peers. Try to assess their knowledge and experience of New Age phenomena such as tarot cards, reflexology, crystal healing and astrology.

WWWebtask

Go to the website of the Cult Information Centre (www.cultinformation.org.uk). To what extent do you think their accounts of 'cults' are biased? Explore some of the organisations and incidents mentioned. Use the 'links' part of the site to explore the role of the sociologist Professor Eileen Barker in cult controversies.

EXAM PRACTICE

Extract from AQA-style question

New religious movements can appear at any time. However, they seem most likely to emerge during periods of rapid and unsettling change. Such circumstances can lead to social dislocation, to a feeling of being uprooted and to anomie.

Source: Taylor *et al.*, (1995) *Sociology in Focus*, Ormskirk: Causeway Press

a Describe and briefly explain two characteristics of new religious movements. (8 marks)

b Examine the view that the emergence of new religious movements is a response to social disorganisation and change. (12 marks)

OCR-style AS question

a Identify and explain two differences between sects and cults. (15 marks)

b Outline and discuss the view that indicates renewed interest and belief in religion and therefore a religious revival. (30 marks)

The Waco siege

The siege of the headquarters of the Branch Davidian sect in Waco Texas in 1993 provides an interesting example of the dynamics of the relationship with world rejecting movements and the wider society. The sect predicted the end of the world and separated itself from the wider society. Its leader, David Koresh, was seen to be a charismatic 'God incarnate'. Membership involved whole families as well as people who had left their families to join. The wider societies' view was that Koresh had captured and indoctrinated people and was sexually abusing them. The group had also armed themselves in preparation for the 'end' and this became the excuse for police, military and FBI involvement. A 51-day stalemate between federal agents and members of the cult ended in a fiery tragedy after federal agents botched their assault on the sect's compound. About 80 Branch Davidians, including Koresh himself and at least 17 children, died when the compound burned to the ground in a suspicious blaze in September 1993. The FBI claim that the fire was a mass suicide attempt by members of the sect whilst survivors claim that the FBI fired an incendiary device. Earlier, on February 28, four agents were shot to death in a failed attack on the heavily armed compound, hence, as some argue, motivating the assault. Jurors in the criminal trial of surviving cult members were unable to determine who fired the first shot. Cult apologists and surviving members, many of whom still believe that Koresh will return, continue to criticise the Federal government both for its religious intolerance and selective application of gun controls in a state which generally defends the right to possess firearms.

Adapted from: N. Jorgensen *et al.* (1997) *Sociology: An Interactive Approach*, London: Collins Educational and Britannica.com

Read Item A and answer the following questions.

1 Use Wallis's typology of new religious movements to classify the Branch Davidians.

   Explain your answer.

2 Identify the key causes of the Waco siege? Who do you believe was responsible?

   Why?

3 How does the tragedy illustrate problems in the relationship between world-rejecting movements and the wider society?

The 'New Age'

The NAM 'is an eclectic collection of psychological and spiritual techniques that are rooted in Eastern mysticism, lack scientific evaluative data, and are promoted zealously by followers of diverse idealized leaders claiming transformative powers,' (Michael D. Langone, Ph.D., *Cult Observer*, Volume 10, No. 1, 1993)

There are four main streams of thought within the NAM:

1 the 'transformational training' stream, represented by groups such as *est* and *Lifespring*;
2 the intellectual stream, represented by publications such as *The Tao of Physics*;
3 the lifestyle stream, represented by publications such as *Whole Life Monthly*, and organizations such as the Green Party; and
4 the occult stream, represented by astrology, Tarot, palmistry, crystal power, and the like. It is important to keep in mind that within this diversity there is much disagreement. Many intellectual new agers, for example, deride adherents of the occult stream of the new age.

The NAM, then, is too 'fuzzy' and disparate to constitute a great conspiracy, as some have claimed. Nor is it a cult, although cults exist within the NAM. The NAM is, in essence, a world view, that has attained a high enough level of popularity to challenge the two world views that have been in competition through most of this century – the Judeo/Christian tradition and the secular scientific tradition.

The NAM is similar to traditional religions in that it posits the existence of a supernatural realm, or at least something beyond 'atoms and the void.' But the NAM adherent believes that spiritual knowledge and power can be achieved through the discovery of the proper techniques. These techniques may be silly, as in crystal power. But they may be very sophisticated, as in some forms of yoga. Its concepts have permeated our culture in a quiet, almost invisible way. For example, a Gallup survey of teenagers, several years ago, found that approximately one third of churchgoing Christian teenagers believed in reincarnation, a fundamental new age belief. Reincarnation is antithetical to Christianity. Yet, one third of church going Christian teenagers believe in it!

Professor Arthur Dole, University of Pennsylvania, *Cultic Studies Journal*, Vol. 7, No. 1, 1990

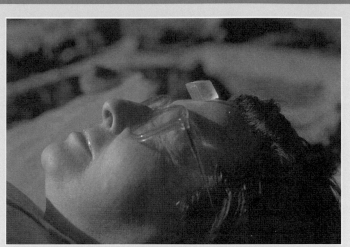
Spiritualist resting with crystal on forehead

Tarot cards

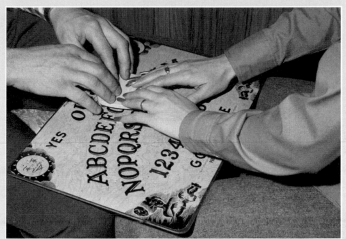
Using a ouija board

4 'The New Age is a mix and match of religions, therapies and astrologies which are claimed to have transformative powers'. Illustrate this statement with reference to Items B and C.

5 Use the passage and any other information to show how 'New Age concepts have permeated (seeped into) our culture in a quiet, almost invisible way'.

Church persists with sexual apartheid, say women priests

Women clergy yesterday accused the Church of England of discrimination and prejudice against them nine years after the church voted in favour of female ordination. They accused bishops of bending over backwards to accommodate the few parishes which still refused to accept women priests and they said sexual apartheid persisted.

A report by the female pressure group GRAS – the group for the rescinding of the act of synod – said: 'There are a number of reasons – fear of conflict, misogyny, the bishops' wish to present a united front to the world, a devotion to the old boy network or, in some cases, to a closeted gay network, laziness, indifference, an excessive concern about what Rome thinks and a habitual stance of not taking women seriously.'

A fifth of the ordained clergy in the Church of England – 2,000 – are women but some claim they are accused to their faces of being witches. Some male clergy decline to be touched by female priests during ordination, claiming they are tainted. John Broadhurst, the Bishop of Fulham, said this year that 'proper women would not think of becoming priests'.

GRAS is pressing for the church's parliament to abolish regulations giving those opposed to women's ordination special treatment. The Rev Mary Robins, the group's coordinator, said: 'We live in a country which supports human rights but has a state church which discriminates against women.'

Christina Rees, a member of the Archbishops' Council – the Church's executive – said: 'There is deep prejudice against women and it seems to be perfectly all right for certain people to behave towards women in ways that would not be acceptable in other professions. They are called witches and priestesses with the tribal, pagan connotations that implies.'

The *Guardian*, Thursday October 25, 2001

Gender and church attendance in Britain and Northern Ireland

Attendance	Britain		Northern Ireland	
	Men	**Women**	**Men**	**Women**
Frequent	37	63	39	61
Regular	35	65	57	43
Rare	48	52	49	51

Source: *British Social Attitudes Survey* (1991) quoted in S. Bruce (1995) *Religion in Modern Britain*, Oxford: Oxford University Press

1 What reasons are suggested for the existence of 'sexual apartheid' in the Church of England?

2 Summarise the patterns of church attendance given in the table above.

3 Look at both pieces of information above. Why might you expect the Church of England to have a rather more positive attitude to women?

4 Suggest reasons why women appear to be more religious than men?

The decline of the goddess

Women have not always been subordinate to men where religion is concerned. In fact, until about 4,000 years ago, the opposite appeared to be so. Large numbers of **effigies** of a naked, pregnant mother, goddess figures have been uncovered by archaeologists across Europe and Asia. In the days when people worshipped the gods of nature (who were believed to provide sustenance to those entirely reliant upon them for good weather, fertile land, abundant food to harvest, healthy offspring and so forth), the female sex was seen as closer to nature. They represented the mysteries of life and fertility. As Armstrong (1993) put it:

The Earth produced plants and nourished them in rather the same way as a woman gave birth to a child and fed it from her own body. The magical power of the Earth seemed vitally interconnected with the mysterious creativity of the female sex.

Armstrong argues that male aggression exhibited through the invasion of these societies by more male-dominated cultures from the Northern hemisphere and the Middle East, needed a **patriarchal rationale** in order to justify such behaviour. Male gods became increasingly important, introducing a more aggressive spirituality. **Monotheism** – the belief in one God rather than many (**Polytheism**) – was the final death knoll for the goddess and the major world religions have all adopted the same male god.

Images of God in different religions

Although there is only one god for most contemporary religions, men and women tend to view him differently. Davie (1994) showed that:

- women see God more as a god of love, comfort and forgiveness
- men see God more as a god of power and control.

Suggest reasons why men and women may view God in rather different ways?

This implies a situation whereby, God has preferred, gendered characteristics according to the sex of the believer. A tacit recognition of the female connection to spiritual influence can also be seen in the Jewish religion whereby a person can only be Jewish if their mother is. But, on the other hand, some orthodox Jewish men include the following words in daily prayer:

> *Blessed art thou O Lord our God that I was not born a slave*
> *Blessed art thou O Lord our God that I was not born a woman*

Christianity is also inherently patriarchal with men made in 'the image and glory of God' and women made 'for the glory of man', as the following passage from the New Testament shows:

> *Wives be subject to your husbands, as to the Lord. For the husband is the head of the wife as Christ is the head of the church (Ephesians 5:22–24)*

> (*The Holy Bible: New International version. Inclusive Language Edition*, (1996) London: Hodder & Stoughton)

There are many female characters in the biblical texts, and some are portrayed as acting charitably or bravely, but the prime parts are reserved for males. There is no female equivalent to Moses, for example, and in the New Testament all the apostles are men.

The most prominent females in the Bible, Eve and Mary mother of Jesus, serve to reinforce patriarchal ideas regarding the dangers of female sexuality and the virtues of motherhood. Similarly the Qur'an, the sacred text of Islam contends that 'men are in charge of women'. Even Buddhism (in which females appear as important figures in the teachings of some Buddhist orders), is dominated (like Christianity) by a patriarchal power structure in which the feminine is mainly associated with the secular, powerless, profane and imperfect.

Sexuality and religion

Women's bodies and sexuality are also felt to be dangerous by many religions. Because women menstruate and give birth they are considered to have a greater capacity to 'pollute' religious rituals. In addition, their presence may distract the men from their more important roles involving worship.

Bird (1999) points out that sexuality is an important issue in many religions. Roman Catholic priests are expected to be **celibate**, while (some interpretations of) Christianity and Islam (amongst others) are opposed to homosexuality. Turner (1983) suggests that a disciplinary role with respect to sexuality is central to religion. The widespread importance of **asceticism**, a self-disciplined existence in which pleasure (especially physical pleasure) does not predominate, means that in order to properly carry out priestly duties, there needs to be a degree of policing of the body – and the presence of women makes this more difficult.

Women in religious organisations

Patriarchal attitudes have meant that women have been barred from serving as priests in many of the world's great religions until recently and the more traditional factions continue to do so. Islamic groups, Orthodox Jews and the Roman Catholic church continue to exclude women from the religious hierarchy.

Although women ministers have long been accepted in some sects and denominations, the Catholic and Anglican churches persisted in formally supporting inequalities of gender. However, in 1992 the Church of England voted to make the priesthood at last open to women. Many groups opposed the decision, including the organisation Women Against the Ordination of Women. According to this group, the full acceptance of women is a **blasphemous** deviation from biblical truth.

There have been some challenges to the patriarchal structure of organised religion. Judaism, for example, has long elevated women to the role of Rabbi in its non-orthodox denominations. Gender-neutral language has been introduced in many hymns and prayers and the requirement to love, honour and *obey* is now optional in the Christian marriage ceremony.

Suggest some other situations where it has been argued that language creates and reinforces prejudice and inequality.

Feminism and religion

Many Christian feminists argue that there will never be gender equality in the church so long as notions of gender are attached to the understanding of God. Mary Daly (1973;1978) goes as far as to suggest that Christianity itself is a patriarchal myth. Although herself originally a Catholic, she argues that the Christian story eliminated other 'Goddess' religions. She

Exploring images of God

Item A

Ancient fertility goddess

Item B

1 How do the images in Items A and B reflect changes in religion?

argues that Christianity is rooted in male 'sado-rituals' with its 'torture cross symbolism', and that it embodies women-hating.

Simone de Beauvoir in her pioneering feminist book *The Second Sex* (1953) saw the role of religion in a similar way to Marx. However, she saw it as oppressive to women in particular. Religion is used by the oppressors (men) to control the oppressed group (women). It also serves as a way of compensating women for their second-class status. Like Marx's proletariat, religion gives women the false belief that they will be compensated for their suffering on earth by equality in heaven. She concludes: [Religion] … gives her the guide, father, lover, divine guardian she longs for nostalgically; it feeds her daydreams; it fills her empty hours. But, above all, it confirms the social order, it justifies her resignation by giving hope of a better future in a sexless heaven'.

El Sadawi (1980), a Muslim feminist does not blame religion in itself for its oppressive influences on women but the patriarchal domination of religion that came with the development of **monotheistic** religions. Such religions she argues 'drew inspiration and guidance from the patriarchal and class societies prevalent at the time'. Men wrote their scriptures, and the interpretation of them was almost exclusively male-orientated. This has on many occasions enabled men to use religion as an abuse of power. In the fourteenth century, for example, the Catholic church declared that women who treated illnesses without special training could be executed as witches. This, of course, had nothing to do with the fact that traditional remedies administered by women threatened the authority of the emerging male-dominated medical profession!

 Identify two types of feminism and explain their similarities and differences.

Is religion necessarily patriarchal?

It should not be assumed that all religions are equally oppressive to women. Even in Catholicism becoming a nun can be viewed as either oppressive or highly liberating. Holm and Bowker (1994) go as far as to suggest that religious organisations developed exclusively for women are the forerunners of the modern women's movement in that they separate women from men (and therefore oppression) and they enhance women's sense of identity.

Today, Women's orders, show a considerable diversity in their beliefs and modes of life. In some convents, sisters dress in full traditional habit and keep to established routines. Other communities, by contrast, have dropped many of the old regulations. Restrictions on talking at certain periods of the day have been relaxed, together with rules about dress and the position of the body, (such as walking with the hands folded).

Judaism has allowed women to become rabbis since 1972, and even some Christian religions, particularly Quakerism, have never been oppressive to women. According to Kaur-Singh (1994) Sikh gurus pleaded the cause for the emancipation of Indian womenhood, fully supporting them in improving their condition in society.

Some writers highlight how there are signs of hope developing. Gross (1994) detects signs of a post-patriarchal Buddhism developing in the West which does not differentiate roles for male and female members. Leila Badawi (1994) has noted aspects of Islam that are positive for women, such as being able to keep their own family name when they marry. In fact, most converts to Islam are female. Numerous writers have highlighted how veiling (the covering of the entire face in the company of men outside the family) rather than being a submission to patriarchy, is in fact a means of ethnic and gender assertiveness. Leila Ahmed (1992) suggests that the veil is a means by which Muslim women can become involved in modern society whilst maintaining a sense of modesty and correctness. As she puts it: 'it [Islamic dress] is a uniform of both transition and arrival signalling entrance into and determination to move forward in modern society'.

Why are women more religious than men?

Whatever women's influence and status may have been in religious organisations, studies have consistently shown that women are more religious than men. Miller and Hoffmann (1995) report that women:

- are more likely to express a greater interest in religion
- have a stronger personal religious commitment
- attend church more often.

These patterns appear to hold true throughout life, irrespective of the kind of religious organisation (cult, sect or church) or religious belief (astrology, magic, spirits, and so on).

One explanation for the more religious orientation of women is offered by Greely (1992). He argues that before women acquire a partner and have children, their religiosity is not dissimilar to men's (although slightly more committed). But, 'Once you start "taking care" of people, perhaps, you begin implicitly to assume greater responsibility for their "ultimate" welfare'. Greeley contends that women are more involved in caring than in practical responsibilities. Caring, it seems, tends to be associated with a more religious outlook.

Using evidence from other aspects of your studies, give two pieces of evidence that indicate that 'women are more involved in caring than practical responsibilities'.

Miller and Hoffmann (1995) identify two main explanations for such gender differences.

Differential socialisation

Females are taught to be more submissive, passive, obedient and nurturing than males. These traits are compatible with religiosity as such characteristics are highly esteemed by most religions. By the same token, men who internalise these norms tend to be more religious than men who do not.

Differential roles

Females have lower rates of participation in paid work and this, it is argued, gives women more time for church-related activities, and more need for a source of personal identity and commitment. They also have higher rates of participation in child-rearing which also increases religiosity because it coincides with a concern for family well-being.

Women and new religious movements

Sects

Women tend to participate more in sects than men. Bruce (1995) has suggested (although difficult to estimate) the ratio of female to male involvement is similar to that in established religion at about 2:1.

Explain why it is difficult to collect accurate figures on participation in sects and new religious movements.

Women are more likely than men to experience poverty and those who experience economic deprivation are more likely to join sects. As Thompson (1996) notes 'they may not have the economic and social standing of others in society, but sect members have the promise of salvation and the knowledge that they are enlightened'.

Glock and Stark (1969) identify a number of different types of deprivation in addition to the economic, all of which are more likely to apply to women. They suggest that people who form or join sects may have experienced one or even a number of these.

- *Social deprivation* – this may stem from a lack of power, prestige and status. For example, if people experience a lack of satisfaction or status in employment they may seek it via a religious sect. Those in unsatisfying lower-middle-class jobs (mainly occupied by women), may find satisfaction in the **evangelical goals** set by **conversionist** sects such as Jehovah's Witnesses or Mormons.

Give examples of 'lower-middle-class jobs performed mainly by women that are often "unsatisfying"'.

- *Organismic deprivation* – this is experienced by those who suffer physical and mental problems (again more likely among women than men). For example, people may turn to sects in the hope of being healed or as an alternative to drugs or alcohol.
- *Ethical deprivation* – people may perceive the world to be in moral decline and retreat into an **introversionist sect** which separates itself from the world, for example Jim Jones' People's Temple. Again, women tend to be more morally conservative than men.

In the nineteenth century many sects were initiated by women: Ellen White set up the Seventh Day Adventists, Mary Baker Eddy founded Christian Science, Ann Lee founded the Shakers and the Fox sisters began the Spiritualist movement.

Cults

Cults involve a highly individual, privatised version of religious activity. This is mainly (although not exclusively) involved with the promotion of a notion of personal 'improvement'. Even where wider issues are addressed (such as social problems like crime, unemployment, the environment), the solutions offered tend to be couched in personal terms (meditation, greater consciousness, etc.). This 'private sphere' of cult activity relates to traditional gender roles for women which are based in the 'private' arena of the home. Women are also more inclined to see in themselves a need for self-improvement.

Give two examples of social issues that may have been 'hidden' because they take place in the 'private arena of the home'.

New Age movements

Historically, wherever Nature is conceptualised the role of women has been seen in terms of their 'essential femininity', that is, as being naturally different creatures to males – more attuned to the supposed natural rhythms of life. Thus, within the philosophies of New Age cults, women tend to be afforded a much higher status than men. This is one reason that may explain higher female involvement in NAMs. Many New Age movements emphasise the 'natural' such as herbal and homeopathic remedies, aromatherapy and massage.

Women and fundamentalism

The resurgence of religious fundamentalism over the past decade has played a major role in attempting to reverse the trend of women's increasing autonomy and their pursuit of fulfilment beyond motherhood.

- In America, opposition to women controlling their fertility through abortion has sometimes ended in violence with right-wing, religious fundamentalist pro-life groups adopting near terrorist tactics to close clinics down.
- Despite India's long history of reform and modernisation, the rise of Hindu fundamentalism has made it difficult for governments there to intervene in family life or encourage greater freedom for women despite their commitment to preventing the oppression of members of certain lower castes.
- Fundamentalist groups in Iran, Israel, Afghanistan and parts of the former Soviet Union similarly insist on ruthlessly conserving or reinstating women's traditional positions.

Cohen and Kennedy (2000) suggest that 'the desire to restore fundamentalist religious values and social practices is associated with the fear that any real increase in women's freedom of choice and action will undermine the foundations of tradition, religion, morality and, it could be argued, male control'.

Women's traditional roles centre around child-rearing and the home. They are thus responsible for transmitting religious values from one generation to the next and upholding all that is most sacred in the lives of family members. Fundamentalism, both in the West such as the **Christian Right** or the **Nation of Islam** in America and elsewhere, has often emphasised the significance of protecting and defending women. The spin-off is that this re-empowers men by removing some of the **ambiguities** that have been associated with the modern world. But, as feminists assert, the apparent position of importance such women experience in upholding the faith, brings with it powerlessness and sometimes abuse at the hands of husbands and kinsman.

However, not all women are unwilling victims of the return to traditional roles – as the work on Muslim women and veiling demonstrates. Research by Woodhead and Heelas (2000) shows how women converting to orthodox Judaism in the US are actually attracted by the status in the home that it provides them with. Such women can also be seen as seeking to remove the ambiguities of modernity as they perceive them.

KEY TERMS

Ambiguities – uncertain issues, having more than one meaning.

Asceticism – the practice of severe self-discipline and denial of individual pleasure.

Blasphemous – insulting to religious beliefs.

Celibate – deliberately refraining from sexual activity.

Christian Right – fundamentalist and right-wing Christian groups, particularly powerful in the southern states of America.

Conversionist – see Key Terms in Topic 2.

Effigies – images or statues.

Evangelical goals – the aim of converting others to your faith.

Introversionist sect – world-rejecting sect.

Monotheism – belief in one God.

Nation of Islam – black, radical, American Islamic organisation.

Patriarchal rationale – an explanation of events motivated by a desire for male domination.

Polytheism – belief in many Gods.

1 What evidence is there to show that women were not always subordinate to men in religion?

2 What caused men to dominate religion and religious practice?

3 What evidence for patriarchy is there in the world's major religions:
 a) in terms of their scriptures?
 b) in terms of roles in religious institutions?

4 Why, according to Bird, is sexuality such an important issue for many religions?

5 How do feminists view the role of religion?

6 What evidence is there to show that some religions are not necessarily patriarchal?

7 a) What evidence is there for women's greater religiosity?
 b) What explanations have been given for this?

8 Why is it more difficult to measure the extent of women's involvement in sects?

9 What reasons are given for women's greater involvement in NRMs?

10 How has the resurgence of fundamentalism affected the role of women?

WWWebtask

Go the the Google website http://www.google.co.uk Type in 'The role of Women in religion'. Select an article on women in various religious organisations past and present and summarise it.

EXAM PRACTICE

Extract from AQA-style question

In 1991, in Britain and Northern Ireland almost two thirds of frequent Christian church attenders were women, but not until 1992, after considerable pressure, did the Church of England decide to ordain women, although they still cannot be bishops. The Roman Catholic Church still opposes the ordination of women as priests.

Adapted from: Lawson, Jones & Moores (2000) *Advanced Sociology through Diagrams*, Oxford: Oxford Revision Guides

a Identify and explain two reasons why church attenders are predominately female. (8 marks)

b Examine the extent to which religion acts as an agent of social control over women. (12 marks)

Extract from OCR AS question

Outline and discuss the view that religion, in general, has negative consequences for women.
(30 marks)   *OCR, Jan 2002*

Item A

movement to be able to communicate without being on show'. She found that far from being invisible it made her stand out as a Muslim and also helped her to avoid 'lecherous stares or worse' from men. The second women, Maryam, was a middle-aged Algerian living in France. Upon moving to France she felt it more appropriate to wear a veil. She commented that 'it is difficult enough to live in a big foreign city without having the extra burden of being molested in the street because you are a woman'. The Islamic revolution in Iran had also made her more aware of the importance of Islam and she felt her conduct set a good example for the future generation. The third respondent, Fatima, was an older woman. She was less positive about veiling, seeing it as 'just a trend' but recognised that to turn against some of the less desirable western values, e.g. the over-emphasis on women as sex objects, was a good thing. Although she felt that modest conduct was important, in her opinion veiling should be a matter of choice.

Adapted from: 'Women and the Veil: Personal responses to Global Process' in L. Ahmed and I. Donnan (eds.) (1994) *Islam, Globalisation and Postmodernity*, London: Routledge

Read Item B.

1 What criticisms could be made of Watson's research?

2 How does Watson's work serve as a caution to sociologists who interpret the practices of unfamiliar religions in simplistic terms?

Item B
The meaning of veiling

According to the Qu'ran, women should exercise religious modesty or *hijab* because their seductiveness might lead men astray. Many writers, including some Islamic feminists, have argued that this has been misinterpreted by men to mean that women must cover their bodies and faces in the presence of men who are not relatives, with the patriarchal motive of controlling women. Western commentators also are critical of the practice, seeing it as evidence of repression. As Julie Burchill (2000) writing in the *Guardian* commented, 'such women carry round with them a mobile prison'.

Watson (1994) however, demonstrated that the veil has the potential to liberate. She interviewed three Muslim women who had alternative perspectives on the practice of veiling (covering the face and hair). Nadia, a second generation British Asian woman studying medicine at university chose to start wearing a veil at 16. She commented, 'It is liberating to have the freedom of

Item C
Jewish women seeking traditional gender roles

Despite feminist criticisms of the prescriptive roles ascribed to women by many religions, significant numbers of women continue to be attracted to such religions. Davidman (1991) explored the reasons why culturally advantaged North American women were converting to Orthodox Judaism. Davidman's conclusion is that it is precisely because such religion maintains a clear distinction between the sexes that it becomes attractive to women who in an increasingly dislocating world, value domesticity and their future role as wives and mothers. In contrast to the feminist goal of sexual liberation, careers and variation in family patterns, Orthodox Judaism offered clear gender norms, assistance in finding partners and explicit guidelines for family life. It legitimated their desires for the traditional identity of wives and mothers in nuclear families. Also, women are seen as central in the Jewish religious world and are given special status. In contrast to the liberal feminist goal of equality such women seek the alternative of equity – the idea of equal but separate roles.

Adapted from: L. Woodhead and P. Heelas (2000) *Religion in Modern Times: An Interpretive Anthology*, Oxford: Blackwell

3 Why do the women described in Item C want to convert to Orthodox Judaism?

4 What might such women say has been the disadvantage of 'Women's liberation'?

Women in religious organisations

The theme of gendered approaches to caring roles has been researched in the context of female clergy by Simon and Nadell (1995). They refer to their earlier in-depth interviews with 32 female Jewish rabbis. They asked, 'As a rabbi who is also a woman, do you think you carry out your rabbinical role differently than a male rabbi who is the same age as you are and who was ordained from the seminary?' Almost all the women rabbis said yes. These women described themselves as less formal, more approachable, more egalitarian, more inclined to touch and hug, less likely to intrude their egos, and less likely to seek centre stage. Some of them used the phrase 'own the ritual', by which they meant they wanted ceremony participants to take charge of fulfilling rituals rather than residing over all of the rituals themselves. Simon and Nadell also reported that 17 out of 27 Protestant clergy who were women described themselves as less formal, more people oriented, more into pastoral care, and less concerned about power struggles than male clergy.

Adapted from: R. J. Simon and P. S. Nadell (1995) 'In the Same Voice or is it Different? Gender and Clergy' *Sociology of Religion*, 56 (1).

5 How might the researchers in Item D argue that women can make better religious leaders than men?

Getting you thinking

Membership in the United Kingdom (thousands)

Group	1970	1980	1990	2000
Christian: Trinitarian* of whom:	9,272	7,529	6,624	5,917
Anglican (C of E)	2,987	2,180	1,728	1,654
Catholic	2,746	2,455	2,198	1,768
Free Churches	1,629	1,285	1,299	1,278
Presbyterian	1,751	1,437	1,214	989
Orthodox	159	172	185	235
Christian: Non-Trinitarian**	276	349	455	533
Buddhist	10	15	30	50
Hindu	80	120	140	165
Jewish	375	321	356	383
Muslim	130	305	495	675
Sikh	100	150	250	400
Others	20	40	55	85

*Trinitarian churches – are those which accept a view of God as the three eternal persons: God the Father, God the Son and God the Holy Spirit. These are the great majority of Christian churches.

**Non-Trinitarian churches accept a range of different views of God. These include sects such as: Christian Scientists, the Church of Scientology, Jehovah's Witnesses, Mormons (Church of Jesus Christ of Latter Day Saints), Spiritualists and the Unification Church (Moonies).

Adapted from: P. Brierley (ed.), *Religious Trends* 2000, London: HarperCollins

1 What is the overall trend in the membership of Trinitarian churches?

2 What do the figures tell us about ethnicity and religious practice?

3 In what ways does religion influence the way that you lead your life?

4 How important is it to you that children practise their faith or that they pass on their religious heritage to their children?

5 Does religion give you a personal motivation and strength that helps you to cope with the stresses and difficulties involved in society?

It is likely that most 'white' members of the class would have had little to say with regard to the role of religion in their lives. On the other hand, students from different ethnic backgrounds may have said a great deal more. The statistics above show the continuing importance of religion in the lives of many minority groups in Britain. Why this is the case is much more difficult to explain and this is even harder when you take into account differences between first generation immigrants and their children who were born in Britain.

The United Kingdom in the twenty-first century is a multi-faith society. Everyone has the right to religious freedom. A wide variety of religious organisations and groups are permitted to conduct their **rites** and ceremonies, promote their beliefs within the limits of the law, own property, and run schools and a range of other charitable activities. For the first time in the UK since 1851, the 2001 Census included a question on religion. When the answers to this question have been analysed, they will provide extensive official information on patterns of religious identity in the United Kingdom.

What is the Census? What problems are associated with finding out people's religious beliefs using this method?

Religion and community solidarity

A study by the Policy Studies Institute found that 74% of Muslim respondents said that religion was 'very important'. This compared with around 45% for Hindus and Sikhs. In contrast, only 11% for white people described themselves as belonging to the Church of England. Amongst Muslim men over the age of 35, four in five reported that they visit a mosque at least once every week.

Immigrants to Britain have placed a greater emphasis on religion than the indigenous population for a number of possible reasons.

- People had high levels of belief before migration, and (as Weber has suggested), as members of deprived groups, tended to be more religious. Religion provides an explanation for disadvantage and offers hope possibly of salvation, if not elsewhere then in the afterlife.

● Religion helps bond new communities – particularly when under threat. As Durkheim has argued, it provides members with a sense of shared norms and values, symbolised through rituals that unite them as a distinctive social group.

 *According to functionalists, which other social institutions provide members with 'shared norms and values'? How?*

However, religion has also become a basis for conflicts between cultures. The dominant culture often sees minority cultures in a negative light as there is the feeling that newcomers to British society should **assimilate**. This view is characterised by such statements as 'when in Rome, do as the Romans do'. Ethnic-minority issues such as arranged marriages, the refusal of Sikhs to wear motor-cycle helmets and the growth in the number of religious temples and mosques (whilst many Christian churches have closed) suggest an unwillingness to assimilate and have created resentment from the host community. However, many second, and third, generation ethnic-minority Britons were born in this country and their refusal to fully assimilate has led to a re-evaluation of what being British actually means. Racially motivated riots in northern towns in the summer of 2001 highlighted the continuing difficulties experienced by ethnic minorities.

In studying religion and ethnicity it is clear that religions offer much more than spiritual fulfilment and each in their way re-affirm the ethnic identity of their adherents, albeit in uniquely different ways. Before examining specific cultural and religious groupings, we need a brief overview of the main ethnic-minority religions in the UK.

Apart from religion, what other social influences are there on identity?

Religion and ethnic identity

Whilst there are significant differences in **religiosity** within the Asian and African-Caribbean communities it is possible to make some initial generalisations about them. First, Caribbeans were mainly Christian on arrival in Britain but were unable to access the existing religious institutions here. However, Hindus, Sikhs and Muslims, (for whom religion was part of their 'difference') had virtually no existing religious organisations and places of worship in Britain to join. From this flowed different experiences. On the one hand, the Caribbeans tried to join existing religious institutions and had to come to terms with the fact that the Church and its congregations were aligned to the general pattern of racism in British society.

What is the difference between institutional and individual racism? What factors might cause racism in a society?

On the other hand, Asians had to make a collective effort to establish and practise their faith in a radically new social setting. Modood *et al.* (1994) point out that whilst for Asians their religion was intricately connected with their status as an ethnic group, this was not the case for Caribbeans (see figure below). Even for those who saw their Christianity as part of family tradition and culture, their religion was not significantly part of their sense of ethnic difference. However, distinctively Caribbean forms of Christian spirituality in both the mainstream churches and in the black-led churches have mushroomed in the past couple of decades, as some Caribbeans have sought to establish their own churches and styles of worship.

Differences in the significance of religion for first generation Asian and African-Caribbean migrants to Britain

	African-Caribbean	Asian
Role of religion	Religion is used as a means of coping with the worries and the pressures of life through the joyful nature of prayer, as much through its immediacy and mood-affecting quality as its long-term contribution to personal development.	Asian groups tended to speak of control over selfish desires and of fulfilling one's responsibilities to others, especially family members. Prayer is seen in terms of duty, routine and the patterning of their lives.
Religion and family life	Used to develop trust, love, mutual responsibilities and the learning of right and wrong within the context of the family. Caribbeans express an individualistic or **voluntaristic** view of religion. Children should decide for themselves whether they maintain religious commitment into adulthood.	Used in a similar way but Asians tend to adopt a collective or conformist approach. The expectation of parents is that their children would follow in adulthood the religion they had been brought up in; not to do so was to betray one's upbringing or to let one's family down.
Religion and social life	Little importance beyond fostering and maintaining a spiritual, moral and ethical outlook. The church offers opportunities to socialise and to organise social events in an otherwise privatised community of member families.	Muslims tend to see conformity to Islamic law and Islam as a comprehensive way of life affecting attitudes to alcohol, food, dress and choice of marriage partner. The influence of religion is less extreme for most Sikhs and Hindus but its importance for the first generation is still considerable.

Adapted from: T. Modood, S. Beisham, and S. Virdee, (1994) *Changing Ethnic Identities*, London: Policy Studies Institute

Religious commitment amongst second-generation members of ethnic minorities

When examining the position of members of ethnic minorities born in Britain, Modood (1994) found that there appears to be an overall decline in the importance of religion for each group.

- In each ethnic group fewer second-generation than first-generation respondents said that religion was of personal importance to them, and fewer said they observed the various rules and requirements, (for example, the prohibition of alcohol).
- Some second-generation Asians spoke of having to go to the temple for certain family or community functions and of fasting and praying out of fear of the criticism that would otherwise be incurred; and of marrying within their faith in order to avoid conflict with their parents and families.
- Most second-generation respondents did not regularly attend a place of religious worship and even those who said that religion was important wished to interpret their religious traditions and scriptures flexibly.

Modood found that the simple contrast between Caribbeans and Asians no longer holds for the second generation. Muslims appeared the most religiously committed Asian group, Caribbeans followed and Sikhs were the least religiously committed. When asked how they saw themselves, virtually none of the second-generation Punjabis spontaneously said 'Sikh'. However, in the early 1980s Beatrice Drury studied a much larger sample of 16 to 20 year old Sikh girls and found that, if prompted, all replied positively. (Drury, 1991).

Religious practice and belief for many Asian young people may have become of secondary importance to the identity-giving role that religion provides. Johal (1998) has pointed out how in a country such as Britain where **religious pluralism** is still a long way off, many British Asians have chosen to preserve and uphold the religious and cultural doctrines of their parents as a means to assert a coherent and powerful identity and to resist racism. As Johal puts it 'holding on to these doctrines can provide a kind of **empowerment** through difference'. He also notes that many second-and third- generation Asians carefully negotiate their associations with religion. Issues such as choice of marriage partners, intra-ethnic marriage and diet '… often lead to the adoption of a position of selective cultural preference, a kind of code-switching in which young Asians move between one culture and another, depending on context and whether overt "Britishness" or pronounced "Asianness" is most appropriate'.

It certainly appears to be the case that Muslim women, often commented on for their apparent submissiveness and repression, have actually adapted well to the challenge of maintaining their cultural and religious identity whilst becoming effective, well-integrated members of mainstream society. A number of studies such as of Butler (1995) have explored this **cultural hybridity**. Indeed, many Asians have sought to separate culture from religion in an attempt to

maintain religiosity whilst moving on culturally. Many see their parents as stuck in a time-warp from which they wish to escape intact in terms of their religiosity. Recent research shows how veiling and the wearing of traditional dress actually give Muslim girls greater freedom from patriarchal attitudes experienced by many white girls. (This is discussed further in Topic 4.)

Item A

Voluntary-aided schools 1998

These schools receive 85% of their building costs from the government and all of their running costs are paid for by the local authority.

Denomination	Number of Schools
Church of England	1,875
Roman Catholic	1,817
Jewish	17
Methodist	4
Seventh Day Adventist	1
Muslim	1
	TOTAL 3,715

Students at an Islamic Primary School.

1 Look at Item A. Refer back to the table in 'Getting you thinking' and compare the proportion of different religious schools to the proportion of members of different religions. How fair is the current distribution of religious schools?

2 What are the arguments for and against the existence of religious schools?

3 To what extent do you agree that there should be more religious schools for ethnic-minority religions?

4 Should religious education be compulsory in schools? What should be taught in religious education?

Apart from religion, what other agents of socialisation are likely to influence the gender identity of Asian girls born in Britain? What images of gender are they likely to be exposed to?

Case study 1: Muslims in Britain

Although early migrants saw themselves as temporary visitors, successive changes to immigration laws encouraged them to settle. The subsequent restructuring of manufacturing industries in the 1970s and the disappearance of many of the jobs in northern Britain for which South-east Asians had originally been recruited, encouraged a large number of South-east Asians to become self-employed in the service sector. This was also affected by religious and cultural factors. A survey in the 1990s (see Metcalf *et al.* 1996) found that two thirds of self-employed Pakistani people mentioned that being their own boss meant it was easier for them to perform their religious duties, and suggested that their strong religious faith gave them confidence to set up on their own despite a lack of formal qualifications and poor access to finance.

As both a reflection and a reinforcement of the transition to seeing themselves as settlers, in the 1960s Pakistanis and Bangladeshis established a wide range of community organisations. They began at the same time to be more self-consciously Muslim and more observant in the practice of their faith. Factors affecting this strengthening of religious belief and practice included:

- the desire to build a sense of corporate identity and strength in a situation of material disadvantage, and in an alien and largely hostile surrounding culture
- the desire, now that communities contained both children, on the one hand, and elders on the other, to keep the generations together, and to transmit traditional values to children and young people
- the desire for inner spiritual resources to withstand the pressures of racism and **Islamophobia**, and the threat to South-Asian culture and customs posed by Western materialism and permissiveness.

What norms and values might be associated with 'Western materialism and permissiveness'?

The increased influence of Islam in the politics of Pakistan and Bangladesh in the 1970s, and the increased influence of oil-exporting countries in international affairs, most of which were Muslim, contributed to Muslim self-confidence and assertiveness within Britain. In addition, a sense of community strength grew through the 1980s from successful local campaigns to assert Muslim values and concerns – for example, for **halal food** to be served in schools and hospitals. Events such as the Rushdie affair (see 'Exploring ethnicity and religion') and the recent bombing of the Twin Towers have served to promote even greater assertiveness. One key consideration in discussing the experience of Muslims in particular, concerns their younger age profile than all other groups. Around 70 % of all British Muslims are under the age of 25.

Case study 2: Pentecostalism

Immigrants from the Caribbean have settled throughout Britain but are concentrated in inner-city areas. Many have established strong, culturally distinctive communities in urban areas such as Brixton in South London. However, whilst religious institutions are central to Asian communities, this is not necessarily the case where African-Caribbeans are concerned. The more individualist relationship that committed Christian Caribbeans have had to their religion has meant that the issue of identifying with a wider culture associated with Asian religions is less extreme. African-Caribbean culture gives more choice about whether to be religious or not and those that *are* see their involvement as one aspect of their lives rather than central to all aspects. Moreover, many African-Caribbeans are fully assimilated into British society and do not see the loss of religion as a threat to their identity. Indeed, like many white Britons, many do not ascribe any significance to religion in their lives.

Many African-Caribbeans belong to racially mixed Christian denominations. However, the largest distinctively African-Carribean churches comprise of the Pentecostalist and the **charismatic** or '**house church**' movements. These churches have a distinctive style of worship with its roots in the Caribbean, Jamaica in particular. According to Stuart Hall (1985), when white Anglican missionaries met ex-slaves whose Jamaican folk religion included magical beliefs and behaviours, Christianity was assimilated into folk beliefs to form an 'Afro-Christianity'. Common features were **ecstatic trances**, night gatherings, processions led by a 'captain' to the sound of muffled drums. Afro-Christianity gave key biblical events high prominence and some struck a chord within the African heart. The story of Moses, for example, liberating the Israelites to lead them to the promised land, echoed a desire for many to return to Africa. (Rastafarians have also picked up on this biblical theme.) Whilst the literal reading of the Bible characterises many African churches, they also maintain distinctively African folk traditions. '**Speaking in tongues**' is believed to involve languages specifically given by God to improve communication with God, and divine healing is thought to prove God's power to redeem the people from sin.

Differences in styles of worship

Whilst Anglican churches are dominated by older people and women and require limited formal involvement of the congregation in worship, Pentecostal church congregations are comprised of every age group and an equal balance of the sexes. There is a greater emphasis on religious experience than **religious dogma**, and worship is concerned to demonstrate publicly the joyous nature of religious conversion and the power of religion to heal people both physically and mentally. Considerable involvement is required from worshippers in the form of dancing and call and response between congregation and clergy.

Bird (1999) suggests that Pentecostalism has played a dual role for African-Caribbean people.

1 For some it has enabled them to cope with and adjust to a racist and unjust society. It serves as an 'opium' for the people, as Marx has suggested.

What does the term 'ideology' refer to? According to Marxists, how does ideology help people adjust to unequal and exploitative societies?

2 For others such as Pryce (1979), it encourages hard work, sexual morality, prudent management of finances and strong support of the family and community. In this sense it reflects the protestant ethic that Weber saw as essential in the development of capitalism (see Topic 1).

There are many other ethnic-minority religions, all of which help to define and maintain a cultural identity, traditions and customs whilst others provide direction and enable their members to cope in a racist and unjust society (e.g. **Rastafarianism**). Some religions or religious factions are antagonistic to society and the ambiguities of modernity. They offer solutions that may involve resistance and/or a return to fundamental principles felt to have been eroded through spiritual and moral decline. Such **fundamentalism** is discussed further in Topic 2.

WWWebtask

Using the categories in the diagram in the Research activity, find evidence of Islamophobia using the website of the Muslim News (http://www.muslimnews.co.uk)

1 Give two reasons why immigrants to the UK have placed a greater emphasis on religion.

2 Give an example of how the phrase 'when in Rome, do as the Romans do' might have been used to criticise ethnic minority behaviour.

3 a How did the experience of Asian and African-Caribbean groups differ when they originally came to Britain?
b How did this affect their sense of identity?

4 Suggest in your own words three differences in the significance of religion for first generation Asian and African-Caribbeans.

5 According to Modood, what changes have there been for the second generation?

6 Why have many second generation Asians chosen to hold on to their religious identity?

7 Give examples of how recent world events have served to re-affirm religious commitment for many minority groups.

8 What are the reasons for the growing popularity of Pentecostal churches?

9 What role does Pentacostalism play for African-Caribbean adherents?

KEY TERMS

Assimilate – blend in and integrate.

Charismatic – a church in which the preacher has a powerful influence through their beauty of speech which can sway the congregation by the power of language. (John Wesley, leader of the Methodists in the late eighteenth century, was noted in this way to have reduced congregations to tears and caused epileptic fits.)

Cultural hybridity – to mix and match different cultural influences.

Ecstatic trances – an apparently hypnotic state where worshippers appear overwhelmed by their religious experience and unaware of the immediate physical world around them.

Empowerment – to be given greater power and recognition.

Fundamentalism – see Key Terms in Topic 1.

Halal food – food prepared and blessed according to Islamic law.

House church movement – a church body which doesn't assemble in an established church building but in the homes of its members. By their very nature, house churches tend to be smaller in size and counter-cultural in many ways, i.e. have a sect-like, world-rejecting quality. They exist all over the world from USA to China.

Islamophobia – obsessive fear and hatred of Islam and Muslims.

Rastafarianism – Rastafarians (Rastas) worship Haile Selassie I, (know as Ras [Prince] Tafari) former emperor of Ethiopia, considering him to have been the Messiah and the champion of the black race. Rastas believe that black people are the Israelites reincarnated and have been persecuted by the white race in divine punishment for their sins. They will eventually be redeemed by exodus to Africa, their true home and heaven on earth.

Religiosity – see Key Terms in Topic 2.

Religious dogma – rules and regulations, commandments and formal requirements of a particular religion.

Religious pluralism – where a variety of religions co-exist, all of which are considered to have equal validity.

Rites – customary religious practices, e.g. baptism.

Speaking in tongues – when people speak in languages new to them, that is, languages they had not learned or used until that time and believed to be a gift from God and referred to in the gospels. 'And these signs shall follow them that believe; In my name they shall cast out devils; they shall speak with new tongues' (Mark 16:17).

Voluntaristic – a matter of individual choice.

Research idea

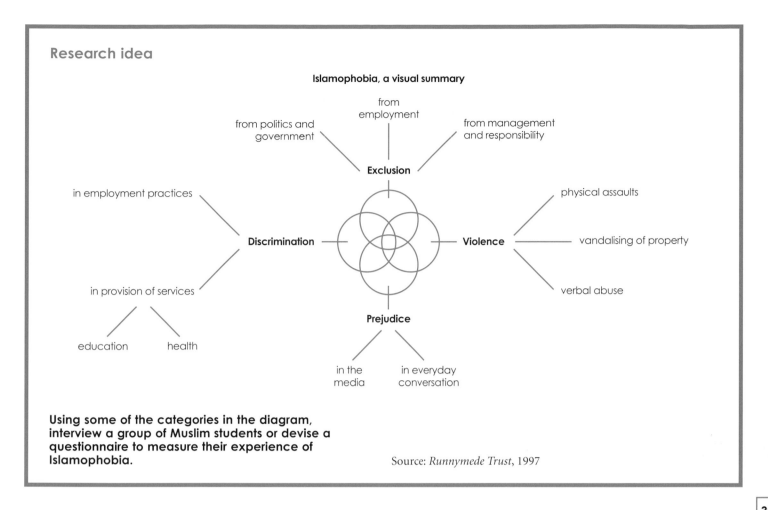

Islamophobia, a visual summary

Source: *Runnymede Trust*, 1997

Using some of the categories in the diagram, interview a group of Muslim students or devise a questionnaire to measure their experience of Islamophobia.

EXAM PRACTICE

Extract from AQA-style question

Item		
UK Membership of non-Christian religions in thousands		
	1975	**1985**	**1995**

	1975	1985	1995
Muslims	400	853	990
Sikhs	120	185	390
Hindus	100	130	140
Jews	110	110	110
Jehovah's Witnesses	80	102	120

a Identify and describe two consequences of a 'multi-faith' society for the sociology of religion. (8 marks)

b Examine the significance of the trends in the Item. (12 marks)

OCR-style AS question

a Identify and explain two reasons why some ethnic minorities are more committed to religion than the non-ethnic population. (15 marks)

b Outline and discuss the view that religion continues to have a significant effect on the lives of ethnic minority groups in the contemporary UK. (30 marks)

Item A

Pressures and influences on young Muslims

1) *The family.* Muslim families, like all families, vary in their approaches to child-rearing and in the freedoms they permit to teenagers. However, the generation gap may be wider as children may clash with parents who have a stronger affiliation to the culture in which they were reared. They may be impatient or critical regarding some of their parents' loyalties and priorities which they feel have not moved on since emigrating from the 'mother country'.

2) *The mosque.* Up to the age of 14 most Muslim children attend a local mosque school. The teaching style is typically different from that which they encounter at their mainstream school, for it puts much emphasis on learning the Qur'an in Arabic by heart and on oral repetition (*tartil/tajwid*), and gives relatively low priority, in the first instance, to discussion and intellectual understanding. The imams and other teachers at the mosque schools mostly received their own education, both secular and religious, outside Britain. There is an increasingly widespread perception in Muslim communities that imams are not equipped by their own training to help young British Muslims cope with issues such as unemployment, racism and Islamophobia, drugs, the attractions of Western youth culture, and so on. At the very time when they may become more devout and observant in their own personal Muslim beliefs and in their determination to live according to Muslim principles, they feel that the mosques and imams are often unable to respond to their particular needs and concerns.

3) *Extremist Muslim organisations.* Their position is frequently anti-western and they have closed and hostile views of other religions. Their references to Judaism and Israel are indistinguishable from crude antisemitism. Their phobic hostility to all things western is a mirror image of western Islamophobia and indeed helps to feed it. Their simplistic messages can be attractive to young people, since they appear at first sight to give a satisfactory picture of the total world situation (the West is the root of all evil) and appear to have a clear practical agenda (resistance and struggle). However, they have far fewer active supporters than the mainstream media claim.

4) *The Islamophobic messages of the mass media.* These often have the effect of undermining young people's self-confidence and self-esteem, their confidence in their parents and families, and their respect for Islam. The distorted image portrayed by the media is so profound, it is believed by Muslim elders that 60–80% of young Muslims will never practise Islam 'other than ... rituals.' Islamophobia makes extremist organisations, however, even more attractive.

5) *The largely secular culture of mainstream society,* encountered through the education system and the mass media, and in employment and training. Mainstream western culture is largely indifferent to all forms of religious commitment, not only to Islam. Also, at the same time, it seems distinctively hostile to Islam, since so many Muslims meet rejection when they apply to mainstream employers for jobs, and since so many are unemployed. The Policy Studies Institute's recent research showed a clear decline in religious observance amongst younger Muslims. Vertovec's (1993) sample of young Pakistanis in Keighley were not interested in practising Islam ('I will be a proper Muslim when I'm old' was the prevailing attitude) but were emphatically proud to be Muslims.

6) *The street culture of the young people themselves.* There are trends amongst young British Muslims, particularly those who are unemployed or who expect to be unemployed, towards territoriality and gang formation, and towards anti-social conduct, including criminality. In the prison population of England and Wales the numbers of Muslims increased by 40 per cent in the period 1991–1995. Such trends exist everywhere in the world where young people feel dispossessed and disadvantaged. Amongst other things social exclusion is a fertile seedbed for extremists.

Source: *Islamophobia: A Challenge For Us All*, compiled and published by the Runnymede Trust in 1997

1 What threats to continued commitment to Islam among young Muslims are suggested in Item A?

2 What pressures exist which could create more extreme commitment to Islam for young Muslims?

Item B

Islamophobia since September 11th

- Sixth form students of Asian and Arab/European parentage at the state Comprehensive Boys School in East Finchley, London, were accused by white pupils of being 'terrorists' and they murmured 'Get those bastards'.
- At a Roman Catholic School, in Islington a 13-year-old boy, was verbally abused, 'Your family has done this, what happened in America.'
- In Tooting, south London, graffiti was daubed on the wall of the mosque, 'Murdering bastards'. Similar incidents have been reported as far afield as Belfast, Wales and in Scotland.

- Britain's first state funded Islamic School, Islamia Primary School, Brent, was forced to close, after threatening telephone calls.
- In Southend, Islamophobes went a stage further and actually attacked a mosque. The Imam's daughter, Siddiqah Awan, told *The Muslim News*, 'We live upstairs and were woken up by the smashing of the windows. We were devastated, that a holy place was desecrated'.
- In Oldham and Bolton mosques were also attacked – Jamia Alavia Islamic Centre in Bolton had 2 or 3 petrol bombs thrown against it as 20 people (including children) inside were praying Isha (evening) prayers.
- More seriously still, there have been serious attacks on individual Muslims and people who look like Muslims (e.g., Sikhs). For instance, in the North East, a 20-year-old Bangladeshi man suffered a broken jaw after being beaten and kicked by a gang of youths. In Swindon, a woman aged 19 wearing Hijab, was attacked by two unknown white males. No arrests have been made; the police are appealing for witnesses.
- A 20-year-old university student on September 12 at 6pm, in Longsight, Glasgow, was going to her sister's house by bus. During the journey, a white man sitting behind her said 'You Muslim bastard' and then he hit her over the head with a glass Tizer bottle.
- Most seriously of all, an Afghani taxi driver has been left paralysed from the neck down after an argument over a fare led to a vicious assault where, it is believed, the man's origin was a factor in aggravating the attack. Police have arrested three men on suspected GBH on Hamidullah Gharwal (28). The incident took place in Twickenham in SW London.

Source: *Islamophobia in the West (A Report from Britain)* by Sarah Sheriff in http://www.islamweb.net, 2000

Legislating against religious hatred

In the wake of the 11 September, some British Muslims were attacked. The UK government wanted to introduce a ban on incitement to religious hatred in its Anti-terrorism, Crime and Security Bill. This would have carried with it severe penalties for perpetrators. Current legislation mitigates against incitement to *racial* hatred which offers some protection to distinctive racial groups but does not protect Muslims because they are so racially diverse.

Opposition members of the House of Lords forced the government to back down. They said the proposal needed more debating time and should not be rushed through with emergency anti-terror laws. There were worries too that the planned new offence could prevent legitimate arguments over religion thus impeding freedom of speech. Opponents of the plans also drew a distinction between race, which people could not change, and religion, which they chose for themselves.

The dropping of the plans has disappointed those groups which argued strongly for the law change especially when some British Muslims were attacked in the wake of 11 September. Yousef Bhailok, General Secretary of the Muslim Council of Britain, said the onus was on the government to give parliamentary time for the measure, especially as other parties said they would examine it positively.

Announcing his climbdown on the religious hate laws, Home Secretary David Blunkett said the anti-terror act did include some protection for people of particular faiths.

That was a reference to the new law which means the courts must treat religion, like race, as an aggravating factor when dealing with incidents of violence or intimidation.

Source: BBC World Service, January 2002

3 Which of the Islamophobic incidents in Item B might have been covered by a new law against racial hatred (see Item C) in addition to current legislation?

4 Which, if any, would the police have been able to see as serious offences?

Getting you thinking

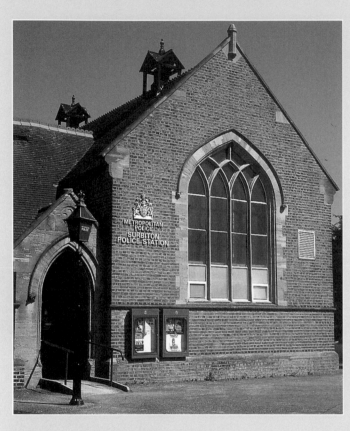

'Christianity will go. It will vanish and shrink. I needn't argue with that – I'm right and I will be proved right. We're more popular than Jesus now. I don't know which will go first – rock 'n roll or Christianity.'

Source: John Lennon (The Beatles), *London Evening Standard*, March 4, 1966

1   What kinds of values do the pictures of ex-churches suggest may have replaced religious values?

2   Why do you think that John Lennon's comments caused international uproar, especially in the United States?

What is secularisation?

The idea of 'secularisation' suggests that religion is becoming less prominent in society and its institutions less important and influential in the lives of individuals. One group of writers believe it is happening, whilst others consider it to be a myth and that religion is merely changing. The problem with the debate is that writers use different definitions of religion. As Hanson (1997) points out, such definitional diversity leads to 'much misunderstanding and talking past one another'. Even before it starts the debate can never be conclusive.

There are two main ways in which religion is defined.

- **Substantive definitions** – These define a religious belief system as involving relations between the 'natural' and 'supernatural' spheres. This includes beliefs in God or gods, the afterlife, heaven, spirits, prophecy, and so on. Thus religion is defined in terms of the structure and content of people's beliefs rather than what religion does for them.
- **Functional definitions** – Functional definitions characterise religion in terms of the functions it performs for individuals and society. These definitions are also called **inclusive** because they include beliefs that have a religion-like influence but which theorists from the substantive camp would not include. For Marx, religion was the 'opium of the masses' and for Durkheim a form of 'social cement'. The same 'religious' functions may be now performed by television, going to a football match or civil ceremonies such as the Queen's Golden Jubilee celebrations. Using the functional definition, all these could be considered 'religious'.

The relationship between these two senses is clearly a problem. But as Wilson (1982) has pointed out, those who define religion in substantive terms are more likely to support the **secularisation thesis** because they can show that religious belief has declined as people accept other more **rational** explanations of the world. But those who see religion in functional terms are more likely to reject the secularisation thesis. If the functions of religion are essential to the smooth running of society, they argue, even though religion may change, these functions still need to be fulfilled. What we call religion, must simply remain in some form or another to fulfil them.

Which sociological perspective is likely to focus on the 'smooth running of society'? Explain your answer.

Practice and belief

It is also important to consider changes in the ways people practise religion. Do they still attend church regularly and, if not, does this indicate a reduction in **religiosity**? They may still believe, but are too busy to attend, or see churches as inappropriate these days because they think that religion is a private matter. On the other hand, those who attend church may do so for reasons other than religion, to appear respectable or to make new friends. Making comparisons with the past can be difficult too as it is impossible to know exactly what people's motives for religious commitment were back then.

What is the evidence for secularisation?

One of the most influential supporters of the secularisation thesis, Wilson (1966), defines secularisation as 'the process by which religious institutions, actions and ideas lose their social significance'. He suggests that this is mainly reflected statistically in declining church attendance and membership but he also argues that religion is losing influence over public life and affairs. Wilson mainly focuses on statistical evidence relating to religious institutions and their activity.

What problems would a sociologist face in testing the idea that religion is losing influence over public life?

Attendance

The strongest evidence for secularisation in Britain comes from church-attendance statistics. According to the 1851 Census approximately 40% of the population attended church. By 1950 this had dropped to 20% and was less than 7.5% in 2000 (Brierley, 1999). Sunday school attendance is also in decline.

Membership

Hamilton (2001) also points out that fewer people are church members – see figure below.

Critics of the secularisation thesis point to the growth of new churches and the fact that ethnic-minority churches have pretty much held their own. However, it is clear that the big organisations such as the Church of England and the Catholic church have declined badly, whereas those that have stayed stable or grown are the smaller ones (see Topic 2).

Church membership in the United Kingdom 1900–2000

Year	Members (Thousands)	Population (Thousands)	Members as % of population	% of Population attending Sunday School
1900	8,664	32,237	27	55
1920	9,803	44,027	22	49
1940	10,017	47,769	21	36
1960	9,918	52,709	19	24
1980	7,529	56,353	13	9
2000	5,862	59,122	10	4

Source: P. Brierley (ed.) (2000) *Religious Trends 2000*, London: HarperCollins

Age bias

Brierley also points out that the gross figures of decline hide a trend even more worrying for the future of Christianity in Britain: age bias. For each of his three English surveys (1979, 1989, 1999), he estimates the age profile of the various groups of denominations. With the exception of the Pentecostal churches, he notes that church-goers are considerably older than non-churchgoers – see the figure below.

It would seem that fewer and fewer younger members are attending church – suggesting that eventually many congregations may die out altogether.

Suggest reasons why older people are more likely to participate in religion than the young.

Percentage of churchgoers aged over 65, 1979–1999

Church	1979	1989	1999
Anglican	19	22	29
Catholic	13	16	22
Methodist	25	30	38

Source: P. Brierley (ed.) (2000) *Religious Trends 2000*, London: HarperCollins

Reduced moral influence

Church weddings now only make up approximately half of marriages compared with about three-quarters 30 years ago. This fact, together with the rising divorce rate, increase in cohabitation and the proportion of children born outside marriage, is seen as evidence that religion and its moral value system exert little influence today.

If religion is decreasing as a source of moral values, what social institutions might be replacing it? Explain your answer.

Lower status of clergy

As the number of clergy has fallen, their pay and status have declined. As Bruce (2001) states, the size of the clergy is a useful indicator of the social power and popularity of religion. In 1900, there were over 45,000 clerics in Britain, this had declined to just over 34,000 in 2000, despite the fact that the population had almost doubled.

What is the evidence against secularisation?

Many interpretivist sociologists suggest these statistics should be treated with caution.

Why do interpretive sociologists often question the accuracy of official statistics?

Statistics relating to the previous century are unreliable because reliable data-collection practices were not in place. Martin (1978) claims that relatively high attendance figures from the Victorian age may be a reflection of non-religious factors such as the need to be seen by social superiors. As Hamilton (2001) points out, the notion of an 'age of faith' is an illusion partly created as a result of concentrating on the

Exploring religious behaviour

Item A

Evangelical Christian Service

Regents Park Mosque, London

Footballers praying before a match

1 How do the photographs above challenge the statistical evidence in favour of secularisation?

2 What types of religion in Britain appear to be declining and which thriving?

religious behaviour of the elite, about which we have more information than the vast majority of ordinary people. This may mean that the past was no more or less religious than the present.

Contemporary statistics, too, may not be reliable because different religious organisations employ different counting methods. The validity of such statistics is also in doubt because people who attend church are not necessarily practising religious belief whilst those who do believe may not see the need to attend. Religion is a private experience for many and consequently may not be reliably or scientifically measured. Grace Davie (1995) has characterised the situation in Britain as 'believing without belonging' and there may even be a case for suggesting that church attendance in the UK reflects 'belonging without believing'.

Religious belief

Despite very low levels of church attendance and membership, surveys show that there seems to be a survival of some religious belief. According to the 1998 British Social Attitudes survey, 21% of those surveyed agreed to the statement 'I know God exists and I have no doubt about it' whereas only 10% said that they did not believe in God at all. However, there may be a moral connotation attached to such surveys such that people feel more inclined to answer 'yes' whether they do believe in God or not.

Other aspects of secularisation

Bryan Wilson (1966) and others, notably, Bruce (1995) and Wallis (1984), cite evidence for secularisation in addition to statistics. They argue that secularisation is a development rooted in **modernity** and focus on three key processes:

- rationalisation
- disengagement
- religious pluralism.

Rationalisation

First, they suggest that rational thinking in the shape of science has replaced religious influence in our lives because scientific progress has resulted in higher living standards. Moreover, science has produced convincing explanations for phenomena which was once the province of religion, e.g. how the world was created, etc. Further, drawing on the work of Weber who saw rationalisation as being linked to the Christian tradition, Berger (1973) has suggested that Christianity has ultimately been its own gravedigger. Protestantism focused attention on this life, work and the pursuit of prosperity, rather than on the domain of God and the after-life.

Disengagement

The **disengagement**, or separation, of the church from the wider society is an important aspect of secularisation. The church is no longer involved in important areas of social life such as politics. Moreover, Wilson argues, religious belief is no longer central to most people's value systems or personal goals. People are now more concerned with their material standard of living rather than with spiritual welfare and are more likely to take moral direction from the mass media than the church. Hamilton (1995) has suggested that churches themselves have secularised in an attempt to compromise with those who have rejected more traditional beliefs. For example, he argues the Church of England no longer supports ideas of the virgin birth, hell or even God as a real external force.

Criticisms

- There is evidence that people prefer 'religious' explanations for random events such as the early death of

New 'rational' religions?

Replacement for religion	For	Against
Science	A common view is that science has replaced religion. It gives factual explanations for phenomena such as earthquakes and illness, previously explained by religion.	Many people seem sceptical of its claims and increasingly aware of its failures, e.g. foot and mouth disease, BSE. There is less trust in scientific 'experts'.
Medicine	Turner (1983) argues that people in modern societies used to turn to religion when ill. Now the focus is on the medical profession to provide explanations and cures. The medical and spiritual advice is often combined in tribal societies in the role of 'witch doctor'.	Medicine still struggles with AIDS, cancer, etc. Many still turn to some form of prayer when medicine offers no hope.
Psychotherapy	Lasch (1980) and Gellner (1985) see psychotherapy as having taken over the role from religion of curing the innerself. Therapies rather than church attendance help people to 'get better'.	Psychotherapy is only used by a wealthy elite. It has failed to become widespread in society although 'self-help' books remain popular.

loved ones. Many people still subscribe to the concept of 'luck' or 'fate', as evidenced by the growth of gambling opportunities such as the National Lottery.

- There is no doubt that religion plays less of a political role but religion is still a major provider of education and welfare for the poor. Moreover, national debates about issues such as the age of homosexual consent, the family, abortion and so on are given a moral dimension by the contribution of religious leaders. The media still shows a great interest in issues such as women priests and religious programmes such as 'Songs of Praise' still attract large audiences (7–8 million viewers). Some sociologists, notably Parsons (1965), have argued that disengagement is probably a good thing because it means that the churches can focus more effectively on their central role of providing moral goals for society to achieve.

Give one other example of a social institution that Parsons argues has become more 'streamlined'.

- According to Hamilton (2001), decline in religious practices may be part of a more general decline in organisational membership and increased privatisation. For example, less people join trade unions or political parties. It may be that they still 'believe' but are more committed to family or individual priorities.

- Thompson (1996) suggests that the influence of the new Christian evangelical churches is underestimated. In the absence of mass political campaigning, such church-inspired campaigns have a high media profile especially in the United States. Many New Right policies on abortion, media violence and single parents are, he argues, influenced by the evangelical churches.

Religious pluralism

Bruce (1995) argues that industrialisation has fragmented society into a marketplace of religions. Wilson argues that as a result religion no longer acts as a unifying force in society. He points to the **ecumenical movement** (where churches band together) as an attempt by institutionalised religion to reverse secularisation because such unification only occurs when religious influence is weak. In particular, the growth in the number of sects, cults and new religious movements has also been seen by Wilson as evidence of secularisation. He argues that sects are 'the last outpost of religion in a secular society' and are a symptom of religion's decline. Competition between religions is seen to undermine their credibility as they compete for '**spiritual shoppers**'.

Criticisms

Unlike functionalists who focus on the functions of religion for society, Stark and Bainbridge (1985) see religion as meeting the needs of individuals. All individuals seek rewards, many of which may be physically unattainable. They therefore seek compensators in the absence of the rewards themselves. For example, a Marxist may want social and economic transformation, but can compensate for the absence of it happening, by believing a future revolution is inevitable. An A-level student, burning the midnight oil, while revising for a sociology exam, can compensate for their stress with the promise of a university place and a well-paid career! Stark and Bainbridge argue that sometimes individuals want rewards which are so great that the possibility of gaining them can only be contemplated alongside a belief in the supernatural, e.g. answers to our most fundamental questions, or a life after death.

Only religion can answer these questions and provide **religious compensators** to meet universal human needs. In their view therefore it can never disappear nor seriously decline. Furthermore, the more religious organisations move away from the supernatural, the more people will turn to different organisations that continue to emphasise it. Hence, the relative success of traditional Orthodox and New churches at holding on to their congregations, relative to the modernising established churches, as well as the growth of new religious movements. The quest to re-discover more spiritual religion has, they argue, led to greater **pluralism**.

However, Bruce and Wallis point out that neither new religious movements nor those churches that have increased their membership have recruited anywhere near the numbers of those lost from the established churches. Brierley (1999) estimates that the growth of non-Trinitarian churches of half a million members, amounts to about only one-sixth of those lost to the main churches.

Studies by Greeley (1972) and Nelson (1986) argue that the growth of new religious movements indicate that society is undergoing a religious revival. G.K. Nelson (1986) argues that, in the 1980s, institutional religion lost contact with the spiritual needs of society because it had become too ritualised and predictable. In this sense, Nelson agrees with Wilson that established religion is undergoing secularisation. The young, in particular, are 'turned-off' by such religion. However, Nelson argues that a religious revival is underway, and is being helped by the success of evangelical churches. These churches offer a more spontaneous religion which is less reliant on ritual and consequently more attractive to the young.

The secularisation myth?

Many writers have pointed out that secularisation has tended to be seen in terms of the decline of organised established churches in Western industrialised countries. However, if one looks at the world globally, then religion is as overwhelming and dominant a force as ever. As Berger (1997) comments, 'the world today with some exceptions is as furiously religious as it ever was and in some places more so than ever'. Religious revival among Christians in the USA, Jews in Israel and Muslims throughout the world has gone unexplained by proponents of the secularisation thesis. Hervieu Leger (1993) suggests that what **secularisationists** see as religious decline is merely the reorganisation of religion so that it better suits the needs of modern societies. He suggests that religion now serves to support emotional communities in increasingly impersonal societies by providing a focus for cultural identity. Whilst established religion may appear to be in decline in Western countries like Britain, the growth of their immigrant populations is causing an increase in religiosity. Islam is the fastest growing religion in Britain and non-Trinitarian church membership has mushroomed.

Why should religion particularly appeal to immigrant communities?

Postmodernists, too, see the development of New Age beliefs, what Heelas (1996) calls a '**cultic milieu**', as a rejection of science and modernity in the postmodern age. The true extent of New Age beliefs cannot be known, but the number of internet sites feeding such interests indicates that they are widespread. This new explosion of spirituality doesn't at first seem to detract from the secularisation thesis because these private beliefs don't impact upon the way society runs. But, as postmodernists argue, consumption is the way society runs now, or is at least a very significant factor. So this is precisely where we should look to find openings for religious activity.

Secularisation – an over-generalisation?

The general picture painted by secularisationists disguises some important variations. Even institutionalised religion is not necessarily dying in some modern societies.

- The increasing influence of the Christian Right in America should not disguise the fact that the USA has a much more committed religious population than any other

Western country with 40% of the adult population regularly attending church. About 5% of the US television audience regularly tune in to religious TV and 20 million watch some religious programming every week.

- Religious participation also varies between social groups, with some who have continued to be extremely religiously committed – and in many cases have become more so. As we saw in Topic 5, this is true of many ethnic-minority groups in Britain and elsewhere.
- If we accept the view of Bellah (1967) that civil religion has increased in influence (see Topic 1), then this too constitutes a new form of religiosity.

As far as the UK is concerned, it is fairly obvious that profound changes are occurring in institutional religion. However, whether these changes can be described as secularisation is difficult to ascertain. Religious participation through organised religion has declined but the extent and nature of continuing belief still proves difficult to determine. Further, increased globalisation has meant that **religio-political events** elsewhere have global significance and this is bound to have an impact upon religious influence in Britain. Baumann (1997) and Giddens (2001) for example, argue that religion is becoming more important in the late modern/postmodern world. According to Giddens:

Religious symbols and practices are not only residues from the past: a revival of religious or more broadly spiritual concerns seems fairly widespread … not only has religion failed to disappear; we see all around us the creation of new forms of religious sensibility and spiritual endeavour.

Give two examples of global 'religio-political events'.

KEY TERMS

Cultic milieu – the melting pot of novel interpretations of sacred matters out of which new religious communities take shape.

Disengagement – the increasing separation of the institutions of the church from the state and government and their reduced influence in wider aspects of social life.

Ecumenical movement – where churches come together in joint worship, each seeing the other as having something to offer.

Inclusive – all encompassing.

Modernity – the modern age, based on science and reason.

Pluralism – co-existence of a variety of religious positions.

Rational – based on reason, logic and science.

Religio-political events – instances of religion coming into conflict with governments which have national and sometimes international consequences.

Religiosity – see Key Terms in Topic 2.

Religious compensators – aspects of religion that provide temporary answers to fundamental queries about the nature of existence and satisfy universal needs.

Secularisationists – those who support the secularisation thesis.

Secularisation thesis – belief in the declining influence of religion in society.

Spiritual shoppers – a postmodern idea that people consume religion in much the same way as any other product.

CHECK YOUR UNDERSTANDING

1 What does Hanson mean when he says that definitional diversity leads to 'much misunderstanding and talking past one another'.

2 Why are those who support substantive definitions likely to support the idea of secularisation whilst those who adopt functionalist definitions reject it?

3 What evidence on religious participation does Wilson give to support the secularisation thesis?

4 How do anti-secularisationists refute this?

5 What impact is modernity said to have had on religiosity?

6 a) What evidence is there that disengagement has occurred?
   b) How is this evidence refuted?

7 What according to Stark and Bainbridge has been the impact of the churches' changing role in providing religious compensators?

8 How do secularisation theorists challenge this view?

9 In what ways does a more global perspective demonstrate that secularisation is a 'myth'?

10 How do postmodernists view the secularisation thesis?

Item A

There is a story told by Australian Aboriginals of a mighty river that once flowed across the land. Generations were sustained by its flow but gradually it ceased to flow. Some waited for its return but others went to see what had happened. It turned out that the river still flowed but had changed course upstream creating a billabong on the curve where the Aboriginals still sat. The river still flowed, but elsewhere. Religious life in postmodern times has not dried up as predicted by the theorists, but it is being relocated. Patterns of religious behaviour are being restructured. The river is flowing elsewhere.

Source: McGrath, cited in D. Lyon (2000) *Jesus in Disneyland: Religion in Postmodern Times*, Cambridge: Polity Press

1 Explain the message of the story in Item A, using examples to illustrate the points it is making.

Item B

Brown (2001) suggests that participation has mainly declined in the established churches because of the changing role of women. Where female church-attendance and participation was high, the same was true for both children and men. Women, their domestic and maternal roles heavily emphasised in both secular and religious literature right down to c.1960, were the primary churchgoers, with children in tow and husbands – sometimes reluctantly – following suit.

Brown further suggests that from the 1960s, feminism and the media presented women with other ways of understanding their identities, their sexuality and their lives generally than traditional Christian notions. 'British women secularised the construction of their identity, and the churches started to lose them (and their husbands and children).'

Adapted from: C. G. Brown (2001) *The Death of Christian Britain: Understanding Secularisation 1800–2000*, London: Routledge

Read item B.

2 How were women's roles emphasised in both secular and religious literature?

3 What caused women to leave the church?

Item C

Predicting religion globally

a Across the globe, religions which can accommodate democracy, greater personal freedom and empowerment will do well.

b Religions of difference will fare well in developing countries when they integrate some elements drawn from religions of humanity – in particular the emphasis on human rights (as in Eastern Europe, Bangladesh and Indonesia).

c Religions which serve to undergird (support or strengthen from beneath) emerging endangered local, ethnic or national identities will do well. In the west, often as pockets of protest.

d Particularly outside the West, modernising religions will do well, i.e. religions which encourage the development of modernity and adaptation to a global capitalist economy without following a western secularising model and so losing their distinctive traditions, identities and faiths.

e Spiritualities of life will not fare as well as many have predicted because they fail to provide a clear framework for living focusing solely on the Self which may not be strong enough to sustain belief.

f In contrast, experiential religions (where there is active participation in the spiritual quest rather than passive acceptance of the word of those in authority), both of humanity and difference but especially of difference will do better because they cater for the Self and the relational and the different and the universal.

g Religions that do best will be those which are able to mobilise the most resources, both financial and human. The accumulation of wealth over a long period of time may sustain older faiths that might otherwise have disappeared.

Adapted from: L. Woodhead and P. Heelas (2000) *Religion in Modern Times: An Interpretive Anthology*, London: Blackwell

4 What does the extract suggest about the religious commitment of churchgoing men, women and children before 1960?

5 Provide examples of religions to illustrate at least four of the points in Item C.

Using a search engine such as Google www.google.co.uk, type in 'Keep Sunday Special Campaign'. Summarise the main objections Christian groups have to the secularisation of Sunday. Evaluate their arguments. How relevant are they to the majority of the population today?

Research idea

Interview parents/grandparents and other older relatives to ascertain the level of belief and participation in religion, both past and present, in your family. Design a questionnaire measuring religious belief and practice to compare with your own age group. Collate the results for the whole class, and compare them.

EXAM PRACTICE

Extract from AQA-style question

'It is difficult to regard religious institutions as central to modern society.'

Evaluate the arguments and evidence for this view. (40 marks)

OCR-style AS question

a   Identify and explain two ways in which religion continues to be a significant influence on society. (15 marks)

b   Outline and discuss the view that the influence of religion on UK society is declining. (30 marks)

World Sociology

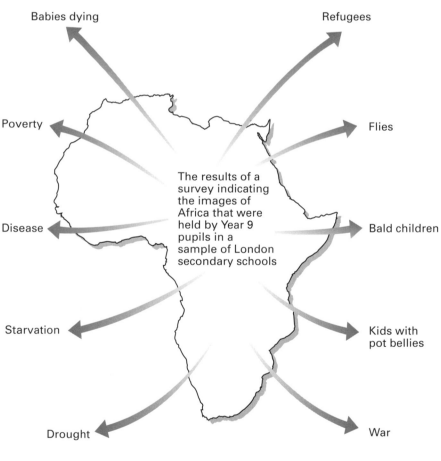

Babies dying

Refugees

Poverty

Flies

Disease

Bald children

Starvation

Kids with pot bellies

Drought

War

The results of a survey indicating the images of Africa that were held by Year 9 pupils in a sample of London secondary schools

The simple but tragic fact: there are just too many people and not enough being grown to feed them all

1 Look at each of the images of the children opposite in turn and explain what feelings each picture provoked in you. Suggest reasons for the predicament of each child. How would you go about improving their chances of survival into adulthood?

2 Examine the results of the survey into children's images of Africa. Do these images reflect the dominant images in your head? What other images might you add to this list? Where do people get such images from?

3 What does the cartoon tell us about our perception of problems in the developing world?

Surveys generally indicate that the sorts of images of children used opposite provoke two distinct sets of feelings among young people in the UK.

● First, some of you will have felt compassion and pity, and perhaps an overwhelming need to help. If you felt this way, you probably constructed a detailed list of solutions that focused on how we in the West might help these children out of poverty. In this case you are probably the type of person who gives generously to charities that target children in the developing world such as Comic Relief.

● Second, some of you may have felt indifference. The likelihood is that you have seen these types of images so many times now that you have become immune to their emotional content. You are experiencing what is known as 'compassion fatigue'. Such feelings are likely to be accompanied by nagging questions such as 'why do we always need to put our hands in our pockets?' and 'why don't these people sort themselves out?'

You are likely to find both these sets of feelings present in your sociology class. Neither set is right or wrong. Both groups of people share similar characteristics in that they both have their images of places like Africa which are similar to the ones held by the children in the survey opposite. Note how negative these images are. They are generally images of Africa starving, Africa as victim of natural disasters such as drought and volcanoes or man-made disasters such as war, and Africa over-populated with too many babies. Such images are the product of **value-judgements** that we make about how people should live their lives. They are constructed relative to our own experience. Our standard of living in the UK generally ensures that most children in the UK survive healthily into adulthood. We therefore should not be too surprised that our ideas about how societies like these in Africa should change or develop are based on our own Western experiences. Moreover, some of us will quite naturally jump to the conclusion that their problems are created by their failure to adopt our way of life.

We should not underestimate the role of the mass media in constructing our perceptions of other parts of the world and the explanations and solutions available to their problems. Few of us have had actual experience of these parts of the world and consequently our perceptions are ultimately formed by the images we see in the media. Media analysis may be partial and selective, as the cartoon indicates.

Using examples from other topics you have studied, explain how media coverage might be partial and selective.

It is important to understand that our perception and media representations of developing countries reflect a wider academic and political debate about how sociologists, politicians and aid agencies should define development. As we shall see, the dominant definitions of development that exist involve the same sorts of value-judgements that informed your reaction to the poverty and suffering of children in the developing world.

What is a value-judgement? Give examples from other parts of your studies.

Affluence and destitution

World sociology is concerned with explaining the relationship and, in particular, the economic and social differences between different countries and peoples of the world. World sociologists aim to explain why the nations of the world exist in a hierarchy of affluence which ranges from utter destitution to immense wealth (Harris 1989). For example, in 1997 the richest fifth of the world's population enjoyed an income 78 times as great as the poorest. Most of this wealth is concentrated in the industrialised world – North America, Western Europe, Japan and Australasia. Most of the destitution is concentrated in the less developed world – which consists mainly of most of Africa, South and Central America, the Indian subcontinent and most of East Asia.

This Unit will generally distinguish between the rich and poor regions of the world by using the terms 'developed world' and 'developing world'. However, these terms are themselves not without problems because world sociologists are not in total agreement as to how development should be defined and therefore measured. Moreover, even within these two worlds there are enormous differences in terms of wealth, poverty, health, education, etc.

Development: the terminology problem

This topic area uses the terms 'developed' and 'developing' worlds but there are a confusing range of terms used by world sociologists and textbooks. Up to the 1990s, the terms 'First World' (i.e. the West), 'Second World' (i.e. communist countries) and 'Third World' (i.e. the developing world) were in common use but the collapse of communism has largely rendered such terms redundant. Some sociologists divide the world into 'North' (i.e. the industrialised world) and the 'South' (i.e. the developing world) but if you look at a map you will see this is not geographically very accurate. Others prefer the terms 'rich' and 'poor' worlds. The situation is complicated by the diversity of economic and social progress found in the developing world today. This has prompted the use of the following terms which acknowledge the hierarchical character of the world:

- *MEDCs: more economically developed countries*, i.e. the developed world of the West.
- *NICs: newly industrialised countries*, i.e. countries such as Singapore which have achieved economic success despite having only industrialised in the past 40 years.
- *FCCs: former communist countries* who are struggling to convert their economies along capitalist lines.
- *LEDCs: less economically developed countries* mainly dependent on agriculture and raw materials.
- *LLEDCs: least economically developed countries* – the poorest countries in the world, e.g. Ethiopia, Bangladesh, etc.
- *Fourth World*: this term is used by feminists to describe all women in the patriarchal world.
- *Fifth World*: a term used by feminist Gloria Steinem to describe the female part of the population used as cheap labour and that has the least control over capital and technology.

Generally speaking, dominant definitions of what constitutes development have been based on the experience of Western nations. For example, the major catalyst of social change in the West was industrialisation and this has brought economic

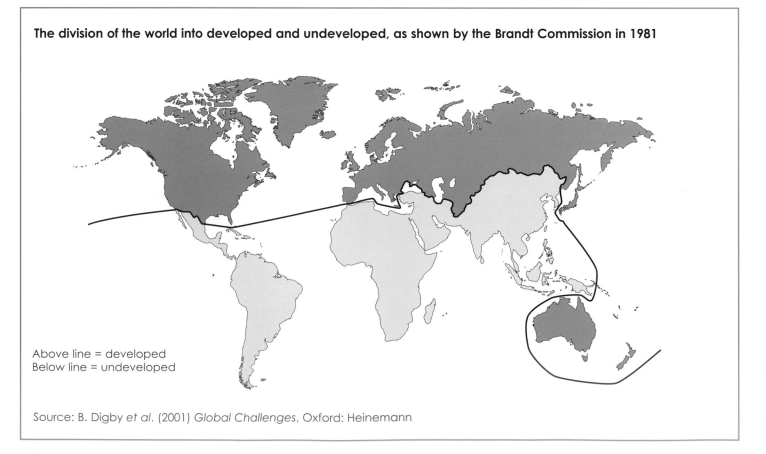

The division of the world into developed and undeveloped, as shown by the Brandt Commission in 1981

Above line = developed
Below line = undeveloped

Source: B. Digby *et al.* (2001) *Global Challenges*, Oxford: Heinemann

and social benefits to the populations of the developed world. For example, the majority of people in the UK enjoy good living standards, access to consumer goods, free education, easy access to welfare services, long life expectancy, etc. Therefore we should not be surprised that 'development' has become associated with the economic success of industrial capitalism and Westernisation, and that it is generally assumed to be a desirable goal, a sign of progress and something all countries should strive for. As we shall see in Topic 2, some sociologists and economists have been unable to resist equating development with modernisation along Western lines.

Measuring development

Development as economic well-being

Sociologists and economists who subscribe to the industrial–capitalist model of development tend to favour economic measurements of development such as Gross National Product (GNP). This is the total economic value of goods and services produced by a country over the course of a year available for consumption in the marketplace. The total value of GNP is divided by the total population of a country to give a figure per head (i.e. known as 'per capita').

What other possible measures of wealth could be used? What problems are associated with their use?

Gross National Product (GNP) for selected countries, 1992, 1997

Country	Per capita GNP (US$) 1992	Per capita GNP (US$) 1997
Brazil	2,770	4,720
The Gambia	390	240
Italy	20,510	20,120
Nigeria	320	260
USA	23,120	28,740
Japan	28,220	37,850

Source: World Development Report, 1992, 1999

The use of GNP figures illustrates the enormity of the gap between the developed and developing worlds. For example, in 1997, GNP per capita in the USA was $28,740 whilst in Nigeria it was only $240. However, GNP as a measure of development is unsatisfactory for the following reasons.

- There are inconsistencies in the way countries collect such data so we cannot be sure of its reliability or its value as a comparative tool.
- Production in developing countries is often geared to subsistence rather than for consumption in the marketplace. Such production (which is mainly carried out by women) does not normally have a monetary value because the domestic unit consumes it in order to survive. It is therefore not included in GNP statistics.

- GNP gives us little insight into either the standard of living of a population or how wealth and income are actually distributed within a society. Therefore the $28,740 GNP figure for the USA quoted earlier gives a false impression because it disguises the fact that some social groups in the USA, mainly African-Americans and Native-Americans, experience disproportionate poverty. Economic growth in terms of GNP, therefore, does not necessarily result in economic development for all members of a population. In fact, GNP has actually grown in some societies whilst the majority of people in them have experienced greater levels of poverty and inequality.

Development as social well-being

Development experts working for non-government organisations (NGOs), such as charities like Oxfam, argue that the measurement of development should focus on social rather than economic indicators of development. As a result, NGOs have focused on the concept of 'basic needs' such as food, shelter, drinking water, sanitation, health and education. These needs can be converted into statistical measurements relatively easily and without controversy. Most of us agree that these are worthwhile goals. Moreover these basic needs also have economic benefits in that they produce a healthy and literate workforce. This approach, which is based on a desire for social justice and welfare, has dominated NGO thinking on development.

What problems are created in attempting to identify 'basic needs' across a range of societies?

In 1990, the United Nations constructed the Human Development Index (HDI) which aims to measure aspects of human welfare, e.g. adult literacy, life expectancy at birth, the number of doctors per 100,000 population, etc. In 1998, the HDI showed that, in the USA, 99% of the adult population was literate whilst average life expectancy was 76.4 years. However, in Nigeria, only 57% of the population was literate and average life expectancy was 51.4 years.

In 1997, the Human Poverty Index (HPI) was introduced in order to measure three essential dimensions of deprivation – life expectancy, knowledge and living standards – in both the developed and developing world. The HPI confirms the picture of destitution expected in the developing world, e.g. 34% of the people of Ethiopia are not expected to survive to

Human-needs-centred development

Development as social well-being tends to focus on eight targets:

- low levels of poverty
- low levels of unemployment
- relative equality
- democratic ways of thinking
- good literacy and educational levels
- relatively equal status for women
- sustainable ability to meet future needs
- human security

Source: World Bank website

the age of 40, 64.5% are illiterate, 75% have no access to safe water and 54% have no access to health services. However, interestingly, the findings of the HPI also undermine the superiority of the industrial–capitalist model of development. They suggest that 7–17% of the population in developed countries are poor – approximately 100 million people whilst nearly 200 million are not expected to survive beyond the age of 60.

Development as global well-being

In the 1980s and 1990s there was an increasing realisation amongst agencies such as the World Bank that development had a global dimension and that it should be targeted at what Korten (1995) calls the 'the global threefold human crisis' of deepening poverty, social disintegration and environmental destruction. Development strategies in the 1990s, therefore, focused on ameliorating problems which might otherwise threaten chaos at a global level.

In 1987, the World Commission on Environment and Development (WCED) concluded that economic development in both the West and the developing world should be compatible with greater responsibility for the global environment. The Commission advocated the policy of **sustainable development.** A central component of this idea is that poverty in the developing countries may be a major cause of global environmental problems such as global warming. For example, developing countries such as Brazil and Indonesia have engaged in major deforestation policies in order to raise foreign exchange and pay debts. The Commission argued that the construction of a more equitable economic relationship between the developed and developing world would reduce the need for the developing world to over-exploit their environments and consequently slow down environmental destruction. Moreover, the WCED argued that rich countries should aim to reduce pollution and put clean air before higher living standards. In the 1990s, 178 UN member states agreed to pursue sustainable development.

However, in recent years, there are signs that sustainable development may be faltering because commitment from the more developed countries, especially the USA, has been distinctly lacking. Moreover, some critics argue that the goal of sustainable development is impossible to achieve if

governments or other international agencies do not regulate **transnational corporations** because such companies are primarily responsible for creating the global environmental problems that we experience today.

The developing world: its distinguishing features

Developing countries, in contrast with the developed world, are likely to have the following features:

- a colonial past
- economies based on agriculture (especially the export of cash crops) and the extraction of raw materials, rather than manufacturing industry
- low economic growth (e.g. a large proportion of income from exports is likely to be used to service foreign debt)
- vast inequalities in ownership of and access to land
- large sections of the population may be unemployed or under-employed
- a subsistence standard of living, e.g. the World Bank estimates that 800 million people live in absolute poverty in the developing world
- a young and fertile population that is growing rapidly
- high rates of child malnutrition
- low life expectancy
- high rates of infant mortality
- death from preventable and treatable diseases such as measles due to a lack of basic medical provision, e.g. the number of doctors, hospitals and clinics per head of population is low
- high levels of adult illiteracy
- lack of access to free schooling
- lack of basic infrastructure and services including telecommunications, roads, electricity supply, clean water and sanitation etc.

The influence of Westernisation on definitions of development

There is considerable evidence that countries are often unable to choose their own development path. Despite the NGOs' attempts to focus on social development by meeting basic needs in the 1980s and 1990s, development strategies initiated by powerful Western countries and agencies such as the World Bank have focused on stimulating or tinkering with the economic organisation of such societies. The potential to develop, therefore, often depends on them adopting the Western model of industrial–capitalism because Western governments control access to scarce resources essential to development such as capital investment, aid, foreign exchange, oil and manufactured goods. What this means in practice is that countries in the developing world are often strongly encouraged to abandon traditional values or alternative development strategies in return for access to these resources, (see, for example, the concept of structural adjustment programmes in Topic 4).

However this Western model of development is problematical for several reasons.

1   It is a **value-laden** concept which is rooted in **ethnocentrism** – the view that Western forms of

---

The World Bank's development goals

- to reduce poverty by one-half by 2015
- to reduce infant mortality by two-thirds and mortality in childbirth by three-quarters
- all countries to have primary education by 2015
- all countries to have comprehensive family-planning services
- all gender disparities in primary and secondary education to be eliminated by 2015
- all societies to have sustainable development strategies in order to reverse the current loss of natural resources such as rain forests by 2015.

Source: World Bank

civilisation are technically and morally superior and that all other types of culture are deficient in some respect.

2 It often involves making negative value-judgements about developing societies. Often such societies are defined as 'backward' if they insist on retaining some elements of traditional culture and belief and/or if they adopt **fundamentalism** as a way of life. Carmen (1996) argues that such an approach is demeaning, dehumanising and results in dangerous delusions because often the people of the developing world internalise the myth that they are incapable, incompetent, and the problem. As Sankaro notes, their minds end up being colonised with the notion that they should be dependent and should look to the West for direction. Galeano (1992) concludes 'they train you to be paralysed, then they sell you crutches'.

3 There is an assumption running throughout the Western model of development that industrialisation only brings benefits. This ignores the social problems that are unique to industrial–capitalist societies.

Using ideas from other parts of the course, identify five possible negative effects of industrialisation.

4 Western-style **democracy** is often cited as an indicator of development by Western sociologists and politicians. However, this indicator is probably the most value-laden and therefore contentious aspect of development. The emphasis on it up to the 1990s was very much a product of the ideological conflict between the free West and the Soviet Bloc, i.e. the Cold War. Western models of development generally tend to assume that democratic forms of development are more suitable than communist or socialist models of development – which are often dismissed as extremist and dangerous. There is evidence that Western governments and agencies such as the World Bank and International Monetary Fund (IMF) have distributed aid on the condition that socialist/communist policies were jettisoned. In practice, this has meant that policies that have positive benefits for people in developing countries, such as collective farming co-operatives, land reform and welfare benefits have been cut back or abandoned altogether because of the stringent political conditions attached to Western aid.

5 There is evidence that Western models of development create problems for the populations of developing societies. For example, **indigenous** peoples have been forcibly removed from their homelands, aggressive advertising and marketing have created **false** (and ultimately harmful) **needs,** grave environmental damage has been done to rainforests and child labour has been exploited – all in the name of progress towards the industrial–capitalist model of development. Marxist and post-development sociologists refer to this process as **under-development** and suggest that development strategies are essentially aimed at maintaining exploitative practices such as ensuring cheap labour for transnational corporations and new markets for Western products. Development therefore may not be positive progress if it means increasing social and economic divisions and inequalities within a country.

6 Ethnocentric interpretations of development tend to exclude contributions from sociologists located in the developing world. Consequently the notion that development needs to be **culture-specific** – i.e. that it needs to be adapted to the particular needs of particular societies, rather than being universally imposed in an **homogeneous** fashion – is neglected. Carmen argues that development is a 'Trojan horse' and acculturation, i.e. the taking over of indigenous cultures by Western culture, is 'at the heart of the development business' (p.42).

7 Critics of Western models of development such as Sachs (1992) and Esteva (1992), known as the 'post-development school', argue that development was always unjust, that it never worked and that it has now clearly failed. They suggest that development is a 'hoax' in that it was never designed to deal with humanitarian and environmental problems. Rather it was simply a way of allowing the industrialised world, particularly the USA, to continue its dominance of the rest of the world. They point out that the poor have actually got poorer in the developing world despite forty years of development.

Allen and Thomas (2001) acknowledge that development has not always succeeded but they challenge this

Balance sheet of human development

Indicator	Development	Deprivation
Health	Over the last 36 years life expectancy at birth for developing countries has increased (by over a third) from 46 to 62 years. Four out of five people in the developing world have access to health services.	In 1997 31 million people were living with HIV, up from 22.3 million the year before. 880 million people worldwide still have no access to health services.
Children	Nearly 90% of one-year olds in developing countries are now immunised against tuberculosis.	109 million primary-school-age children are out of school.
Education	Between 1970 and 1995 the adult literacy rate in developing countries increased from 48% to 70%.	885 million adults (aged 15 or more) worldwide are illiterate.
Women	Between 1970 and 1992 the female education enrolment ratio in developing countries rose from 38% to 68%.	6–8 hours a day are spent by rural women in the developing world gathering fuel and fetching water.
Politics and conflict	In the 1990s, two-thirds of the world's people live under fairly democratic regimes	13.2 million people worldwide are refugees.

Adapted from: T. Allen and A. Thomas (2001) *Poverty and Development in the 21st century*, Oxford: Oxford University Press

post-development position. They point to the economic success of the Asian **tiger economies** and China. They also suggest that the evidence in regard to reductions in mortality and increases in literacy also support the view that development on balance has made a difference in the developing world.

Alternative definitions of development

There is now an increasing recognition especially among sociologists in the developing world that industrial–capitalist development is not the only development path available to them despite pressures from the West.

- Korten argues that development should be aimed at the realisation of human potential. He argues that development needs to be more 'people-centred' and suggests that 'authentic development' should be guided by three principles of justice (i.e. 'a decent human existence for all'), sustainability (the resources of the Earth need to be used in ways that ensure the well-being of future generations) and inclusiveness (every person must have the opportunity to be a recognised and respected contributor to family, community and society). Similarly, Amartya Sen (1987) argues that development needs to be about restoring or enhancing basic human capabilities and freedoms, giving people real choices and power over their daily situations. However, as Allan and Thomas note, such definitions of development are often over-romanticised. For example, Sahlins (1997) argues that people in the developing world may have few possessions but they are not poor. Poverty is a social status and, as such, it is the invention of civilisation.
- Such radical models of development have focused on the need of people in the developing world to reassert autonomy and control over their destinies. However, the problem with this approach is that it has failed to construct models of development in which the poor can realistically do things by themselves and for themselves.
- Ironically liberation from the consequences of Westernisation such as neo-colonialism and economic dependency on the West is now seen by some sociologists in the developing countries as their ultimate development goal. In some countries, such as India, resistance to Western forms of development has resulted in protest movements based on violent separatist agendas whilst globally, in recent years, we have seen a rise of an international new social movement based on a radical critique of the global economy and the Western institutions that underpin it.
- Some Islamic societies regard development as the need to apply Muslim principles to all aspects of their societies, i.e. government, law, education, art, etc. and consequently have adopted fundamentalist ways of life. However, as Said notes, Western commentators tend to regard such interpretations of development as a product of irrational fanaticism.

How does the reaction to the events of September 11 2001 confirm Said's observations?

- The experience of Cuba suggests that socialist models of development can have positive benefits. Despite decades of enforced isolationism (the USA has imposed a trade embargo on Cuba which has made it extremely difficult for it to export its goods), Cuba has achieved literacy rates, infant mortality rates and life expectancy comparable to those experienced in the West.
- What is now increasingly recognised by development agencies is that the countries that make up the developing world have specific problems and needs which are the result of geographical, religious, ethnic, cultural, political, economic and social factors unique to them which interact with global economics and culture. Models of development may therefore have to be individually tailored in order to reflect each country's individual circumstances whilst acknowledging the impact of global influences. Carmen argues that terms such as 'development' in this context are incapable of reflecting global reality. He suggests the alternative term of 'maldevelopment' which he defines as the global process involving all countries in which some are suffering from lack of resources whilst others are wasting them.

So what is 'development'?

The lesson to be learned from this topic is that the concept of development is about social change. However, we have seen that defining what form that social change should take is not an easy, straightforward process. Despite the continuing dominance of Western models of development, there are signs of resistance in the form of critiques of the industrial–capitalist model and alternative development strategies put forward by sociologists in the developing world and the NGOs. Most of the debate about what development means in 2002 now recognises the concept of globalisation. It is suggested by many world sociologists today that culturally, socially, politically and economically, national and regional boundaries are less important than ever. As a result, we now have to consider definitions of development and 'consequently' the inter-relationship between the developed and developing world within the context of global economics, culture and communications. This theme will be examined in depth in Topic 7.

Development as liberation

For people who have been slaves or have been oppressed, exploited and disregarded by colonialism or capitalism, 'development' means liberation. Any action that gives them more control of their own affairs is an action for development, even if it does not offer them better health or more bread. Any action that reduces their say in determining their own affairs or running their own lives is not development and retards them even if the action brings them a little better health and a little more bread.

Source: Rweyemamu, quoted in *Sociology: New Directions*, M. Haralambos (ed.) (1985), Ormskirk: Causeway Press

Culture-specific – characteristics that are unique to a particular society and not shared by others.

Democracy – a political system involving governments produced by the people voting in free elections.

Ethnocentrism – a set of beliefs, values, behaviours, etc. that lack objectivity in that they are based on the view that some cultures are superior whilst others are deficient.

False needs – the outcome of intensive advertising that persuades people that a particular consumer item is vital to their social well-being despite it being potentially harmful in the long term.

Fundamentalism – the belief, usually religious in origin, in the need to subscribe or return to traditional values and practices.

Homogeneous – sharing the same or similar characteristics.

Indigenous – native to a particular country or region.

Industrial–capitalist – the economic system of the West: this is based on an industrial mode of production (i.e. factory system) and is underpinned by unregulated (free market) economic competition.

Non-government organisations – organisations such as charities like Oxfam which work independently of governments in the developing world.

Sustainable development – development that is not dependent on using up the world's resources.

Tiger economies – term used to describe fast-growing economies in south-east Asia.

Transnational corporations – global businesses that produce and market goods and brands across both the developed and developing worlds.

Under-development – term used to describe the process whereby capitalist countries have distorted and manipulated the progress of less developed countries to their own advantage.

Value-judgements – positive or negative statements about, for example, the behaviour of others, which are shaped by our own subjective experiences.

Value-laden – bias in favour of a particular cultural point of view.

CHECK YOUR UNDERSTANDING

1 Identify five key differences in the living standards of the developed and developing world.

2 Identify two reasons why the terms 'first world' and 'third world' are now thought to be obsolete.

3 What economic process brought about development in the West?

4 Why can Western models of development be seen as ethnocentric?

5 Identify three negative consequences of Western forms of development for people in the developing world.

6 Why are economic indices of development seen as unsatisfactory as measures of development?

7 What are the main characteristics of 'basic needs' development?

8 How does the HPI index of development undermine the industrial capitalist model of development?

9 Why are models of development that incorporate gender measurements controversial?

10 In addition to the industrial–capitalist model of development, what four alternative types of development are identified in the course of this topic?

Item A   A baby girl born in one of the least developed countries can expect to live barely 44 years – 2 years more than a baby boy. Her problems begin before birth since her mother is likely to be in poor health. She has a high probability of being malnourished throughout childhood. She has a 1 in 10 chance of dying before her first birthday and a 1 in 5 chance of dying before her fifth. She will be brought up in inadequate housing under insanitary conditions and will have a good chance of contracting diarrhoeal disease, cholera and tuberculosis. She will have a 1 in 3 chance of ever getting enough schooling to learn how to read and write. She will marry in her teens and may have 7 or more children close together unless she dies in childbirth before that. She will be in constant danger from infectious disease from contaminated water at the place where she bathes, washes clothes and collects her drinking water. As well as caring for her family she will work hard in the fields, suffering from repeated attacks of fever, fatigue and infected cuts.

Adapted from: B. Digby *et al.*, (2001) *Global Challenges*, Oxford: Heinemann, p.200

Item B   Absolute poverty describes a situation in which people are barely existing, where the next meal may literally be a matter of life or death as the cumulative effect of malnutrition and starvation enfeeble all, particularly children, whose weakness gives them the tragic distinction of having the highest mortality rate for any group anywhere in the world. Thus in these circumstances poverty takes on an 'absolute' status since there is nothing beyond or 'beneath' it except death. Many in the developing world are close to this very vulnerable position, relying on aid, food relief or their own meagre returns from squatter farming, scavenging on refuse tips, prostitution, street hawking, and so on. For such people, statistics about relative GNPs can have no meaning or worth.

Adapted from: A. Webster (1990) *Introduction to the Sociology of Development*, Basingstoke: Macmillan, p.16

Item C

Human Poverty Index (HPI-2) for selected developed countries, 1998

Countries	% of people not expected to survive to age 60	% of people aged 16-65 who are illiterate	% of pop. in poverty	% of labour force long-term un-employed
Sweden	8	7.5	6.7	1.5
Germany	11	14.4	5.9	4.0
Belgium	10	18.4	5.5	6.2
UK	9	21.8	13.5	3.8
USA	13	20.7	19.1	0.5

Source: *Human Development Report* (1998), United Nations Development Programme, New York: Oxford University Press

Item D

Crying shame

'Nice to see you, Will. Just take us to the thinnest child – it'll save a lot of time.' With these words, a British TV reporter greeted aid worker Will Day in 1985 on arriving at Wadkouli in the Sudan where 100,000 famine-stricken refugees were encamped. Emotive pictures of dying children have been a staple part of television news reporting of Africa and other parts of the developing world since the 1960s. It has been suggested that the dominance of such disaster images may hinder public understanding of the causes of problems like famine. Critics note that pictures of the dying degrade their subjects and only serve to convince people in the West that the people and governments of developing countries like Ethiopia, Bangladesh, Mozambique etc. have brought the problems upon themselves and that improvement is impossible. As Jon Snow, the anchorman of Channel 4 News says, the more people see these images, the more pessimistic they feel about remedies. Moreover television coverage of famine in the developing world mainly focuses on the short-term effects of disasters or on graphics-friendly causes such as natural phenomenon. There is rarely any discussion of long-term causes (e.g. colonialism, the dominance of world trade by the West, the failure of official aid etc.) or long-term effects (e.g. debt) which may be a product of their relationship with the West.

Adapted from: L. Marks (1991) 'The Crying Shame of How the West sees Famine', *The Observer* 25/5/91

1 Identify three reasons why infant mortality rates are so high in the developing world according to Item A.

2 What is the relationship between absolute poverty and infant mortality?

3 Examine Item B and explain why statistics about relative GNPs can have no meaning or worth.

4 Identify two reasons why statistics relating to poverty in both the developed and developing world are probably not comparable.

5 Summarise the main trends of the statistical data shown in Item C. How might such statistics contribute to the debate about what constitutes development?

6 Using Item D as a starting point, suggest reasons why public understanding of the causes and effects of the problems that characterise the developing world is so poor.

Research ideas

1 **Conduct a survey which investigates the general public's images and understanding of the developing world. You should ask questions about:**
   a **the origin of their images**
   b **what they think are the causes of problems in the developing world**
   c **how they see the developing world solving its problems and**
   d **whether they see the West, and especially the UK, making a contribution in terms of causes and solutions.**
   What do your results tell you about which model of development the general public might subscribe to?

2 **Choose one of the following countries: Ethiopia, Somalia, Bangladesh, Laos, Malawi, Mozambique, Bolivia, Zambia, Honduras or Nepal. Using the box from earlier in the Topic entitled 'The developing world: its distinguishing features', research and construct a development biography for your chosen country. Contact some aid agencies via e-mail and find out whether they currently have development projects in that country.**

WWWebtask

- Visit the United Nations Development Programme website: www.undp.org
  This contains an impressive range of information about development projects across hundreds of countries being carried out by United Nations agencies. You should think about carrying out the following tasks.

- You can visit the UN sites of particular countries to see what is happening practically in terms of development projects. Click on Country Office websites on the right-hand side of the page and choose a country.

- Click on the Human Development Report 2001 (HDR) on the left-hand side of the page. You can enter any human development indicator into the search engine along with your country of choice.

- Click on 'Statement by Lead Author', (right-hand side of the HDR page) to access the introduction of the HDR by its director Sakiko Fakuda-Parr. Read this through and work out the model of development subscribed to by this author.

EXAM PRACTICE

Extract from AQA-style question

Briefly examine some of the problems in judging whether a particular country is more or less developed. (12 marks)

Getting you thinking

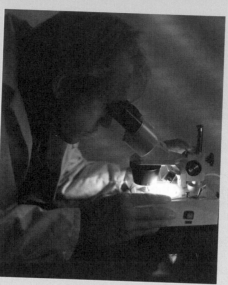

It is very likely that you associated the images showing science and technology with the developed world. This is not surprising as you are probably aware that your rather comfortable standard of living (compared with that experienced by 17-year-olds in developing societies) is underpinned by scientific discovery and constantly evolving technology. You are probably also aware, having seen countless images in the media, that parts of the developing world lack our taken-for-granted access to such technical support. It is easy to put this down to poverty but there are those who believe that it has more to do with beliefs, values and attitudes. In other words, aspects of the culture of developing worlds (such as religious beliefs) will always prevent progress. As we shall see, there are those who strongly believe that it is not enough to inject aid in the form of money into the developing world but that physical and material development can only come about if attitudinal development occurs as well. However, the images may also have reminded you that having the 'right' attitudes can come at a terribly expensive environmental price.

Modernisation theory

After World War II (1939–45), it became clear that many countries in Africa, Asia, Latin America and the Caribbean were remaining poor despite exposure to capitalism and the rational and scientific ways of thinking that underpinned this economic system. This observation was coupled with a concern among the leaders of wealthier countries that widespread poverty, encouraged by the strong mass appeal of **communism**, could lead to social unrest across the world – particularly in the ex-colonies of the European powers that had recently acquired their political independence. Crucially, such political instability was thought likely to limit the growth of the economy of the United States. In response to these potential developments, American economists, sociologists and policymakers developed the theory of modernisation.

Modernisation theory can be seen to have two major aims.

- It attempts to explain why poorer countries have failed to develop by focusing on the process of development: how traditional societies could evolve into modern developed societies. Huntington (1993), for example, describes modernisation as an **evolutionary** process that brings about **revolutionary** change.
- It aimed to provide an explicitly non-communist solution to poverty in the developing world by suggesting that economic change (in the form of capitalism) and culture could play a key role in bringing about modernisation.

Before we begin to examine the mechanics of modernisation theory, it is important to understand the profound influence this theory has had (and is still having) on the relationship between the developed and developing worlds. No other sociological theory can claim to match its influence on global affairs – not even Marxism which, of course, has steadily declined in credibility since the collapse of the Soviet Bloc in the early 1990s. Much of Western, especially American, foreign-aid policy is underpinned by the principles of modernisation theory.

1 Which of the images above do you associate with development and why?

2 Which of the images above symbolise lack of development and why?

3 Some people argue that even if we could eradicate poverty tomorrow in the developing world, these countries would still fail to develop. What do you think is the basis of this argument? Look at the images for clues.

The process of development

Walt Rostow (1971) suggested that development should be seen as an **evolutionary** process in which countries progress up a development ladder of five stages:

Rostow's evolutionary ladder of development

5 The age of high mass consumption

4 The drive to maturity

2 Pre-conditions for take-off: the West assists development through aid and industrial investment

3 Take-off

1 Traditional society

He argued that at the bottom of this evolutionary ladder were traditional societies whose economies are dominated by **subsistence farming**. Such societies have little to invest and consequently have limited access to science and technology. Industrialisation is therefore basic or non-existent, and economic output and growth low.

Other modernisation thinkers suggest cultural factors are more important than economic factors in explaining poverty in the developing world and are interested in why such countries have been unable to acquire the capital and technology needed to modernise.

From other parts of your studies, provide two examples of the importance of cultural factors in explaining a social phenomenon.

Talcott Parsons (1964) argued that such societies are often dominated by traditional values that act as obstacles to development. People are committed to customs, rituals and practices based firmly on past experience and consequently they are often fatalistic about their future. Inkeles (1969) noted that such people are unwilling to adjust

to modern ideas and practices, i.e. to entertain the notion of social change.

What sociological perspective is associated with Talcott Parsons? Give examples of his contribution to sociology.

Parsons was particularly critical of the extended kinship systems found in many traditional societies. He argued that these hinder **geographical mobility** which he claimed is essential if a society is to industrialise quickly and effectively. They also encourage traditional values and norms such as **ascription**, **particularism** and **collectivism** which undermine modernity by discouraging individual incentive, achievement and therefore, social change.

What is the difference between norms and values? Give examples of each.

Modernisation and social engineering

Modernisation theorists see the West as playing a crucial role in assisting and guiding the development of poorer countries. A number of 'motors' of development emanating from the West are thought to be essential in bringing about the social organisation and values necessary for development.

1   Rostow and others argued that traditional societies needed to encourage Western companies to invest in building factories and to train the local population in technical skills. Moreover, official aid programmes could supplement this process by paying for technical expertise and specialist equipment, as could borrowing from both the World Bank and the commercial banking sector. It was argued that the wages paid to the local labour force would **'trickle-down'** and stimulate the economy of the developing nation by creating demand for manufactured goods.

2   Bert Hoselitz (1964) argued that the introduction of meritocratic education systems (paid for by official aid and borrowing) would speed up the spread of Western values such as universalism, individualism, competition and achievement measured by examinations and qualifica-

The right to intervene: of beneficiaries and benefactors

Thank God for that. A panel of experts.

Source: *New Internationalist*, January 1993

tions. These values are seen as essential to the production of an efficient, motivated, geographically mobile factory workforce. Similarly, Lerner (1958) argued that Western values could more effectively be transmitted to developing societies if the children of the political and economic elites of these countries were educated in Western schools, universities and military academies. It is suggested that these future leaders of the developing world could then disseminate Western values down to the mass of the population.

How might Western values be spread to the mass of the population?

3 Inkeles (1969) argued that the mass media was a crucial agent in bringing about modernity because it rapidly diffused ideas about the need for geographically mobile, nuclear-family units, family planning, secular beliefs and practices and the adoption of the democratic process – all essential components of modern development.

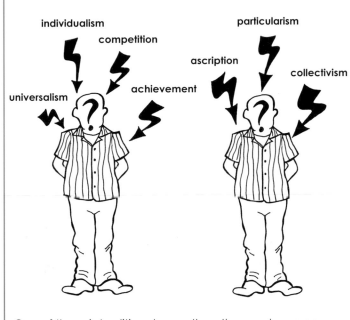

individualism
competition
particularism
ascription
universalism
achievement
collectivism

One of these is traditional man, the other modern man. Explain which is which and why.

4 Hoselitz argued that urbanisation should be encouraged in the developing world because:

- it is easier to spread Western ideas and values amongst a concentrated city population than a thinly dispersed rural population
- in the city, the individual is free from the obligations and constraints found in rural areas
- cities have a cultural effect on the rest of society. Malcolm Cross (1979) notes that 'the city is the key entry point for Western values and ideas to undeveloped societies; the city is the nucleus for the cultural penetration of the modernising society'.

Modernisation theory believed that these motors of development would produce a new capitalist **entrepreneurial** middle-class who believed in change, and who were willing to take risks and therefore drive progress forward. As Timmons Roberts and Hite (2000) note, 'in a traditional society the entrepreneur is a social deviant because he is doing something new and different; in a modern society change is routine, innovation is valued, and the entrepreneur esteemed'.

What is meant by 'deviance'? Explain, using examples from your studies, how deviance is relative to time, place and social context.

Rostow believed that the pinnacle of such modernity was 'the age of high mass consumption' in which the majority of citizens live in urban rather than rural areas, work in offices or in skilled factory jobs and enjoy a comfortable lifestyle organised around **conspicuous consumption**. Life expectancy is high and most citizens have access to a welfare state that includes healthcare and free education.

Some general criticisms of modernisation theory

1 Some commentators claim that modernisation theory is ethnocentric in three ways.
- It implies that the traditional values and social institutions of the developing world have little value. This is certainly true of early modernisation theorists such as Parsons but neo-modernisation theory argues that capitalist culture can make use of traditions within societies in order to bring about modernisation. Edwards (1992) suggests that the economic success of the Asian tiger economies and China is due to a successful combination of the Chinese Confucian religion and Western rational thinking and practices. Religion in these societies has encouraged the emergence of a moral and authoritarian political leadership that demands sacrifice, obedience and hard work from its population in return for prosperity. This has paved the way for an acceptance of Western economic and cultural practices such as widespread respect for **meritocratic** education for both men and women, discipline and the acquisition of technical skills.
- It ignores the crisis of modernism in both the developed and developing worlds. In the developed world there are problems such as inequalities in the distribution of wealth, poverty, homelessness, high rates of crime, drug abuse and suicide. In the developing world poverty has not been eradicated and the resulting disillusion may lead to non-Western societies resisting modernisation because they equate it with Western or American **cultural imperialism** or exploitation.
- It smacks of Western propaganda and ideology. Rostow actually described communism as a disease. Moreover, Malcolm Cross points out that Inkeles' modern man is essentially an individualised version of the American Dream. However, in defence of modernisation theory, it rightly celebrates American capitalism as a success. It may be interested in opening up new markets for its products but it also genuinely believes that capitalism can bring benefits to the developing world. Moreover, Herb Thompson (2001) argues that in general industrialising societies are not becoming like the United States. He argues that the United States is a deviant case because its people hold more traditional

values and beliefs than those in other equally prosperous societies.

2 It has been argued that education only benefits a small section of developing societies. There is evidence that educated elites monopolise top positions and restrict upward mobility, create vast inequalities in wealth through corruption and the siphoning-off of aid into their own bank accounts, and engage in human-rights abuses in their desire to hold onto power. However, in defence of modernisation theory, it can be argued that education has some of these effects in all societies.

Suggest ways in which elites in Britain may restrict upward mobility.

3 Modernisation has **ecological** limits. The existing process of modernisation cannot be extended to all societies because of the limits of the planet. For example, for all nations to enjoy similar standards of living would involve a six-fold increase in global consumption and unsustainable pollution. There are already signs in some developing societies that such modernisation is a problem. As Esteva and Austin (1987) notes: 'In Mexico, you must either be numb or very rich if you fail to notice that "development" stinks. The damage to persons, the corruption of politics and the degradation of nature which until recently were only implicit in "development" can now be seen, touched and smelled.'

4 Cross argues that modernisation theory assumes that all societies will advance in the same way through a fixed set of changes. However, this can be challenged in two main ways.
   ● There is no reason to assume that traditional societies share the same features or that capitalism will mould societies in the same fashion. The evidence suggests that there exist a diversity of both traditional and capitalist societies. Modernisation theory has been slow to understand that value systems and institutions tend to be **culture-specific**. For example, Ethiopia and Somalia may be neighbouring countries but their cultures are quite different from one another and they each require different development programmes.
   ● Traditional societies cannot develop in the same way as modern Western societies because they exist within a global economy dominated by Western interests. For example, it may not be in the industrialised world's interest to let poorer countries develop manufacturing industry that may compete with their own.

5 The assumption that cultural ideas can initiate economic growth is challenged by **empirical** evidence collected by Inglehart and Baker (2000) based on a study of 61 pre-industrial societies. They found that all the pre-industrial societies for which they had data placed a strong emphasis on religion and male dominance in economic and political life, deference to parental authority and traditional gender roles and the importance of family life. Such societies were also authoritarian, found cultural diversity threatening and were generally opposed to social change. Advanced industrial societies tended to have the opposite characteristics. However, Inglehart and Baker's data suggests that

such cultural characteristics were the product of economic insecurity and low levels of material well-being rather than the cause of it. Culture therefore may be less important than differential access to scarce resources.

The influence of modernisation theory today

Despite these empirical and theoretical problems, modernisation theory still exerts a considerable influence.

The 'people first' aid policies of non-governmental agencies which aim to help the rural poor by helping them take control of agricultural projects through training and education are based on the quite distinct modernisation principle of 'intervention'. As Burkey (1993) notes 'the poor are seldom able to initiate a self-reliant development process without outside stimulation. An external agent must therefore be the catalyst'. Critics of this modernisation approach are keen to describe it as **paternalistic** but they very rarely offer alternatives that are not idealistic in their view of what the poor can achieve on their own.

Neo-liberal theories of development, dominant in the 1990s, were strongly influenced by aspects of modernisation theory, despite their championing of the free market and rejection of intervention of any sort. In particular, neo-liberals argue that tradition (especially systems of obligations found in traditional kinship systems) impede the proper working of the economic market.

The work of the neo-modernisation theorist, Samuel Huntington (1993) has been very influential in recent years. He strongly affirms the importance of culture as the primary variable for both development and the conflict generated by that development. He asserts that the world is divided into eight major 'cultural zones' based on cultural differences that have persisted for centuries. These zones were shaped by religious traditions that are still powerful today, despite the forces of modernisation. The zones are Western Christianity, the Orthodox world, the Islamic world, and the Confucian, Japanese, Hindu, African, and Latin American zones.

Huntington sees future world confrontations and conflicts developing between these cultural zones. He suggests that the roots of this conflict lie in the exceptional values and institutions of the West that have brought it economic success and which are lacking in the rest of the world. Huntington argues that non-Western civilisations resent this success and what they see as the West's attempts to impose its version of **modernity** upon them through control of institutions like the United Nations and the World Bank. Huntington concludes that resistance to Western forms of modernisation are now more likely to take the form of a return to **fundamentalism** in the Arab world and the sponsorship of international terrorism against Western interests and targets. Huntington's ideas seem particularly significant in the USA after September 11, 2001.

The contribution of modernisation theory

Early modernisation theory can rightly be criticised for dismissing the culture of the developing world as irrelevant. However, it is often too easy and 'politically correct' to blame the problems of developing societies on colonialism, world trade, debt, global capitalism, etc. These factors are important but modernisation theory has probably been right (and certainly unpopular) in insisting that in order to reduce poverty, we need to understand culture or at least take it into account when assessing development progress. As we shall see, this once deeply unpopular view is again in fashion as seen in some postmodernist accounts of development that suggest culture is and always has been more important than economics in encouraging social change.

KEY TERMS

American Dream – a set of ideas associated with the USA which suggests that if you work hard you can be an economic success regardless of social background.

Ascription – the occupying of jobs, authority within the family and political roles on the basis of inheritance or fixed characteristics such as gender and race.

Collectivism – the notion that members of the family/tribal unit put the interests of the group before self-interest.

Communism – a political system and set of beliefs that stresses shared ownership of property by the group or community.

Conspicuous consumption – consuming goods for status reasons, e.g. wearing designer labels.

Cultural imperialism – global dominance of American culture such as McDonalds and Disney.

Culture specific – relevant to a particular culture.

Ecological – concerned with the environment.

Empirical – based on first-hand research.

Entrepreneurial – willing to take risks in investing money in business and to compete with others for markets.

Ethnocentrism – see Key Terms in Topic 1.

Evolutionary – gradual change or progress that is the result of natural accumulation.

Fundamentalism – see Key Terms in Topic 1.

Geographical mobility – being able to move around the country easily to meet economic demands for particular skills.

Individualism – the notion that individual self-interest should come before the interests of the group.

Interventionist – believing in the need to take an active role to change a situation.

Meritocratic – rewarding people on the basis of their intelligence, ability, effort, qualifications, etc., i.e. merit.

Modernity – the state of being modern or fully developed.

Neo-liberal – view that the free market is the best way of organising societies. Against government intervention in society.

Particularism – loving someone or treating someone in a certain way on the basis of them being a member of your family regardless of their level of achievement outside the family group.

Paternalistic – patronising. Not believing others are capable on their own.

Revolutionary – radical or extreme change that can come about both gradually or swiftly.

Subsistence farming – producing crops in order to subsist or survive only.

Trickle-down – view that wealth will 'drip' down to benefit the less well-off.

Universalism – the idea that occupational roles be allocated on the basis of universal norms such as achievement measured by examinations and qualifications.

Urbanisation – the growth of cities.

CHECK YOUR UNDERSTANDING

1 What are the two major aims of modernisation theory?

2 What are the economic characteristics of traditional undeveloped societies according to Rostow?

3 Identify four cultural values or institutions that allegedly hold up development.

4 How are geographical mobility, kinship systems and modernisation inter-connected?

5 What is the role of aid, debt and transnational investment in development?

6 How might education and urbanisation help accelerate modernisation?

7 What characteristics does Rostow's final stage of development have?

8 Explain what is meant by the two meanings of 'crisis of modernism' in terms of their critique of modernisation theory.

9 Why is modernisation theory criticised for being ideological?

10 How do Cross and Inglehart and Baker challenge modernisation theory?

11 What influence does modernisation theory have today?

12 Why is there conflict between the West and Islamic world according to Huntington?

Exploring modernisation

Item A

The 'modern' man was one who scored highly on a scale of 'activism' as opposed to fatalism according to the modernisation theorist, J. A. Kahl. The 'modern man' experienced a relatively low degree of integration with extended kin but a high level of individualism, contact with the mass media and a pronounced interest in urban living. 'Modern' men also saw the occupational structure as open and regarded the sacrifices of occupational effort as worthwhile. The 'modern man' is stimulated by the city and urban life, 'he sees it as open to influence by ordinary citizens like himself'. Furthermore 'he sees life changes or career opportunities as open rather than closed; a man of humble origins has a chance to fulfil his dreams and rise within the system. He participates in urban life by actively availing himself of the mass media. He reads newspapers, listens to the radio, discusses civil affairs'. Not surprisingly, the thesis is advanced that the more modern one's men, the more likely a society is to develop and modernise, that is to converge towards the goal of 'development' reached by the United States.

Adapted from: M. Cross (1979) *Urbanisation and Urban Growth in the Caribbean* quoted in M. O'Donnell (1983) *New Introductory Reader in Sociology*, London: Nelson Harrap, pp.242–243.

Item B

The education system is like a train which travels on a single track bound for one destination, but which ejects most of its passengers, without stopping, at several points along the route. In other words, the system favours a small minority who are believed to be the most able academically, at the expense of the vast majority of others. By doing so, it promotes a spirit of selfish competition, rather than co-operation. It breeds individualism, élitism and class consciousness, since material wealth and the comfortable life seem to be the goal at the end of the academic ordeal.

Republic of Zambia, Ministry of Education, 1976 quoted in R. Carmen (1996) *Autonomous Development: Humanising the Landscape*, London: Zed Books, p.62

Item C

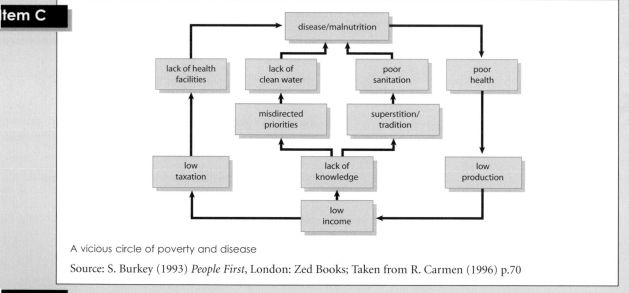

A vicious circle of poverty and disease

Source: S. Burkey (1993) *People First*, London: Zed Books; Taken from R. Carmen (1996) p.70

Item D

Islamic fundamentalist projects have emerged in all Muslim societies and among Muslim minorities in non-Muslim societies. These projects have originated as a socio-cultural movement of protest and frustration of a generation of youth that has been excluded, economically and politically, from the accelerated modernisation of Muslim societies and their partial and disjointed view of the global economy. Oliver Roy argues that today's masses who follow Islam are not traditionalists. Instead, they live with the values of the modern city. They are fascinated by the values of consumerism. They live in a world of movie theatres, cafes, jeans, video and sports, but they live precariously from menial jobs or remain unemployed in immigrant ghettos with the frustrations inherent in an unattainable consumerist world. These people see themselves as the outcasts of a failed modernism and, for reasons to do with the cultural history of Islam, their exclusion from modernity takes a religious meaning. Militant resistance to modernity and what is perceived to be its source, i.e. the secular West becomes the central component of Islamic identity.

Adapted from: A. Hoogvelt (2001) *Globalisation and the Post-colonial World*, Basingstoke: Palgrave, pp.212–215

1 Using Item A, outline the main features of a modern developed society.

2 Using Item B and other material, assess the role of education in development.

3 How does Item C support modernisation theory?

4 What policy solutions for the problems seen in Item C would agencies influenced by modernisation principles suggest?

5 Using Item D and other material, outline and assess the view that modernisation theory and its policy solutions have failed the developing world.

WWWebtask

Visit the World Bank web-site, www.worldbank.org/ and using the search facility, look for policy statements or documents that focus on culture, poverty, population growth, education, etc. What aspects of World Bank policy endorses the view that it supports an industrial–capitalist or modernisation model of development?

EXAM PRACTICE

Extract from AQA-style question

Examine the strengths and weaknesses of modernisation theory. (40 marks)

Research ideas

1 Modernisation theory has been profoundly influenced by the theories of social change advocated by classical sociologists such as Durkheim, Weber and Tonnies. You should think about investigating these theories in order to enhance your understanding of modernisation theory.

2 Think about your own experience of modern society. Using the knowledge obtained from this Topic, make a list of development-friendly values, attitudes and agencies. Follow this up with a mini-survey of your friends and family to see how many of them subscribe to the traditional values, e.g. community, co-operation, particularism, etc. so disapproved of by some modernisation theorists.

Getting you thinking

What do you think the cartoon symbolises about the relationship between the developed and developing world?

The message from the cartoon is clear – the wealthy nations of the world got rich on the backs of the poorer nations. This is essentially the message of the Marxist-based 'dependency theory'.

The Marxist economist-sociologist, Andre Gunder Frank has provided the major critique of the principles underlying modernisation theory. Frank (1971) argues that developing countries have found it difficult to sustain development along modernisation lines (see Topic 2) – not because of their own deficiencies, but because the developed West has deliberately and systematically **under-developed** them in a variety of ways, leaving them today in a state of dependency. Hence, Frank's theory is known as **dependency** theory.

The world capitalist system

Frank argues that since the sixteenth century there has existed a world capitalist system which is organised in a similar fashion to the unequal and exploitative economic or class relationships that make up capitalist societies. This world capitalist system is organised as an interlocking chain comprised of **metropolis** or **core nations** (i.e. the developed world) which benefit from the economic surplus of **satellite** or **peripheral countries** (i.e. the developing world). These peripheral countries 'have low wages, enforced by coercive regimes that undermine independent labour unions and social movements. The metropolis exploits them for cheap labour, cheap minerals and fertile tropical soils' (p.12). This results in the accumulation of wealth in the developed world and in stagnation and destitution in the developing world. For dependency theory, then, under-development in the periphery is the product of development in the centre and vice versa. In turn, the elites of the developing world situated in their own urban metropolis (i.e. cities) and sponsored by the core countries exploit those living in rural regions or the periphery of their own countries. Foster-Carter (see Haralambos, 1985, p.96) suggests that the ultimate satellite is a landless rural labourer, who has nothing and no one to exploit and is probably female.

The origins of dependency

Slavery

Frank argues that dependency and under-development were established through slavery and colonialism, both of which helped kick-start Britain's industrial revolution. Over a two-hundred year period (1650–1850), the triangular slave trade shipped approximately nine million Africans aged between 15 and 35 across the Atlantic to work as an exceptionally cheap form of labour on cotton, sugar and tobacco plantations in America and the West Indies, mainly owned by British

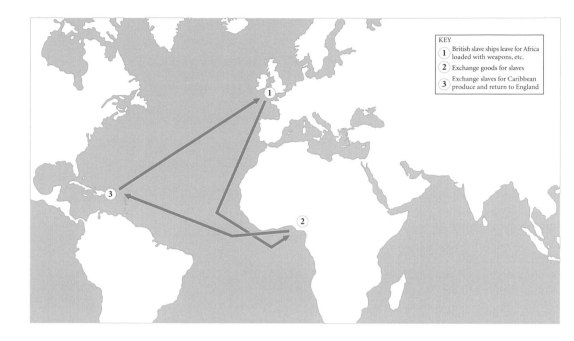

The 'Triangular Trade': the slave route

KEY
1) British slave ships leave for Africa loaded with weapons, etc.
2) Exchange goods for slaves
3) Exchange slaves for Caribbean produce and return to England

Source: A. Webster (1990) *Introduction to the Sociology of Development*, Basingstoke: Macmillan

settlers. This generated tremendous profits for both the British slave-traders and the plantation owners. Britain also enjoyed a virtual monopoly over raw materials such as cotton, tobacco and sugar which benefited industrial expansion such as that found in the Lancashire/Yorkshire textile industry.

Using the terms 'ascribed' and 'achieved status', compare slavery and the allocation of jobs in Britain today.

Colonialism

Colonialism locked much of Africa, Asia and Latin America even further into an exploitative relationship with the capitalist West. During the period 1650–1900, using their superior naval and military technology, European powers, with Britain at the fore, were able to conquer and colonise many parts of the world. As Harrison (1990) argues, this **imperial** expansion was to work the greatest transformation the human world has ever seen. The principal result of European rule was the creation of a global economy. Consequently, colonialism had a number of effects that benefited the world capitalist system.

● Colonies were primarily exploited for their cheap food, raw materials and labour.
● The most fertile land was appropriated for growing cash crops for export to the West.
● New markets were created for the industrial world's manufactured goods.
● Local industries, especially manufacturing, which attempted to compete with those of the colonial powers were either destroyed or undermined by cheap imported manufactured goods from the West.
● Divisions and conflicts were created or reinforced between indigenous peoples as the colonial powers sponsored some

tribes and social groups, giving them wealth and power as a reward for acting as their agents of social control.
● Arbitrary borders were imposed on countries (especially in Africa) which are partially the cause of civil wars and refugee problems today.

A case study of Jamaica carried out by Elliott and Harvey (2000) supports Frank's thesis. They conclude that Jamaica's development problems will never be solved by policies that ignore the vast inequalities in power arising from Jamaica's political, social and economic history. They suggest that the root of Jamaica's contemporary problems lie in the creation of the plantation economy by the British which resulted in vast inequalities in ownership of land that persist to this day. Today the Jamaican economy continues to serve the needs of the Jamaican ruling class rather than those of the masses.

Contemporary forms of dependency: neo-colonialism

Many colonies have achieved political independence today but dependency theory argues that their exploitation continues via **neo-colonialism**. New forms of colonialism have appeared which are more subtle but equally destructive as slavery and colonialism.

The term 'neo' means a new version. Identify other examples from your studies where old ideas have been updated to create new versions.

Neo-colonial exploitation and world trade

World trade is one aspect of neo-colonialism. Despite political independence, the legacy of colonialism means that the economies of developing countries are still dependent upon the developed nations in a number of ways.

- Developing nations are still dependent for their export earnings upon a small number of cash crops or raw materials. This over-concentration on **primary products** (often a single commodity) was the result of the colonial powers reorganising societies after conquest in order to produce one or two particular crops or materials required by their industries.
- Over-production of the primary products or any fall in demand caused by variation in Western tastes and lifestyles can have a severe negative effect upon their economies. This situation is made worse by the fact that their markets often consist of only a few metropolitan countries rather than many – with the main one usually being the colonial mother country.
- Western nations can limit the amount of goods, especially manufactured goods, imported from the developing world by imposing tariffs (a type of import tax which results in the good becoming more expensive than home-produced goods) and quotas.
- Western inflation means that, over the past thirty years, the prices of manufactured goods produced by the West have risen rapidly whilst the prices of the primary products mainly produced by the developing world have actually fallen. Hayter (1981) notes that cash crops are 'false riches' because countries have to produce more and more of them to get the same amount of manufactured goods in return. In 1960 the earnings from 25 tons of natural rubber would buy four tractors but today it is not enough to buy one. As Hayter notes 'in their desperate search for foreign exchange, under-developed countries produce more and more, thus setting up a vicious circle of over-production and declining prices'.

The exploitation of this export-orientated primary production found in developing countries is often made easier by a class alliance between the agents of the developed world, i.e. the transnational companies and the local landed elite. The power and economic interests of the latter often derived from colonialism. As Hoogvelt (2001) notes, their 'economic interests became increasingly intertwined with those of the advanced capitalist states, and their cultural lifestyles and tastes were a faithful imitation of the same'. Cardoso (1972) points out that these elites paved the way for the penetration of **transnational** companies into developing countries on favourable terms for Western capitalism (see Topic 7) and economically benefited themselves from the related trade and banking arrangements. In some extreme cases, these elites, who are often military in origin, have even removed threats to foreign interests by violence and their repressive powers in terms of their use of police and military serves to assure the co-operation of the masses.

Examples of countries reliant on a limited range of agricultural produce in their exports, 1990

Country	Type of produce	Named produce as % of agricultural exports	All agricultural produce as % of merchandise exported
Réunion	Sugar	93.3	79.2
Cuba	Sugar	92.3	88.2
Uganda	Coffee	92.2	86.4
Ghana	Cocoa	85.8	41.2
Jamaica	Coffee	81.2	19.9
Swaziland	Sugar	78.3	38.1
Martinique	Bananas	66.4	60.8
Sri Lanka	Tea	66.2	39.0
Bangladesh	Jute	64.8	12.7
Ecuador	Bananas	60.0	28.7

Source: J. Chrispin and F. Jagede (2000) *Population, Resources and Development*, London: HarperCollins

How can elites control populations other than through the use of the police and miltary services? Give examples from your studies.

Neo-colonialism, the World Trade Organisation and transnational exploitation

In 1994 the World Trade Organisation (WTO) was set up by the rich and powerful nations in order to reduce national trade barriers and to liberalise trade. At the heart of the WTO are the transnational companies (TNCs) which control two-thirds of world trade. Neo-Marxists accuse such companies of exploiting developing countries for cheap labour, cheap raw materials and new markets. It is suggested that such companies wield economic and political power far in excess of that wielded by governments of developing nations. Moreover, they are unaccountable and this has led to TNCs abusing their power by interfering politically in the affairs of democratically elected governments as well as behaving unethically in regard to environmental destruction and aggressive marketing of harmful products. We will explore the arguments and evidence for and against the WTO and TNCs in Topic 7.

Neo-colonialism, aid and debt

Dependency theory argues that official aid and the international debt crisis that has stemmed from borrowing money from Western governments and multilateral organisations such as the World Bank and IMF is the third major component of neo-colonialist exploitation. This will be examined in detail in Topic 4.

Urbanisation

The modernisation focus on encouraging urbanisation as the focus for development planning and policy has been criticised by dependency theory. In contrast, dependency theory suggests urbanisation in the developing world is not acting as an effective force for development – rather it is likely to sustain under-development. Dependency theorists note that modernisation theory based its view of urbanisation on the European experience. However, European urbanisation was a response to industrialisation when people migrated to towns and cities to take work in factories. In developing societies, people have migrated to cities leaving behind land which provided **subsistence** but jobs are not available because transnational investment tends to be in highly mechanised forms of production. Moreover, urban populations in developing countries are disproportionately young and fertile so the growth of populations in these cities is more rapid than the European experience.

Over-urbanisation is now a major problem in the developing world because their housing and basic services are unable to cope. In many cities **shanty towns** have become the norm. These suffer from a range of major social problems such as unemployment, poverty, overcrowding, disease, etc. due to a lack of clean water and sanitation, malnutrition, high infant mortality and high crime and suicide rates.

Take any two of these 'social problems' and suggest how they could be measured. Identify problems involved in their measurement.

However, the urban elite – the successors of those put into power by colonial rule – own and control a disproportionate share of wealth and monopolise political power in the city. Consequently the city is often the focus of repressive social controls and human rights abuses because such elites see the concentration of the poor and disprivileged as a threat to their power.

Exploring urbanisation

Item A

A city in a developed country

Item B

A city in a developing country

1 Compare the two cities using the photographs provided.

Solutions to dependency

Timmons Roberts and Hite (2000) argue that there are two sets of views when it comes to ideas for fixing these situations of dependency.

1   The first view argues that 'under-development is not a phase but a permanent, inescapable position. In other words, the only way this situation of dependency can be escaped is to escape from the entire capitalist system' (p.13). Frank's theory of dependency suggests that the peripheral or satellite countries can never develop in a sustained way so long as they are stuck in what Paul Baran (1957) calls an 'imperialist' stage of capitalism and remain part of the world capitalist system. One solution is 'isolation' as in the example of China (although even that country is now adopting capitalist free-market principles and trading extensively with the West). Another solution is to 'break away' at a time when the core or 'metropolis' country is weak, as in times of war or recession. This may involve a socialist revolution in order to overthrow the local elite – as in Cuba in the early 1960s. However, Frank is pessimistic about this and believes that, sooner or later, the global capitalist economy will reassert its control through denying the rogue country access to free world trade, applying sanctions to countries that attempt to trade with it and through the threat of military force. This has been Cuba's experience for the past forty years.

2   The second view argues that despite dependency, there is some scope for what has been called 'associate development' or 'dependent development' through nationalist economic policies such as Import Substitution Industrialisation (ISI). ISI basically involved industrialisation which was aimed at producing consumer goods that would normally be imported from the developed world. ISI transformed the economies of South America, as Green illustrates:

By the early 1960s domestic industry supplied 95% of Mexico's and 98% of Brazil's consumer goods. From 1950 to 1980 Latin America's industrial output went up six times. (quoted in Hoogvelt (2001) p.243)

However, ISI eventually failed because:

- It neglected to address the issue of class and income distribution – that is, the existing elites controlled ISI and this led to further deepening of income and wealth inequalities in these societies.
- It was still dependent on the West for technical expertise, spare parts, oil, etc.
- The export-orientated form of industrialisation adopted by the Asian tiger economies was seen as more successful.

Despite these difficulties in coming up with realistic solutions, Hoogvelt argues that the influence of dependency theory on the political ideologies of many developing countries in the 1960s and 1970s shouldn't be underestimated. She notes that political leaders, particularly in Africa, used the principles of dependency theory to argue for development as liberation (see Topic 1) from Western exploitation. Political and social movements in Africa in this period consequently stressed nationalism, self-reliance and delinking as a means of countering neo-colonialism.

Criticisms of dependency theory

Frank's biggest problem is that he fails to be precise in his use of terms. 'Dependency' is extremely difficult to operationalise and therefore test or measure empirically. Some sociologists such as Myrdal (1968) have attempted to measure the amount of investment put into the developing world and compare it with the amount of profit taken out. However, it is generally agreed that this is a crude and imprecise method that does not necessarily measure dependency, exploitation, and subordination.

What is meant by 'operationalising' and 'measure empirically'? Give examples from your studies of other concepts that are difficult to operationalise and measure empirically.

Clearly, modernisation theory would argue that Western aid and transnational corporations do bring benefits to developing nations. For example, the economic success of the Asian tigers can be partly attributed to the role of Japanese aid and transnational investment. However, in reply, neo-Marxists point out that these societies are heavily in debt whilst their industrial base is largely controlled by Japanese TNCs. Their economies have also demonstrated instability in recent years as the Japanese economy has faltered and foreign investment has been withdrawn. In 1997, Thailand, Indonesia and South Korea had to accept Western rescue packages. Moreover, the economic success of these economies is founded on people working very long hours for very low wages. Economic growth may have been rapid but it has only benefited the top 10% of these societies.

John Goldthorpe (1975) and other liberals have argued that colonialism had the positive benefits of providing developing countries with a basic infrastructure. Moreover, it provided people with wage-labour and made more efficient use of land. He also points out that those countries without colonies (such as Germany and Japan) have performed economically better than those with empires, whilst countries such as Afghanistan and Ethiopia, which were never colonised, face severe problems of development because they lack the infrastructure provided by the colonial powers.

Timmons, Roberts and Hite note that Frank's version of dependency theory fails to explain why there appear to be greater levels of exploitation over time or why there are significant differences among poorer countries. Later dependency theorists such as Gereffi (1994) and Evans (1979) have addressed these issues by noting that the influence of the core is not always homogeneous and that differences among elites in the periphery can explain different political regimes, economies and class relationships within the peripheral countries.

World systems theory

Some sociologists, notably Chase-Dunn (1975) and Gereffi (1994), argue that the overly descriptive nature of dependency theory means that it does not have much explanatory power. These sociologists subscribe instead to a variation on dependency theory called world systems theory, which was a response to criticisms of dependency theory. The founder of world systems theory was Wallerstein (1979). His theory has four underlying principles to it:

1   Individual countries or nation states are not an adequate unit of sociological analysis. Rather, we must look at the overall social system which transcends (and has done for centuries) national boundaries. Capitalism is responsible for creating the world order or Modern World System (MWS) because capital from its beginning has always ignored national borders in its search for profit. At the economic level then, the MWS forms one unified system dominated by the logic of profit and the market.

2   Wallerstein builds upon dependency theory by suggesting that the MWS is characterised by an economic division of labour consisting of a structured set of relations between three types of capitalist zone: the core, semi-periphery and periphery. The 'core' or developed countries control world trade and monopolise the production of manufactured goods. The 'semi-peripheral' zone includes countries like Brazil and South Africa which resemble the core countries in terms of their urban centres but also have extremes of rural poverty. Countries in the semi-periphery are often connected to the core because the latter contract work out to them. Finally, Wallerstein identifies the 'peripheral' countries (such as much of Africa) which are at the bottom of this world hierarchy. These countries provide the raw materials, e.g. cash crops to the core and semi-periphery and are the emerging markets in which the core countries market their manufactured goods.

3   Wallerstein argues that countries can be upwardly or downwardly mobile in the hierarchy of the MWS although most countries have not been able to move up. This obviously partially solves one of the weaknesses of dependency theory, i.e. the fact there is such tremendous economic variation in the developing world. It could be argued that the Asian tiger economies have moved up into the semi-periphery. Some have argued that the UK may now be a semi-peripheral economic power rather than a core one. Wallerstein's model, therefore, is more flexible than Frank's because it allows us to look at the world system as

a whole and to explain changes in the fortune of individual countries.

4   The processes by which surplus wealth is extracted from the periphery are those already described by dependency theory, i.e. historically through slavery and colonialism and contemporaneously through forms of neo-colonialism.

Wallerstein goes on to suggest that this MWS is constantly evolving in its search for profit. The signs of this are constant **commodification** (attaching a price to everything), **de-skilling**, **proletarianisation** and mechanisation. Wallerstein shows his Marxist roots by insisting this will lead to the **polarisation** of class. It will supposedly generate so many dispossessed, excluded, marginal and poor people that in the long term the world economy will be located within a socialist world economy.

What is polarisation? Can this term be applied successfully to modern Britain?

Evaluation of world systems theory

The main problem with world systems theory, as with Marxism generally, is that it is too **economistic**. It assumes that the economy is driving all other aspects of the system, i.e. politics, culture, etc. Bergesen (1990) argues that it was military conquest and political manipulation of local peoples that imposed economic dependency on developing nations rather than the logic of capitalism. Wallerstein has also been accused of being vague about how challenges to the established capitalist order can be mounted and how the socialist world economy will come about.

What other criticisms have been made of Marxist perspectives?

Wallerstein is also criticised by modernisation theory which accuses him of neglecting the importance of internal factors especially cultural factors in the failure of LDCs to develop. For example, his critics point out that he ignores the corruption of LDC elites and their wasteful spending.

The most important criticism, however, is of Wallerstein's methodology. The theory, like Frank's, is highly abstract. It is also rather vague in its definitions of concepts such as 'core', 'peripheral', etc. and many of its propositions cannot be measured or tested.

However, despite these criticisms, Wallerstein's work was one of the first to acknowledge the 'globalisation' of the world (although he himself never uses the word). He drew attention to the international division of labour which some see as the basis of global inequality. Lately, however, sociologists working from a globalisation perspective have noted that relationships within the world system are far from one-way. Economic inter-dependence can also mean that problems in the developing world (such as financial crises caused by debt) may have profound ripple effects on the economies of core countries thereby causing unemployment and destabilisation of Western currencies. These themes will be explored in greater detail in Topic 7.

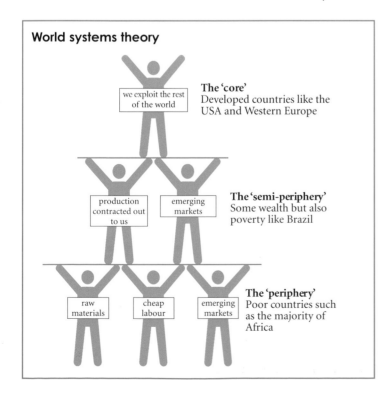

World systems theory

we exploit the rest of the world

The 'core'
Developed countries like the USA and Western Europe

production contracted out to us

emerging markets

The 'semi-periphery'
Some wealth but also poverty like Brazil

raw materials

cheap labour

emerging markets

The 'periphery'
Poor countries such as the majority of Africa

Item A

Colonial powers laid the foundation of the present division of the world into industrial nations on the one hand, and hewers of wood and drawers of water on the other. They wiped out indigenous industry and forced the colonies to buy their manufactures. They undermined the self sufficiency of regions like Africa and transformed it into a source of raw materials for Western industry. Sometimes they forced locals to grow the desired crops. Sometimes they bought land or just seized it to set up their plantations, drafting in cheap labour to work them. In this way the colonial powers created the world economic order that still prevails today, of industrial centre and primary producing periphery, prosperous metropolis and poverty-stricken satellites. Apologists of empire – and there are some, even today – point to the benefits it often brought; education, science and technology, the rule of law, efficient administration and so on. However, despite this, almost all the imbalances that now cripple the economies, societies and politics of the developing world had their origins in colonialism.

Adapted from: P. Harrison (1990) *Inside the Third World: The Anatomy of Poverty*, (2nd edition), Harmondsworth: Penguin

Item B

There are a number of serious theoretical weaknesses that can be identified in Frank's account of dependency. Firstly, like the concept of modernisation, the concept of dependency is much too vague to be of use. It tells us very little other than that economies are not autonomous but depend on each other for growth. This is not unique to developing countries. Kitching (1982) argues that the only real measure of dependency is the assessment of the amount of money that is invested and the amount over and above this that is taken out by the metropolitan centre. But simple measures of the net transfer of money say nothing about the possible benefits that may have arisen from the initial investment – the spin-off perhaps from the construction of a railway.

Adapted from: A. Webster (1984) *Introduction to the Sociology of Development*, (2nd edition), Basingstoke: Macmillan, p.86–87

Item C

From the beginning the world economy has been stratified into three layers: core, periphery and semi-periphery. The dynamic quality of the world system is that it allows for the upward and downward mobility of nations. It is during world economic recessions that most of the relative shifting of positions occurs. Theoretically it is not possible for all states to develop simultaneously. The rise of some nations always occurs at the expense of others that decline. Successful strategies of national upward mobility include 'promotion by invitation', 'self-reliance' and 'seizing the chance'. The successful strategy is, however, unsuccessful from the point of view of achieving national economic independence. Some world sociologists have used the world system to make sense of the reversal of fortunes evidently experienced by the newly industrialised countries that were upwardly mobile, and some of the core countries (notably Britain) demonstrably in decline by any measure of international statistical comparison.

Adapted from: A. Hoogvelt (2001) *Globalisation and the Post-colonial World*, Basingstoke: Palgrave, p.59–60

1 Using Item A and other material, outline the effects of colonialism on the economies of developing nations according to dependency theory.

2 Describe how critics of dependency theory generally view the role of colonialism in developing countries.

3 Explain why dependency theory believes that world trade penalises the developing world.

4 Identify and explain the three agents of neo-colonialism allegedly engaged in exploiting the developing world.

5 Using Item B and other material, explain why some sociologists are not happy with the concept of 'dependency'.

6 Using Item C as a starting point, compare and contrast how Frank and Wallerstein explain the role of capitalism in the world order.

KEY TERMS

Colonialism – the take-over and exploitation of countries, usually by means of superior military force.

Commodification – applying an economic value to a range of human activities.

De-skilling – breaking down expensive complex occupational skills into routine and simple tasks.

Dependency – the state of being dependent on more powerful countries for investment, trade, aid, debt relief, charity, etc.

Homogeneous – see Key Terms in Topic 1.

Imperial – empire-building.

Metropolis or core nations – terms used by Frank to describe the developed world.

Neo-colonialism – modern forms of exploitation of poorer societies by rich societies which are usually dressed up as beneficial, e.g. aid, world trade and transnational investment.

Polarisation – the Marxist idea that the experience of workers will become so alienating that they will see the need for socialist revolution.

Primary products – crops and mineral extracts.

Proletarianisation – the process by which professional, managerial and white-collar workers experience convergence with working-class conditions of work, service, etc.

Satellite or peripheral countries – terms used by Frank to describe the developing world. The terms indicate its dependence on the 'core' nations.

Shanty towns – very poor 'towns' with almost no sanitation, facilities and proper housing that develop outside cities in some developing countries because people are drawn to the city but find there is nowhere to live or that they cannot afford anywhere.

Subsistence – see Key Terms in Topic 2.

Tariffs – taxes on imports to protect a country's own industries.

Transnational – see Key Terms in Topic 1.

Under-development – see Key Terms in Topic 1.

CHECK YOUR UNDERSTANDING

1 Define 'under-development' and 'dependency'.

2 Outline Frank's theory of the world capitalist system.

3 Who is at the very bottom of this system according to Foster-Carter?

4 How did the triangular slave trade result in a super-accumulation of capital for Britain?

5 What advantages did colonialism have for Western capitalism?

6 How are the economies of the developing world locked into and dependent upon the developed nations today?

7 What role have some elites of developing countries played in the world capitalist system?

8 Apart from world trade, what two other forms of Western intervention are described as neo-colonialist today?

9 How does dependency theory criticise the modernisation view that urbanisation is a catalyst of positive change in the developing world?

10 What solutions does Frank offer for dependency?

11 How does the solution of dependent development differ from that offered by Frank?

12 Identify the similarities and differences between the theories of Frank and Wallerstein.

Research idea

Bananas are a really interesting topic to research if you want to understand the way that world trade is loaded in favour of the developed world. Recently a 'trade war' has broken out between Europe (which supports bananas produced by a confederation of Caribbean countries) and the USA (which supports bananas produced by American transnationals in Latin America). Find out as much as you can about this. Speak to your school or college Geography department and see whether they have any information. In particular, they may have copies of the following books: *Global Challenges* edited by Bob Digby (Heinemann, 2001) or *Population, Resources and Development* by Jane Chrispin and Francis Jegede (HarperCollins, 2000) that you could look at. Your research should try and comment on the following:

● the role of past colonial relations

● the role of TNCs

● tariffs

● trade blocs

● the role of the World Trade Organisation

● the impact on both Caribbean and South American

WWW Webtask

Follow bananas and world trade generally on the net by accessing 'Unpeeling the Banana Trade', Fairtrade Foundation on their web page: http//www.fairtrade.org.uk

See the Caribbean Banana Exporters Association side of the story on: http://www.cbea.org/

Also, check out the websites for the following charities/pressure groups and note their comments on world trade.

Traidcraft: www.traidcraft.co.uk/ – click on 'factsheets'

Christian Aid: www.christian-aid.org.uk

World Development Movement: www.wdm.org.uk/ – click on 'The Tricks of the Trade'

Actionaid: www.actionaid.org.uk

EXAM PRACTICE

Extract from AQA-style question

Examine the different ways in which sociologists have explained the relationship between development and the growth of cities. (40 marks)

Getting you thinking

Fact: The £20 billion that Britons pocketed in 1997 in windfall payments from building societies would cancel the entire debt of the lowest income countries in the developing world.

Fact: The £750 million cost of the Dome would cancel the entire debt of the eight countries that the United Nations ranks as 'least developed'.

Fact: The £16 billion Britain is spending on 232 Eurofighters would cancel the entire debt of South Asia and Sub-Saharan Africa.

Ali the sieve-maker's daughter, Zenithou, has half a face, the rest has been eaten by a sickness called the Grazer or Noma which eats through the muscles, the tissues and bones. In Niger where they live, there is no war, famine or pestilence but the Grazer is kept supplied with children by the starvation diets and a collapsing health system caused by pressure of international debt. In Niger, the poorest country in the world, they spend three times more money paying off foreign debt than on health and education. Debt means that they have no money to buy the antiseptic cream and mouthwash Zenithou needs to treat the Grazer. As a result, the World Health Organisation estimates that 80,000 children will die from this very treatable disease in this region. Niger owes Britain £8 million. If we cancelled this debt, Niger could inoculate 750,000 children from measles which kills nearly one in three children in Niger before they are five years old.

Adapted from: 'Suffering from Plague – The Plague of Debt' by Maggie O' Kane, *The Guardian*, May 11, 1998

1   Look carefully at the facts accompanying each of the pictures above. What is your view of the morality of the spending decisions above? Do you believe that we should take a lead in helping developing nations out of debt or even in cancelling it altogether? Try and list your reasons for and against such actions.

2   In your opinion, do we have a moral obligation to help children like Zenithou? What should the UK do about the Niger debt? How would we feel if 80,000 British kids died because of measles?

Many people believe that debt is of one's own making and that interference by assisting in any way or cancelling the debt is only going to encourage countries to become over-dependent on Western help. However, some of you may have suggested that debt is not the fault of the debtors. You may have argued that the cause of the problem lies with the developed world (and especially the desire of Western banks to lend money in order to make profit) and the organisation of world trade. The truth lies somewhere in between. Whatever 'truth' we go with, the facts tell us that children like Zenithou are suffering early death because of debt. Imagine how people would feel if any child died in the UK because of debt to building societies and banks. And yet Zenithou who has since died and eighty thousand other children, have done

so indirectly because the Niger owes the UK money. This section therefore explores some of these issues and looks at the inter-connectedness of British aid, world trade, the debt of the developing countries and children's deaths.

Aid

'Aid' refers to any flow of resources from developed countries to the developing world which may take the form of:

● a financial grant or material gift that does not have to be paid back
● a loan with interest.

Aid mainly involves the transfer of capital (i.e. money) but may also be made up of expertise (i.e. experts are sent and their wages are paid by the donor country), science and technology, medicines and contraceptives, weapons, and so on.

Types of aid

There are essentially four broad types of aid:

1 **Bilateral aid** involves governments in the developed world giving aid to governments in the developing world. This is known as 'official development assistance' and in the UK is administered by a branch of the Foreign Office, i.e. the Department for International Development (DfID) formerly the Overseas Development Agency (ODA). Bilateral aid accounted for about 51% of the DfID budget in 2000–2001.

2 **Multilateral aid** involves the UK donating capital (46% of the DfID budget in 2000/01) to agencies such as:

- **the World Bank:** This institution was set up after World War II by Western governments. Although all countries can join, US economic interests dominate its policy. It makes loans to member states at interest rates below those of commercial banks in order to finance **infrastructure** development projects such as power plants, hydro-electric dams, roads, etc. It is also the world's largest funding source for agricultural development. The Bank's International Development Association makes soft loans, i.e. with no or very low interest rates to the poorest countries
- the International Monetary Fund (IMF)
- the European Community: the UK, along with other member states, contributes to a European aid fund which allocates grants rather than loans to developing countries. Food aid has also been an important aspect of EC aid
- the United Nations: a small proportion of the UK's aid budget is allocated to UN agencies such as UNICEF (i.e. the UN's Children's educational fund).

3 Commercial banks lend money to developing countries at commercial rates of interest. In 2000–2001 private flows from the UK to developing countries were estimated at £1.4 billion.

4 Non-governmental organisations (NGOs), e.g. charities such as Oxfam, Save the Children Fund, etc. aim to raise donations from the general public by raising awareness of problems in the developing world. NGO fundraising is usually matched by donations from the DfID.

Top five recipients of DfID aid in 2000/01 (millions)		
1.	India	£105
2.	Uganda	£86
3.	Ghana	£73
4.	Bangladesh	£70
5.	Tanzania	£67

However, aid raised by NGOs is minute compared with bilateral and multilateral aid. The NGOs in the UK raise approximately £50 million annually (remember 50% of this comes from the DfID) which is less than one tenth of DfID official aid. NGOs prefer to target the 'poorest of the poor' and consequently tend to work with voluntary groups rather than the governments of developing countries on small-scale aid projects such as irrigation, and boring wells as well as rural health and education schemes.

The record of the UK government in terms of aid

In 1969, a UN commission recommended that 0.7% of rich countries' GNP (i.e. less than 1%!) should be given in aid. This excludes both loans and military aid. However, very few rich countries, including the UK, have managed to meet this target. For example, the UK official aid total in 2000–2001 totalled £2.8 billion – which sounds a lot but is only 0.32% of Gross National Income (formerly GNP). Excluding humanitarian need (i.e. responses to disasters, etc.), Sub-Saharan Africa received 54% of all bilateral aid in 2000–2001 whereas Asia only got 29%.

Modernisation and aid

As we saw in Topic 2, modernisation theory believed that official aid was a crucial component required for take-off into industrialisation. This was a view shared by policymakers after World War II and especially the World Bank. Consequently, aid was spent by countries receiving it on importing Western technicians and experts to develop industry and modernise agriculture. Moreover, aid aimed to change cultural attitudes by setting up meritocratic education systems focused on literacy, and family-planning programmes targeted at freeing women from the powerlessness and dependency caused by the patriarchal family system.

What is meant by the phrase 'patriarchal family system'? How could you research the claim that the family in Britain is patriarchal?

These early aid strategies acknowledged that elites in the developing world would be the primary beneficiaries of aid but it was argued that the poor would benefit in the long run as wealth 'trickled down' from the better off to the local economy and stimulated local production and markets. This modernisation approach did generate some early successes, as shown by the fact that the large quantities of aid distributed in the 1950s meant that global levels of infant mortality, life expectancy, literacy levels, etc. improved slowly but surely. In the 20 years following independence many African nations experienced economic growth.

However, the aid bubble is generally perceived to have burst in the late 1970s. Both absolute and relative (i.e. the gap between rich and poor) poverty in the developing world has actually increased in the past 30 years.

What is the difference between absolute and relative poverty? What other issues have you studied where the difference between absolute and relative rates are important?

Diseases of poverty like tuberculosis and malaria, once thought to be under control have returned with a vengeance and today are major killers of children in the developing world. Moreover, despite fantastic amounts of aid pouring in, countries such as Bangladesh have actually become poorer in the 1980s and 1990s. Such trends have led some sociologists and economists to talk about the 'poverty of aid' and 'the end of development'.

Dependency theory and aid

Neo-Marxists, in particular, have questioned the functions of official aid. They reject the view that the primary function of aid is to assist development. Rather, they suggest that it functions to bring about and sustain under-development and to benefit Western monopoly of wealth, consumption and political power. Other critics have suggested that organisations like the World Bank and IMF have adopted inappropriate and ineffective aid strategies that have primarily served the interests of the transnational corporations that dominate global capitalism. Theresa Hayter (1981) argues that official aid is a form of neo-colonialism because the development promoted by aid is aimed at reproducing, maintaining and legitimating the interests of the capitalist metropolis.

What is meant by 'legitimating'? Using your previous studies, give two other examples of this process.

The political agenda of aid

The allocation of UK and US aid has depended on whether the political ideology and practices of the developing country have met with Western approval. This was most obvious during the Cold War when the regimes of developing countries were rewarded with aid for aligning themselves with the capitalist world whilst others were punished for adopting socialist policies or for being seen as too close to the Soviet Union. The effects of the famine in Ethiopia in 1985 (which led to Band Aid, Live Aid and Comic Relief) were probably worsened by the fact that despite extensive warnings of potential famine by the UN, both the USA and UK refused aid on the grounds that Ethiopia had a Marxist government.

The focus on anti-communism can also be seen in the US military-aid programme. By the end of the 1950s there was a 4:1 proportion of military to economic aid in terms of US spending. Much of this was sent to South and Central America where it was used by right-wing governments to repress groups fighting for a more just social order. The result of such aid was often the creation of vast inequalities in wealth and land ownership between elites and the rural poor.

However, the fall of communism in the 1990s has not diluted the political character of both US and UK aid. There has merely been a shift in emphasis as new political threats are identified. Developing countries are rewarded with aid today for supporting Western strategic interests, e.g. Kenya was rewarded with aid for providing US forces with port facilities during the Gulf War in 1991. In 2001, there are signs that developing nations will be rewarded for assisting the USA's war against international terrorism. This policy will have negative economic implications for the poorest countries who have little or no political, strategic or commercial advantages for the developed world.

The economic agenda of aid

Neo-Marxists argue that there is an economic motive at the heart of all official aid and that this is the expansion of global capitalism. Aid is aimed at opening up new markets for Western goods and services. The evidence strongly supports this argument because approximately 75% of British aid is tied, i.e. the recipient country has to spend the grant or loan in the UK. Such aid stimulates the economy of the UK in the following ways.

- A substantial number of jobs in the UK depend on the orders placed by developing nations using official aid. Oxfam suggests that the UK aid programme often appears to be more concerned with supporting ailing or inefficient sectors of British industry than the poor of the developing world.
- The DfID can also control what the money is spent on, e.g. they may insist that the aid is spent on infrastructure or technology that the UK supplies. For example, British aid to India has resulted in the purchase of millions of pounds worth of helicopters and airport-surveillance equipment. Oxfam notes that such projects very rarely benefit the poor.
- There is evidence that the British government has given aid to countries such as Indonesia and Malaysia in return for securing weapons, aircraft and construction contracts for British industry. John Major, the British Prime Minister at the time, was upfront about British motives and said 'here is the British government backing British business in achieving orders abroad and maintaining billions of pounds of British exports in Malaysia'.
- Tied aid creates artificial markets because the developing country will need spare parts and technical expertise from the donor country for many years to come.

In 2001, Clare Short, the Minister in charge of the DfID, announced that she was bringing tied aid to an end. However, in 2002, the UK announced that Uganda was buying an air-traffic control system from British Aerospace using DfID grants.

The debt crisis

By the mid-1990s it was apparent that a debt crisis existed in the developing world. In 1980, the developing world owed the West $600 billion but by 1998, this had increased to $2.2 trillion. Most of the countries in real trouble are extremely poor African states, e.g. in 1998 Sub-Saharan Africa owed $222 billion which made up 71% of its national earnings whilst Mozambique and Ethiopia spent almost half their export earnings servicing their debts. Nearly a quarter of the aid African countries receive this year will be immediately given back to the West in the form of debt repayments. The problem is not unique to Africa. Mexico, Brazil and, most recently in 2002, Argentina, have struggled to repay their foreign debts resulting in political and economic instability in these countries.

Item A | Examples of Aid Projects

TANZANIA

The World Bank financed the Narmeda Dam project costing £2,300 million. However, those who benefited were landowners and rich farmers, while tribal people, who were struggling to make a living, lost their access to land. Compensation to the tribal people to aid fishing schemes, co-operative shops and clinics would have cost less than 1% of the total spent on the project.

BANGLADESH

The British government paid £38 million to extend the electricity supply in Dacca, the capital. This was intended to encourage new industry. However, it has mainly benefited those who can afford to use it – the well-off.

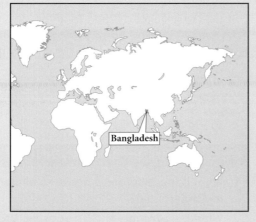

Source: *Teaching Development Issues*

INDIA

The Swedish government paid for a rural water supply project. At first it used steel pipes and diesel pumps. As they proved too expensive, aid was then used to pay for bamboo pipes, shallow wells and hand-pumps. This project has improved the incomes of small farmers.

COULD BE ANYWHERE

A development agency decided to stop putting its money into well digging for agricultural projects. The reason they gave was that the 'community' would not co-operate. Even after prolonged discussion with the men in the area, the agency fieldworkers could not persuade the men to dig deeper when the first sight of water appeared and, so, the wells dried up in the dry season. A visiting woman researcher asked: 'But why are you only talking to the men? They're not the ones who go to the well every day, year in and year out, and who actually observe the water level going up and down according to the season: the women do.'

FOREIGN AID: WHEN YOU TAKE THE MONEY FROM THE POOR PEOPLE IN A RICH COUNTRY AND GIVE IT TO THE RICH PEOPLE IN A POOR COUNTRY

WILEY'S DICTIONARY

1 Look at Item A. Read the brief case studies and look at the cartoon. Identify the factors that make aid projects successful or unsuccessful.

Dependency theorists argue that the debt crisis has been brought about by a number of factors:

- Colonialism resulted in the economies of developing countries being over-dependent on the production of a few major cash crops or raw materials. However, the prices of such commodities, and therefore export earnings, have fallen sharply in the past two decades whilst the price of oil and manufacturing goods needed for development have risen steeply. Therefore developing countries have needed to borrow money to make up the difference. In their search for greater profits Western banks were happy

to oblige in the belief that countries never go bust.

- Little of the money borrowed was spent on effective economic development. It generally went on oil (as prices rose again) and about 20% went on weapons. Much of it was stolen by corrupt post-colonial elites or it was squandered on projects like international airports which were totally inappropriate for the needs of developing countries. Even the successful or appropriate projects such as irrigation schemes were too slow in generating income to match both repayments and interest. David Landes (1998) argues that too much was expected of political leadership in Africa. He notes that since it took Europe centuries to get good government why should Africa do so in mere decades, especially after the distortions of colonialism?

- In the 1980s recession in the West increased interest rates. The effect on the developing world was that they were forced to keep borrowing in order to pay the interest on old debts. Western banks were happy to lend because they were making record profits through the interest charged.

Solutions to the debt crisis

Some commentators have suggested that Western solutions to the debt crisis have actually worsened the problem. Ransom (1996) notes that when the debt crisis first appeared in the 1980s the World Bank and IMF tied aid to prescriptive 'structural adjustment programmes' known as SAPs. These required developing societies to make internal political and economic adjustments. In practice, this meant that they were forced to privatise any public ownership of industry or agriculture, e.g. (collective or co-operative farming), cut public expenditure in the fields of health, welfare and education and increase their exports by opening up their economies and markets to transnational companies. However, it is generally agreed that SAPs did not work. Ransom notes that SAP principles 'are by definition, indifferent to the eradication of poverty; they are largely responsible for its creation'. SAPs, then, involved the West in imposing its values with regard to 'good governance' on developing nations.

The overall effect on the developing world of the debt crisis has been devastating. Debt has actually increased infant mortality rates and lowered life-expectancy because essential capital which should be used for developing health care has been diverted to servicing debt. According to Oxfam, more than 100,000 Ethiopian children die each year from easily preventable diseases but debt repayments are four times more than health spending in that country.

Western solutions to this crisis have therefore produced mixed results. The main lender countries have written off or re-negotiated over $300 billion worth of debt. However, this has made little impact as symbolised by the fact that debt is at such a level that every baby born into the developing world in 2000–2001 will owe $482. In 1996, the IMF and World Bank created the Highly Indebted Poor Countries initiative (HIPC). Under HIPC, all creditors have agreed to reduce debt so that the 41 worst affected countries should not have to pay back more than 20–25% of their export earnings. However, to receive such debt relief, the country has to stick to IMF economic reforms, similar to SAPs for six years in total. The aid charities and supporters of the global social movement Jubilee 2000 argue that this process takes too long and are campaigning to have all debts wiped out. In 2000 many Western governments, including the UK, announced they were looking at ways in which debt could be cancelled or at the very least reduced further.

So is aid a good or a bad thing?

There is no doubt that aid, especially that associated with loans from commercial banks and the World Bank, has created tremendous problems within the developing world. Similarly, despite being solutions, SAP and HIPC may also be part of the problem of underdevelopment. Some critics have gone as far as to describe the debt crisis as a new form of slavery.

In what ways can aid be compared to slavery?

However, it is not all bad news. Robert Cassen's study (1985) of bilateral aid to seven developing countries indicates that aid can be effective in improving railways, roads, telecommunication and power facilities, in setting up rural community-health schemes and in setting up rural credit-schemes for the poor in agricultural areas. However, Cassen does acknowledge that these successes are under threat from policies such as SAP and HIPC and consequently there is much room for improvement.

KEY TERMS

Bilateral aid – official aid that goes from the government of one country to the government of another.

Infrastructure – the basic services that underpin a society such as roads, communications, electricity, gas and water supplies.

Irrigation schemes – schemes that create water supplies to areas which suffer from lack of water.

Military aid – aid in the form of weapons or troops.

Multilateral aid – aid that is given to international agencies (such as the World Bank) to distribute.

Tied aid – aid that is dependent on the recipient taking a particular course of action. i.e. usually buying products manufactured by the donor country.

The World Bank – set up after World War II by Western governments to make loans to member states at interest rates below those of commercial banks in order to finance development projects.

CHECK YOUR UNDERSTANDING

1 What is the difference between bilateral and multilateral aid?

2 What percentage of GNP does the UN recommend should be given by developed countries to the developing world and how does the UK measure up?

3 How does modernisation theory view the process of aid?

4 How might aid be used as a political weapon?

5 Why might aid benefit the economies of the developed world?

6 How has colonialism contributed to debt today?

7 In what ways was aid spent inappropriately in the 1970s and 1980s?

8 What is structural adjustment and what have been its effects on the developing world?

9 How does debt impact on children?

10 What solutions have been suggested by the West to alleviate debt?

11 What is the relationship between aid and debt?

12 Has aid made any positive difference in the developing world?

Item A

In the 1970s the international community authored a developmentalist or modernisation model in the developing world, and especially Africa, that effectively set up autocratic state regimes. Such state-led development intervened in the economy in order to encourage economic competitiveness, introduced subsidies on staple foods and petrol and provided social and welfare services such as education and health to promote 'modern' attitudes. However, all this was beyond the financial capacity of such countries and consequently a mountain of debt was built up as such countries were encouraged to catch up with the West. By the end of the 1970s, private lending to Africa by commercial banks outstripped bilateral and multilateral aid by 3:1. However, this 'borrowing culture' also encouraged a kleptocratic elite and corruption at all levels, and led to millions being wasted on inappropriate aid schemes.

Adapted from: A. Hoogvelt (2000) *Globalisation and the Post-Colonial World: The New Political Economy of Development*, (2nd edition), Basingstoke: Palgrave, p.177

Item B

In Britain there would be an outcry if the government were to introduce charges for education, leave children without desks and roofs on their classrooms, or let hospitals and clinics run out of basic drugs. In the developing world, it happens every day of every year, as money is siphoned off to pay foreign debts. In Africa, as a whole, one out of every two children does not go to school but governments spend four times more in debt repayments to the developed world than they spend on health and education.

Larry Elliott, 'Why the Poor are Picking up the Tab', *The Guardian* May, 11 1998

Item C

Africa needs firm commitment on the key trio of debt, aid and trade. There is a wide misperception that debt has been solved, yet only a handful of African countries have so far received debt relief. Debt continues to distort African economic development as government revenue is swallowed up by interest payments. Britain may have increased its aid budget but it is still less than the UN target; Africa's poverty is such that it cannot attract the foreign investment nor generate the capital for its own development. Its inadequate transport infrastructure strangles growth and only huge aid flows can meet that shortfall. Moreover, trade barriers cost Africa at least $2bn a year in a global economy in which the odds have been against Africa since colonial times: economies were structured to extract resources and grow cash crops for the benefit of the West. That has left many countries vulnerable to collapsing commodity prices – for example, Uganda's benefits from debt relief have been virtually wiped out by the recent fall in the coffee price. What Africa needs is not just charity, but also justice.

Extracted from: 'Blair's African Safari', editorial in *The Guardian*, February 4, 2002

1 Using Item A and other material, assess the success of the 'developmentalist' approach to aid encouraged by the international community.

2 Outline the causes of the debt crisis that faces the developing world today.

3 What is Item B saying about Western attitudes towards problems like debt in the developing world?

4 What are the real consequences of the debt crisis for the developing world?

5 Using Item C as a starting point, outline and assess the view that what the developing world needs now 'is not just charity, but also justice'.

Research ideas

1 **Try and find out which countries are the Top Ten recipients of DfID aid and what their GNP is. You could do this by visiting the DfID website at www.dfid.gov.uk or by visiting the Geography department in your school or college. Construct a graph showing the relationship between debt and GNP.**

2 **Visit the website of a newspaper such as *The Guardian* and find out which countries have had an economic crisis in the past year because of debt.**

EXAM PRACTICE

Extract from AQA-style question

Despite increased aid and debt relief there is a persistence of marked inequalities between developed and under-developed societies of which life expectancy is but one stark example.

Describe and explain three such persistent inequalities between societies other than that mentioned in the passage above. (12 marks)

WWW Webtask

Update yourself on recent crises caused by debt, and on the campaign for the cancellation of the debt of the developing world by visiting the following sites:

● www.dropthedebt.org – this site contains a counter at the top of the page which documents the number of children who have died because of debt since you started reading the page. Its flash introduction featuring Bono from U2 is quite impressive.

● www.debtchannel.org – one feature of this site is to allow you to research debt by country. It is also excellent on the latest debt news.

● www.jubileedebtcampaign.org.uk – excellent site documenting British efforts to have debt cancelled.

● www.jubilee-kids.org/ – my favourite site. It contains a really great cartoon movie lasting four minutes called 'The Debt Monsters' which explains in a really clear fashion (i.e. it's for kids!) how the debt crisis came about. You can even have a go at killing the monsters with the Slingshot or create your own debt monster. Highly recommended.

● www.cafod.org.uk/campaign – excellent site documenting clearly and in detail the debt crisis and possible solutions.

Getting you thinking

Region or country	Pop.Total (millions) 1980	Pop.Total (millions) 1997	Pop. average annual growth rate (%) 1990–1997	Under 5 mortality rate (per 1000) 1996	Total fertility rate (births per woman) 1996	Maternal mortality ratio (per 100,000 live births) 1990–96
Developing world	3,600	4,903	1.6	80	3.0	
Developed world	825	926	0.7	7	1.7	
Bangladesh	87	124	1.6	112	3.4	850
Brazil	121	164	1.4	42	2.4	160
China	981	1227	1.1	39	1.9	115
Ethiopia	38	60	2.3	177	7.0	1,400
India	687	961	1.8	85	3.1	437
Indonesia	148	200	1.7	60	2.6	390
Kenya	17	28	2.6	90	4.6	650
Mozambique	12	19	3.8	214	6.1	1,500
Uganda	13	20	3.1	141	6.7	550

(Left) Source: 'Population: Whose Problem?' *New Internationalist* cover, No 74, September 1979

1 What do the above statistics tell us about population growth in both the developed and developing world?

2 Which countries seem to be experiencing the most rapid population growth?

3 Look closely at the figures for death of children (under 5 mortality rate), births per woman and deaths in childbirth (maternal mortality ratio). What are the trends here? Do these have any effect on the reasons why population growth in some of these countries may be so high?

4 How does the *New Internationalist* cartoon view the 'population problem'?

It is not surprising when we look at the statistics on population growth that some people conclude that the developing world has a 'problem' and this may be the cause of other problems such as famine, malnutrition and shortage of resources. However, as sociologists, we should attempt to avoid making such **value-judgements**. Hopefully, objective examination of other statistics above (especially infant mortality) will have alerted you to the possibility that there may be a rational context in which this population growth is taking place.

Which research methods are most likely to produce data that is value free? What problems are there in being 'objective'?

The sociological study of population change is known as '**demography**'. Sociologists believe that it is important to study demographic trends such as those associated with birth, fertility, infant mortality, death and migration because they can produce insights into why societies experience social change.

Explain how analysis of demographic trends has contributed to two areas of social life.

The demographer's toolkit

- **Crude birth rate:** this measures the number of live births per 1,000 members of a population in a given year. For example, the Kenyan rate was 53.8 in the mid-1980s compared with 15.3 in the USA.
- **The fertility rate:** the number of live births per woman over her lifetime. The USA and Europe show very low fertility rates in the mid-1980s, i.e. approximately 1.2.
- **The crude death rate:** this measures the number of deaths per 1,000 of the population. In the USA it was 8.7 in 1987 whilst in Chad, it was 44.1 in the same year.
- **The infant mortality rate:** the number of deaths among infants aged below one year per 1,000 of the infant population. In the USA, it is 10 whilst in Ethiopia, it is 229.
- **Life expectancy:** the number of years projected as remaining to an average person of a certain age. Most developed societies have life expectancy of 70+ whereas it is 41 in Malawi.

Adapted from R. Cohen and P. Kennedy, (2000) *Global Sociology*, Basingstoke: Palgrave

---

World population growth

On October 12 1999, the United Nations declared that the population of the world had reached six billion people. There is no doubt that the world has experienced a massive rise in population, as can be seen in the figure on the right. Two aspects of this rise stand out:

- Much of the increase has occurred this century, e.g. there were only two billion people in 1925. Another way of thinking about this is to consider that the fifth billionth human born is about 12 years old, the fourth billionth is about 25 years old whilst the third billionth is approximately 40 years old. The increase in world population, then, has been phenomenally rapid.

- Most of this increase has occurred in the developing world. World population increases by about 83 million people annually. Ninety-nine percent of this increase occurs in the less developed regions of Africa, Asia, Latin America and the Caribbean. For example, Africa's population, despite the AIDS epidemic, has tripled since 1960 to 767 million whilst Asia's population has doubled in the same period to 3.6 billion. Six countries account for half of the increase in world population: India, China, Pakistan, Nigeria, Bangladesh and Indonesia. In contrast, the population of the developed world has fallen.

Population: future projections

The United Nations forecasts that by 2050 the world's population will hit 9.3 billion. The population of less developed countries is expected to rise from 4.9 billion in 2001 to 8.2 billion in 2050. Nine out of every ten people in 2050 will live in a developing country. In contrast, only three of the more developed countries, the United States, Russia and Japan, are expected to remain amongst the most populous by 2025 (see figures overleaf). In particular, population levels in Europe are projected to decline sharply.

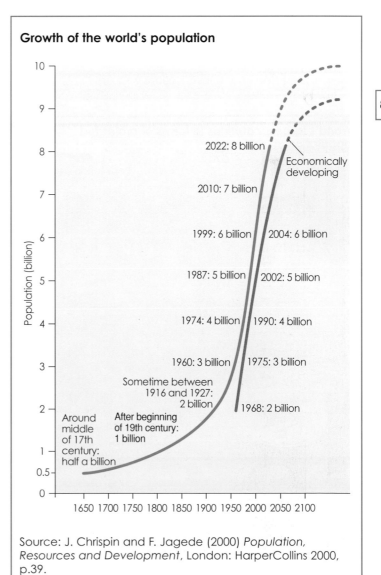

Growth of the world's population

Source: J. Chrispin and F. Jagede (2000) *Population, Resources and Development*, London: HarperCollins 2000, p.39.

Top 15 largest countries in 2001

Rank	Country	Population (millions)
1	China	1,273
2	India	1,033
3	United States	285
4	Indonesia	206
5	Brazil	172
6	Pakistan	145
7	Russia	144
8	Bangladesh	134
9	Japan	127
10	Nigeria	127
11	Mexico	100
12	Germany	82
13	Vietnam	79
14	Philippines	77
15	Egypt	70

Source: Extracted from United Nations website

World's largest countries in terms of projected population in 2025

Rank	Country	Population (millions)
1	China	1,431
2	India	1,363
3	United States	346
4	Indonesia	272
5	Pakistan	252
6	Brazil	219
7	Nigeria	204
8	Bangladesh	181
9	Russia	137
10	Mexico	131
11	Japan	121
12	Ethiopia	118
13	Philippines	108
14	Congo, Democratic Republic of (Zaire)	106
15	Vietnam	104

Source: Extracted from United Nations website

Sociological explanations: neo-Malthusian modernisation theory

In his *Essay on the Principle of Population* in 1798 Thomas Malthus (1766–1834) argued that populations increase in size at a much faster rate than the ability of those same populations to feed themselves. He concluded that these limits on food supply would lead to natural checks on population such as famine and malnutrition – and perhaps even war – as people fought over scarce resources. Such checks limit population because they increase death rates. Malthus also argued, however, that we should attempt to avoid over-population by delaying marriage and abstaining from sex.

Malthus' ideas have been adopted by the biologist Paul Ehrlich who, in his book *The Population Bomb* (1968), argued 'the battle to feed all humanity is over' after studying the figures for birth rates and death rates and comparing them with food production and malnutrition rates. Ehrlich argues that the high birth rates of developing countries has led to a 'population explosion' which has put too much strain on their limited resources of food and energy. This, allegedly, is responsible for problems in the developing world such as famine, malnutrition, poverty, war, **desertification** (because of over-use of land), **deforestation** (because more land is required for housing) and increasing environmental pollution. He concludes that 'the birth rate must be brought into balance with the death rate or mankind will breed itself into oblivion'.

Sociologists sympathetic to the modernisation approach to development have seized upon these arguments with some relish. Over-population has been cited as yet another internal obstacle preventing countries from adopting Western forms of development. It is argued that the economic growth necessary for industrial development is difficult to achieve because any spare capital is unlikely to be re-invested in developing industry. Instead it is likely to be spent feeding the population in order to avoid civil unrest and political instability. In addition, the infrastructure of such societies, especially their health and education systems (which are already basic) are stretched to the limit.

Blaming the victims

The modernisation approach to development sees religions such as Islam and Roman Catholicism as responsible for the high birth rates in the developing world. Paul Harrison's *Inside the Third World* (1990) notes that 'the areas with the fastest population growth rates lie preponderantly in the Moslem belt from North Africa, through South-West Asia to Pakistan and Bangladesh, and in Roman Catholic Central and South America'. Harrison points out that the **theologians** of the Islamic world are divided about family planning whilst the Koran does permit some forms of birth control. However, Harrison notes that ordinary Muslims are often opposed to any form of family planning because they fear that contraception will lead to 'promiscuity' and 'pre-marital sex'. Harrison suggests this 'could undermine the entire sexual politics of society from arranged marriages and parental authority, to fathers' control over daughters and men's control over women'. In other words, it is the patriarchal nature of Muslim societies that prevents 'progress' in the form of family planning. Harrison also points out that often the only way a woman can gain status and power in developing societies is by producing sons – who are regarded as more valuable than daughters because they attract **dowries**.

Harrison is particularly critical of the stance of the Roman Catholic Church on contraception. The Pope is opposed to effective family planning and Harrison notes that priests in Latin America have rigidly enforced this line among the poor.

To what extent is religion a conservative force in society?

Moreover, the Church has found an ally in the 'powerful **machismo**' of the Latin male which views contraception in all its varied forms as a threat to masculinity. As Harrison argues 'the macho (South American) male wishes to prove his virility not only to himself and his wife, but also, and perhaps primarily to other men. The only verifiable way of doing so is by getting women pregnant'.

To what extent does evidence suggest that the values associated with masculinity are changing? To what extent does this depend on the culture of countries or social groups?

Solutions to over-population

The modernisation perspective is very keen on using official aid and even economic trade sanctions to persuade the governments of developing countries to adopt family-planning and health-education policies. There is some evidence that this view has strongly influenced the US government and that the receipt of aid from the USA has been dependent on introducing such policies. A massive amount of Western aid has been pumped into population control. In 1980 USAID and other agencies donated $476 million, which had increased to $2034 million by 1995. Other countries such as China and Singapore have adopted policies that are a variation on this theme and economically rewarded those parents who choose to have fewer children.

Meanwhile, Ehrlich has suggested that men with three or more children in developing nations should be forcibly sterilised! Followers of this perspective have also argued in favour of educating women so that they will abandon patriarchal beliefs and practices and take advantage of the employment offered by transnational companies. It is suggested that such work will offer alternative sources of status, delay marriage and limit the period of fertility.

The critique of neo-Malthusianism

One major problem with neo-Malthusian statistical analysis is that the statistics we have are unreliable. Most of these

How effective are adverts encouraging birth control?

population statistics are collected by governments using a census questionnaire which requires heads of household to complete a form. There are all sorts of methodological problems associated with collecting census data in the developing world as the figure below indicates.

Another source of statistics is registration data. In the developed world, there is a legal obligation to register births, deaths and marriages. However, similar registration data in the developing world is inconsistently gathered. As Chrispin and Jagede (2000) note: 'those people who do register may not be representative of the whole population. Often, they are better educated, wealthier and they understand the need and procedures for vital registration.'

Selected reasons for unreliable census data

- Households may be omitted due to incomplete mapping of enumeration areas
- Lack of trained staff to administer the census
- Nomads and the homeless may be difficult to record
- Transport difficulties in remote rural areas (often made worse by seasonal weather patterns, e.g. monsoon)
- In northern India and the Middle East, male enumerators are not allowed to interview women
- Language barriers, e.g. in Cameroon there are 30 major language groups
- In areas where there are low literacy levels, some people have difficulty filling in the forms
- Age misreporting: a person may not have a birth certificate and in some cases the enumerator may have to guess ages; people may describe themselves as being younger or older than they actually are, e.g. teenage girls and older women shift their ages into the fertile age band; where status is associated with age, people may give an older age.

Source: J. Chrispin and F. Jagede (2000) *Population, Resources and Development*, London: HarperCollins

What problems are associated with the use of official statistics in Britain? Give examples from your studies.

Cohen and Kennedy (2000) argue 'it would be foolish to deny that there is cause for concern' in regard to world population-growth. However, they suggest that neo-Malthusians may be guilty of overstating their case and distorting their statistical analysis. Cohen and Kennedy point out that predictions of population explosions and world collapse are usually based on present trends (i.e. from the period the author is writing). However, these are often wrong because 'people change their conduct in response to earlier plausible warnings'. The slowing down of the annual growth rate of the world's population from 2 per cent in 1980 to 1.5 per cent in 2000 would support this view.

Brian Carnell (2000) is critical of Ehrlich for similar reasons: 'Why did Ehrlich's predictions fail to come true? Because the model he used was basically flawed. In a nutshell what Ehrlich did was take population growth for the 1960s and **extrapolate** it out through the 1970s, but he insisted production of food and water were at their limits – both would likely decline and certainly not increase. However, food production not only increased, but increased faster than population growth because of advances in technology'. In the developed world, farmers are actually paid by governments *not* to produce food because in the past they have produced too much. Carnell, then, is critical of the selective bias in Ehrlich's examination of the statistics.

A third critique of the statistical analysis approach suggests that there has been too much attention paid to birth rates. This focus has made it relatively easy for positivist demographers to blame the rising population on the 'irresponsible' behaviour of people and governments of the developing world. However as the demographer Nick Eberstadt (see Carnell, 2000) says in relation to population growth: 'It's not because people starting breeding like rabbits. It's that they stopped dying like flies'. In other words, population growth mainly stems from the decline in infant mortality and general death-rates and the rise in life expectancy in the developing world. The irony here is that this is the result of scientific progress in the fields of medicine, (especially the advances made in controlling diseases such as smallpox and malaria), public hygiene and the processing of food.

In defence of positivist approaches to population, they have highlighted a crucial dimension of population growth – that is, the fact that in developing countries, the majority of the population are aged under 25 years old, e.g. in Mexico, 45% of the population is aged under 15. Consequently, the period of fertility is longer and may produce greater numbers of children.

Sociological explanations – socialist anti-Malthusian

Sociologists working from Marxist or socialist perspectives are very critical of the neo-Malthusian idea that developing countries are responsible for the poverty they experience and that this is the result of their inability to control their family size.

- Mamdani (1996) notes that the economic inequalities that characterise social and economic relationships within developing countries are neglected. These are often the legacy of colonialism and/or shaped in the contemporary world by the terms of world trade which favour the developed West. Access to land in developing nations is often controlled by local elites who were put into place by the colonial powers. For example, in South America, 47% of the land is owned by just 2% of the population. Land is also monopolised by Western multinationals in order to produce cash crops for export to the West. For example, Lappe and Collins (1977) note that Mexico (which experiences high rates of child malnutrition) provides the USA with most of its winter and spring vegetables. Such processes mean that the rural poor often have to make do with less efficient marginal land which is often over-farmed. Webster therefore argues that land-reform programmes would probably be more effective in relieving world hunger than population control policies.
- Neo-Malthusians, like Ehrlich, tend to ignore the social context of fertility. Adamson (1986) argues this is because of a fundamental misunderstanding of the relationship between poverty and population. Ehrlich makes the mistake of supposing that population causes poverty. However, Adamson argues that poverty causes high population because in developing societies, children are economic assets in terms of their labour-power and the extra income they can generate. For example, in Bangladesh, boys are already producing more than they can consume by the age of 10. Moreover, in developing societies which lack a welfare infrastructure such as pensions, children are vital for old-age security. The decision to have lots of children is rational in this context especially if infant mortality rates are high. For example, in Sub-Saharan Africa, a couple have to bear 10 children in order to be certain of producing a son who will survive to the age of 38. There are signs that economic prosperity slows down birth rates because the costs of supporting a child increase and, consequently, dependency theorists argue that birth control programmes will always fail if poverty is not tackled. Moreover improving healthcare systems in developing countries will reduce infant mortality rates and so reduce the need for what Cohen and Kennedy call 'insurance children'.

How do ideas about childhood differ in the developing and developed worlds?

The UK experience of population change in the nineteenth century supports the view that development is the best contraceptive. Improved living standards and the introduction of public health had the effect of dramatically decreasing the UK death rate, especially the infant mortality rate as improved diet led to greater resistance to disease. The introduction of mass education and the trend towards urbanisation led to a natural fall in the birth rate as children were more likely to survive into adulthood and also became more expensive to raise.

- Adamson (1986) argues that by focusing on over-population we run the risk of ignoring the major cause of poverty and its associated problems in the developing world which is the unequal global distribution of resources such as food and energy between the developed and the developing world. In particular, Adamson argues that we should be focusing on the over-consumption of the world's resources by the West and the wasteful nature of Western standards of living. For example, the average American consumes 300 times as much energy as the average Bangladeshi. *New Internationalist* magazine points out that (Adamson 1986) 'the 16 million babies born each year in the rich world will have four times as great an impact on the world's resources as the 109 million born in the poor world'. The USA which has 6% of the world's population consumes 40% of its resources. Moreover, Western industries rather than the peoples of the developing world have caused the most environmental pollution. Adamson argues that much of the neo-Malthusian concern with population is unconsciously racist because it reflects white Western concerns that black and brown-skinned people may start to demand a fairer share of the world's resources and this may impact on white affluence. Family-planning policies, from this perspective, therefore end up 'substituting condoms for justice'.

The neo-Malthusian approach, despite its 'doom and gloom' predictions, has given us a valuable insight into the cultural context of population growth and, despite its ethnocentric judgements, it has rightly drawn our attention to problems which arise out of factors such as the patriarchal control of women. There is no doubt, as Jonathon Porritt (1985) argues, that family planning is important in the short term because economic changes in regard to standards of living can take years to take effect. Anti-Malthusians are important because they have drawn attention to the influence of global inequalities on population growth. They suggest that our concerns about population growth and the implication that this is deviant and irresponsible behaviour may stem from our concerns about whether we can continue to consume the world's resources at our present rates. They also point out that economic prosperity is the most powerful influence on reducing birth rates in the developing world – followed by education, (especially of women), better healthcare facilities and a welfare state rather than birth control. As Cohen and Kennedy argue, 'birth rates are only likely to decline if people in the developing world have the following questions answered: Where is my next meal coming from? Will my family have a future? Are my children likely to survive?'

KEY TERMS

Demography – the sociological study of population.

Deforestation – destruction of forests.

Desertification – increasing spread of deserts.

Dowry – a sum of money paid by a bride's parents to a bridegroom's family in return for marrying their daughter.

Extrapolate – take a pattern or idea and apply it to wider or future situations.

Machismo – an exaggerated sense of masculinity mainly found in Latin America.

Theologians – religious thinkers.

Value-judgement – See Key Term in Topic 7.

CHECK YOUR UNDERSTANDING

1 How does population change in the past thirty years compare across the developed and developing worlds?

2 What did Malthus predict in regard to population growth and the world's resources?

3 Identify six problems identified by Paul Ehrlich which are allegedly a consequence of the population explosion.

4 In what ways, might the value system of some developing countries contribute to high population growth?

5 What solutions do neo-Malthusians offer for high population growth?

6 Identify three reasons why population statistics may be unreliable.

7 What is the reason for population growth in the developing world according to Nick Eberstadt?

8 In what ways might inequalities in wealth and access to land contribute to high population?

9 Compare and contrast the neo-Malthusian and anti-Malthusian approach to the relationship between poverty and high population.

10 What lessons do we learn about population from the experience of the UK in the nineteenth century?

11 Why is Adamson convinced that birth control strategies in the developing world encouraged by Western aid are essentially racist?

12 In your view, is the problem over-population or over-consumption? Explain the rationale for your choice.

Item A

	Pop. mid-2001 (millions)	Births per 1000 of pop.	Deaths per 1000 of pop.	Rate of natural increase	Projected pop. change 2001–2050 (%)
World	6,137	22	9	1.3	47
More developed	1,193	11	10	0.1	4
Less developed	4,944	28	9	1.9	75

Source: Population Reference Bureau, 2001

Item B

A cancer is an uncontrolled multiplication of cells; the population explosion is an uncontrolled multiplication of people. Treating only the symptoms of cancer may make the victim comfortable at first, but eventually he dies, often horribly. A similar fate awaits a world with a population explosion if only the symptoms are treated. We must shift our efforts from treatment of symptoms to the cutting out of the cancer. The operation will demand many apparently brutal and heartless decisions. The pain may be intense. But the disease is so far advanced that only with radical surgery does the patient have a chance of survival. We have to understand that people have no sacred legal 'right' to have children. Governments should be able to tell you precisely how many children you can have and should be able to clap you in jail if you exceed that number. Compulsory sterilisation in some nations may have to become a fact of life.

We should stop food aid to those nations that experience chronic food shortages if their populations are out of control. If these nations refuse to introduce population controls, we should be willing to let the people in those nations starve.

Source: adapted from: P. Ehrlich (1968), *The Population Bomb*, New York: Ballantyne Books

Item C

REASONS FOR HAVING CHILDREN

	Birth rate	Economic support (%)	Love, etc. (%)	Other (%)
Mexico	High	72	16	12
Singapore	Medium	19	65	16
USA	Low	4	73	23

Source: East-West Population Institute quoted in *New Internationalist* http://www.newint.org/

Item D

The more people there are, the more resources they will consume. This seems obvious – at first glance. But when I stopped to think about it, it was equally obvious that 15 people might not make any more impact than 10, if the 15 lived frugally and the 10 were big spenders. In fact, the 10 might consume far more. Paradoxically, fewer people could make more environmental damage than many people. The key lay not in numbers but in choice: how much each person chose to consume – and how much the world at large chose to enable that person to consume. But surely, although hundreds of millions of people in the developing world are very poor, the sheer weight of their numbers would make their consumption catch up with the consumption of us few in the developed world. But the developed world consumes five-sixths of the world's resources and each person in the developed world consumes around 20 times as much as a person in the developing world. This is really a remarkable ratio. It means that 80 average people in the developing world are managing to live their lives consuming no more than my husband, my two children and I consume. Even with population in the developing world projected to double to 9 billion people, the 20:1 consumption ratio means we will always be consuming twice as much as them.

Source: Adapted from: 'Consuming Passions' in *New Internationalist* magazine, Issue 235, September 1992

1 Using Item A, compare and contrast population trends in the 'more developed' and the 'less developed' worlds.

2 What is the relationship between births, deaths and projected population change within the 'less developed world' seen in Item A?

3 Identify three solutions to the population explosion identified by the extract from Ehrlich in Item B.

4 How does the data in Item C challenge the view that high population may be responsible for poverty in the developing world?

5 What impact might high population in the developing world have on international migration patterns?

6 How do the arguments contained in Item D challenge the neo-Malthusian theory of population growth?

Research idea

Conduct a social survey to find out what view of population is held by a representative sample of people. Ask people on a scale of 1–5, 1 being *strongly agree* and 5 being *strongly disagree*, whether they agree or disagree with the following statements.

- They have too many babies in the developing world.
- The world's population is out of control.
- We consume more than our fair share of resources in the West.
- The developing world needs more contraception.
- The world just cannot support all these extra mouths.
- High population results in more poverty.
- There are simply not enough resources to go around.
- The cause of high population in the developing world is poverty.
- The world's food resources are not fairly distributed.
- Obesity in the developed world is linked to starvation in the developing world.

WWWebtask

There is a fantastic selection of web-sites on the internet which are concerned with population. We recommend that you and your class tour around the following and work out whether they are neutral, neo-Malthusian or anti-Malthusian:

- www.census.gov/main/www/popclock.html
- www.peopleandplanet.net
- www.prb.org
- www.undp.org/popin/wdtrends/6billion
- www.2pg.org
- www.populationaction.org
- overpopulation.com
- overpopulation.net
- www.popnet.org/
- www.oneworld.org/ni/

EXAM PRACTICE

Extract from AQA-style question

Examine the causes and social consequences of population changes in Third World Countries in the last fifty years. (12 marks)

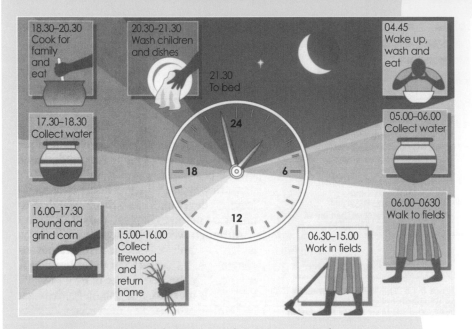

Source: J. Chrispin and F. Jegede (2000) *Population, Resources and Development*, London: HarperCollins

Quotes from poor women in Bangladesh

'When I can, I give my husband and sons more. Men don't understand if food runs short, so I wait till they have eaten.'

'A good wife is one who makes sure her husband has enough to eat.'

'If a woman eats before her husband, she shortens his life.'

'Men work harder than women, they need to eat more.'

'How can I explain to children that there is not enough food? When my son cries, I feed him. It is easier to make my daughter understand.'

'If there is less, I eat less. You have to feed the men more or they beat you. Even my son beats me if there is not enough food.'

1 Examine the diagram and work out the following.

   a How many hours are there in a typical African woman's day?

   b How many hours a day do African women work in the fields?

   c How many hours a day do African women spend on domestic labour?

   d Compare an African woman's day with that of a Western mother. How do the lifestyles differ?

2 Examine the quotes and answer these questions.

   a What seems to be the character of gender relationships in Bangladesh?

   b How do the gender relationships you form differ?

The two sources above illustrate that developing societies may be characterised by patriarchal institutions and values but that the character of these differ across different societies. The developed world, too, is characterised by patriarchy but it is of quite a different character – as this topic will illustrate.

Women in developing countries

Despite women in the developed world lagging behind males in terms of pay, we can see that across a range of criteria such as education, health, access to jobs and legal rights, women in the West enjoy opportunities that suggest greater equality

with men. Patriarchy is not dead and buried in the West, but it is no longer all-powerful. However patriarchal control in the developing world is generally all-consuming and exerts control which can actually threaten women's lives.

Madeleine Leonard (1992) notes that 'while most women in the world, like most men, lead humble lives, being mainly concerned with economic survival, nonetheless, what is very striking is how different women's ordinary lives are from men's ordinary lives. No matter which country we focus on throughout the world, women are worse off than men. Women have less power, less autonomy, do more work, earn less money, and often have more responsibility. Women everywhere have a smaller share of the pie, and if the pie is very small (as it is in developing countries) than their share is smaller still. Women in rich countries have a higher standard of living than women in poor countries, but nowhere are women equal to men'.

Give three examples from your studies of ways in which women are disadvantaged compared with men in Britain.

Leonard goes on to argue that 'the conditions of under-development – dependency, powerlessness, vulnerability and inequality of income – are experienced by women to a greater extent than men'.

Explanations for the position of women in developing countries

Cultural explanations

Some cultures, and especially the religious ideas which underpin the values, norms, institutions and customs of the developing world, **ascribe** status on the basis of gender. In practice, this means that males are accorded patriarchal control and dominance over a range of female activities and, consequently, women have little status in many developing societies.

Women in the developing world

Work

- In 1995, the United Nations conducted a survey of 17 developing countries and found that women's work hours exceeded men's by approximately one third. This confirmed previous studies which had long concluded that women do more work than men in subsistence societies. Leonard (1992) notes that in many developing countries, women grow, harvest and prepare all the food consumed by their families.

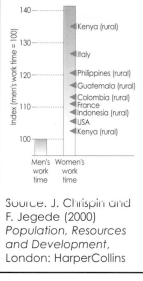

Source. J. Chrispin and F. Jegede (2000) *Population, Resources and Development*, London: HarperCollins

- Hay and Stichter (1984: see Leonard, 1992) who found in Africa that women perform 60–80% of all agricultural work confirm this. Paul Harrison actually refers to women in developing nations as 'the poorest of the poor' because, in general, they spend eight hours or more on formal work outside the home and spend the equivalent on domestic labour. The latter is very different to that experienced by Western women and includes tasks such as fetching water and gathering firewood as well as nursing children.

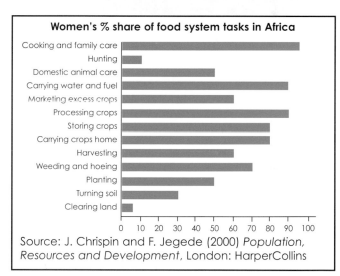

Source: J. Chrispin and F. Jegede (2000) *Population, Resources and Development*, London: HarperCollins

Health

- Half a million women die each year as a consequence of pregnancy and childbirth. Of these deaths, 99% are in the developing countries, e.g. the maternal death rate in developing countries is 479 per 100,000 live births compared with 27 in developed countries.

Education

- 90 million girls receive no education at all in the developing world. Two thirds of the 960 million illiterate people in the world are women.

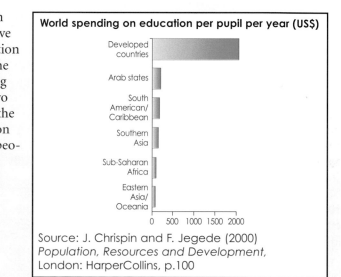

Source: J. Chrispin and F. Jegede (2000) *Population, Resources and Development*, London: HarperCollins, p.100

Women's lack of power and status in developing societies

Women often lack **reproductive rights**. They do not have the power to decide whether to have children, when to have them and how many they should have. They are often prevented from making rational decisions about contraception and  abortion. Men make all these decisions. Instead, women are strongly encouraged to see their role and status as tied up with being a mother and being dependent upon the male head of household. This lack of reproductive rights is one of the main causes of high maternal death-rates in the developing world.

Foster-Carter (see Haralambos, 1985) notes that **purdah** is practised in many Islamic countries (in West and South Asia, and North Africa). This is the custom of making women wear clothing that covers them from  head to toe. This often prevents them from playing an active role in social, economic and political life. As Foster-Carter (1985) notes, 'women's participation in public life ranges from limited to non-existent. Often, even to enter the public domain (e.g. walk in the street) requires varying degrees of veiling'. Most people are now familiar with how the Taliban treated women in Afghanistan but they are unaware that these rules about women's dress codes apply in varying degrees across a range of developing societies.

There is evidence that religious stress on the importance of male children is encouraging the infanticide of female babies in India and China. Moreover, in Africa, it is estimated that 6,000 girls every day are subject to genital cutting or female circumcision in order to enhance their future husband's enjoyment of sex. Moreover, there is evidence that in rural India, between five and ten women a day die because of dowry-burning whereby husbands kill wives so that they become free to marry again and attract a dowry.

The emphasis on women marrying and becoming mothers means that cultures and families may not regard the education of female children as a priority.

Observations about cultural practices such as those above are controversial because the experiences of Western women tend to be used as the yardstick in terms of quality of life for women in developing countries. However, such views may be guilty of ethnocentrism and therefore of imposing Western values on such societies. For example, it is often assumed by Western feminists that aspects of patriarchy in developing countries are morally wrong, repressive, exploitative and barbaric, etc. Development is often associated with bringing these cultural practices to an end. This, of course, assumes a moral superiority among Western feminists and simplistically dismisses such cultural behaviour as being the product of ignorance. However, some Muslim women argue that Islam values and empowers them. For example, the wearing of the **burkha** ensures that women control how men perceive their bodies.

How might feminists argue that the wearing of a burkha is positive for women?

Modernisation theory

In relation to gender in the developing world this theory would argue that the low status of women in developing societies is another obstacle to development because their potential contribution to the economy is not being fully realised and their status as mothers contributes to over-population. Boserup (1970) called for greater educational opportunities for adolescent girls in order to break the cycle of early childbearing. Modernisation theory believed that the creation of industrial jobs by multinational companies would encourage female economic independence from men. Moreover, family planning, health education and a sympathetic media transmitting Western values would reinforce female liberation and sexual equality which (modernisation theory argues) are essential components of the Western-industrial model of development.

The marginalisation thesis

Give two examples of groups who might be considered to be marginalised from British society?

This perspective on development suggests that the introduction of capitalism in developing societies has led to women being increasingly excluded from economic life, restricted to the home and being forced to be dependent upon men. A number of observations can be made to support this thesis, which is similar in tone to dependency theory.

- Colonial powers and missionaries brought with them, and imposed upon indigenous peoples, traditional Western values about males and females, e.g. a woman's place is in the home. Abbott and Wallace (1997) note: 'Western notions of femininity and the family have been imposed upon other models of gender and rendered them "peculiar", "heathen", "unliberated" or "sexually exotic"'.

What social institutions have contributed to the creation of this ideology of femininity in Britain? How?

Colonialism probably introduced new forms of inequality which re-affirmed the ascribed roles encouraged by religion. As Leonard (1992) argues, the colonial powers introduced a 'money economy, based on wage labour and cash crops, into Africa and Asia. Men were absorbed into the cash economy while women were left with all the work associated with subsistence food production'. However, there is evidence that colonialism challenged some aspects of ascribed gender roles that were harmful to women, e.g. the British made **female circumcision**, infanticide, suttee (the burning of wives after the death of their husbands) and dowries illegal.

- Leonard notes that the emphasis on exporting **cash crops** in the developing world today has resulted in men rather than women being employed as agricultural labourers. Moreover, many men migrate to other regions in search of such work leaving women to subsist without male help on the smaller and poorer plots of land not taken by elites or multinational companies for cash-crop production.
- The modernisation view that men's wages will trickle down to women rarely occurs in practice. Moreover, Leonard notes that in Africa many men are unused to the status of being a wage-earner and consequently they see their wage as their own money rather than as a means of supporting their families.
- Aid projects also marginalise women. Information collected from 46 African countries showed that only 3.4% of trained government workers providing agricultural advice to people in rural areas were women. The introduction of modern agricultural technology is primarily aimed at male tasks and used almost exclusively by men.
- Leonard's review of official aid programmes concludes that aid is not gender neutral. Rather, it comes with Western values attached – values that are often male-dominated and male-orientated. Aid workers bring with them the patriarchal prejudices about women and technology found in their own societies. For example, science and technology are considered masculine activities in the West because women are not supposed to understand technical

matters. As a result technical aid in terms of training and equipment tends to be aimed at men rather than women despite the fact that women play a greater role in the production of food than men. Even irrigation systems are seen to be a male domain – men are trained to use pumps, wells and filtering systems despite the fact that women play the central role in supplying water to fulfil the household's needs. Moreover, aid planners tend to neglect other aspects of female work such as domestic tasks because they do not consider this 'real work' because it is unwaged or because they undervalue the role of women.

The exploitation thesis

This view is essentially a Marxist-feminist position. It suggests that modernisation is about imposing an exploitative global system of capitalism on developing societies.

What types of feminism exist? How do they differ?

Many Western transnational companies (TNCs) have relocated their mass-production assembly lines producing electronic equipment, textiles, sports shoes, etc. to export-processing zones or centres (EPZs) mostly in developing countries. TNCs are attracted to these zones by governments offering benefits such as tax privileges, cheap labour, restrictions on the activities of trades unions and limited or non-existent health, safety and environmental regulations. The work exported to the EPZs is generally standardised, repetitive, calling for little technical knowledge and labour-intensive. The majority of workers in these factories are young women who are employed because the TNCs regard them as cheap, pliable and docile. The exploitation of these women takes several forms:

- Low pay – women workers in the EPZs are paid lower rates than male workers. Wages are often only about 10% of those in developing societies and working hours are often 50% higher. Consequently, women in the EPZs are producing more for less pay.
- Western owners do not invest a great deal in training female workforces. The work is generally regarded as unskilled despite high skill-levels being evident. However, because girls have already learned these skills in the home (e.g. sewing) the skill is downgraded.
- TNCs take advantage of what Elson and Pearson (1981) call 'women's material subordination as a gender', i.e. the fact that women will put up with lower wages or accept oppressive working conditions. They do this because either there is no alternative or the patriarchal conditions of their society mean the job is only temporary until they achieve the cultural goal of marriage and childbearing. Consequently TNCs are able to control socially their female workforces with little protest, e.g. sacking them when they become pregnant, minimising toilet breaks, bullying by management, etc.

Leonard and others therefore conclude that TNCs aim to exploit female labour rather than provide it with training, fair pay and job security. However, in criticism, we have to acknowledge that the wages earned from such work are superior to the subsistence living eked out of rural existences. Also, it does allow some escape from the powerful forms of patriarchy found in the countryside such as arranged marriages. Such developments, alongside urban living and access to education, constitute major changes for women. However, as Foster-Carter points out, such changes often bring with them new forms of exploitation 'in which the price of gaining some measure of autonomy and income of one's own is often submission to long hours, low wages and the advances of chauvinist male bosses'.

Solutions to gender inequalities in the developing world

Marxist-feminists argue that socialism is committed to dismantling patriarchal regimes in the developing world. Molyneux's (1981) study of societies that were both Marxist–Leninist and Islamic found that such regimes were willing to challenge traditions such as child marriage and the veil as well as being fully committed to maximising women's education and job opportunities. However there was little sign of change within the home. As Elwood (New Internationalist, 1986) said of the old Soviet Union 'women can fly to the moon but they still have to do the ironing when they get home again'.

The international feminist movement, too, has not always understood the nature of the developing world. The radical-feminist insistence that men were the enemy failed to address what women in developing nations saw as their main problem, i.e. uneven development and neo-colonial exploitation. Women's subordination only formed part of this. Feminists in these regions argued that their immediate task was to join with men to fight such exploitation and oppression. Moreover, women in the developed world have different priorities to those in developing nations. Whilst women in the developed world were campaigning against the trivialisation of women in the media, women in the developing world were focusing on acquiring the reproductive rights that women in the West took for granted. Moreover, women in the developing world were physically at risk from male violence for even daring to campaign for such rights. In other words, it was recognised that nationality, social class, ethnicity and religious identity were just as important, (and in some cases, more important) than gender as a source of inequality.

Cohen and Kennedy (2000), however, point to a second wave of postmodern feminism that appeared in the 1990s made up of feminists from both the developed and developing worlds who share a more global agenda. It was generally agreed that the globalisation of the world had led to common problems for women, such as:

- sex tourism and prostitution
- environmental degradation – eco-feminists such as Shiva (1989) argue that women are more inclined towards nature than men and therefore more protective of the natural world
- Christian, Hindu and Islamic forms of religious fundamentalism have led to attempts to reverse the progress made by women in the past 50 years. Attempts have been made to restrict women's reproductive rights (e.g. by reversing abortion legislation) and to return women to the home.

What is religious fundamentalism? Give examples of its influence.

- Economic globalisation – TNCs tend not to recognise national differences any more when it comes to exploiting workforces. Women in both the developed and developing world are likely to be exploited in the search for profit.
- The international debt crisis – feminist action groups have supported the 'breaking the chains' of debt movement because they appreciate that women and children in the developing world bear the brunt of debt in terms of less spending on health and education.

Pearson (2001) notes that since the mid-1990s the major development agencies have responded positively to the critique that women's issues were neglected by development policy. Consequently gender has been incorporated into the indices of development used by multilateral aid agencies such as the UK's Department for International Development, the World Bank and United Nations. For example, the Gender Empowerment Measure (GEM) indicates whether or not women play an active part in economic and political life across both the developed and developing world. All these agencies now check, as a matter of course, that gender is considered across a range of projects including civil engineering works and famine relief. In particular, NGOs have championed a number of projects aimed at alleviating the feminisation of poverty. For example, micro-credit schemes in countries such as India and Bangladesh make small amounts of credit available to the poor to cover subsistence needs so that they can invest in livestock, equipment, fertiliser, etc. These schemes are seen to particularly empower women (who are often responsible for domestic production).

There has also been a growing realisation in development theory that the concentration on women in recent years has led to the neglect in understanding of men and masculinity. In the developed world, this has resulted in sociologists investigating a so-called 'crisis of masculinity'.

What reasons have led some commentators to argue that a crisis of masculinity is occurring?

Consequently, researchers have begun to focus on examining how masculinity is constructed in the developing world in order to understand the nature of patriarchal gender-relations. However, it is important to acknowledge that all these changes in perspective in regard to gender are still in their infancy.

The future?

The prognosis for women in the developing world is at best mixed. On the plus side, the expansion of both education and family planning does constitute progress. Adamson (1986) argues that there is now a generation of women in the developing world who see education as the norm and not the exception. These women will demand more input into political and domestic decision-making. When they have daughters, they will pass down these modern attitudes and so positive change will continue to occur. Foster-Carter is a little more pessimistic. He notes the growing influence of fundamentalism, especially in India and some Islamic societies such as Pakistan and Algeria. In some societies, industrial capitalism has led to women's social and material positions being worsened because women have been forced into peripheral areas of the global economy (i.e. into low-paid, low-skilled jobs which are not good for their health or into the sex industry). Finally, even in our own, so-called 'modern society', sexual equality is still a little way off. In other words, patriarchy is still a global social fact.

KEY TERMS

Ascribe – see Key Terms in Topic 2.

Burhka – long enveloping garment worn by Muslim women in public.

Cash crops – crops grown to sell rather than to use.

Crisis of masculinity – the notion that masculinity is under threat because of the rapidly changing nature of work and that this has undermined men's sense of their role and power in the world.

Eco-feminists – feminists who link the social position of women to environmental issues.

Female circumcision – removal of the clitoris.

Infanticide – the practice of killing unwanted children, usually female children, at birth.

Postmodern feminism – a branch of feminism that suggests that there is a diversity of female experience in the world and that no one feminist theory is capable of explaining the range of culture-specific patriarchal experiences that women have.

Purdah – Muslim custom of keeping women in seclusion by requiring them to wear clothing that shields them from public view.

Reproductive rights – rights relating to women's choice to have children and control their bodies.

CHECK YOUR UNDERSTANDING

1 Identify four aspects of patriarchal inequality in the developing world.

2 What are reproductive rights and how do women in the developed and developing world differ in access to them?

3 What is the relationship between religion and patriarchy in the developing world?

4 Why might Western critiques of cultural and religious practices be ethnocentric?

5 What is the key to women's development according to Boserup?

6 What effect did colonialism have on the social status of women in the developing world?

7 Why is aid not gender-neutral?

8 What forms does exploitation of female labour by transnationals take in the developing world?

9 Why might exploitation of women by transnationals be acceptable for many women in the developing world?

10 Why has the international feminist movement not always understood the nature of the developing world?

11 What international problems are thought to be shared by women today?

12 What is the future of women in the developing world likely to be?

Item A

The received wisdom used to be that modernisation benefits women as well as men and that women in the developing world face the same problems as men: technological and institutional backwardness, poverty, illiteracy, malnutrition and ill health. However this is a misconception: development projects which benefit one section of society (men) do not automatically benefit the other (women). They hurt rather than help women in the long term and impose increased burdens. The general drift of development projects, both in the technology they transmit and in the training they provide, benefit men and make women even more invisible than they were.

Adapted from: R. Carmen (2000) *Autonomous Development: Humanising the Landscape: An excursion into Radical Thinking and Practice*; London: Zed Books

Item B

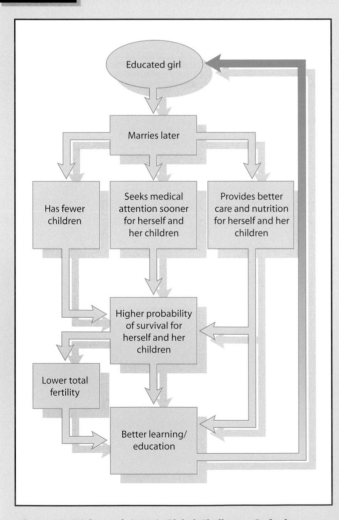

Source: B. Digby *et al.* (2001) *Global Challenges*, Oxford: Heinemann, p.200

Item C

Maria del Rosario Garcia

Maria is 42 years old and a single parent living in the Mexican border town of Matamoros. Maria used to work for Kemet, a US electronics components manufacturer, but she was sacked just two days before completing 20 years' service which would have entitled her to a payment of a pension for life. The practice of sacking workers just before they are entitled to pensions and other benefits is a common practice among US transnational companies. Maria used to earn $60 a week – a tenth of what employees in Texas get for doing the same work. Women like Maria are employed in factories because they have greater manual dexterity than men and are willing to work long hours. In an eight hour day, Maria only had one break of ten minutes and one of twenty minutes.

Adapted from: C. Flint and D. Flint (2001) *Urbanisation: Changing Environments* London: HarperCollins, p.92

Item D

There is a long way to go to overcome women's subjugation in the developing world, perhaps most acutely and appallingly represented by the ritual practice of the genital mutilation of young girls in many African countries: it is estimated that 74 million women are suffering psychological and physiological damage as a direct result of this ritual. Why do mothers require their daughters to undergo such horrific and harmful operations, usually performed by the old women of the village, with knife, razor blade or glass? In one form or another, it has existed for many hundreds of years. There may be some quasi-religious motives for the operation. The evidence suggests that it is practised by Muslims, Catholics and Protestants in certain African countries. Many believe that without the ritual women will be 'impure' as though they carry some 'original sin'. Finally, the practice has been used as a symbol of Africa's cultural identity. Some African leaders have denounced Western attempts to stop the mutilations as yet another example of Western imperialism.

Adapted from: A. Webster (1990) *An Introduction to the Sociology of Development*, (2nd edition) Basingstoke: Macmillan, pp.106–107

1 Using Item A and other material, explain the view that modernisation 'benefits men and makes women even more invisible than they were'.

2 Using Item B as your guide, outline the benefits of investing in female education in the developing world.

3 Examine Item C. Why are female workers like Maria so attractive to Western transnational companies.

4 How might both education and transnational employment impact positively on population growth?

5 According to Item D, what is the relationship between patriarchy and culture?

6 Using Item D and other material, outline and assess the view that Western feminist attempts to improve the lot of women in the developing world is 'another example of Western imperialism'.

Research ideas

1 **Find out how three of the major British aid agencies, e.g. Oxfam, Cafod, Christian Aid are specifically targeting women's development in the countries in which they are involved.**

2 **Visit the website of the Department for International Development – access through www.dfid.gov.uk – and see whether any of their policy statements specifically target women.**

WWW Webtask

● Visit the New Internationalist website – www.oneworld/ni/ – and access the Magazine mega index and click on 'W'. This will give you access to all the articles on women in the developing world published by the magazine in the last ten years. Their search engine is also worth using because they monitor articles on women in the developing world produced by a host of other agencies such as Amnesty International.

● Compare the treatment of women across the world at Human Rights Watch – www.hrw.org.

Two feminist websites worth a visit are:

● www.womensedge.org/development/usaidgenderplan.htm – this gives a very interesting insight into how American aid-policy deals with gender issues.

● The Feminist majority foundation – www.feminist.org/ – has some good material on the Taliban's treatment of women in Afghanistan

EXAM PRACTICE

Extract from AQA-style question

Assess the view that educating women is a major catalyst for change in the developing world.
(12 marks)

Getting you thinking

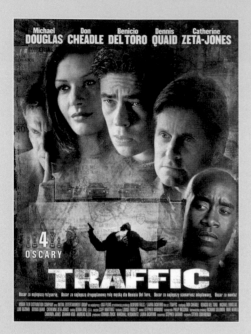

Americans consume more cocaine than any other industrialised country. Over 22 million say they have tried it and between two and three million are addicted to it. In 1989, around 2,500 Americans died from it. In 1990, one in five people arrested for any crime were hooked on cocaine or crack. Americans spend $110,000 million a year on drugs ($28,000 million on cocaine): more than double the profits of the USA's top 500 companies put together.

Juan Paredes worked as a tin-miner in Bolivia until the late 1980s. In the early 1980s, 79% of his country's export earnings came from tin. However, technological advances in the West meant that large Western companies such as Coke, Pepsi and Heinz switched to substitutes such as aluminium. In

October 1985, the worldwide price of tin set by speculators at the London Tin Exchange fell from £8,000 to £4,000 per ton putting thousands of miners like Juan out of work. Juan turned to farming instead and managed to obtain the title to four hectares of land. Very soon, he was attracted to the growing of a crop that yielded up to four or five harvests a year, which had a seemingly limitless demand and which earned him far more than tin-mining ever did. That crop was coca. By 1991, Bolivia was the largest producer of the coca leaf in the world and the second ranked producer of refined cocaine.

Adapted from: R. Cohen and P. Kennedy (2000) *Global Sociology*, Basingstoke: Palgrave; and J. Chrispin and F. Jegede (2000) *Population, Resources and Development*, London: HarperCollins

1 In what ways are the USA's domestic problems such as crime tied to global processes?

2 What two global processes led to Juan Paredes becoming a coca farmer?

3 How would you go about persuading Juan Paredes not to produce coca?

You will probably have realised from doing the above exercise that crime in the USA cannot be analysed in isolation from global processes. The problems faced by the USA in terms of drugs are very much related to economic globalisation – especially the fact that countries like Bolivia and Colombia desperately need American dollars to pay their debts to Western banks. However, because their economies are tied up with a single crop or raw material, any fall in demand or price in the global market place is going to result in poverty in this part of the world. This means that poor farmers will be tempted to produce illegal crops in order to survive. The coca leaf therefore is a global crop in that it links the poorest in the poor countries together with the most desperate in the West.

Defining globalisation

Cohen and Kennedy (2000) suggest that the function of sociologists today is to provide a 'sociology for one world', i.e. a global sociology which investigates and analyses the increasing interconnectedness and interdependency of the world.

What other functions might sociology have? Give examples from your studies to show its uses.

Cochrane and Pain (2000) (in Held 2000) illustrate these ties that bind us together:

Drugs, crime, sex, disease, people, ideas, images, news, information, entertainment, pollution, goods and money now all travel the globe. They are crossing national boundaries and connecting the world on an unprecedented scale and with previously unimaginable speed. The lives of ordinary people everywhere in the world seem increasingly to be shaped by events, decisions and actions that take place far away from where they live and work.

Source: D. Held, (ed.) (2000) *A Globalising World: Culture, Economics, Politics*, London: Routledge

What Cochrane and Pain are describing is '**globalisation**' – the emergence of a global economic and cultural system which, allegedly, is incorporating the people of the world into a single global society. Cohen and Kennedy argue that globalisation needs to be understood as a 'a set of mutually reinforcing **transformations**' of the world. These include the following:

- *Changes in the concept of time and space*: Developments such as the mobile phone, satellite television and the internet mean that global communication is virtually instantaneous, whilst mass travel enables us through tourism to experience a greater range of other cultures.
- *Economic markets and production in different countries* are becoming **inter-dependent** because of the growth in international trade, the new international division of labour, the growing influence of transnational corporations and the global dominance of organisations like the World Trade Organisation.
- *Increasing cultural interaction* through developments in mass media (especially television, films, music and the transmission of news and international sport). We can now encounter and consume new ideas and experiences from a wide range of cross-cultural sources in fields such as fashion, literature and food.
- *Increasingly shared problems*: These may be:
  1 *Economic*: We are becoming much more aware that the economic decisions we make about our lifestyle preferences and leisure pursuits may cause problems such as unemployment, debt and the loss of livelihoods for workers and peasants thousands of miles away. Similarly, the financial problems experienced by the Asian tiger economies in 1998–1999 led to unemployment in the UK.
  2 *Environmental*: The Chernobyl nuclear disaster of 1986 demonstrated quite vividly that ecological disasters do not respect national boundaries – today acres of land in the Lake District and Wales still experience high levels of radiation because of the fall-out from this accident thousands of miles away. Environment degradation is not only caused by Western industry and **consumption** but also by unwitting damage caused by the poor in the developing world engaging in over-cultivation and deforestation. The resulting global climate change has implications for everyone in the world.
  3 Other common problems include world-wide health problems such as AIDS, international drug-trafficking and the sort of international terrorism practised on September 11 2001.

Kennedy and Cohen conclude that these transformations have led to 'globalism', a new consciousness and understanding that the world is a single place. Giddens (1999) notes that most of us perceive ourselves as occupying a 'runaway world' characterised by common tastes and interests, change and uncertainty and a common fate.

However, as sociologists we also need to be cautious in our use of the term 'globalisation' – as Wiseman indicates: 'Globalisation is the most slippery buzzword of the late twentieth century because it can have many meanings and be used in many ways' (quoted on p.12 of Held 2000). We can illustrate this by looking closely at the theoretical interpretations of the concept.

Theories of globalisation

Cochrane and Pain (2000) note that three theoretical positions can be seen in regard to globalisation:

1 Globalists believe that globalisation is a fact that is having real consequences for the way that people and organisations operate across the world. They believe that nation-states and local cultures are being eroded by a homogeneous global culture and economy. However, globalists are not united on the consequences of such a process.
(a) Optimists or positive globalists welcome such developments and suggest globalisation will eventually produce tolerant and responsible world citizens.
(b) Pessimistic globalists argue that globalisation is a negative phenomenon because it is essentially a form of Western (and especially American) imperialism peddling a superficial and homogeneous mass form of culture and consumption. Such a view focuses on the dangers of what has variously been called the 'McDonaldisation' or 'Coca-Colonisation' of the world (see later in this Topic).
2 Traditionalists do not believe that globalisation is occurring. They argue that the phenomenon is a myth or, at best, exaggerated. They point out that capitalism has been an international phenomenon for hundreds of years. All we are experiencing at the moment is a continuation, or evolution, of capitalist production and trade.
3 The transformationalists occupy a middle ground between globalists and traditionalists. They agree that the impact of globalisation has been exaggerated by globalists but argue that it is foolish to reject the concept out of hand. This theoretical position argues that globalisation should be understood as 'a complex set of interconnecting relation-

True national Independence: a condition for development

'Here, Señor Carter, is the statue of Simón Bolívar, who liberated Latin America from foreign domination!'

Source: T. Allen and A. Thomas (2001) *Poverty and Development in the 21st century*, Oxford: Oxford University Press

ships through which power, for the most part, is exercised indirectly'. They suggest that the process can be reversed, especially where it is negative or, at the very least, that it can be controlled.

Economic globalisation

It is in the area of economic globalisation that the debate between traditionalists and positive globalists can most obviously be seen. Thompson (2000) notes that the globalist position claims there has been a rapid and recent intensification of international trade and investment such that distinct national economies have dissolved into a global economy determined by world market-forces (pp.88–89). This view has attracted two forms of criticism. Firstly, neo-Marxists accept that a strong globalisation process has occurred but condemn it as an extension of global capitalist exploitation. Secondly, traditionalists argue that the international economy has not gained dominance over national economic policies.

We can observe three major economic trends seen to symbolise globalisation.

The New International Division of Labour (NIDL)

The neo-Marxist, Frobel, notes that from the 1970s onwards, we have seen substantial movement of industrial capital from the advanced industrialised world to the developing world. This movement was due to rising labour costs and high levels of industrial conflict in the West which had reduced the profitability of transnational corporations (TNCs). TNCs were attracted by the large supply of cheap labour available in the developing world. Moreover, developments in manufacturing meant that labour could be fragmented into a range of unskilled tasks that could be done with minimal training, whilst computer-controlled technology enabled production to be automatically supervised.

This new international division of labour (NIDL) is thought by positive globalists to benefit world consumers by

The elements of free trade zones

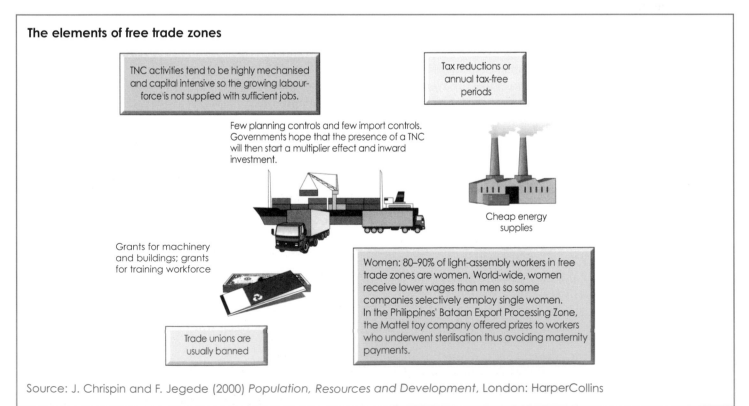

TNC activities tend to be highly mechanised and capital intensive so the growing labour-force is not supplied with sufficient jobs.

Tax reductions or annual tax-free periods

Few planning controls and few import controls. Governments hope that the presence of a TNC will then start a multiplier effect and inward investment.

Cheap energy supplies

Grants for machinery and buildings; grants for training workforce

Women: 80–90% of light-assembly workers in free trade zones are women. World-wide, women receive lower wages than men so some companies selectively employ single women. In the Philippines' Bataan Export Processing Zone, the Mattel toy company offered prizes to workers who underwent sterilisation thus avoiding maternity payments.

Trade unions are usually banned

Source: J. Chrispin and F. Jegede (2000) *Population, Resources and Development*, London: HarperCollins

enhancing competition and thus keep the prices of goods reasonably low. However traditionalists like Frobel see the NIDL as merely a new form of neo-colonial exploitation. In addition to exploiting peasants who grow cash crops for Western consumption, the TNCs are now exploiting wage labourers (especially women) in factories throughout the world. Pessimistic globalisers share these concerns. They point out that as TNCs relocate production in their search for lower costs and higher profits so the prospects of employment in the West decline. Wages in the UK will need to be kept sufficiently low so that TNCs see investment in the UK as an attractive option.

McDonaldisation

George Ritzer (1993) argues that another aspect of economic globalisation is McDonaldisation, 'the process by which the principles of the fast food restaurant are coming to dominate more and more sectors of American society as well as the rest of the world'. Ritzer argues that McDonaldisation has impacted upon economic production and consumption in four ways:

- efficiency: producing and consuming burgers is likened to an assembly-line experience
- calculability: achieving maximum quantity with minimum input
- predictability: standardisation of product, service and environment
- control: tasks are de skilled through technology.

Give examples of areas of society that may have been 'McDonaldised'.

Ritzer sees the process as essentially dehumanising both for workers and consumers. Moreover, he suggests that it is essentially another form of US economic and cultural imperialism. Spybey (1998), however, rejects this argument and suggests that McDonalds are a true symbol of genuine globalisation because they accommodate local culture and customs wherever they set up business. Spybey points out that true globalisation is actually a combination of global and local influences – there is 'inter-penetration' between the two. For example, burgers in McDonalds in India contain no meat because of local Hindu beliefs. In this sense, the global McDonalds has an effect upon the local (i.e. by setting up a fast food outlet) but the local has an effect upon the global too.

Transnational corporations (TNCs)

Another symbol of globalisation are the transnational corporations that have appeared in the past twenty years or so. These share the following characteristics.

- They usually operate in more than one country and have no clear home or national base. They therefore produce and market in a genuinely international sense.
- They seek competitive advantage and maximisation of profits by constantly searching for the cheapest and most efficient production locations.
- They have geographical flexibility in that they can easily shift resources and operations across the world.

- They are responsible for three-quarters of world trade and about one-third of all global economic output.

If we look at a league table of the world's top 100 most important economic units, we will see that half are nation-states and half are TNCs. Approximately 130 nation-states, (mainly in the developing world) have economies smaller than the top 50 TNCs. It is argued by neo-Marxists and pessimist globalists that TNCs exercise power without responsibility. TNCs have been accused of acting immorally and illegally in their pursuit of profit in the following respects.

- Shell in Nigeria and RTZ in Angola have exploited natural resources with ruthlessness and indifference. Indigenous people have had their land forcibly seized and despite international protests, have been removed at gunpoint from their homelands by local elites working on behalf of these TNCs.
- The sweatshop conditions of factories in the EPZs have been criticised, especially for use of child labour and exploitative rates of pay.
- TNCs have been responsible for ecological damage in countries like Nigeria.
- TNCs have refused to take responsibility for the welfare of local people killed or injured by their factories and plants. The explosion at Bhopal in India at the Union Carbide plant killed 2,800 people and injured 28,000 people in 1984. The company has not paid a cent in compensation.
- TNCs have influenced tastes and consumption patterns in the developing world in negative ways. For example, Nestlé has been criticised for its aggressive marketing of baby-milk powder in areas without easy access to clean water. Other TNCs have been criticised for their marketing of high-tar cigarettes and drugs and pesticides banned in the West for being dangerous to health.
- There is evidence that TNCs have interfered in the internal politics of developing countries and have even financed military coups against leaders they don't like.

Using a Marxist position, explain why TNCs are rarely made accountable for their illegal and immoral acts.

Global controls

The activities of TNCs illustrate a lack of global control by national governments and agencies such as the United Nations. Quite simply, there is no international law in place to regulate the activities of such organisations despite their blatant and consistent infringement of human rights. This lack of control is not unique to the activities of TNCs.

Globalisation also results in opportunities for cross-border crime which is thought to be worth $500 billion a year. International criminal activity includes people-trafficking, computer fraud, illegal arms-dealing, smuggling, violating patents and copyright agreements, and drug trafficking. The latter is particularly profitable. The world turnover in heroin went up twenty times between 1970 and 1990, whilst cocaine turnover went up 50 times. As described earlier, drug-trafficking is truly a global phenomena because it is linked to the poverty of certain countries which is a result of their position within the global capitalist system. The international trading system means that poor farmers in countries like Bolivia, Nepal and Jamaica cannot survive on the income provided by legitimate cash crops and turn instead to the production of coca or poppies.

Globalisation also increases the possibility of white-collar crime because of more open borders and international computer link-ups.

Why is it difficult to find accurate statistics about white-collar crime?

Drug money is also often '**laundered**' through legitimate global banking operations. Finally, violence is also taking on a global dimension as international drug gangs compete with each other for global dominance. Terrorism, too, has also moved beyond national boundaries. Osama Bin Laden's Al Queida group has recruited from a range of Arab, Asian and European nations.

The globalisation of culture

The global growth and spread of cultural goods (especially cinema, television, radio, advertising, music and the internet) in recent years has been phenomenal. McKay (2000) notes that the total number of television sets in the developing world has grown so rapidly that it has had a globalising effect on people in the developing world.

Positive globalisers see the global media as beneficial because it is primarily responsible for diffusing different cultural styles around the world and creating new global hybrid styles in fashion, music, consumption and lifestyle. It is argued that in the postmodern world such cultural diversity and **pluralism** will become the global norm.

The onslaught of Disney

Source: New Internationalist, December 1998 (taken from D. Held (ed.) (2000) *A Globalising World: Culture, Economics, Politics*, London: Routledge

Pessimistic globalisers, in contrast, are concerned about the concentration of the world's media in the hands of a few powerful media corporations. Media conglomerates, mainly American (such as Disney, Microsoft, Time Warner and AOL) and Japanese (such as Sony) have achieved near monopolistic control of newspapers, film archives, news programmes, television and radio, advertising and satellites. It is suggested that media moguls are able to influence business, international agencies and governments and consequently to threaten democracy and freedom of expression.

It is also argued that such media corporations are likely to primarily **disseminate** Western forms of culture. For example, most films released by these organisations are Hollywood produced and consequently of a certain **formulaic** type. There have been concerns that these Western forms of culture reflect a cultural imperialism that results in the marginalisation of local culture. Mass advertising of Western cultural **icons** like McDonalds and Coca-Cola may result in their logos becoming powerful symbols to people in the developing world (especially children) of the need to adopt Western consumer lifestyles in order to modernise. There is a fear that this may undermine and even destroy rich local cultures and identities. Some commentators refer to this as 'coca-colonisation.'

However, transformationalists are critical of cultural-imperialist arguments for three reasons.

- They make the mistake of suggesting that the flow of culture is one way only – from the West to the developed world. This focus fails to acknowledge how Western culture is enriched by inputs from other world cultures and religions.
- It assumes that people in the developing world are consumer dopes. In fact, their involvement in global culture may result in them accessing a wider range of choices.
- It underestimates the strength of local culture. As Cohen and Kennedy observe: 'On occasions, some inhabitants of Lagos or Kuala Lumpur may drink Coke, wear Levi 501 jeans and listen to Madonna records. But that does not mean they are about to abandon their customs, family and religious obligations or national identities wholesale even if they could afford to do so, which most cannot' (p.243).

Responses to globalisation

There are a number of social and collective responses to the phenomena of globalisation.

- Robertson (1992) notes that we select from the global only that which pleases us and then alter it so that it is adapted to our local culture or needs. He calls this 'glocalisation'. Cohen and Kennedy refer to this as 'indigenization', i.e. the local 'captures' the global influence and turns it into an acceptable form compatible with local tastes. For example, the Indian film industry in the form of 'Bollywood' combines contemporary Western ideas about entertainment with traditional Hindu myth, history and culture.
- We may mix global ingredients to produce new fused inventions – some world music mixes Western dance beats with traditional styles from North Africa and Asia. Cohen and Kennedy call this 'creolisation'.

- Global communication means that it is now difficult for people to avoid reflecting on world events or acknowledging that we live in a world characterised by 'risk'. This may result in a broadening of our identities, especially if we choose to champion a particular global cause related to issues such as the environment or debt relief. Such choices may be partly responsible for the rise of the anti-globalisation movement especially among young people.
- Our knowledge of the global may heighten our awareness of and loyalty to the local – our sense of Britishness may become stronger, for example.
- Some religious and ethnic groups may resist globalisation because they interpret it as Western imperialism and as an attack upon the 'purity' of their own cultural or religious beliefs. There is some evidence that this rationale may underpin Islamic attitudes towards the West.

Is globalisation actually occuring?

How might the term 'globalisation' be operationalised in order to test the theory that it is occurring?

The answer to the question in the heading depends on what theoretical position you decide to take. The problem with neo-Marxists and traditionalists is that they tend to over-focus on economic globalisation and neglect the globalisation of culture. They also make the mistake of viewing globalisation as a one-way process and as a form of cultural imperialism. They consequently tend to see globalisation as leading inevitably to **dystopia.**

Pessimistic globalisers like Barber and Schulz (1995) fear that we are turning into a 'McWorld' in which cultures and consumption will be standardised. However, the limited evidence we have so far suggests that **hybridity** – cultural borrowing and mixing – rather than uniformity may be the outcome of global cultural change. Cohen and Kennedy optimistically state that globalisation will lead to an extension in human rights, universal access to education and communications and multicultural understanding. However, we must remember that the phenomenon of globalisation is fairly young and, as Cohen and Kennedy soberly note, 'globalisation has so far done little to diminish the blight of poverty and wretchedness in which about half of the world's inhabitants is forced to live' (p.372).

KEY TERMS

Bollywood – Indian film industry based in Bombay.

Consumer dopes – are easily manipulated into spending their money.

Consumption – consuming material and cultural goods and resources.

Disseminate – transmit.

Dystopia – a future characterised by disaster and negative events.

Formulaic – predictable.

Globalists – those who believe that globalisation is occurring.

Globalisation – the increasing interconnectedness and interdependency of the world.

Hybridity – new cultural forms resulting from a mixture of different cultural influences.

Icons – symbols.

Imperialism – see Key Term in Topic 3.

Laundered – process of transferring money gained illegally into respectable accounts.

McDonaldisation – a term coined by Ritzer to describe the process by which the principles of the fast food restaurant are coming to dominate more and more sectors of American society as well as the rest of the world.

Pluralism – variety of groups.

Transformations – social changes.

White-collar crime – crime committed by the middle and upper classes in the context of corporate life.

CHECK YOUR UNDERSTANDING

1   What are the four transformations of the world that have led to globalisation according to Cohen and Kennedy?

2   What is globalism?

3   What is the difference between a positive globalist and a pessimistic globalist?

4   What is meant by the phrase 'coca-colonisation of the world'?

5   How does the New International Division of Labour differ from previous forms of capitalist production?

6   Why are transnationals attracted to EPZs?

7   What is McDonaldisation?

8   Identify four criticisms of TNC activity in the developing world?

9   Why are some sociologists anxious about the globalisation of culture?

10   What is globalisation?

11   Why might globalisation be leading to greater awareness of the world's problems and a desire to change the world for the better among young people?

12   Why are some sociologists like Wiseman sceptical about the use of the term 'globalisation'?

Item A

Globalisation implies that the boundaries between nation-states become less significant in social life. One example of this can be seen in economic life, where world trade is increasingly dominated by transnational corporations and capital can be moved rapidly by investors from one country to another as the international financial markets are connected by computerised technology. Globalisation can also be seen in culture where television programmes, films and books are made for an international market. This cultural globalisation can also be seen in the worldwide spread of tastes in food; for example, hamburgers, pizzas and curries, while identified as American, Italian or Indian, can be found in restaurants all over the world.

Extracted from: P. Taylor (1997) *Investigating Culture and Identity*, London: HarperCollins, p.128

Item B

To many living outside Europe and North America, globalisation looks like Westernisation or even Americanisation since the US is now the sole superpower, with a dominant economic, cultural and military position in the global order. Many of the most visible cultural expressions of globalisation are American – Coca-Cola, McDonalds, etc. Globalisation, some argue, destroys local cultures, widens world inequalities and worsens the lot of the impoverished. It creates a world of winners and losers, a few on the fast track to prosperity, the majority condemned to a life of misery and despair. In the last decade of the 20th century, the share of the poorest fifth of the world's population in global income has dropped from an already miserable 2.3% to 1.4%. Global corporations sell goods in the developing world that are controlled or banned in the West. Some argue that this is less of a global village and more like global pillage.

Adapted from: Lecture 1, 'Runaway World', one of the BBC Reith Lectures, BBC Radio 4 given by Anthony Giddens (1999)

1 Using Item A and other material, outline the evidence for economic globalisation.
2 Using Item A as a guide, assess the impact of economic and cultural globalisation on your lifestyle.
3 Outline in detail, using a range of materials, the criticisms of the concept of globalisation contained in Item B.
4 Describe, using Item C, the strengths and weaknesses of the relationship between the developing world and transnational companies.
5 Examine Items B and C, and assess what theoretical positions these sources take in regard to globalisation.
6 Using Item D and other materials, assess the methodological value of the concept of globalisation.

Item C

The theory behind EPZs [Export-Processing Zones] is that they will attract foreign investors who, if all goes well, will decide to stay in the country, and the zones' segregated assembly lines will turn into lasting development. To lure the TNCs [Transnational Corporations] in, the governments of poor countries offer tax breaks, lax regulations and the services of a military willing and able to crush labour unrest. To sweeten the pot further, they put their own people on the auction block, falling over each other to offer up the lowest minimum wage, allowing workers to be paid less than the real cost of living. Integration with the local culture and economy is kept to a bare minimum. As one International Labour Organisation report puts it, the EPZ 'is to the inexperienced foreign investor what the package holiday is to the cautious tourist: Zero-risk globalisation'. However, as critics of EPZs are quick to point out, the global economy has become much more competitive. Today seventy countries are competing for TNC investment. The incentives to lure investors are increasing and consequently wages and standards are being held hostage to the threat of TNC departure. The upshot is that entire countries are being turned into industrial slums and low-wage labour ghettos.

Source: N. Klein (2000) *No Logo*, London: Flamingo

Item D

It is undoubtedly true that, on a planet in which the same fashion accessories (such as designer training shoes) are manufactured and sold across every continent, one can send and receive electronic mail from the middle of a forest in Brazil, eat McDonald's hamburgers in Moscow as well as Manchester, and pay for all this using a Mastercard linked to a bank account in Madras, then the world does appear to be increasingly 'globalised'. However, the excessive use of this term as a sociological buzzword has largely emptied it of explanatory and analytical value.

Extracted from: G. Marshall (1998) *A Dictionary of Sociology*, Oxford: Penguin, p.259

Research idea

Construct a questionnaire that operationalises the concept of cultural globalisation in terms of the use of global brands and logos, transnational services like McDonalds, Burger King, Starbucks, clothing, trainers, tastes in film, music and television programmes, etc. in order to assess the influence of globalisation in your own life. Contact schools abroad via e-mail and ask students to fill in your questionnaire.

WWWebtask

- Visit the *Guardian* website and research the arguments for and against globalisation contained in the special report (www. guardian.co.uk/globalisation). This site contains over two dozen links to a range of excellent websites on globalisation. Most of them are critical such as:

- Corporation watch (www.corpwatch.org) which keeps an eye on the activities of transnational corporations.

- www.mcspotlight.org/ aims to track the activities of McDonalds.

- www.nosweat.org.uk/ looks critically at those companies allegedly running sweatshops in the EPZs.

- www.resist.org.uk/ is a site that co-ordinates the anti-globalisation movement.

- Finally, if you are cheesed off with the way that Harry Potter has been transformed into yet another global commercial brand, visit www.barrytrotter.com/ to read the latest instalment 'Harry Potter and the fight against global capitalism'.

EXAM PRACTICE

Extract from AQA-style question

Assess the view that 'globalisation is both necessary and inevitable'. (40 marks)

Power, Politics and Protest

Getting you thinking

A police officer arrests a suspect

George W. Bush

Osama Bin Laden

Madonna

Sven-Goran Eriksson

Bill Gates, owner of Microsoft

All of the people shown above exercise some sort of power.

1 What type of power do you think they exercise?

2 How do these types of power differ from each other?

3 Rank these individuals in hierarchical order on the basis of how much power they exert over your life.

4 How might Madonna's success have equipped young females today with more power than their mothers?

The above exercise should have shown you that power can take several different forms and can be exercised in a number of direct and indirect ways. For example, you are unlikely to meet George Bush or Osama Bin Laden but they still exercise considerable power over your life. Similarly it can be argued that if you are a female, Madonna's success impacts directly on your capacity to exercise power. You exercise more power than your mother because Madonna's career over the years has led to an acceptance of a wide range of activities for women that were once considered deviant.

Give examples of two activities that might have been considered deviant for women fifty years ago that are now widely accepted.

Max Weber and power

In the most general sense, power refers to any kind of influence exercised by individuals or groups on others – for example, Max Weber defined power as the chance or probability of an individual or group of people imposing their will on others despite resistance, i.e. if A has power over B to the extent that A can get B to do something that B would not otherwise do. This conception of power – **the zero-sum view of power** – implies that the exercise of power involves negative consequences for some individuals and groups because it involves repression, **coercion** and constraint. Weber believed that such power could be exercised in a range of social situations.

Positions of power can emerge from social relations in a drawing room as well as in the market, from the rostrum of a lecture hall as well as the command post of a regiment, from an erotic or charitable relationship as well as from scholarly discussion or athletics. (see Lukes, 1986).

Why is it difficult to operationalise the concept of power?

Max Weber's types of authority

Weber argues that legitimacy can be derived from three sources.

- *Charisma*
  Some individuals are able to direct others on the basis of powerful personalities alone.

- *Tradition*
  Power can be derived from historical precedent such as that embodied in the succession of the Royal Family in the UK.

- *Rational–legal*
  Most authority in Britain, whether that of the prime minister, a police officer or a teacher, derives from formal rules which often take the form of laws. Such authority is thought to be impartially applied to everyone and enforced without bias. Consequently people consent to obey this type of power, which is usually administered by a hierarchical bureaucracy. Morgan (1999) refers to this as 'the routinisation of obedience'. The option of force still exists but it is used only as a final resort.

Weber distinguished between two main types of [...] this bill.

- Coercion is force, usually in the form of [...] military resources.
- **Authority** depends upon consent – that [...] that the power is **legitimate**.

Some sociologists have highlighted other for[...] power halfway between coercion and authority, e.g. influence (where people are persuaded to change their minds) and manipulation (where individuals are cynically deceived perhaps through control over education, knowledge, information and news).

Functionalism and power

The functionalist conception of power sees power as a positive resource and, as such, characterised by consensus and legitimacy. Talcott Parsons (1963) argued that power results from the sharing of collective resources in order to achieve social and cultural goals. If A and B work together, they will both increase their power as well as benefit society. Power is a functional resource working for the benefit of the social system. It helps maintain social order and strengthens social solidarity.

Explain what is meant by 'social order'. Give an example of a social institution that helps maintain social order. How does it achieve this?

Marxism and power

Marxists argue that power arises out of the social **relations of production** that characterise the economic system of production found in capitalist societies. The dominant class is defined by its control over the **means of production**, such as capital, land, factories, technology and raw materials. This control, argue Marxists, is the basic resource for power in society. The lack of power experienced by the proletariat or working class is a product of its weak position in the social structure. Its only resource is labour power: the ability to work for others. However, the social relations that characterise the **bourgeoisie**–proletariat relationship are exploitative and unequal as the **capitalist class** acquires wealth by appropriating the surplus value generated by the labour power of workers (the proletariat).

Identify two criticisms of the Marxist perspective.

Hegemony

Class domination and economic power is maintained through coercion (although this tends to be used as a last resort) and ideological **hegemony**. Hegemony, according to Bocock (1986), occurs when the intellectual and moral leadership provided by the dominant class provides the fundamental cultural outlook for the whole of society. Marxists such as Althusser (1971) argue that this cultural dominance is achieved through the bourgeoisie using its economic power to define what counts as knowledge, ideas, art, education, news, and so on. The role of institutions that make up the

...ture of society is to transmit such ruling-class ... so that it is accepted by the mass of the population ... 'ormal' or 'natural' and so gain the active consent and ...pport of society in general for the capitalist dominance of society. These institutions include the education system, the legal system, the political system, the mass media and religion.

Exploring Giddens and power

Leading sociologist Anthony Giddens (1968) is critical of functionalist analyses of power. He suggests that power is part of all social relations and interactions.

Item A

What slips away from sight almost completely in the Parsonian analysis is the very fact that power is always exercised over someone! Parsons virtually ignores, quite consciously and deliberately, the hierarchical character of power, and the divisions of interest which are frequently consequent upon it. However much it is true that power can rest upon 'agreement', it is also true that interests of power-holders and those subject to that power often clash.

Item B

All interaction involves the use of power because all interaction is concerned with the production and reproduction of structure, drawing upon rules and resources. Power relates to those resources which actors draw upon in interaction, in order to 'make a difference'.

Source: Both Item A and Item B taken from: A. Giddens (1968) '"Power" in the recent writings of Talcott Parsons', *Sociology* 2 (3).

1 Explain Giddens' criticism of Parsons in your own words.

2 In Item B, Giddens argues that all interaction involves power. Explain how power might be involved in:

   a a group of friends talking
   b a family deciding what TV programmes to watch in the evening
   c a doctor–patient interaction
   d a parents' evening at school.

Take any one example of a social institution from the list above. How do Marxists argue that it transmits ruling-class ideology?

Westergaard (1996) argues that the result of hegemonic power is that workers fail to understand their own structural position correctly – that is, they fail to realise their true interests as exploited workers. This false class-consciousness means that they rarely realise their potential power for bringing about revolutionary change. The Frankfurt School of Marxism in a similar analysis argue that the working class has become 'ideologically **incorporated**' into capitalist society. Marcuse (1964) argued that this incorporation took the form of encouraging 'one dimensional thought': the general population was encouraged to indulge in uncritical and sterile forms of entertainment or mass culture that reduced their appetite for critical and creative thought and action that might challenge hegemonic power.

According to Gramsci (1971), hegemony, and the resulting consent of the people, has enabled the ruling class to deal with any threats to its authority without recourse to force. However, hegemony does not mean that subordinate classes will always lack power or that the power of the dominant class is absolute. Power is potentially available to the subordinate classes if they become sufficiently class-conscious and politically organised to seize or to challenge the control of the means of production.

Neo-Marxists such as Stuart Hall (Hall and Jefferson, 1976) have developed **relational conceptions of** power, that is, they recognise that power is a process which involves **ideological struggle** between the capitalist class and groups such as working-class youth. The capitalist class is normally able to impose cultural hegemony and so obtain the consent of most of the people to rule. However, pockets of **symbolic resistance** among sections of the working class indicate that power is not a one-way process. Gilroy (1982 a) suggests that working-class crime may well be political, a means by which subordinate groups can enjoy some power through hitting back at the symbols of capitalist power such as wealth and property. The work of the Birmingham Centre for Contemporary Cultural Studies similarly suggests that working-class deviant youth subcultures may be symbolically resisting hegemonic definitions of respectability by adopting forms of style and behaviour that set out to shock.

Criticisms of the idea of a dominant ideology

Abercrombie *et al.* (1980) are dismissive of claims that a dominant ideology characterises contemporary society. They put forward three key reasons.

- Capitalism today is characterised by conflicts *between* capitalist interests such as small businesses, finance capital, industrialists, multinational companies and state corporations. This conflict undermines the idea that the capitalist class is transmitting strong and unified ideological messages.
- Moreover they point out that the subordinate class often rejects the so-called dominant ideology – as can be seen in surveys of working-class people who recognise that we live in a class society characterised by inequality. Such workers

Exploring hegemony and resistance

Item A

Item B

Item C

1 Explain how the people in Items A and B could be seen to be symbolically resisting hegemony.

2 In what ways might Jim Royle (Item C) fit Marcuse's definition of 'one dimensional' thought?

may express resistance through strikes and membership of trade unions.

● The simple fact that workers have to work in order to preserve their standard of living leads to their co-operation and participation. People conform, not because of ideological hegemony but quite simply because they fear unemployment and poverty.

Post-structuralism and power

Foucault (1980) rejects the link between social structure and power. Foucault suggested that power is part and parcel of everyday life. In particular, power plays a major role in the construction of identity.

According to Foucault, there is a significant relationship between power, knowledge and language. He argued that there exist bodies of knowledge and language which he terms '**discourses**'. These dominate how society sees, describes and thinks about how we should live our lives in terms of family, sexuality, health and illness, and so on.

Foucault showed how, during the eighteenth century, there was a shift away from coercive forms of power associated with physical punishment to what he calls '**disciplinary power**'. This type of power saw a move to identify and categorise 'normality' and 'deviance' in the form of discourses in the fields of criminality, sexual behaviour and illness. Bauman (1983) notes how this type of power is based on the construction and imposition of **surveillance** (watching for deviation from normality), routine and regulation. 'It wanted to impose one **ubiquitous** pattern of normality and eliminate everything and everybody which the pattern could not fit.'

Foucault's conception of disciplinary power, i.e. discourses that control everyday behaviour via surveillance and discipline, first developed in state institutions such as prisons and asylums. However, during the course of the twentieth century it has become part of the organisational fabric of institutions such as schools and factories.

Give two examples of how either schools or factories 'control everyday behaviour'.

Foucault identified a second conception of power which he termed '**bio-power**'. Bio-power is concerned with controlling the body and how it is perceived by the general population. Foucault sees bio-power as especially influential in structuring discourses on sexuality. He claims that, from the nineteenth century onwards, discourse on sexual behaviour has rapidly become dominated by professionals working in the fields of psychiatry, medicine and social work. He argues that this discourse on sexual behaviour has power over all of us because it defines what is and what is not 'normal' and 'what is and what is not available for individuals to do, think, say and be' (Clegg, 1989). This power to impose definitions of 'normality' has become part of institutionalised life and may result in individuals being criticised, treated prejudicially and punished for being different, i.e. for indulging in behaviour or for holding attitudes that challenge the discourse. Moreover, this type of power is all pervasive since it influences our own sense of identity because unconsciously we may internalise aspects of the discourse and engage in self-discipline. We avoid behaviour and attitudes that are likely to provoke even more surveillance and discipline from official agencies.

Foucault's work has been criticised for not being empirical in a conventional research sense. He tended to support his arguments with selective historical examples rather than systematically gathered contemporary data. Moreover, his work tended to be overly descriptive at the expense of explanation – for example, it is not entirely clear why disciplinary power and bio-power evolved nor who exercises these types of power. Foucault did argue that no one group dominates disciplinary power but it may be unrealistic to suggest that no one group benefits more than others from exercising this type of power.

Gender and power

Westwood (2002) notes that feminist thinkers who focused on the concept of patriarchy insisted that the key issue in gender relations was power. Feminism saw itself 'as fighting for a reversal of the status quo in which men were seen to be dominant'. However, Westwood argues that this type of approach was crude and alienated women because it cast women as powerless subordinates, oppressed and exploited by patriarchal power.

What do feminists mean by 'patriarchal power'?

Westwood argues for the development of 'post-feminism' in which sociologists use Foucault's work on discourse to show how women can take control of their lives and identities. She cites Rubin who argues that females can exercise power through a series of strategies focusing on the micro-processes of power. Women can use their bodies, intuition and control

---

Exploring Foucault, gender and power

Item A

Item C

Item B

In all her supposed powerlessness, Diana was more powerful than she had been as the wife of the future monarch, demonstrating the importance of visibility and the confessional mode. 'Diana as victim' actually displayed her powers and, through the medium of television, managed to seduce vast numbers of people. She recreated herself and became an icon against the institutional power of the monarchy and the legitimation of the hereditary principle in Britain.

S. Westwood (2002) *Power and the Social*, London: Routledge.

1 Explain how Princess Diana became such a powerful figure.

Item D

Dominant discourses celebrate thinness and ... locate beauty with the fragile frame and almost androgynous shapes of highly paid models. This aesthetic exercises a powerful discipline on women's bodies which have constantly to be policed, watched, weighed, creamed, made over.

S. C. Bartkey (1992) 'Reevaluating French Feminism', *Critical Essays in Difference, Agency and Culture* (eds.) N. Fraser and S. C. Bartkey, Bloomington: Indiana University Press

2 How could the growing incidence of anorexia in young girls be explained through the idea of a dominant discourse about women's bodies?

of gestures to gain power and to construct their identities. Westwood uses the example of Diana, Princess of Wales to demonstrate how the micro-processes of power can be amplified through the media. Westwood concludes that Diana was able to subtly exercise power through presenting herself as a victim of both adultery and institutional power, by making herself highly visible through the media and by using her role as the mother of the future king to ensure her voice was heard. She argues that the Diana story raises many of the issues seen in a Foucauldian reading of power relations. For

example, Diana's struggle for p...
attempts to construct an identi...
odds with a discourse which sta...
obedient subject of the monarch...
attempts to discipline her and co...
disciplinary power eventually fail...
was able to develop visibility and ...
processes of power (especially in t...
which monarchy and society could...

KEY TERMS

Aesthetic – matter of taste.

Androgynous- sexually unclear.

Autonomy – having control over your own life.

Bio-power – term used by Foucault to describe concern with controlling the body and its perception.

Bourgeoisie – Marxist term describing the ruling class in capitalist society.

Bureaucracy– form of organisation associated with modern societies. Consists of a hierarchy of formal positions, each with clear responsibilities.

Capitalist class – social class that owns the means of production, i.e. factories etc.

Coercion – force.

Disciplinary power – the power to identify and categorise what is 'normal' and what is 'deviant'.

Discourse – ways of talking and thinking that dominate how society sees, describes and thinks about how we should live our lives.

Hegemony – situation where the ideology of the dominant class becomes accepted as the shared culture of the whole of society.

Ideological struggle – cultural conflict between the capitalist and subordinate classes.

Incorporated – sucked in.

Legitimate – justified and accepted.

Means of production – Marxist term referring to the material forces that enable things be produced, e.g. capital, land, factories.

Relational conception of power – power seen as a process that involves ideological struggle between the capitalist class and subordinate groups.

Relations of production – Marxist term referring to the allocation of rules and responsibilities among those involved in production.

Superstructure – Marxist term used to describe the parts of society not concerned with economic production such as the media, religion and education.

Surveillance – watching for deviation from normality.

Symbolic resistance – rebellion which takes an indirect form.

Ubiquitous – universal, everywhere.

Zero-sum view of power – idea that power involves one person or group gaining and another person or group losing.

CHECK YOUR UNDERSTANDING

1 How does the 'zero-sum of power' model define power?

2 What is the difference between coercion and authority?

3 What type of power is exercised by the prime minister?

4 What is the function of power according to Parsons?

5 Where does political power originate according to Marxists?

6 What is the function of the superstructure in regard to power?

7 According to Gramsci, how is the consent of the people gained by the ruling class?

8 Suggest two ways in which subordinate groups can acquire power according to Marxists.

9 What is a discourse?

Research idea

1 Construct a flow diagram with a box in the centre symbolising yourself. Draw lines to other boxes which contain the names of significant people in your life, e.g. friends, brothers and sisters, parents, other relatives, teachers, employers, workmates. Use a different colour pen to symbolise the type of power relationship you have with these people – for example, if the relationship is based on authority draw a red line, as you would from you to your teacher. Some of your relationships may be based on coercion, persuasion, influence, manipulation, even ideology – use different colour lines to symbolise these. You may have to add categories or adapt existing ones.

2 Ask a small sample of other people (try to include people of different ages, gender, ethnic and class backgrounds) to construct similar diagrams. Compare the diagrams. What similarities and differences do you find?

...ciologists of different persuasions tend to emphasise one ...ype of power at the expense of the others. For example, some have stressed that owners of factories have important economic power, although the effects of their power may be indirect. For example, investment decisions made by a Board of Directors can create jobs in some areas and destroy them in others. In the past, military power has been a crucial aspect of British society and, while still important, it is much less visible than it was in the past. The exception to this is, of course, Northern Ireland, where military power is an everyday experience for many citizens. In postmodern society, cultural power is seen as the most important aspect of power, as it is the manipulation of images in the media which is claimed to 'create' reality and have political consequences in the postmodern world. Power need not be as a result of formal position, but rather it is networked in all social situations. It is shifting and filled with reversals and resistances. For example, labels which attempt to stigmatise a social group can be taken by that social group and be used to reaffirm identity and create new cultural forms of power out of the label, e.g. the Black Movement in the USA used the phrase 'black is beautiful' in very positive ways.

Adapted from: T. Lawson (1993) *Sociology for A-Level*, London: HarperCollins

Item C

Michael Mann (1993) believes that in order to understand social life, sociologists need to study the way that humans enter into social relationships which involve the exercise of power. Mann sees power as the ability to pursue and attain goals through mastery of the environment. Power, in this sense, can take two separate forms. Distributional power is power over others especially the power to get others to help you pursue your own goals. In contrast, collective power is exercised by social groups. Collective power may be exercised by one group over another, e.g. when one nation colonises another. Mann goes on to explain the two different ways in which power can be exercised. Extensive power is the ability to organise large numbers of people over an extensive area, e.g. an empire. Intensive power is the ability to organise tightly or command a high level of loyalty. In the final part of Mann's analysis, he identifies a difference between authoritative and diffused power. Authoritative power is exercised when conscious, deliberate commands are issued and people make a conscious decision to follow them. Diffused power spreads in a more spontaneous way and operates without commands being issued, e.g. market forces may force a company to close.

Adapted from: M. Holborn and M. Haralambos (2000) *Sociology: Themes and Perspectives*, London: HarperCollins

Item B

Power on its own is raw and often relies on the threat or use of violence or other unpleasant sanctions. Legitimate power, however, carries – indeed becomes – authority. It rests on the acceptance of the people under its sway. Legitimacy is a claim to power that people accept. Naked power is often that of the bully or tyrant. Legitimate power is the authorised holder of office. In most societies, a balance is struck between the use of coercion and persuasion and, in that respect, force is the armour plating rather than the norm. Moreover, force is only permissible if it's used according to law. Authority is an effective form of 'power' because it gains the consent of those who are subject to it. Used by corporate bosses and politicians, authority can be a soft form of social control, a gentle subjugation that uses ideology (the collective outlook of a group) to coax rather than cajole.

P. Stephens *et al.* (1998) *Think Sociology*, Cheltenham: Stanley Thornes

Item D

Foucault defines society in terms of a multiplicity of fields of knowledge or discourses which are characterised by specific rules which enable specialists and experts (doctors, teachers, scientists) to produce statements about a specific practice (such as mental illness). A discourse is everything written or spoken about a specific practice based on specialist knowledge and bodies of experts which has the effect of controlling those who lack knowledge (such as the patient). In this way normalising judgements are made and experts make decisions on who is to be defined as mentally ill, criminal or sexually deviant. Discourse is thus effectively a form of power exercised by particular social groups.

Adapted from: A. Swingewood (2000) *A Short History of Sociological Thought*, Basingstoke: Macmillan

1 Using Item A only, define what is meant by cultural power.

2 Which theory argues that owners of factories have important economic power?

3 Using Item B and other sources, outline the relationship between coercion, authority and legitimacy.

4 Using Item C only, describe with examples Mann's six types of power.

5 Using Item D and other sources, explain how discourse works as an agency of power.

WWWebtask

Visit the website of the *Guardian* newspaper – www.guardianunlimited.co.uk. Enter 'power lists' into the search engine and access the Channel 4/Observer top 100 powerful individuals. What is the basis of the power of those who make up the list?

EXAM PRACTICE

Extract from AQA-style question

Evaluate competing sociological theories of the nature of power. (12 marks)

OCR-style question

Outline and assess the view that the exercise of power inevitably involves negative consequences for some individuals. (60 marks)

Getting you thinking

Imagine you are attending a Public Inquiry into whether a new road should be built between the port of Grimsby and the A1. There are two proposed routes. Route A will cost £210 million and will run straight through the only known habitat in the north of England of the rare wide-mouthed frog. It will also involve the blasting of a tunnel through the Lincolnshire Wolds, an area of outstanding natural beauty. Route B will cost £160 million but will run through the greenbelt around the historic city of Lincoln, as well as involve great disruption to traffic in the area while a by-pass is especially built to take traffic away from the city centre. Five groups will give evidence to the Inquiry.

Lincoln Chamber of Commerce: we favour Route B. The motorway will bring extra business and trade to the city which is good for our members. Hauliers and builders will especially benefit. In particular, it will increase the tourist trade to the city. The motorway will affect the surrounding countryside but there is plenty of it to enjoy that will not be affected. (Report prepared by John Smith of Smith Road Haulage Ltd and Stephen Brook of Brook Building Quarries Ltd.)

Dept. of the Environment: we approve of Route B for cost reasons. It will also attract foreign investors to the area because of the fast road-links to London. It will increase the status of the area and attract commuters in from London who can take advantage of rail links from Lincoln. Employment opportunities will increase, leading to full employment and higher wages. However, the department is also content with Route A because the Department of Defence requires a fast road from the Grimsby area to facilitate the efficient movement of nuclear waste in and out of RAF Binbrook. (This information is highly confidential and should not be disclosed to the Inquiry.)

Friends of the Earth: we oppose both routes on the grounds that both wildlife and the countryside will suffer. We are particularly concerned about the survival of the wide-mouthed frog which is in danger of extinction across the country. Both roads will be a blot on the landscape. Existing rail services can easily deal with the container traffic from the port of Grimsby.

North Lincolnshire Ratepayers' Association: we oppose both routes. We are concerned that the natural beauty of the area will be ruined. We are concerned about the danger to children from more traffic, especially in terms of accidents and pollution. There may be an influx of new people into the area. Some of these may be undesirables and bring crime to the area. The value of our properties may fall considerably.

National Farmers' Union: we favour Route A. This route involves less damage to the environment compared with Route B. The danger to the wide-mouthed frog is over-estimated. It can be moved to another habitat. The land around Route B currently attracts about £200 million in EU subsidies – the NFU estimates that we would only receive about £70 million from the Ministry of Transport if the land is compulsorily purchased whereas our members would receive approximately £90 million for the less fertile land around Route A.

1 Look carefully at the five briefs. If you were representing these organisations what information would you disclose to the Inquiry? What would you hold back and why?

2 What does this exercise tell you about the decision-making process?

The point of this exercise is to demonstrate that decision-making is not a straightforward process. You will have noticed that four of the groups had a vested interest in either one or both routes. Moreover, they probably made decisions not to divulge all of the information they had because it might have prejudiced the Inquiry against them. The Inquiry, then, was basing its conclusions on incomplete information. There were three groups who would have benefited enormously whatever road had been built. Only one group had nothing to hide. Ironically, this group, the Friends of the Earth was most likely to lose. What this exercise tells us is that decision-making is not an open process. Rather there are hidden dimensions to it that we rarely see. It is important to examine the distribution of power if we want to gain insight into the decision-making process in modern societies.

Pluralism

Robert Dahl (1961) carried out an **empirical** study of decision-making in New Haven, USA of three contentious issues. He employed a range of methods which he believed would precisely measure the exercise of power.

These included:

- looking at changes in the socio-economic background of those who occupied influential political positions in the community
- measuring the nature and extent of the participation of particular socio-economic groups
- determining the influence of particular individuals
- randomly sampling community-based activists and voters
- analysing changing voting behaviour.

Suggest two problems that Dahl may have encountered in conducting his research.

Dahl's research concluded that:

1 Power in modern societies is **diffused** and distributed among a variety of community elites who represent specific interests in fairly unique areas. No one group exerts influence in general.
2 Moreover, each group exercises **countervailing power** – that is, each serves as a check on the others thus preventing a monopoly of power.
3 Power is also **situational**, tied to specific issues. If one group does succeed in dominating one area of policy, it will fail to dominate others.
4 All elites are **accountable** because they rely on popular support and must constantly prove they are working in the public interest rather than in their own.

Dahl concludes, therefore, that societies are characterised by democratic **pluralism**. Power is open to all through political parties and pressure groups. No interest group or individual can have too much of it.

Pluralism: the critique

Dahl was criticised by Newton (1969) who notes that about 50–60% of the electorate fail to vote in US presidential elections. It is therefore not enough to assume that inclusion within a community is evidence of sharing in the power process. Newton suggests that Dahl overstates the 'indirect influence' that voters have over leaders by virtue of voting for four reasons.

- Votes are cast for aggregate packages of policies and personnel. Observing the whole range of these factors is difficult, sorting them out is extremely difficult, and measuring their influence is impossible.
- Indirect influence via the medium of voting assumes voters' interests are similar and that these are clearly communicated to politicians. It is also assumed that they are represented by selfless politicians. All these things are difficult to measure empirically.
- The needs of groups like the poor can be ignored because they lack the economic and cultural power to be heard or to have influence over politicians.
- The power of elected officials may be severely constrained by permanent officials such as civil servants.

Why is it easy to ignore the interests of social groups such as the poor?

Dahl did acknowledge that political apathy, alienation, indifference and lack of confidence among the poor and ethnic-minority sections of US society did create obstacles to effective participation in political life.

Bachrach and Baratz (1970) note that Dahl only looks at what Lukes (1974) calls the 'first dimension of power': decisions that can be seen and observed. Dahl consequently neglects the second dimension of power – the ability to prevent issues from coming up for discussion at all. Power, then, is not just about winning situations but confining decision-making to 'safe' issues that do not threaten powerful interests. In short, power may be expressed through '**non-decision-making**'.

Lukes takes this critique further by identifying a third dimension of power. Those that benefit from decision-making may not be the ones making the decision. It is therefore important to identify who benefits in the long term from

---

Non-decision-making

Non-decision-making can work in three ways.

1 The powerful may ignore the demands of the less powerful. If these demands do gain admission to the political agenda they may effectively be undermined via fruitless discussion in endless committees and public inquiries.
2 The 'rule of anticipated reaction' may come into effect when issues are not raised simply because opposition is anticipated.
3 **Mobilisation of bias** occurs. This refers to those situations where dominant interests may exert such a degree of control over the way in which a political system operates (and over the values, beliefs and opinions of the less powerful within it) that they can effectively determine not only whether certain demands come to be expressed but even whether such demands will cross people's minds.

Exploring pluralism

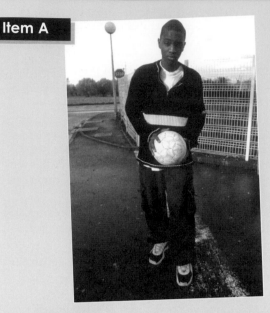

Abercrombie and Warde (2000) argue that the pluralist view of power in Britain is undermined by four processes.

1 Many interests are not represented by pressure groups and political parties – for example, fewer than half the workforce is represented by trade unions and groups such as the poor, single mothers, women in general, ethnic minorities, and young people lack specific groups that represent their interests in the political arena.

2 Some interests (in particular finance capitalism and employers) are over-represented in terms of powerful interest groups working on their behalf.

3 Many campaigning groups are undemocratically organised and dominated by self-perpetuating oligarchies.

4 There is evidence that key institutions in the UK are run by elites who share similar economic, social and educational backgrounds.

1 What is meant by the pluralist view of power?

2 How do the photographs illustrate some of the points made by Abercrombie and Warde?

particular decisions. Powerful groups may pursue policies that they genuinely believe will benefit the whole community but that actually benefit the powerful more than others. Lukes argues that this is the most potent type of power because it is never questioned or challenged.

Saunders' *et al.* (1979) study of two policies in a rural community illustrates this point. The two policies were the preservation of the environment and the maintenance of low **rates** and, would appear to be in everybody's interests.

However, the first ensures that private housing is scarce and expensive and council house-building is restricted, thereby forcing farm labourers into tied housing and therefore dependence upon their employers. No new industry was allowed to develop and this resulted in farmers being able to maintain the low wage levels paid to their employees. Low rates meant that little was spent on services that would benefit the poor such as public transport, welfare and education provision.

Elite theory

Classical **elite** theory stresses that power is concentrated in the hands of an elite – a closed minority group. Pareto (1935) argued that concentration of power is an inevitable fact of life. In any society, power is exercised by the active few who are better suited to such a role than the passive masses. Pareto saw power as a game of manipulation between two dominant elites who compete with each other for power – the foxes (who used cunning and guile) and the lions (who exercise power through force). Pareto argued that all states are run by these elites and all forms of government are forms of elite rule. Political change is merely the replacement of one elite by another.

Give an example of an agency of social control that can be seen as a 'lion' and an agency that can be seen as a 'fox'. Explain your answers.

Similarly, Mosca (1939) argued that the masses will always be powerless because they don't have the intellectual or moral qualities to organise and run their societies. He argued that elections are merely mechanisms by which members of the elite have themselves elected by the voters. Mannheim (1960) argued that democracy did not work because the masses were 'irrational', and therefore not capable of decision-making. 'Cultured' and 'rational' elites were essential to maintain civilisation.

Some critics have suggested that this is a very simplistic view of power and politics because real differences between governments are dismissed. Both socialism and democracy are seen to conceal elites. However, no criteria is provided by which we can measure the so-called superior qualities of elites. It is merely assumed that the masses are inferior and that the elite is superior.

C. Wright Mills: the power elite

The American sociologist C. Wright Mills (1956) regarded the USA as a society characterised by elite rule. He argued that three key elites monopolise power in modern societies like the USA:

- the economic or business elite, symbolised by the growth of giant corporations controlling the economy
- the political elite which controlled both political parties and federal and state governments
- the military elite.

Mills argued that the activities of each elite were inter-connected to form a single ruling minority or '**power elite**'. The cohesiveness of this group is strengthened by their similarity of social background, i.e. white, male, Protestant, urban and sharing the same educational and social class background. Moreover, there is interchange and overlap between these elites in that company directors sit on government advisory committees, retired generals chair business corporations, and so on. Such unity, argued Mills, means that power elites run Western societies like the USA in their own interests and the bulk of the population is manipulated by the elite through their control of education and the media.

Design a piece of research that aims to discover if Britain is controlled by a 'power elite'.

Marxism and the distribution of power

Marxists believe that elites constitute a ruling class whose major aim is the preservation of capitalist interests. Marxists argue that exploitation of the working class has led to the concentration of wealth in the hands of the few. For example, most stocks and shares are in the hands of a minority whilst over 50% of the top 250 companies are owned and controlled by individuals or families. This economic elite is united by common characteristics such as inherited wealth and public school and Oxbridge connections. Marxists argue that the class structure is of central significance because those who own what Abercrombie and Warde (2000) call 'property for power' – the means of production such as finance capital, land, technology and factories – are able to exert power over everyone else.

Explain why Marxists believe that the capitalist system exploits the working class.

Direct and indirect rule

Miliband (1970) argues that the capitalist class rules both directly and indirectly in the UK.

- It rules directly by forming Conservative governments. He argues that direct and open rule by the ruling class is common in history, as is their willingness to confront working-class dissent and protest.
- Miliband suggests that the ruling class also rule indirectly by occupying powerful positions in the **civil service** and **judiciary**. Miliband argues that the upper levels of the civil service (responsible for advice and policy) are mainly drawn from the same background as the economic elite. Like other members of this elite, their outlook tends to be conservative and suspicious of change.

Miliband argues that the groups that constitute the political elite (i.e. members of the Government, politicians in general, top civil servants, etc.) and the economic elite share similar educational backgrounds in terms of public school and Oxbridge experience. They often have family connections and are members of the same London clubs. They are therefore similar enough to constitute a ruling class. Moreover elite members often 'swap' roles. For example, top civil servants on retiring often take up directorships in business whilst prominent businessmen often appear on government committees.

Marxists also suggest that economic power results in ideological power. The ruling class exerts influence over the ideas transmitted through a range of social institutions. Miliband, for example, focuses on the role of the media in promoting the view that the national interest is best served by capitalist interests. This can be seen in advertising campaigns that promote companies such as BP as symbolising 'security, reliability and integrity'. Television programmes and tabloid newspapers reinforce capitalist values by encouraging people to see the way to fulfilment as being through the acquisition of material goods. Such ideological power leads to hegemony or cultural domination. People accept that the culture of capitalism (based on consumerism, materialism and individualism) is good for them and so consent to power being held by the capitalist class or its representatives, who are seen to manage the economy effectively and thus maintain their standard of living.

Provide two examples of social institutions that have 'ideological power' other than the mass media.

Divisions within the capitalist class

Miliband therefore argues that the ruling class rules but does not necessarily govern – instead it rules the government by the fact of common background and therefore class interest. If we examine the statistical evidence in regard to social and educational backgrounds we can see that it supports Miliband's argument, i.e. elite occupations do share characteristics and there is considerable overlap between these groups. Scott (1991) refers to this overlap as 'the establishment' and claims it monopolises the major positions of power and influence.

Other sociologists have pointed out that government economic policy has generally failed to benefit those groups who dominate capitalism. Some actually suggest that the economic elite is characterised by conflict and division. Scott points out that the the interests of industrialists may be different from those of finance capital. He notes the existence of 'power blocs' within the capitalist class which form alliances to promote their interests. He notes how different power blocs dominate the political and economic decision-making process at different points in history in Britain. For example, manufacturing capital was dominant in the 1950s, finance capital (i.e. the City) was dominant in the 1980s and 1990s whilst it could be argued that power today is dominated by transnational companies and currency speculators as economies become increasingly globalised.

Explain what is meant by the term 'globalised'. Give two examples to show how globalisation has affected culture in Britain.

Poulantzas: power and the capitalist system

Poulantzas (1973) suggested that the common social background of the ruling class is less important than the nature of capitalism itself. It does not matter whether elite groups rule directly or indirectly because the ruling class will always benefit as long as capitalism exists. Most governments across the world, whether they are on the right or left of the political spectrum, accept that economic management of their economies involves the management of capitalism in such a way that they do not lose the confidence of international investors or The Stock Exchange. Moreover, legislation in favour of subordinate groups such as pro-trade union or health and safety laws benefit the capitalist class in the long term because it results in a healthy, fit and possibly more productive workforce.

Poulantzas argued that the capitalist class will always ultimately benefit unless the whole system is dismantled. The capitalist class does not have to interfere directly in decision-making – the fact that the decision-making process is happening within a capitalist framework will always benefit it.

In summary, then, the overall evidence seems to support the view that elites dominate decision-making in both Britain and the USA. There is no doubt that these elites share some elements of a common social background and culture. However, this is not the same as suggesting that these elites constitute a unified ruling class. At best, the evidence for this is speculative.

KEY TERMS

Accountable – those in power can be held responsible for their decisions and actions.

Civil service – paid officials who work in government.

Countervailing power – an alternative source of power that acts as a balance to the prevailing power source.

Diffused – spread widely.

Elite – small, closed dominant group.

Empirical – based on first-hand research.

Establishment – informal network of the powerful, linked by shared social, economic and educational backgrounds.

Judiciary – judges.

Mobilisation of bias – a situation where dominant interests control the way in which a political system operates in such a way that some issues are never actually discussed.

Non-decision-making – the power to prevent some issues from being discussed.

Oligarchy – control by a small elite.

Pluralism – the theory that power is shared amongst a range of different groups in society.

Power elite – a few small, closed dominant groups that are inter-linked and that control society.

Rates – a tax that used to exist on property (now replaced by Council Tax).

Situational – holders of power vary from issue to issue, no one individual or group is dominant.

CHECK YOUR UNDERSTANDING

1 What does Dahl mean when he says that power is diffused?

2 What does Lukes identify as the three dimensions of power?

3 Explain what is meant by 'mobilisation of bias'.

4 What is the most potent type of power according to Lukes?

5 Outline the contribution of 'foxes' and 'lions' to our understanding of power.

6 What is the power elite?

7 In what ways does a ruling class rule both directly and indirectly according to Miliband?

8 What is meant by the 'establishment'?

9 Why are the common social backgrounds of elites not that important according to Poulantzas?

Item A

Robert Dahl believes that elections play an important part in controlling government and he also cites a second major means by which leaders are made answerable to the people. The other method of social control is continuous political competition among individuals, parties or both. Elections and political competition vastly increase the size, number and variety of minorities whose preferences must be taken into account by leaders in making policy choices. Above all, elections, or the certainty that an election must come, means that a governing party must always conduct itself in a way that will ultimately appeal to the majority of the electorate. There is evidence that widespread retrospective voting does occur: many voters do remember major features in the overall performance of administration, and this acts as a check upon it. When the election comes, the government knows that, to win, it must have the backing of a 'majority of minorities'.

Adapted from: M. O'Donnell (1992) *A New Introduction to Sociology*, (3rd edition), London: Nelson

Item B

Recent research by Stern (1988) makes interesting reading. Money is probably the most important factor in someone becoming and staying elected in the United States. Senators and congressional members have to raise enormous sums of money not only to be in a position to win office but also to retain it once there. Consequently, newcomers in general have a more difficult task ahead of them than do those who are already established, particularly where the former have no access to either personal or sponsoring sources of wealth. Because of this, there is a persistent influence accruing to those who regulate access to political donations. Political contenders who espouse issues detrimental to the agenda of the major contributors, whether they are corporate or labour organisations, are unlikely to see these issues gain much support nor be articulated into the political process through alternate means such as the media.

Adapted from: S. Clegg (1989) *Frameworks of Power*, London: Sage

Item C

There are three pieces of evidence that support the ruling class thesis. Firstly, no elected government in Britain has sought to abolish the capitalist economy based on private ownership. Nor has any government seriously tried to reorganise industry so that firms are managed by their workers. Nor has any government in Britain extended welfare services so that they provide adequate provision for all the population from the cradle to the grave. Secondly, business interests are not merely one group amongst a number, but are the best organised. Business interests are the wealthiest of all groups and were able, as in the early 1970s, to mount extensive newspaper campaigns against nationalisation. Thirdly, the best organised social grouping within Britain is finance capital, popularly known as the City of London. British economic policy has been mainly devoted to protecting finance capital through keeping a strong value of the pound sterling enabling these institutions to invest abroad on a massive scale.

Adapted from: N. Abercrombie and A. Warde (2000) *Contemporary British Society*, (3rd edition) Cambridge: Polity Press

1 Using Item A only, identify two ways in which governments are kept in check by minority groups.

2 Using Item A and other sources, outline the pluralist theory of power.

3 Identify two criticisms of pluralist theory identified by Clegg in Item B.

4 Outline the three pieces of evidence of a ruling class according to Item C.

Research idea

Interview a small sample of teachers about the distribution of power at your school or college. You could ask them to explain one or two recent decisions and how they were taken. To what extent does the evidence you have collected support pluralist or elite theories?

WWWebtask

Find out the names of the politicians who constitute the Cabinet and Shadow Cabinet, Examine the biographical data of each politician by looking at the biographical details part of the Houses of Parliament website. In particular, investigate the educational and occupational backgrounds of the elite to see whether they share any common ground.

EXAM PRACTICE

Extract from AQA-style question

'Power is more fairly measured by who benefits than by who decides.'

Assess this statement concerning the distribution of power in the modern world. (40 marks)

OCR-style question

Outline and assess the view that power is concentrated in few hands in the UK. (60 marks)

Getting you thinking

The Bank of England

A prision warder locks a cell

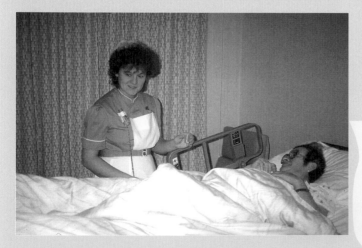

1 What do all these images have in common?

2 What role do the people in these occupations play in your life?

3 Do you think the role they play is an important one?

4 Who pays for these people and institutions? How?

All the people pictured in these images are servants or employees of the state. Another way of looking at this is to understand that each of these people is working on your behalf because the state serves the society of which you are a member. All these occupations play a crucial role in your life whether you realise it or not. The police protect you from crime. The army exists to ensure you are defended if the country is invaded by a foreign army. Prison officers ensure that dangerous criminals are kept away from your door. Doctors and nurses are dedicated to keeping you alive and healthy. The Bank of England is dedicated to making sure the pound in your pocket is worth something, whilst a postman ensures that your mail reaches its destination. All of these things come courtesy of the state!

What is the state?

Abercrombie and Warde (2000) note that the state is made up of a combination of major social institutions that organise and regulate British society.

> *The state consists of that set of centralised and interdependent social institutions concerned with passing laws, implementing and administering those laws, and providing the legal machinery to enforce* **compliance** *with them. These institutions rest upon the state's monopoly of legitimate force within a given territory, which means that most of the time the laws of Britain are upheld. The powers of the state ultimately rest upon this threat of legitimate force.*

A state, then, is a central authority exercising legitimate control over a given territory and which can use political violence against either its own citizens or other states to enforce that control.

Explain what is meant by 'legitimate control'.

Abercrombie and Warde argue that the British State is characterised by six significant and far-reaching powers.

- It has an almost unlimited ability to make and enforce law, although final appeals can now be made to the European Courts.
- It is able to raise large sums of money via taxation.
- It employs about one-fifth of the UK's total labour force.
- It is a major landowner.
- It controls instruments of economic policy especially control over currency exchange and interest rates.
- It regulates the quality of provision of both services and commodities on behalf of the general public. OFSTED, for example, inspects the quality of schools on behalf of the state.

We can add another power which has increased in recent years: surveillance and recording. Supporters of human rights have become very concerned at the state's ability to observe our behaviour via CCTV and about its accumulation of information about its citizens through birth, marriage and death registration data, taxation and social security details, criminal records, etc. Human-rights campaigners are concerned at the possibility that the British state may one day require all citizens to carry ID cards. In 2002, the police announced that all genetic samples taken from citizens, whether they were guilty of a crime or not, would be kept on police file.

What contribution has Foucault made to our understanding of 'surveillance'?

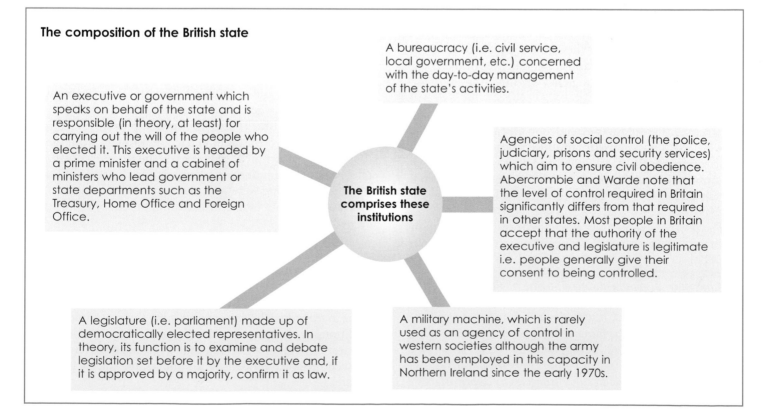

The composition of the British state

A bureaucracy (i.e. civil service, local government, etc.) concerned with the day-to-day management of the state's activities.

An executive or government which speaks on behalf of the state and is responsible (in theory, at least) for carrying out the will of the people who elected it. This executive is headed by a prime minister and a cabinet of ministers who lead government or state departments such as the Treasury, Home Office and Foreign Office.

The British state comprises these institutions

Agencies of social control (the police, judiciary, prisons and security services) which aim to ensure civil obedience. Abercrombie and Warde note that the level of control required in Britain significantly differs from that required in other states. Most people in Britain accept that the authority of the executive and legislature is legitimate i.e. people generally give their consent to being controlled.

A legislature (i.e. parliament) made up of democratically elected representatives. In theory, its function is to examine and debate legislation set before it by the executive and, if it is approved by a majority, confirm it as law.

A military machine, which is rarely used as an agency of control in western societies although the army has been employed in this capacity in Northern Ireland since the early 1970s.

Organisations controlled, regulated and administered by the state

Education
The state finances institutions such as schools, colleges and universities and has played a vital role in defining the content and assessment of the curriculum.

The state controls, regulates and administers the activities of a range of organisations.

Communications
The BBC is essentially also part of the state. It was set up by Royal Charter. Its political independence is supposedly guaranteed by not being dependent upon the state for its finance, the main bulk of which comes from the licence fee. However, the cost of the licence fee is decided by the state. Parliament must vote on this. Moreover the executive is responsible for appointing the BBC's Chairman and Governors.

Health
The National Health Service (NHS) is the product of the state's decision to take responsibility for the health and welfare of its citizens.

Economic bodies
The Bank of England is part of the state despite its relative autonomy from the Treasury. The state provides a range of economic services to the general public such as the Post Office, and regulates the economic activities of those industries that were once under state control such as the railways, gas, electricity and water.

A brief history of the British state

The state as it is today is the result of a long historical process in which power has been effectively transferred from the monarchy to the people. The nineteenth century, in particular, saw the power of the House of Commons increase as the vote was extended to the middle classes. This led to the emergence of distinct political parties with distinct ideologies and high-profile leaders. Elections resulted in the party with the largest share of the vote forming governments and leaders of political parties becoming the prime minister of the day. Nineteenth-century governments generally adhered to *laissez-faire* policies (meaning that they were generally reluctant to interfere in the daily social and economic lives of their citizens). Consequently, state policy involved minimal legislation.

During the twentieth century, elections became even more important as the vote was extended to all citizens aged 21 and over in 1928. Political parties produced manifestos of their policies in order to attract voters and consequently governments once in power saw it as the state's responsibility to manage the economy and look after the welfare of its citizens.

The post-war period saw a massive transformation in the size, range and power of the state. As Abercrombie and Warde (2000) observe:

> It has at its disposal enhanced powers of observing, recording and repressing the population (particularly through computer databases). It provides a wide range of services administered by large bureaucracies (both the civil service and local authorities). And it plans and acts on behalf of society as a whole, since, if matters were left to each individual, many would suffer unnecessary deprivation.

For example, the Labour government of 1945–51 extended the role of the state in a number of extraordinary ways.

- It **nationalised** key industries such as the railways, mines, iron and steel.
- It set up the National Health Service (NHS).
- It extended state services in regard to social welfare and the alleviation of poverty.
- The 1944 Education Act extended state control over all aspects of education with the exception of the private sector.

Give one example of a state policy introduced by the Labour government 1945–51.

Up to 1979, a consensus existed between the main political parties on welfare and economic policy. State management by both these parties when in government was remarkably similar. However, Mrs Thatcher's leadership from 1979 on saw a fracturing of this consensus and a commitment from the Conservative government to 'roll back' the frontiers of the state. Nationalised industries were **privatised**, public utilities and council housing were sold, taxation was lowered and there were attempts, albeit unsuccessful, to reduce the size of the welfare state.

The Labour Government which came to power in 1997 has committed itself to a so-called '**third way**' which seems to mean the state taking **paternalistic** responsibility for the '**socially excluded**' whilst encouraging the general population to take responsibility for their own actions. The third way also seems to extend to the state maintaining the economic conditions in which economic investors and transnational corporations are satisfied (although as we shall see later in this section, global influences can undermine state actions in this area).

What is meant by 'social exclusion'? Give an example of the way the term has been used from any area of your studies.

Theories of the modern state

Pluralist theories of the state

As we saw in Topic 2, pluralists like Robert Dahl (1961) argue that modern democratic societies are pluralist – they are characterised by power being dispersed between a plurality of elite groups as represented by political parties and pressure groups. However, although these elites share a basic consensus on social values and goals (e.g. they agree that violence is not a legitimate strategy) they are often in conflict with each other. The function of the state, according to pluralist theory, is to act as a neutral, independent referee or 'honest broker' whose role is to reconcile and accommodate competing interests. Aron (1967) sees the state as in the business of compromise. Resources such as power and capital are primarily in the hands of the state and its role is to distribute such resources to deserving causes on the basis of public or national interest. The state therefore regulates competing interest groups and operates to ensure that no one group gets its own way all of the time. The state and its servants such as the civil service are neutrally serving the needs of all by ensuring all competing interest groups have some influence on government policy.

Marxist vs. pluralist beliefs about the state

'I'm completely neutral and judge every incident on its merits.'

Pluralist approach to the state

'I take the side of the powerful. If Manchester United claim a penalty in the last minute, I'll give it.'

Marxist approach to the state

Marxist theories of the state

Marx (1876) described the state as a 'committee for managing the affairs of the whole bourgeoisie'. Marxists argue that the state gives the illusion of serving the general will of the people but in reality (they argue) it serves class interests. Althusser (1971) noted that agencies of the state are essentially ideological apparatuses that function to cultivate a picture of the state as being above any specific interest. However, the reality is that the state serves to reproduce, maintain and legitimate capitalism, ruling-class interests and therefore class inequality.

What is meant by an 'ideological apparatus'? From your studies, give one example of an ideological apparatus and describe its ideological role.

There are, however, variations in the Marxist approach.

Instrumental Marxism

Miliband (1970) and other 'instrumental Marxists' see the state as an instrument controlled directly and indirectly by the ruling class. This view argues that the state is manned and controlled by those representing the interests of capitalism. Miliband argues that the view that the civil service and judiciary are neutral institutions is an ideological one aimed at disguising their true function – to protect the economic interests of the ruling class. Instrumental Marxists argue that political and economic elites are unified by social and educational background and therefore constitute a ruling class.

Explain how elites might be 'united by social and educational background'.

Structural Marxism

Structural Marxists like Poulantzas (1973) argue that the social backgrounds of those that occupy key positions doesn't really matter. The state is shaped by the economic structure of capitalist society and therefore its actions will always reflect the class relations built into the structure of capitalism. The social relations of capitalism are characterised by class inequality so the state will always reproduce such inequality unless capitalism is dismantled. However, Poulantzas does argue that in order to fulfil its role unchallenged the state needs to be relatively autonomous or free from the direct control of the ruling class. There are a number of reasons for this.

- The bourgeoisie have their own internal conflicts. The state must be free of interference from these in order to represent their interests as a whole.
- The state may need to make concessions to subordinate classes every now and then in order to prevent social disorder. These concessions may not benefit the ruling class in the short term although they are likely to benefit their objective interests in the long term.
- The state can promote the ideology that it represents the national interest or consensus.

> *Give one example of what Marxists might see as a concession made to subordinate classes in order to 'prevent social disorder'.*

Hegemonic Marxism

Hegemonic Marxists point out that the mass of the population consent to the state managing capitalism, despite the fact that it mainly benefits the ruling class rather than society in general. Gramsci (1971) argued that the ruling class were able to manage the state in such a way that hegemony – cultural and ideological domination – is achieved. People accept the moral and political leadership of high-status groups without question.

> *Explain why people might 'accept the moral and political leadership of high status groups without question'.*

Hall (Hall and Jefferson, 1976) used the concept of hegemony in explaining Mrs Thatcher's victories in three elections in 1979, 1983 and 1987. He argues that her management of the state was characterised by 'authoritarian populism'. She was able to use the ideological apparatus of the media to portray herself as a strong resolute and moral leader – the Iron Lady – and to convince the general public that a good dose of strong economic medicine, whilst painful, was good for them. She convinced a substantial section of the nation that those who dissented from her vision were the 'enemy within' and threatened the security of the nation, the state and the family.

Evaluation of the Marxist view

Despite differences of interpretation all three Marxist positions agree that the state serves the interests of the dominant class. However, as we saw in Topic 2, this is a difficult assertion to prove. We can see economic and social connections between the political elite and members of the economic elite but this does not necessarily mean that they are using the mechanisms of the state to advance ruling-class interests.

Concepts such as 'ideology' and 'hegemony' are difficult to operationalise and to use as a means of measuring degrees of power. It is also unlikely that hegemony is experienced universally. The state has consistently faced opposition in the form of urban riots by the powerless, strikes, new social movements and terrorism over the past thirty years and it has been forced to use coercion and force on a number of occasions.

> *What is meant by 'operationalise'? Give examples from other areas you have studied of two concepts that are difficult to operationalise. Explain why this is the case.*

The view that the British state is an instrument of the capitalist class can also be criticised because a great deal of economic policy has been unsuccessful. The state has been unable to prevent events such as stock market crashes, devaluation of sterling and the decline of heavy industry and manufacturing. If the state is an agent of the ruling class, it is a very unsuccessful one.

Criticisms of the modern state

- Abercrombie and Warde are critical of what they call the 'secret state'. They note that civil servants rarely appear in public to explain or justify their actions. Judges and senior police officers are generally not accountable for their decisions or actions. The security or intelligence services also largely operate outside the law.
- Some commentators have become concerned with the concentration of political power in the hands of the prime minister and his closest advisers. Many of the latter are not elected officials or civil servants. In 2002, Tony Blair was criticised for his presidential approach. It was argued that parliament is now expected merely to rubber stamp presidential and executive decisions.
- New Right sociologists are still critical of what they term the '**nanny state**'. They see state policy as undermining personal responsibility and creating what they label as a '**dependency culture**'.
- State bureaucracy is seen by some as unnecessarily bulky, insensitive to the needs of ordinary people and the puppet of global corporations.
- The state is also accused of institutional racism. The immigration laws are the most obvious example but sociological evidence indicates that institutional racism may be embedded in the everyday practices of the police, the judiciary, the prison service, the NHS – especially the mental-health sector – and in education.

> *What is meant by 'institutional racism'? Choose any one of the institutions above and explain how they have been accused of institutional racism.*

- Feminist sociologists argue that the state is patriarchal. State agencies have until fairly recently been dominated by male personnel. State policy is also accused of being patriarchal, especially in the fields of family welfare and in its failure to get to serious grips with gender inequalities.

> *Give one example of a state policy that has been accused of being patriarchal. Explain why the accusation has been made.*

The future of the state

Recent research (e.g. by Abercrombie and Warde) suggests that the state and its power to act is under threat from a number of trends.

- *Regionalisation* – as a result of increasing regional pressure, the Labour government has devolved some state powers to a Scottish Parliament, Welsh Assembly and Northern Ireland power-sharing assembly.
- *Europe* – the European Union (EU) has some legal authority over the British state especially in the fields of economic policy and trade. There are some concerns that this is eroding the power of ordinary people to take part in the democratic process because the agencies of the EU are not elected.
- *Internationalisation* – British foreign policy is increasingly tied in with that of Europe or the USA. In the aftermath of the events of September 11 concerns were expressed

that Britain had become a 'poodle' of the US administration.

- *Globalisation* – David Held (2000) argues that globalisation threatens the very existence of the nation state for four reasons.
  1. States find it almost impossible to control the international flow of money which can severely affect exchange rates and undermine economies.
  2. Transnational economic behaviour can severely disrupt economic policy by shifting investment and therefore employment between countries.
  3. The global economy means that recession in one part of the world can undermine the economy in another part.
  4. Global communications and the internet have made it difficult for states to regulate the flow of information across borders. There are concerns about transnational media influence, cultural imperialism (in which the indigenous culture is weakened by American mass culture) and the use of the internet to encourage global dissidence.

Held concludes that globalisation challenges the traditional contexts in which states have operated because they are less able to resist external events and forces. He argues for new forms of cross-national institutions to help deal with global challenges and conflicts in the fields of trade and currency, the environment, security and new forms of communication. Held sees a bright future in a more democratic EU and the transformation of the United Nations into a world parliament that would deal both with global issues such as debt, AIDS, refugees, environmental pollution and famine.

KEY TERMS

Compliance – conformity.

Cultural imperialism – situation where one culture dominates and overrides other cultures. American culture is often accused of cultural imperialism.

Dependency culture – a way of life where people become incapable of independence and rely on the state to meet their needs.

Indigenous – native, original.

Laissez-faire – to leave alone.

Nanny state – term used by the New Right to imply that the state acts as a 'nanny' to people by providing for their every need and not leaving them alone.

Nationalisation – policy that involved governments taking important industries (e.g. coal) into state (public) ownership.

Paternalistic – fatherly, tending to be patronising.

Privatisation – selling off previously nationalised industries to the private sector.

Relatively autonomous – term used by Marxists to show that the state can still represent capitalist interests even if it is not made up of capitalists.

Socially excluded – those members of the population who are not a part of mainstream society because of poverty and lack of opportunity.

Third way – political philosophy favoured by New Labour. The 'third way' is a middle way between socialism and capitalism.

CHECK YOUR UNDERSTANDING ✓✓✓✓

1. What is the role of (a) the state executive and (b) the state legislature?

2. In what sense is the BBC a state institution?

3. Identify four ways in which the state was expanded between 1945–51?

4. What is the role of the state according to pluralist theory?

5. What are the key differences between Miliband and Poulantzas in regard to the role of the state?

6. Why is the neo-Marxist notion of 'rule by consent' problematical?

7. Why are Abercrombie and Warde critical of the state?

8. What problems has the state caused according to New Right sociologists?

9. Why is globalisation a threat to the British state?

10. What effect has regionalisation had on the British state?

Research idea

Take a sample of broadsheet newspapers such as *The Guardian*, *The Times*, *Independent* and *Daily Telegraph*. Conduct a content analysis to ascertain the influence of the state on our daily lives. What proportion of articles are concerned with the state or some agency of the state? Is foreign news dominated by accounts of government action? Do the articles indicate consent in regard to the role of the state or are they critical of it?

Charter 88 is a pressure group that aims to reform the British state, especially in terms of its lack of openness and accountability. Visit their website at www.charter88.org.uk. What issues are they raising about the British state? What concerns do they have about the power and openness of government? What are they doing about it?

EXAM PRACTICE

Extract from AQA-style question

'The State is merely a committee for managing the common affairs of the bourgeoisie.'

Critically examine the theories and evidence for and against this view of the State in modern industrial societies. (40 marks)

OCR-style question

Outline and assess the view that the function of the State is to manage competition between elite groups for scarce resources. (60 marks)

Exploring the state

Item A

Just about everywhere we turn in modern life we encounter the State. The State in some form is present when we post letters, use money to buy stamps, watch BBC television, travel abroad bearing passports, go to school or attend further or higher education. The State obliges birth, marriage and death to be registered. It takes a cut from every pound you earn. The roads you walk and drive on belong to the State. The State can declare you insane and institutionalise you. It can kick your door down at five in the morning and arrest you under the Prevention of Terrorism Act. It can conscript you and send you to fight in a foreign land. The State can remove all your belongings if you don't pay your taxes. Clearly the State is a powerful and diverse organisation.

Adapted from: A. Barnard and T. Burgess (1996), *Sociology Explained*, Cambridge: Cambridge University Press

Item B

The agencies of the State are both highly secretive and powerful. Leading judges, who in theory are bound by the laws made by Parliament, are actively engaged in making the law because they are continuously involved in interpreting existing laws. This process of interpretation, particularly through the establishment of precedents, itself creates the law. Likewise, although the social background of the police is very different from that of the other groups considered here, the force similarly attempts to limit its accountability, particularly to local authority representatives. The police are powerful because they have the scope to exercise discretion. Among the millions of law-breakers, the police decide who to stop on suspicion, and they do so in terms of a number of crude stereotypes of possible criminals. The security services also enjoy a very high degree of autonomy in their operations and operate largely outside the law. The elected parts of the State have little idea of the activities of the security services, or of the scale of their operations. On occasions, even the prime minister has not been made aware of the scale of operation of the secret security forces.

Adapted from: N. Abercrombie and A. Warde (2000) *British Contemporary Society* (3rd edition) Cambridge: Polity Press

Item C

David Coates claims that finance capital (the banks, the insurance companies and financial trusts in the City of London) has a particularly strong influence on the British State. He suggests that the State relies to a considerable extent upon the support of financial institutions. If, for example, these institutions choose to sell sterling it can rapidly cause a currency crisis as the value of the pound falls. In comparison to financiers, Coates claims industrial capital (i.e. British owned industry) has less influence over State policy. The Confederation of British Industry failed to persuade the government to reduce the value of the pound and reduce interest rates in the 1980s which would have benefited British industry. Coates concludes that finance capital has had more influence over the British government than industrial capital and the consequences have been the decline of British manufacturing industry and rising unemployment.

Adapted from: M. Holborn and M. Haralambos (2000) *Sociology: Themes and Perspectives* (5th edition) London: HarperCollins

Item D

Offe (1984) provides a detailed picture of the institutional constraints of states in capitalist society. He argues that a number of mechanisms produce a systematic class bias in the operation of the State. In particular he emphasises the mechanism by which the state raises revenue to fund expenditure. The major sources of revenue are taxation based on private production and borrowing from private financial institutions. In order to increase its revenue the state is therefore forced to act in ways which promote the continued financial health of private capitalist accumulation. Offe criticised the notion that the Welfare state can overcome the inequalities that arise from capitalism. The Welfare state is itself highly dependent upon the prosperity and continued profitability of the economy.

Adapted from: M. Kirby (1995) *Investigating Political Sociology*, London: Collins Educational

1 Using Item A only, identify six functions of the British state.

2 Using Item B and other sources, explain why it is a problem that the state is both powerful and secretive.

3 In what ways might the state be both institutionally racist and patriarchal?

4 Using Item C and other sources, outline the instrumental Marxist theory of the state.

5 Assess the view that the state is relatively autonomous from the capitalist ruling class using Items C and D plus other information.

Politicians turn to Pop Idol for voter inspiration

A campaign to encourage young people to vote in high numbers for the forthcoming local elections as they did for the final of Pop Idol was launched today.

The campaign launched outside the Houses of Parliament comes amid fears of voter apathy among the young and follows a record-low turnout at last year's general election. The Electoral Commission said the 'phenomenal' voter turnout for Pop Idol on Saturday proved young people enjoy using their voice to influence decisions if they are presented in an 'appropriate and engaging manner'.

England's 18- to 24-year-olds will be targeted with messages such as 'votes are power' and 'who controls who?' via the internet, mobile phone text messaging and traditional advertising in the run-up to the local elections on May 2. They will be encouraged to register to vote on the internet or vote by post, while the commission will run a Votes Are Power awareness week from April 29. A national newspaper advertising campaign will feature the Votes Are Power campaign slogan, depicting a hand playing with a politician puppet on strings.

The campaign has been launched in response to research compiled by MORI following the June 2001 election which saw the lowest turnout since 1918 – 59% overall and an estimated 39% of young people. However, MORI found that political apathy was an issue for only 10% of young people, while the majority claimed they were interested in politics.

Monday February 11, 2002, *The Guardian* Unlimited © *Guardian* Newspapers Limited 2002

1 Why do you think young people aged 18–25 voted in large numbers for Will Young and Gareth Gates yet failed to turn out in the General Election the year before?

2 Polls of young people suggest that the majority are interested in political issues. What sort of political issues is your peer group interested in and how do these relate to your support for, or apathy towards, conventional political parties?

3 Look closely at the tactics adopted by the Electoral Commission. Do you think these worked?

4 What would motivate you to go out and vote for a political party?

The final programme of ITV's Pop Idol, i.e. the showdown between Will Young and Gareth Gates, attracted an audience of 15 million people on February 9 2002. A total of 8.7 million votes were cast over the telephone, with Will Young emerging as the winner with 53.1% of the popular vote. In contrast, at the general election in June 2001, less than 15 million people voted for the victorious Labour Party and Will Young and Gareth Gates later attracted more votes between them than the Liberal Democrats, the Scottish National Party and Plaid Cymru (the Welsh **nationalist** party) had done nation-wide in the elections.

As we shall see, sociologists who study voting behaviour have tended to focus on the relationship between voting and social class. However, the last two elections in 1997 and 2001 have seen record low turn-outs particularly among young people and this has prompted interest in other variables such as age in an attempt to explain the apathy and indifference that seems to have recently overcome the British voting public.

Suggest two other variables that might be a factor in influencing voting behaviour. Explain why.

Political parties

Politics is the site of a struggle between **belief systems** represented by political parties. In Britain, this struggle has generally been between belief systems or ideologies associated with the 'left' at one extreme (with their emphasis on equality for all and social change) and the 'right' at the other extreme (associated with **individualism**, **free enterprise** and respect for tradition). However, this is an over-simplified view because in the post-1945 period, **consensus** rather than ideological struggle characterised British politics until the 1970s. In addition, traditional right and left ideologies as represented by the Conservative and Labour parties respectively have undergone a political 'make-over' in the last two decades.

The Conservative Party

The **right-wing belief** system that characterises this party is generally focused on preserving tradition and established institutions. Conservatives are particularly concerned with defending the concept of social hierarchy. They believe that inequality is a good thing because it motivates people to adopt **entrepreneurial** skills and work hard. However, Conservatives also believe that a role of government is to provide help for those who are unable to help themselves. This **paternalistic** streak in Conservative thought led to post World War II Conservative governments committing themselves to the concept of the welfare state and the maintenance of full employment as an aspect of economic policy.

An ideological struggle amongst the right in the 1970s led to the emergence and dominance of a **New Right ideology**. This could clearly be seen in practice during the term of Mrs Thatcher's government. This government preached minimal state intervention, the promotion of free enterprise and individual choice and the determination to challenge the power of organisations such as the trade unions. However,

since the fall of Mrs Thatcher, the emphasis has shifted again. The Conservative ideology associated with the premiership of John Major shifted back in favour of paternalism, although under William Hague and Ian Duncan Smith, Conservative ideology has become more **populist** by tapping into people's nationalist fears about Europe taking away British sovereignty and the impact of immigration on British identity.

Give two examples of the influence of New Right thinking from other areas of your studies.

The Labour Party

The **left-wing belief** system has also undergone radical change since 1979. From 1945 to the 1970s the Labour party was generally seen as the party of the working class and its ideology was predominantly socialist in principle. **Nationalisation** of key industries such as coal, steel and the railways, the setting up of the welfare state, (especially the NHS) and the introduction of the comprehensive system in education can all be seen as socialist ideology (**socialism**) put into practice.

However, the party reacted to the election defeat of 1979 by embarking on a re-evaluation of its ideology and a revamp of its image. This resulted in Labour jettisoning many of the overtly socialist principles embodied in its constitution and describing itself as a party aiming to work for all sections of the community, rich and poor. Tony Blair's election to the leadership saw a major shift to the centre in terms of ideology as Labour politicians made statements about New Labour being a social democratic party rather than a socialist one. Labour presented itself as forging a 'third way' towards a common good and being trustworthy and competent enough to look after the economy **prudently**.

Voting behaviour

The sociological study of voting behaviour is known as **psephology**. Generally speaking, studies of voting behaviour can be divided into three broad groups of theories dealing with the periods:

1   1952–1979
2   1979–1997
3   1997 onwards.

However, although sociological theories of voting behaviour tend to be focused on these specific time periods, there are common inter-related themes that have been recycled over and over again.

1952–1979

Early studies of voting behaviour saw a very strong statistical correlation between social class and voting behaviour. This is known as **class** or **partisan alignment**. Butler and Stokes (1971) studied voting behaviour between 1952 and 1962 and discovered that 67% of their **objective** working-class sample (based on the Registrar-General's classification of occupations) voted for the Labour Party. They noted an even stronger relationship between **subjective class** (based on self-evaluation of respondents) and voting behaviour. They found that where subjective evaluation agreed with objective classification 80% of their sample voted Labour. Studies of

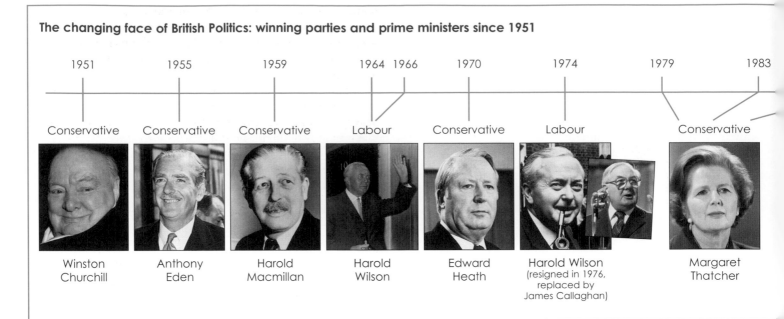

The changing face of British Politics: winning parties and prime ministers since 1951

1951	1955	1959	1964	1966	1970	1974	1979	1983

Conservative	Conservative	Conservative	Labour	Conservative	Labour	Conservative

| Winston Churchill | Anthony Eden | Harold Macmillan | Harold Wilson | Edward Heath | Harold Wilson (resigned in 1976, replaced by James Callaghan) | Margaret Thatcher |

Conservative voters in this period reached similar conclusions: 75%-80% of the middle-class vote went to the Conservative Party. Some sociologists saw these figures as evidence of the institutionalisation of class conflict in that the Labour Party and Conservative Party were seen as representing the natural interests of the working class and middle class respectively.

Early explanations of voting behaviour focused on the existence of so-called '**deviant voters**' – a third of the working class were voting Conservative whilst one-fifth of the middle class were voting Labour. These trends suggested that the relationship between social class and voting behaviour was not so clear cut. McKenzie and Silver's explanation (1968) focused on the working-class **deferential voter** who, they argued, accounted for half of the working-class Conservative vote. They noted that statistically this type of voter tended to be older, have a lower income, be female and reside in rural rather than urban areas. Moreover, attitude surveys of such voters suggested that they subscribed to a world view in which high-status individuals such as aristocratic landowners were seen as naturally superior and destined to rule.

Frank Parkin (1972) argued that the working class are exposed to two types of value systems or ideologies.

● First, the working class is constantly exposed to the dominant value system (DVS) which endorses existing inequalities through agencies such as the media and education system. Workers are particularly exposed to this value system in areas where no alternative value system exists and are therefore unable to resist it. Deferential voters, therefore, were those who had internalised the ideological messages of the DVS.

Give two examples of 'dominant values'. Explain how they are promoted by the media or education system.

● However, many manual workers had access to a subordinate value system (SVS) generated at the level of working-class community. This value system was underpinned by a recognition of class inequality and

hostility towards employers. Workers could see that there was a contradiction between what they were being told in institutions like education and what they experienced for themselves.

McKenzie and Silver argued that many working-class deviant voters were '**secular voters**'. These young, affluent factory workers, like consumers in a supermarket, rationally evaluated the policies of political parties and voted in terms of **individual goals** rather than class loyalty. Other theories also zoomed in on the idea of 'rational choice' being an alternative variable to class. Butler and Rose (1960), for example, linked the emergence of secular voting to '**embourgeoisement**' – the theory that the increased affluence of the working-class in the 1950s was leading them to identify with middle-class values. However, Goldthorpe and Lockwood's (1969a) study of **affluent workers** in Luton found that the working class and middle class actually subscribed to very different value systems.

Suggest two differences in values between the middle and working classes.

Goldthorpe and Lockwood further developed the idea of the working-class secular or consumer voter because they discovered very little deep-seated loyalty to the Labour Party among well-paid factory workers. This study was one of the first to note that class alignment as a factor in voting behaviour was beginning to waver among large sections of the working-class. For example, Goldthorpe and Lockwood's sample voted for Labour not because they were working-class but for '**instrumental**' reasons – as a means to an end, a method of achieving material success.

1979–1997

Explanations focusing on working-class instrumental voters became very popular among sociologists in the light of the Conservative election victories in 1979, 1983 and 1987. In particular, the 1983 result was Labour's worst defeat since 1931 in terms of total votes cast (28%). What was evident was

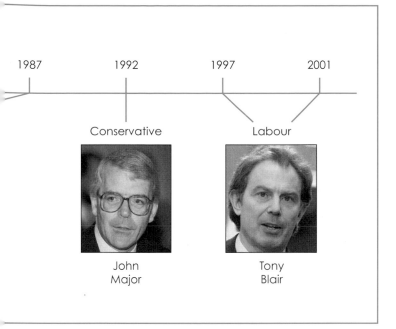

1987   1992   1997   2001

Conservative   Labour

John
Major

Tony
Blair

that the traditional working-class vote had deserted Labour –
little more than half of the manual working class voted for
them.

Ivor Crewe and class de-alignment

The work of Ivor Crewe (1984) produced the most extensive
research on why a substantial proportion of the working class
no longer naturally voted Labour. He identified long-term
structural factors that, he claimed, had fundamentally
changed the composition and character of the working class.
For example, he argued that the proportion of traditional
manual workers in the labour force had declined as older
primary industries such as mining and shipbuilding had been
hit by recession. A consequence of this was a decline in
working-class community as younger workers migrated to the

south in search of work. Crewe concluded that the traditional
working-class manual worker expressing unwavering support
and loyalty to trade unions and Labour along class lines was a
dying breed. Crewe referred to this trend as '**class de-
alignment**'.

Crewe argued that the expansion of the service sector and
high-technology manufacturing in the 1970s had led to the
emergence of a well-paid and non-unionised 'new working-
class', mainly living in the south, who owned their home
(because of the Conservative policy of selling council houses).
This group no longer automatically identified with the
Labour party. Rather, it acted instrumentally and made
rational choices aimed at maintaining its affluent lifestyle.
Crewe referred to this as '**partisan de-alignment**'.

Crewe identifies a number of short-term factors that
shaped the instrumentalism of these voters. Mrs Thatcher's
Conservative party successfully portrayed itself as the homeowners' party of mortgage tax relief and council-house sales.
The Conservatives' promises of tax cuts and reduced public
spending (implying further tax cuts) appealed to the material
interests of this instrumental working class. Crewe concluded
that the Labour vote in the 1980s remained largely working
class but that the working class was no longer largely Labour.
Moreover, class was no longer the main variable influencing
people's voting habits.

Criticisms of Crewe

If we examine Crewe's work closely, we can see that he was
not saying anything radically new. His analysis is essentially a
synthesis of 1960s voting theory. His 'new working-class' is
very similar in character to the affluent workers identified by
Goldthorpe and Lockwood. Their voting behaviour is
instrumentalist and very much based on the notion of 'voter
as consumer' making rational choices on the basis of material
interests rather than class loyalty. Crewe's theory came under
sustained attack from a number of quarters.

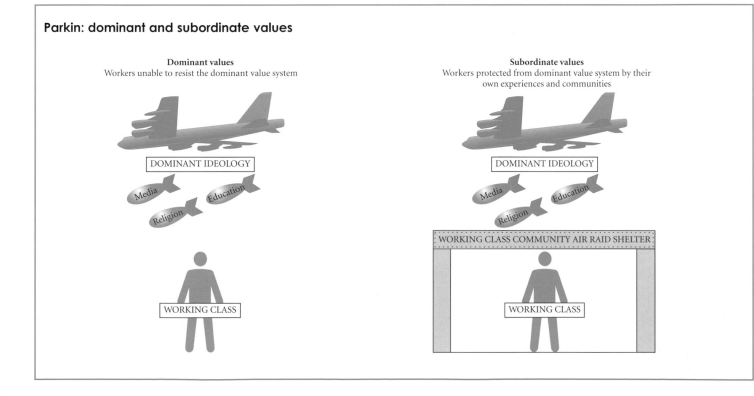

Parkin: dominant and subordinate values

Dominant values
Workers unable to resist the dominant value system

DOMINANT IDEOLOGY

Media   Education
Religion

WORKING CLASS

Subordinate values
Workers protected from dominant value system by their
own experiences and communities

DOMINANT IDEOLOGY

Media   Education
Religion

WORKING CLASS COMMUNITY AIR RAID SHELTER

WORKING CLASS

- His methodology was regarded as rather suspect. Empirically he was rather vague in the use of the concept 'new working-class'. He distinguished between 'old' and 'new' working-class on the basis of such variables as home ownership, trade union membership and living in the south. It is not clear how these variables operationalise long-term shifts in voting behaviour.

Explain how you would construct a questionnaire to test the existence of a 'new working-class'.

- Butler and Kavanagh (1985) believed that Crewe had underestimated the effects of short-term influences such as the wave of patriotic fervour that swept the country following the UK's victory over Argentina in the Falklands War in 1982. They point out that opinion polls showed that Mrs Thatcher was at her most unpopular in the polls prior to Argentina's invasion of the Falklands and the odds were against a Conservative victory. The tabloid media overwhelmingly threw its weight behind Mrs Thatcher because of the Falklands victory. She was portrayed as a resolute, decisive, no-nonsense war leader – the 'Iron Lady' – and Labour leaders were unfavourably compared with her. The Conservative government was able to paint itself as the party of authority while the Labour Party was portrayed as led by weak individuals who could not control in-fighting in their own party, never mind run the country.

- Labour came under sustained attack from the majority of newspapers throughout the 1980s and 1990s until the *Sun* switched to Tony Blair in 1996. The Glasgow University Media Group (1985) documented that the Labour party was constantly presented as a 'divided' party dominated by **'left-wing loonies'** who allegedly threatened the national interest. The hegemonic Marxist, Stuart Hall (Hall and Jacques, 1983), suggests that media coverage reflected the cultural dominance of the capitalist class which saw Mrs Thatcher as someone who would protect their interests. Media-owners such as Rupert Murdoch were happy to sell her brand of **'authoritarian populism'** in return for Conservative government support for his dominance of the British media industry.

- The major critique of Crewe's work came from the sociologists Gordon Marshall and Antony Heath. Marshall (1987) argued that Crewe had exaggerated both class and partisan de-alignment. His research suggested that classes had not withered away and that class identities continue to exert a powerful influence on electoral choice. Marshall's survey-based research indicates that manual workers, whether situated in the north or the south, still think in class terms. Marshall argued that Labour has failed to attract the working-class vote because it had shifted ideologically too far in the direction of the Conservative Party. Cynicism and disillusionment had resulted in working voters switching their votes to the Liberal Democrats, or simply not voting at all.

- Heath *et al.* (1992) looked at voting behaviour between 1964 and 1987 and also concluded that Crewe's class de-alignment theories were wrong. Heath argued that the main reason Labour had lost four elections in a row between 1979 and 1992 was their record of poor political management during this period. They claim that there was very little change in voting behaviour or social and political attitudes between 1979 and 1992. However, they do acknowledge that there have been changes in class structure. For example, the changing shape of the class structure because of the decline in primary industries and manufacturing, and the expansion of the service sector, has decreased the Labour vote by 4.5% and increased the Conservative vote by 3.8%.

Suggest one other effect of the changing occupational structure, other than on voting behaviour.

The 1997 and 2001 elections

The analysis of the 1997 election result – a Labour landslide – suggests that little has actually changed structurally. Most routine and skilled manual workers, council tenants and trade unionists voted Labour whilst the **salariat** and the elderly voted Conservative. Most sociologists now agree that structural changes such as class and/or partisan de-alignment had little bearing on this result. Rather, sociologists have

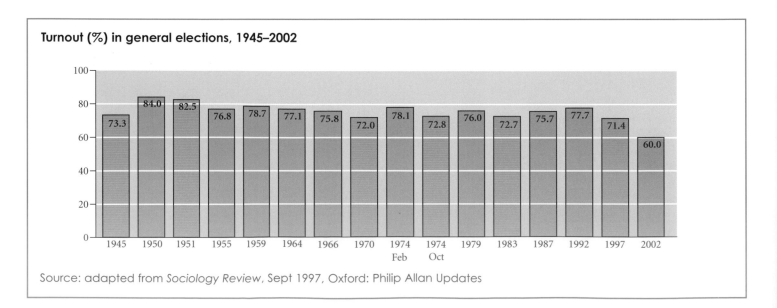

Turnout (%) in general elections, 1945–2002

Year	Turnout
1945	73.3
1950	84.0
1951	82.5
1955	76.8
1959	78.7
1964	77.1
1966	75.8
1970	72.0
1974 Feb	78.1
1974 Oct	72.8
1979	76.0
1983	72.7
1987	75.7
1992	77.7
1997	71.4
2002	60.0

Source: adapted from *Sociology Review*, Sept 1997, Oxford: Philip Allan Updates focused on the changing political environment as the major explanation. The Conservatives were quite simply, extremely unpopular after 17 years of continuous rule. The government was interpreted by the electorate as hopelessly divided over issues such as Europe, as incompetent at economic management and tainted by corruption. On the other hand, the public now had greater confidence in Labour. People could see that the party had modernised, that the leadership had distanced themselves from the trade unions and that the internal dissent of the 1980s had largely gone. Most importantly, there was public confidence in the leadership of Tony Blair and Gordon Brown.

Five important sociological observations can be made on the basis of the 1997 and 2001 election victories for New Labour.

1 The electorate are still committed to fairly stable ideological convictions that reflect the key differences between the Labour and Conservative parties.

2 People seem to be more politically literate than in the past. They have more knowledge about the policies of parties and are now more able to make informed judgements about the past and potential future performances of political parties. So-called 'deviant voters' used this political knowledge in constituencies where Labour is weak to vote tactically to prevent Conservative success by voting for Liberal Democrat candidates. This strategy was the outcome of judging that Labour was more competent to govern than the Conservatives.

3 Regional differences now seem to be an important variable in voting behaviour. The Labour vote is mainly found in urban areas, the North, Wales and Scotland whilst the Conservative vote is largely rural and found mainly in the South. For example, in 1997 the Conservatives did not win a single seat in Wales and Scotland.

4 There are signs that voter apathy may be becoming a problem, especially among young people. In 2001 only 60% of the electorate voted compared with 71% in 1997. Some commentators argue that conventional two-party politics are a turn-off for the younger generation who see very little difference between the messages propagated by the two main parties. Surveys indicate that young people are less willing to trust politicians. Moreover, young people seem more motivated by single issues relating to protecting the environment, animal welfare, etc. and/or issues relating to identity politics than the more conventional issues of defence, health and education. Certainly new social movements draw much of their support from the young (see Topic 5). Governments are often seen by such movements as colluding with global corporations to create what many young people see as the important problems facing the world today.

5 A more cynical view concludes that voter apathy in 2002 was either due to disillusion because New Labour has not achieved more during its period in office or quite simply because if people perceive a result to be a foregone conclusion, they do not see any point in voting.

Exploring the regional distribution of votes in the 2001 General Election

Item A **2001 election results by region**

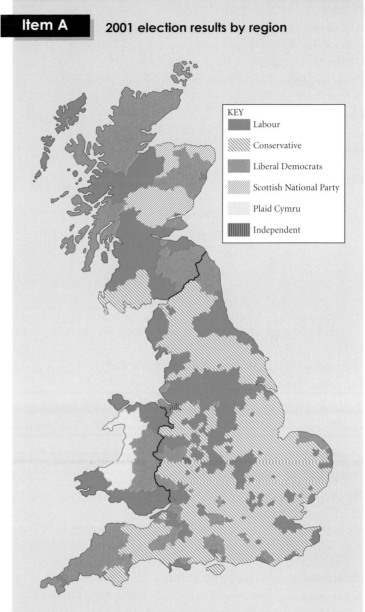

KEY
Labour
Conservative
Liberal Democrats
Scottish National Party
Plaid Cymru
Independent

1 Suggest explanations for the regional distribution of seats in the 2001 General Election.

EXAM PRACTICE

Extract from AQA-style question

Examine the view that fundamental changes have taken place in the relationship between social class and voting behaviour in the United Kingdom in the last twenty-five years. (40 marks)

OCR-style question

Outline and assess the view that Labour's success in the 1997 and 2001 elections challenges the theory of class and partisan de-alignment. (60 marks)

Affluent workers – people in well-paid manual jobs.

Authoritarian populism – the view that strong leaders attract popular support.

Consensus – agreement.

Class alignment – the idea that social class determines loyalty to political parties and therefore voting behaviour.

Class de-alignment – the view that the link between class and voting behaviour has been broken.

Deferential – the feeling that some people are naturally superior and should be looked up to.

Embourgeoisement –the view that the working class and middle class were converging in terms of lifestyle, attitude and voting behaviour.

Entrepreneurial skills – skills required to identify a market demand and then to set up and run a business to meet that demand.

Free enterprise – the idea that the market should determine the success or failure of business.

Identity politics – types of political action that focus on the extension of rights to groups which may be socially different from mainstream society.

Individualism – putting yourself and your family first.

Left-wing beliefs – in sympathy with socialism.

'Left-wing loonies' – abusive term used by tabloid press to describe some Labour councils in the 1980s.

Instrumental voter – a person who votes for a political party because they feel that party will make them better off.

Nationalisation – see Key Terms in Topic 3.

Nationalist – belief that nation-state is the most important political unit.

Objective class – the categorisation by government of people into a social class category. This was traditionally based on occupation.

Paternalistic– see Key Terms in Topic 3.

Partisan alignment – the sense of loyalty to a political party based on awareness of class membership.

Partisan de-alignment – the view that the working class no longer see themselves as naturally loyal to the Labour party.

Populist – attracting mass support, has popular appeal.

Prudently – carefully.

Psephology – the sociological study of voting behaviour.

Right-wing beliefs – in sympathy with conservatism.

Salariat – those who work in white-collar work who are paid a salary rather than a wage.

Secular voters – young affluent voters who rationally weigh up political policies in terms of how they will benefit their own standard of living and vote accordingly.

Social democratic – the view that social injustices should be addressed and that equal opportunities should be promoted.

Socialism – a set of ideas underpinned by belief in a more equal distribution of wealth, income and opportunities.

Subjective class – awareness of one's class position.

CHECK YOUR UNDERSTANDING

1 How did the ideologies of the Conservative and Labour parties diverge after the post-war consensus was fragmented in the late 1970s?

2 What was the main influence on voting behaviour in the 1950s and 1960s according to Butler and Stokes?

3 Identify three characteristics of the deferential voter.

4 Outline Parkin's contribution to our understanding of voting behaviour.

5 In what ways was voting likened to shopping in a supermarket in the 1960s and 1970s?

6 In what ways does Crewe's 'new working-class' differ from the traditional working-class?

7 How do Butler and Kavanagh challenge Crewe's ideas?

8 How do Marshall and Heath view class and partisan de-alignment?

9 Identify three reasons why Labour won the 1997 general election.

10 What are the main variables influencing voting behaviour in 2001?

Research ideas

1 Construct two social surveys:

one aimed at the parents of sociology students exploring the motives underpinning their voting behaviour. The theories of voting behaviour above, (e.g. class and partisan alignment, deference, rational-consumerism, instrumentalism, and so on) should be operationalised in the form of a questionnaire.

one aimed at students in your school or college aged 16+ exploring their perceptions of politicians, political parties and the sorts of issues contained in the party manifestos (these are available from the party websites). Design a set of questions that explore their potential for apathy and the rationale that might underpin it.

You will find copies of the questionnaires used by the British Election Study on their website – http://www.essex.ac.uk/bes – which will assist your survey design.

2 Invite your local MP or a representative from one of the main political parties into your school or college and grill them on how they intend to make politics more young-people friendly.

WWWebtask

Research voter apathy by visiting the following websites and downloading articles and audio and video files.

- http://www.politics.guardian.co.uk/election2001/ – contains a range of articles and letters debating reasons for declining voter turn out.

- http://www.news.bbc.co.uk/vote2001/ contains an excellent audio/video report by Peter Gould which is worth downloading, and details of the Voter Apathy Study.

Exploring voting behaviour

Item A

The rational-voter thesis is based on the idea that people have clear knowledge about specific party-political policies, judge the parties on these in an objective and informed way and then vote. The link is precise and calculating. However, the concept of the voter-consumer engaged in 'rational' voting is flawed in a number of respects. Firstly, there may be no political party that represents an individual's views adequately in terms of its overall package of policies. For example, a voter may agree with the Conservative Party's stance on Europe but might disagree on its policies on the NHS. A second problem is that voting is strongly related to beliefs, and at what point do we say that beliefs are irrational? The rationality model is based on the US experience where the tradition of social class and of parties effectively representing class interests is far weaker than Britain's. In Europe, both social class and ideology are more powerful. Thirdly, the rationality thesis assumes that the media faithfully reflect the truth. However the press in many European countries is highly partisan. Finally, a large proportion of the electorate simply doesn't care about politics. There is no rational response to particular political messages because these are largely ignored.

Adapted from: M. Brynin (1998) 'Why Do People Support Political Parties, *Sociology Review*, November, Oxford: Philip Allan Updates

Item B

Research by Golding, Deacon and Billig at the Communications Research Centre at Loughborough University suggests that campaigning in the 1997 general election was intensely 'presidential' (rather than issues-based) in style, with the two party leaders (John Major and Tony Blair) dominating the campaign and accounting for 43% of all appearances by any candidate in the media. National newspaper coverage – in recent elections slanted towards support for the Conservatives – also seemed much more supportive of Labour in 1997. Remarkably, even the *Sun*, such a strong Tory voice in previous elections, publicly opted for Labour in 1997. In fact, six national dailies with combined sales of over 8 million copies backed Labour this time. Conservative supporters in the daily press could muster only 4.5 million readers between them. But this picture is not all it seems. As Golding *et al.* point out, though the Rupert Murdoch-owned right-leaning *Sun* 'came out' this time, perhaps crucially, as a Labour supporter, this newspaper still ran more pro-Conservative election coverage than any other newspaper.

Adapted from: J. Williams (1997) 'Research Round-Up, Election Landslide', *Sociology Review*, September, Oxford: Philip Allan Updates

Item C

Denver (1989) points out that in 1987 only 16% of voters were 'very strong identifiers' with the Conservative or Labour party. This compares with an average of 40% during the period 1964–70. With more extensive television coverage of politics and increased education, the electorate has become more informed and politically sophisticated. Moreover, the growth in support for third parties provides further evidence of the weakening of the links between class and voting.

Adapted from: I. Morgan (1999) *Power and Politics*, London: Hodder and Stoughton

Item D

The General Election of 2001 was notable for the low level of turn-out. To analyse the dynamics of the likelihood of voting we can utilise the variable of social class to give an indication of the type of person who, in our survey, said they might not vote in the election. We asked respondents how likely they were to vote.

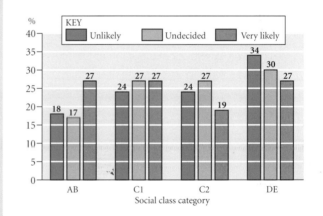

Source: British Election Study 2001 University of Essex (www.essex.ac.uk/bes)

The low turn-out figure is not a feature of this one election. Low turn-out forms part of a long-term trend. Our data clearly shows the working classes to be uninterested and deactivated in terms of turning out to vote.

Adapted from: A. Billinghurst (2001) 'Election 2001: Findings from the British Election Study', *Sociology Review*, November, Oxford: Philip Allan Updates

---

1 Using Item A only, identify in your own words, four problems with the voter as rational consumer theory.

2 Using Item B and other material, outline and assess the influence of the mass media on general elections since 1979.

3 Assess the theory of class alignment that dominated sociological debate about voting behaviour between 1964 and 70. (Item C)

4 Using Item D and other material, identify three reasons why voter turn-out is in decline.

5 Using the information in Items A–D and from elsewhere, outline and assess the view that long-term structural changes in the economy have led to fundamental changes in voting behaviour.

Getting you thinking

A strong rural force

The National Farmers' Union is the democratic organisation representing farmers and growers in England and Wales.

Its central objective is to promote the interests of those farming businesses producing high quality food and drink products for customers and markets both at home and abroad.

The NFU takes a close interest in the whole range of rural affairs and works with politicians and officials – both in the UK and internationally – and other groups and organisations to advance rural interests.

Another key aspect of the NFU's work is encouraging a greater understanding of farming and rural life among school children and the wider public.

As well as representing its members' interests, the NFU provides a wide range of services to them including help with legal, planning and taxation matters, marketing and food promotion.

The Greenpeace mission statement

Greenpeace is an independent non-profit global campaigning organisation that uses non-violent, creative confrontation and public campaigns to expose global environmental problems and their causes. We research the solutions and alternatives to help provide a path for a green and peaceful future. Greenpeace's goal is to ensure the ability of the earth to nurture life in all its diversity.

Greenpeace does not solicit or accept funding from governments, corporations or political parties. Greenpeace neither seeks nor accepts donations which could compromise its independence, aims, objectives or integrity. Greenpeace relies on the voluntary donations of individual supporters, and on grant-support from foundations.

Greenpeace is committed to the principles of non-violence, political independence and internationalism. In exposing threats to the environment and in working to find solutions, Greenpeace has no permanent allies or enemies.

Campaigning to end the factory farming of animals and long distance transport through hard-hitting political lobbying, investigations and high profile campaigns.

Compassion in World Farming was started in 1967 by dairy farmer Peter Roberts. Peter and his wife Anna were becoming increasingly concerned with the animal welfare issues connected to the new systems of intensive factory farming that were becoming popular during the 1960s.

Compassion in World Farming campaign through peaceful protest and lobbying and by raising awareness of the issue of farm animal welfare. We also produce fully referenced scientific reports. Our undercover teams provide vital evidence of the suffering of farm animals.

Thousands of animals are killed in the name of sport in this country. You can help stop this appalling slaughter. Hunt saboteurs take action where it counts in the killing fields using non-violent direct action tactics to save the lives of thousands of hunted animals every season. From using hunting horns and voice calls to run off with the hounds at fox hunts, to standing in front of the shooting butts on the grouse moors, to wading through the rivers at mink hunts, wherever animals are being hunted for fun, hunt saboteurs will be there, protecting our wildlife from the 'sportsmen' who get their kicks from killing.

Animal Liberation – the ultimate struggle. All too often animal liberation is seen, by those who do not understand, as a radical form of animal welfare, it's not about welfare, it's about freedom from oppression, it's about fighting abuses of power and it's about achieving a world in which individuals – irrespective of gender, race or species – are at liberty to be themselves. The state, the establishment and the multinationals seek to control our lives and imprison or kill us when we resist.

They seek to profit from the imprisonment or murder of those from the other species. They seek to own and control the land, the oceans and the skies which should be free to all. Animal Liberation is the struggle – indeed the war – against such tyranny in all its forms. We must fight this tyranny in all its forms. We must fight for the defenceless and the innocent. We must fight for a more compassionate world. We can, we must and we will win the ultimate struggle. When Animal Liberation is achieved we shall all be free... free to enjoy the true liberty that has been denied us for far too long!

Robin Webb, Animal Liberation Front Press Office

Examine the manifestos (statement of beliefs) of the five organisations above.

1 Allocate these organisations to the following categories.

- organisations that conform to mainstream political rules and work within the law to achieve their aims.
- organisations that use both politically acceptable and unlawful means of drawing attention to their cause(s).
- organisations that are generally in confrontation with the authorities.

Under each category, clearly state why the organisation's beliefs and tactics may be acceptable or unacceptable forms of political action.

2 Are any of these organisations influential enough to shape their members' sense of personal identity?

You will have noticed that the organisations above occupy very different positions on a continuum of political protest! At one extreme, we have organisations such as the National Farmers' Union (NFU) who work within the existing political system to represent the interests of their members. The NFU as you shall see, is typical of what we call a '**pressure group**'. You will have noticed that two other organisations also operate within the conventional political world – Greenpeace and Compassion in World Farming (CIWF) but reserve the right to work outside the democratic process in order to draw attention to particular causes. For example, CIWF uses undercover agents in factory-farming enterprises to gather evidence for animal cruelty. Both these organisations qualify as pressure groups but they can also be classed as '**new social movements**' because membership usually involves a type of dedication to a cause which shapes the identity of the member. We can particularly see this in the case of social movements that lie outside the political mainstream. Membership of groups like the Hunt Saboteurs Society and especially the Animal Liberation Front (ALF) involve their members in actively opposing the democratic mainstream. Moreover, the fact of their membership tends to lie at the very heart of the identity of their members – in other words, an Animal Liberationist is likely to see membership of the ALF as a central defining component of his or her existence.

What is meant by identity? Give examples to show how identities are socially constructed.

Pressure groups

Pressure groups are organised bodies that aim to put pressure on decision-makers such as government ministers, and Members of Parliament, and those in the European Union and local government. This pressure may take the form of mobilising public opinion and/or **lobbying** behind the scenes in order to encourage policymakers to make no change to existing policies and practices or, more likely, to insist on reform and even radical innovation. Pressure groups seek to influence rather than to get elected.

Types of pressure group

It is generally accepted by sociologists that two broad types of pressure group exist.

- *Interest or sectional pressure groups* aim to protect the interests of their members or a section of society. This category would include trade unions representing workers, employer and trade associations such as the Confederation of British Industry (CBI) and Institute of Directors, professional associations such as the British Medical Association and the Law Society, and even organisations such as the National Trust and Automobile Association. All of these protect the interests of particular social groups.
- *Promotional pressure groups* focus on specific issues or causes that members feel strongly about. Examples would include Greenpeace and Friends of the Earth which aim to protect the environment, Oxfam which aims to promote greater understanding and sensitivity towards issues like third world poverty and debt, and Gingerbread

which seeks to alleviate the problems and poverty of single-parent families.

However, this distinction is not watertight. For example, some interest pressure groups such as trade unions may pursue causes that are in the public interest such as the need for greater corporate responsibility in terms of health and safety. Professional associations such as the British Medical Association have drawn attention to the need to increase public spending in regard to health risks such as specific types of cancer.

In addition, Morgan (1999) identifies the following types of pressure groups.

- *Ad hoc or 'fire brigade' groups*: formed to deal with specific new proposals such as the building of a motorway. These are often disbanded once their aims and objectives are achieved.
- *'Idea' or think-tank groups*: aim to provide an ideological rationale or to carry out research for the aims and objectives of specific causes or issues. For example, the Fabian Society has provided the intellectual rigour that has underpinned socialism and the actions of trade unions whilst the Adam Smith Institute has provided much of the New Right philosophy underpinning those organisations in favour of free-market government policies. Groups such as the Joseph Rowntree Foundation often provide the research and evidence in anti-poverty campaigns.
- *'Political cause' groups*: seek to change the organisation of the political system. For example, Charter 88 aimed to change the nature of democracy in the UK. It can be argued that the Human Rights Act in 2001 was a direct consequence of their campaign.
- *'Latent' groups*: those which have not yet fully evolved in terms of organisation, representation and influence. There are some social groups such as the poor and ethnic-minority groups who experience a 'poverty of politics or protest' in that they have no formal organisations to speak out on their behalf. However, their 'representatives' may be consulted by the government or media, especially when moral panics develop around 'problems' perceived to be associated with such groups.

What do sociologists mean by 'moral panics'? Give two examples.

However, Morgan's typology is also by no means comprehensive or watertight. In recent years we have seen the evolution of the 'celebrity' pressure group in which rock stars like Sir Bob Geldof, Sting and Bono have used their celebrity status to raise the public profile of issues such as famine, the degradation of the Amazonian jungle, and debt in the developing world respectively to influence governments to change or modify their policies.

Insider and outsider status

Another useful way to look at pressure groups is to work out whether they have 'insider' or 'outsider' status when it comes to exercising power over the decision-making process.

Insider pressure groups
Pressure groups with insider status are often invited to send representatives to sit on official committees and to collaborate on government policy papers. Civil servants and ministers regularly consult with them. Such groups tend to use 'political brokers' or professional lobbyists who have inside knowledge of how the political process works and/or have official and non-official access to influential politicians and public servants. Such groups prefer to keep a low profile. This is not surprising because as Duverger (1972) notes, some of these pressure groups, especially those representing the interests of capital, have 'unofficial power' – 'they actually have their own representatives in governments and **legislative bodies**, but the relationship between these individuals and the groups they represent remains secret and circumspect'.

What is 'capital'? How would Marxists explain the influence of 'those representing the interests of capital'?

Outsider pressure groups
Outsider groups, on the other hand, do not enjoy direct access to the corridors of power. Such groups attempt to put government under pressure by presenting their case to the mass media and generating public opinion in their favour. Their campaigns are likely to involve demonstrations, boycotts and media campaigns, writing to those with influence and occasionally giving evidence to government committees. Some pressure groups have gone further than this and either disobeyed the law or challenged the law through the courts.

Pressure groups and the distribution of power

Sociological theories of power have generally allocated pressure groups a central role in debates relating to the social distribution of power.

Pluralists see competition between pressure groups for the attention of policymakers as evidence of '**polyarchal democracy**'. In other words, modern democracies like the USA and Britain are seen as being characterised by many sources of power and influence. Pressure groups are seen as part of a diffused power network and are regarded as a force for democracy because they give ordinary people and minority groups an effective voice in the political process. It is suggested that pressure groups increase awareness of issues among the general public and that this prevents complacency among politicians. In this sense pressure groups are a vehicle for social change which governments dare not ignore if they are to retain public support.

However, this view has been criticised for a number of reasons.

- **Neo-pluralists** suggest that pluralism exaggerates the openness of democratic societies. They argue instead that Britain is a '**deformed polyarchy**' meaning that some pressure groups have more influence than others because they are strategically better positioned to bargain with policymakers. Their control over scarce resources such as labour, skills, capital and expertise may mean that they always have insider status and can use threats of withdrawal of such resources to ensure substantial influence over decision-making. It was believed that trade unions had such power until the late 1970s, whilst pressure groups representing capital may use their powerful influence over levels of financial investment to shape government economic policy.

- The Marxist critique of polyarchal democracy is not dissimilar to neo-pluralism except they argue that powerful capitalist interests dominate competition between pressure groups and thus decision-making. However, as we have already seen in Topic 2, it is relatively easy to identify these groups but generally impossible to prove the extent of their influence on the decision-making process. Moreover, analysis of economic government policy over the last fifty years indicates that these economic power blocs have not always benefited from such policy.

Suggest reasons why it is difficult to prove the extent of the influence of powerful capitalist interests on the decision-making process.

- New Right analysts claim that the existence of pressure groups threatens to destabilise democracy. They argue that there are too many of them vying for political influence. Such hyper-pluralism makes it increasingly difficult for governments to govern. For example, it is argued that in the 1970s governments were weakened by competing demands (especially from trade unions) and this led to political stagnation and national decline.
- Recently there has been concern about the disproportionate influence that global transnational corporations might be exercising over the domestic decision-making of national governments.

New social movements

Recent political sociology has moved away from the study of pressure groups to examine the emergence of '**new social movements**'.

Hallsworth (1994) defines the term new social movement (NSM) as the:

wide and diverse spectrum of new, non-institutional political movements which emerged or (as in the case of feminism) which re-emerged in western liberal democratic societies during the 1960s and 1970s. More specifically, the term is used to refer to those movements which may be held to pose new challenges to the established cultural, economic and political orders of advanced (late twentieth century) capitalist society.

Sociologists differentiate between NSMs and 'old social movements' (OSMs). The latter refer to older, more established political organisations such as the socialist movement or organisations representing working-class alliances such as trade unions or employers associations. OSMs mainly focus on bringing about economic change and tend to be class-based organisations that are organised in a formal and centralised way.

Types of new social movement

Hallsworth argues that if we examine the ideological values underpinning the activities and philosophy of NSMs, we can see two broad types.

- Defensive NSMs
- Offensive NSMs.

Defensive NSMs

These are generally concerned with defending a natural or social environment seen to be under threat from unregulated industrialisation and/or capitalism, impersonal and insensitive forms of state bureaucracy and the development of **risk technology** such as nuclear power or genetically modified crops. Examples of such NSMs would include animal-rights groups, environmental groups and the anti-nuclear movement. Such groups call for an alternative world order characterised by forms of **sustainable development** and social justice for all.

A variation on defensive NSMs is a new form of association that Hetherington (1998) calls the **bunde**, made up of vegetarian groups, free-festival goers, dance culture, travellers, and so on. This social network of groups has characteristics similar to defensive NSMs. They generally resist the global marketplace, are anti-capitalist and are focused on opposing the rituals and conventions that modern societies expect their members to subscribe to such as settling down in one permanent place or abiding by social standards of hygiene. The bunde therefore create their own spaces such as 'Teepee valley' in Wales and gather in 'tribes' at key events and places such as Stonehenge and Glastonbury to celebrate symbolically their alternative lifestyles. The bunde normally experience intense hostility from society. For example, traveller convoys are subjected to regular surveillance and harassment from the police.

Offensive NSMs

These aim to defend or extend social rights to particular groups who are denied status, autonomy or identity, or are repressed by the state. Examples would include anti-racist, human-rights and gay-liberation movements. Hallsworth argues that such NSMs are concerned to expose institutional discrimination and to advance the social position of marginalised groups such as women, gays and ethnic minorities.

Explain what is meant by the term 'marginalised group'.

Whether they are defensive or offensive, NSMs are generally concerned with promoting and changing cultural values and with the construction of identity politics. People involved in these groups see membership of the NSM as a defining factor in their personal identity. NSMs provide their members with a value system which stresses 'the very qualities the dominant cultural order is held to deny' (Hallsworth, 1994). This value system embodies:

- *active participation*: people genuinely feel that they can help bring about change as opposed to feeling apathy and indifference towards formal politics

- *personal development*: members want personal as opposed to material satisfaction
- *emotional openness*: they want others to see and recognise their stance
- *collective responsibility*: they feel social solidarity with others.

The organisation of new social movements

Often the organisational structure of NSMs is very different to that of other political organisations. OSMs are often characterised by high levels of bureaucracy, oligarchic control by Elite groups, limited participation opportunities for ordinary members and employment of full-time officials. Hallsworth notes that the internal organisation of NSMs is often the diametric opposite of this. NSMs are characterised by low levels of bureaucracy, the encouragement of democratic participation at all levels of decision-making for all members and few, if any, full-time officials. Often such organisations are underpinned by local networks and economic self-help, both of which deliberately aim to distance their activities from traditional political institutions and decision-making.

The social characteristics of the members of new social movements

Research into the social basis of support for NSMs suggests that members and activists are typically drawn from a restricted section of the wider community, specifically from the youth sector. Typical members of NSMs are aged 16–30 and tend to be middle class in origin. For example, a typical member of a NSM is likely to be employed in the public and service sector of the economy (in teaching, social work, and so on) or they are born to parents who work in this occupational sector. Other typical members are people who are likely to be **peripheral** to the labour market such as students and the unemployed. However, Scott (1990) points out that it is difficult to make accurate generalisations about the membership of NSMs. For example, many of the anti-veal export campaigners at Brightlingsea in Sussex were middle-aged or retired.

Suggest reasons why those who identify with NSMs are often young and middle class.

New social movements and political action

The mode of political action adopted by NSMs deliberately differs from the activities of OSMs and pressure groups. The latter generally work within the existing framework of politics and their last resort is the threat of withdrawal of whatever resource they control – for example, labour or capital investment. NSMs tend to operate outside regular channels of political action and tend to focus on '**direct action**'. This is a form of political action which operates outside the formal political process and includes demonstrations, sit-ins, publicity stunts and other obstructive action. Much of this action is illegal but it often involves fairly mild forms of mass civil-disobedience such as anti-roads protestors committing

mass trespass in order to prevent bulldozers destroying natural habitats, the Reclaim the Streets movement disrupting traffic in the centre of London, and Greenpeace supporters destroying fields of genetically modified crops. However, there have been instances of action which has involved more serious forms of illegal and criminal action – for example, damaging nuclear-weapons installations or military hardware, fire-bombing department stores that sell fur goods, breaking into animal-testing laboratories and attacking scientists with letter and car bombs.

The nature of politics

Many sociologists (e.g. Scott) argue that the emergence of new social movements in the 1960s indicates that the nature of political debate and action has undergone fundamental change. It is suggested that both political debate and action were dominated until the 1960s by political parties and pressure groups which sought either to protect or challenge the economic or material order. In other words, politics was dominated by class-based issues. However, the emergence of the women's movement and the civil-rights movement led to a recognition that wider social inequalities were of equal importance and resulted in a concern to protect, and even celebrate, the concept of 'social difference'. It was argued that affluence in Western societies meant than economic issues became subordinated to wider concerns about long-term survival reflected in increased interest in social movements related to anti-nuclear technology, peace, the environment and global issues such as debt.

Give three examples of 'wider social inequalities' referred to in the passage above.

Theories of new social movements

The Marxist Habermas (1979) saw membership of NSMs as arising out of the nature of post-capitalism in which the majority of people enjoy a good standard of living and are supposedly therefore less interested in material things. In such societies priorities change – economic matters are of less importance than issues such as protecting human rights and democracy from an ever-encroaching state bureaucracy. NSMs, therefore, are a means by which democratic rights are protected and extended.

Touraine (1982), another Marxist, agrees and argues that NSMs are a product of a post-industrial society that stresses the production and consumption of knowledge rather than materialism, consumerism and economic goals. The focus on knowledge has led to a critical evaluation of cultural values, especially among the young middle class who have experienced greater periods of education. NSMs are therefore concerned with the promotion of alternative cultural values that encourage quality of life, concern for the environment and individual freedom of expression and identity. Touraine sees NSMs as at the heart of a re-alignment of political and cultural life. He suggests that they are in the process of replacing political parties as the major source of political identity.

Marcuse (1964) argues that NSMs are the direct result of the **alienation** caused by the capitalist mode of production

Item A

In life he was a nobody, a failed dustman turned firebomber. But in death Barry Horne will rise up as the first true martyr of the most successful terrorist group Britain has ever known, the Animal Liberation Front (ALF). Horne, who was convicted of arson in 1997 and sentenced to 18 years, died last week after months of being on hunger strike. Horne was a dedicated animal rights terrorist. He was convicted after being caught red-handed with incendiary devices that he had used to set light to department stores for daring to sell fur coats. In another attack he burned a branch of Boots on the Isle of Wight – causing £3m worth of damage – for selling animal-tested medicine. To his fellow activists, his lone firebombing campaign was part of a liberation war. Horne was a freedom fighter on behalf of those who could not fight for themselves: animals.

Kevin Toolis, Wednesday November 7, 2001 *The Guardian* Unlimited
© *Guardian* Newspapers Limited 2002

Item B

YOU'RE RUNNING
BECAUSE YOU WANT THAT RAISE,
TO BE ALL YOU CAN BE.
BUT IT'S NOT EASY.
WHEN YOU
WORK
SIXTY HOURS A WEEK
MAKING SNEAKERS IN AN
INDONESIAN FACTORY
AND YOUR FRIENDS
DISAPPEAR
WHEN THEY
ASK FOR A RAISE.
SO THINK
GLOBALLY BEFORE YOU DECIDE
IT'S SO COOL
TO WEAR
NIKE

Spoof Nike advert from 'Adbusters'
(www.adbusters.org)

Item C

6 April 2002, Mexico City Greenpeace swimmers blocked the harbour entrance of the port of Veracruz, Mexico today to stop the ship 'Sea Crown' transporting 40,000 tonnes of genetically engineered (GE) maize from the United States. Greenpeace repeated its call for a ban on all US GE maize imports as they are the most likely source of the genetic contamination discovered over six months ago in a country that is the world's most important centre of origin and diversity for maize.

Greenpeace website (www.greenpeace.org)

Item D

Anti-globalisation protest, Genoa, 2001

Item E

Demonstration against the export of live animals

1. In your opinion, was Barry Horne (see Item A) making a legitimate or illegitimate form of protest in firebombing department stores?

2. Would you describe him as a terrorist? Is a hunger strike to the death taking political protest too far?

3. Compare the forms of direct action in Items A–E.

4. Which form of direct action do you think is most effective? Explain your answer.

5. Are the forms of direct action depicted above justifiable? Explain your answer.

and consumption. Marcuse argued that capitalism produces a superficial **mass culture** in order to maximise its audience and profits. However, the emptiness of this culture has led some middle-class students whose education has given them critical insight, to reject materialism. NSMs are a form of **counter culture** which aim to encourage people to focus on emotional and personal needs such as concern for other people or the environment.

Other writers believe that NSMs are the product of a search for identity rather than the product of common political ideology or shared economic interests. Alberto Melucci (1989) argues that the collective actions and political campaigns associated with NSMs are not organised in a formal sense. It is this informality or looseness that appeals to its membership. This belonging to a vast unorganised network is less about providing its members with a coherent and articulate political manifesto or ideology than about providing a sense of identity and lifestyle. In this sense, Melucci argues that new social movements are cultural rather than political phenomena. They appeal to the young in particular because they offer the opportunity to challenge the dominant rules whilst offering an alternative set of identities that focus on fundamentally changing the nature of the society in both a spiritual and cultural way.

Commentators like Ulrich Beck (1992) and Anthony Giddens (1991) note that in a world dominated by global media and communications there is a growing sense of **risk** – people are increasingly aware of the dangers of the world we live in. In particular, there is a growing distrust of experts such as scientists who are seen as being responsible for many of the world's problems. Giddens uses the concept of increasing **reflexivity** to suggest that more and more people are reflecting on their place in the world and realising that their existence and future survival increasingly depends on making sure that key political players like governments and global corporations behave in a responsible fashion.

Global social movements

There is evidence that NSMs are becoming increasingly globalised. Klein, in her book *No Logo* (2001) suggests that global capitalism and its strategy of **global branding** and marketing is responsible for the alienation that underpins an emerging global anti-corporate movement.

Klein argues that young people's disillusion with capitalism is the result of a realisation that what counts as youth identity in modern society is increasingly a product of corporate branding rather than individual choice. People now see governments of all political persuasions in collusion with global corporations or ineffective in the face of corporate global power. What unites all these people, argues Klein, is their desire for a citizen-centred alternative to the international rule of the brands and to the power that global corporations have over their lives. Consumer boycotts of environmentally unfriendly goods, goods produced by child labour or regimes that regularly engage in human-rights abuse are examples of this alternative. Moreover, the global anti-corporate movement has provided networks in which high-profile NSMs such as Greenpeace and Oxfam have been able to collaborate and exert pressure on governments and transnational companies.

Explain how it can be argued that 'youth identity in modern society is increasingly a product of corporate branding rather than individual choice'.

There has undoubtedly been a fantastic interest in new social movements in the past thirty years but it is a mistake to conclude that this indicates the end of class politics. An examination of the distribution of power, studies of voting behaviour and the activities of pressure groups indicates that class and economic interests still underpin much of the political debate in Britain. It is also important not to exaggerate the degree of support that new social movements enjoy. Most people are aware of such movements but are not actively involved in them. However, conventional political parties and pressure groups can still learn a great deal from such movements, especially their ability to attract the educated, articulate and motivated young.

CHECK YOUR UNDERSTANDING

1 What are the main differences between sectional and promotional pressure groups?

2 What is the difference between an 'insider' and an 'outsider' pressure group?

3 How do pluralists and neo-pluralists differ in their attitudes towards pressure groups?

4 Why are Marxists critical of pressure groups?

5 Identify three differences between old social movements and new social movements.

6 What are the main differences between defensive new social movements and offensive new social movements?

7 What is the bunde?

8 What is meant by identity politics?

9 In what ways might membership of new social movements be related to anxieties about post-industrial society?

10 How do Marxists like Marcuse explain the emergence of new social movements?

11 How is the notion of 'increasing reflexivity' related to membership of new social movements?

12 What evidence is there that new social movements have become globalised?

WWWebtask

www.resist.org.uk/ is the co-ordinating site for most of the organisations that make up the anti-globalisation social movement. Click on their website and go to the 'Links' page. This lists all the organisations/issues that are affiliated. Choose a sample of organisations and find out their aims and tactics.

KEY TERMS

Alienation – an inability to identify with an institution or group to which you might belong.

Bunde – term used by Hetherington to describe new form of association made up of vegetarian groups, free-festival goers, dance culture, travellers, and so on.

Counter culture – a culture that is in opposition to authority.

Deformed polyarchy – situation where some pressure groups have more influence than others because they are strategically better positioned to bargain with policymakers.

Direct action – political action that operates outside the formal political process (e.g. demonstrations, sit-ins) and which is often illegal.

Global branding – attempts by global corporations to make their image and products recognisable world-wide.

Global order – the world political and economic system.

Hyper-pluralism – a situation where there are too many pressure groups competing for influence.

Identity politics – see Key Terms in Topic 4.

Legislative bodies – The state, parliament, the judiciary, i.e. agencies that have the power to make laws.

Lobbying – a means by which pressure groups and new social movements inform politicians and civil servants of their concerns and/or pass on information that will assist their cause. Pressure groups often employ lobbyists to promote their cause in parliament.

Mass culture – a superficial entertainment culture propagated by the mass media which undermines people's capacity for critical thinking.

New social movements – loosely organised political movements based around particular issues which have emerged since the 1960s.

Neo-pluralists – writers who have updated the idea of pluralism.

Peripheral – on the margins.

Pluralists – see Key Terms in Topic 2.

Pressure group – organised body that aims to put pressure on decision-makers.

Reflexivity – the ability to reflect on your experiences.

Risk technology – technology that poses danger to society such as nuclear power.

Socialism – see Key Terms in Topic 4.

Sustainable development – strategies for modernisation for the developing world that result in a fairer distribution of wealth and resources.

EXAM PRACTICE

Extract from AQA-style question

'As voting in elections has declined, other forms of political action have increased to give the poor and powerless more of a voice in the political arena.'

Evaluate the extent to which theories and evidence support this statement. (40 marks)

OCR-style question

Outline and assess the view that the beliefs and activities of new social movements do not differ significantly from the beliefs and activities of pressure groups. (60 marks)

Item A

According to Crook *et al.*, 'old' politics has largely given way to a 'new' politics which is very different. New politics is less concerned with sectional interests such as those associated with social class. Rather it is more concerned with moral issues that affect everyone. For example, a concern with animal rights, world peace or ecology is not confined to particular classes but is based upon a universal appeal to moral principles or choice of lifestyle. The new politics is less reliant on elites. Rather, in the new politics, social movements encourage everyone to become involved in campaigns over certain issues. The State too is less important because the focus of new politics is to convince civil society that it must change. Finally, the new politics often involves a total counter-cultural way of life. Choosing to live in a particular way is a political statement and a form of political activity.

Adapted from: M. Holborn and M. Haralambos (2001) *Sociology: Themes and Perspectives*, London: Collins Educational

Item B

It has been suggested that by the late 1960s people had become disillusioned with established political parties and this led to the growth of the new social movements and also of pressure groups. Coxall (1981) argues that the 1960s and 1970s witnessed an explosion of pressure group membership. He cites the examples of Shelter, which by 1969 had more than 220 affiliated branches, and the Child Poverty Action Group, which by 1970 had over forty. He argues, however, that despite this growth they still mobilised only a minority of the population. In the 1980s, groups such as CND went into decline but others, notably those concerned with the environment and animal welfare, rose to take their place. Pluralists argue that such growth and decline is a sign of a healthy democracy. Their assumption of inertia means they believe people only become involved in pressure group activity if the issue affects them personally. The fact that only a minority of the population is involved in such political action is taken by pluralists as evidence that most people are happy with the existing governmental arrangements.

Adapted from: M. Kirby (1995) *Investigating Political Sociology*, London: Collins Educational

Item C

Membership of the ALF (Animal Liberation Front) is like membership of an extraordinary fundamentalist religion. Since its foundation in 1976, animal rights terrorists have targeted butchers' shops, science laboratories, fur farms, live exports, dog breeding farms and high-street chemists. Most animal rights activists begin their career around the family kitchen table as young teenagers by refusing to eat meat, and then going on to become vegans – who reject the use of all animal products, such as milk, cheese or leather. This rejection is based not on taste but the moral conviction that killing animals for human consumption is wrong. In their own minds, ALF members are possessed of a blinding religious truth: our society is built on the unnecessary killing of animals and they are morally bound to use all means, including violence, to stop the daily holocaust of animal lives.

Source: Kevin Toolis, *The Guardian*, Wednesday November 7, 2001

Item D

Naomi Klein suggests that the global anti-globalisation social movement is truly a people's movement. 'Its members are young and old; they come from elementary schools and college campuses suffering from branding fatigue and from church groups worried that corporations are behaving 'sinfully'. They are parents worried about their children's slavish devotion to logo tribes and they are also the political intelligentsia who are concerned with the quality of community life'. What unites all these people, argues Klein, is their desire for a citizen-centred alternative to the international rule of the brands and to the power that global corporations have over their lives. They no longer want to be identified as just consumers. Quite simply, they want their identity back.

Source: Steve Chapman (2002) 'No Logo', *Sociology Review*, April, Oxford: Philip Allan Updates

1 Using Item A only, summarise the difference between old social movements and new social movements.

2 How does pressure group activity differ from the activities of new social movements?

3 Using Item B and other material, outline and assess pluralist theories of pressure groups and new social movements.

4 How does Item C support the view that new social movements reflect a new politics which is mainly about finding an identity?

5 Critically assess Klein's view in Item D that new social movements are truly people's movements.

Getting you thinking

Anti-globalisation demonstration, London, 1999

Brixton riots, 1981

Youths attack police in the Ardoyne area of Belfast

Protestants clash with police in north Belfast as they tried to stop catholic school children from attending the Holy Cross Primary School

1 Look at each photograph carefully. What types of people do you think riot?

2 What do you think motivated each of the groups above to take to the streets?

3 What types of crimes constitute rioting?

4 Is rioting ever a legitimate form of protest?

5 Do riots ever achieve anything positive?

Riots are a form of **direct action**. They can generally be defined as a type of collective urban disorder. They usually involve some degree of violence, especially against property and this most commonly takes the form of confrontation with the police. Such street disorders tend to be focused in inner cities characterised by high levels of social and economic deprivation. Rioting may be perceived as being the only option available to some social groups who lack access to legitimate means of political protest. Mainstream political parties, pressure groups and trade unions fail to represent their interests. Street riots may be the only means by which grievances can be voiced so that they are noticed.

It is important to understand that riots are not a modern phenomenon. John Beynon (1986) points out that the history of Britain has been characterised by frequent outbursts of urban disorder. In June 1780 a total of 285 people died in the Gordon Riots (anti-Catholic riots), and serious riots occurred throughout the nineteenth century in cities such as Bristol, Manchester, Birmingham, Nottingham, Derby and London. In 1887, three people were killed and 200 injured in Trafalgar Square after the police clashed with unemployed people. In 1910 troops were called in to deal with violent disorder in South Wales at Tonypandy whilst four people were shot by troops in Liverpool and Llanelli. In 1919 people were shot dead in race riots in Cardiff. The 1930s were also years of considerable disorder.

What sources of data might have provided data about urban disorder in the past? What problems do sociologists face in using this data?

Much of the sociological explanation that has evolved to explain rioting came about as a result of urban disorder that occurred in the 1980s. In 1980 and 1981 riots broke out in the St Paul's area of Bristol and in Brixton and Southall in London. In 1985 serious rioting broke out in Handsworth, Brixton and Broadwater Farm in Tottenham. The latter resulted in the death of a police officer.

The conservative perspective

This perspective is made up of a number of interlinked explanations that tend to focus on law and order issues in that they very clearly see no excuse for what is interpreted as criminal and immoral behaviour. Such theories take a number of forms.

● Some conservative writers and commentators see urban disorder as an expression or symptom of social change. It is argued that rapidly changing values have brought about a moral decline in behaviour. This view sees the inhabitants of inner-city areas as morally corrupt, and consequently it is suggested that those who take part in urban riots see themselves as being outside the moral and legal restraints of wider society.

● Poor or inferior socialisation is often linked to this moral decline. Conservative commentators suggest that the main responsibility for the criminal behaviour of youth lies with parents who either do not care about what their children do or who cannot control them. It has even been suggested by some that the black community suffers from a 'weak' family structure compared with the white community.

What is socialisation? Which social institutions are responsible for primary and secondary socialisation?

● Some conservative sociologists suggest that urban disorder is the product of 'alien' values imported into Britain through immigration. It has been suggested that ethnic minorities have a more confrontational attitude towards law and order than whites. Solomos (1993) notes that young blacks were seen by some right-wing politicians as carriers of negative cultural values that resulted in them adopting a '**ghetto mentality**'.

● The New Right position associated with Charles Murray suggests that inner-city areas in the UK are inhabited by an 'underclass', that is, a distinct lower-class grouping

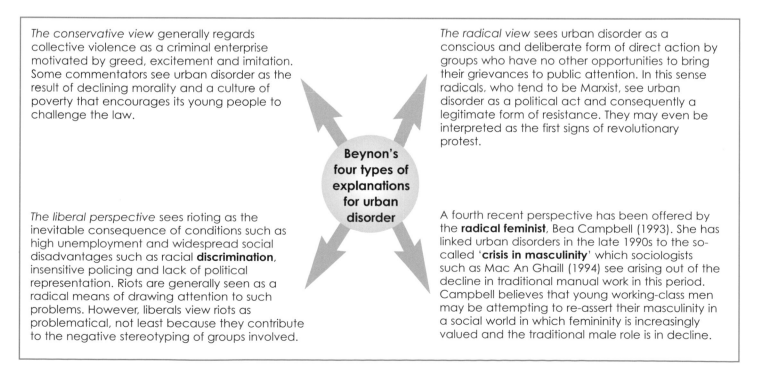

The conservative view generally regards collective violence as a criminal enterprise motivated by greed, excitement and imitation. Some commentators see urban disorder as the result of declining morality and a culture of poverty that encourages its young people to challenge the law.

The radical view sees urban disorder as a conscious and deliberate form of direct action by groups who have no other opportunities to bring their grievances to public attention. In this sense radicals, who tend to be Marxist, see urban disorder as a political act and consequently a legitimate form of resistance. They may even be interpreted as the first signs of revolutionary protest.

Beynon's four types of explanations for urban disorder

The liberal perspective sees rioting as the inevitable consequence of conditions such as high unemployment and widespread social disadvantages such as racial **discrimination**, insensitive policing and lack of political representation. Riots are generally seen as a radical means of drawing attention to such problems. However, liberals view riots as problematical, not least because they contribute to the negative stereotyping of groups involved.

A fourth recent perspective has been offered by the **radical feminist**, Bea Campbell (1993). She has linked urban disorders in the late 1990s to the so-called '**crisis in masculinity**' which sociologists such as Mac An Ghaill (1994) see arising out of the decline in traditional manual work in this period. Campbell believes that young working-class men may be attempting to re-assert their masculinity in a social world in which femininity is increasingly valued and the traditional male role is in decline.

which subscribes to 'deviant' rather than mainstream values which it transmits to its children. Murray suggests that this class is characterised by commitment to a life of unemployment, dependency on benefits, **fatalism**, criminality, hostility towards the police and authority, poor parenting, ill-disciplined children and immoral behaviour. This theory is often invoked to explain urban disorder, especially that which characterised white council estates in cities and towns like Newcastle, Sunderland, Oxford and Lincoln during the mid-1990s.

What criticisms have been made of the idea of an 'underclass'?

Solomos points out that the conservative approach has been extremely influential in shaping the general public's perceptions of inner-city riots. One reason for this is that the mass media, especially the tabloid press, have tended to take a conservative view of urban disorder. This has had two consequences.

- The **criminalisation** of the problem – the social and sociological reasons for such behaviour have been neglected and society at large has been persuaded that such problems are the product of an 'alien' minority, and consequently not typical.
- The **racialisation** of the problem – it is suggested that this type of urban disorder is a racial problem, i.e. it arises out of the unique culture of black people, rather than being a legitimate or understandable reaction to poor social conditions.

The liberal perspective

Lord Scarman's (1982) report into the Brixton riots of that year is typical of the liberal response to the social problem of urban disorder. Scarman highlighted three crucial causes of these riots.

- *Insensitive policing of young people in Brixton*
  The use of 'stop and search' tactics and racist language had led to great hostility among young blacks towards what they perceived as a racist police force.

- *Social and economic disadvantage*
  Scarman concluded that young blacks in Brixton experienced higher than average levels of unemployment, poor housing and amenities, and widespread racial discrimination. Although black people experienced the same type of deprivations as whites, they experienced them more acutely.

What problems do sociologists face in attempting to measure the extent of racial discrimination in Britain?

- *Feelings of rejection*
  Young blacks felt rejected by British society. Such feelings of frustration, deprivation and **marginalisation** were reinforced by what they perceived as police harassment and the non-existent level of black political representation.

Scarman concluded that these factors created a set of social conditions which 'create a **predisposition** towards violent

protest'. He noted that many young blacks believed with justification that violence was an effective means of protest because it attracted the attention of the media, thus allowing them to get their message across.

Scarman's conclusions are not dissimilar from the theory of **left realism** associated with John Lea and Jock Young (1993) (see Unit 5 Topic 11). This theory argues that some working-class and black youth turn to street crime and urban disorder because of **relative deprivation**. In comparison with their peers (middle-class and white youth), they feel deprived in terms of education, jobs, income and standard of living. They feel they have little power to change their situation, that they are picked on by the authorities and that nobody listens to them. As a result, some young people may resort to **collective responses** such as criminal subcultures or collective social disorder such as urban rioting. Young and Lea note that the former response is more likely but particular circumstances may come together to precipitate urban disorder. For example, Young and Lea are very critical of the **'military-style' policing** tactics that were adopted by the London Metropolitan Police in the 1980s. Such policing involved saturating the local community with officers on the beat, stopping and searching young blacks and engaging in dawn drug-raids in which excessive violence was used. These tactics allegedly raised tension in Brixton, Toxteth and Broadwater Farm immediately prior to the outbreak of urban disorder.

Other liberal explanations have focused on political exclusion. Bachrach and Baratz (1970) conclude that riots are the 'ballot boxes of the poor' and are attempts to force onto a political agenda demands that otherwise would be neglected or ignored. The poor, therefore, have no other way of being heard. Wedderburn (1974) notes that mainstream political parties have little time for the poor because they are perceived as exerting little power compared with the articulate and wealthy middle-classes.

Sociological research indicates that liberal explanations are supported by strong evidence of institutional forms of racism across many areas of British society. For example, the Macpherson Report (1999) into the death of the black teenager Stephen Lawrence suggested that there are still serious concerns about police officers' treatment of ethnic-minority citizens (see Unit 5 Topic 10). Macpherson concluded that the Metropolitan Police Service was institutionally racist, which he defined as follows:

The collective failure of an organisation to provide appropriate and professional service to people because of their colour, culture or ethnic origin. It can be seen or detected in processes, attitudes and behaviours which amount to discrimination through unwitting prejudice, ignorance, thoughtlessness and racist stereotyping which disadvantage minority ethnic people.

MacPherson noted that institutional racism could be seen in stop and search tactics which were disproportionately used against black youth. Moreover, it was reflected in the lack of confidence black people had in the police in relation to reporting racist attacks against them. Moreover, Mason (2000) points out that there have been widespread and persistent reports of police officers acting unjustly and with unnecessary violence towards ethnic-minority citizens, as well as claims of racial abuse and harassment. There is also evidence that policing practices, especially definitions of what constitutes 'suspicious' or 'criminal' may be shaped by stereotypes about black people.

Beynon documents a range of other evidence that supports the view that extreme forms of economic and social deprivation may be underlying causes of urban disorder.

- Ethnic unemployment is high and especially affects the young. Moreover, there is evidence that black rates of unemployment are significantly higher than the national average. For example, on the Broadwater Farm estate, youth unemployment was 60%.
- Housing occupied by the poor, especially black families in inner cities is often substandard. There has been a lack of adequate investment in council housing in many inner-city areas. Moreover, many of these areas lack adequate and appropriate youth amenities.
- Schools in inner-city areas are often short of funds, experience a high turnover of staff and consequently compare badly in terms of examination results when compared with suburban schools. Moreover, there is some evidence of institutional racism in the form of teacher attitudes towards African-Caribbean boys which may be reflected in the disproportionate number of school exclusions experienced by this group.

Apart from institutional racism, what other explanations may be put forward to explain the disproportionate number of school exclusions experienced by African-Caribbean boys?

- Racial discrimination by employers is still fairly common.
- Racist abuse, harassment and attacks are a fact of life in many parts of Britain.
- The poor and especially ethnic minorities are very rarely in a position to influence decisions made about them. They are very rarely consulted. Surveys indicate that they feel they are not listened to.

The radical approach

The Marxist approach to urban disorder generally sees riots or urban disorder in terms of resistance and rebellion, even uprisings. Urban disorder is presented as a legitimate reaction against an oppressive and racist state. This approach is very similar to that of the 'new criminology' which saw crime as a conscious political act (see Unit 5 Topic 4). Taylor, Walton and Young (1973) suggested that working-class people choose to commit crime or riot because of their experience of the injustices of capitalism. It is a deliberate and conscious reaction to being placed at the bottom of the socio-economic hierarchy. Paul Gilroy (1982b) argued that black participation in urban disorder is political in that it is a conscious and deliberate reaction to young black people's anger at the way white society has historically treated black people via slavery, colonialism and everyday prejudice and discrimination.

The Marxist view has been criticised as naive and over-romantic. It would make sense if affluent areas were being attacked and capitalist property was being destroyed. However, the victims of urban disorder tend to be other poor people as it is property and amenities in the inner cities that are destroyed.

The 'flashpoints' model of urban riots

This analysis essentially combines liberal and radical approaches. It emphasises the relationship between a precipitating incident (such as over-policing) and existing and longstanding grievances.

The 'flashpoints' model

This model sees a range of factors as influencing the potential for riot.

1 Structural factors
Rioters experience inequalities in power, resources and life-chances. Inner city residents may feel relatively deprived and frustrated because the state seems uninterested or unwilling to relieve their problems.

2 Political/ideological factors
Rioters lack political representation. They feel that no one cares and that they have little to lose.

3 Cultural factors
The police and other agencies of social control may not be able to relate to young people's culture such as hanging around in the street. If the groups have different or incompatible definitions of a situation, then the potential for conflict is increased.

4 Contextual factors
Those who riot may be responding to a past history of conflict between themselves and the authorities. Media rumour and prediction may lead to siege mentalities and self-fulfilling prophecies about disorder.

5 Situational factors
Riots may evolve spontaneously to a particular situation, such as what is seen as a wrongful arrest.

6 Interactional factors
The quality of interaction between police and members of a community may be poor. 'Flashpoints' occur as some actions, especially by the police, may be seen by participants as breaking unwritten rules governing behaviour – for example, unfair arrests and excessive police violence.

Recent riots

In 2001, the towns of Oldham, Burnley and Bradford saw violent confrontations between young Asians and the police. Kundnani (2002) has identified a number of possible explanations for these riots:

- High Asian unemployment has stemmed from the closure of textile mills. Young Asians in towns across Lancashire and Yorkshire experience unemployment rates of about 50%.
- Local-council housing policies mean that whites dominate council estates in these areas. For example, only 2% of Bradford's stock of council housing has been allocated to

Asians. Asians have had to buy or rent cheap housing in particular areas which have then become dominated by Asian families. Whites and Asians therefore live in mutually exclusive areas.

What problems may be created by the residential segregation of ethnic groups?

- Segregation in housing has led to segregation in education. In some districts school catchment areas contained nearly 100% populations of just one ethnic group. This has produced Asian ghetto schools in which institutional racism in the form of expectations of failure and negative assumptions about Asian culture by white teachers is common. The growing popularity of **faith schools** has encouraged mutual distrust between the white and Asian communities.
- Young Asians born and bred in Britain are less willing to be the victims of racial attacks and are fully prepared to take the law into their own hands in order to protect their

areas. Violent confrontations between racist whites and Asians attracted police attention but young Asians feel that the police generally tend to criminalise them for defending themselves. Moreover, Asian areas have become increasingly targeted by the police who believe Asian gangs are getting out of control.
- The leaders of Asian communities have sold their communities short. They are more concerned with being seen as members of the respectable middle class than with serving the real needs of their communities.

Kundnani argues that the Labour government has reacted in a conservative way to these riots. 'Blair spoke of thuggery, refusing to look beyond a narrow law-and-orderism, refusing to see in the riots the reflection of his own failed ambitions to tackle 'social exclusion''. Even the community leaders blamed the riots on a lack of discipline, a decline in Muslim values and the undue influence of Western values. He concludes that the mistakes of the past are being repeated because nobody is consulting the young Asians who took to the streets.

KEY TERMS

Collective response – a group or gang response.

Criminalisation – shaping the perception of the general public so that they always see the activities of a particular group as criminal or potentially criminal.

Crisis of masculinity – the idea that young working-class men are experiencing anxiety as traditional jobs disappear and women take over the breadwinning role.

Direct action – see Key Terms in Topic 5.

Faith schools – religious schools.

Fatalism – the feeling that nothing can be done about the future.

Ghetto mentality – feeling under siege.

Marginalisation – lacking power, being forced to live at the edge of society.

Military-style policing – confrontational policing in large visible numbers.

Predisposition – natural inclination towards doing something.

Racial discrimination – the practice of refusing to give people jobs, promotion or housing on the basis of skin colour or other 'racial' characteristics and/or the physical and verbal abuse of people from ethnic minorities through racially motivated attacks and name-calling.

Racialisation – shaping the perception of the general public so that they always associate a particular social problem with black people.

Radical feminist – a school of feminist thought that sees society as being divided into two biological and cultural classes: men and women.

Relative deprivation – feeling of being poor arising from a comparison with a peer group.

Social exclusion – see Key Terms in Topic 5.

CHECK YOUR UNDERSTANDING

1 Explain what is meant by a riot.

2 What is the alleged relationship between family, culture and urban disorder according to Conservative thinkers such as Charles Murray?

3 In what way can Conservative theories of inner-city rioting be seen as racist?

4 What effect has Conservative thinking on inner-city riots and mass-media representations of them had on the general public's perception of this problem?

5 What were the three causes of the inner-city rioting of 1981 according to Lord Scarman?

6 In what ways is the left realist theory of urban disorder similar to the conclusions of the Scarman Report?

7 What is meant by Bachrach and Baratz when they describe riots as the 'ballot boxes' of the poor?

8 Identify five types of economic and social deprivation that may trigger urban unrest.

9 Explain how police institutional racism may provoke inner-city unrest.

10 Why do Marxists use the term 'uprising' to describe inner-city rioting?

11 What six elements go to make up the 'flashpoints' theory of urban disorder?

12 What were the main causes of the 2001 rioting according to Kudnani?

Research idea

Using either your local library or the internet, access newspapers such as the *Guardian, Daily Telegraph, The Times, Independent* and *Yorkshire Post* for July/August 2001. Conduct content analysis of the language and images used by journalists to describe the riots that occurred in Bradford, Burnley and Oldham. In particular, look closely at headlines, photographs and editorials. Who or what do these newspapers blame? Are there differences in their interpretation of events? Are they taking a conservative, liberal or radical line?

WWWebtask

Access the *Socialist Worker* newspaper's reports on the 2001 riots on www. socialistworker.co.uk/1780/08.pdf. How does its coverage of the riots differ from mainstream newspapers?

Extract from AQA-style question

'In all societies there are accepted ways of making decisions affecting the whole group. Usually such ways become institutionalised and legitimate power comes to lie with only a few. Eventually such institutions seem to exclude many of the population and then it may seem necessary to express political opinions in ways outside these institutions of the state. Such extra-institutional expression may occur either because people dispute the legitimacy of the state institutions, much as Gandhi did, or because they have no expectation of participating in such Institutions, like the majority population in Apartheid South Africa.

From street demonstrations to suicide bombers extra-institutional actions are the preserve of the disenfranchised, the powerless, the dispossessed of the earth'.

Examine the role of extra-institutional political actions in modern societies. (12 marks)

OCR-style question

Outline and assess the view that urban riots are the result of the frustration caused by extreme economic and social deprivation rather than criminality. (60 marks)

Item A

Conservative reactions to the disorders in 1985, as in 1980 and 1981 ascribed the riots to criminality and greed, hooliganism and 'mindless violence', extremists and subversives, imitation, base impulses in human nature and general evil, or to a failure in education and a breakdown in family life and proper values. Douglas Hurd (the then Home Secretary) said after the Handsworth disorder that it was 'not a social phenomenon but crimes': it was 'not a cry for help but a cry for loot'. Mr. Norman Tebbit, Conservative Party Chairman, said after the Tottenham riots that they were the result of 'wickedness', and he later suggested that the moral degeneration was a legacy of the permissive society of the 1960s. Police officers, on the other hand, favoured explanations drawn from the basic social and political flaws category. The Chief Superintendent of Police in Tottenham said that social disadvantage and unemployment were important factors. Black community leaders blamed police harassment and abuse, as well as racial discrimination and disadvantage.

Adapted from: J. Beynon (1986) 'Turmoil in the Cities', *Social Studies Review*, January, Oxford: Phillip Allan Updates

Item B

It is possible to argue that the riots shared certain features. First they challenged, and signalled the bankruptcy of colour-blind social policies that relied on the assumption that black people would assimilate into British culture. Second, they were almost always triggered to some degree by community responses to some action of the police. Thirdly, they all constituted in some measure an attempt by members of local communities to assert a degree of control over the urban space they occupied. This might be in response to what were seen as outside intrusions (such as those by the police or by members of extreme right-wing groups), in protest against urban deprivation and unemployment or as a symbolic demonstration of control and resistance. It is instructive that the response of government was to develop more closely targeted measures aimed more explicitly than hitherto at the perceived needs of the communities concerned.

Extracted from D. Mason (2000) *Race and Ethnicity in Modern Britain* (2nd edition), Oxford: Oxford University Press

Item C

Racism has remained more or less constant since the Second World War yet the first-generation migrants did not take to the street. Why did so many of their sons and daughters do so? However, given the persistence and scope of racism in recent years, the inequality to which it has contributed and the conflict it has inspired, another more relevant question might be 'why has there not been more rioting?' In my opinion, there are four constructive consequences to urban disorder. Firstly, there is a catharsis function – riots provide a spontaneous outlet for built-up emotional energies. Riots for young blacks are occasions for symbolic revenge against a system they despise. Youth, in burning the property of their own neighbourhoods were attacking symbols of their entrapment in the ghettos. Secondly, riots heighten public awareness of social and economic deprivation. Young blacks are often denied access to conventional means of protest. Politicians show little interest in them. A riot gets their attention. Thirdly, riots are often the catalyst for educational reform. It is recognised that urban violence was partially the result of prolonged unemployment which in turn is linked to poor school performance. Fourthly, riots result in the prompting of an economic revitalisation of the inner cities as governments pour funds in to attract business and therefore jobs.

Adapted from: E. Ellis Cashmore (1989) *United Kingdom? Class, Race and Gender since the War*, London: Unwin Hyman

Item D

The summer of race riots on British streets in Oldham, Burnley, Bradford and Leeds was fuelled partly by resentment among local groups who believed other races were being favoured for Government grants, a groundbreaking official report says. The report paints a picture of dangerously fragmented communities, with ethnic groups segregated into virtual 'ghettos' at home and at school for fear of racist attack if they tried to move away from what was regarded as their territory. Political and community leadership was alarmingly weak, making little effort to bridge the divide or to listen to young people who have become increasingly disenfranchised, according to the review. White and Asian inner-city areas ended up 'pitted against each other, competing for resources', with jealousy and suspicion on both sides. Areas with high ethnic minority populations often scored highest for deprivation and received more funding. When a mainly white estate saw an Asian estate receiving funding, or vice versa, suspicions were swiftly aroused. A Home Office source said 'with regeneration money, because the communities have become so distant and because they are not talking to each other, you end up with rumours about "that side of the fence getting lots more money" and so on.'

Gaby Hinsliff, Sunday December 9, 2001, Society *Guardian*.co.uk
© *Guardian* Newspapers Limited 2001

1 Using Item A only, identify six reasons given for inner-city riots.

2 Using Item A and other material, outline theories of crime that suggest the blame lies with the perpetrators.

3 Using Item B, in your own words, identify the four features common to rioting, according to Mason.

4 In Item C, Cashmore expresses surprise that there has not been more rioting. Why?

5 Using Item C, outline four positive functions of rioting.

6 Using Item D, outline the view that recent rioting may be the result of competition for scarce resources.

Theory and Methods

Getting you thinking

One of the people above is saying that they are very sorry but you are seriously ill and are going to die, there is nothing that can be done about it, and it would be better to enjoy your remaining few months than to undergo pointless further treatment. The other is saying that they can cure you completely if you undertake a treatment they suggest. One of them is correct.

1 Which do you think is more likely to be telling 'the truth'?

2 Explain your answer carefully.

Most of you will probably have decided in the above activity that the modern Western doctor is more likely to be providing an accurate picture of your health. This is not surprising as modern Western medicine is based on science, and scientific explanations dominate modern societies.

For at least a hundred years, sociologists have argued amongst themselves over whether or not sociology is a science. For most students coming to the subject for the first time, this seems a fairly pointless debate – after all, who cares how you classify the subject, just get on with doing it!

But the issue is important. Indeed, the very existence of sociology as an academic subject was for a long time tied up with it being accepted as a science. Even today, sociology still needs to wrap itself in the cloak of science if it is to retain its status in the general academic world.

The status of sociology

The status of sociology as a science has been related to two important factors – funding and prestige.

Funding

Subjects receive funding for research from government departments, charities and commerce if they are seen to be 'scientific' and therefore useful in producing reliable data. Subjects that are not seen as being useful (such as astrology, **parapsychology** and fortune-telling) are not likely to receive the financial support of these organisations.

Give two examples of research which the current government might be interested in funding. Explain why.

Prestige

This is closely connected with funding. For over two hundred years the status of 'science' has been head and shoulders above any other method of understanding the world. The result of this prestige is funding, availability of the subject at A level and university and academic posts for people to learn it, and so on.

Within sociology itself, this issue has been important as it has influenced what subjects have been studied and what methods have been regarded as acceptable for research. The tussle between those who see sociology as a science and those who do not, largely reflects the difference in approach between **positivists** (who prefer surveys and statistical tools), and **interpretive** sociologists (who prefer to use observational studies and less structured interviews) (see Topics 2 and 3).

However, in recent years the significance of the status of sociology as a science has become less importance as science itself has declined in prestige – which is just part of the movement away from modernity in the latter parts of the twentieth century to a late-modern society in which experts and their views have gradually become viewed as **contestable**.

What is a science?

The 'march of progress' approach to science argues that there are certain key components to a science which have emerged over time. These are that science is:

- empirical
- testable
- theoretical
- cumulative
- objective.

Empirical

By empirical we mean, in the strictest sense, 'knowable through our senses'. In practice, it means that the information can be counted or measured. The tradition comes from the philosopher Locke who lived and wrote in the seventeenth century. He was arguing against metaphysical explanations of the world which relied solely upon assuming that objects and powers existed beyond the 'physical realm'. Magic, some areas of religion and astrology are all metaphysical ways of explaining the world that cannot be proven (or disproved) and so cannot be empirical.

Testable

This leads us on to the crucial importance of empirical knowledge – that it can be tested and revisited as many times as needed. This means that the knowledge gained is open to **verification** or **refutation** by others.

According to Karl Popper (1959) once knowledge is put forward for scrutiny, it should be possible to engage in the process of **falsification** – that is, that the empirical model can be tested with the aim of showing it to be false. Only if all tests have been applied and it still seems accurate, can scientists assume that it is the best existing explanation. (We discuss this in more detail in Topic 2 'Positivism and sociology'.)

Theoretical

Many students comment that good investigative journalism is the same as sociology in that it searches out 'the truth' behind events. This is not true, however, as one of the main distinguishing features of sociology is that of theory construction. A theory seeks to uncover **causal relationships** between phenomena rather than simply describing these phenomena.

 Using any area of sociology you have studied, give an example of a hypothesis that suggests a causal relationship between two phenomena.

Cumulative

Scientific theory, it is claimed, builds on previous knowledge, so that there is an ever-growing, empirically testable body of such knowledge which moves us forward in our understanding of the world.

Objective

We discuss this in some detail in the Topic on values (Topic 6), but the key issue here is that science blocks out personal prejudices and political views in its search for empirically testable propositions about the world.

What are values? Provide two examples.

The process of science

Scientific methodology has developed into a clear set of procedures. These include the following steps.

1. A phenomenon is observed and noted by a scientist through observation.
2. An **hypothesis** or initial explanation for the phenomenon is suggested.
3. A form of experimentation is devised in which the key **variables** which (it is believed) explain the phenomenon are placed in a situation where they can be controlled in some way.
4. The experiment or data collection is carried out.
5. The resulting data are examined and analysed.
6. The hypothesis is then accepted, amended or rejected.
7. Finally, a theory is formed on the basis of the research, which is then open to examination by other scientists.

Sociology and science

The scientific tradition in sociology

We have seen that science has five components and a methodological process that is followed in ideal circumstances. So, how does this relate to sociological methods?

Traditionally, sociology has sought to be recognised as a science, and one school of sociology – the positivist one – has modelled its approach as closely as it can on the **physical (or natural) sciences**. The tradition began with the work of Comte and Quetelet, two founding fathers of sociology. They argued that philosophising about the world was not enough. Statistics needed to be gathered so that cause and effect could be properly proven.

Similar to those studying the natural sciences, they believed that there were general laws that explained the nature of society which could be uncovered. Extreme examples of this approach to understanding the social world include the work of Durkheim (for example, his study of suicide) see Unit 5, Topic 12), and also Karl Marx. Indeed, Marx's work was a lifelong attempt to show that there were laws of economics that would inevitably lead to a communist society.

Give an example from your studies of Durkheim's contribution to an understanding of any aspect of social life.

Much later, the main sociological opposition to Marxist ideas came from Talcott Parsons and the **structural–functionalist school** he founded. Once again, Parsons was intent upon showing that society existed as a structure and that there were forces and social laws that existed independently of individuals. Throughout this and any other textbook of sociology, you will find endless examples of studies that are based on generalised statements about how humans will act in certain circumstances and what factors cause this. Explicitly or not, these approaches are supporting the view of sociology as a science.

How has the perspective of functionalism been criticised?

The work of Durkheim and Marx combined theory with a search for the evidence to support their ideas. However, a third tradition that was highly sympathetic to the vision of sociology as a science was developed in the nineteenth century through the study of working-class life in Britain. This empirical work, which first emerged in the writings of Mayhew (1851) and Rowntree (1901), formed the basis of the **British empirical tradition**. (Here information is gathered about various social phenomena – for example, the lives of the poor – for its own sake, or to influence social policy.) However, the work never set out to be theoretical. This tradition has remained and is still the most common form of sociological research – today, there are innumerable studies looking at success and failure in education; at drug use; at health patterns, and so on.

How do these writers justify sociology as a science?

In order to understand this, we need to go back to the elements of science we looked at earlier.

Theoretical
Scientists who are dubious about sociology's claim to scientific status point out that natural objects are predictable as they simply react, whereas people have free will and are therefore not predictable. This thus makes a theoretical statement that involves making a general prediction (if X occurs then Y will act in this way) impossible in sociology. However, although we cannot predict how individuals will act, we can predict how *groups* will act. For example, Durkheim claimed that there are clearly distinguishable patterns of suicide with certain groups having distinctive rates over a number of years.

From your studies, give two further examples of 'clearly distinguishable patterns' in society.

Empirical and testable
Natural scientists argue that in the physical world, there are phenomena that exist independently of the scientists. The scientist merely has to measure these phenomena. But, they argue, society on the other hand is created by people and there are no phenomena 'out there' waiting to be measured.

For those sympathetic to the view that sociology is a science, this is an unfair criticism. They argue (that although ultimately the creation of society), there are a wide range of phenomena that do exist separately from individuals, and that constrain and limit our behaviour (again, a possible answer to critics regarding free will). All of these are in Durkheim's words 'social facts' which exist independently and can be measured in an objective way. Theories can thus be tested to see whether they are true or false.

Cumulative
Again, like all sciences, knowledge is cumulative. Sociologists have built up knowledge over time and accumulated a stock of knowledge about society (and it is this cumulative information that forms the current-day sociology that you are studying).

Objective
A major criticism of sociology as a science is that if it deals with issues and concerns about which we all have strong feelings, then how is it possible for sociologists to be objective? Won't their values emerge in their choice of subject and their methods of study? This is a complex subject, so much so that we have a Topic devoted to it (Topic 6). However, positivist sociologists argue that it is possible to be value-free by rigorously adhering to the methodological process that is discussed below.

The methodological process in sociology
We saw earlier that there is a traditional process followed by physical scientists. Many of them argue that sociology is simply unable to follow this. We look at this in detail later in the Topic on positivism (Topic 2), but critics have particularly concentrated on the difficulty of undertaking experiments in sociology. Sociologists have answered this by arguing that the sociological equivalent of an experiment is the comparative method (or multi-variate analysis), as used by Weber to explain the emergence of capitalism in Britain (see Unit 1, Topic 1) and Durkheim in his study of suicide (see Unit 5, Topic 12). The comparative method involves comparing societies to find out key differences that might explain different social phenomena.

Is science a science?

Increasingly natural science itself has come under fire for not matching the criteria of science discussed above.

The paradigm critique

Kuhn (1962) argues that one crucial element of science – that of cumulative progress – cannot be true. Kuhn argues instead that *normal science* operates within a **paradigm** (or accepted framework of concepts regarding a particular area of knowledge). This framework includes assumptions regarding what is important, the correct procedures, and the right sort of questions to be asking. This paradigm dominates scientific thinking, and traps thought and investigation within it. Any attempt to step outside the accepted conventions is usually ignored and rejected.

Science changes in a series of scientific revolutions which create their own new paradigms, rather than through the accumulation of knowledge. Kuhn suggests that over time there is a gradual build up of evidence which does not fit into the accepted paradigm and out of this unease emerges a distinctively new explanation that can accommodate the previous inconsistencies. A new paradigm is born and the process begins again. Kuhn calls this the 'process of scientific revolutions'.

Kuhn is himself not free from critics, however. Lakatos (1970), for example, has argued that Kuhn's idea of paradigms is too simplistic and only applies to the past, in relation to the abandonment of ideas regarding the earth being flat, or being the centre of the universe. Modern science is largely open and much more sophisticated in its thinking. Rarely in modern science have central ideas been abandoned.

Experiments and open/closed systems

Sayer (1992) has pointed out that the model of the physical sciences presented to the public may be misleading. He argues that we need to distinguish between **open and closed systems**.

Sciences such as chemistry or physiology operate in closed systems, in which all variables can be controlled. This allows experiments to be carried out. However, other physical sciences such as meteorology and **seismology**, operate in open systems, in which the variables cannot be controlled. These sciences recognise unpredictability. Seismology cannot predict when earthquakes will occur, though it does understand the conditions leading to earthquakes. Meteorologists can explain the forces producing weather, but the actual weather itself is difficult to predict. So, certain sciences therefore do not necessarily follow the process which it is claimed is a hallmark of science.

From Sayer's viewpoint (known as **realism**) the social sciences are no different from many physical sciences. Their aim ought to be the uncovering of the relationship between the wider structures that determine the way we relate to other people in everyday life. For example, we can only understand the relationship between a student and teacher by referring to the education system, inequalities of power, the aim of education, and so on.

Modernity, postmodernity and science

Science and modernity have gone hand in hand, according to Rorty (1980), with the belief that rationality, truth, and science are all bound together, and that other ways of knowing the world are inferior.

Postmodernists challenge this view. For Rorty, scientists have simply replaced priests as the sources of truth. We want someone to be the experts and to make sense of the world for us. Science has taken on this role. Yet we now know that, despite the advances in science there may well be concepts and questions that it can never answer – questions about the origins of the universe, the concept of infinity, and so on.

Lyotard (1984) has also shown that the nature of language limits and channels science because if provides a framework to approach an understanding of the world. Language both opens up possibilities and closes down others since we think within language and are unable to conceive of something that is outside our linguistic framework.

What is meant by modernity? What has led some sociologists to suggest that this period is ending?

Science and values

We have noted before that sociology has problems in disentangling values from the research process. However, so, too, does science. Scientists do not work in an ideal world. Those who fund their research lead the direction of the work, and not all science necessarily benefits the world. Cigarettes are the result of 'science', yet are the biggest killer of adults in the more affluent societies. Pharmaceutical companies have produced numerous drugs that have been directly harmful to society, including heroin, thalidomide and barbiturates. Beck (1992) has pointed out that science has actually *created* new

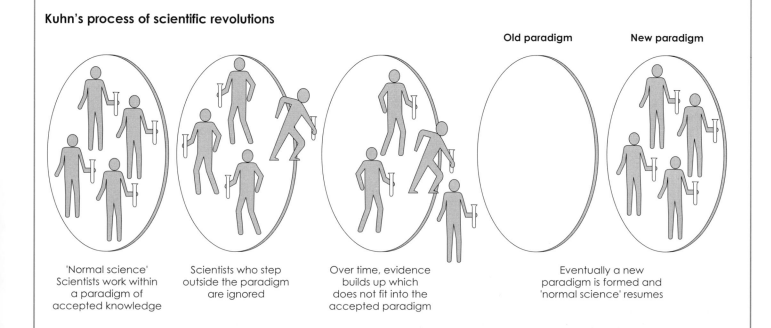

Kuhn's process of scientific revolutions

Old paradigm　　　New paradigm

'Normal science' Scientists work within a paradigm of accepted knowledge

Scientists who step outside the paradigm are ignored

Over time, evidence builds up which does not fit into the accepted paradigm

Eventually a new paradigm is formed and 'normal science' resumes and serious risks for society – for example, pollution and global warming.

Sociology and science: the debate in a nutshell

Our discussion so far has suggested the following.

- Sociology has sought scientific status in order to obtain status and acceptance as an academic subject.
- Critics from the traditional sciences have argued that sociology does not meet the criteria of science both in terms of the *components* (theory, objectivity, etc.) and in terms of the *process* (hypothesis, experiment, etc.)
- One group of sociologists – who have been called positivistic sociologists – have rejected this criticism and have claimed that sociology can and does achieve the criteria to make it a social science.
- However, if we look critically at the nature of science itself, it would appear that the natural sciences also fail the criteria of being a science.
- Postmodernists argue that the whole debate itself is a

reflection of outdated notions of a fixed, knowable world out there, waiting to be discovered. They argue instead that all knowledge is relative to the world of those who seek it, and that it is bounded by constraints of language and of culture.

So is sociology a science?

There is no simple answer to this question. According to writers such as Bhaskar (1986) and Sayer (1992), sociology can be as scientific as the natural sciences by adopting certain procedures. At the other extreme, postmodernists such as Rorty (1980) or Bauman (1978) would argue that the real question is why sociology would *want* to be seen as a science. They go on to say that the whole debate reflects the process of modernity – a period which we are now leaving.

Somewhere in the middle lie the bulk of sociologists who accept that there is a debate over the scientific nature of sociological study, but who get on with their research, attempting to make sense of society in the best and most honest way they can.

KEY TERMS

British empirical tradition – an approach to the study of society that largely ignored theory and simply collected data.

Causal relationship – a relationship between two factors in which one causes the other.

Comparative method – a method that involves comparing societies to find out key differences that might explain different social phenomena.

Contestable – open to challenge.

Empirical – refers to the ability to measure physical and social phenomena.

Falsification – the process whereby scientists seek to disprove their hypotheses, rather than prove them.

Hypothesis – an initial plausible guess concerning the causal relationship between events.

Interpretive sociology – an approach that stresses the role of people in constructing the society around them.

Metaphysical explanations – explanations that rely on assuming that objects and powers exist beyond the 'physical realm'.

Open and closed systems – in closed systems all variables can be controlled, in open systems (like society) they cannot.

Paradigm – a framework of thought that provides the way in which we approach and understand an issue.

Parapsychology – a disputed branch of psychology which studies a range of experiences such as mind-to-mind communication.

Physical/Natural sciences – the scientific study of the physical world. These include chemistry, physics, biology, botany, etc.

Positivists – those advocating an approach that supports the belief that the way to gain knowledge is by following the conventional scientific model.

Postmodernism – refers to a belief that we have moved into a period in which the dominance of rational, scientific thought and the significance of experts is being challenged.

Realism – the view that sociology should aim to uncover the relationship between the wider structures that determine the way we relate to other people in everyday life.

Refutation – showing something to be false.

Seismology – the study of earthquakes.

Structural-functionalist school – a version of society that starts by asking what function for a society a social phenomenon performs, for example 'what does the family do for society?' Associated with Talcott Parsons.

Theoretical – a general explanation of cause and effect between two or more phenomena.

Variable – a social phenomenon that changes in response to another phenomenon.

Verification – showing something to be true.

1 Why has it been considered important that sociology should be classified as a 'science'?

2 What are the elements of a science?

3 What do we mean by 'falsification'?

4 What do we mean by the 'British empirical tradition'?

5 What was Kuhn's criticism of the cumulative element of science?

6 Explain the difference between closed and open systems of science.

7 Why is an understanding of modernity and post-modernity relevant to this debate on the nature of science?

Research idea

Identify a range of behaviour and beliefs in phenomena that science cannot fully explain. You might think about religious and supernatural beliefs, fortune-telling, astrology, superstition and alternative therapies, for example. Use interviews to discover the extent to which a sample of people believe in or have used these non-scientific approaches. What do your results tell us about trust in science today?

WWWebtask

Search for the websites of two pressure groups dealing with the issue of smoking: Ash (anti-smoking) and Forest (defending smokers' interests). Examine the research they refer to regarding cigarette smoking – are there crucial differences between them? By the way, Forest receives about 90% of its funding from the cigarette companies. What does this debate tell you about science, values and research?

EXAM PRACTICE

Extract from AQA-style question

Assess the view that sociology can and should be seen as a science. (40 marks)

(Topic not in OCR specifications)

Item A

In 2001 relatives of Donald Schell who murdered his wife, daughter and granddaughter before committing suicide, took GlaxoSmithKline, a major pharmaceutical company, to court. They claimed that the company's best-selling antidepressant drug, Seroxat had caused Schell to commit the murders.

In its defence, the company cited published research papers which stated that Seroxat did not increase suicidal tendencies amongst those who took it. However, of the three researchers who produced this information, one never saw the original research data, and simply accepted information provided by the drugs company. A second author was employed by the company. The third, an eminent doctor, has refused to respond to requests by newspapers about what data he actually saw, or where it came from.

According to a research doctor who provided evidence for the relatives, the original data of the tests does show a substantially increased risk of suicide by people taking Seroxat.

Based on: 'Scandal of Scientists who take Money for Papers Ghostwritten by Drug Companies', Sarah Boseley, February 2002, *The Guardian*

Item B

Scandal of Scientists who take Money for Papers Ghostwritten by Drug Companies

'Scientists are taking large sums of money from drug companies to put their names to articles endorsing new medicines that they have not written…

Marcia Angell, former editor of the *New England Journal of Medicine*, wrote that when she ran a paper on antidepressant drugs treatment, the authors' financial ties to the manufacturers…were so extensive that she decided to commission an editorial about it and [she] spoke to research psychiatrists, but 'we found very few who did not have financial ties to drug companies that make antidepressants'…

Researchers serve as consultants to companies whose products they are studying, join advisory boards and speakers' bureaux, enter into patent and royalty arrangements, agree to be the listed authors of articles ghostwritten by interested companies…allow themselves to be plied with expensive gifts and trips to luxurious settings…'

Based on: 'Scandal of Scientists who take Money for Papers Ghostwritten by Drug Companies', Sarah Boseley, February 2002, *The Guardian*

1 Why might there be some lack of trust in the opinions of the three scientific researchers referred to in Item A?

2 What does Item B tell us about the relationship between science and business?

3 How might a close relationship between science and business influence the work of scientists?

4 What do the two extracts tell us about the claims of science to be 'value-free'?

Topic 2 Positivism and sociology

Getting you thinking

Design a survey aimed at finding how happy young people are in Britain today.

1 Write down a detailed, step-by-step plan of what you are going to do.

2 How are you going to define and measure happiness?

3 To what extent do you think the results of your survey will give you an accurate picture of the distribution of happiness?

4 What problems are involved in trying to represent concepts like 'happiness' in figures?

We saw in the previous topic that there is considerable debate between sociologists over the scientific status of sociology. However, the fact is that (in order to do their job) sociologists have to put this aside and get on with their research. Rather than splitting them into two completely irreconcilable camps, it is perhaps better to think of sociologists as being either *more sympathetic* to the use of traditional scientific methods (positivists) or *more sceptical* that this is the most useful way to proceed (interpretive sociologists). This Topic deals with the first of these two positions.

The hypothetico-deductive method

Positivists seek to follow the **hypothetico-deductive** research method: a series of steps providing what is regarded as the most scientific method of finding information.
As we saw in Topic 1, they consist of:

- background reading and personal experience
- formation of a hypothesis
- devising the appropriate form of study to isolate the key variables
- collecting the data
- analysing the data
- confirming, modifying or rejecting the hypothesis
- theory formation or confirmation.

Defining the term hypothetico-deductive

Hypothetico	Refers to an hypothesis, which Punch (1998) defines as 'a predicted answer to a research question'. An example is the fact that people routinely think that there is more violent crime than there really is. My *research question* is 'why is this?' And my *predicted answer* (or hypothesis) is that it is 'because the media focus on violent crime and exaggerate the extent of it'.
Deductive	Refers to the fact that the hypothesis is drawn from a *broader framework* of observation, possibly from an existing theory. **Deductive** refers to the process of working something out from the general to the particular.

Identify any one study you have come across in your studies that uses the approach outlined above. Explain why you think it meets these criteria.

An alternative pattern of thinking is that of **inductive reasoning**, which builds up a picture by working from the small to the large. Detectives use this form of reasoning – starting from particular 'clues' they then work up to larger conclusions. In sociology, inductive reasoning is used by those engaging in observational studies, and most forms of interpretive research.

Identify any one study you have come across in your studies that uses inductive reasoning. Explain why you think it meets these criteria.

This hypothetico-deductive model is an **ideal type** and most real research programmes are rather more complex and overlapping than this. Nevertheless, it provides the model that positivistic sociologists seek to follow.

We shall look at an example of the hypothetico-deductive model later, but for the moment, we will examine some of the key issues it raises. These are:

- model of society
- variables
- indicators
- reliability
- validity
- falsification.

Model of society

Positivists generally support a theoretical model of society that is based on the idea that there is some form of structure that exists independently of individual views, perceptions or desires – the structural model of society. This structure guides and forms our behaviour.

Give two examples from topics you have studied of how social structure may 'guide and form' our behaviour.

There are two and a half (!) theoretical approaches which are most closely linked with positivism and all of them base their

Exploring deductive and inductive reasoning

Item A

1 Why is Watson wrong about the detective work of Sherlock Holmes?

approaches on the idea of structure. Functionalism, Marxism and – the half – empiricism. Empirical approaches are not based on any explicit theory, but simply seek 'the facts'. Implicitly, they therefore assume that there is a structure and that there are facts out there waiting to be discovered. The term used by Durkheim was social facts.

This concept of 'structure' has been criticised and to some extent superseded by a range of sociological theories which dispute the idea of a structure 'out there' which constrains and controls our lives. Alternative models such as Giddens' **structuration theory** (1984), postmodernism and **symbolic interactionism** all offer alternative models which suggest that it is impossible to separate out the facts in an objective way (see Topic 3).

Variables

The purpose of research is generally to find out and explain the relationship between two or more variables, and that is what a theory does. By **variables** we mean any specified social phenomena that change in relation to each other. So when one variable changes it brings about a change in the other. The variable that causes the change is known as the **independent variable** and the one that is changed is known as the **dependent variable**. The usual outcome of research is to uncover the independent variable and then find out and explain its relationship to the dependent variable.

However, interpretive sociologists have argued that it is difficult, if not impossible, to isolate variables, in some clear way, given the complexity of society. According to them there must be many variables that we simply do not know about. This criticism echoes the debate on open and closed systems that we looked at in Topic 1 on science and sociology. For interpretive sociologists, it is simply impossible to imagine a closed system, with clear and controllable variables.

Indicators

We have just seen that positivist sociologists follow the hypothetico-deductive model which involves isolating variables and looking at the relationship between them in order to construct a theory. However, these variables may not be clear, or they may not be in a form in which they can be tested. The positivist must therefore find a way of making them clear enough so that they can be researched. This is what an 'indicator' does. Take the concept **alienation**, first used by Karl Marx in his analysis of the working class under capitalism. The idea as used by Marx is arguably rather unclear. He refers to it as a sense of having a stake in society and yet feeling oppressed by society.

Give more details of Marx's analysis of the position of the working class in capitalism.

When Blauner later decided to use the concept in a study of workers' feelings about their jobs (1964), he had to redefine it in a way that he could measure clearly. He therefore used four indicators to measure alienation. These were: the degrees of powerlessness and meaninglessness in their work, their isolation from colleagues and a sense of self-estrangement (which meant the extent that they viewed employment in terms of wages rather than job-satisfaction). Blauner claimed that all these were measurable and that he could therefore relate the extent of alienation (dependent variable) to the sort of job that people did (independent variable), with those in higher positions being less alienated.

However, interpretive sociologists argue that there are many concepts in sociology that simply cannot be measured via indicators. A good example of this is Blauner's classic study which, they argue, completely distorts Marx's original intention of making a general criticism of capitalism. In Blauner's research the concept simply becomes a measure of work satisfaction and contains no radical criticism. Using real-life indicators to measure an abstract concept that only exists in theory immediately destroys the very concept.

Reliability

One of the most favoured methods of research used by positivists is the survey, in which people are interviewed or a questionnaire is distributed, and where the results are then added-up. But there is always a problem of knowing whether in each questionnaire, or interview, the same event is taking place. Issues of personal dislike of the interviewer by the interviewee, or mutual attraction, differences caused by race, age, class or gender could intervene to a greater or lesser extent in each interview. The content of the interview may be different too – for example, one interview could be conducted in a hurry because the interviewee wants to leave soon, another could be at a leisurely pace. These factors may influence the outcome of the research, because all the results are put together under the belief that each individual component is identical. Positivists are therefore extremely keen to ensure that their work is reliable, otherwise they believe it is impossible to make a generalisation – which is the aim of their research.

Explain what is meant by 'reliability'.

However, interpretive sociologists point out that every interaction is potentially unique and the search for reliability is pointless. We can never know for certain that two interviews are the same or have the same meaning to the participants. Reliability is therefore impossible, they claim.

Validity

Validity takes us back to indicators and variables. Positivists believe that they need to use clear indicators to measure variables. But they also have to ensure that the indicators they are using truly reflect, through behaviour or expressed attitudes, the social phenomenon that they are studying. So, validity refers to the need to ensure that the indicators you use do actually (and accurately) measure what you set out to measure.

The problem faced by positivists is to discover what behaviour and which attitudes can be taken as true measures of the indicator/variable they are studying. Take, for example, Inkeles' (1993) study of the impact of **modernity** on the quality of life of different countries across the world. The problem was how to measure (a) modernity and (b) quality of life. For modernity he effectively substituted 'industrialisation' and for quality of life such things as access to health care, standard of diet and size of housing space per person. But interpretive sociologists argue that there is no 'objective' basis to prove that a measure is valid or not – to a large extent the positivists are merely relying upon their own perceptions and, possibly, biases.

Falsification

The hypothetico-deductive model used by positivists as their guide does not set out to prove a hypothesis as true, but rather to disprove the initial hypothesis. This apparently bizarre idea comes from the work of Karl Popper (1959) who argued that we can never logically prove that something is true, as we can never know what unforeseen circumstances may occur, or what mistakes we have made. However, we can certainly prove that something is *untrue* – because if we can find one exception to the rule, then the exception to the rule disproves it. Popper used the example of the black swans of Australia. For hundreds of years philosophers used as an example of a general rule the statement that 'all swans are white', until one day in Australia, they discovered black swans. We have to accept that the same could be true of any rule – that it is only true given our state of knowledge.

Most sociologists would agree with this – but interpretive sociologists say that the issue only arises because of the positivists' desire to be like a science. Since sociologists using more interpretive methods do not claim their studies hold true for all situations, the issue of falsification is not so important.

Give examples of methods favoured by interpretive sociologists.

Methods favoured by positivist sociologists

Positivists believe that there is a social world 'out there', relatively independent of individuals, that can be uncovered by testing hypotheses using rigorous research-collection techniques. They seek out valid indicators to represent the variables under study in order to study them in a reliable way.

This approach strongly favours certain methods:

1 **Quantitative approaches**
   These use surveys based upon interviewing or questionnaires.

 Explain what is meant by the term 'quantitative'.

2 **Statistical comparative methods**
   Where the sociologist is interested in a particular phenomenon they collect information from different groups or societies in the search for clear statistical patterns. If these are found and they differ in a coherent pattern from one society to another, then the sociologist searches for the relevant social differences (independent variables) that may cause the differences (dependent variables).

3 **Experiments**
   These are relatively rare in sociology because:
   - it is accepted that it is difficult to recreate normal life in the artificial setting of an experiment
   - there are often ethical problems in performing experiments on people – for example, by placing them under stress
   - the results may be influenced by the **experimenter effect**: people respond to what they perceive to be the expectations of the researchers.

However, sociologists have used a form of experiment known as the **field experiment** where researchers will disrupt normal activity in a bid to uncover the phenomenon under investigation. For example, Rosenhahn (1973) sent researchers to psychiatric institutions in the USA and asked them to act their normal ('sane') selves. They found that the staff re-interpreted the researchers' actions in such a way as to confirm the staff's belief that they were suffering from some psychiatric disorder.

Positivism in action

An interesting study that illustrates the positivist approach and combines elements of both statistical analysis and comparative analysis is the work of Need and Evans (2001) on the factors affecting secularisation (the decline in the importance of religion in society – see Unit 1, Topic 6).

Background

Sociologists in Britain have, until recently, believed that the growth in **secularisation** (that is, the decline in organised religion) was a direct result of **modernisation** with its emphasis on rationality and science. However, there has never been a way to actually prove this. But recent changes in the political structures in Eastern Europe provide the chance to study the issue as, in 1990, most communist states abandoned their version of communism and adopted democracy. Part of the new, democratic constitutions allows freedom of worship, where previously there had always been state repression of religion.

Hypotheses

If modernisation was the main reason for the decline in religion then younger people, who had not experienced communist repression at the time of first awareness of religious/moral issues, would have lower rates of religious attendance and higher levels of secularisation.

On the other hand, if repression had been a more important factor and modernisation was not the key, then older people would have lower levels of religious attendance and lower levels of secularisation. This is because, once communism fell, they would have been able to attend church again without fear.

So, Need and Evans wanted to find out which was the more important influence on secularisation: repression of the church or modernisation.

Appropriate form of study

An international comparison was undertaken, using national sample **surveys** of ten post-communist societies. The **sampling frame** were electoral registers, from which people were selected **randomly** by computer.

 Give two examples of sampling frames other than the electoral register. What are their advantages and disadvantages?

Issues of reliability and validity

The surveys were designed in collaboration with the ten countries involved. Extensive cross-comparison of questions by multi-lingual researchers took place to ensure that the questions meant exactly the same in each country. A **pilot study** of 50 100 interviews were conducted to assess the reliability and validity of questions.

 What is a pilot study?

Need and Evans: variables and indicators	
Variables	• repression/ religiosity • age/religiosity
Indicators of religiosity	• church attendance • church membership
Indicator for repression and modernisation	• age

Open/closed systems

Need and Evans recognised that they could not simply isolate their variables from wider factors. They also therefore took into account different ethnic compositions of the societies and different religious traditions. They overcame the problem by using surveys from ten countries – five countries with Orthodox traditions and five with Catholic traditions.

Data collection

The people chosen from each country were then contacted by letter and subsequently interviewed – about 2,000 in each country, with a 90% **response rate**.

Theory modification

The conclusions were not clear cut but, overall, the study found that older people were more likely to go to church and be religious than younger ones. This conclusion supported the modernisation thesis and undermined the repression hypothesis. However, it did seem that religious traditions were significant and that countries with Catholic traditions were more likely to see higher attendance by younger people. Overall, the modernisation theory was supported, although the study concluded that it does need to take into account the importance of the religious tradition of any country.

KEY TERMS

Alienation – according to Marx, a state of disillusionment and unhappiness caused by capitalism. According to Blauner, a lack of work satisfaction.

Deductive – a hypothesis is derived from a theory, then tested.

Dependent variable – a social phenomenon that changes in response to changes in another phenomenon.

Experimenter effect – unreliability of data arising as a result of people responding to what they perceive to be the expectations of the researchers.

Falsification – see Key Terms in Topic 1.

Field experiment – refers to experiments that take place in real life. Usually involves the manipulation or disruption of normal routines to see the effects.

Hypothetico-deductive model – the research process associated with the physical sciences and used by positivists in sociology.

Ideal type – a term first suggested by Weber. In real life, ideas and concepts are often rather unclear and overlap with other concepts. This can lead to confusion. An ideal type is the 'perfect' example which contains all the traits that a concept ought to exhibit. This helps distinguish and clarify the concept, even if it is rarely, if ever, found in this form.

Independent variable – the phenomenon that causes the dependent variable to change.

Indicator – a measurable social phenomenon that stands for an unmeasurable concept.

Inductive reasoning – where theories are generated by small scale study.

Interpretive sociologists – those whose approach to sociology and research emphasises understanding society by exploring the way people see society.

Modernisation/Modernity – refers to the period in history dominated by rational thought, the development of industrialisation, the classification of the physical and social worlds. Generally accepted as having started in Europe in the mid-eighteenth century and arguably began to decline in the latter part of the twentieth century.

Pilot study – a small, exploratory study to throw up any problems on issues, before the main study takes place.

Positivists – see Key Terms in Topic 1.

Random – allocated by chance.

Reliability – the need to show that each repeated questionnaire or interview is truly identical.

Response rate – the proportion of the people contacted who replied.

Sampling frame – the source or list from which the people to be questioned are selected.

Secularisation – decrease in the importance of organised religions.

Social fact – a term used by Durkheim to claim that certain objective 'facts' exist in society that are not influenced by individuals. Examples include the existence of marriage, divorce, work, etc.

Structural model of society – theories based on the idea that society has some 'structure' over and above the interactions of people.

Structuration theory – a theory of society associated with Giddens which seeks to bridge the gap between structural and interactionist approaches, by showing how they are interrelated.

Surveys – where opinions are sought by asking a cross-section of people their views.

Symbolic interactionism – a theorical approach stressing how people construct and respond to symbols in everyday life.

Validity – the need to show that what research sets out to measure really is that which it measures.

Variable – any specified social phenomenon that changes in relation to another.

1 Explain briefly in your own words the six stages of the hypothetico-deductive model.

2 What is the difference between 'deductive' and 'inductive' reasoning?

3 What model of society is positivism based upon?

4 What are 'indicators' used for in sociological research?

5 Explain the concept of 'falsification'.

6 Why is validity a problem in positivistic research?

7 Explain what an 'ideal type' is.

Research idea

Using the positivist criteria, conduct a small study utilising the knowledge you have gained from this topic to find out what changes students would like to see in your school/college.

WWWebtask

Look up the website of the polling organisation MORI (www.mori.co.uk). Look through a selection of survey results.

EXAM PRACTICE

Extract from AQA-style question

Experiments

Despite being widely used and widely respected in the natural sciences, experiments are rarely used in sociology. Some of the reasons for this are ethical, others may be practical. However some of the techniques of experiments are used in sociology and psychology, though sociologists are unable to have the complete control of variables achieved by scientists. They will always face the problem of wanting to study people in society itself rather than in the false situation of a laboratory.

a Explain why experiments are widely used and widely respected in the natural sciences. (8 marks)

b Assess the reason why experiments are rarely used in sociology. (12 marks)

Extract from OCR-style question

A leading chain of supermarkets wants to find out the relationship between social class and the purchase of different items in their stores. You have been asked, as a sociological researcher, to design a research proposal that will target a representative sample of shoppers from the various classes.

a Outline and explain the research process you would adopt in collecting quantitative data on the relationship between social class and supermarket purchases. (16 marks)

b Assess the potential weakness of your research proposal, briefly explaining how you intend to overcome it. (16 marks)

Item A

Poverty is having an **income of less than 50% of average income**.

Three main features of modern society are **industrialisation, urbanisation** and the **development of the nation-state**.

According to the Homes Act 2001, the official priority groups of homeless people are those who are '**unintentionally homeless**'.

Item C

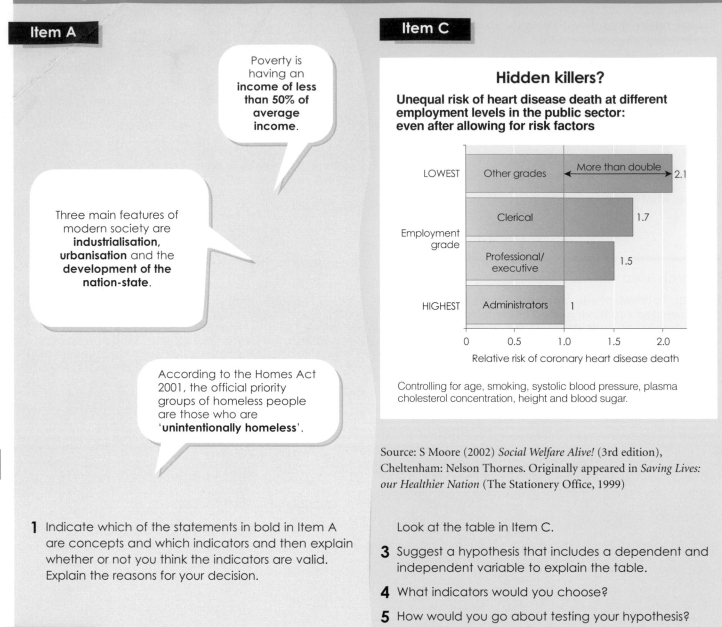

Hidden killers?

Unequal risk of heart disease death at different employment levels in the public sector: even after allowing for risk factors

Relative risk of coronary heart disease death

Controlling for age, smoking, systolic blood pressure, plasma cholesterol concentration, height and blood sugar.

Source: S Moore (2002) *Social Welfare Alive!* (3rd edition), Cheltenham: Nelson Thornes. Originally appeared in *Saving Lives: our Healthier Nation* (The Stationery Office, 1999)

1 Indicate which of the statements in bold in Item A are concepts and which indicators and then explain whether or not you think the indicators are valid. Explain the reasons for your decision.

Look at the table in Item C.

3 Suggest a hypothesis that includes a dependent and independent variable to explain the table.

4 What indicators would you choose?

5 How would you go about testing your hypothesis?

Item B

When natural scientists carry out their research in laboratories, the issue of controlling variables is of crucial importance... More specifically, experimentation usually involves manipulating one independent variable and creating change in the dependent variable...What is important of course is that all other factors are held constant (or controlled) and are not allowed to contribute to any change which might occur.

M. Moores (1998) 'Sociologists in White Coats' *Sociology Review*, Feb. Vol. 7, No. 3

2 Look at Item B. Can sociologists control 'all other factors'? Explain why this is a problem.

Getting you thinking

Ethnographers usually live in the communities they study and they establish long-term, organic relationships with the people they write about. In other words, in order to collect 'accurate data', ethnographers violate the canons of positivist research; we become intimately involved with the people we study...

... I spent hundreds of nights on the street and in crackhouses observing dealers and addicts. I regularly tape-recorded their conversations and life histories. Perhaps more important, I also visited their families, attended parties and intimate reunions ... I interviewed and in many cases befriended, the spouses, lovers, siblings, mothers, grandmothers ... of the crack dealers featured in these pages.

P. Bourgois, (1995) *In Search of Respect*, Cambridge: Cambridge University Press

1 What research method is associated with **ethnography**?

2 How do ethnographers violate the 'canons of positivist research'?

3 What insights might Bourgois have gained from his approach that would not have been possible using a different approach?

Methods in sociology reflect sociologists' theoretical assumptions. As you have seen throughout your course, the various theories start from very different beliefs about the nature of society.

Give an example of how two sociological perspectives start from 'very different beliefs about the nature of society'.

Essentially, there are two ways to start analysing society. One is to begin by looking at *society* and how it influences people. To take this starting point reflects the belief that there really is a society 'out there' that is influencing our behaviour and directs us into routine patterns of action.

A second way of starting an analysis is to begin by looking at the *individual*, and then working one's way up to the social level. In starting here, the researcher is seeing individual perceptions and ideas as the building blocks of any larger social analysis.

It would be nice if the ideas of those who start at the bottom and work up and those who start at the top and work down met 'in the middle', but, sadly, this is not so. Indeed, the different starting points lead to quite different explanations of what society is like and how it operates.

In the last Topic we looked at the methods used by those who start at the top. These positivistic methods are all based (explicitly in the case of functionalism and Marxism, and implicitly in the case of most quantitative research) on the idea that a society exists in such a way that it can be counted and gauged. In this Topic we are going to look at the methodology of those who believe that analyses ought to start at the bottom – that is, with theories that stress how people perceive the world and interact with one another. These theories include **interactionism** (and labelling theory, which is a version of it) and there is also an overlap with postmodernism. These various approaches are typically referred to as **interpretive** or **phenomenological approaches**.

 What is labelling theory? Give an example of the contribution of labelling theory to an understanding of any one area of social life.

Theory and interpretive research

Bryman, (2001) has argued that if there is one distinction to be made regarding the different aims of positivist and interpretive research, it is that while positivist research sets out to *explain* human behaviour through analysing the forces that act upon it, then interpretive sociology sets out to *understand* varieties of human behaviour by being able to empathise with it.

Weber and *verstehen*

The division can be traced back at least as far as Durkheim and Weber. As we have seen in earlier topics, Durkheim's attitude was that society could be treated as a 'thing' that existed beyond the individual and could be explored in a similar way to the physical sciences. For Weber, however, society was very different from an inanimate object. It consisted of thinking, purposeful people who acted as a result of a variety of influences which could not be understood except by looking through the eyes of the individual actors. Weber used the term '**verstehen**' (similar to the English word 'empathy') to describe the sociological process that looking through the eyes of the individuals involved. In fact, Weber defined sociology as a 'science which attempts the interpretive understanding of social action in order to arrive at causal explanations' (1947).

 Give a further example from your studies of a contribution made to understanding society by Durkheim or Weber.

Structuration theory

More recently, Giddens has argued in his **structuration theory** (1984) that there is a form of structure that exists beyond the control of individuals and which does constrain human action. However, Giddens argues that these structures only exist in so far as people make them exist. So, families exist only as long as people choose to stay within the particular set of relationships which define a family. Research, according to Giddens, must therefore understand the motivations and actions of individuals, before it can see how structures can 'exist'.

A good example of the difference between objective facts and perception of facts is Foster's (1995) ethnographic study of a housing estate (consisting mainly of blocks of flats) in East London. Objectively, the estate had a high crime-rate – at least according to official statistics. However, residents did not perceive the estate to be particularly threatening. Of particular significance was the existence of 'informal social control'. People expected a certain level of crime, but felt moderately secure because the levels were contained by informal controls and by a supportive network. Neighbours looked after each other and they believed that if any trouble should occur, they could rely upon neighbours to support them. Furthermore, because of the degree of intimacy and social interaction on the estate, most people knew who the offenders were, and felt that this knowledge allowed them some degree of protection, because they could keep an eye on the troublemakers.

Official statistics portrayed this estate as having major problems – yet ethnographic research showed that the estate actually provided a secure environment in which most people were happy.

 What are the advantages of using official statistics in sociological research?

Interpretive approaches and method

Interpretive researchers largely reject the use of quantitative methods (that is, statistical surveys and other positivist approaches) and prefer instead **qualitative** research. Qualitative research methods refer to any approach in sociology that sets out to uncover the **meaning** of social action rather than measure it through statistics.

Interpretive researchers prefer qualitative methods for the following reasons.

Meaning

As we have just noted, qualitative research allows sociologists to search for the meaning for participants of events, situations and actions in which they are involved. This reflects the belief of interpretive approaches that only by understanding how individuals build up their patterns of interaction can a full understanding of society be presented.

Context

Interpretive research usually studies small-scale groups and specific situations. This allows the researcher to preserve the individuality of each of these in their analyses, (in contrast to positivistic research which is based on large samples). Interpretive-based research provides the researcher with an understanding of the events, actions and meanings as they are influenced by specific circumstances. It is only within the contexts that action makes sense.

Unanticipated phenomena and influences

Positivistic research tends to fall into a format whereby researchers look for evidence to back up a hypothesis and then amend or reject it. In other words, positivistic researchers tend to anticipate certain outcomes – research does not start in a vacuum, but is based on a fairly clear idea of what should happen if variables react as expected. In qualitative research, the researcher does not necessarily have to have a clear idea of what they are looking for – researchers often start with an interest in a particular area and absolutely no idea of where it might lead. Without the 'blinkers' of the hypothetico-deductive model, researchers are much more open to the unexpected, and to fresh ideas.

Process

Positivistic forms of research are generally interested in outcomes (what happens if), however qualitative research is more interested in the process (what is happening). This reflects a belief by positivists that they are looking for patterns that can be generalised across society – they are not interested necessarily in the details of the actual processes that lead to the outcome. Interpretive sociologists, on the other hand, will be interested in the actual dynamics of the situation – the process. If 'bad parenting' causes crime according to positivists, then interpretivists want to explore what 'bad parenting' actually is, and the specific dynamics of family life.

Developing causal explanations

Qualitative research is largely inductive – that is, moving from specific situations and contexts to larger ones. Qualitative researchers argue that their approach is superior to positivism in that by using an inductivist model, they provide explanations that are rooted in the actual events and processes of social interaction. The deductivist positivist approach starts with a hypothesis and then imposes this framework on the research data.

An example of this is Davies' (1999) work on young people with learning disabilities. In the course of a series of qualitative interviews with these young people, Davies noticed how often the subject of 'food' was mentioned by them. At first, she did not think it had any significance and just used the topic as a way of getting chatting to them. However, over time, she began to realise just how important food was for them as a way of expressing themselves. In fact, their comments on food and eating were a way of expressing their anxieties – particularly about the way that their carers were trying to control them. It turned out that debates over food were their way of resisting control. This is a good example of inductive research – where the specific issue generated the wider concept of resistance exhibited through eating. Deductive research, which would come to the data with an already existing theoretical framework, would have missed this.

What ethical problems are involved in researching young people with learning disabilities?

Varieties of interpretive research

There are a considerable number of ways in which interpretive sociologists carry out their research, and in fact a high proportion of sociological research combines both qualitative and quantitative elements. But there are some elements that are specific to qualitative research.

Grounded theory

Grounded theory is an approach to interpretive research that was first suggested by Glaser and Strauss (1967). In this, the

authors argue that by beginning research with a clear hypothesis and then testing this, many alternatives are closed off. They claim instead that researchers should simply begin to study an area of interest, with an open mind, and then as they explore the issue, certain features emerge. By linking and categorising the recurring features of the particular social interaction, the researchers can start to build up a theoretical framework that is directly emerging from the research and that is not imposed upon it.

Grounded theory therefore challenges traditional views of finding and then researching a problem, by virtually reversing the process.

Action research

Action research has become particularly common amongst professionals dealing with social problems, such as nurses and social workers, but it also overlaps with feminist research. In action research, the researcher and the 'subject' collaborate together to define a problem or issue and then engage in research with the specific intention of solving that problem. The researcher becomes part of the research process, as a full participant.

Feminist research

Qualitative research methods have been particularly favoured by feminist writers. According to Mies (1993) quantitative research suppresses the voices of women, either by ignoring them or by submerging them in a torrent of facts and statistics. Secondly, she argues that the typical research process **disempowers** women as they simply become objects of research and have no ownership of it. This reflects their position in society. Finally, the typical tradition of value-freedom in research actually means that women are unable to get their views across. In Mies' view, feminist research should be for the benefit of women – and should specifically set out to be so.

What is meant by value-freedom? Why might the desire for value-freedom mean that women might not be able to get their views across?

According to Mies, qualitative research is much more sympathetic to feminist concerns. It allows women's voices to be heard, and their views expressed. Secondly, the research should be conducted in such a way that the researcher and participant are equal and engage in defining and conducting the research together. Feminist research should never impose categories or meanings upon women.

Participant observation/ethnography

The most common form of research reflecting interpretive ideas is 'participant observation' or ethnography. For the purposes of this book we will use the terms interchangeably. Both approaches involve the researchers immersing themselves in the lives of the people under study, generally joining in as much social activity as possible, so that they could gain an in-depth understanding of the lives of a particular group.

Ethnography does, however, have a built-in problem, in that it sets out to uncover the rules and activities and that the very best way to do this is to immerse oneself completely in the culture. Yet sociologists who do this have found that the very task they set out to do gets lost, as they are drawn ever more closely into the values, attitudes and activities of the group and so fail to notice important issues. On the other hand, the further away from the group the researcher's stance, the lesser the chance of understanding key issues.

Criticisms of research methods associated with interpretive sociology

Positivist sociologists have not been shy in criticising qualitative methods. These criticisms include the following.

Values

Positivists argue that although a value-free sociology may not be possible, there are reasonable limits to observe. Qualitative research is shot through with issues related to value bias, and it is almost impossible to untangle the personal biases of the researcher with the research 'insights' generated. The approach taken by feminists such as Mies (see above), which commits itself to a particular value approach, is seen as going beyond the acceptable limits.

Transferability

Qualitative research is often small scale and specific to a particular group. Positivists claim that it is difficult to transfer the results of research in one specific situation to others – that is, there are problems with transferability.

Generalisability

Generalisability follows from transferability. To what extent can general statements be made from highly localised and specific studies that aim to uncover the meaning of the interaction of a group in a specific situation? Interpretive approaches to sociology have generated a range of sophisticated methods that can justifiably claim to provide extremely useful insights into the nature of social action. Interpretive approaches seek, above all else, to understand how people perceive the world about them and how this influences their actions – and the consequences of these actions for both themselves and others. The nature of the questions asked by these approaches therefore leads interpretive sociologists to use qualitative methods, rather than qualitative ones. Whether qualitative approaches are 'better' or 'worse' than qualitative approaches is like asking whether in theory, structural approaches are 'better' or 'worse' than interpretive approaches. There is no simple answer, except to say that each approach asks different questions which need to be studied in different ways.

Gold's Classification of participant observer roles

Involvement ⟵――――――――⟶ Detachment

| Complete participant | Participant-as-observer | Observer-as-participant | Complete observer |

Source: R. L. Gold (1958) 'Roles in Sociological Fieldwork' *Social Forces*, 36: pp.217–23.

KEY TERMS

Action research – research in which researcher and subject define a problem and then jointly set about researching it in order to provide a solution.

Disempowers – makes powerless.

Ethnography – approach involving the researcher immersing themself in the lives of the people under study, so that they can gain an in-depth understanding of the lives of a particular group; small-scale qualitative research.

Generalisability – the extent to which general statements can be made from highly localised and specific studies.

Grounded theory – an approach to theory construction in which theory is generated during research.

Interactionism – theory associated with G. H. Mead and H. Blumer which argues that people constantly work via symbols (language, writing, and so on) to construct society through the process of social interaction.

Interpretive or phenomenological approaches – approaches such as interactionism which stress how people perceive the world and interact with one another.

Meaning – the sense people make of a particular situation.

Qualitative research – sets out to uncover the meaning of social action rather than measuring it through statistics (quantitative research).

Structuration theory – see Key Terms in Topic 2.

Transferability – the ability to transfer the results of research in one specific situation to others.

Verstehen – term first used by Weber in sociology, to suggest that the role of sociology is to understand partly by seeing through the eyes of those who are being studied. Similar to 'empathy' in English.

1 What two ways are there for starting an analysis of society? What terms do sociologists use for these approaches?

2 Explain the meaning of *verstehen*. Why is it different from Durkheim's approach to sociology?

3 Identify and explain three reasons why interpretive sociologists prefer the use of qualitative methods in research.

4 What is meant by 'grounded theory'?

5 Why do some feminist researchers prefer qualitative methods of research?

6 Why do interpretivist-based approaches have a difficulty with *generalisability*, according to positivist critics?

Research idea

Design a research strategy using positivist ideas to discover why some young people are attracted to illegal drugs and alcohol. Now, design an alternative piece of research using interpretive ideas. How is the research different? How could each piece of research be criticised?

Extract from AQA-style question

'Sociologists should always consider the meaning and interpretations that people have of the events in their lives.'

Assess the effect this belief would have on sociological research methods. (40 marks)

Extract from OCR-style question

A leading drugs charity needs to collect qualititative data to find out what smoking cannabis means to regular users of the drug. You have been asked, as a sociological researcher, to design a proposal that will target a sample of cannabis users.

a Outline and explain the research process you would adopt in collecting qualitative data from a sample of regular cannabis smokers. (16 marks)

b Assess the potential weaknesses of your research proposal, briefly explaining how you intend to overcome them. (16 marks)

WWW**ebtask**

Go to the Joseph Rowntree website at www.jrf.org.uk. Select a summary of one piece of research Why do you think the researchers used the particular methods they did?

Item A

Hobbs conducted a famous study of minor criminals and policing in East London. In this study Hobbs needed to spend large amounts of time in pubs, in the company of the criminals. Hobbs comments that 'I often had to remind myself that I was not in a pub to enjoy myself, but to conduct an academic inquiry and repeatedly woke up the following morning with an incredible hangover, facing the dilemma of whether to bring it up or write it up'.

D. Hobbs, (1988) *Doing the Business: Entrepreneurship, the Working Class and Detectives in the East End of London*, Oxford: Oxford University Press

Item B

Skeggs engaged in a 12 year, longitudinal, study of 83 white, working-class women living in the North-West of England. The research included three years' participant observation and followed the women's enrolment in a Social Care course in a local college, through their changing jobs, educational experiences and family changes. Skeggs' work set out specifically to give a voice to the women. The research demonstrated the context within which the women constructed their images of themselves. Skeggs argues that her relationship with them was not exploitative, but enabled the women's self-worth to be enhanced by 'being given the opportunity to be valued, knowledgeable and interesting'.

Adapted from B. Skeggs, (1997) *Formations of Class and Gender*, London: Sage

Item C

Kelly (1985) conducted a research project which, as a result of discussions with teachers, focused on the issue of how few girls were taking science and technology in schools. The researchers then collected the views of girls on science subjects and fed these back to the teachers. The researchers and teachers then formulated various strategies together to raise female students' interest in science and technology. The research differed from traditional research in that the researchers were fully involved and engaged in a cross-flow of information and views with the teachers on how best to resolve a problem which had emerged in discussion rather than imposed by the researchers.

A. Kelly, (1985) 'Action Research: What Is It and What Can It Do?' in R. G. Burgess (ed.) *Issues in Educational Research: Qualitative Methods*, London: Falmer Press

Item D

Orona (1997) was interested in the decision-making process that led relatives to place sufferers from Alzheimer's Disease in an institution. After interviewing many relatives, she realised that there was no real issue to be explored, as all the relatives were in a situation where the problems they were encountering were so bad that they felt they had no choice but to place the sufferers in an institution. But what emerged from her interviews/discussions was the completely unexpected concept of 'identity loss'. She discovered that all the relatives began to speak in terms of the sufferer 'before' as the real person and the individual suffering from Alzheimer's was regarded as not the same person. Orona arrived at this idea by constantly revisiting her notes of conversations and interviews and saw that the idea of 'identity loss' emerged in speech and behaviour of all the relatives.

C. J. Orona, (1997) 'Temporality and Identity Loss due to Alzheimer's Disease' in A. Strauss and J. M. Corbin (eds.) *Grounded Theory in Practice*, Thousand Oaks, California: Sage

Each of the pieces of research in Items A, B, C and D illustrates a particular style of interpretive research. Identify which of the following styles is represented by each extract and explain your reasoning.

1 Grounded theory

2 Action research

3 Feminist research

4 Participant observation/ethnography

Getting you thinking

1. Write down what you think makes someone attractive.

2. Look at the photos. Rank them in order of attractiveness.

3. Compare your results with others. Is there general agreement or disagreement?

4. Now compare what criteria you use for attractiveness?

5. Which criteria are objectively correct?

6. What does this tell us about 'attractiveness' as a concept?

7. What might this also tell you about other 'concepts' and ideas?

One of the most exciting developments in sociology over the past twenty years has been the emergence of postmodernism. In many ways this is rather strange, as apparently one of the key messages of postmodernism is that it rejects the very project of understanding society – the aim of sociology itself! However, some sociologists have enthusiastically taken on board some of its messages and have incorporated them into what they see as a consequently revitalised and radical sociology.

In this Topic we look at the impact of postmodernism on research methods and explore how, by influencing methods, postmodernism has also led sociology into studying new areas that were previously considered outside the domain of sociology.

Modernism, positivism and sociology

Modernity refers to a period of time which began around the end of the seventeenth century and which, some sociologists argue, began to wane in the latter part of the twentieth century. The term is used to refer to a period in history dominated by rational, scientific thought manifested in the search for an understanding of how the physical and social worlds function.

Give three examples of social phenomena that developed as a result of modernity.

Sociology was also a product of modernity. Writers such as Durkheim believed that the rational, scientific study of society would provide a full understanding of its 'mechanisms', and the subject was therefore born on the basis of scientific or positivistic methods. Much of sociology has continued within the framework of positivism. We have discussed these in some detail in Topics 1 and 2, but three key elements stand out in terms of method.

- Positivistic sociology claims that society exists 'out there', separate from and influencing our lives. The task of sociology is to study social facts without letting our personal, academic or political views influence us.
- The methodological tools to do this exist already in the natural sciences. By sensibly adapting them and then scrupulously applying the correct research methods, the information will be found.
- Theories can be constructed that will provide the basis for social scientific 'laws' which will be true for all societies. This knowledge will allow us to improve societies by solving a range of social problems.

Perhaps the most famous theoretical approach to society that emerged in modernity and which illustrates perfectly these elements is that of Marxism. Karl Marx claimed to have uncovered an explanation for the functioning of society, based entirely on sober, unbiased and empirical scientific research, which would allow a whole new form of society – communism – to be constructed and thereby to eliminate all social problems.

Explain how some feminists and functionalists have made similar claims.

Postmodernism and the rejection of positivism

Postmodernists such as Bauman (1990), Lyotard (1984) and Baudrillard (1998), argue that the coherent 'picture' of the social and physical worlds drawn by modernists, is no more 'true' or 'real' than the picture previously painted by the religions that dominated thought processes before modernity. Postmodernists see a fragmented, discontinuous world in which the desire for order has led people to impose a framework which ignores those things that do not fit neatly into the classifications and theories which have been constructed.

This idea of artificial structures imposed on a fragmented world has also been applied to sociology itself. Postmodernists argue that the nature of sociological theorising is rooted in this false idea of structure and order. Not only this, but the methods used by sociologists are also a reflection of the mistaken belief in an organised, structured social world out there.

The postmodern critique of sociological methods has three strands:

- **relativity**
- knowledge as control
- narrative and discourse.

Relativity

As you know, the assumption underlying positivism, is that there is an objective, world 'out there' waiting to be uncovered by research. Postmodernists dispute this. They see, instead, many different, competing 'worlds' that exist only in particular contexts and at particular times. There is, quite simply, no objective reality waiting to be discovered. The objective, scientific analysis based upon a scrupulous following of the rules does not produce knowledge about the world – it simply produces another relative version of society.

What is meant by 'objectivity'?

Knowledge as control

Scientists and other professionals and academics are not objective intellectuals engaged in a struggle to find the truth. According to Foucault (1963/1975), they, like any other group in society, are engaged in a struggle to have their concept of knowledge (as opposed to other, competing ones) accepted as reality. The reason for engaging in this struggle is that whoever has control over what is regarded as knowledge, and how to obtain it, gains considerable power in society. Scientists and professionals are therefore not disinterested and objective, but key players in a power struggle. A particularly good example of this can be found in medical knowledge. Despite the fact that about 20% of people in hospital actually contract another illness or are medically harmed in some way by the very 'healing process', doctors have gained control over the task of healing and of defining what is or is not a healthy body. Other ways of dealing with health have been labelled as 'complementary medicine' or 'alternative therapies', and denied equal status on the grounds that they are not scientifically rigorous.

Narrative and discourse

We have seen that sociologists are yet another group seeking to impose their form of knowledge on society and that they do so by claiming expert knowledge based on sociology as a form of science.

The outcome of sociological research is the production of explanations or theories that explain social phenomena. Postmodernists call these explanations 'narratives'. The implication is that they are no more than stories, giving a partial account.

Where sociologists have provided large-scale 'grand-theory', which claims to provide a full and complete explanation for human behaviour, the term used by postmodernists is **meta-narrative**. The reason for the dismissal of these theories is that, as we explained before, there is no world out there waiting to be explained. All explanation is partial and grounded in the context of people's lives and experiences.

Give examples of two sociological perspectives which could be seen as 'meta-narratives'. Explain your answers.

Linked to narrative is the concept of discourse. Discourse can be seen as the framework of language within which discussions about issues occur. Discourse therefore limits and locates discussion.

Postmodernist research

Postmodernism has also been a positive force in three main ways relevant to research.

- It has introduced new methods and approaches to research.
- It has introduced different topics to study.
- It has encouraged people to speak for themselves, thereby allowing their narratives to stand without necessarily interpreting them.

Deconstruction: a new method

Postmodernism argues that all knowledge is relative and that some knowledge is more powerful than others. So, postmodernist writers such as Baudrillard (1998) argue that these 'narratives' about what we consider to be knowledge crucially affect how we act. But they do not influence us in the way that Marxists or functionalists would argue, rather they interact with people to create new and fragmentary patterns of thought and behaviour which alter according to place, time, and an unknowable range of other factors. The task of postmodernists is to try to uncover the linkages and possible patterns that underly these narratives.

Foucault suggests this process of **deconstruction** is like the activities of an archaeologist in that the sociologist carefully digs down layer after layer to explore the construction of narratives. The postmodern researcher is, however, not concerned to give the 'truth' but to look instead at how particular narratives emerge at different times and in different

contexts. Furthermore, they are not seeking to make claims for anything beyond the particular area studied.

One particular area to which deconstruction is applied is the subject of sociology itself, so traditional concepts are taken apart and looked at in new ways.

Transgression: new areas of study

The second innovation that postmodernism brought to research was that of topic areas. Traditionally sociologists have divided the subject matter of society into various categories and classifications – so we study religion, work, social divisions, crime, and so on. If there is no world out there, and if sociology is just one narrative amongst many others (with no claim of superiority) then we also need to look critically at the sociological enterprise itself. Why do we have these divisions? They don't actually exist and we don't divide ourselves into separate chapters as we live our lives!

Postmodernists suggest that we should **transgress** classification boundaries and think in new ways. Take criminology, for example. Traditionally this studies people who commit crime. But the category 'crime' covers a massive range of actions which sociologically have little in common. Crimes are just what some people manage to have made declared illegal, no more, no less. A different way of looking at the area is to study why people do harm to others – irrespective of what form that takes. Immediately, torture by the state, low wages, child labour and a million other forms of harmful activity enter the area of study – thus transgressing traditional boundaries.

Why might these 'new' areas not be included in conventional approaches to crime and deviance?

Furthermore, if all areas of knowledge are equally relative, then how do we know what is more important or relevant than anything else? This has liberated sociologists to study issues such as the body, sexuality, eating, and time – all areas which traditionally have been seen as marginal to sociology.

Examples of postmodern research

The first thing to say is that, in terms of traditional ideas of research, there are not that many clear examples of postmodern research. Rather, postmodern ideas have percolated throughout sociology, enriching the subject by, on the one hand, providing us with a new way of looking at traditional problems, and, on the other, by giving us new subjects to explore.

Reanalysing sociological concepts

Foucault and knowledge

In *The Birth of the Clinic*, Foucault reanalyses texts that describe the emergence of the medical profession. Instead of accepting their ideas, he uses them to illustrate the way that new forms of thinking emerged with the development of medicine. The new forms of thinking or discourses then moved out into the wider society as the predominant way of thinking. As this scientific, rational thought came to dominate, it also ensured the importance of doctors and other professionals. Foucault's analysis challenged the traditional functionalist, Weberian and Marxist ideas of power and knowledge. Postmodernist research can thus involve a critical deconstruction of existing sociological concepts.

 Explain the traditional functionalist or Marxist view of 'power and knowledge'.

Youth culture

The study of youth culture has been dominated by critical sociologists who have seen it as a form of resistance by young people. The search by these sociologists has been to find the meaning of youth culture and to explain what is the significance of the clothes and music.

Postmodernists, such as Redhead (1993) have challenged this view and argued that youth culture has 'no meaning' as such but is simply a complex and ever-changing mixture of influences – ranging from resistance, through constructions of what looking-good means, to the manipulation of media companies, overlaid with genuine innovation. According to Redhead, to seek the meaning of it all is completely mistaken. Redhead uses secondary data in his work but also uses the writing of young sociology students, drawing upon their current experiences of clubbing.

How representative of young people is Redhead's sample likely to be?

New areas of study

Tourism

Urry (1990) has examined tourist attractions and argued that certain places have been constructed so that they are seen and experienced as places of leisure and tourism – rather than for any other characteristics. When people visit, they do so through a 'tourist gaze'. This tourist gaze may screen out certain unwanted characteristics and focus solely on the socially constructed tourist image. The Lake District becomes more than a mountainous (and rainy!) place, and instead becomes a place of tranquillity, poetry and beauty. Walkers go there not just to walk, but to experience these additional elements. Spain becomes a place for clubbing, sunshine and beaches, or possibly a retirement dream, rather than a modern, industrialised country with a full range of social problems.

Food

Baudrillard (1998) has looked at the idea of food, arguing that in affluent Western societies most people do not eat to satisfy hunger, rather eating carries with it numerous symbols. We are almost literally what we consume. In a world where the fixed structures of class, sexual identity and ethnicity have been challenged and become more fluid, consumption then becomes one way of defining who we are. Where we eat and what we eat makes statements about us, in much the same way as our clothes do. For example, eating small amounts of food, in fashionable, expensive restaurants clearly indicates our success and aspirations.

KEY TERMS

Deconstruction – the breaking down of a taken-for-granted subject to uncover the assumptions within it.

Discourse – the linguistic framework within which discussion takes place.

Gaze – a postmodern concept which refers to a particular way of seeing an issue, people or place.

Meta-narrative – a large-scale theory which purports to be generalisable across societies.

Modernity – a period in history with specific ways of thinking largely based on rational, scientific thought applied to both the physical and social worlds.

Narrative – an accepted explanation or theory for some occurrence.

Postmodernists – see Key Terms in Topic 1.

Relativity – the idea that there is no fixed truth 'out there' waiting to be found. All knowledge is relative to a particular situation.

Transgress – to cross accepted academic boundaries.

CHECK YOUR UNDERSTANDING

1 Give two examples of meta-narratives in sociology.

2 Why does the postmodernist stress on the relativity of knowledge imply criticism of positivism?

3 Explain in your own words what is meant by 'discourse'. Give an example.

4 How do postmodernists view experts and professionals?

5 What do postmodernists do when they deconstruct a concept or theory?

6 Give one example of:
   a a traditional subject looked at in a new way by postmodernists, and
   b a new subject brought into the domain of sociology by postmodernists.

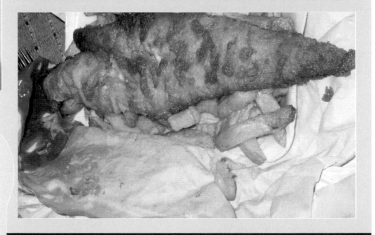

Baudrillard argues that eating in Western societies makes statements about us and helps create our identities. Explain how this may be the case in each of the situations above.

Research idea

Redhead (see 'Youth Culture' earlier in Topic) used the writing of sociology students to uncover their feelings and emotions about clubbing. Get a small sample of students who have experience of clubbing to do the same. What can you learn from their written accounts? What do you think are the advantages and disadvantages of this approach to research?

EXAM PRACTICE

Extract from AQA style question

'Postmodernism is less concerned with researching reality than in declaring that reality is dead.'

Evaluate the influence of postmodernism on sociological research. (40 marks)

WWWebtask

Search the web for tourist information about a particular place. What impression of the place do they create? To what extent do the images and information about the places reflect Urry's idea of the 'tourist gaze'?

Getting you thinking

By now, you will have been studying sociology for some time. Perhaps it is time to reflect on what it means to you, if anything!

Rave

Palestinian youths throwing stones at Israeli soldiers

Burglary

This is a quote from a well-known sociologist explaining why he likes sociology.

> *For me, the attraction and promise of sociology has always been its capacity for illuminating aspects of our lives which we rarely stop to examine for ourselves. Personal experiences can be reinterpreted and our understanding of them enriched, by siting them in a broader social context which makes sense of why we do certain things, how other things happen to us and what the unforeseen consequences of our actions are likely to have been.*

P. Saunders (1990) *A Nation of Home Owners*, London: Unwin Hyman

A classroom

1 In your own words, explain what you think Saunders means.

2 Take any one situation from the photos above. How can your studies in sociology provide you with insights into what is happening?

3 Take another situation you have personally experienced. How can your studies in sociology provide you with insights into this and other aspects of your own life?

In this topic we try to bring together a number of the issues concerning sociological methods. If the aim of research is to generate an understanding of the social world around us, then it is the duty of researchers to ensure that what they say is as accurate as possible. Few sociologists claim they are telling 'the truth', what they do claim is that they have done the very best they can to be accurate and honest.

We have selected four examples of research to illustrate key problems in studying society.

Bias in research: *A Nation of Homeowners*, P. Saunders

Values

Saunders is very happy to admit the reasons for writing his book (1990) were partly political, partly sociological and partly personal.

- They were personal in that he was interested in the way that home ownership had altered his parents' lives, in terms of the 'wealth' they had accumulated simply by purchasing their own home rather than renting. As prices rose they soon outstripped the **mortgage** which his parents had on their house. This was a typical experience for a whole generation of people from the 1950s onward.
- Politically, Saunders is one of the few '**libertarian**' sociologists who is not sympathetic to sociology's leanings towards feminism and 'left-wing' ideas. In fact, he argues that sociologists have become out of touch with the experiences of ordinary people.

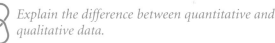
What is meant by left wing? Identify one view you have come across during your course that is not left wing. Explain your answer.

- The sociological reasons were that he was interested in the consequences for British society of the growth of home ownership. Saunders wanted to challenge the general sociological orthodoxy that home purchase had harmed society.

The methodology

Secondary sources
Saunders used a wide variety of secondary sources, including official statistics and the work of other sociologists – most of whom he disagreed with.

Sample survey
The main research method was to use household **surveys** of 500 people in three towns – Burnley, Derby and Slough. Saunders chose these towns because they represented a cross-section of towns in Britain (Burnley – declining industrial; Derby – successful industrial; Slough – prosperous new industries). They also included a high proportion of ethnic minorities.

Sampling
The sample consisted of 522 individuals living in 450 households. **Clusters** of roads were selected according to a quota of different specific forms of housing and then households were selected randomly from within these roads.

Quantitative and qualitative information
Letters were sent to the households explaining the research, and respondents were then interviewed by Saunders and his researchers. The interviews used a questionnaire comprising a mixture of open and closed questions. The information obtained was therefore both quantitative and qualitative.

Explain the difference between quantitative and qualitative data.

Findings
Saunders found that over 90% of respondents expressed a preference to buy a home over renting one. The financial incentive and the desire for a home of one's own were the major reasons given for this. Those living in council houses could see no advantage in renting and expressed considerable degrees of dissatisfaction. Overall, Saunders disagreed with the argument that a division existed between public and private owners. However, he did identify a new underclass consisting of those living in the worst housing in the most disadvantaged estates.

Avoiding bias
The researchers working with Saunders all had different viewpoints on the social significance of housing. According to Saunders these differences in opinions prevented one particular value position being taken.

Saunders is open about his political beliefs that home ownership is good for society. However, on a number of occasions (according to Devine and Heath (1999)), his claims about the benefits of home ownership are not actually borne out by the research findings.

Surveying sensitive issues: *Sexual Behaviour in Britain*, K. Wellings et al.

The research here was concerned with the rather delicate and private area of our lives concerning sexual activity. There are real problems concerning **validity** here – that is, can the research truly measure the types and extent of sexual practices of the British population?

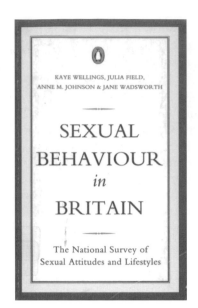

The researchers were well aware that there might be some degree of embarrassment in relation to this reference, and that people might not be too keen to disclose very personal information to researchers they did not know. They were also concerned over the language used. What sort of words would people feel were appropriate – clinical language or commonly used slang? Would it be better to let people complete questionnaires by themselves or should they be interviewed? Would respondents be convinced that their answers really were going to be confidential?

The researchers decided to carry out a small pilot survey consisting of interviews to find out just how much information people were prepared to give before they felt that things got too personal, and to check on the most appropriate form of language to use. As a result, Wellings *et al.* (1994) decided to use the following format.

- The research was to be conducted face-to-face, rather than by telephone. This would allow the researchers to put people at their ease.
- A combination of self-completed questionnaire and interview was chosen. The interview dealt with less personal issues such as family background, early sexual experiences and sex education.
- The self-completed questionnaire asked about more private issues including visits to prostitutes and details of sexual activity. The interviewers used 'cards' for some of the questions. These cards listed the possible answers and the respondent could indicate the number or letter rather than saying the words – the idea here was to save embarrassment.

What are the advantages of self-completion questionnaires, other than avoiding embarrassment?

- The form of language used was a matter of considerable debate, but in the end, the researchers used more formal language – 'sexual intercourse' rather than 'making love' (or more potentially offensive terms). However, they still had problems over this, as sexual intercourse was interpreted in a variety of ways by respondents.

Politics and the issue of sexuality

Although the researchers used the neutral term 'sexual partner' to refer to the person(s) that the respondents were engaging in sexual acts with – there was considerable criticism that the study underestimated the extent of same-sex sexual activity as a result of inadequate methods and inaccurate reading of the findings. The survey suggested that about 1% of men and about 0.3% of women engaged in 'sexual experiences' which were 'mostly or only homosexual', and that 5.2% of men and 2.6% of women had at least one experience of homosexual activity. Many pro-gay campaigners felt that this grossly undercounted the numbers of same-sex sexually active people. Tatchell, a well-known gay campaigner, for example, argued that the true figure of homosexuality is 10% of the male population (see Lawrence 1994).

Why might people be less likely to admit to gay sex than heterosexual sex?

This might just appear to be a debate about the accuracy of the research, but there is a lot more to it than first appears. For Tatchell and other pro-gay campaigners, the greater the number of gays in the population, the more they could justifiably claim support for legal changes, on the one hand, and on the other, the greater their argument against those who claim that homosexuality is 'abnormal' . The research findings therefore ran unintentionally into a debate about equal rights, and was seen by some as providing ammunition for those who did not wish to give equal rights to gays and lesbians.

Triangulation: *Negotiating Family Responsibilities*, J. Finch & J. Mason

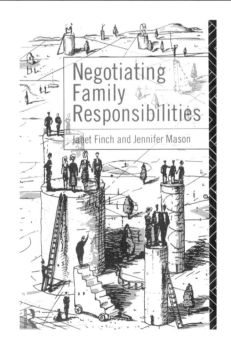

Finch and Mason's study (1993) wanted to move away from traditional areas of family studies and so set out to explore two related but distinct issues.

- What British people thought that the family *ought* to do for its members.

- What family members actually *do* for each other, in reality.

The aim, then, was to find out if publicly expressed beliefs about family responsibilities were actually carried out in real life.

Different methods were used to find out different types of information.

The research

In order to find out about public attitudes, Finch and Mason conducted structured interviews with a random sample of 978 adults. To find out about what people did in practice, they carried out qualitative semi-structured interviews with 88 people (though because they interviewed some people more than once, there were actually 120 interviews).

Questionnaires
In order to find out what attitudes were towards family responsibilities, Finch and Mason used 'vignettes', that is, short, hypothetical situations which the respondents were asked to give their opinion on. For example:

'If an elderly person, who has become very frail, and can only move around with help, can no longer live alone, should she or he move into an old people's home or go and live with relatives?'

The advantage of the vignette model is that the question asked is distanced from the respondent, so that they do not feel they are being quizzed on their own behaviour – which might lead them to be defensive or to give the answer they thought the interviewer expected.

What emerged from the research was that there was a considerable variety of responses. But overall, people tended to think that:

- family members should be helped only if they deserved it, not automatically because they were family members
- that help should be given when it was not too onerous
- that children/parents had special responsibilities to each other.

Why should children and parents have 'special responsibilities' towards each other?

Interviews
The next stage of the research consisted of the qualitative interviews. Here interviewers found that there were many complex and unquantifiable rules regarding when it was right or when it was unjustified to expect help from another family member.

Three themes emerged:

- *Reciprocity*: if one family member helped another, then they could expect help back.
- *Legitimate excuses*: if assistance was refused, the person failing to give the assistance needed to have an acceptable reason – otherwise their failure to help was regarded as unfair.
- *Moral reputation*: people were very aware of what others thought about them in giving or refusing help.

Triangulation

Finch and Mason's work is a good example of a technique known as **triangulation**. In this, more than one method of research is used both to generate different data, and to provide different approaches to similar information. Using different methods also provides a check on the validity of the other approach's results. Triangulation or multi-method approaches provide a range of data that one particular approach could never manage to uncover.

What are the similarities and differences between structured and unstructured interviews?

The result of using two different methods of analysis, in this survey, was that contradictions emerged in the research. They found that most people believed that after separation, a couple's in-laws ought to maintain a reasonable relationship with their daughter-in-law or son-in-law, particularly if there are children involved. However, in the interviews, this was rarely found in practice.

Grounded theory

Rather than Finch and Mason viewing this as contradiction, they saw it as a chance to generate a theory about how relationships with the wider family were maintained or curtailed after the break-up of the relationship. This idea of generating theory in the middle of research is known as **analytic induction** and is closely linked to the writings of Glaser and Strauss on **grounded theory** (see Topic 3).

Theoretical sampling

In order to generate theory, according to the rules of grounded theory, Finch and Mason needed to delve deeper into this 'contradiction' and so they used a technique known as **theoretical sampling**, which consists basically of seeking out a situation that is most likely to deliver a theoretical breakthrough – in this case it was of a family where good relationships were maintained after separation. What they found was that a good relationship between married partners and in-laws needed to exist before the breakdown, and also that there was not a strong issue of 'divided loyalties' constraining the in-laws.

Give examples of two other types of sampling. What are their advantages and disadvantages?

Ethnography and values: *Doing the Business*, D. Hobbs

In his book (1988) Hobbs studied the local CID and the petty criminals whom they were policing. However, the book is primarily concerned with the way that these both exist within a specific East London, working-class culture. Hobbs argues that East London culture is characterised by a spirit of **entrepreneurship**, with locals 'getting by' through numerous scams and marginally legal activities. It is within this cultural background that the CID officers and the petty criminals need to be understood.

DOING THE
BUSINESS

Entrepreneurship, The Working Class,
and Detectives in the East End of London

DICK HOBBS

The petty criminals are sometimes successful, sometimes not – but they all share a willingness to get an income from outside the traditional employment route, opting instead for whatever opportunities might arise. The entrepreneurial culture also affects the CID, according to Hobbs – who claims that they barter information from criminals for turning a blind eye to some scams and they search endlessly for 'a good result' (a successful arrest – particularly of an important 'villain').

Access

Hobbs' work was based on detailed ethnographic study, which was helped by the fact that he came from the East End of London, was a male and enjoyed going to pubs. These attributes allowed him to fit into the culture of both detectives and petty criminals.

Explain how the fact that Hobbs was male may have helped his research.

However, these attributes were not enough to actually get him inside the police and in contact with petty criminals. The breakthrough, as far as the CID were concerned occurred through his involvement as a coach of a local youth football team. One of the youths playing was the son of a local CID officer and so this gained him his trust and the CID officer, 'Simon', effectively became his **key informant**, introducing him to his circle of colleagues and regular pubgoers. His entry to the petty criminals was through his friends and family. Over the time of his study, new contacts were made through drinking in pubs and other social activities.

Why are key informants often so important to participant observers?

Whose side are we on?

Hobbs' ethnographic style was not to approach the study of the CID through the police service, but to try to understand the officers through informal, friendly relations. This is important as their view of him was as 'one of them', rather than an official researcher. This enabled him to get very close to the officers and to see the world through their eyes. However, it also led him to identify very strongly with them, as opposed to the uniformed branch of the police and also to the bureaucratic structures of the police. Despite this, Hobbs was also on the side of the petty criminals, and saw both sides of the law as sharing a common culture, which he liked and respected. He argues throughout the book that he is on the side of the East End working-class as a whole, and this included both petty criminals and the CID.

This leaves Hobbs open to criticisms of bias – he identifies and describes police corruption and malpractice but regards this as simply evidence of the entrepreneurial spirit of East London. This was particularly important because at the time of writing, the Metropolitan Police were doing their best to stamp out corruption, which had led to a number of cases of innocent people being sent to prison. Hobbs actually criticises the Metropolitan Police for doing this, closely reflecting the views of the CID officers he studied.

Hobbs' research is an interesting illustration of how difficult it is to put into practice Howard Becker's (1967) famous advice for sociologists – that they should be on the side of the 'underdog' (see Topic 6) in their research, and act as a mouthpiece for them. Hobbs clearly feels that both the CID officers and the petty criminals were the underdogs, equally deserving of his support. However, little sympathy (and few words) were spent on discussing the victims of crime or miscarriages of justice. Furthermore, in this case the more powerful group (the Metropolitan Police) which Becker advised us to be against, was actually engaged in an activity that most people would support – in this case stamping out corruption amongst CID officers.

Involvement and morality

Hobbs' ethnographic research into illegal activities meant that he was drawn into areas of illegal activity and he held information on crime that might have been useful to the police. However, he decided that if he was to do his research then he had to become involved in most of these practices where necessary. Although Hobbs treats all this rather lightly, there are nonetheless moral issues involved when a researcher has knowledge of illegal activities – especially when they may have harmful consequences for some people. The only ethical line that Hobbs did draw (and made quite clear to those he encountered) was that of racism, and he would actively object to racist speech or actions. Because of the extent of racism, however, he did acknowledge that the objections threw up a barrier in some areas to obtaining information.

To what extent do you think Hobbs is justified in ignoring corruption and crime but objecting to racism?

Validity

As with much ethnographic research, there is no way in which we can ever know how accurate a description and analysis of East London Hobbs' work provides us with. Much of the research was conducted in pubs and consisted of drinking sessions written up the following day. Hobbs himself comments a number of times on the extent of his drinking and we can never know how this might have impacted upon his recollections or ability to remember events accurately.

Not all of Hobbs' work was in pubs, however; he did also conduct formal interviews with senior CID officers, and spent considerable time in other non-alcoholic settings with detectives (such as the court canteen). However, he never observed police officers at work. We cannot, therefore, be sure that the informal discussions with the police actually reflected what they did at work.

Hobbs' research brings to life the activities of the CID and the petty criminals he studied. It is typical of most ethnographic research in that, in the end, any insights or understanding emerge through the viewpoint and experiences of one person. We can never know if these are accurate or if they apply to other, apparently similar, situations.

KEY TERMS

Analytic induction – refers to a research approach where theories are generated *during* the research.

Clusters – in surveys it is too difficult/expensive to spread out the sample across the country, so sampling is done in geographical 'clusters' – for example in a few streets.

Entrepreneurship – the ability to innovate and create new business opportunities.

Grounded theory – see Key Terms in Topic 3.

Key informant – key member of group being studied that the participant observer befriends.

Libertarian – a description used by some sociologists to suggest that they are not conservative nor politically left-wing. They tend to believe in individual freedom as being most important.

Mortgage – loan taken out to buy a house.

Qualitative – see Key Terms in Topic 3.

Quantitative – see Key Terms in Topic 3.

Representativeness – refers to how representative of the overall population the sample is.

Sample – the cross-section of people chosen in research to represent the views of the majority.

Surveys – where opinions are sought by asking a cross-section of people their views.

Theoretical sampling – a form of sampling which takes place during the research process where people are chosen on the basis that studying them, in particular, would be useful for generating theory.

Triangulation – where more than one method of research is used in order to provide a balanced picture.

Validity – see Key Terms in Topic 2.

Vignette – a small story used to stimulate a response.

CHECK YOUR UNDERSTANDING

1 **Give an example of how political sympathies affect choice of research topic?**

2 **Why is the choice of language so important when researching sensitive issues?**

3 **Give two examples of the problem of validity.**

4 **Explain in your own words what sociologists mean by 'triangulation'.**

5 **How might the funding of a research project have an important impact upon it?**

6 **Explain why it might be difficult to decide who the 'underdog' is in Hobbs' research.**

7 **Give an example from the text of moral problems that researchers might have to face.**

EXAM PRACTICE

Extract from AQA-style question

Assess the usefulness of questionnaires in researching sensitive areas of social life. (40 marks)

Extract from OCR-style question

Finch and Mason's research examines family obligations – the sense that one is obliged to provide help and assistance to family members. They conducted a large-scale survey and in-depth qualitative interviews. The survey was intended to discover people's beliefs about their relationships with their family, not the actual patterns of these relationships. The subject of the qualitative study was the actual behaviour in families: 88 people from 11 families were interviewed, some more than once. The interviews provided a fuller account of negotiations within families from the perspectives of more than one member. Respondents were asked to talk about relationships within their own families, concentrating on examples of support and assistance and their sense of responsibility to relatives.

Adapted from N. Abercrombie and A. Warde (1994) *Family, Household and the Life-course*, Lancaster: Framework Press

Identify and explain two strength of combining quantitative and qualitative methods when studying family obligations. (8 marks)

Item A

...I was willing to skirt the boundaries of criminality on several occasions, and I considered it crucial to be willingly involved in 'normal' business transactions, legal or otherwise. I was pursuing an interactive, inductive study of an entrepreneurial culture, and in order to do so I had to display entrepreneurial skills myself.

D. Hobbs, (1988) *Doing the Business: Entrepreneurship, the Working Class and Detectives in the East End of London*, Oxford: Oxford University Press

1 Looking at Item A, explain what the term *inductive* study means. What method of research normally uses this?

2 What alternative way of theorising is there?

3 What approach is the researcher taking to illegal activities in his research?

4 What differing views do sociologists take to the relationship between values and research?

Item B

The sampling was carried out in the Greater Manchester area among a representative random sample of adults aged 18 and over. The response rate among those who were eligible for interview was 72%. Sampling was executed using a two-stage, stratified, cluster sampling technique. Forty-five electoral wards in the Greater Manchester region were selected from a list... using a random start number and a fixed interval (between them). Within each ward, thirty-five addresses were selected...

J. Finch and J. Mason, (1993) *Negotiating Family Responsibilities*, London: Routledge, (Appendix A)

5 Sociological research is often divided into positivist and interpretivist research. Where would you locate the research project described in Item B? Explain the reasons for your decision.

6 What do we mean by stratified, cluster sampling? What problems are there with stratified sampling? What alternative approach is there?

Item C

Researching this subject [serious crime] is of course both practically and ethically difficult, just like real life. Yet numerous writers have succeeded in engaging with deviant populations through some variant upon ethnographer-participant observation...However, a detailed analysis of the utility of these research tools as part of a study of professional crime will not be a feature of this book. Such analyses have a habit of lapsing into apologetic justifications of a technique that, no matter what is written, will be criticised by those of alternative methodological and theoretical dispositions.

D. Hobbs, (1995) *Bad Business*, Oxford: Oxford University Press

7 The writer of Item C is wittily refusing to discuss his research techniques. Why do most sociologists regard it as very important to engage in a detailed discussion?

Research idea

Use triangulation to try to find out the difference between people's attitudes and behaviour. You could combine questionnaires (to find out attitudes) and observation or unstructured interviews (to find out behaviour). One example could be a comparison of educational and career ambitions with the amount of work actually done outside school or college. Another could be males' attitudes to females, compared with their actual behaviour.

WWW Webtask

Go to the website of the Joseph Rowntree Foundation (www.jrf.org.uk). Look up summaries of research that may have raised key issues in research such as the role of values, personal or political bias, researching sensitive issues, triangulation and ethical issues. How have the researchers dealt with these issues? How successful have they been?

Item D

Research methods are important, but sociology still requires the researcher to maintain a clear perspective on what is happening around them, and the context of their research.

8 Suggest reasons why sociologists have to be aware of wider political and social events.

Getting you thinking

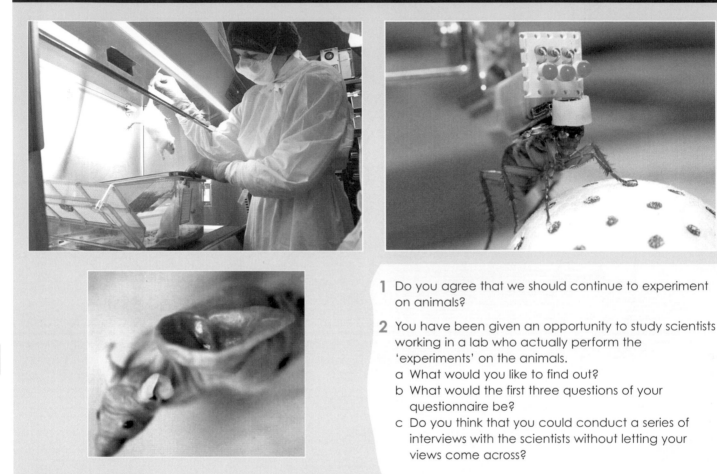

1 Do you agree that we should continue to experiment on animals?

2 You have been given an opportunity to study scientists working in a lab who actually perform the 'experiments' on the animals.
  a What would you like to find out?
  b What would the first three questions of your questionnaire be?
  c Do you think that you could conduct a series of interviews with the scientists without letting your views come across?

One of the most bitterly contested concepts in sociology has been over the question of the place of personal and political values in theory and research. Three distinct positions can be identified on this issue.

1 On one end of the debate are those sociologists who argue that if sociology wants to make any claim to scientific status then it has to be free of personal and political biases. This is known as **value-freedom** or **objectivity**.

2 A second position is that ideally our personal values should not intrude into our sociological studies, but that in practice it is simply impossible to keep them out – sociology as value-laden.

3 At the other extreme from value-freedom are those who argue that anyone doing sociology must surely use their studies to improve the condition of those most oppressed in society. Sociology is therefore more of a tool that helps bring about social change than just an academic subject studying society – committed sociology.

From any previous topic you have studied, give one example of a situation where it has been claimed that values have influenced sociological ideas.

Value-free sociology

As we see in Topics 1 and 2, there is a significant current of opinion in sociology (deriving from Emile Durkheim) that argues that we should seek to copy the methodology of the physical sciences such as biology or chemistry. One of the key ideas that these sociologists, or **positivists**, have taken from the physical sciences is that of the importance of objectivity in research.

Positivists argue that the nature of sociological research is no different from that of the physical sciences – both branches of science (the physical and the social) study a series of phenomena, that exist totally independently of the scientists, and which can be measured and classified. On the basis of this, theories can be constructed and tested.

From any previous topic you have studied, give one example of a theory and suggest ways in which it might be tested.

The 'social facts' positivists refer to are the statistics obtained by surveys and possibly from official publications. Properly constructed, these should be a perfect reflection of the subject under study. The evidence to show that surveys are objective and accurate exists in the accuracy of opinion polls on a range of subjects including voting and general elections; market research; extent of drug use and even sexual behaviour. According to O'Connell Davidson and Layder (1994), personal biases and political opinions of researchers are irrelevant as long as the research is well designed and there is no attempt to distort or alter the findings. Finally, to ensure that no biases have inadvertently intruded, there is the check coming from publication of the research findings which will include a discussion of methods used. The publication will be read and possibly criticised by other researchers.

Sociology as value-laden

This second school of thought believe that whether it is desirable or not, sociology cannot be value-free and it is a mistake to see it as such. They further claim that sociologists arguing that sociology *is* value-free are actually doing a disservice to the subject and identify a number of issues as evidence in support of their position.

Historical context

Gouldner (1968) has pointed out the argument for a value-free sociology is partially based in a particular historical context. Weber has traditionally been associated with the idea that personal and political values should be excluded from research. Yet Gouldner claims that Weber was writing at a time when the Prussian (now German) government was making a strong attack on intellectual freedom. According to Gouldner, Weber was merely trying to prevent the government from interfering in sociology by claiming it was value-free. So, Weber was simply protecting sociology by this strategy.

Give one example of a situation where it has been claimed that a government has influenced social research.

Paying for research

Sociological research has to be financed and those who pay for the research usually have a reason why they want it done. Sociologists working for British government departments for instance, usually have to sign an agreement that if the department does not like the ideas or findings, then it has the right to prevent publication.

In *Market Killing*, Philo and Miller (2000) have argued that, increasingly, all sciences are having their critical researchers silenced through a combination of targeted funding by those who only want research undertaken into the topics of benefit to them and by the intrusion of commercial consultancies into research. This means that scientists benefit financially from certain outcomes and lose out if other outcomes are uncovered. They also point out that scientists allow their findings to be manipulated by public relations companies, operating for the benefit of the funders – even when the findings do not necessarily support the funder's claims.

Career trajectories

All sociologists have personal ambitions and career goals. They want to publish, get promoted, become renowned in their field. These desires can intrude either knowingly or subconsciously into their research activities.

Personal beliefs and interests

Sociologists are no different from other people, in that they hold a set of values and moral beliefs. They might set out to eliminate these as best they can, but, ultimately, all our thoughts and actions are based on a particular set of values and it is impossible to escape from these. The best that can be done is to attempt to make these values clear to both ourselves and to the readers of the research.

Similarly, sociologists find certain areas of study 'interesting'. Why are they drawn to these areas in the first place? The answer is that often they reflect personal issues and a desire to explore something important to them. This makes it more difficult to extricate personal values from the research process itself. An example of this is the work of Ken Plummer, who has published widely on sexual issues. In an interview in *Sociology Review*, he makes it plain that his own sexual preference encouraged him to become interested in gay issues:

So, in a sense, I was actually exploring my own life side by side with exploring sociological theory. And I suppose that has shaped the way I think about these things today.

Source: Sociology Review, 9 (4), April 2000

Give a further example of how a sociologist's personal interests have led them to study a particular issue.

The domain of sociology

Sociology does have academic status and has been accepted today as a 'social science'. As a subject it has developed a range of accepted ways of exploring the world, of sensible questions to be asked and reasonable research methods. It has joined other subjects in rejecting other non-orthodox approaches that claim to provide knowledge. For example, Collins and Pinch (1998) studied parapsychology and found that other social scientists believed that parapsychology was simply fantasy, therefore any research conducted by parapsychologists was dismissed out of hand. Any positive outcomes were simply regarded as the result of poor experimental methods or quite simply fraudulent.

Quite why social scientists simply reject alternative, non-orthodox approaches can be explained by postmodernism and by the work of Foucault outlined below. A good contemporary example is discussed by Mark J. Smith, who points to the great difficulty that environmental or 'green' sociology has had in getting its concerns over the environment accepted by the sociological 'establishment' – so that green concerns are seen as peripheral to the subject.

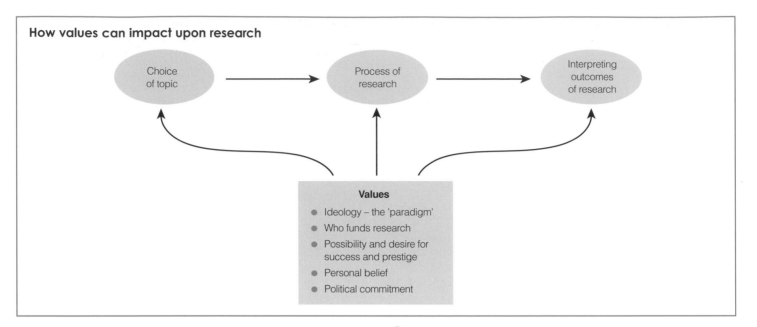

How values can impact upon research

Choice of topic → Process of research → Interpreting outcomes of research

Values
- Ideology – the 'paradigm'
- Who funds research
- Possibility and desire for success and prestige
- Personal belief
- Political commitment

The postmodern critique

Postmodernists such as Lyotard (1984) and Baudrillard (1988) argue that the whole process of sociological and scientific thinking is itself based on a series of values about the nature of society. As we saw in our discussion of the growth of scientific thinking (Topic 1), science itself is a product of modernist thought.

Postmodernists dispute the assertion that rational thinking based upon verifiable evidence is superior to any other approach to understanding the world. They argue that, in fact, scientific thinking is just one of many possible ways of approaching an understanding of the world and that it is not inherently better – nor does it provide any superior 'truths'. Quite simply, the process of science is based upon a set of values and all that a sociologist does is derived from a set of values – which are no 'truer' than any other set of values.

Foucault

A similar argument is put forward by Foucault in his analysis of knowledge. Foucault (1977) argues that what is considered to be knowledge reflects the ability of more powerful groups to impose their ideas on the rest of society. By gaining control over the production of knowledge (methodology) one also gains knowledge over what is considered knowledge. In a very similar argument to postmodernists, Foucault therefore argues the very 'value-free' process itself is actually based on a set of values.

Committed sociology

The third approach comes from those who argue that sociology should not be value-free and instead should have some explicit values which should guide its approach to study (i.e. it should be **committed**). The most ardent advocates of this approach are feminist writers and **critical** (or Marxist) **sociologists**. It has also been used by writers who are challenging racism and discrimination against people with disabilities. However, it was two sociologists from rather different traditions who started this approach.

From any topic you have studied, give an example of a piece of research which is 'committed'.

Whose side are we on?

In the 1970s a famous debate took place between Howard Becker and Alvin Gouldner. Both sociologists agreed that sociology should not be value-free but the debate that followed went on to ask: 'well, if we are going to be committed, then what side shall we be on?'

Becker (1970) started the debate by arguing that sociology (or at least the study of deviance, his speciality) had traditionally been on the side of the more powerful, and so had looked at issues from the viewpoint of the police officer, the social worker or the doctor, rather than from those of the criminal, the client or the 'mental patient'. Becker called for sociology to look instead from the viewpoint of the 'underdog'. By examining issues from their perspective, new questions and 'facts' could emerge. This sort of approach is the one that was taken by **labelling theorists** such as Becker (see Unit 5 Topic 5).

Gouldner (1968) attacked Becker for this argument, claiming that it did not go far enough – and, indeed, merely strengthened the status quo. Gouldner argued that Becker's work still focused on the less powerful. After all what *real* power do police officers, social workers and doctors actually have? According to Gouldner, sociology needs to study the *really* powerful, those who create the structures of oppression of which police officers are merely unimportant agents.

Apart from Gouldner's view, in what other ways has the idea of labelling been criticised?

Marxist view

Exactly this sort of argument was taken up by critical sociologists or Marxists. They argue that the role of sociology is to uncover the ways in which the ruling class control the mass of the population. In doing so, they hope to achieve the breakdown of capitalism by exposing the truth of how it operates to the benefit of a few.

A good example of this comes from the Critical (Marxist) criminologists Taylor, Walton and Young who argued in *The New Criminology* (1973) that 'radical criminological strategy…is to show up the law, in its true colours, as the instrument of the ruling class… and that the rule-makers are also the greatest rule-breakers'.

Feminist view

Feminist writers, such as Spender (1985), would agree with the idea of exposing the workings of an oppressive society, but also argue that the key is to explore how males dominate and control society. Again, the aim is exposing the truth, but the *result* is to free women from patriarchy.

There are four elements to feminist research, according to Hammersley (1992) – all of which demonstrate a rejection of searching for objectivity.

- Feminist research starts with the belief that the subordination of women runs through all areas of social life.
- Rather than seeking to exclude women's feelings and personal experience, these should form the basis of all analysis.
- The **hierarchical** division between the researcher and the researched should be broken down so that the subjects of research should be drawn in to help interpret the data obtained. This would help the research belong to the women under study.
- As the overall aim of feminist research is the emancipation of women, the success of research should only be measured in this, not solely in terms of academic credibility.

Within sociology, feminist writers accuse it of traditionally being '**malestream**', that is, interested in male views and concerns, rather than trying to include views of both males and females.

Give examples of particular areas of sociological thought which have been criticised as 'malestream'.

Feminist writers such as Cain (1986) and Smart (1990) also argue that the categorisation by sociologists into areas of study (criminology, social class, politics, and so on) has failed to show the pattern of oppression that women face in all these areas – only by **transgressing** these categories can feminists gain a real view of their situation and of patriarchy.

Research ethics

By **ethics** we are referring to the moral dilemmas that sociologists face when undertaking and writing up their research. Research ethics are closely interwoven with the debates over value-freedom and objectivity, although there are distinctive concerns which go beyond the value-freedom debate.

Whatever the view of the researcher regarding the importance of values in research, no sociologist would wish the actual procedure of research to harm those being studied or to produce a piece of research that was not as 'true' to the facts uncovered as possible. Ethical procedure is so important to sociologists that the British Sociological Association – the

official body of sociology in Britain – has actually issued a guide to ethics that all researchers are expected to follow. Punch (1994) has summarised the main ethical concerns of sociology as:

- *Harm*
  Any research undertaken must not cause any harm either directly or indirectly to those being studied (although a further question arises: what should a researcher do if the people under study are going to harm someone else?).
- *Consent*
  Any person or group being studied, wherever possible, should give their consent to being the subject of research. This usually involves an honest explanation of the research being undertaken and the future use of the material obtained.
- *Deception*
  The researcher should, wherever possible, be clear about their role to those being studied.
- *Privacy and confidentiality of data*
  The information obtained should not breach the privacy of the person being studied, and nothing should be published that the person regards as confidential. Research therefore should not provide the real name or address of a person being studied.

These ethical concerns may seem necessary but following them can pose great difficulties for sociologists engaged in certain research methods such as covert **participant observation**. Difficulties also arise in certain areas of research – for example, amongst young people, those engaged in criminal or deviant activities and those with learning difficulties or suffering from mental illness.

What are the advantages and disadvantages of covert observation?

An example of both of these fine lines between acting ethically and crossing the boundary can be found in Hobbs' study of East End criminals and the CID (1988) – see Topic 5. Hobbs engaged in an **ethnographic** study of East End villains and local CID officers. During his study he found out about many illegal activities committed by both villains and police officers, including acts of violence. Hobbs decided not to pass any information from one group to the other, and despite knowing about criminal activities he decided that the most 'ethical' thing to do was not to interfere in any way.

Hobbs also mixed a covert style of research with the police with an overt one. Overtly, he was conducting research through interviews, but covertly he befriended a number of police officers and carefully studied them in their social lives without telling them what he was doing. Hobbs' work can be questioned for its rather dubious ethics in terms of condoning law-breaking behaviour (which was sometimes serious) and in researching the detectives informally without their consent. However, in doing both these activities, he produced a more vibrant and possibly more accurate piece of research than if he had adhered to the 'correct procedures'.

KEY TERMS

Committed – where an approach is open in its support of one particular approach, usually used with reference to Marxist sociologists, feminist sociologists and those wishing to confront racism and discrimination against people with disabilities.

Covert participant observation – when the researcher joins a group as a full member, and studies them, but does not tell them that he or she is a researcher.

Critical sociology – another term used for Marxist approaches in sociology.

Ethics – refers to issues of moral choices.

Ethnographic – see Key Terms in Topic 3.

Hierarchical – some people are regarded as more important than others.

Labelling theory – a theoretical approach, derived from symbolic interactionism, which looks at the consequences of having a particular social typing or label placed on an act, group or person.

Malestream – originally a feminist term implying criticism of traditional sociology for excluding women from the subject both as sociologists and as the subjects of research.

Positivism – an approach to sociological research which aims to use the rigour and methods of the physical sciences.

Transgressing – to cross the boundary of one subject area of sociology to another.

Value freedom or objectivity – the exclusion of values from research.

Research idea

Design two questionnaires aiming to discover young women's views of feminism. The first must discover that feminism is still important and relevant to young women, the second that it has gone too far and young women do not support it. What different questions could you use to get these different results? Could you interpret answers in different ways?

WWWebtask

Go to the MORI website (www.mori.co.uk). This contains a wide range of opinion surveys. Take a few examples of their surveys. Check who is sponsoring the research and see if you can identify any evidence of the intrusion of values, for example in the motives for the research and in the sorts of questions asked.

CHECK YOUR UNDERSTANDING ✓✓✓

1 What is meant by 'positivism'?

2 How do positivistic sociologists think how the problem of values can be overcome?

3 How can the funding for research influence its content, according to Miller and Philo?

4 Compare the views of Becker and Gouldner on values in sociology.

5 Why do postmodernists see it as impossible to even try to overcome the issue of values?

6 What do we mean by 'committed sociology'? Give two examples.

7 Identify and explain three ethical issues faced by sociologists.

EXAM PRACTICE

Extract from AQA-style question

'Values must inevitably enter research in many ways.' Explain and discuss this view. (40 marks)

Extract from OCR-style question

Kelly's research sample was a voluntary one of 60 predominantly white British women with a considerable range with regard to age, class of origin, marital status, work experience and sexual identity. She interviewed three groups, each of ten women, who volunteered because they had experienced rape, incest and domestic violence respectively. Kelly also interviewed a comparison group of 30 other women, whose previous experience was unknown before they were interviewed.

Summarised in A. Warde and N. Abercrombie (1994) *Family, Household and the Life-course*, Lancaster: Framework Press (L. Kelly (1988) *Surviving Sexual Violence*, Oxford: Blackwell)

Identify and explain two ethical problems that might arise from Kelly's research. (8 marks)

Exploring values and ethics

Item A

In the mid 1930s, John Steinbeck, a famous campaigning journalist and author, visited squatters' camps in California. These had been set up by desperately poor farming families who had been forced out of their farms in Oklahoma and other mid-western states by the economic downturn in the US economy. The following is an extract from one article he wrote.

The squatters' camps are located all over California. Let us see what a typical one is like. From a distance it looks like a city dump…You can see a litter of dirty rags and scrap iron, of houses built of weeds or flattened cans or of paper. It is only on close approach that it can be seen that these are homes.

Here is a house built by a family who have tried to maintain a neatness. The house is about 10 feet by 10 feet and is built completely of corrugated paper. With the first rain the carefully built house will slop down into a brown, mushy pulp. The spirit of the family is not quite broken for the children, three of them, still have clothes and the family possesses three old quilts and a soggy lumpy mattress. But the money so needed for food cannot be used for soap nor for clothes…in a few months the clothes will fray off the children's bodies, while the lack of nourishing food will subject the whole family to pneumonia when the first cold comes.

[And in another home] There is more filth here. The tent is full of flies clinging to the apple box that is the dinner table…This family has been on the road longer than the builder of the paper house…two weeks ago there was another child…but one night he went into convulsions and died…They know pretty well that it was a diet of fresh fruit, beans and little else that caused his death. He had had no milk for months.

Taken from: S. Shillinglaw, and J. J. Benson, (eds.) (2002) *Of Men and Their Making: The Non-Fiction of John Steinbeck*, Harmondsworth: Penguin. (This extract from the *Guardian*, Saturday Review, p.2 February 2 2002)

1 The extract in Item A is factual, but the author's values emerge. How?

2 What comments would the following make about the place of values in the text?
 a Positivists
 b Critical sociologists

Item B

Feminist knowledge is based on the premise that the experience of all human beings is valid and must not be excluded from our understandings, whereas patriarchal knowledge is based on the premise that the experience of only half the human population needs to be taken into account and the resulting version can be imposed on the other half.

D. Spender, (1985) *For the Record: The Meaning and Making of Feminist Knowledge*, London: Women's Press. p. 5

Item C

This article argues that this social disadvantage reflects discriminatory social attitudes and barriers that result in social exclusion. Policy for disabled people should be aiming to change society and sociological knowledge developed within disability studies has a key role to play in this progress of social change.

M. Hyde, (2001) 'Disabled People in Britain today'. *Sociology Review*, 10 (4) April

3 What implications for the study of sociology emerge from the quote in Item B?

4 Using all the sources, discuss whether it is:
 a possible to keep personal values out of sociological research?
 b desirable to keep personal values out of sociological research?

Getting you thinking

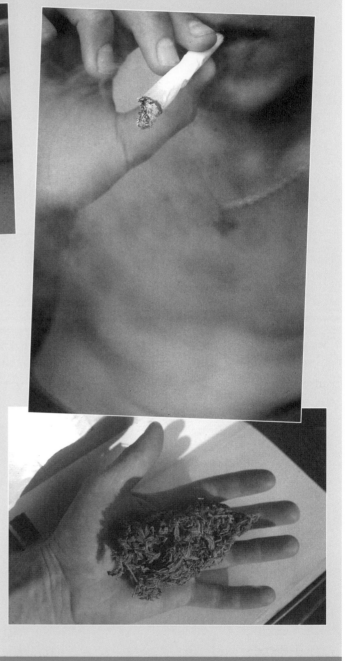

Multiple sclerosis sufferer Colin Davis is arrested outside Britain's first cannabis café in Stockport, Great Manchester.

1 There has been much discussion about the legalisation or de-criminalisation of cannabis. Explain your own view on this issue.

2 Why do you think that the government has not legalised its possession and use as yet?

3 Do you think that if sociological and medical researchers got together to provide the facts, this would change the mind of the government and the public? Explain the reasons for your view.

Sociology is first and foremost an academic subject that sets out to explore the way in which society operates and how it influences our lives – and for many sociologists, that is all they are interested in. For others, particularly those working in universities and research centres, sociological research is undertaken wholly or partly to inform and influence government social policy. This is particularly the case where the government or a pressure group provides the funding for the research.

The information obtained in research can have quite significant effects on social policy. In fact, so important has this applied branch of sociology become that there has recently been a considerable growth in an applied version of sociology – the academic subject known as **social policy** which only concerns itself with studying and influencing how governments respond to social problems.

Applying sociology

According to Giddens (2001), there are four practical benefits of studying sociology:

- understanding social situations
- awareness of cultural differences
- assessment of the effects of policies
- increase in self-knowledge.

Understanding social situations

The most obvious outcome of sociology is that it allows us to understand the world around us, providing us with knowledge and insights. This understanding can take two forms:

- *factual*: factual knowledge provides us with the 'facts' which allow us to form a judgement or develop a theory.
- *theoretical*: theoretical knowledge provides people with an explanation as to why something is happening

Understanding society and poverty
An example of the way factual and theoretical understanding of social situations can influence social policy is the sociological study of poverty.

Factually
By the late 1960s politicians believed that they had eliminated poverty. The welfare state had been in existence for almost twenty years and everyone was guaranteed a minimum income, some form of housing and free healthcare; the issue of poverty gradually lost its political importance. However, a series of reports by Townsend (1979) and later by Mack and Lansley (1985) in the 1980s and 1990s showed that poverty remained a huge but hidden problem in Britain, with over 11 million people living in poverty.

Research not only demonstrated the extent of poverty, but also the specific groups at risk of poverty – for example, women and children emerged as the poorest groups. This implied that policies to combat poverty had to look after women and children before anyone else.

Explain why women and children might constitute two of the groups most likely to experience poverty.

Theoretically
The facts on poverty, however, can only be understood in relation to theory. Sociologists uncovered the extent of poverty by devising more sophisticated ways of measuring it. In particular, they brought in a 'relative deprivation' model of poverty, proving that poverty can only be understood in terms of what people normally expect to have in a society – even if this was well above the levels of **destitution**. This new way of defining poverty thereby allowed a whole new insight into the nature of poverty in advanced, affluent societies.

Explain what is meant by relative deprivation. From your studies, give an example of its use in understanding any one aspect of society other than poverty.

Furthermore, sociologists were able to put forward a range of explanations for poverty based on their research which identified a range of possible explanations for poverty. The result of these researches indirectly led to policies such as the **Minimum Wage**, which guaranteed a minimum hourly pay level; the **New Deal** which introduced training programmes to get people back into work; and greater support for lone mothers and for low-paid parents with dependent children.

Awareness of cultural differences

A second important practical benefit, according to Giddens, is the way in which sociology can help people to see others' viewpoint, looking beyond the boundaries of their particular group. Lack of awareness of the activities and beliefs of other groups can lead to prejudice and discrimination. The information that sociology provides therefore allows us to respond to others' views in an informed and relevant way.

An outcome of this is the way that the recent governments have tackled discrimination in the areas of disability and race.

Disability
Disabled people often face very significant discrimination as a result of a stereotyping of their potential. They experience particularly high levels of unemployment, are discriminated against in many areas of social life and are much more likely than the majority of the population to be living in poverty. For example, they are seven times more likely to be unemployed than the average, and over 50% of families with a disabled male adult were living in poverty. This discrimination both ruins the lives of the people involved and at a political level, costs the government over £100 billion each year in state benefits.

What methods could be used to assess the extent of discrimination against people with disabilities?

Apart from having a higher chance of living in poverty, disabled people also have to cope with the stigma attached to disability, with people reacting to them in a patronising or negative manner. Over time, sociological studies have built up a picture of the social and economic exclusion suffered by disabled people and this has led them to set up groups such as the Disability Alliance, Disablement Income Group and the British Council of Disabled People to demand better treatment. On the other side, their work and the work of sociologists has led to a greater public awareness and sympathy, resulting in the 1995 Disability Discrimination Act, which was followed by the Disability Rights Commission Act in 1999. Just as importantly, there has been a gradual shift in public opinion towards acknowledging the rights of disabled people.

Race
Opinion polls over the past thirty years have shown a consistent decline in expressed racism on the part of the majority population. The reasons for this are complex, but certainly one of the contributing factors has been the growth in understanding of the variety of cultures in Britain, and the problems that ethnic minorities face. Early sociological studies tended to emphasise the issues causing conflict, but increasingly sociologists and others have demonstrated the variety and positive nature of the contribution of ethnic minorities to British life. 'White' people are more informed and aware of the variety of ethnic groups and are less likely to stereotype them as happened in the past. This awareness, plus

the acceptance of a plural Britain has led to the introduction of Race Equality legislation (1976 and 2000) to enforce equality.

Assessment of the effects of policies

Once politicians have recognised that a particular social problem exists, they are then able to develop policies to combat it. If sociological knowledge is used in doing this then the policies adopted may be those that appear to be most effective in combating the problem. However, it is actually extremely difficult to judge just how effective a policy has actually been, and this leads us to another use of sociology – that of evaluating the effects of a particular policy initiative.

Today, virtually all government initiatives are evidence-based – that is, when the government provides funding for new social projects, it requires evidence from the people actually running the programme to provide clear evidence that there is some benefit coming from that particular programme. Sociology is the key subject in providing this sort of research into the relevance and effectiveness of policy initiatives.

A good example of evaluation has been the way in which cost–benefit analyses of health care have been introduced in the NHS. Much of this work was pioneered by the University of York, where analyses were conducted to find out just how effective certain medical procedures were in terms of better quality of life for patients and cost to the NHS. The government has developed this form of analysis to pharmaceuticals, and introduced a **National Institute for Clinical Excellence** which started in 1999 and which dictates what drugs and procedures the NHS is prepared to provide.

Increase in self-knowledge

For many sociologists this is the single most important aim of the subject. Sociology allows people to reflect upon their own experiences of life and in doing so 'liberates' them. Self-knowledge allows people to challenge images of themselves (perhaps currently stereotyped in the media) and to initiate policies that are more sympathetic to them.

Certain groups such as those with disabilities, ethnic minorities and the feminist and gay movements have all benefited greatly from this aspect of sociology. Sociological research has demonstrated the extent of discrimination against all these groups and this knowledge has empowered them because they are able to show the results to the government and demand action. The result of this has been a wide range of anti-discrimination laws. The publication of research has also allowed groups who have traditionally been discriminated against to become aware of their own shared identities and to take a pride in them. For example, sexual practices surveys showed that sexual activity between same-sex partners was not as infrequent as traditionally believed and opinion polls demonstrated that there was support for equal rights for gay people. This helped the gay community to have the courage to demand equal rights and to feel able to assert their own identities rather than having to hide their sexuality.

What is meant by 'identity'? How are identities formed?

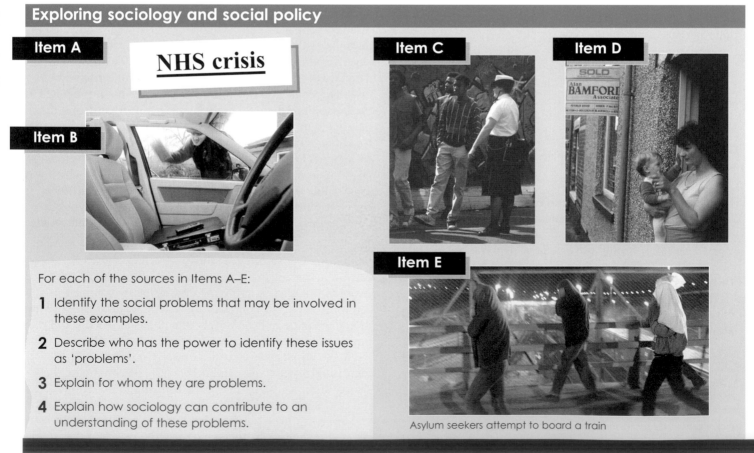

Exploring sociology and social policy

Item A

NHS crisis

Item B

Item C

Item D

Item E

Asylum seekers attempt to board a train

For each of the sources in Items A–E:

1 Identify the social problems that may be involved in these examples.

2 Describe who has the power to identify these issues as 'problems'.

3 Explain for whom they are problems.

4 Explain how sociology can contribute to an understanding of these problems.

Radicalism, sociology and policy

However, the relationship between social policy and sociology has been criticised by a number of writers. In particular, it sees sociology as having been '**colonised**' by governments and thus its radical potential as having been tamed.

Critical criminology

For those belonging to the **critical sociology** tradition based on Marxism, the fault with much of sociology is that it has become too closely linked with the capitalist system – which to them is the main cause of the social problems and discrimination. Therefore sociology is not fulfilling its role as being a provider of knowledge that could liberate people, but actually serving the interests of powerful groups who could then impose their wishes in even more sophisticated ways.

From any aspect of your studies give an example of the Marxist argument that capitalism can be the 'cause of social problems and discrimination'.

A good example of this is the debate between **realist criminologists** and **critical criminologists**. Realist criminologists, such as Lea and Young (1993), argue that sociological surveys indicate that the people who really suffer from crime are the poor and the powerless. It is therefore the duty of the government to introduce policies to prevent crime occurring against these groups, and to improve the quality of their lives. They should do this by better policing, better social conditions and by tackling the social and economic marginalisation of the young males who commit most street crime.

Critical criminologists reject this, saying that the approach deals with the symptoms of crime, not the causes. For writers such as Scraton (and Chadwick) (1991), it is a mistake to focus on the street crime committed by young men. These people engage in crime precisely because they are marginalised and brutalised by the capitalist system. Critical criminologists argue that realism ignores the very real damage committed by corporations. For them, realists have been caught up in the very system, that should itself be attacked.

Feminism

The debate between feminists very much reflects that between the realist and critical criminologists. Radical and socialist feminists criticise liberal feminists for their research and close ties with government. Liberal feminists have been content to point out the way in which society discriminates against women in terms of employment, state benefits and within the family. Their aim has been to introduce anti-discrimination legislation and to change the attitudes of men to women. They would argue that they have largely succeeded in this. However, radical and socialist feminists argue that this misses the point – the current patriarchal society is actually based on the exploitation of women and therefore only by dismantling it and bringing about fundamental change can women achieve any form of liberation.

Summarise the similarities and differences between radical, socialist and liberal feminists.

Postmodernists and policy

Postmodernists such as Bauman (1990) take a position which is radically different from more traditional sociological approaches. They argue that sociology has no contribution to make to policy. Rational, scientific approaches to sociology using surveys or qualitative studies have often been used by government to introduce policies. But postmodernists claim that this is a waste of time, the existence of an orderly and manageable society 'out there', that we can understand and then manipulate is a comforting illusion. They would argue therefore that there can be no link between sociology and social policies. For postmodernists the role of sociology is simply to allow people to seek out an understanding of their personal lives.

Politics and social policy

The assumption underlying much of traditional **empirical sociology** is that if research shows up social problems, then governments will respond by seeking to solve the problems on the basis of the evidence. However, this is not necessarily true for four key reasons.

1 Governments act only when there are groups powerful enough to have their views taken into account by politicians. Gay people are now seen as a potential source of votes and as a group who occupy important positions across society. On the other hand, some of the poorest groups in society have little access to power, and may well be ignored by government.
2 Governments are limited by financial constraints. To eliminate poverty amongst retired people would be simple – raise the state pension by a significant amount. Yet governments regard this as simply too expensive.
3 Some policies will meet too much opposition from entrenched groups. The 'roads lobby', pharmaceutical and cigarette companies have all been very effective in protecting their interests despite evidence to show that many of their practices are harmful.
4 Governments rarely engage in radical or long-term changes. In a democracy, governments operate within fairly short timetables based on election periods and are more concerned with popularity at the time of an election than introducing longer term changes. They also are reluctant to commit themselves to very dramatic social change which could lead to upheaval – preferring to operate within the status quo.

So, although sociology can uncover the extent of social problems and also suggest the causes – transferring this into policy does not necessarily happen.

We can see from the discussion above that there is no agreement amongst sociologists about whether sociology ought to be applied or not. For many sociologists the whole point of the subject is to use the knowledge to improve the quality of life for the majority of the population – however, these then split into two warring factions. One group argues that it is best to influence government policy to bring about reforms, whilst the other group argues that the insights sociology provides should help us to replace the current political and social system. Finally, there are those who argue that the point of sociology is that it is an academic subject and has no need to make any claim beyond its ability to throw light upon the nature of society and its relationship to the lives of individuals.

KEY TERMS

Colonised – taken over.

Critical criminologists – refers to sociologists who study crime and deviance from a Marxist-based perspective.

Critical sociology – a term used for sociology influenced by Marxism.

Destitution – lacking the minimum resources necessary for food, clothing and housing.

Empirical sociology – refers to sociologists who tend to conduct quantitative studies and tend not to theorise.

Minimum wage – a government initiative in 1998 to provide a minimum hourly wage.

National Institute for Clinical Excellence – a government body set up in 2001 to decide what could or could not be provided by the NHS.

New Deal – the name for a wide-ranging review of the state benefits system.

Plural – refers to the fact that British society is now composed of a number of different cultures.

Realist sociology – a term used for sociologists, broadly sympathetic to the left, who wish to influence government policy – particularly in the area of crime.

Social policy – has two meanings. It can refer to government policy to solve social problems or the academic subject studying social problems.

CHECK YOUR UNDERSTANDING

1 Identify Giddens' four links between sociology and policy.

2 Give an example from the text which shows how sociology has influenced policy.

3 How can an awareness of disability issues influence policy?

4 Explain what evidence-based policymaking is.

5 Explain what is meant by sociology having been 'colonised' by government.

6 How do postmodernists view the relationship between sociology and policy?

7 If sociologists provide the 'facts' why don't governments always base their policies upon these facts?

Research idea

Conduct a survey among sociology students at your school or college to discover which social issues they feel most strongly about. Have these issues been covered during your course? Are they included in the specifications of your examining board? To what extent has your study of sociology been relevant to the values and experiences of students?

WWWebtask

Choose any one of the following government websites which most interests you: the Home Office, NHS, Department for Education and Skills, Work and Pensions. Look up the sorts of research being undertaken. What is the aim of research? Do you think that the criticisms of radical sociologists that sociology is 'colonised' are justified?

EXAM PRACTICE

Extract from AQA-style question

Evaluate the idea that 'sociological research has had no important effect on social policy'. (40 marks)

(Topic not included in OCR specifications)

Item A

Perhaps the most fruitful distinction with which the sociological imagination works is between the 'personal troubles of milieu*' and the 'public issues of social structure'. This distinction is an essential tool of the sociological imagination…

In these terms, consider unemployment. When, in a city of 100,000, only one man is unemployed, that is his personal trouble, and for its relief we properly look to the character of the man, his skills and his immediate opportunities. But when, in a nation of 50 million employees, 15 million men are unemployed, that is an issue and we may not hope to find its solution within the range of opportunities open to any one individual.

C. Wright Mills, (1959) *The Sociological Imagination*, Oxford: Oxford University Press.

* the particular social situation a person is in.

(NB this was written in the late 1950s when it was normal to make what we would now regard as sexist assumptions.)

Item B

Deeply immersed in our daily routines, though, we hardly ever pause to think about the meaning of what we have gone through; even less often have we the opportunity to compare our private experience with the fate of others, to see the social in the individual, the general in the particular; this is precisely what sociologists can do for us. We would expect them to show us how our individual biographies intertwine with the history we share with fellow human beings.

Z. Bauman, (1990) *Thinking Sociologically*, Oxford: Basil Blackwell

Item C

Women appear in a sociology predicated on the universe occupied by men…its methods, conceptual schemes and theories have been based on and built up within the male social universe.

D. Smith, (1973) 'Women's Perspective as a Radical Critique of Sociology', *Sociological Inquiry*, 44.

Item D

…our role [as sociologists] is not first and foremost to be received as useful problem-solvers, but as problem raisers…but equipped with our special training in scientific methods and theory, it is our obligation as well as pleasure to penetrate these problems…we will probably [as it is] have to keep a constant fight going against being absorbed, tamed, and made responsible, and thereby completely socialised into society…

Nils Christie, (1971) 'Scandinavian Criminology faces the 1970s' in N. Christie *et al.* (1971) *Scandinavian Studies in Criminology*, London: Tavistock

1 In Item A, C. Wright Mills distinguishes between 'private troubles' and 'public issues'. Explain this distinction in your own words.

2 Which sociological perspectives are represented by the writers of Items B, C and D?

3 Read each of the Items and then suggest what view the author might take regarding the role of sociology.

4 Discuss the arguments for and against the view that sociology should simply be an academic subject and not seek to influence policy.

Unit 5

Crime and Deviance

Getting you thinking

The Walk for Capitalism was the brainchild of the right-wing Prodos Institute in Australia. Robert Groezinger, organiser of the Bath walk, which attracted a total of six people, said: 'How is it possible in our society that people who are the achievers and make all of our lives worth living by achieving for all of us, cannot openly be proud of their achievements?'

Source: 'Business Snubs Pro-Capitalism Demo', *The Big Issue* (2001), December, 17, p.4

1 Do you think people are 'naturally', greedy and self-seeking, or do you believe that they are essentially generous and good?

2 What do you think would happen if we had less police and fewer laws?

The social responsibility quiz

1 You see someone chucking a used McDonald's burger carton on the pavement. What do you do?
a Do you tell them to pick it up?
b Ignore it?
c Pick it up yourself and put it in the nearest bin?

2 You pass a homeless person begging in the street. Do you:
a Give them some money (at least to the value of 20p)?
b Pretend you haven't seen them?
c Tell them to 'get a job'?
d Say to them that you won't give them money, but you will buy/give them a sandwich and a coffee if they want it?

3 A particular student is always being made fun of (bullied?) by other students in your year. Do you:
a Join in bullying them?
b Feel sorry for the person, but do nothing?
c Confront the bullies?
d Tell a tutor or person in authority?

Scoring

Q1 a 5   b 1   c 2   Q2 a 2   b 1   c 0   d 5
Q3 a 0   b 1   c 5   d 3

Results

Less than 5: You are a horrible person, aren't you! Change to Business Studies immediately!

6–10: You are someone who cares about other people – shame you don't actually do anything about it!

11–14: Caring, helpful and, may I add, a little bit smug!

15 – Very impressive, but a bit dangerous. Learn to keep your mouth shut and not to confront people, if you wish to live to an old age.

Durkheim

For Durkheim, crime and deviance were central to any understanding of how society functions. He identified two different sides of crime and deviance for the functioning of society. First, a positive side which helped society change and remain dynamic; second, a negative side which saw too much crime leading to social disruption.

Give examples of the positive functions of other social institutions.

Positive aspects of crime

According to Durkheim (1982), crime – or at least a certain, limited amount of crime – was necessary for any society. He argued that the basis of society was a set of shared values that guide our actions, which he called the **collective conscience**. The collective conscience provides a framework with boundaries, which distinguishes between actions that are acceptable and those that are not. The problem for any society is that these boundaries are unclear, and also that they change over time. It is in clarifying the boundaries and the changes that a limited amount of crime has its place. Specifically, Durkheim discussed three elements of this positive aspect.

Reaffirming the boundaries

Every time a person breaks a law and is taken to court, the resulting court ceremony and the publicity in the newspapers, publicly reaffirms the existing values. This is particularly clear in societies where public punishments take place, where a murderer is taken out to be executed in public, or an adulterer is stoned to death.

What are values? Give examples of how they guide social action?

Changing values

However, every so often when a person is taken to court and charged with a crime, a degree of sympathy occurs for the person prosecuted. The resulting public outcry signals a change in values and, in time, this can lead to a change in law in order to reflect changing values. An example of this is the change in attitude towards cannabis use.

Give other examples of how changing values have led to changes in the law.

Social cohesion

A third function of crime, according to Durkheim, is to strengthen social cohesion. Durkheim points out that when particularly horrific crimes have been committed, the entire community draws together in shared outrage, and the sense of belonging to a community is thereby strengthened. This was noticeable, for example in the USA following the September 2001 attacks on the World Trade Centre.

The negative aspects of crime

However, Durkheim stressed that it was a certain, limited amount of crime that performed positive functions for society. Too much crime, on the other hand, had negative consequences. Perhaps his most famous concept was that of 'anomie', which has been widely used and adapted in sociology.

Suggest some negative consequences of crime for society.

Anomie

We saw before that, according to Durkheim, society is based on people sharing common values (the collective conscience), which form the basis for actions. However, in periods of great social change or stress, the collective conscience may be weakened. In this situation, people may be freed from the social control imposed by the collective conscience and may start to look after their own selfish interests rather than adhering to social values. Durkheim called this situation **anomie**. Where a collapse of the collective conscience has occurred and anomie exists, crime rates rocket. Only by re-imposing collective values can the situation be brought back under control.

Durkheim's concept of anomie was later developed and adapted by Merton, who suggested Durkheim's original idea was too vague. Merton argued that anomie was a situation where the socially approved goals of society were not available to a substantial proportion of the population if they followed socially approved means of obtaining these goals. According to Merton, people turned to crime and deviance in this situation.

Hirschi: bonds of attachment

Hirschi (1969) was also heavily influenced by Durkheim's ideas. Durkheim's concept of anomie suggests that if people are not 'controlled' by shared social values, then they look after their own short-term interests without concern for others. This led Hirschi to turn around the normal sociologist's question of 'why people commit crime?' to another, equally intriguing one: 'Why *don't* people commit crime?'

By asking this question, Hirschi focuses sociologists' attention on what forces hold people's behaviour in check, rather than what propels them into crime. Hirschi argued that criminal activity occurs when people's attachment to society is weakened in some way. This attachment depends upon the strength of the social bonds that hold people to society.

Give examples of social institutions that help bond the individual to society. How do they do it?

According to Hirschi, there are four crucial bonds that bind us together:

- *Attachment*: to what extent we care about other people's opinions and wishes.
- *Commitment*: refers to the personal investments that each of us makes in our lives. What have we got to lose if we commit a crime?
- *Involvement*: how busy are we? Is there time and space for law-breaking and deviant behaviour?
- *Belief*: how strong is a person's sense that they should obey the rules of society?

The greater a person's attachment to society, the lower their level of crime.

The family and crime

Probably the most important agency that socialises us and therefore provides the values that either strengthen or weaken the bonds Hirschi refers to, (or the 'collective conscience' of Durkheim) is the family.

Give examples of socialisation in the family.

Cambridge Study in Delinquent Development

The most famous study of the family is a piece of **longitudinal research** by Farrington and West (1990) in which 411 'working class' males born in 1953 were studied until their late 30s. The study found that:

- Extent of offending – by the age of 25 one-third of them were recorded offenders.
- Concentration of offending – less than 6% of the total sample accounted for 50%+ of all convictions.

What are the advantages and disadvantages of longitudinal studies?

The research demonstrated that there were consistent correlations between family traits and offending. In particular, offenders were more likely to come from homes with poor parenting – especially when the fathers themselves had criminal convictions. Furthermore, offenders were also more likely to come from poorer and single-parent families.

What is the difference between a correlation and a cause? Why might this difference be important?

Family and morality

For some writers, the research of Farrington and West underlined their belief that the family was the key to understanding the causes of crime. Writers such as Dennis (1993) argue that the correlation between crime and certain family characteristics is a reflection of a much wider change in society. In particular, the traditional three-generation family structure had provided stability and a place in which moral values and a sense of community belonging had been passed on. However, over the past thirty years a series of changes in the family has weakened the **external patterns of social control** based on families and communities (where community members felt able to restrain extreme behaviour or young offenders) and also undermined the **internalised forms of social control** that had traditionally occurred through family socialisation.

The specific changes that Dennis blames are:

- *The changing role of women in the family*
  The increasingly dominant role of the mother in the household has led to the marginalisation of the father.
- *Increase in fathers leaving their families*
  Dennis argues that there has been a decrease in the moral condemnation shown towards men who leave their families.

The result of these two factors is that young males do not have role-models to base their behaviour upon and they also do not face the discipline at home that a father might provide.

- *Cohabitation*
  The growth of cohabitation has undermined the belief that a partnership is for life, as is supposed to occur in marriage. This weakens the general moral 'fabric' of society and demonstrates that values and commitments are not fixed and permanent, but flexible. This, in turn, weakens the idea of strong central values which form the basis of society and strengthens the view that morals are relative and negotiable – even moral stands on issues such as crime.

What perspective/political view is represented by the ideas of Dennis. Identify another perspective that is critical of this view of the family. How is it critical?

The underclass and the community

The family may be the most important agency providing socialisation to young people, but the family exists within a particular community. Farrington and West's research not only pointed to the importance of the family, but also to the social network in which the family is located.

The close relationship between family, community and offending was taken up by the American writer Charles Murray (1990), who argued that over the past thirty years there has been an increase in what he terms '**the underclass**'. By underclass, Murray refers to a clearly distinguishable group of young people who have no desire for formal paid employment, preferring to live off benefits and the illegal economy; who have a range of short-term sexual liaisons; and where children are routinely born outside serious relationships so that fathers do not see their offspring as being their responsibility.

The children of these people are brought up with little or no concern for the values of the society in general, so that there is now a generation of young people who do not share the values of the wider society and who are much more likely to commit crime. Poorer communities are being destroyed by the underclass, who are driving out the law-abiding majority, and thus the members of the underclass are becoming ever more isolated and confirmed in their behaviour.

Where else in your studies have you come across the idea of an underclass?

Dennis and Murray's writings link very closely with the work of the right realists (see Topic 11), including James Q. Wilson's 'broken windows' thesis (Wilson and Kelling, 1982). This argues that most communities consist of a balance between those who would commit offences, given the freedom to do so, and those members of the community who are essentially law-abiding and who constantly apply pressure to conform on the potential offenders. The fulcrum of the balance is the ability of the conformists to feel able to make comments against the potential offenders and to impose informal sanctions on them. Wilson argues that it is particularly important that potential offenders should be forced to obey most of the minor, civil obligations – such as picking up litter, respecting people and property and keeping noise levels down. If these are not enforced, then the anti-social behaviour will extend to more serious crimes. Local, informal control of minor matters is therefore crucial for maintenance of law and order. Wilson's arguments can clearly be traced back to Durkheim.

Etzioni: crime and communitarianism

One of the most influential writers in the USA is Amitai Etzioni, who has developed a theoretical and political argument known as **communitarianism**. For Etzioni (1993), changes in modern society have pushed decision-making further and further away from local communities. The conclusion of this process has been for people to lose interest in controlling their community. They regard themselves as powerless and this simply reinforces their acceptance that it is not their job to control others, but the role of the police and the state. Etzioni argues forcefully that only by taking back control and by engaging in direct action in a variety of ways to control local offenders and to provide support for those in need locally will social control be reconstituted.

Crime and control: a Marxist perspective

What are the key elements of Marxist analysis?

Steven Box (1983) argues for a Marxist approach to crime and control. Box agrees with the more right wing writers in that it is release from social control that propels people into committing crime. However, his starting point is not that people are basically bad, but that capitalist society controls and exploits workers for its own ends – or, rather, for the benefit of the ruling class. When people are released in some way from direct control, then they are much more likely to commit crime because they see the unfairness of the system.

Box argues there are five elements that can weaken the bonds of capitalist society and propel individuals into committing crime.

1   *Secrecy*

   If people are able to get away with a crime, especially by not having it noticed in the first place, then they are more likely to attempt to commit crime. According to Box, this is one key factor that helps explain why white-collar crime (such as fraud) takes place. The majority of white-collar crime simply goes undiscovered.

2   *Skills*

   Most people are simply unable to commit serious crime. Minor offending and anti-social behaviour generally occurs on the spur of the moment. Serious crime, however, requires planning and knowledge – plus the skill to carry it out.

3   *Supply*

   Even knowledge and skill are not enough by themselves. The potential offender must also be able to obtain the equipment and support to be able to carry out most serious crimes. For example, a burglar needs a 'fence' to whom to sell his (burglary is an overwhelmingly male activity!) stolen goods.

4   *Symbolic support*

   All offenders must have some justification for their activities. An excellent example of this are the techniques of neutralisation suggested by Matza (1961) (see Topic 3).

5   *Social support*

   Directly coupled with the idea of symbolic support is the need for others who share similar values to support and confirm the values that justify crime. (Social support is another way of describing a subculture – see Topic 3.)

KEY TERMS

Anomie – a term, first used by Durkheim, to describe a breakdown of social expectations and behaviour. It was later used in a different way by Merton to explain reactions to situations where socially approved goals were impossible for the majority of the population to reach by legitimate means.

Collective conscience – a term used by Durkheim to describe the core, shared values of society.

Communitarianism – approach linked with Etzioni, which claims that social problems should be sorted out by local people rather that by central government or their agencies (e.g. the police).

Correlations – refers to a statistical relationship between two or more social events.

Critical criminology – a term used to describe criminologists influenced by Marxist thinking.

Externalised patterns of social control – social control imposed by people on potential or actual offenders.

Internalised patterns of social control – social control that the person imposes upon themselves via their conscience – which is, in turn, largely the result of their upbringing.

Longitudinal research – sociological research method involving studying a group over a long period of time.

Social bond – in control theories, these refer to the forms of social control preventing people acting in a deviant way.

Underclass – a term used by Charles Murray to describe a distinctive 'class' of people whose lifestyle involves seeking to take what they can from the state and living a life involving petty crime and sexual gratification.

Box is arguing therefore that control theory can be applied from a left-wing perspective and is not necessarily conservative in its approach. For Marxists, social control operates for the benefit of the ruling class and once this is weakened, it is possible that people will turn to crime to express their disillusionment with capitalism. **Critical criminologists** still take this position and argue that criminals are engaging in a form of political act in their crimes, and that if they were made more aware of the circumstances that propelled them into crime, they might well act in a more politically conventional way.

Control theories all share the belief that crime is the result of the restraints imposed by society being weakened. The overall approach is a very conservative one which stresses that if it were not for the family or local community then people would resort to their natural greedy and unpleasant selves. The underlying message of the approach is that the decline in the traditional family is potentially very dangerous for society.

The only, rather maverick, exception to this argument is Box's version of critical criminology which agrees that crime results from the weakening of social control – but sees social control as a bad thing, operating for the benefit of the ruling class.

CHECK YOUR UNDERSTANDING

1 Give two examples of the positive aspects of crime according to Durkheim.

2 Explain how crime could be negative for society.

3 Explain the terms: 'attachment', 'commitment', 'involvement' 'investment' and 'belief'. Use an example of your own to illustrate each term.

4 What correlations did Farrington find between the family and criminal behaviour?

5 What is the 'broken windows' thesis?

6 According to communitarian theory, how could crime be stopped?

7 What five elements can weaken the bonds of society, according to Box?

8 What theoretical approach influences Box's writing?

Research ideas

1 Conduct your own social-responsibility survey as described in the activity at the start of this Topic. Compare your findings with the ideas in this Topic.

2 Collect the tabloid newspapers for one week. At the end of the week, see whether you can use them to illustrate Durkheim's ideas on both the positive and negative aspects of crime.

WWWebtask

The *News of the World* has been seeking to have a law passed that would enable people to find out if a paedophile lives locally. This is referred to as 'Sarah's Law' (after the murder of Sarah Payne in July 2000). Find out as much as you can about this campaign using the worldwide web. How does it illustrate the ideas of Durkheim and Etzioni?

EXAM PRACTICE

Extract from AQA-style question

Assess the view that crime is functional, inevitable and normal. (40 marks)

OCR-style question

Outline and assess sociological explanations of the role of social control in society. (60 marks)

Item A

(*Left*) Nadeem Butt, a notorious drug seller, is publicly beaten by police in Lahore, Saturday February 10, 1998

A public execution in Afghanistan

Item B

For those on the right, the family is the key institution in the generation of law-abiding behaviour. Here discipline is learnt, impulse curbed, respect instilled and the grounding of civilized behaviour laid down in childhood to inform the adult throughout the future exigencies of life. Politicians of the right extol the family, criminologists of that persuasion whether it is Travis Hirschi, Charles Murray or James Q. Wilson, all pinpoint the early years as formative and predictive of future delinquency or conformity. But for those on the left, in the recent period, focus on the family is seen as a red herring. Thus it is argued that not only is the type of family irrelevant to the aetiology (causes) of crime and delinquency... For it is not the family which is the locus (location) of the causes of delinquency but the wider social forces of economic deprivation, racism and other forms of social injustice which are its source. If we wish to reduce crime we must tackle injustice – all else concerned is scapegoating and mistargeting.

J. Young (1999) *The Exclusive Society*, London: Sage

1 How does Item A illustrate Durkheim's analysis of crime and social control?

2 Read Item B. What is the key agency of social control according to the criminologists of the right?

3 Why do Marxists disagree with this?

4 If we wished to eliminate crime, how would the policies of the right and the left differ?

5 Explain the last sentence of Item B in your own words.

215

Unit 5 Crime and Deviance

Getting you thinking

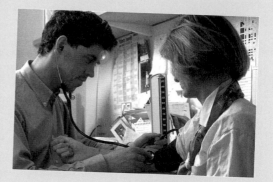

1 How does each of the photographs above represent an example of the way people are controlled?

2 What different types of control are being used?

3 Who is responsible for the control?

Social control

Societies can only exist if there is a degree of order and predictability, otherwise there would simply be chaos. This order is unlikely to arise spontaneously and so societies (or the more powerful members of society) develop methods to control those who fail to stick to the rules. They do so by a mixture of:

- **informal social control** based upon a range of **sanctions** such as negative comments, looks and exclusion
- **formal social control** based upon organisations that exist solely or partly to enforce 'order'.

Give examples of formal and informal social control from other areas of sociology you have studied.

The exact mixture between informal and formal control mechanisms used depends upon the type of society – for example, smaller and less complex groups with strongly shared values might rely more upon informal methods, whilst large complex and multicultural societies generally have to use specific organisations.

Approaches to understanding social control

As we have just seen, all societies need to impose control on their members, in order to ensure predictability of behaviour and stability. On this sociologists agree, but beyond that there is considerable dispute as to who benefits from this control and about how to explain the form that state control takes.

- Functionalist writers see the criminal justice system as operating to look after the interests of society as a whole. Without control and punishment, society would collapse into a state of **anomie**.
- At the other extreme, Marxist writers argue that the criminal justice system operates for the benefit of the ruling class. The law and the police are the agents of the ruling class and exist to eliminate opposition.
- Foucault (1977) put the issue of social control at the centre of his writings, and argued that any society is a battleground between competing interests. A key to gaining power is to control what is considered to be knowledge, and the methods of gaining knowledge. Those who succeed in having their definition of knowledge accepted gain power, and in turn will use it to enforce their view of the world. The criminal justice system and particularly the forms of punishment used play a crucial role in this by imposing the values of the powerful.

Changes in social control

Stan Cohen (1985) has suggested a number of key themes in the changing nature of the formal control in Western societies.

Penetration
Historically, societies had fairly simple forms of control – with the state passing a law which was then haphazardly enforced by whatever authorities existed at the time. However, Cohen argues that increasingly the law is expected to penetrate right through society, and that conformity and control are part of the job that schools, the media and even private companies are supposed to engage in.

Size and density
Cohen points out the sheer scale of the control apparatuses in modern society, with literally millions of people working for the state and other organisations involved in imposing control – and over a period of time, millions having that control imposed upon them. For example, approximately one-third of all males under thirty have been arrested for a criminal

offence. Cohen points out that the range of control agencies is increasing and as they do so, they 'process' ever larger numbers of people.

Identity and visibility
Cohen argues that control and punishment used to be public and obvious, but more recently there has been a growth in subtle forms of control and punishment. Closed-circuit TV (CCTV), tagging, legally enforceable drug routines for the 'mentally-ill' and curfews are all part of an ever-growing and invisible net of control. He also notes that the state has handed over part of its monopoly of controlling people to private organisations. So there has been a growth in private security companies, doorstaff at nightclubs and even private prisons.

Feeley and Simon: actuarialism

Feeley and Simon (1992) have suggested another element of contemporary social control, which they term **actuarialism**. The term derives from the insurance industry, where the people who work out the chances of a particular event happening (and therefore the price to charge for insurance) are known as actuaries. Simon and Feeley argue that in contemporary society, the stress of social control has changed from controlling deviant behaviour, to controlling potentially deviant people. Therefore, agencies of social control work out just who is likely to pose the greatest risk of deviance and then act against them. The police patrol working-class and ethnic-minority areas, whilst the private-security companies police the shopping developments, monitor people who enter and exclude the potential troublemakers – defined as the poor, the young and the homeless.

They extend Cohen's argument that other agencies as well as the state are involved in social control and argue that there is a process of **privatisation** of social control agencies, with increasingly large amounts of surveillance and control of the population by for-profit companies.

What other areas of social life have been subject to increasing privatisation and the introduction of market forces? What political viewpoint is represented by these changes?

Finally, Feeley and Simon argue that there has been a growth in new, more subtle forms of social control which they call **disciplining**, where people are helped in a non-coercive way to do what the organisation wants. For example, Disney controls tens of thousands of people each day in its parks in subtle ways, but this still result in people behaving as Disney wishes.

Davis: Control of space

Davis in the very influential book *City of Quartz* (1990) studied Los Angeles and pointed out that there is an increasing division between the affluent, living in segregated and (privately) protected areas, and the areas lived in by the poorer majority. The role of the police is to contain the poor, segregating them in their ghettos.

Punishment

A key component of social control is punishment. This has therefore been an area of interest to sociologists, as it helps us to resolve in whose interests social control operates and also to tell us about the extent and nature of formal social control.

Durkheim

As discussed in Topic 1, Durkheim (1960) believed that societies could only exist if the members shared certain common, core values, which he called the **collective conscience**. These common values dictate acceptable behaviour. However, many other values exist too which have rather less general acceptance (ranging from ones generally accepted to those that are openly in dispute). Thus a system of law exists that places a boundary line, clearly marking where actions go beyond the boundary of acceptance into behaviour generally regarded as so deviant as to be illegal.

Which sociological perspective is based on the view that shared values exist? What problems exist in claiming shared values exist in contemporary societies?

According to Durkheim, when people act against societal values, then generally a system of *informal* control operates to coerce them back into conformity. However, if their behaviour crosses the boundary into illegal behaviour, then the *formal* system of punishment is generally used. Durkheim argued that both the basis and the form of punishment changes over time. In less complex, **mechanistic societies** punishment is based upon **retribution** – by which savage penalties are imposed upon the wrongdoer in order to demonstrate society's abhorrence at the breaking of the commonly shared values. The punishment will be both public and physical in nature – so people are executed, mutilated and branded.

As societies develop and become more complex (**organic societies**), then the punishment shifts away from public punishment to imprisonment, and the aim of the punishment is more to force the person to make amends for their wrongdoing. He called this **restitutive law**.

Where else in your studies have you come across Durkheim? What themes is he concerned with in his work?

Marxist approaches

Marxist writers such as Rusche and Kircheimer (1939) agree with the general Marxist argument that laws reflect the interests of the ruling class. However, they go further and argue that the forms of *punishment* also reflect their interests. As these interests change so do the forms of punishment. Rusche and Kircheimer claim, for example, that slavery was an early form of punishment because of the need for manual labour, and that in feudalism the state used physical punishment as there was slightly less need for labour, but the peasants still needed to be repressed. With the arrival of capitalism, the prisons served the useful purposes of, first, training workers in the disciplines of long hours of meaningless work (for example, the treadmill) in poor conditions, and, second, of mopping up the unemployed. To support this argument, they pointed out that in times of high unemployment the prison population expands and then contracts in periods of high employment.

Foucault

Foucault's claims (1977) that punishment has changed over time from being physical and public to internalised and intense echo the work of Durkheim. In pre-industrial societies offenders were seen as having offended against God or the rulers and were savagely punished for this. Punishment was conducted in public in order to warn others.

However, over time – as crime came to be seen as deviance from accepted codes of behaviour – the aim of punishment was to bring the person back into society and under control. This is achieved by having 'experts' whose job it is to make sure that the person fully **internalises** the need to conform. The punishment has shifted then from the body to the mind of the offender.

The police

The main agency responsible for the enforcement of social control is the police force. They are the arm of the state whose role it is to maintain public order and to enforce the law. There are two main positions in understanding the relationship of the police to society.

The two main positions for understanding the relationship of the police to society

1. The consensual approach

A consensual approach sees the police having a close relationship with the local area being policed and the role of the police force being to represent the interests of the majority of law-abiding people, defending them against the minority of offenders. Police officers are drawn from the community and reflect its characteristics. Individual offenders are caught as a result of complaints made by the community.

2. Conflict policing

This model of policing has been suggested by Scraton (1985), who argues that the police can best be seen as an occupying force, imposed upon working-class and ethnic-minority communities. Police officers largely patrol working-class and ethnic-minority areas where they impose the law and order that reflects the interests of the more powerful groups. Lea and Young (1984) describe this as 'military-style' policing, which is characterised by the use of large numbers of police officers patrolling an area in vehicles, using advanced technology for intelligence gathering.

Discretion, policing and the law

As we have noted, it is the job of the police to enforce the law. However, there are so many laws that could be applied in so many different circumstances that any police officer needs to use their **discretion** in deciding exactly which laws to apply and in what circumstances. Sociologists have been particularly interested in studying the nature of such discretion, and in seeing the implications for different groups in society. Discretion can also provide evidence to support one or other of the (consensual or conflict) styles of policing we have just discussed.

Reiner (1992) has suggested three ways of explaining the basis of police discretion:

- individualistic
- cultural
- structural.

Individualistic

The explanation for police discretion is that a particular police officer has specific concerns and interests and thus interprets and applies the law according to them. Colman and Gorman (1982) found some evidence for this in their study of police officers in inner London. In particular, they noted individual racist police officers who would apply the law more harshly on certain ethnic minorities.

Cultural

New recruits enter a world that has a highly developed culture – evolved from the particular type of job that police officers must do. Police officers are overwhelmingly white and male. They work long hours in each other's company and are largely isolated from the public. The result of this is the development of a very specific occupational culture – sometimes referred to as a **canteen culture**. According to Skolnick (1966) this has three main components – and we can add a fourth suggested by Graef (1989): that of masculinity.

What do sociologists mean by the term 'culture'?

Suspiciousness

As part of their job, police officers spend much of their time dealing with people who may have committed a criminal offence. As part of their training therefore they are taught to discriminate between 'decent people' and 'potential trouble-makers'. According to Reiner (1992), they categorise and stereotype certain people as a 'police property'. This involves regarding young males and particularly youths from ethnic minorities as potential troublemakers.

Internal solidarity and social isolation

We have just noted how police officers spend large amounts of time in the company of their peers, isolated from the public. They also rely upon each other in terms of support in times of physical threat and when denying accusations from the public.

Conservatism

Those who join the police in the first place are rarely politically radical, and the actual job of policing in itself emphasises a non-political attitude to the job – in which police officers must uphold the law and also the very notion of the state and traditional values. Added to the factors of social isolation and the majority recruitment from white males, this generates a strong sense of conservative values.

What do sociologists mean by values? What are conservative values?

Masculinity

The majority of police officers are male and drawn from the working class. The culture of police officers very much reflects traditional working-class values of heavy drinking, physical prowess and heterosexuality. Racial stereotyping is also heavily emphasised and linked with assuming the role of a police officer.

Structural

A third approach, derived from Marxist theory, stresses that the very definition of law is biased in favour of the powerful groups in society and against the working class. Therefore any upholding of the law involves upholding the values of capitalist society. Police officers' definition of crime in terms of street crimes and burglary (as opposed to white-collar or corporate crime and their repression of the working class) derives from their role as agents of control of a capitalist society. Their internal values simply reflect the job they have been given to do.

Evidence for this view can be found in Tarling's study (1988) which showed that over 65% of police resources are devoted to the uniformed patrolling of public space – particularly poorer neighbourhoods and central city areas. The result is that, as Morgan found out, about 55% of prisoners in police custody were unemployed, and of the rest, 30% were in manual, working-class jobs. Most detainees were young, with 60% being under 25 and 87% of all of those arrested being male. Finally, over 12% were from African or African-Caribbean backgrounds – despite these groups forming less than 3% of the population.

CHECK YOUR UNDERSTANDING

1 What three key changes in social control did Cohen identify?

2 What factors influence the way punishment has changed, according to Durkheim?

3 What explanation do Marxists provide for the development of prisons?

4 Identify and explain what two models of policing have been identified.

5 Identify the components of the police occupational culture.

6 Why is an understanding of police discretion important?

Item A

Images of the police

Item B

A public flogging

A supervised meeting where offenders have to face their victims

Young offenders sentenced to Community Service

Item C

Canteen culture

Item D

Those who are stopped and searched or questioned in the street, arrested, detained in the police station, charged and prosecuted are disproportionately young men who are unemployed or casually employed, and from discriminated-against ethnic minorities. The police themselves recognise that their main business involves such groups, and their mental social maps delineate them by a variety of derogatory epithets: 'assholes', 'pukes', 'scum', 'slag', 'prigs'.

R. Reiner (1997) 'Policy on Police' in M. Maguire, R. Morgan, R. Reiner (eds.) *The Oxford Handbook of Criminology* (2nd edition) Oxford: Oxford University Press

1 What different views of policing are illustrated by the photographs in Item A?

2 Compare the approaches to punishment in Item B. How do these relate to the ideas of:
   a. Durkheim
   b. Foucault?

3 In what way does the occupational culture of the police help us to understand their differing approaches to various groups in society?

4 How might relationships between the police and the groups mentioned in Item D be affected by the language used by some police officers?

Actuarialism – refers to the division of people into potentially deviant groups and controlling them on this basis.

Anomie – see Key Terms in Topic 1.

Arrest rates – refers to the numbers of people arrested for offences. It can be different from the offending rate.

Canteen culture – a term which refers to the occupational culture developed by the police.

Collective conscience – see Key Terms in Topic 1.

Consensual model of policing – policing method based on the consent of the population.

Disciplining – refers to the process of control through non-coercive methods.

Discretion – refers to the fact that the police have to use their judgement when to use the force of the law.

Formal social control – official, organised ways of enforcing conformity.

Informal social control – routine, cultural ways of enforcing conformity.

Internalise – when people come to accept, and possibly believe, some value or rule.

Mechanistic societies – technologically and socially simple societies, as identified by Durkheim in which people are culturally very similar.

Military model of policing – policing which is imposed upon the population.

Offending rates – statistics referring to how many crimes are committed, and by which groups of people.

Organic societies – culturally and technologically complex societies as identified by Durkheim, in which culturally people are different from each other.

Privatisation – giving control from the state to private companies.

Restitutive – a model of law based upon trying to repair the damage done to society.

Retributive – a model of law based upon revenge.

Sanctions – measures taken to control a person or group.

Research idea

Conduct a survey to discover public attitudes to punishment. Some questions can be found at the website of MORI, the polling organisation (www.mori.com/polls/2000/ms000714.htm)

WWWebtask

Search the worldwide web for press stories and campaigns relating to the murder of James Bulger, the young child in Liverpool killed by two ten-year-old boys. What attitudes to punishment do you find? Can you relate these to the different views of punishment covered in this Topic?

EXAM PRACTICE

Extract from AQA-style question

'The police have considerable choice about which crimes and criminals to prosecute'.

Examine the implications of this view for positivist sociological theories of crime. (40 marks)

OCR-style question

Outline and assess the view that policing and punishment in Britain today reflects shared values. (60 marks)

1 Do you think you are going to be successful in life? What do you mean by success?

2 Have you ever failed at something that you really wanted to succeed in? Whose fault was that, in your opinion?

3 If you saw someone drop the large amount of money, what would you do? Pick it up and keep it? Chase after them and give it back? Take it home and phone the police? Explain your answer.

4 Who do you think are more important in influencing your day-to-day behaviour, your family or your friends?

5 If your friends wanted you to do something that you considered acceptable behaviour, but your parents expressly forbade it, what would you do?

Subcultural theories share the common belief that people who commit crime usually share different values from the mass of law-abiding members of society. However, crime-committing people do not live in complete opposition to mainstream values, rather they have 'amended' certain values so that this justifies criminal behaviour – hence the term 'subculture'.

Strain is a term that is used to refer to explanations of criminal behaviour that argue that crime is the result of certain groups of people being placed in a position where they are unable, for whatever reason, to conform to the values and beliefs of society. Many sociologists use the term interchangeably with 'subculture'. Although, strictly speaking, they are not the same thing (for example, Merton is a 'strain' theorist and does not really discuss subculture), we have put them together here because of the degree of overlap between the two approaches.

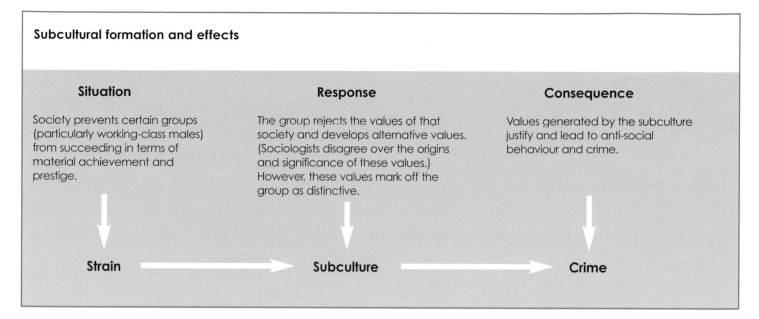

Subcultural formation and effects

Situation	Response	Consequence
Society prevents certain groups (particularly working-class males) from succeeding in terms of material achievement and prestige.	The group rejects the values of that society and develops alternative values. (Sociologists disagree over the origins and significance of these values.) However, these values mark off the group as distinctive.	Values generated by the subculture justify and lead to anti-social behaviour and crime.

Strain → Subculture → Crime

The origins of subculture

Subcultural theories derive from two different schools of sociology – and if you think carefully about each of the later approaches we discuss, you will probably be able to tell which school of thought they derive from.

Appreciative sociology

The first parent-school is that of the University of Chicago, which developed in the early part of the twentieth century, in response to the dramatic social change that was taking place in US cities at that time. Chicago sociologists were determined to appreciate the wide variety of different cultures and lifestyles in Chicago that existed as a result of the huge influx of migrants arriving from all over Europe and southern USA. Chicago sociologists simply wanted to observe and note down the sheer variety and dynamism of urban life. Integral to this was the study of deviant groups, with Frederic Thrasher's *The Gang* (1927) and Whyte's *Street Corner Society* (1943) demonstrating that deviant groups in society had clear norms and values of their own that justified their different behaviour.

 These sociologists pioneered the use of participant observation in their research. What are the advantages and disadvantages of using this method to study deviant groups?

Strain theory

In the 1930s, Robert Merton (1938), tried to locate deviance within a functionalist framework. For Merton, crime and deviance were evidence of a poor fit (or a **strain**) between the socially accepted goals of society and the socially approved means of obtaining those desired goals. The resulting strain led to deviance.

Merton argued that all societies set their members certain goals, and at the same time they also provide socially approved ways of achieving these goals. Merton was aware that not everyone shared the same goals, and he pointed out that in a stratified society the goals were linked to a person's

position in the social structure. Those lower down had restricted goals. The system worked well as long as there was a reasonable chance that a majority of people were able to achieve their goals. However, if the majority of the population were unable to achieve the socially set goals then they became disenchanted with society and sought out alternative (often deviant) ways of behaving. Merton used Durkheim's term **anomie**, to describe this situation.

Merton's strain theory

Responses	Means	Goals
Conformity	+	+
Innovation	–	+
Ritualism	+	–
Retreatism	–	–
Rebellion	+/–	+/–

The following different forms of behaviour then could be understood as a *strain* between goals and means.

- *Conformity* – Here the individual continues to adhere to both goals and means, despite the limited likelihood of success.
- *Innovation* – The person accepts the goals of society but uses different ways to achieve those goals. Criminal behaviour is included in this response.
- *Ritualism* – Here the means are used by the individual, but sight of the actual goal is lost. For example, the bureaucrat or the police officer blindly enforcing the letter of the law without looking at the nature of justice are examples.
- *Retreatism* – Here the individual rejects both goals and means. The person dependent upon drugs or alcohol is included in this form of behaviour.
- *Rebellion* – Both the socially sanctioned goals and means are rejected and different ones substituted. This is the political activist or the religious fundamentalist.

Criticism of Merton

Merton has been criticised by Valier (2001) amongst others for his stress on the existence of a common goal in society. Valier argues that there are, in fact, a variety of goals that people strive to attain at any one time.

Status frustration

Writing in the mid 1950s, Albert Cohen (1955) drew upon both Merton's ideas of strain and also on the **ethnographic** ideas of the Chicago school of sociology. Cohen was particularly interested in the fact that much offending behaviour was not economically motivated, but simply done for the thrill of the act. (This is as true today as it was in the 1950s, for vandalism typically accounts for about 18% of current crime recorded by the British Crime Survey.)

According to Cohen, 'lower-class' boys strove to emulate middle-class values and aspirations, but lacked the means to attain success. This led to **status frustration** – that is, a sense of personal failure and inadequacy. The result was that they rejected those very values and patterns of 'acceptable' behaviour that they could not be successful within. He suggests that school is the key area for the playing out of this drama. Lower-class children are much more likely to fail and consequently feel humiliated. In an attempt to gain status they 'invert' traditional middle class values – behaving badly and engaging in a variety of anti-social behaviours.

Criticisms of A. Cohen

- There is no discussion of females. His research is solely about males.
- The young 'delinquents' need to be brilliant sociologists to work out what are middle-class values and then invert them!
- Cohen fails to prove that school really is the key place where success and failure are demonstrated.

Cohen has been criticised for over-emphasising the influence of education at the expense of other socialising agencies. What are these and what part might they play in the formation of subcultures?

Illegitimate opportunity structure

The idea of strain between goals and means was a relatively minor influence on Cohen, but it did have a very significant impact on the writings of Cloward and Ohlin (1960), who owed much to the ideas of Merton.

They argued that Merton had failed to appreciate that there was a parallel opportunity structure to the legal one called the **illegitimate opportunity structure**. By this they meant that for some subcultures in society a regular illegal career was available, with recognised illegal means of obtaining society's goals. A good contemporary example of this is given in Dick Hobbs' book *Bad Business* (1998). Hobbs interviews successful professional criminals and demonstrates how it is possible to have a career in crime, given the right connections and 'qualities'.

What problems is Hobbs likely to have encountered in ensuring that his data is reliable, valid and representative?

According to Cloward and Ohlin, the illegal opportunity structure had three possible adaptations or subcultures.

Criminal – This adaptation is where there is a thriving local criminal subculture, with successful role-models. Young offenders can 'work their way up the ladder' in the criminal hierarchy.

Conflict – Here there is no local criminal subculture to provide a career opportunity. Groups brought up in this sort of environment are likely to turn to violence usually against other similar groups. Cloward and Ohlin give the example of violent gang 'warfare'.

Retreatist – This tends to be a more individual response and occurs where the individual has no opportunity or ability to engage in either of the other two subcultures. The result is a retreat into alcohol or drugs.

Evaluation of Cloward and Ohlin

This explanation is useful and, as Hobbs' work shows, for some people there really is a criminal opportunity structure. But the approach shares some of the weaknesses of Merton's original theory:

- It is difficult to accept that such a neat distinction into three clear categories occurs in real life.
- There is no discussion whatsoever about female deviancy.

Focal concerns

In the late 1950s Walter Miller developed a rather different approach to explaining the values of crime when he suggested that deviancy was linked to the culture of lower-class males.

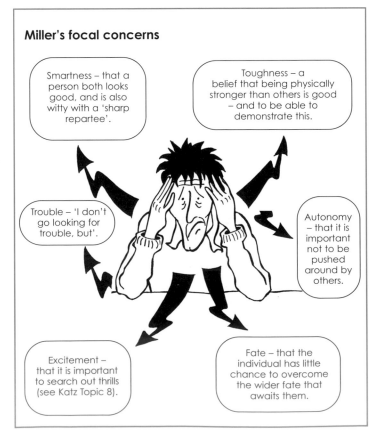

Miller's focal concerns

Smartness – that a person both looks good, and is also witty with a 'sharp repartee'.

Toughness – a belief that being physically stronger than others is good – and to be able to demonstrate this.

Trouble – 'I don't go looking for trouble, but'.

Autonomy – that it is important not to be pushed around by others.

Excitement – that it is important to search out thrills (see Katz Topic 8).

Fate – that the individual has little chance to overcome the wider fate that awaits them.

Miller (1962) suggested that working-class males have six '**focal concerns**' that are likely to lead to delinquency. According to Miller, then, young lower-class males are pushed towards crime by the implicit values of their subculture.

Miller suggests that the values of certain groups of the poor push them to behave in ways that were likely to confirm them in a life of poverty. Have you come across this kind of argument elsewhere during your sociology course? If so, explain the context(s).

Evaluation of Miller

Miller provides little evidence to show that these are specifically lower-class values. Indeed, as Box (1981) pointed out, they could equally apply to males right across the class structure.

Applying subcultural theory: the British experience

The studies we have looked at so far have been American ones. However, subcultural studies were being undertaken in Britain too – though with a variety of results. Howard Parker (1974) successfully applied Miller's focal concerns in his study of working-class 'lads' in inner city Liverpool (although, as we have already noted, he could probably have applied these equally successfully to rugby-playing students at Liverpool University).

On the other hand, studies by David Downes (1966) of young working-class males in London could find no evidence of distinctive values. Instead, Downes suggested that young working class males were 'dissociated' from mainstream values, by which he meant that they were concerned more about leisure than their long-term future or employment, and were more likely to engage in petty crime.

So, in the UK, evidence of distinctive subcultures has been fairly difficult to obtain.

Subterranean values

We have seen that one consistent criticism of subcultural theories was that there was little evidence to demonstrate a distinct set of anti-social values. Even if there were subcultures, were they a response to middle-class values or to a distinctive set of working-class values? Matza (1961) put these criticisms together to make a strong attack upon subcultural theory.

Matza argued that there were no distinctive subcultural values, rather that all groups in society utilised a shared set of **subterranean values**. The key thing was that most of the time, most people control these deviant desires. They only rarely emerge – for example, at the annual office party, or the holiday in Agia Napa. But when they do emerge, we use **techniques of neutralisation** to provide justification for our deviant actions. As we said earlier, the difference between a persistent offender and a law-abiding citizen is simply how often and in what circumstances the **s**ubterranean values emerge and are then justified by the techniques of neutralisation.

Techniques of neutralisation

- Denial of responsibility – The offender denies that it was their fault.
- Denial of victim – The offender claims that in this particular case the victim was in the wrong.
- Denial of injury – Where the victim was not really hurt or harmed by the crime, according to the offenders.
- Condemnation of condemners – Where the offender feels a sense of unfairness of being picked on for something others have done and not been punished for.
- Appeal to higher loyalties – Where the rule or law had to be ignored because more important issues were at stake.

Techniques of neutralisation

Which of Matza's techniques of neutralisation are indicated in these statements?

It was just a laugh.

I was really drunk.

Everybody was doing it – I don't know why they picked on me.

He hit me first.

I was just defending my mates.

Matza's critique of subculture is quite devastating. He is saying that all of us share deviant, 'subcultural values', and that it is not true that there are distinctive groups with their own values, different from the rest of us.

Subculture: the paradox of inclusion

In his book *On the Edge*, Carl Nightingale (1993) studies young black youth in an inner-city area of Philadelphia. For Nightingale, subculture emerges from a desire to be part of the mainstream US culture – that is, subculture emerges from being rejected and marginalised by the mainstream society. Nightingale notes the way that black children avidly consume US culture by watching television with its emphasis on consumerism and the success of violence – yet at the same time they are excluded economically, racially and politically from participating in that mainstream US culture. The response is to overcompensate by identifying themselves with the wider culture by acquiring articles with high-status trade names or logos. Once again, drawing upon Merton's ideas, the subculture reflects the belief that it is not so much how these high-status goods are obtained rather the *fact of possessing* them. In the USA, these are often obtained through violence, expressed in violent gangs and high crime-rates.

Nightingale is suggesting that identification with US culture as experienced through the media, coupled with economic and social exclusion creates a situation of violence and criminality as young blacks seek to identify themselves with this culture by purchasing the symbols (such as expensive clothes) of success.

Similarly, Philip Bourgois' study of El Barrio (1995), looks at the lives of drug dealers and criminals in this deprived area of New York and finds that they, too, believe in the American Dream of financial success. Their 'subculture' is really little different from mainstream values, the only difference being that they deal drugs in order to get the money to pursue an all-American lifestyle.

So, both Nightingale's and Bourgois' versions of subculture take us back to the strain theory of Merton, and Cloward and Ohlin, emphasising that the desire to be included leads to the actions that ensure that they are excluded from society.

Contemporary alternatives to subculture

Postmodernism

What do you understand by the term 'postmodernism'? In what other parts of your studies has this view been influential?

Most of the approaches we have looked at here as well as the Marxist subcultural approaches in the Topic 4, seek to explain deviant behaviour by looking for some rational reason why the subculture might have developed. Recent postmodern approaches reject this explanation for behaviour. Katz (1988), for example, argues that crime is **seductive** – young males get drawn into it, not because of any process of rejection but because it is thrilling. In a similar manner, Lyng argues that young males like taking risks and engaging in '**edgework**' as he puts it. By edgework, he means going right to the edge of acceptable behaviour and flirting with danger.

Masculinity

Subcultural theory is overwhelmingly *male* subcultural theory. The assumptions underlying the vast bulk of the writings we have looked at within this tradition have been discussing masculine behaviour. However, as Collison points out, they may well have missed the significance of this. In order to explain male offending behaviour, it is important to explain the nature of being male in our society and what links masculinity itself has to crime (see Topic 8 on Gender issues and offending).

What norms and values typically associated with masculinity might lead young males into deviant behaviour?

CHECK YOUR UNDERSTANDING

1 What is meant by 'appreciative sociology'?

2 What is 'anomie' and how is the idea used by Merton to explain deviance?

3 How, according to A. Cohen, does school failure lead to the formation of subcultures?

4 What are 'techniques of neutralisation' and how does their existence undermine some subcultural arguments?

5 What do we mean by the 'paradox of inclusion'?

6 Why is the idea of 'masculinity' relevant to understanding criminal behaviour?

Research idea

Interview a sample of friends. If they have ever committed a deviant act, ask them how they justified it. To what extent do their responses reflect Matza's techniques of neutralisation? Also, ask them about their values in general. Do those who have committed deviant acts share deviant values? Use your results to help you evaluate subcultural theory.

KEY TERMS

Anomie – see Key Terms in Topic 1.

Appreciative sociology – similar to ethnography or observational methods i.e. a sociologist who sets out to describe a society through observing the group in action and sometimes joining them.

Edgework – derives from Lyng. Refers to activities of young males which provide them with thrills, derived from the real possibility of physical or emotional harm (e.g. stealing and racing cars; drug abuse).

Ethnographic – form of observational research, in which researcher lives amongst, and describes activities of, particular group being studied.

Focal concerns – term used by Miller to describe key values.

Illegitimate opportunity structure – refers to an alternative, illegal way of life that certain groups in society have access to.

Seductive – beguiling, attractive.

Status frustration – according to Cohen, when young men (and women?) feel that they are looked down upon by society.

Strain – term used by Merton and other functionalists to describe a lack of balance and adjustment in society.

Subculture – a distinctive set of values that provides an alternative to those of the mainstream culture.

Subterranean values – deviant values everyone shares, usually hidden.

Techniques of neutralisation – justifications for our deviant actions.

Item A

Robber Ronnie Knight, far left, with his girlfriend, lived in Spain for a decade before being jailed in London.
Suspected accomplice Clifford Saxe, right, was arrested in Fuengirola in January for the 1983 robbery.
M25 road rage murderer Kenneth Noye, left, absconded to his villa in Andalucía, above.   London Express/PA

Source: *The Observer* (2001) November 18 2001

Item B

I want to place drug dealers and street level criminals into their rightful positions with the mainstream of U.S. society. They are not "exotic others" operating in an irrational netherworld. On the contrary, they are "made in America". Highly motivated, ambitious inner-city youths have been attracted to the rapidly expanding, multi-billion dollar drug economy ... precisely because they believe ... [in] ... the American Dream.

... In fact, in their pursuit of success they are even following the minute details of the classical yankee model for upward mobility. They are aggressively pursuing careers as private entrepreneurs: they take risks, work hard and pray for good luck.

P. Bourgois (1995) *In Search of Respect* Cambridge: Cambridge University Press (p. 326)

1 How do Bourgois' research and the item above illustrate both the ideas of Merton, and of Cloward and Ohlin?

2 Bourgois' study is based on participant observation. Why is this method particularly useful for understanding values?

WWWebtask

Go to the Home Office Website (www.homeoffice.gov.uk/rds/pubsintrol/html). You will find the Research Study 209 on Findings from the 1998/99 Youth Lifestyles Leisure Survey. Look at pp. 34–35 on family and friends and offending. Does this provide any evidence to support or undermine subcultural theory?

EXAM PRACTICE

Extract from AQA-style question

Examine the similarities and differences between subcultural theory and strain theory as explanations for deviant behaviour. (40 marks)

OCR-style question

Outline and assess the view that deviance is the result of strain in society. (60 marks)

Getting you thinking

Angel Isidoro Rodriguez (left), known in banking circles as "El Divino" (The Divine), former head of the Banpais banking group, was extradited from Spain to Mexico June 1, after nearly two years in prison on fraud charges. Rodriguez was allowed to go free after his arrival due to a legal loophole that does not consider white-collar crime "serious".

1 Do you think the release of 'El Divino' was fair? Why do you think he was released?

2 Do you think that the police and criminal justice system treat people equally? What reasons can you suggest for your answer?

3 Look at the photo of the children working in a factory in south-east Asia – they work up to 12 hours a day, earn a very low wage and effectively are robbed of their childhood. It is legal. Do you think it is wrong? Do you think it should be made illegal (as it is in Britain)?

4 On what basis do you think that something should be made a crime?

5 Using your own ideas, can you find any examples of activities that you think ought to be crimes, but are not? Can you suggest why not?

The traditional Marxist approach

Karl Marx himself wrote very little about crime, but a Marxist theory of crime was first developed by Bonger as early as 1916 and then developed by writers such as Chambliss (1975). The overall background to this approach was based on the Marxist analysis of society, which argues that society is best understood by examining the process whereby the majority of the population are exploited by the owners and controllers of commerce and industry. Marxists argue that this simple, fundamental fact of exploitation provides the key to unlock the explanations for the workings of society.

The key elements of the Marxist or critical criminological approach include:

- the basis of criminal law
- the dominant **hegemony** of the ruling class
- law enforcement
- individual motivation
- crime and control.

The basis of the criminal law

The starting point for Marxist analysis is that all laws are essentially for the benefit of the ruling class, and the criminal law reflects their interests. For example, concern with the laws of property ownership largely benefit those with significant amounts of property. For those who are poor, there is little to steal. Personal violence is dangerous, and the ruling class wish to control the right to use violence in society through their agents – the police and the army. Criminal law therefore operates to protect the rich and powerful.

Law creation and the dominant hegemony

In capitalist societies, the ruling class impose their values – that is, values that are beneficial to themselves – upon the mass of the population. They do this through a number of agencies such as the education system, religion and the mass media. (This concept of ruling-class values being imposed upon the population is commonly known as 'hegemony'.)

This dominant set of values forms the framework on which laws are based in a democracy. However, we have just seen that, according to Marxists, the set of values is actually 'forced' on the people. Thus what they believe they are agreeing to as a result of their own beliefs is, in reality, in the interests of the ruling class.

Law enforcement

Despite the fact that the law-making process reflects the interests of the ruling class, many of these laws could provide benefits for the majority of the population if they were applied fairly. However, even the interpretation and enforcement of the law is biased in favour of the ruling class, so that the police and the judicial system will arrest and punish the working class, but tend not to enforce the law against the ruling class.

Individual motivation

Marxist theory also provides an explanation for the individual motivation underlying crime. Bonger, the very first Marxist writer on crime, pointed this out. He argued that capitalism is based upon competition, selfishness and greed, and this formed people's attitudes to life. Therefore crime was a perfectly normal outcome of these values which stressed looking after oneself at the expense of others. But Bonger also said that in many cases, poor people were driven to crime by their desperate conditions

Crime and control

As we saw earlier, the ruling class in capitalism constantly seeks to divert the attention of the vast majority of the population away from an understanding of the true causes of their situation, and to impose their values through the mass media, religious organisations and the education system. These institutions provide alternative accounts of reality justifying the capitalist system as the natural and best economic system. Crime plays a significant part in supporting the ideology of capitalism, as it diverts attention away from the exploitative nature of capitalism and focuses attention instead on the evil and frightening nature of certain criminal groups in society, from whom we are only protected by the police. This justifies heavy policing of working-class areas, 'stop and searches' by the police of young people and the arrests of any sections of the population who oppose capitalism.

An example of the traditional Marxist approach

William Chambliss' study of British vagrancy laws provides an illustration of the ways in which laws may be directly related to the interests of the ruling class. The first English vagrancy laws appeared in 1349, one year after the outbreak of the Black Death plague that was to kill more than one-third of the country's entire population. One result of the catastrophe was to decimate the labour force, so that those who were left could ask for high wages – and many people did this, moving from village to village in search of high pay. To combat this, the vagrancy laws were introduced, requiring every able-bodied man on the road to accept work at a low, fixed wage. The law was strictly enforced and did produce a supply of low-paid labour to help the workforce shortage. For almost 200 years the laws remained unchanged, but in 1530, changes were introduced which altered the emphasis of the laws to protect the concerns of an increasingly powerful merchant class from the many highway robbers who were preying on the traffic of goods along major highways. The vagrancy laws were amended so that they could be used to punish anyone on the road without a job, who was presumed to be a highwayman.

In both cases, the law was introduced and imposed in such a way as to benefit the ruling class – whilst apparently being concerned with stopping vagrants from travelling around England.

Criticisms of the traditional Marxist approach

1 The victims of crime are simply ignored in this analysis. The harm done by offenders is not taken into account. This is particularly important, as the victims are usually drawn from the less well-off sections of the population.

2 The explanation for law creation and enforcement tends to be one dimensional, in that all laws are seen as the outcome of the interests of the ruling class – no allowance is made for the complexity of influences on law-making behaviour.

What else might influence the creation of laws in a society?

The New Criminology

It was partly as a result of these criticisms of what was a fairly crude Marxist explanation of crime, and partly as a result of the influence of interactionism (see Topic 5), that Taylor, Walton and Young attempted to produce a fully social theory of deviance in *The New Criminology* (1973). This became an extremely influential book – possibly because it was a fairly successful fusing of Marxism and interactionism, the two most prominent theories of that time.

The new criminologists argued that in order to understand why a particular crime took place, it was no use just looking at the individual's motivation (e.g. alcohol or jealousy) and obvious influences (e.g. family background), which is what traditional positivist sociology might do. A Marxist perspective must be taken which looks at the wider capitalist society that helps generate the circumstances of the crime and police response to it. It is also important to use interactionist ideas to see how the behaviour of victim, offender, media and criminal justice system all interact to influence how the situation develops.

In what other parts of the course have you come across the influence of interactionism? What contribution has it made?

Ideology and the New Criminology

A further element of the New Criminology was that apart from the actual analysis that is suggested, it also argued that any sociology of crime and deviance had to be critical of the established capitalist order. This meant that instead of accepting the capitalist definition of crime and seeking to explain this, its role ought to be to uncover and explain the crimes of the rich. There was no attempt to be unbiased, rather the approach looked critically at the role of the police, the media and the criminal justice system in general – pointing out how they serve the needs of the ruling class.

Part of this critical approach to crime and criminal justice was to look in a fresh way at the ordinary criminal, who should best be seen as someone who is angry at capitalism and mistakenly expresses this anger through crime, rather than politics.

As we shall see in Topic 11, this later led to debates between '**left realists**' who seek to work within the current system and those who remained true to the ideas of critical criminology.

A good example of critical criminology is the work of Stuart Hall *et al.* (1978) in *Policing the Crisis: The State and Law and Order*. In the 1970s, London witnessed a growth in 'muggings' or assault and robbery of people in the streets. The media focused on this crime and a wave of publicity forced the problem to the top of the political and policing agenda. Although Hall did not exactly follow the model put forward in *The New Criminology*, the general critical criminological framework was used – see table on right.

Criticisms of the New Criminology

1   Traditional Marxists such as Hirst (1975) argued that the New Criminology strayed too far from the Marxist tradition.

2   Others, such as Rock (1988), who were concerned directly in combating crime argued that it gave far too romantic a view of criminals (in later writings, Young echoed this criticism and suggested it was one of the reasons for his development of left realism – see Topic 11).

3   Feminist criminologists, such as Pat Carlen (1988), pointed out that there was absolutely no specific discussion of the power of patriarchy in the analysis, which simply continued the omission of women from criminological discussion.

Marxist subcultural theory

A second strand of thought that developed from Marxism, was a specific explanation for the existence of subcultures amongst the working class. According to *The Centre for Contemporary Cultural Studies* (a group of writers at Birmingham University), capitalism maintains control over the majority of the population in two ways:

● ideological dominance through the media
● economic pressures – people want to keep their jobs and pay their mortgages.

The New Criminology

What a fully social theory of deviance must cover according to Taylor, Walton and Young (1973)	Application of these ideas in Hall et al. Policing the Crisis (1978)
The wider origins of the deviant act	The 1970s was a period of considerable social crisis in Britain, the result of an international downturn in capitalist economies.
The immediate origins of the deviant act	This turmoil was shown in a number of inner city riots, conflict in Northern Ireland and a high level of strikes. The government was searching for a group which could be scapegoated, and attention drawn on to them and away from the crisis.
The actual act	Mugging – which according to the police was more likely to be carried out by those from African-Caribbean backgrounds.
The immediate origins of social reaction	Media outrage at the extent of muggings, linked to racism amongst the Metropolitan Police.
The wider origins of social reaction	The need to find scapegoats and the ease with which young men from African-Caribbean backgrounds could be blamed.
The outcome of social reaction on the deviants' further action	A sense of injustice amongst ethnic minorities and a loss of confidence by ethnic minority communities in the criminal justice system.
The nature of the deviant process as a whole	The real causes of crime were not addressed and were effectively hidden by the criminal justice system.

Only those groups on the margins of society are not 'locked in' by ideology and finance, and thus are able to provide some form of resistance to capitalism. The single largest group offering this resistance is working-class youth.

According to Brake (1980) amongst others, this resistance is expressed through working-class youth subcultures. The clothes they wear and the language they use show their disdain of capitalism and their awareness of their position in it. Brake argues that this resistance, however, is best seen as '**magical**'. By magical, he means that it is a form of illusion that appears to solve their problems, but in reality does no such thing. According to him, each generation of working-class youth face similar problems (dead-end jobs, unemployment, and so on), but in different circumstances – that is, society changes constantly so that every generation

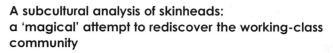

A subcultural analysis of skinheads:
a 'magical' attempt to rediscover the working-class community

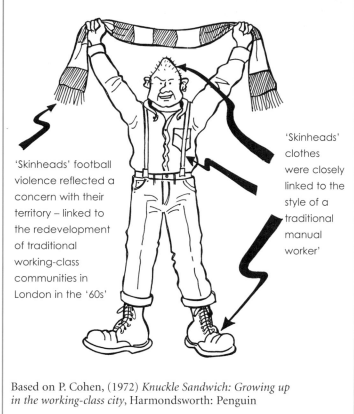

'Skinheads' football violence reflected a concern with their territory – linked to the redevelopment of traditional working-class communities in London in the '60s'

'Skinheads' clothes were closely linked to the style of a traditional manual worker'

Based on P. Cohen, (1972) *Knuckle Sandwich: Growing up in the working-class city*, Harmondsworth: Penguin

Criticism of the Marxist subcultural approach

S. Cohen (1980) pointed out that these writers were simply biased in their analysis. They wanted to prove that working-class youth cultures were an attack on capitalism, and therefore made sure that they fixed the evidence to find this. He pointed out, for example, that there were many different ways to interpret the subcultural style of the groups, and that the interpretation that the Marxist writers had imposed was just one of many possibilities.

CHECK YOUR UNDERSTANDING

1 How does the ruling class impose their values on others?

2 According to Marxists, how neutral is the law?

3 What is Bonger's explanation of individual motivation for crime?

4 How does Chambliss's research on vagrancy support a Marxist view of crime?

5 In what ways does the New Criminology utilise both Marxism and interactionism?

6 Why is it convenient for capitalism to find scapegoats?

7 Why do working-class subcultures develop?

8 How do working-class subcultures resist capitalism?

9 In what way is their resistance 'magical'?

10 How have different Marxist approaches to crime and deviance been criticised?

experiences a very different world, with the one constant being that the majority will be exploited by the ruling class. Each generation expresses their resistance through different choice of clothes, **argot** (slang and patterns of speech), music, and so on. But each will eventually be trapped like their parents before them. An example of this approach is Paul Willis' *Learning to Labour* (1977), a study of working-class boys in a secondary school. They realise early on the sorts of jobs they are going to get and reject school and its concerns. However, their very rejection of school ensures that they are going to fail – thus making their belief come true – but, of course, they have been instrumental in their own failure.

KEY TERMS

Argot – a way of speaking that is specific to a particular group.

Hegemony – the ideas and values of the ruling class that dominate thinking in society.

Left realist – a development from Marxist criminology which argues that it is better to work within capitalism to improve people's lives, than to attempt wholesale social change.

'Magical' – illusory; in this context, something that appears to solve problems, but in reality does no such thing.

Scapegoat – groups in society who are blamed by the powerful for the problems of society. These are usually relatively powerless groups. This draws attention away from the real causes of crime.

Item A The criminal law is thus not a reflection of custom but a set of rules laid down by the state in the interests of the ruling class, and resulting from the conflicts that inhere in class structured societies; criminal behaviour is, then, the inevitable expression of class conflict resulting from the inherently exploitative nature of economic relations.

Criminality is simply not something that people have or don't have; crime is not something some people do and others don't. Crime is a matter of who can pin the label on whom, and underlying this socio-political process is the structure of social relations determined by the political economy.

W. Chambliss, (1975) 'Towards a Political Economy of Crime' *Theory and Society* Vol. 2 (abridged)

Item B

The poster above shows one of the best-selling images ever produced. It is the face of Che Guevara, a Marxist revolutionary who was shot dead in Bolivia in 1967.

1 According to Item A, what is the basis of the criminal law?

2 If we wish to stop crime, according to Marxists what do we need to do?

3 How might a Marxist interpret the display of a poster of Che Guevara in a student's bedroom?

4 Many people have argued that the Marxist explanation of crime is no longer valid today as times have changed, wealth is spread more widely across the nation and social class is no longer important. What is the evidence for and against these criticisms?

Research ideas

Choose any one contemporary subcultural style. What are the favoured clothes, argot, style of music and other distinguishing features (e.g. skateboard)? What explanations can you offer for the origins of these? Interview members of the group to find what meaning they give to their dress, language, and so on.

EXAM PRACTICE

Extract from AQA-style question

Assess the contribution of Marxist theories to an understanding of the relationship between deviance and power. (40 marks)

OCR-style question

Outline and assess Marxist explanations of crime and deviance. (60 marks)

WWWebtask

● Look up the website www.socialistparty.org.uk. To what extent do you think the Marxist analysis contained in it accurately explains today's problems?

● Using the internet, look up newspaper reports and background information about any recent terrorist or criminal event. See if you can use the 'new criminology' framework of Taylor, Walton and Young. At the time of writing, the terrorist attacks on the Twin Towers on September 11th 2001 would be an appropriate subject for this type of analysis.

Marx
Althusser.

1 Are any of the people in the photos above committing a crime?

2 Is their behaviour deviant? If so, which?

3 Will everybody agree about which behaviours are deviant? Why might there be different views?

4 What does this exercise tell us about deviance?

Understanding deviance: reaction not cause

Most approaches to understanding crime and deviance (with the exception of Marxist approaches) accept that there is a difference between those who offend and those who do not. On the basis of this assumption, they then search for the key factors that lead the person to offend.

However, since the early 1950s, one group of sociologists influenced by **symbolic interactionism** have questioned this approach. They argue instead that this approach makes a mistake in its fundamental assumption that lawbreakers are somehow different from the law-abiding. Labelling theory suggests instead that *most people* commit deviant and criminal acts, but only some people are caught and **stigmatised** for it. So, if most people commit deviant acts of some kind, it is pointless trying to search for the differences between deviants and non-deviants – instead the stress should be upon understanding the *reaction* to and *definition* of deviance rather than on the *causes* of the initial act.

 What is interactionism? Give examples of its influence in other topics you have studied.

As Howard Becker (1963) puts it:

> *Deviancy is not a quality of the act a person commits but rather a consequence of the application by others of rules and sanctions to an 'offender'. Deviant behaviour is behaviour that people so label.*

This is a radically different way of exploring crime; in fact, it extends beyond crime and helps us to understand *any* deviant or stigmatised behaviour. Labelling theory has gradually been adopted and incorporated into many other sociological approaches – for example, Taylor, Walton and Young (1973) have used it in their updating of Marxist criminology, and postmodernist approaches owe much to it as well.

Give examples from your studies of how the term 'labelling' has been used by sociologists.

The best-known exponent of 'labelling theory' is Howard Becker. In the book *The Outsiders*, Becker gives a very clear and simple illustration of the labelling argument, drawing upon an anthropological study by Malinowski (1982) of a traditional culture on a Pacific Island.

Malinowski describes how a youth killed himself because he had been publicly accused of **incest**. When Malinowski had first inquired about the case, the islanders expressed their horror and disgust. But, on further investigation, it turned out that incest was not uncommon on the island, nor was it really frowned upon provided those involved were discreet. However, if an incestuous affair became too obvious and public, the islanders reacted with abuse, the offenders were ostracised and often driven to suicide.

Becker, then is saying here that:

1   Just because someone breaks a rule it does not necessarily follow that others will define it as deviant.
2   Someone has to enforce the rules or, at least, draw attention to them – these people usually have a vested interest in the issue. (In the example of the incestuous islanders, the rule was enforced by the rejected ex-lover of the girl involved in incest.)
3   If the person is successfully labelled then consequences follow. Once publicly labelled as deviant, the offender was faced with limited choices – one of which was suicide.

Responding to, and enforcing, rules

Most sociological theories take for granted that once a person has committed a deviant or criminal act, then the response will be uniform. This is not true. People respond differently to deviance or rule-breaking. In the early 1960s when gays were more likely to be stigmatised than now, John Kitsuse (1962) interviewed 75 heterosexual students to elicit their responses to (presumed) sexual advances from gays. What he found was a very wide range of responses from complete tolerance to bizarre and extreme hatred. One told how he had 'known' that a man he was talking to in a bar was homosexual because he had wanted to talk about psychology! The point of Kitsuse's work is that there was no agreed definition of what con-stituted a homosexual 'advance' – it was open to negotiation.

In Britain today, British Crime Survey statistics show that young black males are more likely to be stopped for questioning and searching than any other group. This is a result of the police officers' belief that this particular social group is more likely to offend than any other, and therefore are the subjects of 'routine suspicion'.

Criticism

Akers (1967) criticised labelling theorists for the way he claims they present deviants as being perfectly normal people who are no different from anyone else until someone comes along and slaps a label on them. Akers argues that there must be some reason why the label is applied to certain groups/individual and not others. As long as labelling fails to explain this, then it is an incomplete theory.

The consequences of rule enforcement

As we have just seen, being labelled as a deviant, and having laws enforced against you is the result of a number of different factors. However, once successfully labelled as a deviant various consequences occur for the individual.

The clearest example of this is provided by Edwin Lemert who distinguished between '**primary**' and '**secondary**' **deviance** (Lemert, 1972). Primary deviance is rule-breaking, which is of little importance in itself, and secondary deviance the consequence of the responses of others – this *is* significant.

To illustrate this, Lemert studied the coastal **Inuits** of Canada who had a long-rooted problem of chronic stuttering or stammering. Lemert suggested that the problem was 'caused' by the great importance attached to ceremonial speech-making. Failure to speak well was a great humiliation. Children with the slightest speech difficulty were so conscious of their parents' desire to have well-speaking children that they became over anxious about their own abilities. It was this very anxiety, according to Lemert, that led to chronic stuttering. We see here an example of chronic stuttering (secondary deviance) as a response to parents' reaction to initial minor speech defects (primary deviance).

The person labelled as 'deviant' will eventually come to see themselves as being bad (or mad). Becker used the term **master status** to describe this process – and points out that once a label has successfully been applied to a person, then all other qualities become unimportant and they are responded to solely in terms of this master status.

Rejecting labels: negotiability

However, the process of being labelled is open to 'negotiation', in that some groups or individuals are able to reject the label. An example of this is Reiss's (1961) study of young male prostitutes. Although they engaged in homosexual behaviour, they regarded what they did as work, and maintained their image of themselves as being 'straight' despite engaging in sex with men.

Give two other examples of how reality might be 'negotiated'.

Deviant career

These ideas of master status and negotiability led Becker to devise the idea of a '**deviant career**'. He meant by this all the processes that are involved in a label being applied (or not) and then the person taking on (or not) the self-image of the deviant.

Creating rules

Once labelling theorists began the process of looking at how social life was open to negotiation and that rule enforcement was no different than other social activities, then attention shifted to the creation of rules and laws. Why were they made? Traditionally, sociologists had taken a Marxist perspective that they were made in the interests of the ruling class, or more of a functionalist/pluralist perspective which argued that laws in a democracy reflected the views of the majority of the population. Becker (1963) doubted both these accounts and argued instead that:

Rules are the products of someone's initiative and we can think of the people who exhibit such enterprises as 'moral entrepreneurs'.

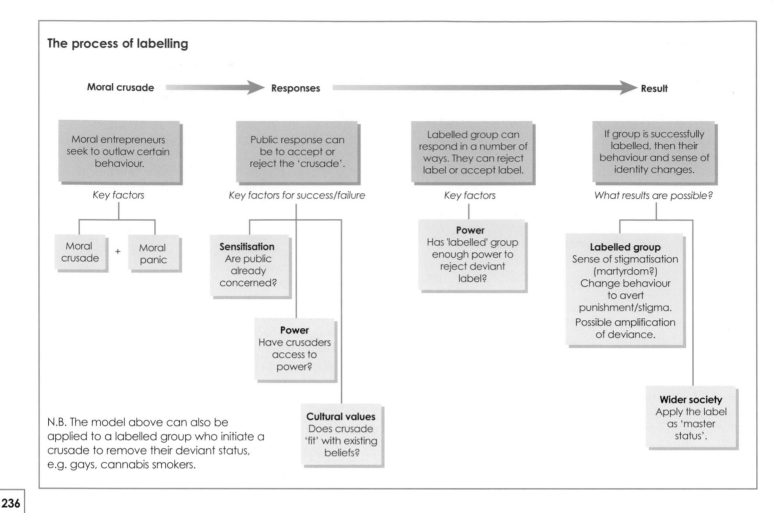

The process of labelling

Moral crusade → Responses → Result

| Moral entrepreneurs seek to outlaw certain behaviour. | Public response can be to accept or reject the 'crusade'. | Labelled group can respond in a number of ways. They can reject label or accept label. | If group is successfully labelled, then their behaviour and sense of identity changes. |

Key factors

Moral crusade + Moral panic

Key factors for success/failure

Sensitisation
Are public already concerned?

Power
Have crusaders access to power?

Cultural values
Does crusade 'fit' with existing beliefs?

N.B. The model above can also be applied to a labelled group who initiate a crusade to remove their deviant status, e.g. gays, cannabis smokers.

Key factors

Power
Has 'labelled' group enough power to reject deviant label?

What results are possible?

Labelled group
Sense of stigmatisation (martyrdom?)
Change behaviour to avert punishment/stigma.
Possible amplification of deviance.

Wider society
Apply the label as 'master status'.

So, labelling theorists argue that laws are a reflection of the activities of people (moral entrepreneurs) who actively seek to create and enforce laws. The reasons for this are either that the new laws benefit the activists directly, or these activists believe that the laws are truly to the benefit of society.

Becker's most famous example is his study of the outlawing of cannabis use in the USA in 1937. Cannabis had been widely used in the southern states of the USA, and its outlawing was the result of a successful campaign waged by the Federal Bureau of Narcotics who, after the repeal of the prohibition laws, saw cannabis as a growing menace in society. Through a press campaign and lobbying of senior politicians, the Bureau was successful in outlawing cannabis growing and use. However, Becker points out that the campaign was only successful because it 'plugged in' to values commonly held in the USA which included:

1 the belief that people ought to be in control of their actions and decisions
2 that pleasure for its own sake was wrong
3 that drugs were seen as addictive and, as such, 'enslaved' people.

The term Becker used to describe the campaign was of a '**moral crusade**', and it is this terminology (along with the concept *moral entrepreneurs*) which sociologists use to describe movements to pass laws.

Criticisms

The idea that there are those who seek to pass laws or to impose rules upon others has been accepted by most sociologists. However, Marxist writers in particular have pointed out that there is a wider framework within which this is placed. Are all laws just the product of a particular group of moral entrepreneurs? If so, then what are the conditions under which some groups succeed and others fail? Labelling theory does not really answer this issue very well. In fact, what is missing is a discussion of the nature of power. Labelling does not address the issue of differences in *power* between groups, which makes some more able than others to get laws passed and enforced that are beneficial to them. In defence of labelling theory, Becker (1970) does suggest in a famous article (*Whose Side Are We On?*) that there are differences in power and that it is the role of the sociologist to side with the underdog. (We explore this in more detail below.) However, no overall theory of differences in power is given.

Labelling and values

We have just mentioned a famous article by Becker, in which he argues that labelling theory has a clear value position – that is, it speaks up for the powerless and the underdog. Labelling theorists claim to provide a voice for those who are labelled as deviant and 'outsiders'.

● However, Liazos (1972) criticises labelling theorists for simply exploring marginally deviant activities as by doing

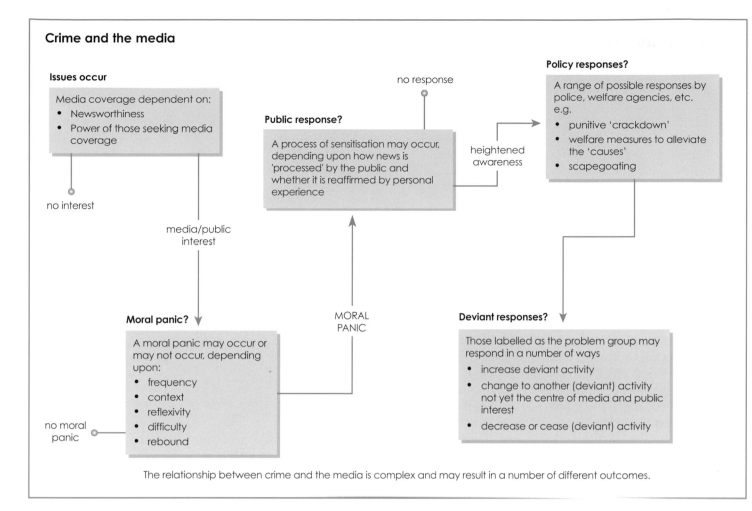

Crime and the media

Issues occur

Media coverage dependent on:
- Newsworthiness
- Power of those seeking media coverage

no interest

media/public interest

no response

Public response?

A process of sensitisation may occur, depending upon how news is 'processed' by the public and whether it is reaffirmed by personal experience

heightened awareness

Policy responses?

A range of possible responses by police, welfare agencies, etc. e.g.
- punitive 'crackdown'
- welfare measures to alleviate the 'causes'
- scapegoating

Moral panic?

A moral panic may occur or may not occur, depending upon:
- frequency
- context
- reflexivity
- difficulty
- rebound

no moral panic

MORAL PANIC

Deviant responses?

Those labelled as the problem group may respond in a number of ways
- increase deviant activity
- change to another (deviant) activity not yet the centre of media and public interest
- decrease or cease (deviant) activity

The relationship between crime and the media is complex and may result in a number of different outcomes.

so they are reinforcing the idea of pimps, prostitutes and mentally ill people as being deviant. Even by claiming to speak for the underdog, labelling theorists hardly present any challenge to the status quo.

- Gouldner (1968) also criticises labelling theorists for their failure to provide any real challenge to the status quo. He argued that all they did in their studies was to criticise doctors, psychiatrists and police officers for their role in labelling – and they failed ever to look beyond this at more powerful groups who benefit from this focus on marginal groups. Gouldner is putting forward a Marxist argument, by claiming that attention is drawn away from the 'real crime' by labelling theorists.

Crime, labelling and the media

What labelling theory alerts us to is the way in which the whole area of crime is dependent upon social constructions of reality – law creation, law enforcement and the identities of rule breakers are all thrown into question. A key element of all three of these processes is composed by the media, as most people's perceptions of crime are actually created, or at least informed by, the media.

Looking back at your studies, what other examples are there of the media playing a key role in constructing reality?

Labelling theory has contributed two particularly important concepts to our understanding of the relationship between the media and crime:

- deviancy amplification
- moral panics.

Deviancy amplification

The term **deviancy amplification** was coined by the British sociologist Leslie Wilkins to show how the response to deviance by agencies such as police and media can actually generate an increase in deviance. According to Wilkins (1964), when acts are defined as deviant, the deviants become stigmatised and cut off from mainstream society. They become aware that they are regarded as deviants, and, as a result of this awareness, they begin to develop their own subculture. This leads to more intense pressure on them, and further isolation, which further confirms and strengthens them in their deviance.

Jock Young (1971) used this concept in his study of drug use in North London, where he showed that increased police activity led to drug use being 'driven underground', and this had the effect of isolating users into a drug subculture, with 'a distinctive style of dress, lack of workaday sense of time, money, rationality and rewards', thus making re-entry to regular employment increasingly difficult – which, of course, made it difficult for them to afford the drugs. The scarcity of drugs drove the price up and this drew in professional criminals who regarded it as worthwhile entering the illicit drug business; criminal rings developed and the competition between them led to violence. It also led to the use of dangerous substitutes and adulterants in drugs by suppliers, interested only in maximising profits, thus creating a situation where users no longer knew the strength of drugs and were consequently more likely to overdose. The process described here caused wide public concern which spurred the police to intensify their clampdown even further, which only served to accelerate the spiral of this 'amplification' process.

Moral panics

The idea of **moral panics** overlaps and complements the concept of deviancy amplification. The term was first used in Britain by Stan Cohen in a classic study (1972) of two youth subcultures of the 1960s – 'mods' and 'rockers'. Cohen showed how the media, for lack of other stories, built up these two groups into **folk devils** – that is, groups who were seen as troublemakers. The effect of the media coverage was to make the young people categorise themselves as either mods or rockers and actually helped to create the violence that took place between them, which also confirmed them as troublemakers in the eyes of the public.

The concept of moral panic and the role of the media in helping to create them, has been widely used in sociology since Cohen's original British work – though perhaps the best adaptation of this is Hall's study of 'mugging' (see Topic 4).

Give two other examples of situations that could be described as moral panics.

Moral panics: an outdated idea?
McRobbie and Thornton (1995) argue that 'moral panics' as described by Stanley Cohen in the 1960s, are outdated and have to be seen in the context of the development of the media and the growing sophistication of the audiences. McRobbie and Thornton make the following points.

Frequency: There has been an increasing number of 'moral panics' – they are no longer rare or particularly noteworthy.

Context: Whereas moral panics would scapegoat a group and create 'folk devils' in the 1960s, today there is no single, unambiguous response to a panic as there are many different viewpoints and values in society.

Reflexivity: As moral panics as a concept are so well known, many groups try to create them for their own benefit. However, the same knowledge means that the media know this and do not necessarily wish uncritically to start a moral panic over an issue.

Difficulty: Moral panics are much more unlikely to start in society because it is far less clear today what is unambiguously 'bad'. Society is too fragmented and culturally pluralistic.

Rebound: People are more wary about starting moral panics as there is the possibility of it rebounding on them. So politicians who start a campaign about family values or drugs have to be very careful about their own backgrounds.

Labelling has been very important in helping to understand the role of the media. However, if what McRobbie and Thornton say is true, then the very success of sociological concepts such as moral panic, have gradually filtered into the wider society, such that journalists and politicians are now aware of the concept and use it in their decisions about what actions to take.

KEY TERMS

Deviancy amplification – when the action of the rule enforcers or media in response to deviance brings about an increase in the deviance.

Deviant career – the various stages that a person passes through on their way to being seen as, and seeing themselves as, deviant.

Folk devils – groups associated with moral panics who are seen as troublemakers by the media.

Incest – sex between close members of a family (other than man and wife).

Inuits – previously known as 'eskimos'.

Master status – when people are looked at by others solely on the basis of one type of act (good or bad) which they have committed. All other aspects of that person are ignored.

Moral crusade – the process of creating or enforcing a rule.

Moral entrepreneur – person or group which tries to create or enforce a rule.

Moral panic – outrage stirred up the media about a particular group or issue.

Primary deviance – the act of breaking a rule.

Secondary deviance – the response to rule breaking, which usually has greater social consequences than initial rule-breaking.

Stigmatised – labelled in a negative way.

Symbolic interactionism – a theory derived from social psychology which argues that people exist in a social world based on symbols that people interpret and respond to. Labelling theorists tend to substitute the term 'label' for 'symbol'.

CHECK YOUR UNDERSTANDING

1 Instead of looking at the cause of crime, what does labelling theory focus on?

2 What theoretical approach does labelling theory derive from?

3 Explain and give one example of what labelling theorists mean when they say that the response to law-breaking is variable.

4 Explain what is meant by the term 'master status'.

5 Explain what is meant by the term 'deviant career'.

6 In what way does the labelling approach to the introduction of laws differ from the Marxist approach?

7 Explain the term 'deviancy amplification'.

8 What criticisms have been made of the term 'moral panic'?

Item A

Item B

Item C

TV clean-up campaigner Mary Whitehouse dies

By Tom Leonard, Media Editor

MARY WHITEHOUSE, the veteran campaigner for broadcasting decency, died yesterday at 91 after a career as the most implacable moral guardian of the airwaves.

John Beyer, director of Mediawatch – the new name for the National Viewers' and Listeners' Association, which Mrs Whitehouse co-founded – said she had continued to scrutinise the television schedules for sex, violence and bad language until the last few weeks before her death.

Her battle against the broadcasters began 38 years ago when as a schoolteacher worried about the effect of television violence on her pupils, she launched the Clean-Up TV Campaign.

Within months, she was addressing rallies attended by thousands, where she blamed the BBC for Britain's "moral collapse". Ridiculed by opponents as a puritan who found fault wherever she looked or listened, her tenacity made her a household name with viewers and a bugbear with broadcasters.

She was responsible for the banning of the film The Last Temptation of Christ in 1976 and the following year she successfully prosecuted Gay News for blasphemy. She also initiated a private prosecution against the sexually explicit play Romans In Britain.

Source: Electronic Telegraph, 24/11/2001

239

1 Use the key concepts from this Topic to analyse the possible experiences of the people in Items A–C. Here is a list of possible concepts: labelling, primary and secondary deviance, master status, deviance amplification.

2 How could Mary Whitehouse (Item D) be described as a moral entrepreneur?

Research ideas

1. **Collect newspaper and other articles about any moral panic of your choice (e.g. concern over film violence, drugs such as ecstasy, underage sex). To what extent can you identify the key features of a moral panic such as media exaggeration, the creation of 'folk devils', the activities of moral entrepreneurs, and so on.**

2. **Conduct a survey to discover young people's perceptions of the elderly. Do their views represent particular labels and stereotypes? Then interview a small number of elderly people. Are they aware of stereotypes and labels? How do they feel about these labels? Do they affect them? Be sensitive in your interviewing technique.**

WWWebtask

- Look up the cases of the ex-pop-stars, Gary Glitter and Jonathan King on the internet. Use these to explore the insights that labelling theory gives us in understanding the response to their crimes, from public, police and judiciary. In particular use them as examples of the concept of 'master status' and moral panic.

- Becker studied the way in which cannabis was made illegal. Search the worldwide web for information about the campaign to make cannabis legal (or at least 'de-criminalised') in Britain. Are there any parallels in your opinion?

EXAM PRACTICE

Extract from AQA-style question

Assess the view that deviance is merely a label applied by some to the actions of others. (40 marks)

OCR-style question

Outline and assess the contribution of labelling theory to an understanding of deviance. (60 marks)

Getting you thinking

1 Have you had any crime (no matter how minor) committed against you in the last year? What was it? Did you report it to the police? Explain the reasons for you reporting/not reporting it.

2 Which of the three people in the photographs is most likely to be the victim of an attack at night on the streets? Explain the reasons for your answer.

3 Which car is more likely to be stolen? Explain your answer.

Our common sense ideas about crime are not always matched by the picture revealed by statistics. Many of us believe that crime is a Robin Hood type of activity, with the less wealthy responsible for crimes against the more wealthy and more vulnerable sections of the community. This view may well have influenced your answers to the questions above. However, police figures indicate that poorer areas have higher crime areas than wealthy areas, that young men are more likely to be the victims of crime than old ladies and that battered Ford Fiestas are more likely to be stolen than the latest executive BMW. But are these figures accurate, and how can we use statistics about crime to help us understand why some people commit crimes?

In order to understand why people commit crime, we need first to find out *who commits crime* and *what sorts of crimes are committed*.

Sociologists use three different ways to build up this picture of crime. Each method provides us with particular information, but also has a number of weaknesses, which need to be identified if our picture is to be accurate. The three methods of collecting information are:

- official statistics
- victim surveys
- self-report studies.

Official statistics

Official statistics are drawn from the records kept by the police and other official agencies, and are published every six months by the **Home Office**.

What perspective is most likely to accept official statistics as an objective and accurate reflection of social reality?

The official statistics are particularly useful in that they have been collected since 1857 and so provide us with an excellent historical overview of changing trends over time. They also give us a completely accurate view of the way that the criminal justice system processes offenders through arrests, trials, punishments, and so on.

Official statistics as social constructions

However, official statistics cannot be taken simply at their face value. This is because they only show crimes that are reported to and recorded by the official agencies such as the police. When we dig a little deeper a lot of hidden issues are uncovered.

*The term '**social construction**' is commonly used in sociology. What does it mean and in what other contexts have you seen it used?*

Crime statistics are not the only official statistics whose accuracy has been challenged. What other examples can you think of?

Reporting crime

Official statistics are based on the information that the criminal justice agencies collect. But crimes cannot be recorded by them if they are not reported in the first place, and the simple fact is that a high proportion of 'crimes' are not reported to the police at all. According to the **British Crime Survey** (1998), we know that individuals are less likely to report a 'crime' to the police if they regard it as:

- too trivial to bother the police with
- a private matter between friends and family – in this case they will seek redress directly (get revenge themselves) – or one where they wish no harm to come to the offender
- too embarrassing (male rape).

Also:

- The victim may not be in a position to give information (for example, a child suffering abuse)
- They may fear reprisals.

On the other hand, people are *more likely to report a crime if*:

- They see some benefit to themselves (e.g. an insurance claim)
- They have faith in the police ability to achieve a positive result.

Recording of crimes

When people do actively report an offence to the police, you would think that these statistics at least would enter the official reports. Yet in any one year, approximately 40% of all crimes reported to the police fail to appear in the official statistics.

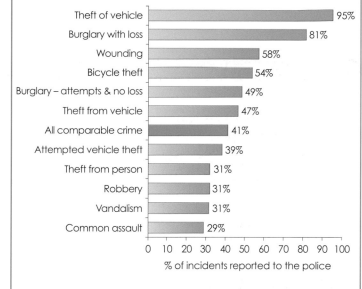

Proportion of offences reported to the police in 1999

	% of incidents reported to the police
Theft of vehicle	95%
Burglary with loss	81%
Wounding	58%
Bicycle theft	54%
Burglary – attempts & no loss	49%
Theft from vehicle	47%
All comparable crime	41%
Attempted vehicle theft	39%
Theft from person	31%
Robbery	31%
Vandalism	31%
Common assault	29%

Source: British Crime Survey, (2000) Home Office

The role of the police

Clearly the police are filtering the information supplied to them by the public, according to factors that are important to them. These factors have been identified as follows:

- *Seriousness* — They may regard the offence as too trivial or simply not a criminal matter.
- *Social status* — More worryingly, they may view the social status of the person reporting the matter as not high enough to regard the issue as worth pursuing.
- *Classifying crimes* — When a person makes a complaint, police officers must decide what category of offence it is. How they classify the offence will determine its seriousness. So, the police officer's opinion determines the category and seriousness of crime (from assault, to aggravated assault for example).
- *Discretion* — Only about 10% of offences are actually uncovered by the police. However, the chances of being arrested for an offence increase markedly depending upon the '**demeanour**' of the person being challenged by a police officer. Anderson *et al.* (1994) show that youths who co-operate and are polite to police officers are less likely to be arrested than those regarded as disrespectful.
- *Promotion and relationships at work* — Police officers, like everyone else, have career and promotion concerns. This involves trying to impress senior officers. However, they also need to get on with other colleagues, who do not like officers who are too keen (as this makes more work for everyone). Arrests reflect a balance between comradeship and a desire for promotion (Collinson, 1995).

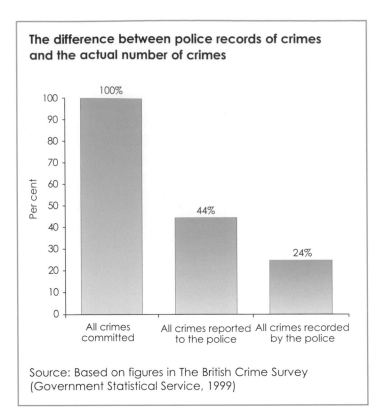

Source: Based on figures in The British Crime Survey (Government Statistical Service, 1999)

spoken agreement, whereby the defence will try to get the charges with the lightest possible punishment put forward by the prosecution. (In the USA this bargaining is far more open than in Britain, and is known as **plea-bargaining**.) The result is an overwhelming majority of pleas of guilty, yet these pleas are for less serious crimes than might 'really' have been committed. The statistics will reflect this downgrading of seriousness.

> *The process of plea-bargaining shows how justice can be negotiated. Which perspective focuses on the negotiation of social reality? What other examples of the negotiation of social reality can you think of?*

The role of the government
What is considered to be a crime changes over time, as a result of governments changing the law in response to cultural changes and the influence of powerful groups. Any exploration of crime over a period is therefore fraught with difficulty because any rise or fall in the levels of crime may reflect changes in the law just as much as actual changes in crime. A good example of this is the way that attitudes to cannabis use have shifted, with an increase in the numbers of people possessing and using cannabis (both of which are a crime) and a decline in the number of arrests for its possession, as the police respond to public opinion. The official statistics might make it look as if cannabis use is actually declining, when it is not.

The role of the courts
Official statistics of crimes committed also reflect the decisions and sentences of the courts. However, these statistics, too, are a reflection of social processes.

British courts work on the assumption that many people will plead guilty – and about 75% of all those charged actually do so. This is often the result of an informal and largely un-

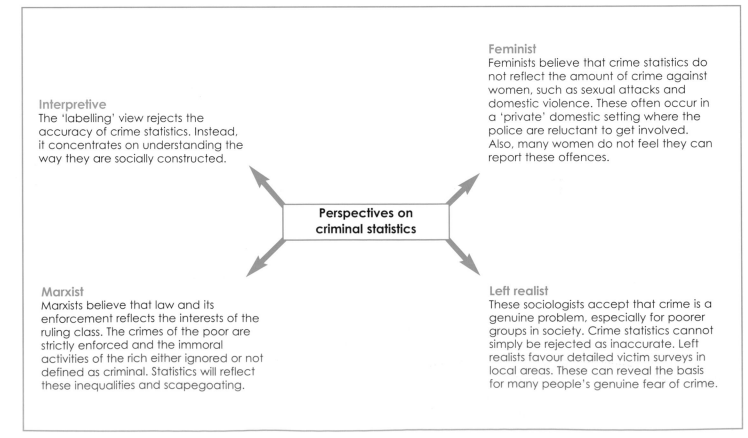

Interpretive
The 'labelling' view rejects the accuracy of crime statistics. Instead, it concentrates on understanding the way they are socially constructed.

Feminist
Feminists believe that crime statistics do not reflect the amount of crime against women, such as sexual attacks and domestic violence. These often occur in a 'private' domestic setting where the police are reluctant to get involved. Also, many women do not feel they can report these offences.

Perspectives on criminal statistics

Marxist
Marxists believe that law and its enforcement reflects the interests of the ruling class. The crimes of the poor are strictly enforced and the immoral activities of the rich either ignored or not defined as criminal. Statistics will reflect these inequalities and scapegoating.

Left realist
These sociologists accept that crime is a genuine problem, especially for poorer groups in society. Crime statistics cannot simply be rejected as inaccurate. Left realists favour detailed victim surveys in local areas. These can reveal the basis for many people's genuine fear of crime.

Victim surveys

A second way of estimating the extent and patterns of crime is that of **victimisation surveys**. In these, a sample of the population either locally or nationally are asked which offences have been committed against them over a certain period of time.

Strengths of victim surveys

This approach overcomes the fact that a significant proportion of offences are never recorded by the police. It also gives an excellent picture of the extent and patterns of victimisation – something completely missing from official accounts. The best known victimisation study is the **British Crime Survey** which is now collected every year and has been in operation since 1982.

Weaknesses of victim surveys

- The problem of basing statistics on victims' memories is that recollections are often faulty or biased.
- The categorisation of the crimes that has been committed against them is left to the person filling in the questionnaire – this leads to considerable inaccuracy in the categories.
- Victim surveys also omit a range of crimes such as fraud and corporate crime, and any crime where the victim is unaware of or unable to report a crime.
- Despite victim surveys being anonymous, people appear to under-report sexual offences.
- The BCS itself suffers from the problem of not collecting information from those under 16 although this is not necessarily a problem of victim surveys as such. The *British Youth Lifestyles Survey* (2000), for example, was carried out specifically to obtain detailed information on crimes against younger people.

Local victim surveys

The BCS is a typical cross-sectional survey, and as such may contain some errors – certainly it does not provide detailed information about particular places. This has led to a number of detailed studies of crime focusing on particular areas. These provide specific information about local problems. The most famous of these surveys were the **Islington Crime Surveys (1986 and 1995)**. These showed that the BCS under-reported the higher levels of victimisation of ethnic-minority groups, and domestic violence.

The media and sensitisation

Victim surveys are dependent upon people being aware that they are victims. This may seem obvious, but in fact this depends very much on the 'victim' perceiving what happens to them as being a crime. The media play a key role in this as they provide illustrations of 'crimes' and generally heighten sensitivity towards certain forms of behaviour. This is known as **sensitising** the public toward (certain types of) activity that can be seen as a crime worth reporting. A positive example of this has been the change in portrayal of domestic violence from a family matter to being a criminal activity.

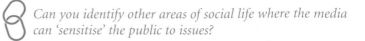

Can you identify other areas of social life where the media can 'sensitise' the public to issues?

Self-report studies

The third method for collecting data is that of **self-report studies**. These are surveys in which a selected group or cross-section of the population are asked what offences they have committed.

Self-report studies are extremely useful as they reveal much about the kind of offenders who are not caught or processed by the police. In particular it is possible to find out about these 'hidden offenders' ages, gender, social class and, even, their location. It is also the most useful way to find out about victimless crimes such as illegal drug use.

Weaknesses of self-report studies

- *The problem of validity*: The biggest problem is that respondents may lie or exaggerate – and even if they do not deliberately seek to mislead, they may simply be mistaken.

Which social groups do you think would be most likely to exaggerate the amount of crime they commit? Can you explain this in terms of their culture and socialisation?

- *The problem of representativeness*: Because it is easy to study them, most self-report surveys are on young people and students. There are no such surveys on professional criminals or drug traffickers, for example!
- *The problem of relevance*: Because of the problem of representativeness, the majority of the crimes uncovered tend to be trivial.

Nevertheless, the only information that we have available of who offends other than the official statistics of people who have been arrested comes from self-report studies, and they have been very widely used to explore such issues as crime and drug use.

Patterns of offending

Using the three methods of gathering information, sociologists have managed to construct an interesting picture of offending and victimisation patterns.

Types of offences

Property crime
According to the British Crime Survey, 62% of crime in 2000 was accounted for by some form of property theft, with burglary and vehicle theft forming the bulk of these.

Violent crime
All forms of violence account for approximately 20% of BCS-reported crime, but the huge majority of these acts of violence – about 68% – consisted only of very minor physical hurt (at most slight bruising). In fact, only about 5% of violent crimes reported involved more than trivial injury.

Patterns of crime: accurate or social construction?

A Official statistics

Official statistics	*Not recorded*
Person defines act of crime →	Fails to define as crime
Person defines as worth reporting →	Not worth reporting
Reports to police →	Fails to report
Recorded by police →	Refuse to record
Categorised by police →	Categorises along guidelines but act redefined to fit into categories
Official statistics	

B Self-report studies

Self-report	*Problems*
Researcher decides on a list of crimes →	How is decision made?
Gives to an available sample →	Never persistent/ professional criminal, usually young people at school
Respondents complete →	May exaggerate Fail to understand Forget Doesn't care Ashamed
Self-report	

C Victim studies: the British Crime Survey

Victim studies	*Problems*
BCS decides on sample →	Accuracy
Respondents given computer to key in offences committed against them →	Categories used are not legal/official ones
	Victim relied upon to define, remember & tell truth
BCS (British Crime Survey)	

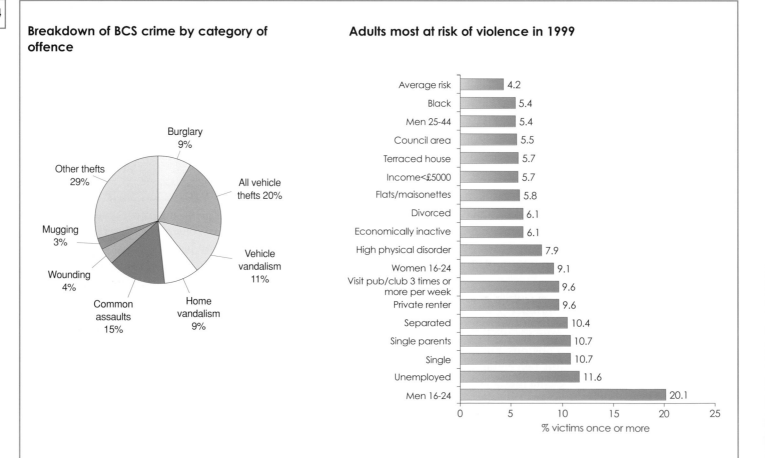

Breakdown of BCS crime by category of offence

Burglary 9%
All vehicle thefts 20%
Vehicle vandalism 11%
Home vandalism 9%
Common assaults 15%
Wounding 4%
Mugging 3%
Other thefts 29%

Adults most at risk of violence in 1999

	% victims once or more
Average risk	4.2
Black	5.4
Men 25-44	5.4
Council area	5.5
Terraced house	5.7
Income<£5000	5.7
Flats/maisonettes	5.8
Divorced	6.1
Economically inactive	6.1
High physical disorder	7.9
Women 16-24	9.1
Visit pub/club 3 times or more per week	9.6
Private renter	9.6
Separated	10.4
Single parents	10.7
Single	10.7
Unemployed	11.6
Men 16-24	20.1

% victims once or more

Source: *British Crime Survey* (2000), Home Office

Source: *British Crime Survey* (2000), Home Office

Types of victims

Victims of violence

Young males, who form the majority of the unemployed or low-waged, have a particularly high chance of being victims. Interestingly, in about 88% of cases of violence, the victim and perpetrator know each other.

Victims of property crime

These are most likely to be low-income households living in poorer areas.

How might Marxists explain the existence of property crime?

Repeat victimisation

Victim surveys demonstrate not only that some people are more likely than others to be victims in the first place, but that a proportion of the victims are likely to be targeted more than once (**repeat victimisation**). Twenty per cent of all households burgled experienced repeat burglaries and one tiny group has a disproportionately high chance of being victimised: 0.4% of householders accounted for 22% of all burglaries.

The statistics suggest that crime does not happen to everyone – it targets the poorer and less powerful groups in society more than the affluent. They also tell us that violent crime tends to happen between people who know each other, even live together.

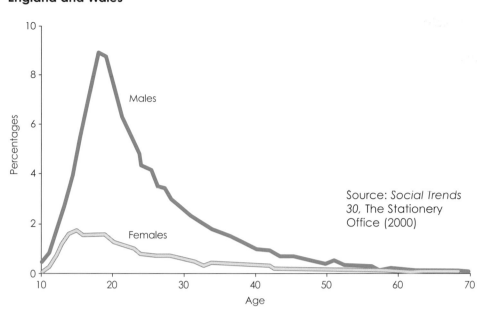

Offenders as a percentage of the population: by gender and age 1997–98, England and Wales

Males

Females

Source: *Social Trends 30*, The Stationery Office (2000)

Types of offenders

According to both official statistics and self-report studies, offenders are most likely to be young and male. The peak age of offending for males is about 18, and for females about 14.

KEY TERMS

British Crime Survey – annual victimisation survey carried out by the Home Office.

Demeanour – appearance, attitude and manner.

Home Office – government department responsible for criminal justice matters.

Islington Crime Surveys – famous local victimisation studies focusing on one area of North London.

Official statistics – statistics released by government agencies.

Plea-bargaining – where there is an informal (sometimes unspoken) agreement that if an accused person pleads guilty to a lesser crime than that of which he or she is accused, the prosecution will agree.

Repeat victimisation – where people are victims of the same crimes more than once.

Self-report studies – where people are asked to note down the crimes they have committed over a particular period.

Sensitising – refers to the extent of disorder or minor criminal activity that people will accept.

Social construction – in this case, refers to the fact that statistics represent the activities of the people constructing the statistics rather than some objective reality.

Victimisation (or victim) surveys – where people are asked what crimes have happened to them over a particular period.

Item A

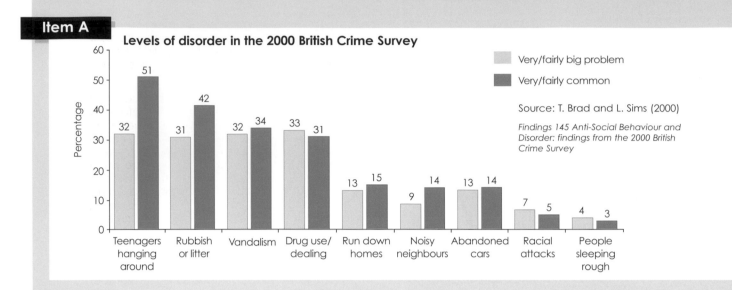

Levels of disorder in the 2000 British Crime Survey

Legend:
- Very/fairly big problem
- Very/fairly common

Source: T. Brad and L. Sims (2000)

Findings 145 Anti-Social Behaviour and Disorder: findings from the 2000 British Crime Survey

Item B

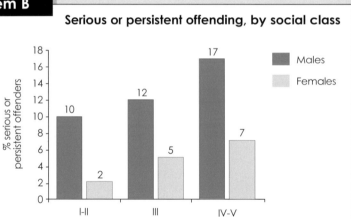

Serious or persistent offending, by social class

Legend:
- Males
- Females

1. The Registrar General's social classification is used to measure social class. The individual's social class is derived from the father's occupation (or their mother's, if father's is unknown or not applicable). I-professional, II-managerial or technical, III-skilled manual and non-manual work, IV-partly skilled, V-unskilled.

Source: *Youth Crime, Findings from the 1998/99 Youth Leisure Lifestyles Survey*, Research Study 209, Home Office.

The table above is based upon a national sample of people aged 16 and over, who were asked to indicate what the greatest problem in their area was.

In deciding whether a specific form of disorder is common or a problem, respondents will be making subjective judgements based on various factors. This means that differences between areas or groups of people may reflect differences in perception, rather than differences in reality.

1 Identify the three greatest problems identified in Item A.

2 What problems are there in accepting this data as an objective reflection of the reality of the situation?

3 Examine Item B, which shows persistent offending by social class. The table is based upon a self-report study. What relationship does it show?

4 Identify two other ways in which sociologists have gathered information on the link between social class and offending.

5 Which method would be most accurate, in your opinion? Explain the reasons for your view.

1 Explain why official statistics give a completely accurate picture of the workings of the criminal justice system.

2 Explain why official statistics do not give an accurate picture of the number and types of crimes committed.

3 Why might official statistics give a more accurate picture of the amount of car theft than the amount of domestic violence?

4 How might a person's 'demeanour' affect their likelihood of arrest?

5 Explain why so many people plead guilty in court.

6 Do reductions in arrests for possession of cannabis reflect a decrease in the use of the drug? Explain your answer.

7 Suggest three crimes that you think people might be willing to admit to being victims of when questioned in a victimisation study.

8 Why might some people exaggerate the amount of crime that they have committed in a self-report study?

9 Suggest two reasons why young males might make up the majority of victims of violence.

10 Explain why repeat victimisation may occur.

Research ideas

1 Undertake a piece of research to discover the factors that influence public reporting of crime. Does it depend on seriousness, whether the crime has a victim or other factors? Does likelihood of reporting correlate with variables such as age or gender?

2 Look at the Item A in Exploring patterns of crime. Conduct a small pilot survey of 14–16 year olds using the categories in the figure. Do your results reflect the results here? Amend the categories and then ask a cross-section of 14–16 year olds. What difference does age make to the identification of social problems?

EXAM PRACTICE

Extract from AQA-style question

In Britain, official statistics on crime are published annually. They provide criminologists, the police, the courts, the media and anyone else who is interested, with two main types of data.

1. They provide information on the total number of crimes 'known to the police'. This information is often taken as an accurate measure of the total amount of crime. The data allows comparisons to be made between crimes, and with previous years. Often the figures receive widespread publicity through the media. The statistics often, though not always, show increases in crime over previous years, and this may lead to concern that the country is being engulfed in a crime wave.

2. The official statistics provide information on the social characteristics of those who have been convicted on offences, such as their age and gender. It is on these figures that a number of theories of crime have been based.

Adapted from: M. Haralambos: London: and M. Holborn, (2000) *Sociology: Themes and Perspectives* (5th edition), London: Collins Educational

Evaluate the accuracy of official statistics of crime. (40 marks)

OCR-style question

Outline and assess methods of discovering information about the amount of different types of crime. (60 marks)

WWWebtask

Find the site of the Home Office (www.homeoffice.gov.uk). Go to the section on Research Development Statistics. Try to find figures about the amount and type of crime using official statistics, self-report studies and victim studies. What similarities and differences can you find? Try to explain the patterns you find.

Getting you thinking

Look at the first two photos.

1 Which do you think has the higher rate of crime? What reasons can you give for your answer?

Look at the second two photographs.

2 What different sorts of crimes might take place in the city during the day and during the night? What reasons can you give for your answer?

3 When you are walking home in the evening, do you feel more concerned than during the day? Are there any precautions you take if you are walking alone at night? What are they?

4 If you see a group of young males standing ahead of you on the street do you alter your behaviour or route in any way? Give reasons for your answer.

(Above right) Piccadilly Circus at night

(Below right) Piccadilly Circus during the day

This topic explores the relationship of crime to places and times. This link is hardly an original idea – since the earliest recorded history people have been warned against going to dangerous places, particularly at night-time. But sociologists have taken this basic idea and explored the links between where people live, work and have their leisure, and crime patterns.

We examine the explanation under two groupings:

● those concerned with locating *offenders*
● those concerned with exploring the location of *offences*.

Explaining offenders

Chicago sociology

The pattern

In the late nineteenth and early twentieth centuries, one of the fastest growing cities in the USA was Chicago. The city also possessed one of the new University departments of sociology, and two of its researchers, Shaw and McKay (1931) began plotting the location of the addresses of those who committed crimes in the city. The results showed that, if they divided the city into **concentric zones**, each of the five zones they identified had different levels of offenders, with zone two (which was nearest the city centre) showing the highest rates.

This was interesting in itself, but they also found that because of rapid social change, the population living in zone two was changing regularly so that although the various zones maintained their different levels of offenders over time, they were *different* offenders. This meant that there was something about the zones that was linked to crime rates, rather than individuals who lived there.

The explanation: social disorganisation

Shaw and McKay suggested that as each successive wave of immigrants arrived in the city they were moved into the cheapest and least desirable zones – that is, the **zone of transition**. Over time, some were successful and they moved out to the more affluent suburbs, while the less successful remained. The places of those who had moved on were taken by newer immigrants, and so the process started again.

This pattern of high population turnover created a state of **social disorganisation**, where the informal mechanisms of social control that normally hold people back from criminal behaviour were weak or absent.

Cultural transmission

In their later writings, Shaw and McKay (1942) altered the meaning of 'social disorganisation' to refer to a distinct set of values that provided an alternative to those of the mainstream society. This amended approach came to be known as **cultural transmission** theory. They argued that amongst some groups in the most socially disorganised and poorest zones of the city, crime became culturally acceptable, and was passed on from one generation to the next as part of the normal socialisation pattern.

Successful criminals provide role-models for the next generation by demonstrating both the normality of criminal behaviour and that a criminal career was possible.

 Which agencies of socialisation are most likely to pass on these deviant values? Why?

Differential association

One criticism of Shaw and McKay and other members of the Chicago School of Criminology was that their theories were too vague and difficult to prove.

What other sociological theories have you come across that could be accused of being difficult to prove? What methods could you use to prove Shaw and McKay's theories?

In response, Sutherland (and Cressey, 1966) introduced the concept of **differential association**. This states that a person is likely to become criminal if he or she receives an excess of definitions favourable to violation of law over definitions unfavourable to violation of law. This simply means that if people interact with others who support lawbreaking then they are likely to do so themselves.

Further tightening his approach in order to avoid criticisms of vagueness, Sutherland suggested that these definitions vary in frequency, duration, priority, and intensity.

- frequency: the number of times the definitions occur
- duration: over what length of time
- priority: e.g. at what stage in life (childhood socialisation is more important than other periods)
- intensity: the status of the person making the definition (e.g. family member rather than a stranger).

The dynamics of community

Most British research failed to reproduce the clear pattern of concentric circles that the Chicago School had identified. Crime rates certainly varied by areas, but in more complex patterns, as can be seen from Item B in the section 'Exploring environmental approaches' at the end of the topic.

Housing policies

One early study by Morris in 1957 led the way. Morris found no evidence that people in areas of high delinquency held a coherent set of values that was any different from that of mainstream society.

The argument that there is a distinct group of people with their own deviant values can be found today in the writings of Charles Murray and his concept of the underclass. What are the arguments for and against the existence of an underclass?

Morris suggested that a key factor in the concentration of delinquents in certain areas was linked to the local council's housing policies. For example, in his study of Croydon, the local council's policy of housing problem families together meant that these areas became, almost by definition, high-crime areas.

The impact of local-authority housing decisions was clarified much later by the work of Baldwin and Bottoms (1976) who compared two similar local-authority housing estates, separated by a dual carriageway. One of the estates 'Gardenia' had a 300% higher number of offenders and a 350% higher level of crimes than the other 'Stonewall'. The difference according to him was the result of a process that he named **tipping**.

Bottoms changed the name of the estates Gardenia and Stonewall. Why do sociologists often change the names of the people, organisations and areas that they research?

Tipping

Most estates consist of a mixture of people from different backgrounds and with different forms of behaviour. Informal social control imposed by the majority of residents limits the offending behaviour of the anti-social minority. However, if

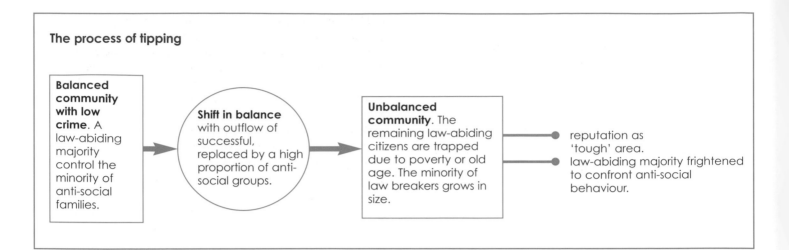

The process of tipping

| Balanced community with low crime. A law-abiding majority control the minority of anti-social families. | → | Shift in balance with outflow of successful, replaced by a high proportion of anti-social groups. | → | Unbalanced community. The remaining law-abiding citizens are trapped due to poverty or old age. The minority of law breakers grows in size. | → | reputation as 'tough' area. law-abiding majority frightened to confront anti-social behaviour. |

for whatever reason (such as local-authority housing policies), the anti-social minority grow in number, their behaviour drives away some of the law-abiding families. Those who wish to enter the estate tend to be relatives of the anti-social families and this leads to a speed up in the law-abiding residents leaving. The estate has 'tipped' and becomes increasingly regarded as a problem estate. Those who are able to flee, do so. In Bottom's analysis Gardenia had tipped whilst Stonewall had not.

Disorder

W. G. Skogan (1990) in the USA has fleshed out this idea of tipping. He suggests that social control breaks down when a combination of *physical deterioration* in local buildings and parks, and *social disorder* in the form of public alcohol and drug use, for example, increase.

This leads to a situation of disorder, which has three consequences:

- It undermines the mechanisms of informal social control and leads people to withdraw, thus undermining the bonds between people.
- It generates worries about neighbourhood safety, so that people avoid going out at night – thus, making it easier for street crime to be committed.
- It causes law-abiding people who can afford it to move out of the area, and leads to a decrease in property values and the growth of housing to let.

How do these ideas link to J. Q. Wilson's arguments on zero tolerance, explored in Topic 11.

Explaining offences

So far we have been exploring theories that look at where *offenders* live and why they have higher levels of offending. However, other approaches have looked at where *offences* take place and why they occur in these places and not others.

This distinction has been highlighted in Wilkstrom's (1991) study of crime patterns in Stockholm. This is particularly important as it demonstrates that the types and extent of offences vary across neighbourhoods. At its simplest, city centres, poorer districts and affluent areas adjacent to poorer districts have higher rates of crime. Within this, crimes of violence are more likely in the poorer districts, while

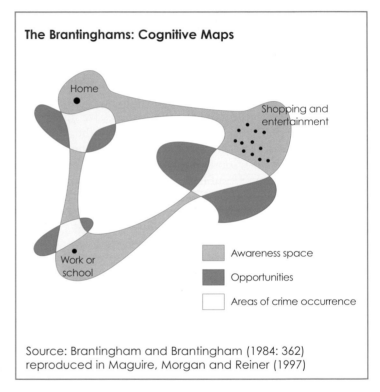

The Brantinghams: Cognitive Maps

Home

Shopping and entertainment

Work or school

- Awareness space
- Opportunities
- Areas of crime occurrence

Source: Brantingham and Brantingham (1984: 362) reproduced in Maguire, Morgan and Reiner (1997)

burglary was more likely in the affluent areas adjacent to poorer districts. This observation shifted environmental theories towards explanations of these different patterns of offences.

Cognitive maps

P. J. and P. L. Brantingham (1991) argue that we all hold **cognitive maps** of the towns and cities where we live, so some parts of our local town are familiar to us and other parts much less known. In particular we know the routes from our homes to where we study or work, and where we go for entertainment.

According to the Brantinghams, offenders are most likely to commit offences where opportunities (e.g. houses to burgle) link with 'cognitively known' areas, and conversely that places that are less 'cognitively known' are less likely to be burgled. This provides an explanation for the patterns of crime we noted earlier for burglary, for example.

Opportunity theory

If crimes are most likely to be committed in areas that offenders know, then the next question must be why, within these areas, are some properties or people chosen and others are not? The answer, according to Clarke's (1995) opportunity theory, is that of *opportunity*.

Opportunity consists of two elements:

- how *attractive* the target is – for example, how much can be gained by committing a crime against this particular place or person and, if it is property, how easy it is to carry away and to sell afterwards
- how *accessible* the target is – for example, how easy it is to commit the crime.

Routine activities

These ideas of cognitive maps, and opportunity were further developed by Cohen and Felson's concept of **routine activities** (1979). They argue that crimes are more likely to occur where the day-to-day activities of victims and offenders are likely to coincide, and where there is little in the way of formal or informal control to prevent an offence taking place. Cohen and Felson have introduced two new issues into the discussion with their definition.

1 They point out that crimes are likely to occur where there is no 'capable guardian', such as a police officer, neighbours or informal social control engendered by a sense of community.
2 They are pointing out that it is not just *place* that is important, but also *time*. For example, the person who is more likely to be 'mugged' is the person returning from work, walking along a quiet street, *in the evening*. We will explore this issue of time later, but first let us summarise what we know so far.

Crime occurs in:

- areas that are familiar to criminals
- targets that are potentially most rewarding
- places where the perceived risk is low – particularly where there is no one to 'guard' the person or property
- these targets and risks are linked to the activities and daily lives of the victims.

The privatisation of public space

Sociologists have always been aware of the distinction between **private space** and **public space**, and its importance on the levels and types of offending. For example, as long ago as the 1960s, Stinchcombe used the term 'the institution of privacy' to illustrate how policing tended to be against deviant activities carried out in public, with much less stress placed on violence and abuse in the home.

Why are the police often reluctant to get involved in 'private' spaces?

However, in recent years, the issue of private and public space has re-emerged as an important debate for sociologists, as changes have taken place in the nature of urban life.

Shearing and Stenning (1983) pointed to the growth of shopping centres and leisure complexes which are both public in that they are spaces where (most) people are welcomed and private in that they are privately owned, and the owners have the power to exclude those they define as undesirable, in housing too, there has been the growth of **gated communities** – housing estates where only residents and guests are allowed.

Shearing and Stenning argue that the owners of these private 'public' spaces have taken over the responsibility for policing them – using **CCTV** and security guards – and this has led to the **privatisation of public space**. The police have been increasingly confined to the more peripheral areas of the city and to the poorer (particularly 'problem') housing estates. The exclusion of undesirable groups (young people, known offenders, beggars) from these private 'public' areas, has simply *displaced* crime to the less affluent public areas.

Time: the nocturnal economy

Earlier, we noted the implication in Cohen and Felson's routine activities theory, that time is a crucial and neglected element in understanding crime. If different *places* have varying levels of crime and different styles of control, then so do different *times*. The busy city centre, filled with families shopping during the day, becomes the location for the young seeking pleasure at night. The same location therefore changes its meaning and possibilities with the closing of the shops and the coming of the darkness.

An interesting example of the significance of time is what Hobbs and Lister (2000) call the '**nocturnal economy**'. They point out that in the last fifteen years there has been a huge growth in pubs and clubs, as Britain's younger people have increasingly embraced the leisure society. This involves, in Britain at least, going out at the weekend to clubs and pubs to consume alcohol (and possibly also drugs) and to enjoy oneself. In 2000, for example, there were over 200 million club admissions to the value of £2.5 billion. This means that there are huge numbers of young people who come together within a very narrow time-band in order to engage in the search for pleasure. Almost three-quarters of all violent incidents in urban areas occur during the weekend between 9pm and 3am, usually by and between groups of young males fuelled by drink and/or drugs.

Interestingly, as we saw before regarding the privatisation of public space, at night-time too, there are relatively few police officers available, so that a medium-sized town might have 15,000 night-time 'revellers' with only 12 police officers on duty. The bulk of the 'policing' is performed by private security companies employed by the pubs and clubs. The high rates of violent crime occurring within this framework of time and space illustrate perfectly the three elements referred to by Cohen and Felson of: offenders, targets, and lack of guardians.

Go to the Home Office website (www.homeoffice.gov.uk). Go to the statistics section and find the results of the latest British Crime Survey. Find out the sorts of people most likely to become victims.

KEY TERMS

CCTV – closed circuit TV.

Cognitive maps – a personal map of a town based on an individual's daily activities.

Concentric zones – widening circles.

Cultural transmission – values are passed on from one generation to the next.

Differential association – a theory which suggests that deviant behaviour is learned from, and justified by family and friends.

Gated communities – housing estates where only residents and guests are allowed.

Nocturnal economy – refers to the way that a leisure industry has developed at night, which provides the location of many offences.

Opportunity theory – that crime occurs when there is an opportunity. Stop the opportunity and crime is less likely to occur.

Private space – areas where entry is controlled.

Privatisation of public space – the way that public areas are increasingly being owned and controlled by companies who police it in such a way as to exclude the undesirables.

Public space – areas where anyone can go.

Routine activities – the normal activities of daily life provide the cognitive maps and opportunities for crime.

Social disorganisation – an area of a city does not have a shared culture, existing over time

Tipping – the process whereby an area moves from being predominantly law-abiding to predominantly accepting of anti-social behaviour.

Zone of transition – the cheapest and least desirable zones of the city.

Exploring environmental approaches: the criminology of place and time

Item A

According to Shaw and McKay Chicago was divided into distinctive 'zones':

Zone I: the central business district. This had very few occupants but was the hub of commerce and banking during the day.
Zone 2: 'the interstitial zone' (or zone of transition). This was once an area of some considerable affluence, but had decayed and was characterised by multi-occupation use. This was the cheapest zone for housing, so new immigrants settled here first.
Zone 3: the respectable working-class district. This was where the solid working class lived.
Zone 4: suburbia. Here were the pleasanter middle-class districts further out of town.
Zone 5: the outer areas on the fringe of the city where the well-off lived.

Cognitive circle model

Factory Zone
I
CBD
II Zone in Transition
III Zone of workingmen's homes
IV Residential zone
V Commuters' zone

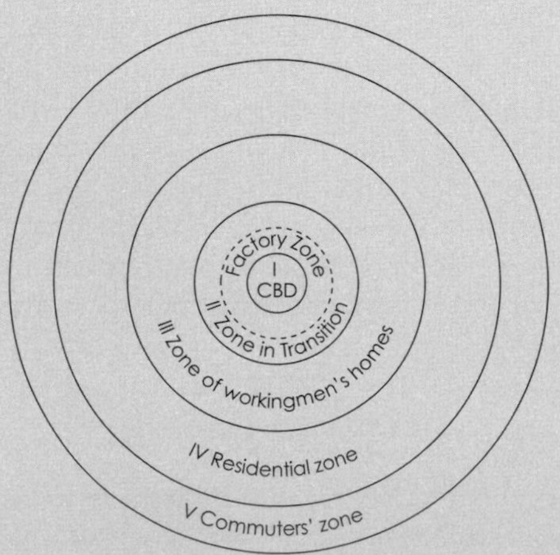

Source: Burgess (1925)

Item B

Area distribution of crimes in Sheffield, 1966

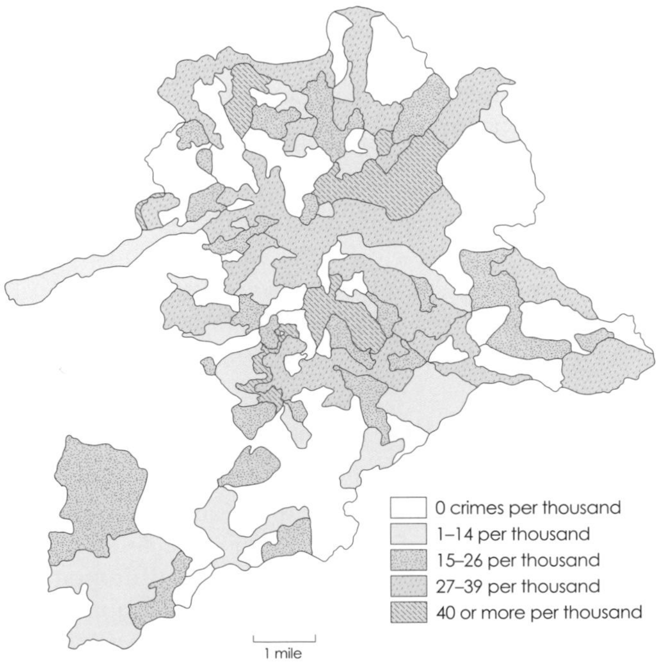

0 crimes per thousand
1–14 per thousand
15–26 per thousand
27–39 per thousand
40 or more per thousand
1 mile

Source: Baldwin and Bottoms (1976: 75)

1 Shaw and McKay suggested two explanations for the behaviour of the people in the zones they identified. What are these explanations?

2 Explain, in your own words, what is meant by the term 'tipping'.

3 What are normally the three key components of a person's 'cognitive map'?

4 What information do 'cognitive maps' and 'routine activities theory' tell us about where and who are more likely to be targeted by offenders?

5 Briefly explain how the privatisation of public space 'displaces' crime.

6 Why is the crime rate likely to rise during the hours of 9pm and 3am?

EXAM PRACTICE

Extract from AQA-style question

Describe the explanations sociologists have offered for why the crime rate is higher in urban areas than in rural areas. (12 marks)

OCR-style question

Outline and assess sociological explanations of the high crime rates in inner city areas. (60 marks)

1 How do Items A and B illustrate the difficulty of applying the Chicago model outside the USA?

2 What factors, other than migration, might influence the number of offenders living in a particular area in Britain?

3 Painter (1992) has argued that a simple way to reduce crime is to introduce street-lights. Her research in a number of cities, including Manchester, seems to support this argument.

4 What explanation(s) of crime provided in this topic would, in your opinion, relate most closely to Painter's research?

5 What form of methodology might be used to prove or disprove Painter's argument? What problems could you foresee with this methodology?

1 Look at the photo opposite. Write down your immediate reactions to it. What do you think are the most common reasons for fighting amongst girls?

2 If it had been a photo of two young men fighting would you have had the same reaction?

3 In your opinion are males more likely to break the law than females? Why do you think that is?

In this Topic we want to explore the relationship that gender has to offending behaviour. Official records show an overwhelming predominance of males compared with females committing crime, and even self-report studies show a less marked, but still noticeable difference between the offending levels of males and females. Given this, there has to be something in the different construction of femininity and masculinity that can help us to explain these differences. In this Topic, we will try to unravel some of the strands of explanation offered.

Before we do so, however, we need to explain why, surprisingly perhaps, there has been relatively little research that explicitly sets out to explain the links between gender and offending. It seems that most sociologists have simply started off with the assumption that males commit more crime and then moved on to explore why it is that only some males commit crime. Explanations offered by sociologists have therefore concentrated mainly on comparing offending males with non-offending males, without first starting to explain why males are more likely to offend in the first instance.

We begin the Topic, then, by exploring just why females have been ignored in the sociology of crime and delinquency; then we examine the explanations for lower rates of female offending, before we turn to an examination of the relationship between masculinity and offending.

Invisible female offenders

Anyone studying the sociology of crime and deviance will notice after a while that it is mainly about male offending. In fact, it would not be unfair to call it the sociology of *male* crime and deviancy. Although it is true that the majority of offenders are male, comprising about 80% of all official statistics on offenders, it is surprising that 20% of all offenders are simply ignored.

Frances Heidensohn (1989) has criticised the male dominance of the subject (known as **malestream** criminology) and has suggested that there are four reasons why it is so.

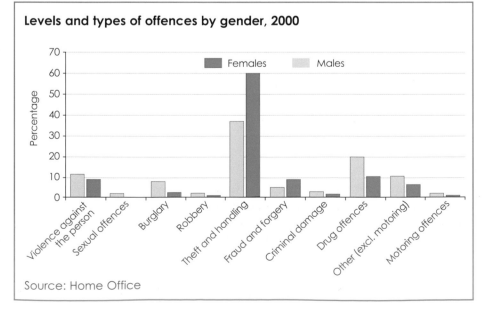

Levels and types of offences by gender, 2000

Source: Home Office

- *Male dominance of offenders*

As the majority of offenders are male, for many sociologists it was therefore most appropriate to study them – rather than the minority of female offenders.

- *Male domination of sociology*

Although the majority of sociology students are women, it has always been the case that the majority of academics have been male. According to Heidensohn, sociological topics of investigation reflect a male view and male interests.

- *Vicarious identification*

This follows from the previous point. What interests males is studied, and, applied to crime, this is most often the lives of the marginal and the exciting, i.e. **vicarious identification**.

- *Sociological theorising*

Male sociologists constructed their theories without ever thinking about how they could be applied to females. Most traditional theories are 'gender blind', that in effect means they ignore the specific viewpoint of women.

Explaining female crime: women's roles

Most theories that explain crime, as we saw earlier, do so by implicitly accepting that males are more likely than females to commit crime and then go on to look at why certain males are more likely than others to commit crime. In the process, criminologists have omitted to explain what it is that makes males more likely than females to commit crime. There have, however, been a number of exceptions to this and we explore these approaches in this section. Three major approaches to explaining the relationship between women and offending are:

- biological explanations
- **sex-role theory**
- transgression.

Biological explanations

This approach has been used by different writers to explain why the overwhelming bulk of women do not offend and conversely why a small minority do. It starts from the belief that women are innately different from men, with a natural desire to be caring and nurturing – both of which tend not to be values that support crime. 'Normal' women are therefore less likely to commit crime. On the other hand, some women writers such as Dalton (1964) have claimed that hormonal or menstrual factors can influence this minority of women to commit crime in certain circumstances.

Sex-role theory

Sex-role theory argues that women are less likely to commit crime than men because there are core elements of the female role that limit their ability and opportunity to do so. There are a number of different versions, all of which can fit quite comfortably together.

Socialisation

According to this approach, girls are socialised differently to boys. The values that girls are brought up to hold are those that simply do not lead to crime. Talcott Parsons (1937) argues for instance, that as most child rearing is carried out by mothers, girls have a clear role-model to follow that emphasises caring and support.

How do the different agencies of socialisation help socially to construct gender differences?

Social control

Females are less likely to commit crime because of the closer levels of supervision that they are subjected to at home in childhood. This control carries on throughout life, with the role of women being more constrained that that of males.

Give examples of ways in which the behaviour of women is likely to be more subject to control than the behaviour of men.

Lack of opportunities

In order to commit crime, a person needs to have the opportunity to do so. The narrower range of roles that women are allowed to have consequently limits their opportunities to commit crime, as they are more confined by their socialisation and social control than men.

The result of these three influences on the lives of females, is to deflect them away from offending and towards conformity.

Socialisation, social control and lack of opportunity

Transgression

The previous two approaches were not popular with feminist sociologists as they felt that they were not really adequate explanations for the differences between male and female causes for offending. Pat Carlen (1992) argued, for example, that these were theoretically weak and represented a sort of 'bolt-on' to existing male criminology.

It was in response to the need for a feminist version of criminology that answered the concerns of women that Carol Smart (1990) introduced the idea of a **transgressive criminology**. By this, Smart was suggesting that criminology itself as a discipline was tied to male questions and concerns and that it could never offer answers to feminist questions. Instead of trying to produce a feminist criminology by asking the question what can feminism offer criminology, feminists should be arguing what can criminology offer feminists? The answer to this question lay in looking at a whole range of activities (both legal and illegal) that actually harm women, and to ask how these came about and how they could be changed. The term 'transgression', in this context then, meant to go beyond the boundaries of criminology. This did lead to feminists (and sympathetic male sociologists) looking more closely at things such as: the way women stayed in at night for fear of becoming victims; at domestic violence; and at how women were treated by the law in issues of rape and harassment (where they form the overwhelming bulk of the victims).

Transgression is a good example of the postmodern influence in sociology, when the traditional boundaries of sociology and the categories used to classify issues are abandoned and new, fresher ways of thinking are introduced.

How has postmodernism influenced other issues you have studied?

Male roles, postmodernity and masculinity

Smart's idea of transgression, linked to the growing importance of postmodern analysis, began to feed back into mainstream criminology. Some sociologists began to go beyond the traditional confines and to revisit the issue of why most crime is *male* crime.

Normative masculinity

The analysis of masculinity began with the Australian sociologist, Bob Connell (1995) who argued that there were a number of different forms of masculinity, which change over time. Although crime was not central to his analysis, the idea of multiple, constructed masculinities was taken up by Messerschmidt (1993).

He argues that there exists a '**normative masculinity**' in society that is highly valued by most men. Normative masculinity refers to the socially approved idea of what a 'real male' is – according to Messerschmidt, it 'defines masculinity through difference from and desire for women'. Normative masculinity is so prized that men struggle to live up to its expectations. Messerschmidt suggests then that masculinity is not something natural, but rather a state that males only achieve as 'an accomplishment', which involves being constantly worked at.

However, the construction of this masculinity takes place in different contexts and through different methods depending upon the particular male's access to power and resources. So, more powerful males will accomplish their masculinity in different ways and contexts from less powerful males. Messerschmidt gives examples of businessmen who can express their power over women through their control in the workplace, while those with no power at work may express their masculinity by using violence in the home or street. However, whatever way used, both types of men are achieving their normative masculinity.

So, it is achieving masculinity that leads some men to commit crime – and in particular crime is committed by those less powerful in an attempt to be successful at masculinity (that involves material, social and sexual success).

The idea that masculinity is the actual basis of crime is reflected in the writings of a number of writers.

Katz: seductions of crime

A postmodern twist on the idea of masculinity is the work of Katz (1988), who argues that what most criminology has failed to do is to understand the role of pleasure in committing crime. This search for pleasure has to be placed within the context of masculinity, which stresses the importance of status, control over others and success.

Katz claims that crime is always explained with reference to background causes, but rarely attempts to look at the pleasure that is derived from the actual act of offending or 'transgression', as he calls it. Doing evil, he argues, is motivated by the quest for a 'moral self-transcendence' in the face of boredom. Different crimes provide different thrills, that can vary from the 'sneaky thrills' of shoplifting, to the 'righteous slaughter' of murder.

Katz argues that by understanding the emotional thrills that transgression provides, we can understand why males commit crime. Katz gives the example of robbery, which is largely undertaken, he claims, for the chaos, thrill and potential danger inherent in the act. Furthermore, in virtually all robberies 'the offender discovers, fantasises or manufactures an angle of moral superiority over the intended victim', such that the robber has 'succeeded in making a fool of his victim'. This idea of the thrill of crime has been used to explain the apparent irrational violence of football 'hooligans', and also the use of drugs and alcohol.

Katz's work is clearly influenced by the earlier work of Matza (1964)(see Topic 3), who has argued that constructing a male identity in contemporary society is difficult. Most youths are in a state of **drift** where they are unsure exactly who they are and what their place in society is. For most young males, this is a period of boredom and crisis. It is in this period of life that any event that unambiguously gives them a clear identity is welcomed, and it could equally be an identity of offender as much as employee. Committing offences provides a break from boredom, pleasure and a sense of being someone – for example, a gang member or a 'hard man'.

Lyng: edgework

A linked argument can be found in the work of Lyng, who argues that young males search for pleasure through risk-taking. According to Lyng, the risk-taking can best be seen as '**edgework**', by that he means that there is a thrill to be gained from acting in ways that are on the edge between security and danger – see Topic 3.

This helps explain the attractiveness of car theft and 'joy riding', and of searching for violent confrontations with other groups of males. By engaging in this form of risk-taking, young men are in Messerschmidt's terms 'accomplishing masculinity', and also proving that they have control over their lives.

Female sex-roles and crime revisited

So far in this topic we have characterised female sex-roles as being more passive and less aggressive than those of males. However, a number of writers including Denscombe (2001), for example, have argued that changing female roles over the last ten years mean that females are increasingly as likely as males to engage in risk-taking behaviour. In his research into self-images of 15-to-16 year olds in the East Midlands in which he undertook in-depth interviews as well as focus groups he found that females were rapidly adopting what had traditionally been male attitudes and this included such things as 'looking hard', of 'being in control', and of someone who can cope with risk-taking. This provides theoretical support for the fact that female crime levels are rising much more quickly than male ones, not just in terms of numbers but also in terms of seriousness of crimes committed.

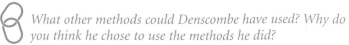 *What other methods could Denscombe have used? Why do you think he chose to use the methods he did?*

Westwood (1999) develops similar ideas when she argues that identities are constantly being reconstructed and reframed. The concept of a fixed female identity has limited our understanding of crime, and so we need to understand how women are reconfiguring their identity in a more confident, forceful way, and the possible link to the growth of female crime

KEY TERMS

Drift – term used by Matza to describe a state where young men are unsure exactly who they are and what their place in society is.

Edgework – see Key Terms in Topic 3.

Malestream – a term used to describe the fact that male ways of thinking have dominated criminology.

Normative masculinity – the socially approved idea of what a real male is. According to Messerschmidt, it 'defines masculinity through difference from and desire for women'.

Sex-role theory – refers to explanations based on the restricted roles women are claimed to have in society.

Transgression – feminist theorists use this term to suggest a need to 'break out' of the confines of traditional criminology.

Vicarious identification – when a person obtains a thrill by putting themselves in the place of another person.

Understanding crime: feminist perspectives

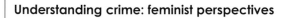

Feminist debates and criminology
Although male sociologists have largely ignored female offending, feminist writers from the various strands within feminism have all sought to include criminological analyses within their approaches.

Liberal feminism
This approach to feminism is based on the idea that by bringing women onto the agenda and by demonstrating how women have been ignored in research, there will be greater understanding of female deviance. In particular, new theories can be developed that will cover both males and females.

Socialist feminism
This approach stresses that the position of men and women in general, and with reference to crime, can only be understood by locating males and females within the context of societies divided by both sexism and by capitalism.

Radical feminism
Radical feminists argue that the only way to understand crime is to see it through a female perspective – and research should be based on the assumption that all men are prepared to commit crimes against women if given the chance. Women should construct their own unique approaches to explaining crime and deviance and this should incorporate the threat from men.

Postmodern feminism
The work of Smart (1990) and Cain (1989) are particularly important since they argue that the very concerns of criminology (burglary/street crime, etc.) are actually a reflection of male concerns, and that women should be looking beyond these to study how harm comes to women in the widest sense possible. The concern of feminist criminology should be looking at the way women are harmed by a whole range of processes and not accept the (male) boundaries of criminology.

Item A

Let us now turn to some of the key theories put forward to explain why some people commit crime. I want to look briefly at Merton's theory of anomie, and labelling theories in order to adequately assess the extent to which they can adequately account for women's participation/non-participation in crime.

Merton's anomie

American society tends to over-emphasise the goals without paying sufficient attention to the means. The pressure to succeed and obtain monetary wealth is so strong that some groups, particularly the working class, will turn to illegitimate means to obtain these goals.

Eileen Leonard argues that women's goals are relational, not financial – they are more concerned with relationships than financial success. In the words of Leonard: 'women have low aspirations and their goals are extremely accessible'.

Labelling Theory:... advocates that deviance theorists should concentrate on studying societal reaction to crime ... Leonard suggests that women who commit crime are often labelled as unfeminine.

Source: M. Leonard (1995) 'Masculinity, femininity and crime' Sociology Review Vol 5 No.1, Oxford: Philip Allan Update

1 Read Item A. Explain in your own words why anomie theory when applied to women might lead to lower crime levels than when applied to males. You can use evidence from any other Topic in this book to illustrate your point.

Item B

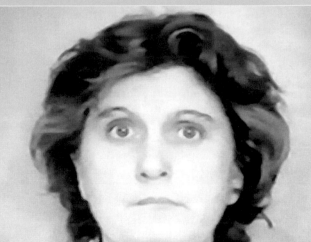

Janet Smith, convicted of the murder of her husband. She stabbed him in both eyes in a fit of jealousy, 9/1/2000.

2 How could it be that women who commit crime could be labelled as 'unfeminine'?

3 Look at Item B. Studies have shown that women tend to murder husbands and lovers while men tend to murder friends and strangers. Women also tend to use less violence than men. They tend to murder in their own homes and use kitchen implements. Explain how this might be related to the role of women in society. You should find evidence from elsewhere in the book to illustrate your point.

1 Why was it that criminology traditionally ignored female crime?

2 Give three examples of sex-role theory.

3 What do we mean by 'transgression'?

4 In your own words, explain the term 'normative masculinity'. How does it help us to understand crime?

5 What is 'moral transcendence'?

6 Suggest three examples of 'edgework'.

7 What implication for the level of female crime is there as a result of the changing role of women in recent years?

Research idea

Devise a simple 'self-report' questionnaire (see Topic 6) with a maximum of ten questions. The offending behaviour or deviant acts should be fairly minor, but common (e.g. starting a fight/smoking cannabis, etc.) Are there any differences between males and females?

WWWebtask

- Conduct an internet search of news media. How are murders by males and females portrayed? How do they differ?

- Go to the Home Office Research and Statistics Publications site. You will find a report on female crime available at http://www.homeoffice.gov.uk/rds/adhocpubs1.html. Find out what sorts of crimes females commit and the proportion of them to males. How many are found guilty and how are they sentenced?

EXAM PRACTICE

Extract from AQA-style question

With reference to material drawn from any part of the course, discuss two social influences that might lead women to become involved in criminal activity. (8 marks)

OCR-style question

Outline and assess sociological explanations of gender differences in crime rates. (60 marks)

Getting you thinking

1 What, in your view, is the difference between an 'accident' which results in someone being harmed and a 'crime' which results in someone being harmed?

The single biggest cause of lung and throat cancer and heart disease appears to be cigarette smoking.

2 Should smoking be made illegal? Justify your view.

(Left) In 1998, in Lanarkshire a local butcher failed to comply with hygiene regulations and to co-operate with local authority enforcement officials. As a result 450 people became ill, some very seriously, and 21 died.

(Right) In 1999, in Glasgow, two students died in a fire in a house converted to small flats. The fire was started accidentally. The flats were not registered with the local authority and had not been inspected.

3 In your view, were the two incidents described above unfortunate 'accidents' or crimes?

4 Each year small children die in Britain because of accidents resulting from playing with unsafe, cheap imitations of more expensive toys. Who is to blame? The children? The parents? The manufacturers? Or are they just unfortunate accidents?

What is white-collar crime?

The study of white-collar crime developed from the original work of Sutherland (1940) in the 1940s. However, Sutherland's work overlapped with the interests of Marxist writers who were interested in the 'crimes of the powerful'. Both approaches share the concern that traditional research into crime centres on such things as robbery and burglary, and in doing so focuses on working-class offenders. People committing offences at the other end of the class structure tend to be ignored.

Although there has been general agreement with Sutherland's argument that crime committed by the powerful needed studying, there remains considerable debate between sociologists about what it is that should be studied under this term.

The problem of offender and victim in white-collar crime

Sutherland (1940) originally defined white-collar crime as:

crime committed by a person of respectability and high social status in the course of his occupation.

The definition is unfortunately very vague and includes within it two, quite different activities; on the one hand, it means crimes *against* the organisation for which the person works, and on the other, crimes *for the benefit of* the organisation for which the person works or which he or she owns.

This has led to two confusing and overlapping traditions.

- First studies of **occupational crime** – how and why people steal from companies and the public in activities associated with their jobs; for example, the employee who claims false expenses from the company or who overcharges customers and keeps the additional amount.
- Much more important as a field of study in sociology is the study of **corporate crime** – crime by corporations or businesses that has a serious physical or economic impact on employees, consumers or the general public. Corporate crime is motivated by the desire to increase profits.

The problem of law and white-collar offending

There is one more problem in the debate about what white-collar/corporate crime actually is. Very often when sociologists talk about white-collar or corporate crime, they may actually not be discussing actions that are illegal – that is, if the company or person is 'caught', no one is likely to go in front of a judge and face the possible personal risk of going to jail. Instead, the crime studied may actually be the breaking of supervisory codes (as in financial services) or technical standards (chemical content of consumer goods) or may refer to a whole range of actions that are, it could be argued, harmful and may even lead to death, but are not strictly speaking illegal – low safety standards at work, but that meet minimum legal criteria, for example. In fact, as Nelkin (1997) points out, the debate about corporate crime is as much about corporate practices and sociologists' biases about what is morally wrong, as it is about breaking the law.

Some writers argue that corporate crime ought to extend to the manufacture of cigarettes or alcohol – both of which are linked to illness and death. Others point out that transnational companies, which manufacture in poorer nations where safety standards are negligible, are engaging in human-rights violations and are therefore committing crime – even if they are acting in a perfectly legal way according to the laws of the country where they are manufacturing.

So, much of the debate about white-collar or corporate 'crime' goes beyond the limits of the law and looks at actions that have harmful consequences – and, in doing so, takes us beyond the limits of conventional criminology, opening up debates about what the sociology of crime and deviance ought to study.

Corporate crime

The impact of corporate crime

Many sociological approaches – particularly that of the left realists – have pointed out the enormous costs of conventional crime to society, as well as the damage it does to the quality of people's lives. Those interested in studying white-collar and corporate crime argue, however, that the costs of conventional crime are actually dwarfed by corporate crime. As Conklin (1977) pointed out about white-collar and corporate crime in the USA.

The direct cost of business crime surpasses the cost of such conventional crimes as larceny, burglary, and auto-theft. (In 1977) the estimated loss from these four crimes was about $3 billion to $4 billion a year. This figure pales in significance when compared with an estimated annual loss of $40 billion from various white collar crimes. Half that results from consumer fraud, illegal competition and deceptive practices.

An example of this was the collapse of the US Stock market (in particular, property and banking corporations) at the end of the 1980s in the USA, the result of financial mismanagement and sometimes downright fraud, has cost in the region of a trillion dollars. Yet, interestingly, this was largely covered by a US government 'loan' that has covered the deficit.

The 'costs' of corporate crime are not just economic. Carson (1970) studied the loss of life in the exploration for oil in the North Sea, resulting from the lack of concern by exploration companies about the safety issues of the workers. This was later tragically illustrated by the loss of 168 lives when the Piper Alpha oil rig exploded.

We pointed out earlier the way that corporate 'crime' can *transgress* the boundaries of crime through acts that may not actually be illegal, but are regarded by sociologists as morally reprehensible and often a violation of certain human rights. Corporations can practise a policy of **law evasion**, for example setting up factories in countries that do not have pollution controls or adequate safety legislation, rather than producing in countries with stricter standards. They may sell goods to poorer countries when the goods have been declared unsafe in the more affluent countries (a fairly common procedure with pharmaceuticals). Box (1983) has claimed that multinationals dump products, plants and practices illegal in industrialised countries on to undeveloped or underdeveloped countries. They are able to do this because the poorer countries do not have the resources to control the large companies and also because officials are likely to accept bribes.

Corporate and white-collar crime are therefore a major problem for society and actually cost societies more than conventional crimes. What is particularly interesting is just how little attention is paid to them and how sanctions against those engaged in this form of crime are relatively minor.

What problems do sociologists face in researching corporate crime? What methods might it be possible to use? Assess their advantages and disadvantages.

Explaining corporate crime

Sociologists have sought to incorporate corporate crime into existing theories – though with varying degrees of success. The approaches include:

- personality-based explanations
- differential association
- subcultural theory
- anomie
- Marxist explanations.

Personality-based explanations

Gross (1978) studied a range of individuals who had been successful in large companies. He found that they shared similar personality traits. They tended to be ambitious, to see their own success in terms of the company's success and most relevant, that they had an 'undemanding moral code', (that we might term 'being unscrupulous'). According to Gross, the more successful they were, the less their sense of obligation to conform to wider social obligations. They accepted that personal and company success was more important than legal constraints.

Differential association

Sutherland (1940) argued that the theory of differential association (see Topic 3) helped account for why business executives committed such enormous amounts of crime that benefited their organisation. Sutherland claimed that the culture of the organisation might well justify committing illegal or dubious acts in order to achieve the organisation's goals. Geis (1967), for example, examined the evidence given to congressional hearings into illegal price-fixing agreements of companies in the USA. He found that people taking up posts in organisations tended to find that price fixing was an established practice and they would routinely become involved as part of their learning process of their jobs.

Subcultural theory

As early as 1952, Aubert studied how rationing procedures had been subverted during World War II by officials and members of food organisations so that favouritism was shown

---

> ### Obstacles organisations need to overcome to make profit, according to Box
>
> Box suggests that there are a number of potential obstacles that organisations may have to overcome in order to achieve their goals. These include:
>
> **The government:** this will impose laws to regulate production and commerce – for example, on **insider trading** in investments, or pollution as a result of productive practices in manufacturing.
> **Employees:** may not wish to work as hard or to perform the sorts of tasks/run the risks the organisation wants.
> **Consumers:** might not wish to purchase certain products if they knew the full facts concerning their production or might not be willing to pay the additional costs to make the product of good quality/safe. An example of this is the food industry that uses a wide range of food-adulterating practices and poor animal-husbandry to produce cheap food.
> **The public:** pressure groups that may want to influence consumers and the government to change or enforce legislation. The proposed regulations might harm the profits of the companies.
>
> Box argues that all of these groups represent potential barriers to companies achieving their goals and these barriers may have to be overcome, possibly in illegal ways.

---

to some groups and individuals (including themselves). Aubert (1952) found that these 'white-collar criminals' had an 'elaborate and widely accepted ideological rationalisation for the offences'. In fact, criminal practices were quite normal. Evidence that such practices continue to this day comes from Braithwaite's (1984) study of the pharmaceutical industry, where bribing health inspectors was regarded as a perfectly normal part of business practice.

Anomie

Merton's anomie approach has also been applied to explain corporate crime. Box, who, as we shall see later, straddles a number of theoretical perspectives, used the idea of Merton's version of anomie (Topic 3) to help explain why organisations break the law. Box (1983) argues that if an organisation is unable to achieve its goals using socially approved methods, then it may turn to other, possibly illegal, methods of achieving its goal of maximising profit.

The idea of anomie was also developed, in a wider way, by Braithwaite (1984) who argued that corporate crime could be seen as:

> *an illegitimate means of achieving any one of a wider range of organisational and personal goals when legitimate means …are blocked.*

He found in his study of the pharmaceutical industry that scientists were willing to fabricate their results in order to have their products adopted by their companies. The motivation for this was often not solely financial greed, but as often as not the desire for scientific prestige.

Marxist explanations

Perhaps the theoretical approach that has most enthusiastically adopted the study of corporate crime is the Marxist tradition. Corporate crime fits the critical criminological view that the real criminals are the rich and powerful. Critical criminologists argue that despite the fact that the powerful are able to use their dominance of society to avoid having the majority of their activities defined as illegal, they will still break the law where it conflicts with their interests. Furthermore, if they are actually caught, then they are less likely to be punished.

Swartz (1975) argues that as capitalism involves the maximisation of corporate profits, then 'its normal functioning produces…deaths and illnesses'. So business crime is based upon the very values and legitimate practices of capitalism. Box (1983) has pointed out the success that the powerful have had in promoting the idea that corporate crime is less serious and less harmful than the range of normal street crimes, violence and burglary. Box describes this as a deliberate process of 'mystification' that has helped keep corporate crime as a minor object of study in criminology.

This theme was taken up by Frank Pearce (1976) who was interested in why there were so few prosecutions against corporations and senior business people. He concluded that they were so rare because otherwise there would be an undermining of the belief that the vast majority of crime is carried out by the working class. If the true pattern of crime came to be known by the bulk of the population then it would create a crisis of legitimacy for the ruling class.

Marxists claim that the working class act as scapegoats as they are held responsible for much crime. Using examples from your studies, what other groups may have acted as scapegoats? For what?

Occupational crime

The impact of occupational crime

Theft by employees is a major source of crime in Britain – though whether the action of depriving an employer of goods, services or money is actually *defined* as theft is a real issue. Ditton (1977) and Mars (1982) have both studied theft by employees and found that in the range of industries they studied – from workers in the tourist industry to bakery delivery drivers – minor theft was regarded as a legitimate part of the job and redefined into a 'perk' or a 'fiddle'. Indeed, according to Mars, fiddling was part of the rewards of the job. For their part, according to Clarke (1990), management generally turned a blind eye to fiddles, accepting them as part of the total remuneration of the job and taking these into account in determining wage structures.

Fraud is a criminal offence covering a wide range of situations, but if we focus only on fraud by employees on employers, Levi (1987) found that in the late 1980s 75% of all frauds on financial institutions such as banks and building societies were by their own employees, and of 56 companies

he surveyed, over 40% had experienced fraud of over £50,000 by employees that year. However, employers were very reluctant to prosecute as they feared that by doing so they could attract negative publicity.

Labelling theory provides the most appropriate avenue for understanding occupational crime and the responses of employers respond to it. Employees build up expectations about what they deserve and what is an appropriate or 'fair' payment for the job and, if they do not receive this, will engage in illegal practices to reach the 'fair' salary.

Labelling theory recognises the importance of the perception of behaviour by others. Where else in your studies have you come across the idea of labelling?

However, writers such as Steven Box have pointed out that the values of capitalism – that, after all, stresses self-interest – do not necessarily support behaving in a law-abiding way. Mars, in his study of the catering industry (1982), explains theft by employees and sharp-practice by restaurant owners by referring to the conflicting values of capitalism:

> There is only a blurred line between **entrepreneuriality** and flair on the one hand and sharp practice and fraud on the other.

KEY TERMS

Corporate crime – crimes committed by companies against employees or the public.

Entrepreneuriality – refers to people who have original ideas for making money.

Insider trading – an illegal act in most advanced economies, where people with particular 'inside knowledge' of important, secret, future company changes, purchase (or sell) shares knowing that the price is about to change. They will therefore make a large profit, or avoid a large loss.

Law evasion – acting in such a way as to break the spirit of laws but technically to conform.

Occupational crime – crimes committed against a company by an employee.

Transgress – to cross over (conventional) boundaries. In criminology it refers to rejecting normal legal ideas of 'crime' and including in crimes, legal acts that are truly harmful to others.

1 Explain the difference between corporate and occupational crime.

2 Which costs society more, white-collar crime or 'conventional' crime? Illustrate your answer with figures.

3 What three obstacles do companies have to overcome, according to Box?

4 How does this lead to corporate crime?

5 Explain how corporations can engage in law evasion.

6 Why are Marxists particularly interested in studying corporate crime?

7 Give two examples of occupational crime from the text.

Research idea

Interview some friends about their part-time work. Do petty pilfering and other minor fraud occur? How is it justified? Are they aware of any examples of illegal or irresponsible business practice in the organisation itself? Emphasise the confidentiality of their responses.

WWWebtask

● Find out all you can about the Hatfield Train Crash that happened on October 17, 2000. (For example, The *Guardian* has a series of reports linked together – www.guardian.co.uk/ hatfieldtraincrash/story). How might this illustrate some of the themes of corporate crime?

● Visit the Serious Fraud Squad website at www.sfo.gov.uk/ publications. Go to the annual review for last year. What does this tell you about the number of cases of fraud under investigation and how many were actually prosecuted. In your view, what proportion of government resources are devoted to combating serious fraud?

● Corporate Watch is a website packed with examples of corporate irresponsibility. (www.corporatewatch.org).

EXAM PRACTICE

Extract from AQA-style question

Examine the problems involved in using official statistics to measure the extent of white-collar and corporate crime. (12 marks)

OCR-style question

Outline and assess the view that white-collar and corporate crime are under-represented in criminal statistics. (60 marks)

Item A

The death of Simon Jones, 24, on his first day at work at Shoreham Docks in April 1998, and last week's court acquittal of his employer Euromin and its general manager, James Martell, for his manslaughter, has made clear the failure of the law in relation to workplace safety.

Simon Jones died when the jaws of a crane grab closed around his head as he was unloading bags from a ship's hold. His death was the result of a dangerous working system: the banksman did not speak English, there was an open grab immediately above the heads of workers, and the grab had not been replaced with a safe hook provided to the company.

Simon's death could have been prevented if the Health and Safety Executive – the body responsible for enforcing safety law in Britain – had found out how the company unloaded cargo and compelled it to operate safely. The Executive is a calamitously under-resourced body.

At the time of Simon's death there was only one HSE inspector responsible for enforcing safety law to cover all the docks in the south of England. That inspector was also responsible for hospitals and local authority, police and Ministry of Defence establishments.

The police investigation did not begin for over six weeks – even though procedures exist that require the CID to start immediate inquiries into work-related deaths. Not until three years had passed did the police finally undertake a full search of Euromin's office and papers, in May 2001.

The government agreed four years ago to reform this archaic law and allow a company to be convicted without the need to prosecute one of its directors or senior managers. But the government has not published a parliamentary bill about this, and has given no commitment when there will be a bill.

Source: David Bergman, The *Guardian* Tuesday, December 4, 2001

Item B

Adidas boycotts EU ethics hearing

Two of Europe's best-known multinationals came under attack yesterday for boycotting a parliamentary hearing that was given graphic evidence of their unethical behaviour in developing countries.

The Swiss and German industrial giants, Nestlé and Adidas, refused to send company representatives to a meeting in the European Parliament in Brussels that heard a litany of accusations against producers of some of Europe's most familiar branded goods. The hearing was told that workers manufacturing Adidas goods in Indonesia were forced to perform more than 50 hours of overtime a week, while being paid less than the legal hourly limit for the work.

Nestlé's sales team in Pakistan was accused of offering anything from small inducements to large items of medical equipment to boost sales of formula milk. The use of breast milk substitutes is discouraged by most aid workers in the Third World because, with the water supply so unreliable, artificially fed infants are about 25 times more likely to contract fatal illnesses.

Despite its Swiss ownership, Nestlé is an object of the parliament's scrutiny because it exports some of its produce from the Netherlands.

By Stephen Castle in Brussels November 23, 2000, *The Independent*

1 Box has suggested that companies have to overcome certain barriers if they are to be successful. Explain the role of the potential 'government' barrier in Item A and how it was overcome.

2 How might a Marxist explanation be used to explain the death of Simon Jones?

3 How does Item B illustrate the difficulty of defining what actually is white-collar or corporate crime?

Getting you thinking

WHAT DO YOU CALL A BLACK MAN IN A BMW?

A POLICE SERGEANT ON PATROL

Officers from all backgrounds play their part in protecting the
If you want a career that makes a difference please contact your local police station for more in

Racism 'rife in justice system'

One of the Home Office's own studies, published today, found that people from ethnic-minority communities were put off joining the police because they anticipated that they would be isolated and subjected to racism. Many also expected to face a level of hostility from their own communities if they joined the police. Members of black and Asian groups sometimes themselves had negative attitudes towards ethnic-minority officers, the study found.

Vikram Dodd, The *Guardian*, Monday March 20

1 What point is being made by the Police Federation poster above?

2 Why do you think this poster was thought necessary?

3 Why do you think that some members of ethnic minorities are 'put off' joining the police?

4 Why do you think that 'black and Asian groups... had negative attitudes towards ethnic minority officers'?

A recurring theme in media reporting of street crime since the mid-1970s has been the disproportionate involvement of young males of African-Caribbean origin. It has partly been on this crime–race linkage that the police has justified the much greater levels of **stop and search** of young, black males, than of white males.

Explain the term 'disproportionate' as it is used above.

Images of Asian criminality have, until recently, portrayed the Asian communities as generally more law-abiding than the majority population. However, slowly at first after the '**Rushdie Affair**' and Ethen more rapidly since the September 11, 2001 attack on the World Trade Centre in New York, a new **discourse** has emerged regarding Muslim youths. The

newer image is of them as being potentially dangerous – a threat to British culture.

Just discussing the relationship between criminality and race is itself a difficult task, and some sociologists argue that making the subject part of the A-level specifications actually helps perpetuate the link. After all, there are no discussions on 'white people and crime'!

Explain in your own words why some sociologists object to the issue of ethnicity and crime appearing on the specifications.

Despite these reservations, sociologists have set out to examine the argument that there is a higher rate of crime by certain ethnic minorities, and the counter claim that the criminal justice system is racist.

Offending, sentencing and punishment

Offending

There are three ways of gathering statistics on ethnicity and crime:

- official statistics
- victimisation studies
- self-report studies.

Official statistics

About 7% of people arrested were recorded as 'black', 4% as Asian. Overall, in 2000 26 whites were arrested per 1,000 of the population, with 113 per 1,000 for 'blacks' and 37 for Asians.

Official statistics tell us the numbers of people arrested by the police. However, they are not necessarily a reflection of offending rates but can be seen just as much as a comment on the actions of the police. If, as some sociologists argue, the actions of some police officers are partly motivated by racism, then the arrest rates reflect this, rather than offending rates by ethnic minorities.

Victimisation studies

Victim-based studies (such as the British Crime Survey) are gathered by asking victims of crime for their recollection of the ethnic identity of the offender. According to the British Crime Survey (1992) the majority of crime is **intra-racial**, with 88% of white victims stating that white offenders were involved, 3% claiming the offenders were 'black', 1% Asian and 5% 'mixed'.

About 42% of crimes against 'black' victims were identified as being committed by 'black' offenders and 19% of crimes against Asians were by Asian offenders. The figures for 'white' crimes against ethnic minorities are much higher – about 50%, though this figure needs to be seen against the backdrop of 90% of the population being classified as 'white'.

Like official statistics, asking victims for a description of who committed the crimes is shot through with problems. For a start, only about 20% of survey-recorded crimes are personal crimes (such as theft from the person), where the victims might actually see the offender. Bowling and Phillips (2002) argue that victims are influenced by (racial) stereotypes and 'culturally determined expectations' as to who commits crime. Certainly, research by Bowling (1999) indicates that where the offender is not known, white people are more likely to ascribe the crime to those of African-Caribbean origin.

Why might white people be likely to 'ascribe the crime to those of African-Caribbean origin', even when the offender is not known?

Self-report studies

Self-report studies use an anonymous questionnaire to ask people what offences they have committed. Graham and Bowling's study (1995) of 14–25 year olds for the Home Office found that the self-reported offending rates were more or less the same for the 'white', 'black' and Asian respondents.

Why has the validity of the findings of self-report studies been questioned?

Sentencing

After arrest, those of African-Caribbean backgrounds are slightly more likely to be held in custody and to be charged with more serious offences than whites. But they are more likely than average to plead, and to be found, not guilty. However, if found guilty, they are more likely to receive harsher sentences – in fact, those of African-Caribbean backgrounds have a 17% higher chance of imprisonment than 'whites'.

Those of Asian origin are also more likely than average to plead not guilty, but more likely than average to be found guilty, but have an 18% lesser chance of being imprisoned.

Sociologists are divided as to whether these statistics mean that members of the ethnic minorities are discriminated against. Bowling and Phillips (2002) summarise the 'patchy' knowledge of sociologists, by saying that the research indicates that both direct and indirect discrimination (types of charges laid, access to bail, etc.) against members of the ethnic minorities does exist.

What is the difference between direct and indirect discrimination?

Punishment

In British prisons, the numbers of African and African-Caribbean prisoners is proportionately (that is, in terms of their proportion of the population as a whole) 7.8 times higher than would be expected, and is 0.77 times higher for those of Asian origin. In 1998 the rate of imprisonment per 100,000 of the general population was 1,245 for black people, 185 for whites and 168 for Asians.

Policing and ethnic minorities

We have already seen that there are considerable differences between the arrest rates for ethnic minorities and those for 'whites', with those of African-Caribbean origins having a four times higher rate of arrest than 'whites'. Sociologists are largely split between those who argue that this reflects real differences in levels of offending and those who argue that the higher arrest-rates are due to the practices of the police.

A reflection of reality?

Sociologists all reject the idea that there is an association between 'race' and crime, in the sense that being a member of a particular ethnic group in itself has any importance in explaining crime. However, a number of writers (Mayhew, Aye Maung and Mirrlees-Black (1993)), argue that most crime is performed by young males who come from poorer backgrounds. This being so then there would be an over-representation of offenders from the ethnic minorities, quite simply because there is a higher proportion of young males in the ethnic-minority population than in the population as a whole. It is also a well-researched fact that the ethnic minorities overall have are likely to have lower incomes and poorer housing conditions. These sociologists would accept that there is evidence of racist practices by certain police officers, but that the arrest rates largely reflect the true patterns of crime.

Identify two reasons why ethnic-minority groups may have lower incomes and poorer housing conditions than the population as a whole.

Phillips and Brown's (1998) study of ten police stations across Britain found that those of African-Caribbean origin were more likely to be arrested than their representation in the community. However, they found no evidence that they were treated any differently during the arrest process, with about 60% of both 'blacks' and 'whites' and about 55% of Asians eventually being charged.

Racist police practices?

A second group of sociologists see the higher arrest rates as evidence of police racism. Within this broad approach there are a number of different explanations.

- *Reflection of society approach*   This approach, often adopted by the police, is that there are some individuals in the police who are racist, and once these 'bad apples' are rooted out, the police force will not exhibit racism. This approach was suggested by **Lord Scarman** (1981) in his inquiry into the inner-city 'riots' of 1981. According to Scarman, the police reflect the wider society and therefore some racist recruits may join.
- *Canteen culture*   The '**canteen** (or working) **culture**' approach argues that police officers have developed distinctive working values as a result of their job. Police officers have to face enormous pressures in dealing with the public: working long hours; facing potential danger; hostility from significant sections of the public; and social isolation. The result is that they have developed a culture in response that helps them to deal with the pressures and gives them a sense of identity. The 'core characteristics' of the culture, according to Reiner (1992) include a thirst for action, cynicism, conservatism, suspicion, isolation from the public, macho values and racism.

  Studies by Smith and Gray (1985), Holdaway (1983) who was himself a serving police officer at the time, and Graef (1989), all demonstrated racist views amongst police officers who, for example, held stereotypical views on the criminality of African-Caribbean origin youths. Most importantly, it led them to stop and search these youths to a far greater extent than any other group. In fact, African-Caribbean people are six times more likely than whites to be stopped and searched by the police.

- *Institutional racism*   After the racist murder of a black youth, Stephen Lawrence in 1993, and after very considerable pressure from his parents, the **Macpherson Inquiry** was set up to look at the circumstances of his death and the handling of the situation by the police. Sir

William Macpherson concluded that the police were characterised by **institutional racism**. By this he meant that the police have 'procedures, practices and a culture that tend to exclude or to disadvantage non-white people' (cited in Bowling and Phillips, 2002).

The key point about institutional racism is that it is not necessarily intentional on the part of any particular person in the organisation, but that the normal, day-to-day activities of the organisation are based upon racist ideas and practice. This means that police officers might not have to be racist in their personal values, but that in the course of their work they might make assumptions about young black males and the likelihood of their offending that influence their (the police officers') attitudes and behaviour.

Theorising race and criminality

Left realist approach

Lea and Young, leading writers in the left realist tradition, accept that there are racist practices by the police (1993). However, they argue that, despite this the statistics do bear out a higher crime rate for street robberies and associated 'personal' crimes by youths of African-Caribbean origin. They explain this by suggesting that British society is racist and that young ethnic-minority males are economically and socially **marginalised**, with lesser chances of success than the majority population. Running alongside this is their sense of relative deprivation. According to Lea and Young, the result is the creation of subcultures, which can lead to higher levels of personal crime as a way of coping with marginalisation and relative deprivation (see Topic 11 for a discussion of Realist criminologies).

What is a subculture? Give one example from your studies of topics other than Crime and Deviance of how the term has been used by sociologists.

Capitalism in crisis

Hall *et al.*'s (1978) study of street crime ('**mugging**') illustrates a particular kind of Marxist approach. According to Hall, the late 1970s were a period of crisis for British capitalism. The country was undergoing industrial unrest, there was a collapse in the economy and the political unrest in Northern Ireland was particularly intense. When capitalism is in crisis the normal methods of control of the population may be inadequate, and it is sometimes necessary to use force. However, using obvious repression needs some form of justification. It was in these circumstances that the newspapers, basing their reports on police briefings, highlighted a huge increase in 'mugging' (street robberies).

According to Hall, the focus on a relatively minor problem, caused by a group who were already viewed negatively, served the purpose of drawing attention away from the crisis and focusing blame on a scapegoat – young African-Caribbean males. This 'moral panic' then justified increased numbers of police on the streets, acting in a more repressive manner.

What is meant by a 'moral panic'? Give two further examples from your studies.

Hall *et al.*'s analysis has been criticised for not making any effort to actually research the motivations and thinking of young African-Caribbean males. What is more, the association between 'criminality and black youth', made by the police and the media, has continued for over twenty-five years, and so it seems unlikely that this can be explained simply by a 'crisis of capitalism'.

Cultures of resistance

A third approach overlaps with the Marxist approach we have just explored. According to this approach, linked with Scraton (1987) and Gordon (1988), policing, media coverage and political debates all centre around the issue of 'race' being a problem. Ethnic minorities have been on the receiving end of discrimination since the first migrants arrived, leaving them in a significantly worse socio-economic position than the 'white' majority.

In response to this, '**cultures of resistance**' have emerged, in which crime is a form of 'organised resistance' which has its origins in the **anti-colonial struggles**. When young members of the ethnic minorities commit crimes they are doing so as a political act, rather than as a criminal act.

There are a number of criticisms of this approach. Lea and Young (1993) have been particularly scathing, pointing out that the majority of crimes are actually 'intra-racial', that is 'black on black'. This cannot therefore reflect a political struggle against the white majority. Secondly, they accuse writers such as Scraton as 'romanticising' crime and criminals, and in doing so ignoring the very real harm that crime does to its victims.

Exclusion and alternative economies

This approach integrates the previous approaches and relates quite closely to the work of Cloward and Ohlin (1960) (see Topic 3). A good example of this sort of argument is provided by Philippe Bourgois' study (1995) of 'El Barrio', a deprived area in East Harlem, New York. Bourgois spent seven years living and researching the street life and economy of 'El Barrio', whose inhabitants were overwhelmingly Puerto Ricans, illegal Mexican immigrants and African-Americans.

What method of research did Bourgois use? How have some sociologists criticised this method?

Bourgois argues that the economic exclusion of these ethnic-minority groups, combined with negative social attitudes towards them, has forced them to develop an 'alternative economy'. This involves a wide range of both marginally legal and clearly illegal activities, ranging from kerbside car-repair businesses to selling crack cocaine. Drug sales are by far the most lucrative employment: 'Cocaine and crack… have been the fastest growing – if not the only – equal-opportunity employers of men in Harlem'.

Running alongside this informal economy has developed a distinctive (sub) culture, which Bourgois calls 'inner-city street culture' – as he puts it, "this 'street culture of resistance' is not a coherent, conscious universe of political opposition, but rather a spontaneous set of rebellious practices that in the long term have emerged as an oppositional style". This subculture causes great damage because the illegal trade in

drugs eventually involves its participants in lifestyles of violence, substance abuse and '**internalised rage**'. Many of the small-scale dealers become addicted and drawn into violence to support their habit. Furthermore, their behaviour destroys families and the community. The result is a chaotic and violent 'community' where the search for dignity in a distinctive culture leads to a worsening of the situation.

You may have studied Paul Willis's study Learning to Labour *(1997) at some point during your course. How are the ideas of Bourgois similar to those of Willis?*

Although this is an extreme lifestyle, even for the USA, elements of it can help us to understand issues of race and criminality in the UK. Exclusion and racism leads to both cultural and economic developments that involve illegal activities and the development of a culture that helps resolve the issues of lack of dignity in a racist society. But both the illegal activities and the resulting culture may lead to an involvement in crime.

CHECK YOUR UNDERSTANDING

1 What different interpretations are there concerning the arrest rates of ethnic minorities?

2 What do we mean when we say that the majority of crime is 'intra-racial'?

3 Identify any two problems with the statistics derived from 'victimisation studies'.

4 What are self-report studies? Do they confirm the statistics derived from the arrest rates?

5 What two general explanations have sociologists put forward for the higher arrest rates of members of the ethnic minorities?

6 Explain the meaning of the term 'canteen culture'.

7 Explain the meaning of the term 'institutional racism'.

8 How do 'left realist sociologists' explain the relationship between ethnicity and crime?

9 What is the relationship between crises in capitalism and police action against 'muggers'?

10 Explain what the term 'culture of resistance' means?

Research idea

Go to the *Guardian* and *Daily Telegraph* websites **www.guardianunlimited.co.uk** and **www.electronictelegraph.co.uk**. Key into the 'search' box the terms 'race and crime' – what sorts of stories can you find? Conduct a content analysis of the stories. You could do this qualitatively or quantitatively by identifying and counting up words that convey particular feelings such as 'black crime' and 'problem'.

Anti-colonial struggles – historically, black resistance to Western attempts to control and exploit black people.

Canteen culture – refers to the set of attitudes and behaviour developed by the police. It is a form of 'occupational culture'.

Cultures of resistance – the term used to suggest that ethnic minorities in Britain have developed a culture that resists the racist oppression of the majority society.

Discourse – a framework of thinking about an issue.

Institutional racism – racism that is built into the normal practices of an organisation.

Internalised rage – term used by Bourgois to describe the anger and hurt caused by economic and social marginalisation.

Intra-racial – *within* a particular ethnic group.

Lord Scarman – in 1981 there were serious inner-city disturbances, particularly in Brixton in London. Lord Scarman led a government inquiry into the causes of these 'riots'.

Macpherson Inquiry – Sir William Macpherson led an inquiry into the events surrounding the murder of Stephen Lawrence (allegedly) by white racists, and the subsequent police investigation.

Marginalised – a sociological term referring to those who are pushed to the edge of society in cultural, status or economic terms.

Mugging – a term used to describe street robbery. It has no status as a specific crime in England and Wales.

Rushdie Affair – Salman Rushdie is a famous novelist. His book, *The Satanic Verses*, was seen by many Muslims as being an attack on their religion. The fundamentalist regime in Iran issued a *fatwah* or death threat to Rushdie who was forced to go into hiding for several years. (The *fatwah* was later revoked.)

Stop and search – police officers have powers to stop and search those they 'reasonably' think may be about to, or have committed, a crime. This power has been used much more against ethnic-minority youths than white youths.

EXAM PRACTICE

Extract from AQA-style question

Examine some of the problems involved in collecting accurate data on crime rates among different ethnic groups. (12 marks)

Extract from OCR-style question

Outline and assess the view that ethnic minorities are over-represented in official crime statistics (60 marks)

WWWebtask

The Home Office produce an on-line publication *Race and the Criminal Justice System*, which contains a wide range of up-to-date statistics. Explore the site and make your own mind up about the way that ethnic minorities interact with the criminal justice system. www.homeoffice.gov.uk/rds/pdfs/s95race00.pdf

Item A

Drug dealing suspects

Smoking crack

1 According to Bourgois, why are some members of ethnic-minority groups in inner cities in the USA attracted to the selling of illegal drugs?

Item B

Despite his public assertiveness, Caesar was ridden with self-doubt over his exclusion from mainstream society. At times, he too shared Primo's fantasies of being a 'normal working nigga.' His tolerance of exploitation, however, was lower than Primo's and his sensitivity towards personal disrespect at work was much more acute… Nevertheless, he too allowed himself to fantasize about 'going legit' when opportunities presented themselves in contexts that were not completely anathema to the norms of street culture. For example, when Ray made his first concerted attempt to launder his crack profits by purchasing the lease on a bodega, Caesar jumped at the chance to work there… During these weeks [when they were killing rats to get the bodega clean] they would come over to my living room in their stinking clothes… in order to sniff speedballs, [and] drink beer…

Caesar: I haven't told 'Buela' (grandma) yet I ain't tellin' no one nothing until I be coming home paid every week (slamming his fist into his palm and then bending over to sniff from the key-tip laden with heroin…) I'm going to get off hard-core drugs (grinning and sniffing heroin again). Well, except for maybe dope and coke…

P. Bourgois, (1995) *In Search of Respect* (1995) Cambridge: Cambridge University Press, pp.133–134

Item C

The notion that increasing youth unemployment, coupled with a high young population in the black community, and the effects of massive, well-documented, racial discrimination and the denial of legitimate opportunity, did not result in a rising rate of real offences is hardly credible… [This] real increase in crime is amplified as a result of police action and police prejudice.

J. Lea and J. Young, (1993) *What is to be Done about Law and Order?* (revised edition) London: Pluto

2 What helped prevent Caesar's exclusion from mainstream employment? To what extent do you sympathise with his views?

3 Which theoretical approach does this extract represent? Explain your answer.

4 Why do you think that he 'fantasizes' about going straight?

5 Does Item C agree or disagree that there is a higher rate of crime in the 'black community'? What evidence do the authors give to support their argument?

Topic 11 Realist criminologies

Getting you thinking

1 Do you think it is ever possible to eliminate crime? Explain your answer.

People on large social housing estates and in the inner cities are having their lives blighted by crime. Imagine you have just formed a new government and you have a choice. You are not sure but you think the real causes of crime are probably poverty and deprivation. You can spend all your money tackling poverty and hope that it has an effect on crime in, say, 20 years or you can spend the money on more police officers, CCTV, better street lighting, and a whole range of other anti-crime measures. You are aware that these may lower the crime rate today, but do nothing to address the 'real' causes.

2 What would you do? (No, you cannot do both!) Give the reasons for your choice.

3 Are there problems with crime in the area where you live? What sorts of crime? What would be your ideal solution if you could do something about it today?

In an earlier topic we looked at criminal statistics. We learned that the victims of crime are, perhaps surprisingly, more likely to be the poor and the disadvantaged than the rich. In the 1980s there was genuine despair that any theory of crime could provide a basis for policies to combat the very real sense of threat that many people felt about crime in inner-city areas and in large social housing developments.

On the one hand, the more **right-wing** policies of ever stricter punishment of offenders did not seem to be lowering the crime rate and, on the other hand, the Marxist-based theories (see Topic 4), seemed to suggest that crime could only be limited by a Marxist 'revolution' – which seemed unlikely to occur. Out of this despair, realist criminology was born.

Realist criminology has two very different and opposing wings:

- **right realism** – deriving from the right-wing theories of James Q. Wilson and emphasising '**zero tolerance**'.
- **left realism** – deriving from the writings of Lea, Young and Matthews who emphasise the importance of tackling

deprivation and of getting policing to respond to the needs of the local population.

Right realism

Right realism originated in the USA with the writings of James Q. Wilson. In *Broken Windows* (1982), Wilson argued that crime flourishes in situations where social control breaks down. According to his analysis, in any community, a proportion of the population are likely to engage in **'incivilities'**, which might consist of such things as dropping litter, vandalism or rowdy behaviour. In most communities, this behaviour is prevented from going further by the comments and actions of other members of the local community. Effectively, the amount and extent of incivilities are held in check by the response of others. However, if the incivilities go unchecked, then the entire social order of the area breaks down and gradually there is a move to more frequent and more serious crime. The parallel which Wilson drew was with abandoned buildings, where he asks whether anyone had ever seen just one window broken? The answer was, of course, that once one window was broken, then they all were.

What agencies are responsible for social control? Identify two examples of social control from elsewhere in your studies.

Once crime is allowed to happen, it flourishes. Wilson was strongly influenced by the work of the American theorist Amitai Etzioni, and his theory of **communitarianism** (1993) – which stresses the fact that only local communities by their own efforts and local face-to-face relationships can solve social problems.

The conclusion that Wilson drew was that the police had a crucial role to play in restoring the balance of incivilities and helping to recreate community. He argued that most police officers engage in *law enforcement* – that is ensuring that the law is not broken and apprehending offenders if they have committed an offence. He argued that this did relatively little to reconstruct communities and prevent crime (after all only about 3% of offences result in successful prosecutions). Police should instead be concentrating on *order maintenance*. By this he means using the law to ensure that the smaller incivilities – groups of rowdy youths, noisy parties, public drug use – are all crushed. According to him, this would help to create a different view of what was acceptable behaviour, and would make public areas feel safe again for the majority of people.

After a version of his ideas were adopted in New York, under the slogan '**zero tolerance**', and there appeared to be a decline in crime, the term was adopted throughout America and to some extent in the UK as a description of a much harsher form of street policing.

What methods could be used to evaluate the success of 'zero-tolerance' policing? What problems would this research face?

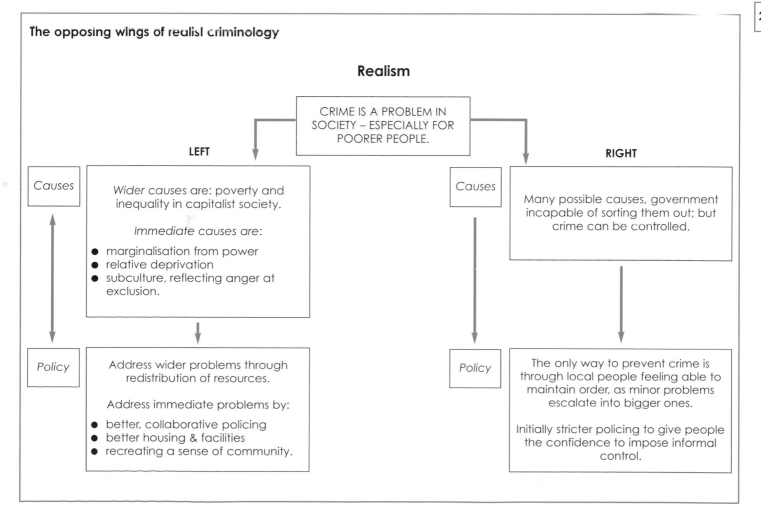

The opposing wings of realist criminology

Realism

CRIME IS A PROBLEM IN SOCIETY – ESPECIALLY FOR POORER PEOPLE.

LEFT

Causes

Wider causes are: poverty and inequality in capitalist society.

Immediate causes are:
- marginalisation from power
- relative deprivation
- subculture, reflecting anger at exclusion.

Policy

Address wider problems through redistribution of resources.

Address immediate problems by:
- better, collaborative policing
- better housing & facilities
- recreating a sense of community.

RIGHT

Causes

Many possible causes, government incapable of sorting them out; but crime can be controlled.

Policy

The only way to prevent crime is through local people feeling able to maintain order, as minor problems escalate into bigger ones.

Initially stricter policing to give people the confidence to impose informal control.

In later writings, Wilson and Herrnstein (1985) explore the 'causes' of crime – although what they actually do is to argue that there are no satisfactory causes of crime that governments can do anything about: crime is just something that is inevitable. However, in so far as causes can be ascertained, Wilson argues that people are more likely to commit crime if they are not socialised into acceptable behaviour in their childhood by their family – so that certain personality traits, such as 'impulsiveness' and 'lack of regard for others', come to the fore. He claims that families that have low intelligence are more likely to be '**discordant**' and are less likely to socialise their children correctly.

What perspective is linked with the view that low intelligence is a key factor in creating social problems? Where else in your studies has this perspective been influential and how has it been criticised?

However, the act of committing a crime depends upon the perception of the person that the advantages of crime outweigh the potential disadvantages.

Criticisms

Right realism has been criticised by Platt and Takagi (1977), amongst others, for the following reasons.

- It concentrates exclusively upon working-class crimes, ignoring the crimes of the powerful and white-collar crime.
- It fails to explain the causes of crime – apart from blaming inadequate socialisation. The approach absolves the government and economic system of any blame.
- The approach ignores ideas of justice and law enforcement and advocates instead the maintenance of social order – even if it is at the expense of justice.

Left realism

Left realism developed primarily as a response to the increasing influence of right realism over the policymakers in Britain and America. In the USA the main writer has been Elliot Currie, and in Britain left realism is associated with Jock Young, John Lea and Roger Matthews.

Young had been one of the founders of 'critical criminology' (see Topic 4) that had introduced elements of interactionist theory into Marxism in order to provide a 'complete' theory of crime. However, Young had become increasingly disenchanted with the Marxist approach that stressed that criminals should be seen as the victims of the capitalist system and that sociological analyses of crime should stress the criminality of the rich and powerful. This disillusionment was generated by a series of local victimisation surveys (in Islington and Merseyside, for example), that showed that the real victims of crime were the poor and the powerless, and that these people viewed street crime and burglary as one of the main social problems they faced.

Young (1984) argued that it was the role of criminology to provide relevant and credible solutions for policymakers to limit the harm that crime was doing to the lives of the poorer sections of the community. We will look at the policy

suggestions of left realism later, but this whole approach led to a bitter debate in sociology with many influential left-wing criminologists attacking Young for selling out. (The implication of Young's new argument is that the role of sociologists is to help the government to combat crime. For Marxists, crime exists because of capitalism and the government represents capitalism.) Young responded by labelling Marxist criminology as 'left idealism', meaning that it was great in theory, but had no practical solutions.

The left realist explanation of crime has three elements:

- **relative deprivation**
- **marginalisation**
- subculture.

Relative deprivation

The concept of relative deprivation derives from the writings of Runciman (1966), who argued that political revolutions only occurred when the poor became aware of the sheer scale of the differences between themselves and the rich. Without this knowledge, they generally accepted their poverty and powerlessness. It is not, therefore, poverty that leads to revolution, but awareness of their *relative* poverty.

Applying this concept to crime, Lea and Young (1984) pointed out that it is not poverty or unemployment that directly causes crime, as despite the high unemployment experienced in the economic depression in Britain from the late 1920s to the 1930s, crime rates were considerably lower than they were in the boom years of the 1980s. According to Lea and Young, the expectations of 1930s youth were much lower than those of contemporary young people, who feel resentful at what they could actually earn compared with their aspirations.

Marginalisation

Marginalisation refers to the situation where certain groups in the population are more likely than others to suffer economic, social, and political deprivation. The first two of these elements of deprivation are fairly well known – young people living in inner cities and social-housing estates are likely to suffer from higher levels of deprivation than those from more affluent areas. The third element – political marginalisation – refers to the fact that there is no way for them to influence decision-makers and thus they feel powerless.

What groups in the population are likely to feel marginalised? Explain your answer.

Subculture

This draws partially upon the Marxist subcultural approach (see Topic 4), but more heavily from the ideas of Robert Merton (see Topic 3). Subcultures develop amongst groups who suffer relative deprivation and marginalisation. Specific sets of values, forms of dress and modes of behaviour develop that reflect the problems that their members face. However, whereas the Marxist subcultural writers seek to explain the styles of dress, and forms of language and behaviour as forms of 'resistance' to capitalism, Lea and Young do not see a direct, 'decodable' link.

For Lea and Young (1984), one crucial element of subcultures is that they are still located in the values of the wider society. Subcultures develop precisely because their members subscribe to the dominant values of society, but are blocked off (because of marginalisation) from success.

The outcome of subculture, marginalisation and relative deprivation is street crime and burglary, committed largely by young males.

The policy implications

Earlier we saw that left realists were heavily criticised by other Marxist writers. In terms of theory, there is no great abandonment of Marxist ideas – Lea and Young (1984) and Matthews (Matthews and Young, 1992) all argue that the elements that lead to crime (subculture, relative deprivation and marginalisation) are the result of the gross inequalities generated by capitalist society. However, the real difference emerges in the policies that the left realists advocate. Marxist criminologists stress that the role of criminology is specifically to support critics of capitalism and to provide evidence of the way that crime is a direct outcome of capitalism. The only logical way, therefore, to eliminate crime is to create a classless, egalitarian society.

For left realists, this is just 'romanticism' – it isn't going to happen in Britain. Left realists therefore propose that the government and local authorities ought to get together and respond directly to the concerns of the victims of crime, whilst tackling as best they can (within the framework of capitalism) the causes of crime.

Left realists therefore advocate committees of local people (and particularly young, local people) to advise the police on what issues of concern they have and how they believe the police should act locally. They suggest that local authorities should go about carrying out audits of crime and then see what they can do about it, by improving street lighting, ensuring that the streets are safe and making social housing developments less subject to vandalism. At a national-government level greater investment should be made in supporting and training young people.

Criticisms

- Marxist or 'critical criminologist' writers have attacked left realism for not actually being realistic. They argue that left realism actually ignores the 'real' causes of crime that lie in the wider capitalist system. All that left realism does is actually help continue the capitalist system and so perpetuate crime in the longer run.
- The approach (like right realism) ignores the crimes of more powerful groups in society and simply concentrates on street crime.
- Feminist criminologists, such as Pat Carlen (1992), have argued that left realist criminology accepts the establishment's view of what crime is and so concentrates its attention on issues to do with street crime and burglary. They argue instead that one role of criminology ought to be exploring the way that society harms women – for example, there ought to be much greater stress upon issues of domestic violence. In reply Young has claimed

that left realism has been very concerned with domestic violence and sees it as one of the main problems that left realism must address.

Both right and left realism have had considerable influence on New Labour policy since 1997, with many of their ideas being brought into law.

Give two examples of policies that either have been, or could be, introduced to combat crime.

KEY TERMS

Communitarianism – an approach to understanding society associated with the US writer Amitai Etzioni. He argues that government should encourage the rekindling of a sense of community. Local communities can then take over responsibilities for local problems.

Discordant – here refers to families who do not provide a loving and stable home background, thereby giving their children anti-social values.

Incivilities – offensive or irritating behaviour.

Left realism – See Key Terms in Topic 4.

Marginalisation – refers to people living on the margins of society, in particular lacking any say over decision-making.

Relative deprivation – people are content if everyone around them is in a similar situation. However, when the most deprived are put in a situation where they can compare their situation with others who are affluent, they become aware of their own relatively disadvantaged state and become discontented.

Right realism – approach to crime deriving from the right-wing theories of James Q. Wilson and emphasising 'zero tolerance'.

Right-wing – refers to approaches that reject the idea of state intervention in health, welfare and educational services to limit the effects of inequalities in wealth and income. Those with right-wing views believe that inequality is good for society and that private companies are more effective in providing services than the government.

Zero-tolerance – using the law to ensure that smaller incivilities (groups of rowdy youths, noisy parties, public drug-use) are all crushed.

1 Make a list of key similarities and differences between right and left realism.

2 What does communitarianism mean and how has it been applied to the fight against crime?

3 According to Wilson and Herrnstein, what are the three 'causes' of crime?

4 What do left realists believe are the causes of crime?

5 Explain the term 'relative deprivation'.

6 In what way can young males who commit offences be said to be marginalised?

7 What are the policy implications of left realism?

WWWWebtask

Go to your local authority website and you should be able to find a section on 'community safety'. (If not you can go to the Home Office Website (www.homeoffice.gov.uk and then click on 'community safety'). Do the activities mentioned link with the ideas of 'realist' sociologists?

Research idea

Conduct a survey of local residents to find out their views about the best ways of reducing crime in your area.

EXAM PRACTICE

Extract from AQA-style question

'Crime is a serious problem that requires practical solutions.'

Examine the solutions offered by the realists. (12 marks)

OCR-style question

Outline and assess realist approaches to crime. (60 marks)

Item A

This was a world where there was a consensus stretching across a large section of informed opinion that the major cause of crime was impoverished social conditions…Anti-social conditions led to anti-social behaviour…Slums were demolished, educational standards improved, full employment advanced, and welfare spending increased: the highest affluence in the history of humanity achieved, yet crime increased.

J. Young, 'Left Realist Criminology: Radical in its Analysis, Realist in its Policy' in *The Oxford Handbook of Criminology*, Oxford: Oxford University Press, pp.482/3

1 Item A is written by Jock Young, a left realist. How do left realists explain the increase in crime described?

2 What does Item B tell us about the victims of crime? Use examples to illustrate your answer.

3 Realists are concerned about discovering the immediate problems that people face and, on the basis of this knowledge, doing something about them. Suggest what research techniques sociologists can use to discover these problems.

Item B

Percentages of different groups who were victims of more than one crime in 2000

Group	Percentage
National average	4.3
Home unoccupied for 5 or more hours	4.6
Flat	5.4
Terraced property	5.6
Asian	5.9
North West	6.1
Black	6.3
Inner city area	6.3
Household income less than £5,000	6.5
Social renter	6.7
Council estate areas	6.8
Head of household unemployed	7.2
Yorkshire and Humberside	7.2
Head of household economically inactive	7.3
Private renter	7.5
Area with high physical disorder	11.1
Single parent	11.7
Head of household 16–24	12

Source: British Crime Survey 2000, Home Office

277

It is possible that some students will find the subject matter of this Topic particularly distressing or disturbing. If you do find this to be the case please talk to your teacher. Alternatively, you can talk in confidence to The Samaritans on 0845 790 9090.

Getting you thinking

Groups at increased risk of suicide

The following table lists the main groups at heightened risk of suicide, together with an estimate of the magnitude of their increased risk in comparison to the general population.

High risk group	Estimated magnitude of increased risk
Males compared to females	× 2–3
4 weeks following discharge from psychiatric hospital	× 100–200
People who have deliberately self harmed in the past	× 10–30
Alcoholics	× 5–20
Drug misusers	× 10–20
Prisoners	× 9–10
Offenders serving non-custodial sentences	× 8–13
Doctors	× 2
Farmers	× 2
Unemployed	× 2–3
Divorced people	× 2–5
People on low incomes (social class IV/V)	× 4

Trends in age and sex specific suicide rates

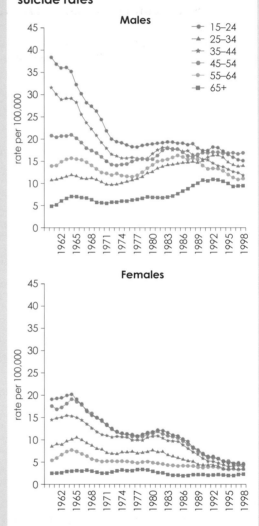

International variations in suicide

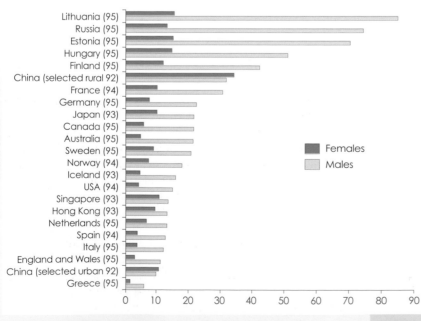

Source of all: National Electronic Library for Health, 2001

1 Why do you think the groups mentioned are at particular risk of suicide?

2 Why do you think the rates of suicides for different ages and genders have changed since 1962?

3 What possible explanations can you suggest as to why some countries have higher suicide rates than others?

You may have already developed some theories of your own as to why people commit suicide and why patterns of suicide exist. Suicide is, in many ways, the ultimate deviant act, as the act destroys the single most important element of society – the people in it. Yet suicide was relatively understudied by sociologists until the 1960s. This was because one major piece of work, by Durkheim in 1897, had so dominated sociological thought that it was believed there was little more to say. Yet, when newer interpretations did come along they carried with them some profound attacks on some of the pillars of theory and research upon which sociology had founded its very claim to be a social *science*.

So, in this topic we study suicide not just because the subject matter is interesting for society, but also as a case study in how applying different theories and methods to the same problem can provide very different and contradictory explanations.

In particular, we can see the deep divisions between the **positivists**, who believe in following the methods of the natural sciences wherever possible, and the **interpretive sociologists**, who prefer to explore the way society is constructed through people's interactions.

Suicide: a positivistic approach

Durkheim (1897/1952) chose suicide as a subject of study not just because it was interesting in itself, but in an attempt to prove that the, then, new subject of sociology could provide an explanation for an act which seemed to be the very opposite of what could be considered as 'social'. By proving that sociology had something useful to say in explaining suicide, Durkheim hoped to secure the status of sociology amongst the newly emerging sciences.

This attempt to locate sociology as a science, with its adherence to 'positivistic' methods of research, is crucial in understanding how Durkheim tackled the issue. Durkheim's chosen method, now called '**multivariate analysis**', consisted of comparing the incidence of various social factors with the known incidence of a particular event – in this case suicide. He therefore studied the statistics of suicide that he collected from death certificates and other official documents and found that there were a number of clear patterns.

What other methods of data collection are favoured by positivist sociologists? Why?

Over a period of twenty years, it could be seen that suicide rates were consistently different across countries and regions within countries; across different religions, and across the married and unmarried. These regularities immediately supported Durkheim's argument that there was a social explanation for suicide, for if suicide was an entirely individual matter, based on individual decisions, no such patterns should emerge.

To explain these patterns, Durkheim returned to the theme of shared values and social cohesion. According to him, people are naturally selfish and do not concern themselves with the problems faced by others, unless, that is, society can force them to do so. Society achieves this by finding ways of making people aware of their social bonds to others. The greater the level of **social integration**, the more harmonious a

society. In fact, society achieves thi[s] drawing people together on the bas[is] taught primarily through the family [and] religion. (It is important to remembe[r] much more influential 120 years ago [than now].)

What perspective emphasises the i[mportance of shared] values? How has the idea that share[d values exist in] modern societies been criticised?

Durkheim suggested that the individuals [most] closely integrated into society are those wi[th] close family relationships. It follows that those without close family ties are the least bonded to society. We shall see the importance of this later.

Religion operated on a broader level, providing people with a moral underpinning for shared values. However, different religions do place varying amounts of stress on individual fulfilment. At one extreme, Protestant versions of Christianity give considerable importance to individual fulfilment, while religions such as Hinduism and Roman Catholicism stress the importance of the group and consider the search for personal happiness relatively unimportant.

What other social institutions help integrate people into society? Give examples of how they do this.

The outcome of the significance of the family and religion in different societies resulted in varying levels of social integration, with Protestant-based societies being less integrated and Catholic/Hindu ones being more integrated. Furthermore, individuals in society vary in their degree of social integration into society, depending upon their membership of family networks.

It was Durkheim's hypothesis that suicide is directly related to the levels of social integration in a society or group within it. Next, he placed societies into four categories depending upon their levels of social integration.

Egoistic

In egoistic societies, individual rights, interests and welfare are heavily stressed and allegiance to the wider group is weak, with people being encouraged to look after themselves and those particularly close to them at the expense of the wider society. As a result, social bonds are weak and there is a low level of social integration. Egoistic societies are closely related to Protestantism, a strand of Christianity that stresses the responsibility of individuals to make their own decisions and to accept the consequences of doing so. Culturally, individual failure or unhappiness are viewed as acceptable grounds for people to take their own lives – **egoistic suicide**. This is typical of contemporary European and North American societies.

However, within this form of society, there are social institutions that counteract the wider egoistic values of society and provide a sense of belonging. These include the family, and other forms of religion such as Catholicism, that stress the importance of an individual's responsibility to the wider church. Durkheim also noted that in times of war or some other form of threat, societies draw together.

Durkheim concluded that there are likely to be relatively

...de in societies with low levels of social ...that that, within those societies, people integrated ...or religious groups that provide greater levels of ...integration are less likely to take their own lives. For ...mple, married people are less likely to commit suicide than single people.

Altruistic

In altruistic societies, the welfare of individuals is viewed as far less important than that of the group. Individual choice or happiness is simply not a high priority. Durkheim therefore argued that there was insufficient motivation for members to commit suicide – with one exception. **Altruistic suicide** occurs when the individual is expected to commit suicide *on behalf of the wider society* – rather than in egoistic societies where the suicide takes place because of individual unhappiness. An example of this today might be suicide bombers prepared to sacrifice themselves for their political or religious cause.

Anomic

Durkheim believed people are naturally selfish and will only look after their own interests unless society restricts their actions. According to Durkheim, societies develop cultural and social mechanisms that provide a clear framework of what is acceptable behaviour. However, if these restraints are weakened, for whatever reason then some people may revert to their natural selfishness, whilst others may simply become bewildered. Social restraints on behaviour are most likely to weaken in periods of dramatic social change (for example, during an economic or political crisis), and therefore Durkheim linked increases in suicide levels to periods of rapid social change – **anomic suicide**.

Fatalistic

This final form of suicide reflects the fact that in extremely oppressive societies people may lose the will to live and prefer to die. Durkheim considered such **fatalistic suicide** a fairly uncommon occurrence, but it could be argued that it accounts for the very high levels of suicide in prisons, for example.

Criticisms of Durkheim

Durkheim's analysis of suicide was used for over seventy years as an excellent example of how to undertake positivistic sociological analysis. During that time there was however a degree of criticism of his approach from those who basically agreed with his approach. These criticisms are known as *internal criticisms*.

However, a second group of writers have criticised Durkheim's analysis as fundamentally flawed and they argue that, rather than being an excellent example of sociological methodology, the research ought to be used as an example of why the use of traditional scientific methods in sociology is a mistake. These criticisms are known as *interpretive* ones.

Internal criticisms

- Durkheim's analysis depends upon the concept of **social cohesion**, for he argues that suicide rates vary with it. Yet, he never provides a clear, unambiguous definition of it, nor is there any obvious method of measuring it.
- He claimed that social integration was linked most closely to religion and family membership. But Durkheim provides no explanation of exactly how this can be verified or falsified. As we see in Unit 4 Topic 1, a key element of science is the ability to carry out some form of research activity that can either prove or disprove a theory. Durkheim's methodology fails this test.
- Durkheim relied largely upon official statistics – yet official statistics are open to dispute – in particular, in Catholic dominated countries and regions, suicide was regarded with great stigma and doctors were very reluctant to certify this as being the reason for death.

What other criticisms are made of the use of official statistics in sociological research? Give examples.

Interpretive criticisms

Interpretive approaches stress the way that society operates through people interacting on the basis of sharing meanings. Interpretive sociologists have paid great attention to exploring the way in that these meanings are constructed and how they influence individual behaviour. As we have pointed out elsewhere in the book, interpretive sociologists reject the idea that society can be studied with methods borrowed from the physical sciences – precisely the approach most favoured by Durkheim.

Two writers in this tradition, Douglas and Atkinson, have been particularly effective in their criticism of Durkheim's explanation.

Douglas – the meanings of suicide

Douglas (1967) argued that defining suicide simply by referring to the *physical* fact of killing oneself misses the central issue, which is that suicide has *different meanings* to those who take their own lives, and their motives vary too. If this is the case, and we can only understand society by studying the meanings through which people understand and interpret the world, then suicide needs much greater exploration regarding meaning than Durkheim provided.

Douglas suggested that those who commit suicide may define their action in at least four ways:

- *as a mean of transforming the self*: a person commits suicide as a means of gaining release from the cares of the world
- *as a means of transforming oneself for others*: the suicide tells others how profound one's feelings are on a particular issue
- *as a means of achieving fellow feeling*: the person is asking for help or sympathy; it includes 'suicide' attempts in that the person hopes to be found
- *as a means of gaining revenge*: the person believes they have been forced into a position where they have to commit suicide.

Douglas: the meanings of suicide

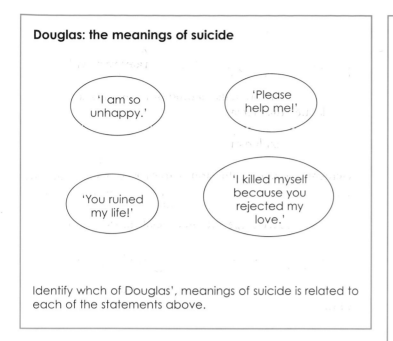

'I am so unhappy.'

'Please help me!'

'You ruined my life!'

'I killed myself because you rejected my love.'

Identify whch of Douglas', meanings of suicide is related to each of the statements above.

So, there is no single act that can be termed 'suicide'. Since the meanings that individuals place upon their acts are so different, it is mistaken to categorise them as the same phenomenon. The only thing they have in common is death. The devastating conclusion, if this argument is accepted, is that *Durkheim's statistical comparisons are worthless.*

Atkinson – the social construction of suicide

Atkinson (1971) further developed this criticism that Durkheim failed to understand that categories such as 'suicide' are really socially constructed. In Britain, for example, before a death can be classified as suicide a coroner must carry out an inquest and, on the basis of this, the death is classified as suicide or not. Atkinson argues that the official statistics therefore reflect **coroners**' decisions rather than any underlying 'reality'.

In order to make a decision, the coroner must piece together a series of 'clues' and then decide whether or not these point to suicide.

Atkinson suggests that the following clues are particularly important:

● *suicide notes*: in about 30% of suicides a note is found, although more may have been written but the family have destroyed them because of the accusations contained in them
● *mode of death*: some types of death are seen as more typical of suicide than others
● *location and circumstances of death*: coroners believe that suicides are committed in places and circumstances where they will not be discovered and where the person is sure the outcome will be successful
● *life history and mental condition*: coroners believe that suicide is often related to depression caused by significant events in the deceased's life. So coroners search for evidence of such events.

Which of the following modes of death do you think coroners are most likely to see as possible suicides? Why?

Road accident

Overdose

Noose

Death under underground train

What Atkinson shows us is that the official statistics forming the basis of Durkheim's work are themselves socially constructed by the activities of coroners.

Integrating positivistic and interpretive approaches

The criticisms made by writers such as Douglas and Atkinson have generally been accepted by sociologists as a useful corrective to the more positivistic approach of Durkheim.

Taylor (1990), however, has suggested that both Durkheim and his critics have missed the significance of **parasuicides**, as in the majority of cases people who attempt suicide do not die. Taylor points out, that when questioned, it seems most attempts at suicide are less a definite decision to finish with life and more of a gamble, in which people leave the outcome in the hands of fate. If they survive then they were not meant to die, and if they die then that was what fate or God intended.

Taylor suggests that parasuicide allows us to widen the discussion of suicide into one of 'risk-taking'. Developing the analysis of Durkheim further, he suggests that successful parasuicides could be categorised into 'ordeal' suicides, which can be related to a profound sense of *anomie*, and the more purposive suicides, similar to Durkheim's *fatalism*. Taylor also supports Durkheim's belief that suicide is more likely in individuals too detached from others in society (egoistic suicides) and those over-attached (altruistic suicide).

The point of Taylor's argument is that it is possible to pull together the wider social factors that Durkheim emphasised with the sense of meaning that Douglas stressed. The two approaches are not necessarily exclusive. Indeed, much of contemporary sociology has been the search for ways of integrating the two traditions.

Can you provide examples of any other research that has attempted to bring together these two traditions in sociology?

Research idea and webtask

Search the worldwide web for suicide statistics. What statistics can you find? What is their source? What possible explanations are there for the patterns shown? How might they be interpreted by positivists and interpretive sociologists?

EXAM PRACTICE

Extract from AQA-style question

Assess the usefulness of Durkheim's theory of suicide in modern industrial society. (40 marks)

(Topic not in OCR specification)

KEY TERMS

Altruistic suicide – Durkheim's term for suicide in societies where people see their own happiness as unimportant.

Anomic suicide – Durkheim's term for suicide in societies where rapid change is occurring.

Coroners – officials who decide on cause of death.

Egoistic suicide – Durkheim's term for suicide in societies where people regard their individual happiness as very important.

Fatalistic suicide – Durkheim's term for suicide in extreme situations where people see their lives as having no value.

Interpretive sociology – an approach to sociology that stresses studying the way that society is based on socially constructed meanings.

Multivariate analysis – a method of gathering statistics from different societies and comparing the patterns to help explain social differences between the societies.

Parasuicide – a term used by Taylor for suicide attempts where the person is not certain whether they want to die or not, and 'gambles' with their life.

Positivists – sociologists who believe that the methods used by the physical sciences can be transferred to the social sciences.

Social cohesion – the extent to which a society is held together by shared culture and values.

Social integration – the extent to which people feel they 'belong' to a society or social group.

Item A

Ziad Zarrah, one of the pilots, prior to the attack, wrote to his girlfriend:

'I did what I had to do and you should be very proud of that...It is a great honour and you will see the result, and everyone will be celebrating.'

Source: Kate Connelly, I did what I had to do, says suicide pilot's last letter, The *Observer*, Sunday November, 18th 2001

Item C

Case 1

A man ingested barbiturates and went to sleep in his car that was parked outside his estranged wife's house. A note to her was pinned on his chest indicating his expectation that she would notice him when she returned from her date with another man. This possibility of being rescued, however, was obliterated by a dense fog that descended around midnight.

Case 2

She became depressed after her marriage of 15 years broke up and was being prescribed anti-depressants. One morning at work she began swallowing the tablets one by one. A colleague at work noticed what she was doing and reported it to a senior. The company doctor was called in and he summoned an ambulance. She was unconscious on arrival at hospital but survived, after intensive medical treatment. She later said that she was unsure about her intentions at the time she was taking the tablets.

Adapted from S. Taylor, *Suicide*, Harlow: Longman (1988)

Item B

Below is the suicide note written by Kurt Cobain, lead singer of Nirvana and partner of Courtney Love, the actress.

To Boddah

Speaking from the tongue of an experienced simpleton who obviously would rather be an emasculated, infantile complain-ee. This note should be pretty easy to understand. All the warnings from the punk rock 101 courses over the years, since my first introduction to the, shall we say, the ethics involved with independence and the embracement of your community has proven to be very true. I haven't felt the excitement of listening to as well as creating music along with reading and writing for too many years now. I feel guilty beyond words about these things. For example when we're backstage and the lights go out and the manic roar of the crowd begins, it doesn't affect me the way in which it did for Freddy Mercury, who seemed to love, relish in the love and adoration from the crowd, which is something I totally admire and envy. The fact is, I can't fool you, any one of you. It simply isn't fair to you or me. The worst crime I can think of would be to rip people off by faking it and pretending as if I'm having 100% fun. Sometimes I feel as if I should have a punch-in time clock before I walk out on stage. I've tried everything within my power to appreciate it (and I do, God believe me I do, but it's not enough). I appreciate the fact that I and we have affected and entertained a lot of people. I must be one of those narcissists who only appreciate things when they're gone. I'm too sensitive. I need to be slightly numb in order to regain the enthusiasm I once had as a child. On our last 3 tours, I've had a much better appreciation for all the people I've known personally and as fans of our music, but I still can't get over the frustration, the guilt and empathy I have for everyone. There's good in all of us and I think I simply love people too much, so much that it makes me feel too fucking sad. The sad little sensitive, unappreciative, Pisces, Jesus man. Why don't you just enjoy it? I don't know! I have a goddess of a wife who sweats ambition and empathy and a daughter who reminds me too much of what I used to be, full of love and joy, kissing every person she meets because everyone is good and will do her no harm. And that terrifies me to the point where I can barely function. I can't stand the thought of Frances becoming the miserable, self-destructive, death rocker that I've become. I have it good, very good, and I'm grateful, but since the age of seven, I've become hateful towards all humans in general. Only because it seems so easy for people to get along and have empathy. Only because I love and feel sorry for people too much I guess. Thank you all from the pit of my burning, nauseous stomach for your letters and concern during the past years. I'm too much of an erratic, moody, baby! I don't have the passion anymore, and so remember, it's better to burn out than to fade away. Peace, Love, Empathy.

Kurt Cobain.

Frances and Courtney, I'll be at your altar

Please keep going Courtney,

for Frances.

for her life will be so much happier

without me. I LOVE YOU. I LOVE YOU

1 What element of Durkheim's analysis, does the letter (and actions) of Ziad Zarrad in Item A illustrate? How?

2 What elements of Durkheim's explanation of suicide might the contents of the suicide note in Item B illustrate? How?

3 In which of the categories of suicide suggested by Douglas would you classify the note? Explain your answer.

4 Use the note to illustrate the 'clues' that coroners look for in order to decide that a death is suicide.

5 Read the cases in Item C. What term is used by Taylor to describe this form of behaviour?

6 How do the cases illustrate the problem of treating official suicide statistics as 'social facts'?

Stratification and Social Difference

Examine the photos above.

1 What factors do you think have enabled the people above to achieve their social position?

2 What factors may have created barriers for them?

3 To what extent do you think society has provided equal opportunities for these people?

Most modern societies pride themselves upon providing opportunities and fairness for their members. However, as we saw above, there are many disparities that exist because people do not start from the same position or have the same level of access to those opportunities. This inevitably leads to some people having more power and privileges than others. Sociologists try to understand how, why and to whom this happens.

Differentiation and stratification

All societies **differentiate** between groups. Men and women, the young and the old, the working class and the middle class, black and white are often perceived to be *socially* different in some way. When these differences lead to greater status, power or privilege for some over others the result is social *stratification*. This term – borrowed from geology – means the layering of society into strata whereby a hierarchy (or ranked order of importance and differences in social influence and advantage) emerge. The degree to which a society has a fixed hierarchy is determined by the degree of opportunity its members have to change their social position.

A person's social importance is referred to as their **social status**. Status can be gained in two ways.

- **Ascribed status** is given at birth either through family (such origin as being a member of the Royal Family) or through physical, religious or cultural factors (such as gender or ethnicity).
- **Achieved status** is the result of factors such as hard work, educational success, special talent or sheer good fortune.

Societies that allow for and reward achievement are called **open societies** whereas those that ascribe social position are referred to as **closed societies**. Politicians tend to see a degree of openness in society as a measure of the freedoms they have helped to create but they may also have a tendency to over-emphasise the extent to which society is open. Modern Britain may have free education for all up to the age of 18 or 19, for example, but those who are rich enough to attend a top public school have significant advantages in life.

In reality, few societies are totally open or closed and each could be placed somewhere along a continuum (see figure opposite). There tends to be more closure in traditional societies as the limited range of roles tend to be fixed at birth and because religion and tradition are more significant. Modern societies, whilst on the face of things more fluid and requiring greater adaptability, may still have significant levels of closure.

Examples of traditional societies based on ascribed status

	The caste system	The feudal estate system
Place and time	Although officially banned in India today, this Hindu system of stratification is still enormously influential.	The **feudal estate system** was found in medieval Europe.
Structure	There are four basic castes or layers, ranging from the Brahmins (religious leaders and nobles) at the top to the Sudras (servants and unskilled manual workers) at the bottom. 'Untouchables' exist below the caste system and are responsible for the least desirable jobs such as sewage collection.	The king owned all the land and, in return for an oath of loyalty and military support, he would allocate the land to barons who, in turn, would apportion parts of it to knights. The majority (95%) were peasants or serfs who had to work the knight's land and in return were offered protection and allowed to rent land.
Restrictions	People are born into castes and cannot move out of them during the course of their lives. There are strong religious controls over the behaviour of caste members – for example, you cannot marry a member of another caste nor can you do certain jobs because these are assigned exclusively to certain castes.	Feudal societies, too, were mainly closed societies – people's positions were largely ascribed and it was rare for people to move up. Marriage between groups was rarely allowed and feudal barons even restricted the geographical movement of the peasants.
Possibility of social mobility	The system is based upon religious purity – the only way people can be promoted to a higher caste is by living a pure life and hoping that they will be reincarnated (re-born) as a member of a higher caste.	On rare occasions exceptional acts of bravery could result in a gift of land.

All societies can be placed somewhere along this line

Openness ——————●—————— Closure

Lots of opportunities to change social position	Equal amount of restrictions and opportunities	No opportunities to change social position

Both of the closed societies outlined above were justified by religious beliefs: Hinduism in the case of the caste system and the 'divine right of kings' in the feudal system. In these cases religion acted as an agent of social control. What other agencies of social control are there?

How do modern societies differ?

The complexity of modern industrial societies requires that a much wider range of roles needs to be fulfilled. In addition, the more dynamic nature of society creates competing, shifting demands on individuals which inevitably lead to inequalities between them. Technological developments in particular help fuel this.

How has technology affected the kind of work people do and their attitudes to that work?

Social class

This is the stratification system mainly found in modern industrial societies such as Britain. Social classes are groups of people who share a similar economic position in terms of occupation, income and ownership of wealth. They are also likely to have similar levels of education, status and power. Class systems are different to previous systems in the following ways.

- They are not based on religion, law or race but on economic factors such as occupation and wealth.
- There is no clear distinction between classes – it is difficult to say where the working class finishes and the middle class begins, for example.
- All members of society have equal rights irrespective of their social position.
- There are no legal restrictions on marriage between the classes.
- Social-class societies are open societies – you can move up or down the class structure through jobs, the acquisition of wealth or marriage.
- Such systems are usually **meritocratic** – that is, people are not born into ascribed roles. We are encouraged to better ourselves through achievement at school and in our job by working hard and gaining promotion.

Just how meritocratic social-class societies really are and to what extent factors, such as race, gender, age, can affect access to opportunity will be a key focus of this unit. But how do sociologists explain social stratification in modern societies? How does it come about? Is it fair?

Functionalism

The classic functionalist view was put forward by Davis and Moore in the 1950s. The figure below outlines both their views and those of their critics.

 Functionalists explain the existence of social institutions in terms of their functions for society. From your studies give two other examples of social institutions and their functions.

The functionalist theory of stratification

Davis and Moore (1945)	Criticisms
All societies have to ensure that their most important positions are filled with the most talented people. They therefore need to offer such people high rewards.	Does this really happen? Lots of occupations can be seen to be essential to the smooth running of society but are not highly rewarded, such as nurses. There are also plenty of idiots in high places!
Class societies are meritocracies – high rewards in the form of income and status are guaranteed in order to motivate gifted people to make the necessary sacrifices in terms of education and training. Educational qualifications, and therefore the stratification system, function to allocate all individuals to an occupational role that suits their abilities. People's class position is a fair reflection of their talents.	Some groups may be able to use economic and political power to increase their rewards against the will of the majority. High rewards sometimes go to people who play no functionally important roles but who simply live off the interest generated by their wealth. Do the 3–5 years of training at college and/or university merit a lifetime of enhanced income and status. Isn't higher education a privilege in itself?
Most people agree that stratification is necessary because they accept the meritocratic principles on which society is based.	There is a substantial level of resentment about the unequal distribution of income and wealth as illustrated by the controversy over 'fat-cat' levels of pay. Unequal rewards may be the product of inequalities in power.
Stratification encourages all members of society to work to the best of their ability. For example, those at the top will wish to retain their advantages whilst those placed elsewhere will wish to improve on their position.	The dysfunctions of stratification are neglected by Davis and Moore. For example, poverty is a major problem for people and negatively impacts on mortality, health, education and family life.

Is stratification really good for society?

A similar view to that of Davis and Moore has been proposed by the New Right. Peter Saunders (1996) points out that economic growth has raised the standard of living for all members of society and social inequality is thus a small price to pay for society as a whole becoming more prosperous. The abandonment in the former Soviet Union of socialism for a free market would seem to bear this position out. However, this perspective, like functionalism, downplays the argument that the disparity of rewards may create resentment and dissatisfaction that could lead to deviance and social disorder.

How can it be argued that crime and deviance occur as a result of social inequalities?

Marxism

An entirely critical view of class inequalities was developed by Karl Marx (1818–83).

According to Marx (Marx and Engels, 1970), the driving force of virtually all societies is the conflict between the rich and powerful minority who control the society and the powerless and poor majority who survive only by working for the rich and powerful. These two classes are always in conflict as it is in the interests of the rich to spend as little as possible in paying their workers.

Lying at the heart of this class conflict is the system of producing goods and services – what Marx called the mode of production. This is made up of two things:

- The **means of production**
  These are the resources needed to produce goods such as land, factories, machinery and raw materials.
- The social **relations of production**
  Resources are not enough on their own. You also need people to be organised to make things. The relations of production refers to the way in which roles and responsibilities are allocated among those involved in production.

Marx described modern Western societies as **capitalist societies**. They consist of two main classes.

- The **bourgeoisie** (or capitalist or ruling class) who own the means of production. These people are the large shareholders in businesses. They control decisions about employment, new investment, new products, and so on.
- The **proletariat** or working or subordinate class. They sell their ability to work (or labour power) to the bourgeoisie. Most people make a living by working for a profit-making business. They have no say in business decisions and rely on the success of the company they work for.

The social relations of production between the bourgeoisie and proletariat are unequal, exploitative and create class conflict. Any extra profit generated by the workforce – what Marx called **surplus value** – is taken by the bourgeoisie who have done no work themselves to justify this. In addition, capitalism's relentless pursuit of profit means that wages are kept as low as possible and that workers lose control over their jobs as new technology is introduced, becoming **alienated** in the process.

So, according to Marx, capitalism is a pretty dreadful kind of society. But if this is the case, why do most people happily accept it – even believing it to be superior to other kinds of societies? Marx had an answer for this, too. Workers very rarely see themselves as exploited because they have been 'duped' by **ideological apparatuses** such as education and the media into believing that capitalism is fair and natural. The people are 'suffering' from **false class-consciousness**.

Marx believed that the conflict in the capitalist system would come to a head because the increasing concentration of wealth would cause the gap between rich and poor to grow and grow. Even the most short-sighted members of the proletariat would see that the time for change had come. Eventually the proletariat would unite, overthrow the bourgeoisie, seize the means of production for themselves and establish a fairer, more equal society – known as **communism**. For Marx, revolution was inevitable.

How can Marxism be applied to other topics you have studied during your course?

Evaluation of Marx

Marx's ideas had a huge influence in the twentieth century. Communist revolutions occurred in many countries such as China and Russia and it could be argued that his ideas have had more impact on more people than have the teachings of Jesus Christ and Mohammed put together. However, his ideas have come in for a great deal of criticism, especially since the communist regimes of Eastern Europe crumbled in the 1990s.

● Marx is accused of being an economic **determinist** or **reductionist** in that all his major ideas are based on the economic relationship between the bourgeoisie and proletariat. However, many conflicts such as those around nationalism, ethnicity and gender cannot be explained adequately in economic terms.
● Marx underestimated the importance of the middle classes. He did recognise a third (in his view, relatively minor, class) made up of professional workers, shopkeepers and clerks that he called the **petit-bourgeoisie**. However, being outside the system of production, they were deemed unimportant in the class struggle. In his view, as the two major camps polarised, members of this class would re-align their interests accordingly with either one.
● Marx's predictions that the working class would experience poverty and misery, the middle class would disappear and that communism would replace capitalism have not come true. The living standards of the working class have risen, the middle classes have grown and communism has been rejected in Eastern Europe at least.
● Marxist ideas do not explain the widely differing circumstances of various groups within the proletariat nor those of the growing middle classes.
● Western class-societies may have problems such as poverty and homelessness but they have a good record in terms of democracy and workers' rights. Perhaps the working class are sensibly reconciled to capitalism rather than 'falsely conscious'.

Although he cannot be blamed for his lack of insight, Marx could not have predicted the ideological power of the bourgeoisie in the age of mass communications. Many **neo-Marxist** thinkers have addressed this deficiency. The Frankfurt School of Marxists, for example, writing since the 1930s, have focused on the role of the media in creating a popular culture for the masses that has focused their attention on trivia that does not threaten the bourgeoisie. The latest soap storylines, or the lifestyles of the rich and famous, are given more priority than political and economic life. Rather

than unite as a class, the proletariat has therefore become isolated and competitive with each other in their drive to acquire and hold on to more consumer items than their neighbour.

The mass media is not the only institution that modern-day Marxists believe plays an important ideological role. Which others have been identified and how has their role been explained by Marxists?

Max Weber

Another classical theorist, Max Weber (1864–1920), disagreed with Marx's view on the inevitability of class conflict. Weber also rejected the Marxist emphasis on the economic dimension as the sole determinant of inequality. Weber (1947) saw 'class' (economic relationships) and 'status' (perceived social standing) as two separate but related sources of power that have overlapping effects on people's **life-chances**. He also recognised what he called **party** as a further dimension. By this he meant the political influence an individual might have through membership of pressure groups, trade unions or other organised interest groups. For Weber, then, class is the most important of three interlinking factors.

Weber identified four main social classes.

1. Manual workers (the working class)
2. The petty-bourgeoisie (the self-employed, managers)
3. White-collar workers and technicians (the lower middle-class)
4. Those privileged through property or education.

Weber's ideas have influenced the way in which social class is **operationalised** by sociologists such as Goldthorpe (1980a) and by the government through the recent NS-SEC scale – see Topic 2.

The significance of status as a dimension of inequality

People who occupy high occupational roles generally have high social status but status can also derive from other sources of power such as gender, race and religion. Weber noted that status was also linked to consumption styles (how people spend their money). For example, some people derive status from conspicuous consumption, e.g. being seen to buy expensive designer products. This idea has been taken further by postmodernists who suggest that in the twenty-first century consumption and style rather than social class will inform people's identity.

Evaluation of Weber

Marxists argue that Weber neglected the basic split between capitalists and workers and argue that class and status are strongly linked – after all, the capitalist class has wealth *and* high status and political power. Weber recognises that these overlap but suggests that a person can have wealth but little status – like a lottery winner, perhaps – or, conversely, high status but little wealth – such as a church minister. Weber's analysis helps explain why some groups may share economic circumstances but have more or less status than others, for example, due to gender or ethnic differences that Weber sees as separate and distinct.

Achieved status – degree of social honour and prestige accorded a person or group because of their achievements or other merits.

Alienation – lack of fulfilment from work.

Ascribed status – degree of social honour and prestige accorded a person or group because of their origin or inherited characteristics.

Bourgeoisie – the ruling class in capitalist society.

Capitalist societies – societies based on private ownership of the means of production, such as Britain and the USA.

Caste system – Hindu system of stratification, now officially banned in India.

Closed societies – societies with no social mobility or movement within each strata.

Communism – system based on communal ownership of the means of production.

Determinist or reductionist – the view that phenomena can be explained with reference to one key factor.

Differentiation – social separation.

Dysfunctions – the negative effects of social actions, institutions and structures.

False class-consciousness – where the proletariat see the society in a way that suits the ruling class and pose no threat to them.

Feudal estate system – stratification system of medieval Europe.

Ideological apparatuses – social institutions that benefit the ruling class by spreading the ideas that help maintain the system in their interests, e.g. the mass media, education system.

Life-chances – opportunities for achieving things that provide a high quality of life such as good housing, health and education.

Means of production – the material forces that enable things to be produced, e.g. factories, machinery and land.

Mode of production – economic base of society that constitutes the entire system involved in the production of goods.

Meritocratic – based on equal opportunities.

Neo-Marxists – those who have adapted Marx's views.

Open society – a society with a high degree of social mobility, with status usually based on merit.

Operationalised – defined in such a way that it can be measured.

Party – term used by Weber to describe political influence.

Petit-bourgeoisie – term used by Marx to describe the small middle class sandwiched between the proletariat and bourgeoisie.

Proletariat – the working class in capitalist societies.

Relations of production – the allocation of roles and responsibilities among those involved in production.

Social class – hierarchically arranged groups in modern industrial societies based on similarities in status, wealth, income and occupation.

Social status – degree of social honour and prestige accorded a person or group.

Surplus value – term used by Marx to describe the profit created by the work of the proletariat but taken by capitalists.

CHECK YOUR UNDERSTANDING

1 What is the difference between social differentiation and social stratification?

2 Why did those at the bottom of the caste system accept their lot?

3 What determined one's position in the hierarchy in the Feudal Estate system?

4 Why are most modern societies more open than most traditional societies?

5 Copy the continuum in the figure showing the position of societies between openness and closure.

   a Place the following societies along the line in terms of your perceptions of their relative openness/closure: Britain, the USA, Taliban-led Afghanistan.

   b Consider the extent to which different groups experience social openness and closure. Try to place

the following groups along the continuum. UK black, US black, UK white, US white, UK male, US male, UK female, US female.

6 Why according to Davis and Moore do some people deserve more rewards than others?

7 Why is social stratification said to be good for society?

8 How might it be argued that social stratification is actually bad for society?

9 What according to Marx determines a person's social class?

10 What stands in the way of the creation of a fair society?

11 What according to Weber determines a person's social class?

12 How does the concept of status help explain gender and ethnic differences?

Exploring social stratification

Item A

Riots caused by resentment about the continuing influence of the caste system in India

1 Why might remaining parts of the caste system in India provoke hostility?

Item B

The Berlin Wall – dividing the communist East and capitalist West – is torn down

2 Suggest two reasons why communism was overthrown in eastern Europe.

Item C

3 Discuss the status, class and influence of the different people in the photographs above.

Research ideas

1 Compare what the idea of class meant to a group of old people (over 70) when they were 40 with what it means to a group of 40 year-olds today. Ask them whether consumption patterns within classes were once/are clearly identifiable. Try to find out whether they were/are able to exercise choice over aspects of their lives such as dress, leisure, standard of living and what they could/can buy above basic needs. Does consumption seem to be more important now than class as an influence on identity?

2 Conduct a survey to discover young people's awareness of Marx and Marxism. Have they heard of communism? Do they know what it is? What is their view, if any, of communist societies? Do they believe that Britain has the sort of inequalities between bosses and workers identified by Marx?

WWWebtask

● Go to one or more of the following sites and investigate in depth the writings on class of the classical sociologists.
http://sosig.esrc.bris.ac.uk/Durkheim/Marx
http://eddie.cso.viuc.edu/Durkheim/
http://msomusik.mursuky.edu/~felwel/http/Weber/home.htm
http://www.anu.edu.au/polsci/marx/marx.htm

● Search the worldwide web to find out about the caste system in India. How did it work and how influential is it today?

EXAM PRACTICE

Extract from AQA-style question

Assess the similarities and differences between Marx' and Weber's theory of class. (40 marks)

Extract from OCR-style question

Assess the view that stratification is both inevitable and beneficial to individuals and society. (44 marks)

Getting you thinking

- Are you bourgeois or proletarian?
- Do you consider yourself to be upper, middle or *lower* class?
- Do you consider yourself to be upper, middle or *working* class?
- Are you a manual or non-manual worker?
- What is the occupation of the head of your household?
- What is your household income?
- Does your current occupation correspond with your class of origin/family background?

Royal Opera House

Bingo Hall

When a random group of respondents were asked to identify the criteria they would use to assess a person's class the results were as follows.

	%		%
Neighbourhood	36	How they talk	17
Job	31	What they wear	15
Pay	29	Parental background	13
Educational background	27	Use of leisure time	11
Wealth (assets such as property and material goods)	22	Political party support	11

Adapted from: G. Hadford and M. Skipworth (1994) *Class*, London: Bloomsbury, p.19

1 Look at each of the questions in the questionnaire. What makes each one:

   a difficult to answer?
   b difficult to use as a way of identifying social classes in Britain?

2 Look at the photographs above. What ways of measuring class do they indicate? To what extent do the people in the table opposite agree with the use of these measures?

3 How much agreement is there among the public on measuring class?

4 Which of the criteria suggested in the table opposite would you use to judge a person's social class? Why?

As you have just seen, measuring social class is not an easy exercise. People define social class in different ways and some even deny its existence altogether. The exercise opposite illustrates some of the following problems in attempting to operationalise the idea of social class.

- Positive and negative values are attached to class positions.
- The terminology is confusing.
- Questions about class can be intrusive and personal.
- Class may be an objective state (as Marx suggested) but subjective observations often have more meaning to people.
- Classifying people in terms of class is a snapshot that does not take account of their life history, past or future.
- Some ideas about class are outdated and don't recognise social changes such as changes in the social position of women.

Sociological approaches to the measurement of class

A neo-Marxist model

A number of theoretical approaches have been suggested that attempt to address changes in the class structure since the times of the classical theorists – in particular, the decline in manufacturing jobs and the growth of the service sector. A neo-Marxist model was proposed by E. O. Wright (1978). He argued that there are now a range of **contradictory class locations** in capitalist society which are 'exploiting' along one dimension but which are 'exploited' along another. For Wright, the social order appears to be more of a 'pecking order'.

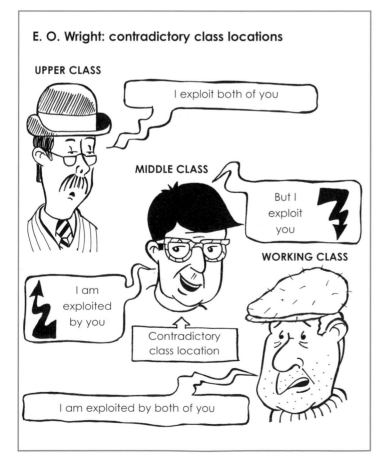

E. O. Wright: contradictory class locations

UPPER CLASS

I exploit both of you

MIDDLE CLASS

But I exploit you

I am exploited by you

Contradictory class location

WORKING CLASS

I am exploited by both of you

A neo-Weberian model

Runciman (1990) proposed a model that introduced the concepts of **marketability** (the perceived value of skills and qualifications) and **control** (management functions). He also recognised the continuing importance of the **ownership of property** (in some ways introducing a Marxist element to his analysis). The seven classes he identified correspond with the commonsense way we generally talk about class in society.

1. *Upper class* – owners, senior managers, those with exceptional marketability (e.g. senior partners in accountancy firms in the City of London).
2. *Upper middle-class* – top professionals and managers.
3. *Middle middle-class* – lower professionals, middle managers, small proprietors (e.g. shopkeepers).
4. *Lower middle-class* – routine white-collar workers.
5. *Skilled working-class* – plumbers, carpenters, electricians, and so on.
6. *Unskilled working-class* – assembly-line workers, shop assistants, cleaners, and so on.
7. *Underclass* – people on benefits and those unable to work.

This hierarchical model, whilst including the upper class and the underclass at each end, does not clearly distinguish within and between its class boundaries. The extent of ownership, control and marketability are also extremely difficult to determine. People may be untruthful about the extent of their wealth or lack of it, may have varying degrees of control at different times and in different places, and marketability is a particularly subjective anyway. It is not at all clear quite how much of each a person needs to have in order to be placed in a particular class group.

The problem with theorising about class is that theories that make sense to sociologists often don't square with ordinary people's experiences of society. Also, many of the theoretical ideas are difficult to **operationalise**. How do you quantify status, marketability or power? How do you define relations of production in practice? How can categories be arrived at that people recognise and agree with? Also, whilst people do recognise what class they personally may belong to, they tend not to adopt a consistent approach when classifying themselves and others.

What other concepts have you studied that are difficult to operationalise?

Why is there a need to measure class?

Various groups such as sociologists, advertisers and government agencies have vested interests in operationalising the concept of social class in a consistent way for a number of reasons.

- For sociologists, class differences in all areas of social life indicate inequalities that need to be addressed.
- Advertisers want to target their knowledge of class and consumption patterns to maximise sales.
- Governments need to address class differences when devising social policy.

Each interest group has tended to operationalise the concept in different ways, each acknowledging both subjective and objective aspects in their analysis. For example, subjectively, class may affect voting behaviour, attitudes and leisure pursuits but objectively it may also affect health, educational achievement and life expectancy.

Whilst criteria such as lifestyle, family background, income and cultural characteristics are common indicators of class, they are all problematic due to the wide range of influential factors associated with each of them. For example, a taxi driver may earn more than a teacher, but the latter may holiday in a cottage in Brittany whilst the former enjoys a golfing holiday (as might a senior executive) on the Costa del Sol.

Although occupation has been adopted as the most significant objective criterion by the government and sociologists, subjective measures based around lifestyle and consumption are still adopted, with differing degrees of seriousness, within advertising and marketing (see figure below).

1980s/1990s Marketing sector acronyms	
BUPPIE	Black Upwardly-mobile/Urban Professional
BOBO	Burnt Out But Opulent (well-off)
DINKY	Double/Dual Income, No Kids (Yet)
FILTH	Failed In London, Try Hong-Kong.
GOLDIE	Golden Oldie, Lives Dangerously
GRUMPY	Grown-up Urban, Mature Professionals
GUPPIE	Green Upwardly-mobile/Urban Professional
JUPPIE	Japanese Upwardly-mobile/Urban Professional
LOMBARD	Lots Of Money But A Right D***head
MIB	Minorities In Business
NIMBY	Not in My Back Yard; (Also: NOTE – Not Over There, Either)
OINK	One Income No Kids
PIPPIE	Person Inheriting Parents' Property
PORW	Post-Retired and Working
PR	Pre-Retired
PUPPIE	Poxy/Poncey Upwardly-mobile Professional
SILKY	Single Income, Loads of Kids
SINBAD	Single Income, No Bird/Boyfriend And/Absolutely Desperate
SITCOM	Single Income, Two Children, Oppressive Mortgage
TOMCAT	Totally Obedient Moron, Cannot Actually Think
WOOPIE	Well-Off Older Person
WE	Women Executives
YUPPIE	Young Urban Professional or Young Upwardly-Mobile Professional

Source: DragonQueen's Humour and Story Site
http://www.Shartwell.freeserve.co.uk

Occupation as an indicator of social class

The single most objectively measurable factor found to correspond best with most criteria associated with class is occupation. It is something that the majority of the population has in common that governs not only their working lives but also a significant range of other aspects of their life such as leisure, housing and education. In addition:

- employment governs a significant proportion of a person's life
- jobs are a good indicator of wealth and income
- different occupations require similar levels of skill or training (i.e. thus creating cultural and intellectual compatibility)
- a person's job is still an important influence on their identity.

How does class influence different aspects of life? Select three examples and explain how they are affected by class.

On the other hand, this still leaves out those who do not work and glosses over the fact that people in similar jobs may have widely varying access to resources, for example, in 2001 a school teacher earned considerably more than a college lecturer. Objective measures using occupation have, however, enabled social class to be measured quantitatively (i.e. statistically). Getting such measures right has proved to be more of a problem and the various occupational scales have all been criticised for failing to present a true picture of the class structure.

Scales of social class

The Registrar General's Scale

This occupational scale was used by the government from 1911 until the 1990s. For its first sixty years, ranking was based upon the alleged **'standing in the community'** of the various occupational groups. For the 1981 census, the criteria altered to **'occupational skill'**.

Criticisms of the Registrar General's Scale

- Assessments of jobs were made by the Registrar General's own staff, hence there was a bias towards middle-class, non-manual occupations, placing them above all manual occupations.
- It failed to recognise those people who do not work – in particular, the unemployed, classifying them according to their last job.
- Feminists have criticised the scale as sexist. The class of everyone in a household was defined by the job of the male head of household. Women were largely ignored, assigning them to the class of their husbands.

Feminists have criticised scales of social class for being 'malestream' – focusing on men and ignoring women. Identify two other cases where sociology has been accused of being 'malestream'.

The Registrar General's scale was the main way in which class was measured in official statistics and much sociological research for most of the twentieth century, being replaced as the official government measure in 1990 by the Standard Occupational Classification.

The Standard Occupational Classification

This scale recognised that class position is determined by qualifications as well as occupational skill. The main criticism of this scale was that it failed to distinguish between the employed and self-employed. This distinction is important as evidence shows that these groups do not share similar experiences. The **black economy** is also much more accessible to the self-employed – for example, they can avoid paying VAT by working at a cheaper rate 'for cash' which is not traceable or by not fully declaring all the work for which they have been paid, thus avoiding income tax. Finally, the scale continued to classify women according to their husband's work.

The Hope-Goldthorpe Scale

Sociologists were often reluctant to use government-inspired scales as they lacked sufficient sociological emphasis. For John Goldthorpe's social mobility studies in the 1970s a more sociologically relevant scale was created that has proved very popular with social researchers. It recognised the growth of middle-class occupations and the self-employed and was based on the Weberian concept of market position (income and economic life-chances such as promotion prospects, sick pay and control of hours worked). It also took account of **work or employment relations** (whether people are employed or self-employed and whether they are able to exercise authority over others). In recognising the growth of the middle classes the scale also acknowledged that both manual and non-manual groups may share similar experiences of work. Hence these groups share the same category where appropriate – in the Intermediate class, in particular. Instead of the basic non-manual/manual divide, Goldthorpe introduces the idea of three main divisions into which the

class groupings may be placed: the **service**, **intermediate** and **working class.**

Despite this scale better reflecting the nature of the British class system, Goldthorpe's analysis of the class structure was still based on the male head of household. Goldthorpe has defended this position by claiming that in most cases the male determines the market situation and lifestyle of a couple.

However, many feminists remain unconvinced by this argument. They argue that scales based on the idea of a male 'head of household':

- overlook the significance of dual-career families where the joint income of both partners can give the family an income and lifestyle of a higher class
- ignore situations where women are in a higher grade occupation than their husbands
- overlook the significance of the increasing number of single working women and single working parents, classifying them by the occupation of their ex-partners or fathers.

A feminist alternative: the Surrey Occupational Class Schema

This scale was developed by Arber, Dale and Gilbert (1986) in an attempt to present a class structure model for sociological research that addresses the criticisms of previous scales (see figue overleaf). Women are classified on the basis of their own occupations whether they are married or not. The gendered nature of work is also taken into account. This is most evident in class 6 that has been divided into 6a (sales and personal services – female dominated) and 6b (skilled manual – overwhelmingly male).

Including women in this way does present some difficulties as women's relationship to employment is generally more varied than men's. More women work part time or occupy short-term occupations, perhaps in a transitory phase between one life stage to another such as being the mother of a small child or children. It is therefore difficult to know

---

The Hope-Goldthorpe Scale

Service class	Intermediate class	Working class
1. *Higher professionals* High grade administrators; Managers of large companies and large proprietors	3. *Routine non-manual* (clerical and sales)	6. *Skilled manual workers*
2. *Lower professionals* Higher grade technicians; supervisors of non-manual workers; administrators; small business managers	4. *Small proprietors and self-employed artisans* (craftspersons)	7. *Semi-skilled and unskilled manual workers*
	5. *Lower grade technicians and supervisors of manual workers*	

Source: J. H. Goldthorpe (1980) *Social Mobility and Class Structure*, Oxford: Clarendon Press
(N.B. The scale was first used in studies conducted in 1972, published in 1980.)

A feminist alternative: the Surrey Occupational Class Schema

1. **Higher professional**
2. **Employers and managers**
3. **Lower professional**
4. **Secretarial and clerical**
5. **Supervisors, self-employed manual**
6a. **Sales and personal services**
6b. **Skilled manual**
7. **Semi-skilled**
8. **Unskilled**

Source: A. Arber, S. Dale and N. Gilbert (1986) 'The Limitations of Existing Social Class Classification of women' in A. Jacoby (ed.) *The Measurement of Social Class*, Guildford: Social Research Association

The National Statistics Socio-Economic Classification (NS-SEC)

Occupational classification	% of working population	Examples
1. Higher managerial and professional	11	Company directors, senior civil servants, doctors, barristers, clergy, architects
2. Lower managerial and professional	23.5	Nurses, journalists, teachers, police officers, musicians
3. Intermediate	14	Secretaries, clerks, computer operators, driving instructors
4. Small employers and self-accountable workers	9.9	Taxi drivers, window cleaners, publicans, decorators
5. Lower supervisory, craft and related	9.8	Train drivers, plumbers, printers, TV engineers
6. Semi-routine	18.6	Traffic wardens, shop assistants, hairdressers, call-centre workers
7. Routine	12.7	Cleaners, couriers, road sweepers, labourers
8. Long-term unemployed or the never-worked		

Source: D. Rose and D. Pevalin (with K. O'Reilly) (2001) *The National Statistics Socio-economic Classification: Genesis and Overview* (provisional title), London: ONS

whether the class assigned provides a meaningful overall description or a very short-term one.

A new scale for the 21st century: the National Statistics Socio-Economic Classification (NS-SEC)

Devised by John Goldthorpe *et al.* (1997), this has fully replaced the Registrar General's scale for official statistics and government research and was used for the 2001 census (see figure opposite).

It is based on:

- **Employment relations** – whether people are employers, self-employed, or employed and whether they exercise authority over others.
- **Market conditions** – salary scales, promotion prospects, sick pay, how much control people have over hours worked, and so on.

Strengths of the NS-SEC

- It no longer divides workers along manual and non-manual lines. Each category contains both manual and non-manual workers.
- Class 8 might be termed the 'underclass'. The Registrar General's scale suffered from the weakness of not having a category that accounted for this group.
- It recognises changes in the occupational structure. In the 2001 review of the classification, for example, teachers were demoted from class 1 because of worsening pay and conditions of service.
- Most important of all, women are now recognised as a distinct group of wage-earners and are no longer categorised according to the occupation of their husbands or fathers.

Potential weaknesses of the NS-SEC

- It is still based primarily on occupation. This may differ from what people understand by the term 'social class' and their subjective interpretation of their own class position.

 What methods could sociologists use to find out someone's objective class position? And their subjective perception of their class?

- There are still significant differences within categories. For example, headteachers are in the same category as classroom teachers.
- Although the underclass are now included, those wealthy enough not to have to work are still unaccounted for.
- Some argue that, being based on employment situation, the scale obscures important differences in status and earning power.

Black economy – illegal ways of increasing income.

Contradictory class locations – concept used by the neo-Marxist E. O. Wright to describe social positions between the traditional Marxist categories (bourgeoisie, petit bourgeoisie and proletariat). Individuals in these locations are both exploited and exploiting.

Employment relations – see 'Work or employment relations' below.

Intermediate class – according to Goldthorpe, a lower grouping of the middle class containing those with the poorer work and market situations than the service class, e.g. clerical workers, small proprietors and lower grade technicians.

Market position or conditions – income and economic life-chances such as promotion prospects, sick pay and control over hours worked and how work is done.

Occupational skill – the level of skill needed to perform a particular job.

Operationalise – see Key Terms in Topic 1.

Service class – according to Goldthorpe, those with the highest work and market situations: the upper middle-class, e.g. large proprietors as well as administrators, managers and professionals who service the economy.

'Standing in the community' – a Weberian idea taken up by the devisers of the Registrar General's scale. It indicates the level of regard in which occupations are held by the general public.

Working class – according to Goldthorpe, manual workers who inevitably suffer from the worst work and market situation.

Work or employment relations – whether people are employed or self-employed and whether they are able to exercise authority over others.

CHECK YOUR UNDERSTANDING

1 How does Wright's schema explain the exploitative nature of modern capitalism more effectively than traditional Marxism?

2 What are the three characteristics that Runciman identifies as the modern determinants of social position? How do they relate to Weber's ideas about class, status and party (see Topic 1)?

3 What is the problem with using theoretical models to define class?

4 What groups need to measure class and why?

5 Pick five of the advertising acronyms from the figure earlier in the Topic. For each, briefly describe what you consider may be their occupation, income and lifestyle. Can you assign them a social class according to the NS-SEC scale?

6 Why is occupation considered to be the most defining characteristic for the measurement of social class?

7 What problems are created by using occupation as the key indicator of social class?

8 What were the strengths and weaknesses of each of the scales used before 2000?

9 How does the NS-SEC scale address the weaknesses of the other scales?

10 How might the NS-SEC scale still be said to be lacking?

Research idea

Undertake a piece of research using a structured interview to measure the class distribution of students on various school or college post-16 courses. Pilot it with a random sample of ten students across the institution. After each interview write down any issues that may affect the validity, representativeness or reliability of the evidence gathered, e.g. did respondents understand the questions, answer truthfully, exaggerate aspects of lifestyle/income? Did they find the questions too intrusive or personal? Were they confused by the terminology you used?

Identify the main problems you encountered in trying to operationalise social class.

What, if any, conclusions can you draw from your findings?

WWWebtask

Use a careers service on the worldwide web such as www.prospects.csu.ac.uk to compare occupations in different social classes. Find out about pay, working conditions and the skills and qualifications needed. Can these explain differences in their position on social-class scales?

Item A

Bob: *Hey folks, I've just been on this great conference about measuring business performance. And do you know what they said? They said that the most important measures aren't to do with how much people spend! They told us that we should be thinking instead about what they are spending their money on, starting with a clear definition of our basic customer segments. Olaf, you're our Planning guru: how could we go about doing that?*

Extract from a series of articles 'Madmen in Authority' written by Robert Bittlestone, in *Accountancy*, the company magazine of Metapraxis Ltd, Business consultants, Hanover House, Coombe Road, Kingston-upon-Thames, Surrey, KT2 7AH, UK. September 1997 Episode 4: Customers Come Last

Olaf: *Well Bob, as you know, in Planning we've been looking at customer segments for some time. We define them as Stinkies, Yuppies, Dinkies, Wrinklies and Wackos. The Stinkies, they're the under-twos, they use our nappy brands and detergents, while the Yuppies, you all know who they are, they buy the cosmetics and the wet-suits. The Dinkies, that's the Dual-Income-No-Kids consumers, they buy detergents and cosmetics, while the Wrinklies, that's the age-disadvantaged group, they seem to go for our pet-food. They just love it; maybe they eat it themselves. Then there's the Wackos, we call them that because we can't categorise them really, they just seem to buy anything or nothing at all, almost at random. Some of our studies put them at 85% of the customer base, but personally I discount that research. Anyway, that's it in a nutshell.*

Item B

A house husband

A dual earning couple

1 In what way is the method of dividing up people into categories in Item A different from the method used by most sociological scales of social class?

2 How do the 'Wackos' highlight a basic problem with measuring the behaviour of 'customer segments' or lifestyle groupings?

3 How might the same problem be said to apply to measuring social class?

4 Look at the photographs (Item B) and read Item C. Why does Giddens (Item C) argue that 'considering the male head of household to be the primary definer of the household experience was indeed flawed for a variety of reasons'?

5 According to Giddens (Item C), what problems arise from assigning class to individuals?

Whilst women now have their own occupational classification and the concept of household has largely been removed from considerations of class, this brings with it other difficulties. The material, cultural and social aspects of the household actually are important considerations in terms of the experiences and life-chances of its interdependent members. Whilst considering the male head of household to be the primary definer of the household experience was indeed flawed for a variety of reasons, what household members bring to the shared experience is still important. The entry of women into paid employment has had a significant impact on household incomes but this has been experienced unevenly and may be leading to an accentuation of class divisions between households. A growing number of women are moving into highly paid professional and managerial positions. As research shows that marriage tends to produce partnerships where both individuals are relatively privileged or disadvantaged, such women tend to have high earning partners. This is creating a gulf between high earner, dual income households on the one hand and single earner or no earner households on the other.

Such a perspective also leaves out the impact of dependents upon earners *within* a household such as full time housewives, the retired, or unemployed. Their individual classification denies the existence of the interplay between the working and non-working in the household and the impact each has on the others' life-chances.

Adapted from: A. Giddens, *Sociology*, (4th edition), Cambridge: Polity Press

EXAM PRACTICE

Extract from AQA-style question

Describe some of the problems involved in measuring social class. (12 marks)

Extract from OCR-style question

Item A

The new NS-SEC classification system reflects changes in society, changes in the structure of occupations, and the fragmentary class structure of late modern society.

It is not intended to depict 'hierarchy' nor is it based on differences in earning power or social status. It is seen as a matter of *social difference* not *social hierarchy*.

Adapted from M. Denscombe (1999) *Sociology Update* Leicester: Olympus books

Using only the information in **Item A**, identify two differences between social difference and social hierarchy. (6 marks)

A 1950s kitchen

A modern kitchen

A miner

A modern call centre

Some argue that de-humanising, exploitative, monotonous jobs have disappeared and working life improved significantly for most of the working class.

A north–south divide?

National statistics showing overall improvement may actually mask regional inequalities. The average household in Britain spent £359 per week in 1999–2000. However, a London household spent about £400 whereas in the North East it was £290.

Adapted from: M. Denscombe (2001) *Sociology Update,* Leicester: Olympus Books

1 Look at the two photographs on the left. What do they suggest has happened to opportunities for moving up the social scale over the past 50 years?

2 Look at the two photographs on the right. Do you think they constitute evidence for or against the view expressed in the caption? Explain your answer.

3 What does the extract tell us about increasing opportunities in Britain?

The movement of individuals up or down the social scale is referred to as **social mobility**. We only need to look around us or to interview older people to see that the population nowadays is generally more affluent and enjoys better working conditions – in other words there appears to have been considerable upward social mobility. However, as the exercise above may have shown, the picture is far less simple once we start taking into account variations caused by factors such as region, ethnicity or gender. These difficulties have not prevented sociologists from attempting to measure social mobility and using their results to comment on the extent to which society is becoming more open or closed.

Types of social mobility

There are two main ways of looking at social mobility.
- **Intergenerational** mobility refers to movement between generations; a son moving further up the social scale than his father, for example.
- **Intragenerational** mobility refers to the movement of an individual within their working life. An individual may start off as an office junior and work their way up to office manager, win the lottery or marry someone wealthy.

A functionalist view

Functionalists, along with many of today's politicians, believe that upward mobility within society provides evidence of greater openness and increased opportunity. They argue that it shows, for example, that the education system is more meritocratic and egalitarian and that the economy is making progress and providing economic prosperity. New Right politicians in the past such as Margaret Thatcher and John Major frequently proclaimed that class no longer mattered and New Labour's claims that we are all middle class now follow similar lines. Such views encourage us to believe the notion that capitalism is a system that is good for all those individuals willing to put the effort in to grasping what's on offer.

Weberians believe that social mobility has implications for class formation and for the boundaries between classes. They highlight how class identity may be changing within particular groups and how class consciousness and solidarity could be affected. For example, a rapid increase in a particular grouping may affect the status of the group as a whole or their sense of cohesion. Large-scale movement down the social scale could create more class solidarity and conflict, for example.

Marxists argue that the minority of the working class who achieve upward mobility help create the myth that capitalist societies are truly open and meritocratic. They are also interested in the downward intragenerational mobility of the lower middle classes who have lost status, career prospects and relative income (see the call-centre workers illustrated in the photo at the beginning of the topic above). Marxists hope that these changes may help this group acquire class-consciousness and revolutionary potential.

What do Marxists believe will eventually happen in capitalist society?

Problems of measuring social mobility

The use of occupation as an indicator of social class creates many problems (as discussed in Topic 2). The earliest studies of social mobility used the Registrar General's scale which, as we have seen, considered an individual's social class solely in terms of the class of the male head of household. In fact, this indicator of class persisted well beyond the period for which it had any relevance at all, mainly because of the comparative nature of social mobility studies. How, after all, can you draw any conclusions about the nature of social movement if it is not possible to compare like with like?

What is meant by operationalising a concept? What other concepts present problems of operationalisation? Give two examples from your studies.

Another key problem is that mobility studies focus on the working population and say nothing about the very rich and the very poor – important groups in society, particularly as the gap between them appears to be increasing.

Social mobility studies

The Oxford (Nuffield) Mobility Study (OMS) 1972

This large-scale study in 1972 led by John Goldthorpe (1980a) found high rates of what is known as absolute mobility. Comparing sons with fathers in their sample, the OMS discovered much greater opportunities for being upwardly mobile into the service class (see Topic 2 for an explanation of the scale of social class they used) than in the 1950s and 1960s.

More recent data from the longitudinal National Child Development Study (Centre for Longitudinal Studies, 1991) gives data about a generation on from Goldthorpe's study.

What are the advantages and disadvantages of longitudinal studies?

When the data is put together we can see how the class structure has been changing. The proportion of the working population in the service class (middle-class jobs with good pay and prospects) is increasing while the intermediate class (lower white-collar jobs) and working class (manual work) are decreasing in size. This means that the sons of those working in 1960 have significantly more chance of getting into the service class than their fathers.

Absolute Mobility 1960–1991			
	Goldthorpe		**NCDS**
	1960	**1972**	**1991**
	%	%	%
Service	14	26	36
Intermediate	31	30	21
Working	55	44	43
	100	100	100

Adapted from: K. Roberts (2001) *Class in Modern Britain*, Basingstoke: Palgrave

Why has absolute mobility increased?

As Goldthorpe pointed out, an increase in absolute mobility is not necessarily the product of meritocracy or evidence of increased openness. He suggests three reasons for this.

- *Changes in the occupational structure*
  The service class had more than doubled in numbers because of changes in the job market created by post-war economic expansion in areas such as the welfare state which led to a greater demand for professionals and administrators in the fields of education, welfare and health. Furthermore, the nature of the economy changed and the financial sector in particular has expanded at the expense of heavy industry.

  What other social changes have occurred as a result of the decrease in traditional heavy industry and an increase in the service sector?

- *Differential fertility*
  The fertility rates of the service class was too low to cope with the growth of service-sector jobs. This sector therefore had no choice but to recruit from other social classes.
- *Educational expansion*
  The introduction of free secondary education in 1944 made this recruitment easier because for the first time people from other social classes, especially the working class, had access to educational qualifications.

The significance of relative mobility

On the face of it, it would appear that there has been a significant amount of social mobility across the generations. However, what such data masks is the *relative chance* that a person from a particular class of origin has of moving upwards or downwards. This is known as **relative mobility**. By comparing the relative mobility chances of different generations, it is possible to determine whether the class structure has become more open. Studies have shown that the percentages of working- and intermediate-class boys reaching the service class have gone up but this is due mostly to changes in the occupational structure. The relative proportions reaching the service class has remained fairly

The significance of relative mobility

Yes, but I've got even more chance of staying here

GOOD JOB WITH PROSPECTS

Great! I've got more chance of getting in there than my dad

constant. In other words, there has been no significant increase in the openness of the British stratification system.

Goldthorpe concludes that the expansion in the education system after 1944 has contributed to increased levels of upward mobility but that influence has been disproportionately in favour of the children of the service class. For example, despite free secondary education and comprehensive schools, three times as many children of the service class go on to higher education compared with the working class.

The Scottish Mobility Study (SMS)

Payne (1987) noted that the potential for social mobility was dependent upon age and region.

The Scottish Mobility Study's Findings

	Age	Location	Region
Associated with high mobility	Young	Urban	South of England
Associated with low mobility	Older	Rural	North and Scotland

Such mobility patterns may lead to a growing **heterogeneous** (mixed) middle class which is underpinned by an increasingly **homogeneous** (similar) working class and underclass, (mainly located in the north of England and Scotland), which experiences few chances of escape from its position. Members of the latter group, particularly young ones, may grow resentful and consequently undermine the 'safety-valve' function of social mobility by, for example, engaging in disruptive behaviour such as inner-city rioting.

More optimistically, Payne stresses that sociologists should be looking at mobility between jobs rather than between social classes. The emphasis on chances of movement between broad class groupings detracts from the fact that there are still generally high rates of upward mobility. In this sense, Payne argues that relative rates of mobility are less important than absolute rates.

The Essex University Mobility Study (EUMS)

This study by Marshall *et al.* (1988) is even more pessimistic than the SMS. The EUMS found that someone starting in the service class rather than the working class had a seven times greater chance of ending up in the service class. One explanation for these continuing disparities is that the expansion of service-class jobs has slowed down and even ended, blocking opportunities for those outside the service class to enter.

Unequal but fair?

The New Right sociologist Peter Saunders is very critical of the findings of most social-mobility studies. Saunders (1995) argues that relative mobility levels are less important than absolute mobility levels and that all mobility studies acknowledge improvements in the latter. This is convincing evidence that capitalism has opened up new opportunities for advancement and brought benefits to the working class.

Saunders claims the stress on relative mobility by Goldthorpe and Marshall indicates a desire by left-wing sociologists to obscure deliberately the fact that capitalism works reasonably well as a meritocratic system. Saunders acknowledges that some elite positions are still quite closed but argues that the rest of society, especially professional and managerial positions, is achievement-orientated. What is more, sociologists like Marshall ignore the possibility that differences in relative mobility between social classes may the result of **natural inequalities**, i.e. genetic or hereditary factors. It may not be the case that talents and abilities are randomly distributed across all social classes as the Oxford and Essex studies assume. Saunders claims that the results of IQ tests indicate that there are genetic differences in ability between social classes and that it is not surprising that middle-class parents pass on genetic advantages to their offspring. Middle-class parenting skills may also be better than those in other social groups.

Where else have you come across biological and genetic explanations during your course? How do sociologists typically criticise these kinds of explanations?

In order to test his claims, Saunders used evidence from the National Child Development Study (see above). Over half of the sample had experienced intergenerational mobility and it appeared that social and economic deprivation had little effect on a child's destination. Ability and motivation levels were much more important than class background in accounting for upward mobility.

Criticisms of Saunders

Saunders has been criticised for excluding the unemployed and part-time workers from his analysis and for his claims regarding the importance of ability and motivation. Educational research has shown there to be a class bias in intelligence tests and that teachers often label working-class pupils negatively, thereby affecting their motivation and leading ultimately to a self-fulfilling prophecy of low achievement. Apparent low ability and motivation may therefore be the product of class.

What perspective is associated with the idea of the 'self-fulfilling prophecy'?

Savage and Egerton (1997) used the same data as Saunders but reached entirely different conclusions. They looked at the destinations of children within each ability group and found that low-ability children with service-class fathers had much more chance of staying in the service class than ending up in other classes. High-ability sons of service-class fathers were much more likely to end up in the service class (75%) than high-ability sons of the working class (45%). This disparity was even greater for working-class, high-ability girls who, it seems, had less than half the chance of their service class counterparts of ending up in that class. Working-class girls need to have higher levels of ability than working-class males if they are to progress into the service class.

Women and social mobility studies

Feminist sociologists have long complained that women have been neglected in social-mobility studies. The major mobility studies have compared sons' with fathers' occupations. There seem to be three reasons for this.

- Surveys that included women would involve larger samples and consequently be more expensive and time-consuming.
- The focus on men in previous studies means it is easier to compare all male samples.
- The nature of men's and women's work is different. For example, women are more likely to be employed part-time and many women are full-time housewives.

Goldthorpe (1980b) claimed that there was no need for any independent study of female mobility since most women take their class from their husband/father. However Abbott (1990) disagrees with this view. She argues that there *is* a need to study female mobility because women's experience of work is different to that of men. Consequently, men and women experience different absolute-mobility rates. Abbott argues that the limited mobility prospects of women actually enhance men's opportunities. For example, if women find it difficult to enter the service class, men's chances of filling these jobs obviously improves.

Women's social mobility patterns

Studies of female mobility have come to several conclusions.

- Women experience less upward mobility than men. The EUMS (which attempted to overcome sexism by using the term 'chief childhood supporter') found that even when their male and female samples had the same qualifications, the destinations of women were less advantageous compared with men.
- Kay (1996) concluded that women were more likely to be downwardly mobile than men because of career interruptions such as pregnancy and childcare. Divorce and the likelihood of being head of a single parent family also impede upward mobility.

A recent study by the Economic and Social Research Council *Twenty-something in the 90s* (1997) looked at a group of 26-year-olds who were born in 1970. It confirmed that class of origin was still a major factor affecting mobility for both men and women. The study noted however, that middle-class women were just as likely as middle-class men to go to university and from there into well-paid jobs. In spite of this, the study found that career development opportunities are still influenced by discrimination from male employers, and primary responsibility for domestic work and childcare forcing women to downplay their careers (see Topic 8).

So, in conclusion:

- Rates of absolute mobility improved considerably in the period 1950–1980. According to Saunders and other functionalist/New Right thinkers, this supports the notion that Britain is moving towards a meritocracy. However, since 1980, there is emerging evidence that rates of absolute mobility have slowed down as the expansion of service-class jobs may have ended.

- Rates of relative mobility between male social groups still continue to demonstrate major social-class differences. The evidence indicates that being born into the service class confers distinct social advantages. Weberians and Marxists would argue that this is evidence that Britain is still characterised by class inequality.

- There are significant differences in the absolute and relative levels of mobility of men and women. In other words, gender may be an important influence on social mobility.
- Studies of social mobility tell us little about the very rich and the very poor – groups without conventional employment.

Exploring social mobility

Item A

Flexible employment

There are an ever-increasing number of flexible working contracts and forms of flexible employment: part-time work, temporary work, fixed-term contract work, seasonal work, shift work, flexi-time, overtime, term time only working (e.g. supply teaching), Sunday working, casual no-contract employment, etc. These are all ways of ensuring that employers can remain competitive in a rapidly changing marketplace and adjust their workforce without having to maintain pay costs for longer than necessary, should a downturn occur. They also in many cases, pass on to the employee other costs such as pensions, sick pay, car allowances and staff training. However, the experience of flexi-workers in terms of their status and job security varies considerably across sectors when compared with permanent workers. Yet mobility studies do not recognise the sometimes precarious nature of these new middle-class occupations. In many ways, it could be said, they really reflect downward mobility as far as security and job satisfaction are concerned. The unskilled worker is the worst affected by flexibility. New technology, in particular, has displaced unskilled workers into apparently higher level occupations – for example, from a factory worker to a call-centre worker. But, new technology also creates new jobs for the skilled workers who can operate it – and such workers are often on flexible contracts, and are able to command high rates of pay and good job security as they are in such demand. Men and women are clearly differentially located within this flexible labour market.

Item B

Changes in male employment 1975–1994

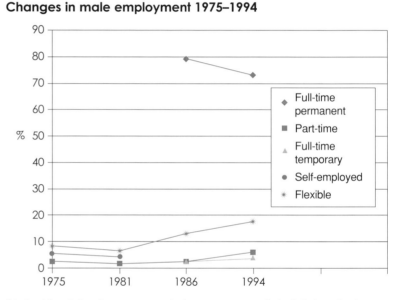

(*Note*: No distinction was made by government statisticians between full-time, permanent and temporary employment until 1986.)

Changes in female employment 1975–1994

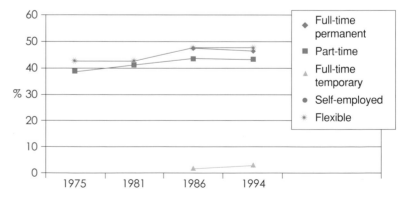

Source: Adapted from *Labour Force Survey* 1975–1994, ONS, London: HMSO

As the tables show, women have always worked more flexibly than men although this has remained fairly constant. Men, however, have tripled the extent to which they work flexibly over the period.

Absolute mobility – the total amount of movement between social classes.

Heterogeneous – diverse.

Homogeneous – the same all the way through (like homogenised milk where the cream is fully mixed with the milk).

Intergenerational – between generations (fathers and sons, for example).

Intragenerational – within a generation (your progress within a career, for example).

Natural inequalities – genetic or hereditary factors.

Relative mobility – the chance one class has of moving up or down relative to another.

Social mobility – the movement of individuals up or down the social scale.

Item C

Too busy earning a living to live

Flexible work means more work and its wrecking our days of rest. For growing numbers of us the phrase 'TFI Friday' no longer signals the end of the working week. Saturday and Sunday working is on the increase and, for some, the seven day week is the norm.

As the demand for 24 hour services increases, the distinction between work and rest is crumbling. The British weekend is under attack from many quarters. White collar workers putting in extra hours to try to get ahead of the pack, lower paid employees who must do overtime to make ends meet and an increasing number of people who do one job in the week and another at the weekend. There are 1.2 million people in the UK with a second job. Double the figure for 1984. Two thirds of them are women.

Adapted from: The *Observer*, October 11, 1998

Item D

Telework – the production line of the 21st century?

Information and communication technologies have developed rapidly since the 1980s and have had a dramatic effect on the nature of work in the finance and service sectors of the economy. Huge databases of information can be accessed electronically at a stroke and people can pay for services using credit and debit cards over their own telephones. Call centres provide customer services and sales more economically than face-to-face facilities which require more staff, and premises with the attendant costs. Call centre staff are also usually casual workers and can be paid very low wages. In 1999 there were between 300,000 and 400,000 people employed in call centres in Britain. Although officially middle class, call-centre workers generally receive low pay, and there is little opportunity for contact with other workers as they are on a call most of the time or at a VDU, often in a personal booth. There is little or no opportunity for creativity in their work, sticking as they do to a prepared script and having their calls monitored. Such working conditions are not unlike those on production lines where, similarly, there is a high turnover of staff – usually women.

Source: Adapted from M. Denscombe, (1999) *Sociology Update*, Leicester: Olympus Books

1 Briefly summarise the trends in male employment between 1975 and 1994 (Item B).

2 How do female employment trends differ? Suggest one reason why this may be so.

3 What problems does Item C raise for measuring:

   a a person's social class?

   b the extent of inter-generational mobility?

   c the extent of intra-generational mobility?

4 Study Item D. Give three reasons why call centres have emerged in recent years.

5 In what ways may call centres be considered to be like 'production lines of the 21st century?'

6 Considering all of the sources (including those in the 'Getting you thinking' exercise at the beginning of this Topic), identify three reasons why it is difficult to measure the real extent of social mobility.

1 Why do sociologists study social mobility?

2 According to Weberians, what is the relationship between social mobility and class identity and status?

3 How might ideas about social mobility make the capitalist system appear fair?

4 Distinguish between absolute and relative mobility.

5 Why has absolute social mobility increased?

6 According to the Scottish Mobility Study, how may the 'safety valve' function of social mobility be being undermined?

7 How does Saunders explain differences in relative mobility?

8 How does Savage and Egerton's work challenge Saunders' claims?

9 Why have women been excluded from mobility studies for so long?

10 What are the main reasons for the patterns in women's mobility?

WWW Webtask

Go to the Government statistical service website: www.statistics.gov.uk. Find out about low pay, the distribution of employment, regional variations in income and expenditure and gender differences in employment. What do they tell us about social mobility?

Research ideas

1 Along with other members of your class, ask your parents what their parents did at the height of their working lives. Note down answers, keeping each gender separate. Consider what you realistically expect you will be doing by the time you are 30. Collate the results for the class as a whole. Quantify the extent of mobility for males and for females. Compare your results with some of the studies discussed in this Topic.

2 Interview a small number of workers (both male and female) in some of the newer jobs in the service sector of the economy: office work, call-centre work, and so on. Ask them about job satisfaction, pay and conditions of work. To what extent are these jobs preferable to manual work?

EXAM PRACTICE

AQA-style question

The growth of low-paid jobs

It is clear that the information age will not eradicate poverty. All predictions of the future suggest that there will be a continuing growth in the number of low-paid jobs. Some of this will be fuelled by demographic trends, primarily the increasing proportion of the elderly in society. Elderly couples do not usually die at the same time. There is thus the likelihood that an elderly single person living alone will need some care either through ill health or infirmity. As families are no longer able to look after elderly relatives as they were in the past, this means that there will be a continuing growth in low-paid care-assistants jobs.

At the same time the growth of the service economy will lead to greater demand for shop assistants, checkout staff, cleaners and a host of other occupations associated with the hotel, recreation, catering, leisure and tourism industries. Because a service economy is labour intensive i.e. has a high turnover and need of staff, wages are low and contracts are often short term. This is why there is a growing demand for women workers, easily exploited in this way as such work is flexible and fits in with child rearing.

Other occupations are emerging in the information age which are as arduous as any to be found in traditional manufacturing. The most obvious of these are the jobs provided by fast food outlets. In these, work tasks are as mechanised, routine and subject to strict supervisory control as in any factory. There is no opportunity to exercise personal discretion, judgement or control.

Adapted from R. Scase (1988) 'The Future of Work – The Coming of the Information Economy', *Sociology Review*, Nov, Oxford: Phillip Allan Updates

Part One

a Identify and briefly discuss why there will be an increase in the number of low paid employees in the future. (8 marks)

b Examine the extent to which it may appear that upward social mobility has occurred against a deterioration in overall standards of living. (12 marks)

Part Two

c Assess the view that Britain is becoming a more meritocratic society. (40 marks)

(Topic not in OCR specification)

Getting you thinking

As well as going to school and university together, young members of the upper classes get plenty of opportunity to meet each other and form relationships.

As well as going to school together, the lower classes have plenty of opportunity to meet each other and form relationships

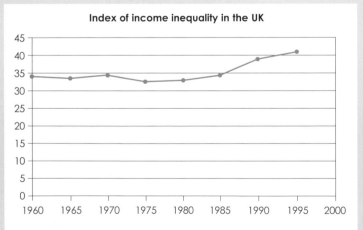

Index of income inequality in the UK

(*Technical note*: If everybody had equal income the value would be 0. If one person owned everything then the value would be 100. The higher the value therefore the more unequal things are.)

Adapted from: J. Hills, (1996) *New Inequalities: The Changing Distribution of Income and Wealth in the UK*, Cambridge: Cambridge University Press

1 How do the pictures above demonstrate that both the upper class and the poor are self-recruiting?

2 Describe the trends described in the graph.

3 What do you think may be the reasons for the trends you have described?

4 The figures in the graph are based on the New Earnings Survey (2000). This includes people in work who have their tax deducted directly from their pay. What people will not be included in these figures? What would be the effect on the index opposite of including them in the figures?

From the exercises above you may have concluded that, because of their common family, educational and social experiences, both the upper and the lower class tend to end up in the same class as their parents because there is little likelihood of them forming relationships with people outside their class. Furthermore, the gap between the rich and poor appears to be widening as the increasing opportunities for those at the top outweigh the decreasing opportunities of those at the bottom. On the face of it, British society seems to be becoming less meritocratic and more closed.

As we saw from some of the sources quoted in the previous topics, there is a common view that class is no longer relevant anyway. Postmodernists have suggested that it is a redundant category in terms of social identity and lifestyle. New Right politicians have also often declared it to be no longer relevant, suggesting that we are all middle class now, sharing similar standards of living and way of life. What both approaches overlook, however, is the fact that lifestyles are significantly influenced by material factors – never more so than at each end of the social spectrum.

Trends in income, wealth and poverty

Whilst there are considerable problems of measurement with regard to all three of the above, a number of observations can be made with regard to the distribution of income, wealth and poverty between 1945–1997.

Income

- Between 1979–1997 income inequality between the rich and poor in Britain widened until it was at its most unequal since records began at the end of the nineteenth century (Marx's time!), and more than in any other western industrialised country.
- Though average income rose by 36% over the period, the top 10% of earners had a 62% rise whilst it fell by 17% for the poorest 10% of earners. In 1997 over a quarter of those working in the UK earned less than £4 an hour.

Wealth

- The twentieth century has seen a gradual redistribution of wealth in the UK. However, redistribution has been very narrow – merely from the very wealthy top 1% to the wealthy top 10% who currently own about half of all marketable wealth – i.e. the redistribution has been to family members in order to avoid paying death duties.
- By 1988, 21% of people owned shares because of the **privatisation** of public utilities (e.g. British Telecom, British Steel). But, the richest 1% of the population still own 75% of all privately owned shares.
- Increased home ownership has, to some extent, redistributed wealth. However, this is wealth that can never be realised as, in order to turn it into money, one has to make oneself homeless.

What problems are there in obtaining accurate figures on the distribution of wealth and income?

Poverty

- The Low Pay Unit (2000) estimated that 45% of British workers were earning less than two-thirds of the average wage. Low-paid workers are often caught in a poverty trap. This means they earn above the minimum level required to claim benefits but the deduction of tax, etc. takes them below it. Similarly, many on benefits could end up even worse off in low-paid work as they would then be no longer eligible for state support.
- New Labour introduced a minimum wage policy in 1999 but it is yet to have a significant impact.
- Treasury figures in March 1999 estimated that up to 25% of children never escape from poverty and that deprivation is being passed down the generations by unemployment and under-achievement in schools. Forty per cent of children are born into families in the bottom 30% of income distribution.

What problems exist in attempting to measure the extent of poverty?

The upper class

It has been argued that the upper class (the extremely wealthy, property owning elite who need not work in order to maintain their lifestyle), especially the aristocratic and traditional rich, have declined in wealth, power and influence over the course of this century. In particular, it has been argued (Roberts, 2001) that high **death duties** (now called **Inheritance Tax**) have resulted in a substantial number of upper-class families losing their **family seats** and experiencing downward social mobility. Some have even been forced to take up salaried employment in the service sector. In other words, it is argued that the upper class is in danger of being assimilated into the upper middle-class. So, how true are these assertions? A number of observations can be made on the basis of the evidence available.

- The upper class is still very wealthy. We saw earlier how the top 1% have got 'poorer', but only because they have made real efforts to avoid Inheritance Tax by transferring their wealth via trust funds to the top 5%. Moreover, the top 1% still own about one-third of the country's wealth.
- The evidence suggests that we should talk about wealthy *families* rather than individuals. In this context, inheritance is very important. In general, individuals or families are wealthy because their fathers were also rich. Inheritance is responsible for most of the inequality in the distribution of wealth.
- Scott (1982) argues that there now exists a unified propertied class which has actively used its wealth to maintain its privileged position at the top of the socio-economic structure. He argues that the core of the upper class – the richest 0.1%, (between 25,000 and 50,000 people) – occupy positions of leadership in manufacturing, banking and finance. He suggests that this core is made up of three groups:
  - *Entrepreneurial capitalists* – this group own (or mainly own) businesses founded by their family.

- *Internal capitalists* – made up of the senior executives who head the bureaucracies that run the big companies.
- *Finance capitalists* – usually own or run financial institutions such as merchant banks and firms of stockbrokers.

- It can be argued that the traditional landed gentry, mainly aristocratic in character, has managed since the turn of this century through investment and marriage to the '**nouveau riche**' to become an integral part of the three groups that make up the core of the modern upper class.

- The upper class is also supported by networks that permeate throughout that class. These may be based on marriage or kinship. For example, there is a tendency for members of the upper class to marry other upper-class individuals. This obviously gives the class a unity based on marriage and kinship, and is instrumental in strengthening business and financial ties between families.

- Membership of the upper class is strengthened by **social closure** – the ability to control mobility into upper-class circles. This is partly achieved by networking and being part of an 'in crowd'. Another major means of ensuring social closure is the emphasis on public school education in generation after generation, especially at those schools seen as the 'great and good', e.g. Eton, Harrow, Winchester, Westminster, Charterhouse, Rugby. The large movement of such pupils into the elite universities of Oxford and Cambridge reinforces such students' belief in their 'difference' from the rest of society. The 'old boy network', based very much on common schooling, results in self-recruitment to the upper class. This means that current members of the upper class are likely to be the offspring of wealthy individuals who attended the same schools and universities, as will their sons and daughters.

- Scott notes evidence relating to **interlocking directorships**. He found that in 1976 eleven people had a total of 57 directorships in the top 250 companies and had many others in smaller companies. Such interlocking directorships provide a powerful network which cement connections between members of the upper class.

- Scott argues that the upper class's influence is not confined to business. There is overwhelming evidence that those in top positions in politics, the civil service, the church, the armed services and the professions come disproportionately from upper-class families. Scott refers to this group as the 'establishment' – a coherent and self-recruiting body of men with a similarity of outlook who are able to wield immense power. However, exactly how this group interacts and whether they do so for their own benefit is extremely difficult to prove.

Which perspective would argue that this group do use power for their own benefit? Explain your answer.

Although the basis of the wealth of the upper class is no longer primarily land, this class still retains many of the characteristics it possessed fifty years ago, especially those such as an emphasis on public school education, thus helping to ensure that social closure continues unchallenged.

The Sunday Times 'Rich list' 2001 is made up of 1012 men and 69 women.

- 759 of the richest 1,000 are self-made millionaires
- 241 inherited their wealth
- 132 are aristocrats.

Source: *Sunday Times* April 2001

What does the 'Rich List' tell us about gender and wealth and the proportion of the very rich who are 'nouveau riche'?

Just how significant are the poor?

Poverty in Britain increased substantially throughout the 1980s (ironically during a period of economic growth) with over 14 million people on incomes below 50% of the national average.

The dramatic increase in single parents has also affected the proportion of children in poverty. Between 1979 and 1997 the numbers of children living in poverty in the UK increased by 40%. A report by the Labour think tank the Institute for Public Policy Studies (Robinson, 2001) suggested that the UK is the worst place in Europe to grow up. The report showed that over a third of children live in poverty in the UK, significantly more than in any other EU country. This prompted the Labour government to prioritise the eradication of child poverty on their public spending agenda in 1999. Although expenditure of several millions is committed to this aim, outside estimates put the real cost of achieving it at £10 billion.

Whilst the increases in unemployed, single parents and children represent the main groups affecting the changing composition of the poor, we have also seen a feminisation of poverty and increasing numbers of ethnic minorities among the poor.

Increases in poverty are evidence of increased closure in society. This may be due to structural problems that affect the extent to which people can participate fully in society or cultural reasons that cause the poor to be deficient in dealing with their situation and thus dependent on others.

How are other areas of social life which you have studied said to be affected by either material or cultural factors?

The question of the underclass

The concept of the **underclass** has entered everyday speech to describe those living at the margins of society, largely reliant on state benefits to make ends meet. However, the concept is rejected by many sociologists due to its negative and sometimes politically charged connotations. Members of the political right such as Charles Murray (1994) in the US have focused on the cultural 'deficiencies' of the so-called underclass, blaming them for their situation, and accusing them of relying on benefits and even manipulating their own circumstances to increase the amount that they can claim from the state. Sometimes, it is also argued, they supplement their income through petty crime, or compensate for deprivation through excessive drug and alcohol abuse. Murray has focused on a black underclass which, he alleges, is to be found in most American cities. Similar points have been made about members of non-working groups in deprived areas of Britain (Dennis and Erdos, 1993).

A matter of choice?

Many New Right commentators (e.g. Saunders, 1995) suggest that a large number of the poor see 'poverty' as a choice, a way of life preferable to work. Young mothers are often cited as examples of this – for example, by having a second child in order to secure a flat that will be paid for by the state. Various studies such as those by Morris (1993) and Gallie (1994) have examined the extent to which the poor possess cultural differences that may account for their situation. They find that there is little evidence of an underclass culture and, if anything, find the most disadvantaged groups have greater commitment to the concept of work than many other groups.

Rather than blaming the cultural deficiencies of the poor, critics of the underclass thesis prefer to use the concept of **social exclusion** to explain poverty. Social exclusion can take many forms, the accumulated effects of which can lead to extreme poverty. Consider the current refugee 'crisis' concerning Eastern European immigrants to Britain. These people are excluded from gaining anything but casual low-paid work, they may be ineligible for state benefits, they have language barriers to contend with and may also be socially excluded due to **xenophobic** attitudes and racism.

What groups in society may experience social exclusion. What areas of social life might they feel excluded from?

It is perhaps understandable that social exclusion may build resentment which can lead to other social ills such as crime or increased suicide rates. Young (1999) suggests that crime rates may be reflecting the fact that a growing number of people do not feel valued or feel that they have an investment in the societies in which they live.

Marx revisited

In one sense Marx was right in predicting that the gap between the top and bottom of the class structure would widen. In many ways the nature of the classes at each end of the continuum resemble the bourgeoisie and proletariat of his time. There can be no doubt that each faction continues to see class as an important influence on their lives.

But what about the rest of us? What Marx did not foresee is the extent to which the remaining majority would become much more heterogeneous, fragmented and difficult to locate in a class structure. But this is not to say that class issues are now viewed as unimportant. Marshall *et al.* (1988) in their survey revealed a continuing and widespread sense of injustice felt by all social classes about the present unequal distribution of income and wealth and the extent of poverty in society.

KEY TERMS

Death duties – see Inheritance Tax.

Family seat – a (usually stately) home which has been in the upper class family since feudal times.

Income – money earned from a job, interest on savings or investments.

Inheritance tax /Death duties – tax payable by the estate of the deceased, paid as a proportion of their total assets.

Interlocking directorships – where a top executive sits on the board of a number of companies who, in turn, are involved at that level in his.

Nouveau riche – new rich, those who have achieved a position of wealth through their own efforts rather than through inheritance.

Poverty trap – earning so little that you are eligible for benefits but unable to escape poverty because receiving more income would reduce eligibility for benefits.

Privatisation – the process whereby previously government-run, publicly owned enterprises were sold to private companies for them to run at a profit to shareholders.

Social closure – exclusive access to those from the right family, school or university background to the exclusion of all others.

Social exclusion – being prevented from full involvement in society because of negatively perceived characteristics or material circumstances.

Underclass – a derogatory term applied to the very poor who are seen to be to blame for their own circumstances and many social ills, e.g. crime.

Wealth – the value of a person's assets.

Xenophobia – dislike/irrational fear of foreigners.

CHECK YOUR UNDERSTANDING

1 How has wealth been redistributed among the wealthy?

2 Give examples of the factions of the upper class described by Scott.

3 How does the upper class maintain its dominance?

4 What is meant by the phrase 'poverty trap'?

5 What is meant by the term 'underclass'? Why is it a controversial concept?

6 What is meant by the concept social exclusion? How does this concept provide a more sociological explanation of poverty?

7 For each of the following groups, list the aspects of social exclusion that may have contributed to their situation: the elderly, women, single parents, many young people, the disabled, the unemployed, the homeless.

The 30–30–40 society

Will Hutton (1995) suggests that the UK has become split into segments of 30%, 30% and 40% based on inequalities in income and wealth. The bottom 30% are the disadvantaged. These are likely to be unemployed and in poverty. The second 30% is made up of marginalised and insecure workers. This includes the growing army of part-timers and casual workers of which 80% are women. It also includes an increasing number of self-employed. Wages earned by this group tend to be less than half average wages. The top 40% are the privileged who have held full-time jobs or been self-employed for more than two years.

Adapted from: M. Denscombe (1988) *Sociology Update*, Leicester: Olympus Books

1 From what you have studied in this Topic, how do you expect that the proportions identified by Will Hutton might change over the next 10 years?

Explain your answer.

2 Study Item B. Considering solely parental choice in education for their children, what do Adonis and Pollard mean when they say 'In Britain's class meritocracy, all children are equal but some are more equal than others'?

3 Why might the percentage of members of the so-called 'Super class' be under-estimated?

4 How might members of this class justify their high incomes?

A Class Act

According to Adonis and Pollard's book A Class Act: the Myth of Britain's Classless Society, *social class is as much in evidence now as it was when George Orwell described England as 'the most class ridden society under the sun'. Indeed, echoing Orwell's famous commandment from 'Animal Farm', they go on to say ' In Britain's class meritocracy, all children are equal but some are more equal than others'.*

Their main point however is to suggest that a new social class is emerging comprising a professional and managerial elite who are separating from other professionals and managers who are lower paid and work mainly in the public sector. This 'Superclass' of higher-salaried people (salariat) has grown considerably in recent years from 7% in 1963 to 12% in 1993 and is currently at about 15%. Whilst the media has touched upon their existence with references to 'fat cat' salaries, Adonis and Pollard suggest that this is just the tip of the iceberg, with many thousands of high fliers in the upper echelons of the finance houses and privatised utilities based in the City of London.

An interesting feature of the Superclass is that it regards its earnings as justifiable and as a reflection of its members' ability. They see themselves as 'worth every penny' of what they receive and regard themselves as a meritocracy. Average boardroom pay in 1995 was over half a million pounds per year. The Superclass also tends to intermarry, thus combining two salaries to create 'super salaries'.

According to Adonis and Pollard, the dominant themes in the life of the superclass include London-based, servants, second homes, the best of private education, health and leisure; exotic foreign holidays, modern art, opera and an almost total separation from public life via private estates and security.

Adapted from: T. Warde (1999) 'A Class Act', *S Magazine*

Research activity

1 Using the definitions provided by Will Hutton (Item A), attempt to assess the make up of your school or college in those terms by asking students the employment profile of their families.

2 How do the proportions of each group in your school or college social profile differ from the proportions suggested by Hutton? Why do you think this is so? Why are inequalities of income and wealth more or less severe than for the nation as a whole?

WWWebtask

Go to the guardianunlimited website http://www.guardianunlimited.co.uk. Search the archive for articles referring to Child Poverty and 'Fat Cat' salaries. To what extent do the differences reflect a class-divided society?

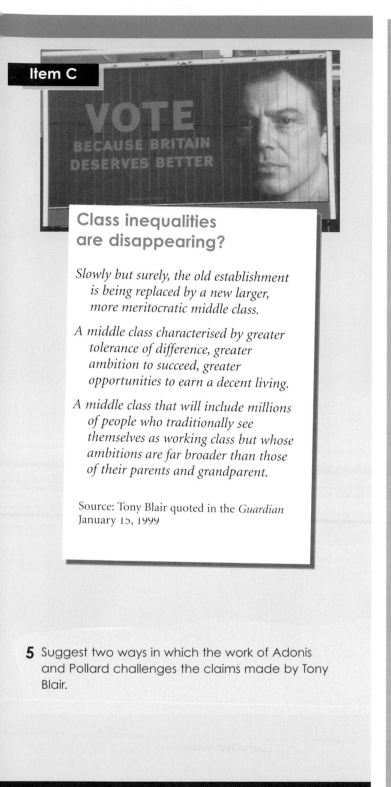

Class inequalities are disappearing?

Slowly but surely, the old establishment is being replaced by a new larger, more meritocratic middle class.

A middle class characterised by greater tolerance of difference, greater ambition to succeed, greater opportunities to earn a decent living.

A middle class that will include millions of people who traditionally see themselves as working class but whose ambitions are far broader than those of their parents and grandparent.

Source: Tony Blair quoted in the *Guardian* January 15, 1999

5 Suggest two ways in which the work of Adonis and Pollard challenges the claims made by Tony Blair.

EXAM PRACTICE

Extract from AQA-style question

'Despite the spread of share ownership the class structure of advanced industrial societies has changed little.' Examine the evidence for and against this statement. (40 marks)

OCR-style question

Item A

Percentage of people whose income is below various fractions of average income 1961–1996

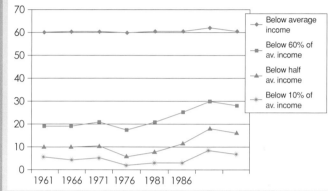

Source: Inland Revenue 1995

Item B

One explanation of poverty is that it is generated by the cultural attitudes and lifestyle of the poor. The culture of poverty argues that poverty cannot be eradicated by giving more money to the poor because they have developed a way of life which does not allow them to improve their position simply by having more money. Their culture is said to be characterised by short term horizons, indifference to work, apathy and feelings of resignation. Furthermore, this culture is said to be transmitted from one generation to another setting up a cycle of deprivation and a culture of dependency.

The culture of poverty thesis is largely discredited because it seemed to ignore structural causes of deprivation.

Source: J. Goldthorpe (1980, 1999), *Oxford Mobility Study*

a   Using only the information in Item A, identify two trends that have occurred with regard to those on below half average income between 1961 and 1996. (6 marks)

b   Using the information in Item B, identify two possible links between culture and poverty. (6 marks)

c   Identify and explain two problems facing sociologists using income statistics from secondary sources. (12 marks)

d   Using your wider sociological knowledge outline the evidence for the growing gap between rich and poor in the contemporary UK. (22 marks)

e   Outline and assess the view that poverty is caused by social exclusion rather than cultural attitudes and lifestyle. (44 marks)

Getting you thinking

1 What do you think are the main differences between the people in the photographs above?

2 Which would you call 'posh' and why?

3 Why do you think Victoria Beckham was often referred to as 'Posh' when she performed with the Spice Girls?

4 Which of the sets of photographs at the top do you most associate the Beckhams with? Explain your answer.

5 What do the terms 'working', 'middle' and 'upper class' mean to you?

6 What factors other than class affect the way people are perceived today?

Your answers to the above questions may demonstrate that class is a difficult thing to define nowadays and that status is no longer simply a matter of being on the right side of the class divide. The old idea of the class structure was that it comprised a triangular shape, with numbers increasing towards the base, which was composed of a vast number of unskilled manual workers providing a strong industrially based manufacturing sector. This model implied a strict hierarchy, with higher levels of income, status and power towards the top. Although this was never actually the true shape (because manufacturing jobs have never accounted for the majority of the workforce), there has been a dramatic shift in Britain's industrial structure with only about 18% of the population working in manufacturing today. At the same time, numbers of those working in **tertiary or service-sector** jobs (those providing services such as transport, retailing, hotel work, cleaning, banking and insurance) has increased dramatically from 25% to 75%.

The idea of a post-industrial economy

Many writers, notably Daniel Bell (1973), have suggested that society is moving from an industrial to a post-industrial stage in which jobs will no longer be characterised by dirty, physical work but will be based more on intellectual creativity. Bell also believed that companies will become less concerned with profit and more concerned with satisfying their workforces through better working conditions and job security, having invested heavily in their training and personal development.

Kumar (1978), however, argues that, even in the nineteenth century, those in the service industries were often substantially worse off in terms of income than those in manufacturing. The ideal of the knowledge-based society seems some way off today (as we will see when we examine further the true plight of the lower middle-classes). Service-sector companies have been struggling to maintain their workforces in the wake of increased competition and the transfer of routine non-manual tasks to computer technology

– for example, consider the impact of on-line banking, insurance and travel on the personnel working in these sectors. It has been argued that the tidal wave of companies **downsizing** in the wake of the September 11 terrorist bombings in New York is in some way the result of executives using that event as an excuse to do what they would have otherwise found more difficult had the events not occurred. However, as Roberts (2001) points out, there are many non-manual operations now performed which simply would not previously have been possible (e.g. telephone banking, flight/holiday booking, car insurance quotations, etc.). This may have led to some increases in the service sector, albeit at the lower end (in most cases in '**call centre**' work).

Another striking development has been the feminisation of the workforce which has not only affected status differences in the workplace, but has also, for most households, had a massive effect on household income. This has, in turn, made a major difference to the lifestyle and consumption patterns of all classes.

Using examples from other topics you have studied, explain some effects of the increased number of women in the workforce.

The middle classes in modern Britain

The expansion of the middle classes

In 1911 80% of workers were in manual occupations. This number fell to 32.7% in 1991 and is approximately 25% today. Non-manual workers (traditionally seen as middle class) have therefore fairly recently become the majority occupational group in the workforce. As Savage (1995) points out, there are now more university lecturers than coal miners.

Reasons for the expansion

The number of manual jobs in both **primary** and **secondary industries** has gone into decline since the 1970s. The decline

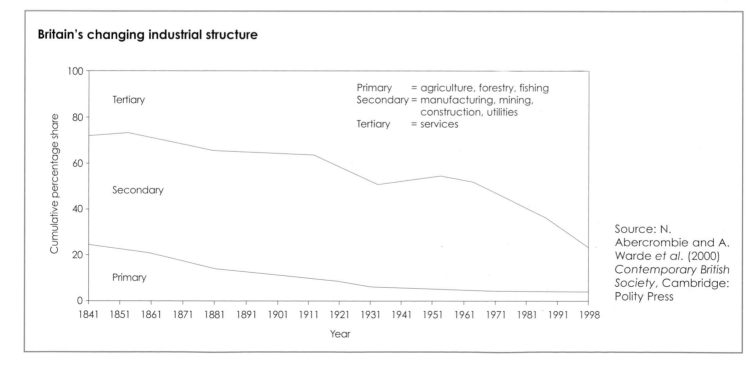

Britain's changing industrial structure

Primary = agriculture, forestry, fishing
Secondary = manufacturing, mining, construction, utilities
Tertiary = services

Source: N. Abercrombie and A. Warde et al. (2000) Contemporary British Society, Cambridge: Polity Press

has been caused by a range of factors such as new technology, the oil crisis and globalisation (the same raw materials and goods can be produced more cheaply in the third world). Some writers have suggested that the **mass production** techniques introduced by Henry Ford had fallen into crisis. Consumers no longer want the same standardised product. Instead, they demand to be able to tailor products to their individual needs.

Sociologists who accept this view are often referred to as **post-Fordists**. They argue that capitalism has had to devise new models of regulating society in order to ensure continued profitability. These included more flexible working patterns and the promotion of specialised small-scale production units to replace mass production.

The tertiary or service sector of the economy that is focused around education, welfare, retail and finance has expanded hugely in the past 20 years. Mass secondary education and the expansion of both further and higher education have ensured the existence of a well-educated and qualified workforce. The service sector is made up of a mainly male professional workforce at its top end but, as a result of changes in women's social position, the bulk of workers in this sector are female.

Fordism and post-Fordism

The Model T Ford was available in one model and any colour 'so long as it was black'. The Ford saloon of today is available in 26 options including a range of engine types, sizes and body shapes. Black is one of the 22 colours available.

The boundary problem

Studying the middle classes can be problematic because not all sociologists agree who should be included in this category. This is the so-called '**boundary problem**'. Traditionally, differentiating between the middle class and working class was thought to be a simple task involving distinguishing between white-collar or non-manual workers on the one hand and blue-collar or manual workers on the other. Generally, the former enjoyed better working conditions in terms of pay, holidays and promotion possibilities. Today, however, this distinction is not so clear cut. It is generally agreed that many **routine white-collar workers**, who are mainly women, now have similar conditions of work and pay to manual workers and therefore cannot be seen as a higher class.

 Using examples from other areas of the specification you have covered, give examples of other 'boundary problems' in sociology.

A fragmented middle class

The term 'middle class' covers a wide range of occupations, incomes, lifestyles and attitudes. Roberts *et al.* (1977) argued that the middle class was becoming fragmented into a number of different groups, each with a distinctive view of its place in the stratification system. They suggest that we should no longer talk of the middle class but of the 'middle classes'. Savage *et al.*, (1992) agrees that it is important to see that the middle class is now divided into strata and can be seen in terms of 'class fractions'. He identifies a number of **class fractions** – higher and lower professionals, higher and middle managers, the petit bourgeoisie and routine white-collar workers.

Professionals
Savage *et al.* (1992) argue that higher and lower professionals mainly recruit internally – in other words, the sons and daughters of professionals are likely to end up as professionals themselves. The position of professional workers is based on the possession of educational qualifications. Professionals usually have to go through a long period of training – university plus professional examinations before they qualify. Savage argues that professionals possess both **economic capital** (a very good standard of living, savings, financial security) and cultural capital (they see the worth of education and other cultural assets such as taste in high culture) which they pass on to their children. Furthermore, professionals have strong occupational associations such as the Law Society and the British Medical Association that protect and actively pursue their interests (although the lower down the professional ladder, the weaker these associations/unions become). The result of such groups actively pursuing the interests of professionals is high rewards, status and job security.

 What other social advantages may be gained from the possession of cultural capital?

Savage concludes that professionals are aware of their common interests and quite willing to take industrial action to protect those interests. In this sense, then, professionals have a greater sense of class identity than other middle-class groups. However, as the public sector has become increasingly privatised, many professionals are facing an increased threat of **redundancy** and reduced promotional opportunities due to **de-layering** (a reduction in the number of promotional 'tiers').

Managers
Savage *et al.* (1992) suggests that managers have assets based upon a particular skill within specific organisations. Such skills (unlike those of professionals) are not easily transferable to other companies or industries. Many managers have been upwardly mobile from the routine white-collar sector or the skilled working-class. Often they lack qualifications such as degrees. They may even have worked their up through an organisation. Their social position, therefore, is likely to be the result of experience and reputation rather than qualifications. Savage notes that most managers do not belong to professional associations or trade unions. Consequently, they tend to be more individualistic in character and are less likely to identify a common collectivistic interest with their fellow

managers – these are much more likely to be seen as competitors. Savage argues that managers encourage their children to actively pursue higher education because they can see the benefits of a professional career. However, managers, despite being well-paid, are less likely to have the cultural capital possessed by professionals.

Savage argues that job security differentiates professionals from managers – managers are constantly under threat from recession, mergers and downsizing. Savage points out that it is middle managers more than higher managers whose jobs are under threat. Higher managers are likely to be on spectacular salaries and to have share options worth millions – as we will see in Topic 6, it is argued that some are part of a 'superclass'. (These higher managers are Company Directors or members of a Company's managerial team who make strategic rather than operational decisions.) However, middle managers such as bank managers may find themselves unemployed or downwardly mobile.

The self-employed

Between 1981 and 1991, the number of people **self-employed** or '**petit-bourgeois**' has risen from 6.7% of the workforce to over 10%. Research by Fielding (1995) examined what the self-employed in 1981 were doing in 1991. He showed that two-thirds of his sample were a relatively stable and secure part of the workforce in that they remained self-employed over this ten-year period. However, the character of the self-employed has changed in some respects too. The number of managers who prefer to work for themselves (for example, as consultants) rose considerably in the 1980s especially in the finance and computer industries. Some writers argue that many firms now prefer to contract services to outside consultants rather than employ people themselves. A large number of people, again mainly managers, have businesses 'on the side' whilst continuing to be employees.

Routine white-collar workers

Marxists such as Harry Braverman (1974) argue that routine white-collar workers are no longer middle class. Braverman argues that they have been subjected to a process of **proletarianisation**. This means that they have lost the social and economic advantages that they enjoyed over manual workers such as superior pay and working conditions. Braverman argues that in the past twenty years employers have used technology, especially computers, to break down complex white-collar skills such as book-keeping into simplistic routine tasks. This process is known as **de-skilling** and is an attempt to increase output, maximise efficiency and reduce costs. Control over the work process has therefore been removed from many non-manual workers.

These developments have been accompanied by the parallel development of the feminisation of the routine white-collar workforce (especially in the financial sector) because female workers are generally cheap to employ and are seen by employers as more adaptable and amenable to this type of work. Braverman concludes that de-skilling means that occupations that once were middle class are today in all respects indistinguishable from those of manual workers.

Braverman represents a Marxist view. Why might Marxists support the idea of poletarianisation?

Marshall *et al.* (1988) challenged the idea of proletarianisation. In a national random sample of female workers, they found that it was mainly manual workers who claimed that their work had been de-skilled. Over 90% of non-manual workers felt that little had changed, and that they were as likely to identify themselves with the middle class as they were with the working class. Finally, they were more likely to vote Conservative than Labour. As far as Marshall *et al.* were concerned, proletarianisation among routine white-collar workers was not taking place.

New-technology workers

In further contrast to Braverman however, Clark and Hoffman-Martinot (1998) highlight the growth of a technological elite of 'wired workers' – new professionals who are as productive through the use of technology as entire offices of routine non-manual workers, spending most of their days behind computers working in non-hierarchical settings. They enjoy considerable **autonomy**, are paid extremely well, often working flexibly, engaged in dynamic problem-solving activities. Such workers can be found in a wide range of new occupations regarded as part of the 'infotech sector', jobs such as web designers, systems analysts, in e-commerce, software development, graphic design and financial consultancy. At the lower end of this sector, however, are growing numbers of casual workers who spend all day on the telephone in front of a VDU, often working in very poor conditions.

What was once the minority, perceived as a class apart from the working class in terms of income, lifestyle, status, and culture, has become a much larger, more **heterogeneous** body whose internal diversity can be demonstrated on all fronts.

The working class

Changes in class solidarity

Fulcher and Scott (1999) point out that until the late twentieth century the working class had a strong sense of their social-class position. Virtually all aspects of their lives including gender roles, family life, political affiliation and leisure were a product of their keen sense of working-class identity. Lockwood's (1966) research found that many workers, especially in industrial areas, subscribed to a value system he called '**proletarian traditionalist**'. Such workers felt a strong sense of loyalty to each other because of shared community and work experience. Consequently workers were mutually supportive of each other. They had a keen sense of class solidarity and consciousness. They therefore tended to see society in terms of conflict, in terms of 'them versus us'. Later research has claimed that this type of class identity is in decline because the service sector of the economy has grown more important as the traditional industrial and manufacturing sectors have gone into decline. Recession and unemployment has consequently undermined traditional working-class communities and organisations such as trade unions.

Middle-class lifestyles?

In the 1960s Zweig argued that a section of the working class – skilled manual workers – had adopted the economic and cultural lifestyle of the middle class. This argument became known as the '**embourgeoisement** thesis' because it insisted that skilled workers had become more like the middle class by supporting bourgeois values and the Conservative party as well as enjoying similar income levels.

This view was investigated in Goldthorpe and Lockwood's famous study of a car factory in Luton (1969). They found little evidence to support Zweig's assertion. Economically, whilst wages were comparable to those of members of the middle classes they did not enjoy the same working conditions or fringe benefits, such as expense accounts, company car, sick pay, company pensions, etc. They had to work longer hours and had less chance of promotion. They did not readily mix with members of other classes either inside or outside work and 77% of their sample voted Labour. They did, however, argue that there were signs of '**convergence**' between working-class and middle-class lifestyles but concluded that rather than an increase in the middle class, what had emerged was a new working class.

What research methods could be used to test the idea of embourgeoisement? What problems might be faced by the researchers?

Privatisation

Goldthorpe and Lockwood identified a new trend, the emergence of the 'privatised instrumentalist' worker who saw work as a means to an end rather than as a source of identity.

These affluent workers were more home-centred than traditional working-class groups and were less likely to subscribe to the notion of working-class community and 'them versus us' attitudes.

Fiona Devine (1992) undertook a second study of the Vauxhall plant at Luton in which she argued that Goldthorpe and Lockwood's study may have exaggerated the degree of working-class privatisation. She found that workers retained strong kinship and friendship links and were critically aware of class inequalities such as the unequal distribution of wealth and income.

Although the concept of embourgeoisement is now rarely used, it is frequently argued that the working class have fragmented into at least two different layers.

- The traditional working class in the north of England as shown, for example, in films like *Brassed Off* or *The Full Monty*.
- A new working class found in the newer manufacturing industries mainly situated in the south who enjoy a relatively affluent lifestyle but still see themselves as working class.

False consciousness?

Marxists reject the view that there is a fragmented working class. They argue that there is still a unified working class made up of manual workers – both black and white, male and

KEY TERMS

Autonomy – freedom to organise one's own workload.

Boundary problem – the constantly shifting nature of work makes it more difficult to draw boundaries between classes of workers.

Call centre work – work in a large office devoted to answering telephone queries and complaints.

Class fractions – subdivisions within particular mass groupings.

Convergence – coming together.

Cultural capital – social advantages associated with the middle classes.

De-layering – reducing the number of tiers of management in an organisation.

De-skilling – reducing the skill needed to do a job.

Downsizing – reducing the size of the permanent workforce.

Economic capital – money in shares (and so on) which generates more money.

Embourgeoisement – the idea that the working class are adopting the attitudes, lifestyle and economic situation of the middles classes.

False class consciousness – see Key Terms in Topic 1.

Fordism – a manufacturing system based upon the most cost-efficient and quick systems of production, usually mass production, assembly-line techniques.

Heterogeneous – see Key Terms in Topic 3.

Mass production – producing identical products in large numbers using a production line.

Post-Fordism – after the collapse of Western manufacturing economies in the 1970s producers had to become more flexible, diverse and focused upon consumer choice in the face of competition. Quality, diversity and small batch production replaced mass production.

Primary industries – those involved in extraction of raw materials, e.g. mining, agriculture, fishing.

Proletarianisation – a tendency for lower middle class to become de-skilled and hence to share the market position of members of the working class.

Proletarian traditionalist – members of the working class with a strong sense of loyalty to each other because of shared community and work experience.

Redundancy – losing your job because a company is downsizing.

Routine white-collar workers – clerical staff involved in low-status, repetitive office work.

Secondary industries – those involved in producing products from raw materials.

Self-employed/petit-bourgeois – owners of small businesses.

Tertiary or service sector – jobs providing services such as transport, retailing, cleaning, banking and insurance.

female, and routine white-collar workers. They would argue that the sorts of divisions discussed above are the product of ruling-class ideology which attempts to divide and rule the working class. The fact that some groups do not see themselves as working class is dismissed by Marxists as **false class-consciousness**. They would argue that in relation to the means and social relations of production, all so-called 'class fractions' are objectively working class because they are alienated and exploited by the ruling class whether they realise it or not.

Does class identity still exist?

Postmodernists argue that class identity has fragmented into numerous separate and individualised identities. Social identity is now more pluralistic and diverse. Pakulski and Waters (1996) argue that people now exercise more choice about what type of people they want to be. Gender, ethnicity, age, region and family role interact and impact with consumption and media images to construct postmodern culture and identity. However, postmodern ideas may be exaggerated as recent surveys indicate that social class is still a significant source of identity for many (e.g. Marshall *et al.*, 1988). Members of a range of classes are still aware of class differences and are happy to identify themselves using class categories.

CHECK YOUR UNDERSTANDING

1 What evidence is there to suggest that Bell's view of post-industrial society may be inaccurate?

2 What was Fordism? What caused its 'collapse'?

3 How according to Post-Fordists has capitalism had to adapt?

4 Why do some writers suggest that 'we should no longer talk of the middle class but of the "middle classes"'?

5 How do managers differ from professionals?

6 What evidence is there for 'proletarianisation'?

7 What was the 'embourgeoisement thesis' and how was it challenged?

8 How do Marxists challenge the view that the working class has fragmented?

9 What do postmodernists like Pakulski and Waters argue has happened to class identity?

10 Why is it no longer possible to draw a clear line between the middle and the working class?

Research ideas

1 Ask a sample of adults across a range of occupations how 'flexible' their work is. Ask them about their job security, the sort of tasks they do, their working hours, how much freedom they have, and so on.

2 Conduct a survey of your peers in casual part-time employment to find out the conditions of work they experience.

WWW Webtask

● For an interesting discussion of the impact of globalisation and consumer demand on manufacturing, visit the Ford website http://www.ford.com/en/ourCompany/heritage/theFordStory.htm

Item A

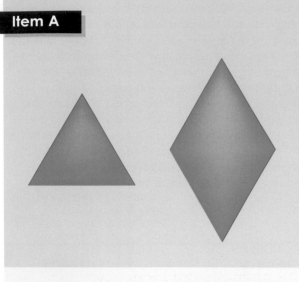

1 How could it be argued that these two shapes represent the changing occupational structure?

Item B

There is a new working class employed typically in hypermarkets, restaurants and hotels and in other businesses connected with leisure, sport and tourism. Such work is usually mundane and low paid, low level, part-time and casual. However, because of their visibility to the client group such often young (attractive) people are required to supply aesthetic labour – looking right to boost the company's image and appearing human and interested in their commitment to customer satisfaction. Such work can be stressful and demeaning. There is more work in call centres, with security firms, in fast food outlets such as McDonalds and with contract cleaners. This new working class is fragmented. Their work is often part-time and insecure and likely to be at odd, variable hours.

Source: K. Roberts (2001) *Class in Modern Britain,* Basingstoke: Palgrave

Item C   A new casualised working class in the 21st century

2 Using the photographs and the ideas in Items B and C, explain how the working class today could be said to be 'fragmented'.

3 What evidence is there in Item B that employers see attributes other than educational qualifications and experience as more important credentials for an increasing number of jobs? What are the implications of this for defining class?

Extract from AQA-style question

Assess the view that a classless society now exists in Britain rather than the polarised society predicted by Marx.
(40 marks)

Extract from OCR-style question

Item A Globalisation

The expansion of manufacturing capability all over the world, in the Far East in particular, has meant that high quality products can be produced cheaply due to very low labour costs. Trans-national companies have emerged to capitalise on both the wider markets available and the possibility of cheaper production costs. Sometimes decisions about particular products being produced in particular places can mean widespread good fortune to a particular region or sudden misfortune when a labour market becomes comparatively expensive to maintain. This cuts both ways. It is as likely that a foreign manufacturer will move into or out of an area of the UK as a British manufacturer will in the Far East. Governments often tip the balance with subsidies or other incentives to reduce unemployment or the cost of it.

Item B Fordism and post-Fordism

In the system of mass production created by Henry Ford, work was fragmented into small tasks which could be carried out repeatedly by low skilled labour with very little training. There was a clear division between a mass of semi-skilled workers and a small number of skilled workers carrying out key tasks. A centralised management sharply separated from the workers controlled production. Many active unions represented the divided groups. Whilst people wanted all the new products from vacuum cleaners to cars (and indeed there did seem to be an almost insatiable demand) this system of providing mass-produced average quality products worked fine. However, once the market became saturated, and competition increased, quality, product diversity and innovation became the crucial characteristics in the marketplace as consumer choice became more influential.

To accommodate to this, sociologists have suggested that a new way of organising production has emerged – post-Fordism. This has brought with it changes to the organisation of work. Small batch production has replaced mass production to maximise market opportunities by responding to diverse demand. Workers need to be more flexible, motivated and multi-skilled and a more cooperative, less conflictual style of industrial management is essential.

Adapted from Fulcher and Scott, (1999) *Sociology*, Oxford: Oxford University Press

a   Using Item A, identify two examples to show how globalised production can de-stabilise the domestic   job market. (6 marks)

b   Using Item B, explain how increased consumer choice has affected the organisation of production. (6 marks)

c   What difficulties might a researcher face in trying to determine the extent to which a workforce is motivated and whether management is co-operative rather than conflictual? (16 marks)

Getting you thinking

The couple pictured are moving from middle-class suburban respectability (above) to the style statement of the inner city-loft apartment (opposite)

Council housing in Charlton, London which is now owner-occupied

The resurgence of cinema has created complexes that integrate social classes socially

1 Consider each set of photographs. How do they suggest that class identity and experience may be less clear cut than it used to be?

2 How do they show that consumption and lifestyle may be becoming increasingly important as definers of identity?

3 How available are the lifestyle choices illustrated above to all social groups? Who may be denied access and why?

You may have concluded from the exercise above that the ground rules regarding the expected behaviour of different social classes are changing. You may also have concluded, however, that material factors still govern lifestyle choices and that these are class related. The previous topic explored the view that the old social divisions based around occupational differences are less clear cut. Class identity has come to depend not only on market situation but on differences and similarities in power, status, and their relationships not only in production but also to consumption and lifestyle.

Postmodernism and consumption

As postmodernists have suggested, the significance of **consumption** is undoubtedly borne out by looking at trends in society as a whole.

The rapid expansion of the service economy as well as the entertainment and leisure industry reflect an increasing emphasis on consumption within modern industrialised societies. The proliferation of style gurus, who represent goods and services to us as something we need to consume in order to be part of the 'it' generation, has produced (for the affluent at least) a growing army of stylists, design consultants, personal trainers and **Feng-Shui** specialists. For the less affluent, there is a fascination with changing rooms, houses and garden with the help of celebrity cooks, gardeners and interior designers.

Postmodern societies have, it is suggested, become increasingly geared towards consumption. In some respects, therefore, a consumer society might be more of a uniform one in which class differences are to some extent over-ridden. After all, everyone has access to the same TV programmes, can drive similar cars or shop in the same clothes stores.

Postmodernists, however, conveniently ignore the view that consumption depends on having a job and a certain level of income. Poverty is certainly going to inhibit any desire to pursue a postmodern lifestyle – although, the desire for consumer goods generated by the mass media can often be such that some young people in particular may turn to deviant means of acquiring them. Note, for example, the increase in the theft of mobile phones from children by other children, or mugging of designer clothes from the backs of some young people by others. Also, just because we all consume similar categories of products, does not mean that we necessarily consume them in the same way. Class differences can become intensified through differences in lifestyle and taste. In other words, consumption and social class are closely related. Fast food for one class may mean a Big Mac, fries and a Coke whereas for another it might be a cream-cheese bagel, and a cappuccino.

However, whilst there may be countless examples of sometimes arbitrary differences in lifestyle choices which illustrate the significance of class or otherwise, it is impossible to ignore the crucial role still played by material as well as cultural factors in the reproduction of social inequalities.

So, does class still matter?

Class position, however measured, has been shown to affect life-chances in almost every aspect of social life. This Topic will highlight the extent to which class can impact not only on cultural but also social and material advantage/disadvantage such that lower socio-economic groups experience significantly reduced life-chances relative to those progressively higher up the class structure. Here we will consider the issues relating to the chances of experiencing good health, education and housing.

Explain how life-chances are unevenly distributed among different classes, genders and ethnic groups using examples from other aspects of your course. If you have studied education, this is a particularly good example to use.

Health

If illness was a chance occurrence we could expect to see rates of illness randomly distributed across the population. However, it is clear from the following that some groups can expect an over-proportionate amount of illness (according to the Department of Health).

- A child born at the bottom of the social scale is twice as likely to die at birth or in the first few months of life as a child born of professional parents.
- The working class experience poorer **mortality rates** and **morbidity rates** than the middle classes. For example, more than 3,500 working-class babies would survive per year if the working-class infant mortality rate was reduced to middle-class levels.
- In general, health across the population is improving but the rate of improvement is much slower for the working class.
- If we compare causes of death we can see that, between 1972 and 1997, death rates for professionals fell by 44% whilst it fell by only 10% for the unskilled.
- Mortality rates are significantly higher for the unemployed and attempted suicide rates eleven times greater.
- Chronic conditions such as asthma and diabetes are actually increasing. Most of the increase is among the lower working class.

Explanations of health inequalities

Lifestyle choices

The New Right are likely to argue that cultural factors rather than material factors cause ill health, i.e. that they are a product of **cultural deprivation**. They suggest that the working class are less likely to eat a healthy diet and more likely to smoke and drink excessively. Research by Warde (1997) examined expenditure on shopping and found that there does appear to be a distinctively working-class diet characterised by a greater proportion spent on bread, tinned food, cooked meats, sausages, fish and chips and sugar and much less on fresh fruit and vegetables.

Roberts (2001) argues that the working class indulge in less exercise and are more passive in terms of their leisure pursuits. According to the Family Spending Survey (1996–7) the middle class spend about twice as much on leisure goods and services than the working-class, although the proportion of household expenditure that this represents is about the same.

Good or bad health, then, may appear to be a matter of choice.

Life-chances

However, it may well be that in the absence of private transport tinned food is a practical alternative to heavy bags of fresh vegetables. What is more, the middle class have more access to recreational facilities. Many modern private housing developments, aimed at the single professional in particular, provide on-site leisure facilities for their residents such as squash courts and a gym. Membership of private gyms is very expensive and affordable only by higher wage earners. Some companies provide facilities or subsidise their employees' sports and leisure activities, encouraging employee loyalty and increased networking between staff in the process. Middle-class employees also have more free time, working on average a much shorter working week than their manual counterparts. Smoking and drinking can be seen as an attempt to relieve stress caused by these kinds of disadvantages.

Poorer sections of the population may also be disadvantaged in terms of access to healthcare. Prescription charges alone can deter some of the low paid from taking medicines that they need. In any case, healthcare facilities vary in quality across areas according to socio-economic factors. Dr Tudor Hart (Hart, 1971) has proposed the existence of an inverse-care law. This states that the greater the need for healthcare, the fewer facilities there are available and the less the need, the greater the availability. Middle-class patients have easier access to healthcare facilities of better quality, with shorter patient lists, and, in their relationship to their doctor, get more time and have their conditions better diagnosed, explained and treated.

Marxists would argue that health inequalities are the result of **material deprivation** and economic disadvantage suffered by the working classes. They become innocent victims of the exploitative conditions suffered in the workplace and society at large.

Using examples from other areas of the course, explain how these two arguments – lifestyle choices or life-chances – can be used to explain class differences in other aspects of social life (again, education could be used here).

Housing

Decent housing is something virtually everyone feels entitled to but changes in government policy have led to a 'ghettoisation' of lower income groups. Whilst government spending on health and education has increased by over 30% since 1981, the reverse is true of expenditure on housing. This has had a significant effect upon the opportunities for decent housing of lower socio-economic groups.

The reduced availability of cheap, good-quality housing

Most public expenditure on housing has supported a **social rented sector** in Britain. At present this comprises council-rented properties managed by local authorities (about 5 million dwellings) and social-rented housing managed by non-profit housing associations (about 800,000 dwellings). Despite active programmes of privatisation by the Conservative governments of the 1980s (which included the

---

Housing tenure changes In Great Britain 1945–2000

	Private renting %	Home ownership %	Social renting %
1945	62	26	12
1951	53	29	18
1961	32	42	26
1971	19	50	31
1981	11	57	32
1991	10	66	24
2000	5	73	22

Source: Council of Mortgage Lenders (2002) *Housing Finance, UK 2001*, London: HMSO

---

sale of council homes under the '**Right to buy initiative**') as well as the transfer of stock to housing associations, local authorities remain the main providers of social-rented housing in Britain. Because of the reduced availability of socially-rented housing, many commentators suggest that there is now a housing crisis. In any case, both local authorities and housing associations have had to develop a more *social* role by allocating housing to those in greatest need. This has had the effect of concentrating socially deprived groups in particular areas, thus creating new class divisions locally and nationally.

It is important to recognise that the tendency for lower income households to be more concentrated in council housing was clearly established well before 1980. However, formerly there was a degree of choice involved in where you wanted to live, giving residential areas a more comprehensive and socially cohesive feel.

The financial incentives and status associated with home ownership and the degree of income inequality in Britain has contributed to divergent patterns of residence, causing the better and worse off to polarise (Murie, 1983). This has led (the figure below illustrates) to the increasing concentration

---

The increasing concentration of those in the lowest 30% of income earners in council housing (approximate figures are quoted for illustrative purposes only)

	1979	2000
No. of council dwellings	8 million	5 million
No. of lowest income households who are council tenants	4 million	4 million
Concentration of those on lowest incomes who are council tenants	= 50%	= 80%

Source: approximate figures taken from *General Household Survey* (2000), London: ONS, HMSO

Percentage of households in lowest 30% income who were council tenants	
	% in lowest 30% of incomes
1963	26.3%
1972	41.1%
1979	47.0%
1991	47.5%
2001	45.0%*

*includes figures for socially rented sector as a whole

Source: Department of Employment (1992; 2001) *Family Expenditure Survey*, London: HMSO

The changing face of council housing in Britain

- Fewer economically active members
- Fewer multiple earner households
- Fewer higher income households
- Declining level of car ownership
- More households with no earners
- Declining role as family housing
- Increase in female-headed households
- Increase in unskilled manual workers
- More elderly people
- Ageing dwelling stock
- Increasing proportion of flats
- Increasing proportion of lettings to the homeless
- Increasing proportion of tenants on state benefits

Source: R. Forrest and A. Hume (1990) *Home Ownership*, London: Unwin Hyman

of low-income households on council estates. Whereas in 1963 only slightly more than 1 in 4 of households with the lowest incomes were council tenants, by 1979 almost 1 in 2 were in that tenure. In the period since 1979 the proportion of low-income households and those on supplementary benefit, (subsequently renamed 'income support') who were council tenants has remained static. But, as the number of council dwellings has declined, this means that the concentration of those with lower incomes in council housing has actually increased, leading to the development of a more coherent 'lower class' in such areas (see figure above).

As councils sold off those properties in the better areas and re-located some families, they avoided placing new tenants in the up and coming areas. This has meant that the comprehensive character of council estates has given way to relatively affluent ex-council home-owning residential areas (as shown in the picture of the house in Charlton in 'Getting you thinking'). On the other hand, less desirable residential areas were used for social renting, creating pockets of deprivation with dysfunctional communities and a disproportionate level of social problems. For example, according to the General Household Survey (2001) 51% of single parent families are council tenants compared to 15% of the general population.

Weak social networks

Low-demand housing areas often have high household-turnover rates as many seek to move on to more desirable areas, while new disadvantaged entrants to the housing market move in. Such areas have weak social networks. This reduces the circulation of information about jobs and community events. Rising unemployment and social polarisation have been more apparent among council tenants than in the population as a whole and council housing has developed a more striking social profile. High unemployment and low income places strains on family life. Crime and juvenile delinquency may undermine the quality of life in the neighbourhood as a whole.

What forms of social exclusion may be experienced by those living in low-demand housing areas?

Rising social inequality has coincided with a major restructuring of **housing tenure**. In part this is due to the

policy that many local authorities have adopted by placing the poorest families all within the same geographical area often within less desirable estates as the better housing stock has been sold off. A greater commitment to providing quality housing in areas which are socially mixed could avoid many of the costly social problems which such policies have caused.

What is a social problem? Why might it be difficult to define this term?

CHECK YOUR UNDERSTANDING

1 What do postmodernists suggest to be the most important determinant of social identity?

2 Suggest two reasons why it is suggested that postmodern claims may be exaggerated.

3 Give three statistical examples of health differences between classes.

4 List three arguments in support of New Right theories of health differences between classes and three against.

5 Why have socially rented housing providers had to adopt a more social role in recent years?

6 What effect has this had on the social make up of some residential areas?

7 Explain why, despite little change in the number of those on the lowest income in council homes, their concentration has increased.

8 What problems do those living in low-demand housing areas face?

9 What evidence is there that council housing is becoming increasingly the domain of the socially deprived?

10 What social problems might this cause?

Consumption – spending on goods and services.

Cultural deprivation – the idea that some cultures are inferior to others and so less able to equip their members to deal successfully with the social world.

Feng Shui – (pronounced Feng shway) an ancient Chinese tradition which focuses on keeping a flow of good energy going to maximise happiness and success. This involves removing blockages to this flow to allow negative energy (sha) out and placing objects appropriately to channel good energy (chi). A specialist in the field will (for several hundred pounds) redesign the layout of your home or office to allow this to happen.

Ghettoisation – the geographical concentration into certain areas of people with similar circumstances and characteristics.

Housing tenure – whether a home is owner occupied, socially rented or privately rented.

Life-chances – likelihood of achieving social, economic and physical security.

Low-demand housing areas – areas where people are reluctant to live.

Material deprivation – the lack of physical resources needed in order to lead a full and normal life.

Morbidity rate – reported ill health per 100 thousand of population.

Mortality rate – number of deaths per 100 thousand of population.

Right to buy initiative – a Conservative government scheme whereby councils were instructed to allow long-term council tenants to buy their rented homes at a fraction of their market value (typically half).

Social rented housing sector – housing that is subsidised to allow those excluded from the housing market to live at a cost considerably lower than that charged in the private rented sector. Mainly provided by local authorities and housing associations.

Research idea

Get an A–Z of your local area. Enlarge a residential area that you know to be a high-demand area. Similarly, enlarge an area in low demand. Annotate each as far as possible to highlight differences in facilities/resources. Conduct a survey of residents in each area to discover the level of services and facilities on offer there. Compare and contrast the two areas to test the extent to which people in low-demand areas suffer a variety of social exclusions.

Exploring life-chances or lifestyle choices

Item A

Spatial exclusion?

Just as disadvantaged individuals are excluded from opportunities and activities that are norms for the rest of society, exclusion can take on a spatial dimension: neighbourhoods vary greatly in terms of safety, environmental conditions and the availability of services and public facilities. For example, low-demand neighbourhoods tend to have fewer basic services such as banks, food shops and post offices than do more desirable areas. Community spaces such as parks, sports grounds and libraries may also be limited. Yet people living in disadvantaged spaces are often dependent on local facilities as they lack the funds and transport which would allow them to use facilities and services provided sometimes more cheaply elsewhere.

Adapted from: A. Giddens (2001) *Sociology* (4th edition) Cambridge: Polity Press

Item B

Social cohesion: the key to better health?

Wilkinson (1996) Unhealthy Societies: The Afflictions of Inequality *surveyed empirical data on health from countries around the world. He found that the wealthiest nations did not necessarily have healthier populations. In fact the key to good national health appeared to be income distribution. The highest levels of good health were in those countries where wealth and income is most evenly distributed such as Sweden or Japan. The United States with its much more noticeable gap between rich and poor had relatively much worse health. In Wilkinson's view the widening gap in income distribution creates resentment, social exclusion in terms of the poor and social isolation where the more wealthy cut themselves off to protect their assets. Social cohesion is affected. People become isolated from their community. People are unable to cope with stress which is reflected in poor health. According to Wilkinson, social factors such as the strength of social contacts, ties within communities, availability of social support, a sense of security are the main determinants of the relative health of a society.*

Adapted from: A. Giddens (2001) p.150

Item C   Cultural and material influences on health

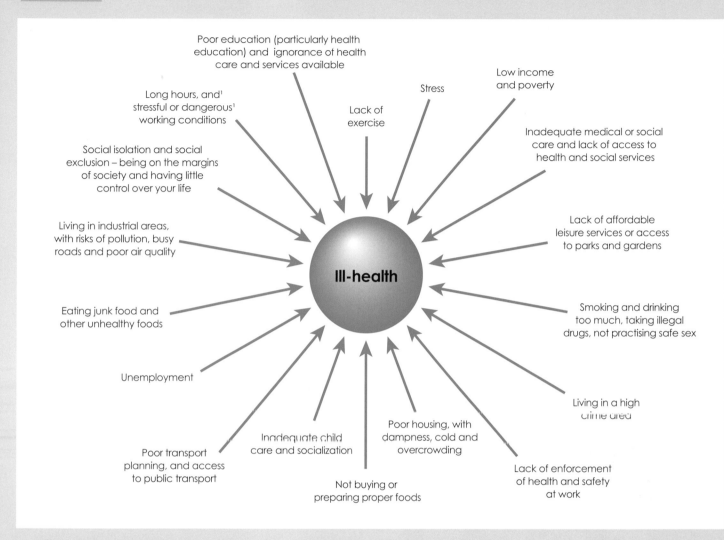

Poor education (particularly health education) and ignorance of health care and services available

Stress

Low income and poverty

Long hours, and[1] stressful or dangerous[1] working conditions

Lack of exercise

Inadequate medical or social care and lack of access to health and social services

Social isolation and social exclusion – being on the margins of society and having little control over your life

Living in industrial areas, with risks of pollution, busy roads and poor air quality

Ill-health

Lack of affordable leisure services or access to parks and gardens

Eating junk food and other unhealthy foods

Smoking and drinking too much, taking illegal drugs, not practising safe sex

Unemployment

Living in a high crime area

Poor transport planning, and access to public transport

Inadequate child care and socialization

Poor housing, with dampness, cold and overcrowding

Lack of enforcement of health and safety at work

Not buying or preparing proper foods

Source: K. Browne (1998) *An Introduction to Sociology* 2nd edition Cambridge: Polity Press

1 Why, according to Item A, are people in low-demand areas 'spatially excluded'?

2 In Item B, Wilkinson asserts that social cohesion is the key factor in a nation's health and that income inequality undermines this. How would you operationalise the concept of social cohesion and set about conducting research in order to test whether this is the case? What problems do you think that you might encounter and how would you seek to overcome them?

3 Study Item C. Create two columns. Head one 'Material factors' and the other 'Cultural factors'. Write each of the factors in the diagram in item B in the appropriate column. For those factors that straddle both columns, write them over the centre line. Annotate each factor in terms of class, for example, if you think that a particular factor is typical of a lower working-class person's experience, write 'lwc'.

- Go to the government statistics site at www.statistics.gov.uk. Select Neighbourhood statistics. Choose your own postcode or the district or postcode where your school or college is situated. You will be able to investigate a variety of indicators of wealth and deprivation. How does your area compare with other parts of the region or with Britain as a whole?

- Many writers are critical of the effect that the growth in consumerism has had on society, suggesting that we have lost sight of any true priorities and that we are destroying our societies, cultures and, even, the planet in the superficial quest for the latest trend. An accessible site which develops such ideas is: http://www.verdant.net/

Use the material to prepare an argument against the idea that 'Class remains the most important influence on society today'.

EXAM PRACTICE

Extract from AQA-style question

Examine the evidence for the idea that, 'life-chances you are born with, lifestyle you choose'. (12 marks)

OCR-style question

Item A

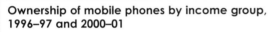

Ownership of mobile phones by income group, 1996–97 and 2000–01

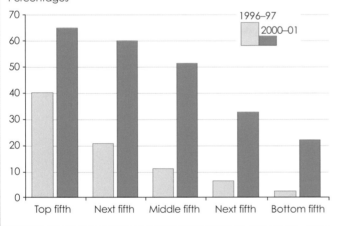

Source: (2002) *Social Trends* 32, p.218, Crown copyright

a   Using only the information in Item A, identify two developments in the use of mobile phones in relation to income group between 1996 and 2001. (6 marks)

b   Using the information in Item B, identify two features of social stratification defined by consumption patterns. (6 marks)

c   Identify and explain two problems facing sociologists attempting to illustrate social stratification using consumption patterns. (12 marks)

Item B

Saunders (1996) argues that differences in consumption and the access that people have to certain goods constitute an independent dimension of social stratification rather than being merely a reflection of class. He calls these differences, or divisions, consumption cleavages. Moreover, Saunders highlights a clear division between the self-sufficient middle mass of consumers and the marginalised and stigmatised minority who are largely dependent on the state, thereby resulting in growing social polarisation. It is the polarization of those who can choose from a range of possible goods to fulfil all their needs, and those whose choices mean going without one necessity in order to buy another that is the major social division in modern Britain. Hence, Saunders argues that it is not class differences but consumption cleavages which form the basis of contemporary political patterns and represent a process of restratification.

Adapted from N. Abercrombie *et al.* (1999) *Contemporary British Society* (3rd edition), Cambridge: Polity Press

d   Using your wider sociological knowledge, outline the evidence for the greater emphasis on consumption in contemporary society. (22 marks)

e   Outline and assess the view that the poor deserve to be poor because of the lifestyle choices that they make. (44 marks)

Getting you thinking

Jane Elliott, a junior school teacher in the USA, began her crusade against racism and discrimination one day after the assassination of Dr Martin Luther King, Jr in 1968. She wanted her students to actually experience racism so she told the blue-eyed students they were smarter, nicer, cleaner and deserved more privileges than the students with brown eyes. The day became a life-changing experience for the children and for Elliott. On the second day of the experiment, Elliott reversed the situation. What she discovered was amazing. Whoever was on top was not only better-behaved, but also more likely to learn. One dyslexic boy even learned how to read for the first time.

Elliott believed that all people are racists, whether they choose to believe it or not.

She was frequently interviewed on TV chat shows as her experiment quickly caught the media's attention. 'I am a racist,' she said. 'If you want to see another racist, turn to the person on your right. Now look at the person on your left.'

Elliott stressed that the world didn't need a colour-blind society, but rather a society that recognises colour. She said people are conditioned to the myth of white superiority. 'Differences are very valuable', she said. 'Start recognising them and appreciating them. They are what make up our world.'

The experiment is commonly used today to raise awareness of discrimination issues with students around the world. The following comments were made by an older group of Dutch students in 1998:

'Today, I have learned what it is to be seen by others as a minority. I did not expect that it would be so humiliating! In the end, I really had the feeling that I was a bit inferior. I was against racism and discrimination already, but now I understand what it really is.'

Karl, 16 years old, brown eyes

'I was one of the blue-eyes today, and I did not find that funny. I felt greatly discriminated against because we (the blue-eyeds) had to shut our mouth and stand still. The brown eyes were treated well. I really understand that people who are discriminated against must feel very angered, like I felt today. It was very much worth it.'

Jardena, 16 years old, blue eyes

'When you feel day by day what I today as a blue-eye felt (especially in the beginning of the day) then your life is rotten… Racism is so very easy to do. Before you realise it happens. As a person, you are powerless, it makes more sense to revolt together.'

Anna, 15 years old, blue eyes

Source: Magenta Foundation (a web-based anti-racist educational organisation based in the Netherlands) © 1999 Amsterdam. www.magenta.nl

1 Why does Jane Elliott believe that all people are racists?

2 Is it racist to treat people differently on the basis of characteristics over which they have no control?

3 Should people have to control their social or cultural characteristics to conform to the requirements of the dominant culture?

4 To what extent can it be argued that it is racist to treat all people in the same way?

Your discussion may have concluded that racism has several dimensions and that it is both racist to treat people negatively on the basis of their perceived physical or cultural differences and, ironically, to ignore such difference. Both aspects can also be seen to operate when examining racism sociologically.

Miles (1989) has argued that a key factor in the positioning of most ethnic minorities at the bottom of the stratification system is racism. This can be seen as a system of beliefs and practices which exclude on the basis of racial or ethnic background. The term 'race' was once used to suggest biological differences between groups but has since been discredited in that sense and abandoned in favour of the term 'ethnicity' or 'ethnic minority'. However, it has re-emerged recently as a useful term for focusing attention on power differences between groups. Ethnicity, meaning cultural grouping, lacks this power dimension. As Kenyatta and Tai, (1999) note:

in abandoning the concept of race, there is a serious tendency to abandon discussions of power, domination, and group conflict … I cannot help but notice in works on ethnicity how quickly the discussion there turns to matters of culture and identity, not at all to questions of economic exploitation, political power, and powerlessness.

Racism

Racism has three key elements.

Cultural attitudes/prejudice

Racism represents a way of thinking that relies heavily on stereotypes which are usually factually incorrect, exaggerated and distorted. These are used to legitimate hostility towards ethnic groups perceived to have negative characteristics.

Prejudice is part of a society's culture and passed from generation to generation through the agencies of socialisation. It is only fairly recently, for example, that children's reading books have begun to reflect ethnic diversity and many offensive racist images are still to be seen. Robertson's Jam for example, only dropped the 'Golly' image from their marketing in 2000, after 90 years.

How might the image of 'Golly' add to racial stereotyping?

How could you conduct research to investigate the extent to which images in children's books reflected a culturally diverse society?

Barker (1982) notes that the New Right, in an attempt to exploit fears about unemployment in the 1980s and 1990s, have focused on the concept of 'cultural differences'. They have suggested that traditional British/English culture is under threat from ethnic minority culture or that ethnic-minorities are not committed to integration. The mass media too, especially tabloid newspapers such as the *Sun* and *Daily Mail*, have tended to portray black people, Muslims and migrants from Eastern Europe as a 'problem' and a threat to the British way of life.

Some of the media coverage of issues related to ethnicity such as asylum-seekers can be termed a 'moral panic'. What does this term mean? Give examples of other situations that might be termed 'moral panics'.

There are many problems with these views:

- They offer an over-simplified view of what traditional English culture is like – for example, warm beer and cricket on village greens.
- They exaggerate the 'strangeness' of other cultures.
- They play down the problem of racism and imply that if the problem does exist, the fault lies with the 'reluctance' of ethnic minorities to adopt a British way of life.

Racial discrimination

This is evident in the discrimination by landlords, building societies and council housing departments that has been well documented. It may take the form of racial attacks – this includes racist name-calling and street violence. The Stephen Lawrence case in 1993, where an 18-year-old black youth died from stab wounds following a racist attack, has brought the enormity of this problem to the British public's attention. This case also highlighted the prejudice of the police officers involved in the enquiry who initially did not take Stephen's injuries seriously enough, did not accept that he was the victim of a racial attack and who mishandled the apprehension of known assailants. At the time of writing, no one has been brought to justice for this crime.

Furthermore many black youths experience police harassment. They are more likely to be stopped and arrested on suspicion than white youth. There is also a body of evidence showing police violence against ethnic minorities and some have suffered injury and even death in police custody.

How can the idea of a stereotype be used to explain accusations that the police are racist?

Institutional racism

Some sociologists argue that racism is a basic feature of the rules and routines of Britain's social institutions such as the police and courts, the immigration service, central and local government, the mass media, the education system, and the employment and housing markets. Racism is taken for granted and is so common that it is not even recognised as racism. For example, chief constables have been accused of being complacent about the amount of racial prejudice among police officers.

Britain's immigration laws are often cited as an example of **institutional racism**. The laws restrict the entry of black people while allowing whiter migrants easier entry. There is also evidence that the laws have been implemented in a racist manner. For example, black visitors are more likely than white visitors to be stopped for questioning by immigration control. Recently both the Home Office and the London Metropolitan Police have admitted that their organisations are institutionally racist (Select Committee on Home Affairs, 1999).

Institutional racism is not conscious nor intentional. That said, it would not be true to say that all members of key institutions are non-racist – they may or may not be. But it is the manner in which some institutions operate that has racist outcomes. Teachers, for example, may be committed to anti-racist education but schools still expel four times as many black pupils as white.

One way of tackling institutional racism is to increase the numbers of ethnic-minority groups working within key institutions, especially in the higher positions. Also, close monitoring of ethnic minority inclusion and exclusion can highlight imbalances which can then be addressed through equal opportunities strategies.

Ethnic minorities and life-chances: empirical evidence

Ethnic minorities are disadvantaged in many areas of social life. However, it is very important to be aware of important differences between the various minorities and the way these inequalities link with gender and class differences (see 'Exploring ethnicity and life-chances' activity opposite).

Explanations of racism and racial inequality

Cultural explanations

Stereotypes associated with cultural racism probably originate in Britain's colonial past. People pick up these stereotypes today in the course of normal socialisation. A great deal of prejudice therefore is the result of faulty stereotypes and a lack of accurate knowledge about the true nature of black people. This is particularly so for those who live outside the inner city where most ethnic-minority groups people reside.

Why are stereotypical views of ethnic minorities more likely outside major cities?

The host–immigrant model
A good example of an early sociological approach that stressed the importance of culture is the host–immigrant model (Patterson, 1965) which shares many of the assumptions of functionalist sociology.

This theory depicted Britain as a basically stable, homogeneous and orderly society with a high degree of consensus over values and norms. This equilibrium was disturbed by the arrival of immigrant 'strangers' who subscribed to different sets of values. Patterson described the

Item A | **Disadvantage and discrimination in Britain today**

Education
● Most Bangladeshi, Pakistani and black pupils achieve less than other pupils at all stages of compulsory education. Black Caribbean children have equal, if not higher, ability than white children on entrance to school. But black Caribbean boys do least well at school.
● African-Caribbean pupils are over four to six times more likely to be excluded than white pupils, although they are no more likely to truant than others. Many of those excluded are of higher and average ability, although the schools see them as underachieving.

Health
● Infant mortality is 100% higher for the children of African-Caribbean or Pakistani mothers than white mothers.
● Pakistani and Bangladeshi people are five times more likely to be diagnosed with diabetes and 50% more likely to have coronary heart diseases than white people.

Housing
● 70% of all people from ethnic minorities live in the 88 most deprived local authority districts compared with 40% of the general population.
● A fifth of the housing occupied by asylum seekers is unfit for human habitation.

Work
● Unemployment is considerably higher among ethnic-minority communities. In 1998, 5.8% of white people of working age were unemployed on average, but among people from ethnic minorities it was more than double that at 13%. It was 20% for Pakistani people and 23% for Bangladeshi people.
● An African-Caribbean graduate is more than twice as likely to be unemployed as a white person with A-levels. African men with degrees are seven times more likely to be unemployed than white male graduates.

Adapted from: (2002) *Disadvantage and Discrimination in Britain Today – The Facts*, Commission for Racial Equality

1 How does the information in Item A illustrate the importance of taking into account gender and class as well as race in explaining inequality? Give examples.

2 Select two of the above points that might be the result of institutional racism. Explain why you think this might be the case.

culture clash between West Indians (boisterous and noisy, and not in the habit of queuing at bus stops!) and the English hosts (who valued privacy, quiet and 'keeping oneself to oneself'). The host–immigrant model interpreted these clashes in terms of understandable fears and anxieties on the part of the host community. The hosts were not actually racist, just very unsure about how to act towards the newcomers. Their confusion sometimes spilled over into suspicion and resentment because the migrants competed with hosts for jobs and houses. But for Patterson the main problem was not so much racism or black-white hostility but cultural 'strangeness'. She was reasonably optimistic about the long-term prospects for racial harmony. She thought Britain's black migrants would eventually move toward full cultural assimilation by shedding their 'old' ethnic values and taking on the values of the host society.

Explain how the 'host-immigrant' model reflects some of the main themes of functionalist sociology.

Criticisms

- The host–immigrant model focuses so much on culture that it tends to end up 'blaming the victim' or scapegoating them by attributing the difficulties of ethnic groups to their 'strange' cultures.
- Racial hostility has not declined as predicted by Patterson. The basic structure of British society remains unchanged and the struggle over jobs, housing and money continues. This may create racial tension.
- Patterson underestimated the persistence and vitality of ethnic-minority cultures.

Today the goal of 'assimilation' has largely been abandoned by policymakers. Instead 'cultural pluralism' (where ethnic minorities retain their own cultures while adjusting to a society which accepts cultural diversity) is the norm.

Weberian explanations

Give examples of the contribution of Weber to other areas of your studies.

Explanations based on the thinking of Max Weber (1864–1920) fall into three categories.

Status inequality

There is not only a class struggle for status, income and wealth but there is also an ethnic struggle. However, status and power is in the hands of the majority ethnic group, thereby making it difficult for ethnic-minority groups to compete equally for jobs, housing, etc. Ethnic minorities who do manual jobs are technically part of the working class but are likely to face prejudice and discrimination from the white working-class because they suffer from status inequality in addition to class inequality. Even middle-class Asians doing professional jobs may experience status inequality in the form of prejudicial attitudes held by members of both the white middle- and working-classes.

Organisation of the job market

Such prejudice and discrimination can be seen in the distribution of ethnic minorities in the labour force. The '**dual labour-market**' theory focuses on ethnic inequalities as

well as gender inequalities in employment. There are two markets for labour – the primary sector characterised by secure, well-paid jobs with long-term promotion prospects dominated by white men, and the secondary sector consisting of low-paid, unskilled and insecure jobs. Barren and Norris (1976) point out that women and black people are more likely to be found in the secondary sector. They are less likely to gain primary-sector employment because employers may subscribe to racist beliefs about the unsuitability of black people – and even practise discrimination against them either when applying for jobs or by denying them responsibility and promotion. Furthermore, the legal and political framework supporting black people is weak. Trade unions are generally white-dominated and have been accused of favouring white workers and being less interested in protecting the rights of black workers. The Race Relations Act 1976 (which is supposed to protect black people from discriminatory practices) is generally thought to be feeble.

Underclass

Rex and Tomlinson (1979) argue that ethnic minority experience of both class and status inequality can lead to poverty, which is made more severe by racism. Consequently, a black underclass may be created which is marginalised and feels alienated and frustrated. Sometimes these feelings may erupt in the form of inner-city riots if young blacks feel they are being harassed by the police and socially excluded.

Explain how Rex and Tomlinson's view of the underclass is more sympathetic towards those in it than the view of the New Right.

In criticism, there is considerable overlap between the white and black population in terms of poverty and unemployment but the constant threat of racism does suggest some sort of break with the interests of the white working-class. In addition, the concept of status inequality does help to explain the apparent divisions between the white and black working-class.

Marxist explanations

Marxists argue that black people are part of the exploited working class and it is this, rather than any lack of status due to ethnicity, that determines their fate in capitalist society. Racial conflicts are usually the symptoms of some deeper underlying class problem.

Marxists suggest that racism and racial inequality are deliberately encouraged by the capitalist class for three ideological reasons.

- **Legitimisation**
  Racism helps justify low pay and poor working conditions because black workers are seen as second-class citizens. Capitalist employers benefit from the cheap labour of ethnic minorities.

- **Divide-and-rule**
  If black and white workers unite then they are in a stronger position to campaign for better wages and conditions. But Marxists such as Castles and Kosack (1973) argue that employers prefer them to be divided by racism so they can played off against one another.

Employers may use the black workforce as a '**reserve army of labour**' to prevent white workers from demanding higher wages.

● **Scapegoating**

When a society is troubled by severe social and economic problems then widespread frustration and aggression can arise. Instead of directing this anger at the capitalist class, whites are sometimes tempted to pick on relatively vulnerable groups. They use black people as scapegoats and it may be blacks who are blamed for unemployment and housing shortages. Scapegoating is in the interests of the richer and more powerful groups because it protects them from direct criticism and reduces pressures for radical change.

Miles (1989) argues that the class position of black people is complicated by the fact that they are treated as socially and culturally different. They become the victims of racist ideologies which prevent their full social inclusion. Miles argues that ethnic minorities are members of '**racialised class fractions**'. Whilst most black people are members of the working-class, they also recognise the importance of their ethnicity. Whilst members of the white working class may stress the importance of ethnicity through prejudice and discrimination, black people may react by stressing their ethnicity in actions such as campaigning for recognition of their need to observe particular religious or cultural traditions.

Miles acknowledges that some ethnic minorities may become part of the middle classes and see their interests lying with capitalism. Furthermore, their ethnicity may be a crucial influence in their business practices and financial success. However, the fact of their ethnicity probably makes it impossible for them to be fully accepted by the white middle class.

Recent approaches

It would be a mistake to think that all black people 'lose out'. Owen and Green (1992) cite Indians and Chinese as two ethnic groups that have made significant economic progress in the British labour market in the 1980s. More generally, evidence suggests that increasing numbers from the minorities are entering the ranks of the professional middle class. Sociologists are also starting to notice the growth of 'black businesses' and the spread of self-employment among minority groups. Even though groups such as Indians are moving into white-collar work, it is quite possible that whites fill the higher status positions within this sector.

However, some sociologists have questioned whether self-employment is really a privileged sector of the economy. Minorities may be forced into setting up their own businesses because racial discrimination prevents them from getting employment. Sometimes these businesses are precarious ventures in extremely competitive markets, offering small returns for long hours and with the owners only managing to survive because they are able to draw upon cheap family labour.

Postmodernist approaches

Postmodernists such as Modood (1992) reject the notions of Weberian and Marxist sociology which seek to generalise and seek blanket explanations for ethnic groups as a whole. They stress difference and diversity among ethnic groups and focus on identity. They argue that the globalisation of culture has led to national cultural identities being eroded. British culture is not immune and all ethnicities, including white, have begun to 'pick and mix', producing an array of new **hybrid identities**. Racial difference becomes a matter of choice and racial disadvantage is impossible to discuss as ethnic identity is not fixed.

The extent and impact of racism will differ from person to person as identities are chosen and interact. Postmodernists argue that once identity is better understood, targeted ethnic disadvantage can be addressed. Once we know that Jamaican boys not born in Britain in a particular area are more likely to drop out of school, for example, then something meaningful could be done to address this problem.

While postmodern ideas are illuminating, they can be accused of neglecting social and economic factors that impact on life-chances.

KEY TERMS

Cultural attitudes/prejudice – a style of thinking that relies heavily on stereotypes which are usually factually incorrect, exaggerated and distorted.

Dual labour-market theory – the view that two labour markets exist: the first has secure, well paid jobs with good promotion prospects and the second jobs with little security and low pay. Vulnerable groups such as women, the young, elderly and ethnic minorities are concentrated in this second sector.

Ethnicity – cultural heritage shared by members of a particular group.

Hybrid identities – new identities created by ethnic mixing.

Institutional racism – where the sum total of an organisation's way of operating has racist outcomes.

Race – variation of physical appearance, skin colour and so on between populations which confers differences in power and status.

Racialised class fractions – term used by Miles to describe splits in the working class along racial lines.

Racism – systematic exclusion of races or ethnic groups from full participation in society.

Reserve army of labour – Marxist concept used to describe an easily exploitable pool of workers drawn from vulnerable groups such as women, ethnic minorities and the old and young.

Extract from AQA-style question

Evaluate the usefulness of the theory of an underclass as an explanation of the social position of ethnic minorities in Britain today. (40 marks)

OCR-style question

Item A

November 2001 saw the 25th anniversary of the Race Relations Act of 1976. It set up tribunals to hear cases of discrimination at work. This discrimination may take a variety of forms: from verbal abuse, intimidatory behaviour and harassment, blocked career development, refusal of a job, differences in pay or conditions. Essentially, as is the case in most institutions, members of ethnic minority groups are treated unfairly in the workplace. Since their introduction, these tribunals have seen a steady increase in the number of cases heard, with 1,365 cases in 1995.

Does this mean, however, that the Act is more successful? Are more people feeling confident that their cases will be heard and that discrimination in the workplace will be tackled? Or, does it mean that more people are being discriminated against?

Proving discrimination at work is notoriously difficult. A very small minority of claims are actually successful. A lot are withdrawn along the way through insufficient evidence that would stand up in court. A few are settled out of court. Of the 1,365 cases in 1995 only 72 were successful in proving racial discrimination in the workplace had occurred.

Adapted from: M. Denscombe (1998) *Sociology Update*, Leicester: Olympus Books

Item B

Race discrimination cases

Source: Labour Research 1996

a Using only the information in Item A, identify two features of racial discrimination in the workplace. (6 marks)

b Identify two possible reasons for the patterns shown by the data in Item B. (6 marks)

c Identify and explain two problems facing sociologists trying to research racial discrimination in the workplace. (12 marks)

d Using your wider sociological knowledge outline the evidence for the view that 'Essentially, as is the case in most institutions, members of ethnic minority groups are treated unfairly in the workplace' (Item A line 8). (22 marks)

e Outline and assess sociological explanations of inequalities experienced by ethnic minorities in contemporary Britain. (44 marks)

335

CHECK YOUR UNDERSTANDING

1 How can it be argued that the term 'race' has more explanatory value than the term 'ethnicity'?

2 Where does racial prejudice come from? Give examples to back up your arguments.

3 Explain why members of organisations deemed 'institutionally racist' may not necessarily be racist individuals.

4 How can institutional racism be tackled?

5 What is wrong with early functionalist explanations of ethnic inequality?

6 Briefly summarise three Weberian accounts of ethnic inequality in the workplace.

7 How do Marxists argue that racism benefits capitalism?

8 Why do postmodernists reject Weberian and Marxist explanations of ethnic inequality?

Research ideas

1 Undertake a piece of research to discover how knowledgeable local people are about ethnic differences. Do people understand the distinctions between the various Asian groups? Do they understand the significance of particular festivals? Do they know of prophets or holy books? Can they point on a world map outline to the countries of origin of the various groups?

2 Assess the extent to which an organisation such as your school or college might be deemed to be institutionally racist. Look at the distribution of ethnic groups on the various courses. Try to acquire statistics on exclusions, achievement rates and progression. What problems might you encounter? How do you propose to overcome them?

WWWebtask

Go to the guardianunlimited website http://www.guardianunlimited.co.uk. Search the archive by typing in 'race equality'. Read the articles highlighting a range of issues from institutional racism, social policy reform to rural racism and racial harassment. Be sure to look at the article 'Promoting race equality should be the norm' by Naaz Coker (February 22, 2001).

Item A

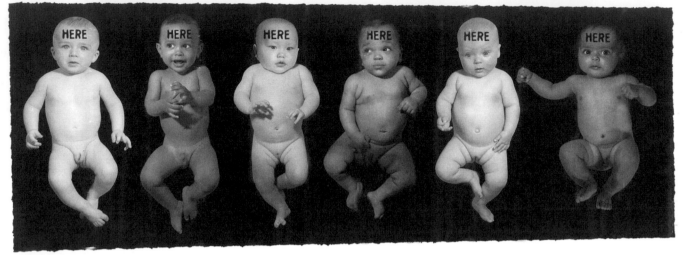

THERE ARE LOTS OF PLACES IN BRITAIN WHERE RACISM DOESN'T EXIST.

1 What point is the poster in Item A making?

2 What social institutions does it imply might be important in reducing racism? Explain your answer.

Item B

English tests for immigrants

Immigrants will have to pass English tests before being given British citizenship under proposals to be unveiled by the government today.

David Blunkett, the Home Secretary, believes that the new rules will help foreigners form closer bonds with their new society.

Immigrants would have to pass tests in written and spoken English and a paper on British customs before being given a passport. They would swear an oath of allegiance to the Queen and promise to respect and uphold British rights, freedoms, values and laws.

Daily Telegraph, February 7, 2000

3 How do the ideas above in Item B reflect the 'host immigrant' model?

4 What are the arguments for and against the government plans? To what extent do you agree with the Home Secretary's ideas?

Item C   Racial incidents (England and Wales 1991)

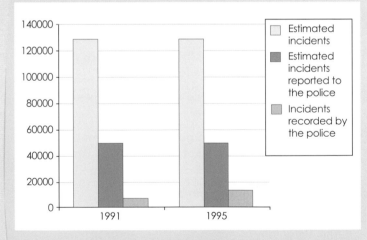

Source: *Home Office Research Findings No. 39*, August 1996

5 Look at Item C. In the light of public awareness of race issues and the police:

a   Why might recorded incidents have gone up?

b   Why might reported incidents have gone down?

Item D — European Anti-Racist Initiative Report

Over recent years, the United Kingdom has taken positive steps to counter racism and discrimination, including: the amendment of the anti-discrimination legislation to cover direct and indirect discrimination by public authorities in all functions and to include an enforceable duty on public authorities to promote racial equality; the strengthening of the battery of criminal law provisions to fight against racist behaviour; the elaboration of a strategy to counter institutional racism in the police in response to the Stephen Lawrence Inquiry Report. Problems of xenophobia, racism and discrimination, however, persist and are particularly acute vis-à-vis asylum seekers and refugees. This is reflected in the xenophobic and intolerant coverage of these groups of persons in the media, but also in the tone of the discourse resorted to by politicians in support of the adoption and enforcement of increasingly restrictive asylum and immigration laws. Racial prejudice in the police continues to constitute an element of concern. Criminal and civil law provisions are not always effective in countering racist, xenophobic or discriminatory behaviour. In their report, ECRI recommends to the British authorities that further action be taken to combat xenophobia, racism and discrimination in a number of areas. These recommendations cover:

- the need to address the hostile climate concerning asylum seekers and refugees
- the need to ensure the effectiveness of criminal law provisions, notably on incitement to racial hatred, and the need to further fine-tune the working of the civil anti-discrimination legislation is also stressed
- ECRI also calls for a swift and thorough application of all policies to address institutional racism in the police. Emphasis is also put on the need to ensure that the educational system meet the demands of a diverse society.

Source: European Commission Anti-Racist Initiative: *Second Report on the UK* 1999

6 a Study Item D. What progress is said to have been made towards eradicating institutional racism?

  b What more still needs to be done?

7 What difficulties might arise in monitoring the effectiveness of the proposals of the ECRI report?

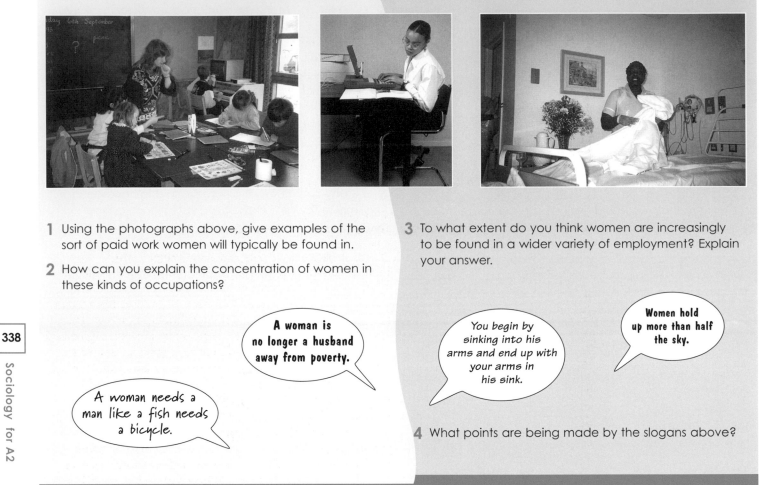

Getting you thinking

1 Using the photographs above, give examples of the sort of paid work women will typically be found in.

2 How can you explain the concentration of women in these kinds of occupations?

3 To what extent do you think women are increasingly to be found in a wider variety of employment? Explain your answer.

> A woman needs a man like a fish needs a bicycle.

> A woman is no longer a husband away from poverty.

> You begin by sinking into his arms and end up with your arms in his sink.

> Women hold up more than half the sky.

4 What points are being made by the slogans above?

You will probably have discussed that the situation for women is far from fair and that they suffer inequality both in the home and the workplace, whether they are married, have children or not. This Topic examines the extent of gender inequality in the UK and examines explanations of why this is the case.

Patterns of inequality

In the past 30 years the number of female workers in the UK rose by 2.45 million whereas the number of males rose by only 0.5 million. The major area of growth in female employment in Western Europe has been in activity among women aged 24–49 – that is, women of child-bearing age. Interestingly having children seems to have less effect on employment than getting married. In 1991, 84% of single childless women in this age group were economically active across the European Union compared with 67% of married childless women in the same age-range.

Employment in the UK 2000 (millions)

	Men	Women
Employment	15.4 (55.2%)	12.5 (44.8%)
made up of:		
Self-employed	2.35 (73%)	0.85 (27%)
Part-time workers	1.4 (20%)	5.5 (80%)
Unemployed	1.04 (61%)	0.66 (39%)

Adapted from: (2000) *Labour Market Statistics*, DfEE London: HMSO

Suggest explanations for gender differences in part-time work and self-employment.

Although the numbers of males and females in employment have been evening out, there are still significant differences in the distribution of male and female workers throughout the occupational structure. Sociologists have noted that the labour market is segregated in two ways.

- **Horizontal segregation**: men and women work in different types of jobs in different sectors of the economy.
- **Vertical segregation**: women occupy the lower levels of pay and status in particular jobs.

Horizontal segregation

A survey by the Equal Opportunities Commission (EOC) in 1996 concluded that women in the public sector were mainly employed in health and education, especially teaching. For example, nursing and primary-school teaching is almost exclusively female all across Europe – about 65% in most countries but as high as 80% in Italy and Portugal. Secondary-school teaching, on the other hand, is shared about equally between men and women whereas higher education is a male preserve with only about 25% of jobs filled by women in this sector. In the private sector women are over-concentrated in clerical, administrative, retail and personal services such as catering whereas men are mainly found in the skilled manual and upper professional sectors.

There is some evidence that horizontal segregation may be in decline because of the general decline in traditionally male sectors. Recent trends in female educational success may further assist the breakdown of this type of segregation. There is also some evidence that men may be moving into traditionally female areas such as nursing and primary-school teaching. This may have negative implications for women in terms of vertical segregation. In 1988, a survey found that while 50% of male primary teachers were head teachers, the equivalent figure for females was 15%.

Vertical segregation

Skill and status

Within each occupational layer, women tend to be concentrated at the lower levels. Even when women have gained access to the upper professional or management sector, they are likely to encounter a '**glass ceiling**' – they can climb the ladder so far but then reach a barrier whereby they can see where they want to go but cannot climb any further. For example, at the end of the twentieth century women constituted only 18% of hospital consultants, 7% of university professors and less than 5% of company directors.

How could sociologists conduct research to investigate the existence of a 'glass ceiling'?

Pay

In 1998 the EOC noted that, in their early twenties, women earn 92% of the male wage. The average gross weekly pay of all women is only 72.5% of men's earnings (84% for full-time working women and 58% for part-time). The EOC conclude that 'Throughout their working lives women earn significantly less than men, whether they are lawyers or sales assistants. At the present rate of change, women will have to wait until the year 2040 to achieve equality in pay.' (EOC, 1999).

Work situation

Women are more likely than men to be employed in part-time work. In 2000 44% of female employees worked part-time compared with only 8% of males. McDowell (1992) argues that the changes brought about by post-Fordism require a core of multi-skilled workers on the one hand and part-time ancillary workers on short-term or part-time contracts on the other. Women mostly make up the latter, with few making it into the core. The majority have part-time temporary work imposed on them for want of alternatives whilst continuing to seek full-time secure employment. The high demand for work (any work) has enabled employers to reduce part-time pay rates which, calculated as a percentage of full time pay, fell from 81% in 1980 to 75% by the end of the decade.

Statistics indicate that male unemployment is higher than female. What problems are involved in collecting accurate official statistics on gender and unemployment? How might the figures exclude some women?

What about men?

Whilst men generally enjoy a greater range of work opportunities, more status and more pay, there is evidence of change in the experience of work for some men. This change is caused by economic recession and unemployment in traditional industries and manufacturing. Some writers suggest that this has led to the development of a marginalised masculinity, causing frustration in men at being unable to fulfill their traditional role as breadwinner and protector. This is exacerbated by the fact that women are more successful at getting the jobs that have replaced manufacturing such as those in the new service sector. In so doing, they are felt to be taking over from men as breadwinners. This is, in turn, threatening marital stability and may be responsible for causing higher divorce rates in such areas. As Mac An Ghaill (1996) has argued, there is a general crisis in masculinity.

Willott and Griffin (1996) have explored this so-called 'crisis'. They researched a group of long-term unemployed men in the West Midlands. Their respondents typified the kinds of men most likely to be marginalised, having little hope of finding steady employment. Whilst their role as provider was undermined, their other masculine characteristics (in particular their sense of authority over their families) remained. Willot and Griffin concluded that rather than there being a crisis of masculinity, as a whole, there was merely a weakening of certain elements of traditional masculinity.

Sociological explanations of gender stratification at work

'Dual labour-market' theory

Barron and Norris (1976) argue that women are more likely to be found in the disadvantaged secondary sector for a number of reasons.

Women's 'unsuitability'

Employers subscribe to stereotypical beliefs about the unsuitability of women for primary sector roles. West and Zimmerman (1991) and Hartnett (1990) note that there are still powerful cultural myths subscribed to by employers in the 1990s, as follows:

- Workers do not like working for a female manager (making them less eligible for promotion to management positions).
- Women are less dependable (and so cannot be trusted to fulfil delegated tasks).
- Women are financially dependent on men (and so need pay rises/promotion less).
- Women will stop work when they marry and have children (and so there is little point investing in their long-term training).
- Working mothers cause their children damage (so for the children's sake women should stay at home – and should not be given management jobs since these can require long or unsociable hours).

Disrupted career development

Jobs with good promotion prospects often recruit people young and require from them several years of continuous service. Few mechanisms exist to enable staff to take time out and return to a similar position. Social pressure to have a family leads to some women finding that child-rearing, even for a couple of years, can mean going back to square one of their career. Caplow (1954) argues that the husband's career may even dictate the geographical movement of the family and wives are sometimes forced to leave their jobs as a consequence, affecting their chances of a continuous career.

Weak legal and political framework supporting women

Both the Equal Pay and Sex Discrimination Acts are ineffective in failing to protect women's employment rights. Coussins (1976) describes the Sex Discrimination Act as 'feeble' as there are many areas of employment to which it does not apply. Further, she doubts the commitment of governments to eliminate gender inequality. There is limited access to nursery care and little support for employers to provide crèche facilities. Recent changes in the legal position of part-time workers have, however, benefited women considerably and some attempt has been made to recognise that men, too, have some responsibility for child-rearing, with the introduction of recent legislation to allow unpaid leave for either partners.

Why might legislation have only a very limited effect in changing the position of women in society?

Evaluation of dual labour-market theory

Dual labour-market theory has two strengths as an explanation of vertical segregation:

- It stresses that the social organisation of work in Western societies is essentially patriarchal with men in the positions of power-making discrimination against women and their lower status appear 'natural'.

- It undermines the popular assumption that better qualifications and increased ambition for women would automatically dismantle gender divisions in employment. Women with the same qualifications as men will continue to be disadvantaged as long as these two sectors are allowed to exist and are underpinned with patriarchal assumptions about the role of women.

However, Bradley (1997) points out that the theory fails to explain inequalities in the same sector. For example, teaching is not a secondary labour-market occupation, yet women are less likely than men to gain high-status jobs in this profession. Whilst 70% of teachers are female, only 35% of senior jobs in teaching are held by women.

Feminism

Liberal feminism

Liberal feminists argue that gender-role socialisation is responsible for reproducing a sexual division of labour in which masculinity is largely seen as dominant and femininity as subordinate.

How does each agency of socialisation reproduce traditional gender roles? Give examples from areas of the subject you have studied.

Ann Oakley (1974) argues that the main reason for the subordination of women in the labour market has been the dominance of the mother–housewife role for women. She argues that ideas such as the maternal instinct have justified male dominance. The fact that female professional workers are three times more likely not to be married than their male counterparts also supports the view that the wife's role is primarily domestic.

In the 1990s, liberal feminists suggested that these processes were coming to an end. Sue Sharpe's work on the attitudes of teenage girls (1994) suggests that education and careers are now a priority for young women, whilst females have also enjoyed great educational success in recent years. Liberal feminists have an optimistic view of the future for women. Both partners will, they suggest, accept equal responsibility for domestic work and child-rearing, and dual-career families where both partners enjoy equal economic status will become the norm. Legislators are also beginning to recognise male responsibility for childcare with the recent increases in paternity rights.

Liberal feminism has been subject to some criticisms.

- Although there is evidence that masculinity and femininity are socially constructed, it does not explain why this leads to men dominating and women being oppressed.
- It also implies that people passively accept their gender identities, underestimating the degree to which women may resist.
- It fails to acknowledge that women's experiences differ according to social class and race.
- In seeing gender equality as simply a matter of time, real obstacles to progress are being overlooked. During World War II when women were required to work in munitions factories, for example, free crèche places were made avail-

Item A

Occupations by hourly pay, 2000

Occupation	Hourly pay (£)	% female
Electrical/electronic trades	9.59	*
Metal machining, fitting and instrument making	9.21	2
Construction trades	7.58	*
Vehicle trades	7.56	*
Clerical and secretarial	7.30	74
Health and related	6.02	88
Childcare and related	5.82	97
Sales assistants/checkout operators	5.50	74
Catering	5.50	62
Hairdresser/beauticians	5.23	90

Note: * denotes less than 10,000. Hourly pay is the average for all full-time employees.

Source: NES 2000 Table A. 12, LFS Spring 2000

1 Summarise the pattern in the table.

2 Does the data illustrate the process of horizontal or vertical segregation? Explain your answer.

341

able. Over half a century later, only a small percentage of workplaces provide this facility.

Marxist feminism

Women's subordination within the labour market is seen by Marxist feminists as suiting the needs of capitalism. Women form a classic example of a 'reserve army of labour', drawn upon by prosperous firms in times of rapid expansion and disposed of when recession sets in. Women constitute a more disposable part of the workforce for a number of reasons.

- They change jobs more frequently than men so they are more vulnerable at times of redundancy.
- They are generally less skilled, relatively under-unionised and often part-time. Consequently it is easier for employers to sack them.
- Capitalist ideologies locate women in the home. The idea that married women have less right to a job than men is common among management, unions and women themselves. Therefore when women are made unemployed

such ideology suggests 'women have gone back to their proper jobs'.

The reserve army of labour theory has been criticised because it does not explain why male and female labour is put to different uses. In other words, it fails to explain why there are men's jobs and women's jobs. It fails to explain why women occupy the mother–housewife role.

Margaret Benston (1972) focused on domestic labour and its role in maintaining capitalist society. The male wage, in fact, pays for two people as the women works for free to create a new labour force. The housewife also provides emotional support for her husband, rejuvenating him sufficiently to enable him to return for the next day's alienated labour. According to Ansley (quoted in Bernard, 1976), she may even soak up his frustration and alienation in the form of domestic violence.

Marxist feminism can be criticised for overlooking the fact that patriarchy can be as influential in its own right – the implication being that once capitalism is abolished gender inequality will disappear.

What other criticisms have been made of the Marxist perspective?

Radical feminism

According to radical feminists, oppressive and unequal relationships between men and women originate not in the wider society but in the intimacy of personal relationships, in sexual partnerships and in families and households of various kinds. Personal relationships are also 'political' in that they are based upon different and unequal amounts of power which are determined by sex and which are reinforced by every aspect of the wider society. Culture, government, tradition, religion, law, education and the media all reflect patriarchal leadership and power.

Take any one of the above list and explain how it can be seen to reflect patriarchy.

Radical feminists focus on the power relationships that are experienced in private – in particular, the significance of sexuality and the use of violence. Patriarchal definitions of women's sexuality are used to control women for the benefit of men. Women are told how to look, dress and behave. When patriarchal ideology fails then women are constantly under the threat of male violence and sexual aggression which limits their capacity to live as free and independent beings.

Radical feminism has been criticised for failing to acknowledge historical change or to take account of divisions between women based on class or ethnicity.

Black feminists have been critical of the **ethnocentricity** of most feminist approaches which have assumed that all women experience partriarchy in the same way. Black feminists have been among the first to point out how different forms of inequality brought about by different oppressions actually intersect. Bhavani (2000) puts the following question: 'When comparing racism to sexism, which is more fundamental?' In her view, the question is unanswerable. It is like asking which number in a multiplication is more important in terms of the answer. Racism and sexism inform each other and both are, in turn, affected by class.

Walby: triple systems theory

Sylvia Walby's 'triple systems theory' (1990) develops the concept of patriarchy to explain gender stratification more fully. She suggests that patriarchy has three elements to it:

- *subordination* – patriarchal institutions like the family, media and education inevitably produce unequal relations between men and women
- *oppression* – women experience sexism because men discriminate against them on the basis of unfounded stereotypes or ideology
- *exploitation* – men exploit women's skills and labour without rewarding them sufficiently.

Walby argues that patriarchy is not only about the interaction of men and women in these three respects but it also intersects with capitalism and racism to produce gender stratification.

Such inequality can be seen in six patriarchal social structures:

- the domestic mode of production where female labour is exploited in the family
- the area of paid work where women experience vertical and horizontal segregation
- the state acts in the interests of men rather than women in terms of taxation and welfare rules, the weakness of laws protecting women at work, and so on
- cultural institutions such as the mass media represent women in narrow social roles such as sex objects and mother–housewives
- in sexuality there is a double standard which values multiple sexual partners for men but condemns the same behaviour in women
- violence against women in the form of sexual assault and domestic violence.

Walby does acknowledge that inequalities between men and women vary over time and in intensity. For example, young women are now achieving better educational qualifications than men. The intensity of patriarchy has to some extent lessened. Nevertheless, women remain disadvantaged. In her recent book *Gender Transformations* (1997) Walby reviews progress made since the 1980s. She notes continuing disparities, particularly for groups of women such as single parents. She also notes that the most powerful positions in all aspects of society continue to be held by men. She concludes that patriarchy continues to exist but that different **gender regimes** affect groups of women differently.

Rational choice theory

Catherine Hakim (1996) is extremely critical of all the previous feminist positions. She argues that feminist theories of patriarchy are both inaccurate and misleading. Women are not victims of unfair employment practices, rather they actively choose part-time work in order to manage childcare and housework which they choose to take primary responsibility for. Moreover, she argues that a lack of available and affordable childcare is not a major barrier to women getting jobs because mothers prioritise child-rearing over employment. In other words, women are not as committed to careers as men and prefer to be supported by someone else while they are doing it – either a husband or the state.

Hakim's work has provoked its own criticism. For example, Ginn *et al.* (1996) point out that all too often it is employer attitudes rather than women's work orientation that confine women to the secondary labour market or the home. Hakim is accused of 'blaming the victim' rather than the structural factors which cause gender inequality. In any case not all women get married and have children yet they still face disadvantages in the workplace.

What other term is used to describe 'blaming the victim'? Give an example of another situation where this idea has been used.

New feminisms
Postfeminism

Postfeminism has two strands:

- The first asserts that feminism is no longer necessary as women have largely won equality and, in any case, went too far in criticising men, the family and femininity. Faludi (1992) sees this first strand of postfeminism (which is not pro feminist) as a male-inspired **backlash**. She highlights how politicians, business leaders and advertisers among others have, on the one hand, recognised women's equality, whilst on the other highlight its cost to women. Magazines in the USA for example claim that professional women are prone to alcoholism, hair loss and infertility whilst women without children suffer more hysteria and depression.

- The second strand abandons the feminist grand theories to adopt a more postmodern position. Brooks (1997) argues that there needs to be a shift from the old debates about equality to debates about difference. Postfeminists (i.e. postmodern feminists) consider that terms like 'patriarchy' and 'women' overgeneralise and ignore the different influences of male ideology in different contexts and among different groups and that all women do not experience oppression in the same way. They consider there to be a range of masculinities and femininities and attack the idea that some characteristics should be preferred over others.

Power feminism

This development advocates a more proactive celebration of women's new found powers and opportunities. Paglia (1992) suggests that instead of adopting a victim mentality, women should confidently assert themselves and enjoy their feminine qualities. In other words, rather than attempt to emulate men, women should become equal but different. The idea of 'girl power' (whether media hype or not) is a recognition of this brand of feminism.

Equality feminism

Natasha Walter (1998) believes that feminism has much the same quest for equality as it always had. However, Walter feels that although most women are aware of this and want equality, they are reluctant to call themselves feminists. In her view they associate this with the negative stereotype of the man-hating miserable women common in the 1970s. They are especially turned off by the slogan 'the personal is political'. Their will and commitment to continuing the fight for equality however makes them worthy of the tag 'new feminism' or 'equality feminism' and Walter is particularly optimistic that they will succeed.

Liberation feminism

Germaine Greer (1999), a major influence on the 1970s Women's Liberation movement, agrees that feminism is still necessary but now takes issue with the quest for equality. Who wants to be equal under patriarchy or equal to men, who in their different ways can suffer oppression of different kinds through their class, race, sexuality and even gender? (for example, when they lose out in custody cases through being automatically seen as the second parent). Greer argues that women should aim for liberation rather than mere equality. Making men and women equal degrades women's (and men's) special qualities and roles, particularly as mothers and carers. The danger of Greer's approach is that differences may come to be used to deny women the same opportunities and freedoms as men. However, if each generation devises their own agenda based upon what they feel is important, wholesale exclusion is less likely and women may achieve the liberation they personally need in order to achieve fulfilment in life.

KEY TERMS

Backlash – term used to describe the reaction against feminism in the 1980s.

Dual labour-market theory – see Key Terms in Topic 7.

Ethnocentricity – the view that your own culture is 'normal' and all others 'abnormal'.

Gender regimes – term used by Walby to illustrate how patriarchy continues to exist but affects different groups of women in different ways.

Glass ceiling – invisible barrier preventing women from gaining high-status positions in employment.

Horizontal segregation – gender division in the workplace whereby men and women work in different jobs in different occupational sectors.

Postfeminism – recent views on gender influenced by postmodernism.

Vertical segregation – gender division in the workplace whereby women occupy the lower levels of pay and status in particular jobs.

CHECK YOUR UNDERSTANDING ✓ ✓ ✓ ✓

1 Explain the difference between horizontal and vertical segregation in your own words.

2 What is the 'glass ceiling'?

3 How it can be argued that changing job opportunities are threatening some marriages?

4 How can dual labour-market theory be used to explain vertical segregation?

5 How does Walby use the concept of patriarchy to explain gender stratification?

6 Explain why Hakim's work has been criticised by some feminists.

7 What does Faludi mean by the 'backlash'?

8 Compare 'power feminism' and 'equality feminism'.

9 Why does Greer argue that equality between men and women is not enough?

Item A

THE PERSONAL IS POLITICAL!

NO REVOLUTION WITHOUT WOMEN'S LIBERATION!

BAN SEX DISCRIMINATION NOW!

Item B   Girl power?

1 Read the slogans in Item A. Identify which is characteristic of:

a Liberal feminism
b Marxist feminism
c Radical feminism

Explain your answers.

2 To what extent do you agree that artists such as Madonna are a positive force for feminism? Explain your answer with reference to feminism and postfeminism.

Research ideas

1 Try to get hold of a staff list from your school or college. Find out which of the staff are in which positions. To what extent does the institution you are studying in reflect vertical segregation?

2 Interview a sample of younger and older women about feminism. What meaning do they give to feminism? To what extent do their views reflect different types of feminism?

WWWebtask

● Find out the range of feminist views on a series of different issues by exploring the site: www.feminism.com

● Find the latest statistics on the position of men and women in British society at the website of the Equal Opportunities Commission.

EXAM PRACTICE

Extract from AQA-style question

Assess the evidence for and against theories that argue gender rather than class is the most important social division in modern industrial societies. (40 marks)

Extract from OCR-style question

a Using your wider sociological knowledge, outline the evidence that shows how women are disadvantaged in any one area of social life apart from the workplace. (22 marks)

b Outline and assess at least one sociological explanation of why women are disadvantaged in the contemporary UK. (44 marks)

Getting you thinking

The elders in tribal societies

Many tribal societies accord the greatest status and power to male elders, e.g. the Tiwi Aborigines of northern Australia. Such societies are known as **gerontocracies**. Others such as the Beaver tribe of North West Canada perceive their elders to be wiser and to possess valuable experience. The status of a male person in tribal society is primarily dependent upon his age because, when young, a male person does not have

enough strength and does not have real skills to combat anything effectively. After gaining strength and skills, a boy becomes a man after a ceremony of initiation. After the initiation, he becomes a Warrior. They are ready to initiate combat at the request of the elders. After becoming too old to do actual combat, a Warrior becomes an elder. The main duties of the elders are promotion and continuance of the personal, economic and spiritual well-being of the entire people under their authority. Primarily, the elders do this through religious rituals. Two factors make the elders the ideal persons for this specific role. Firstly, they are regarded with admiration and dignity by the people, to the extent that they respect them as much as their fathers. Second, the elders are closer to their death than everyone else. Their age and status therefore make them closer to the tribe's ancestors and the people regard their actions as if sanctioned by their ancestors.

L. Mair, (1977) *Primitive Government*, Bloomington: Indiana University Press.

- In 1997–8, 71% of pensioner households depended on state benefits for at least 50% of their income.
- In 1998–9, of pensioners mainly dependent on state pensions and living alone:
  - 81% had central heating, compared to 89% of all households
  - 13% had a car, compared to 72% of all households
  - 91% had a telephone, compared to 95% of all households.

Source: Age Concern Scotland (2001) Fact Card, CAD

Elderly people in industrial societies

Industrialisation pushes living standards upwards and advances medical technology, which, in turn, increases life expectancy. But these same forces simultaneously erode the power and prestige of the elderly. In part, this decline reflects a shift in the prime source of wealth from land (typically controlled by the oldest members of society) to factories and other goods (often owned or managed by younger people). The peak earning years for most workers, for instance, occur around age 50; after that, earnings generally decline. Urban living also separates the generations physically and children depend less on their parents and more on their own earning power. Furthermore, because industrial, urban societies change rapidly, the skills, traditions and life experiences that served the old seem less relevant to the young. Finally, the high productivity of industrial nations means that some members of society do not need to work; as a result, most of the very old and the very young remain in non-productive roles (Cohn, 1982). Over the long term, all these factors are transforming elders (a term with positive connotations) into the elderly (commanding far less prestige).

Adapted from: J. Macionis, K. Plummer, (1988) *Sociology: A Global Introduction*, New York: Prentice Hall

1 Why do elders in many tribal societies enjoy such privilege and status?

2 Why do you think that many of the elderly in the contemporary UK experience low status and few privileges? How do the statistics demonstrate this?

3 Which elderly people have a relatively comfortable lifestyle? Why do you think this may be so?

4 Why do you think youth is so highly esteemed in the contemporary UK?

5 Which groups of young people may not enjoy status and privilege? Why?

Age cuts across all other structural influences such as class, gender and ethnicity and can inhibit the involvement of both the elderly and the young in society. Whilst both groups are affected in different ways, sub-groups of each age cohort may also differ in the extent to which they may be incorporated or marginalised by the wider society.

The elderly

Bradley (1996) refers to age as the neglected dimension of inequality – for example the elderly are one of the most significant groups that comprise the poor. Whilst the experience of the elderly in tribal society gives them status and influence, in Britain many of the elderly are seen as lacking the ability to contribute meaningfully to modern society which is perceived to have 'passed them by'. There are, however, no objective bases for seeing those in old age in negative terms. Rather, differing perceptions of age groups are socially constructed. Nonetheless, these ascribed characteristics serve to exclude many elderly people from full involvement in society. Age also combines with other social characteristics such as class, gender and ethnicity in causing unequal outcomes. For example, the differing pension rights accorded to male and female employees affect their standard of living after retirement. Oppenheim and Harker (1996) found that whilst 73% of male employees receive company pensions this only applies to 68% of female full-time employees and to only 31% of the many female part-time workers.

'Age is an ascribed characteristic but is also socially constructed.' Explain this statement and give an example of another characteristic that can be understood in this way.

The 'demographic timebomb'

The number of people over pensionable age, taking account of the change in women's retirement age, is projected to increase from 10.7 million in 1998 to 11.9 million in 2011, and will rise to 12.2 million by 2021. The increasing number of dependent elderly people has led to much talk of a **demographic timebomb** – crisis for the welfare state, the family and the economy–all of which, it is said, will be unable to sustain the cost of supporting ever increasing numbers of old people against a diminishing working population. After all, the elderly require a disproportionate amount of health care, social services support and housing assistance.

What sort of pressures may be put on families as a result of the 'demographic timebomb'?

However, the notion of a demographic 'timebomb' seems less convincing when we look at the evidence. In terms of the **dependency ratio** (the number of those working relative to those who do not):

- the increase in the elderly has been largely offset by the reduction in the number of dependent children. Also, many immigrant groups who contribute to the Nation's coffers have a much younger age profile than the indigenous population.

- In any case, as Vincent (1995) argues, expenditure on the elderly as a proportion of the national income is relatively low in the UK. Increased financial demands could easily be met by cuts in other expenditure such as education and defence – both of which are projected to make reduced demands on the national income over the coming years.
- Taylor-Gooby (1996) also points out that the number of pensioners increased from 6.5 million in 1951 to 10 million in 1991 without causing major problems. However, some New Right thinkers have argued that the current state of the health service is evidence of problems that lie ahead.

The young

Like the elderly, the young also make up a large sub-group of the poor. Quite apart from the numbers of children living in poverty increasing, many young people of working age face social deprivation caused by low pay, student loans, and in some case ineligibility for benefits and unemployment. In 2001 the unemployment rate for those under 25 was over 20%. Again this is affected by other factors such as ethnicity as, for example, twice as many African-Caribbean males are unemployed as whites.

Declining opportunities for those in vulnerable groups has led to increases in homelessness and financial hardship amongst the young, especially in run-down urban areas. Beatrice Campbell in *Wigan Pier Re-visited* (1985) and *Goliath* (1993) referred to adaptations some young people make in the absence of access to the mainstream routes to adult status. She suggests that some young women use having a baby as a means of acquiring adult status in a society which has increasingly closed down other options for them. Young men, with little prospect of work, on the other hand turn to daring crimes such as car theft and joyriding as alternatives which offer the opportunity to show off their skills. Both motherhood and car theft become public ways of achieving status.

Suggest why young men and women choose such different routes to 'achieve status'.

Most young workers earn relatively little and are given less responsibility and status in almost every occupational sector. Currently, some 235,000 18-to-20-year-old workers earn the minimum wage. Young workers are central to many industries but are generally subjected to the worst pay and conditions and required to be the most 'flexible'. This is particularly evident in retail and catering. More than two-thirds of McDonalds' staff are aged under 20 while the Restaurateurs' Association says that in the commercial sector of the hospitality industry, 31% of staff are aged 16 to 24. Of the nearly two million young people aged between 16 and 24 in full-time education 40.6% are also in paid employment. Two-thirds of Pizza Hut's 'crew' staff are in full-time education, as are one-fifth of Sainsbury's store staff.

Item A

Item B Young people in the 50s and 60s were able to find jobs quickly and were able to earn relatively large amounts. Their spending power made them important consumers and manufacturers responded, creating products that marked youth out as having a distinctive style of clothing and leisure. However, with the changes of the 1970s and 1980s in particular, the *celebration* of youth largely gave way to its *marginalisation*.

The spending power of youth declined because of unemployment and the lengthening of education. The ending of maintenance grants and the introduction of student contributions to higher education fees has led to more dependence on family. The transition to economic independence has become longer and more difficult. Young people are leaving home and marrying later.

Adapted from Fulcher and Scott (1999) *Sociology*, Oxford: Oxford University Press.

1 Using the items and any other information, suggest to what extent the experiences of contemporary youth resemble those of young people in the 50s and 60s.

2 How is the experience of youth influenced by social class?

Theoretical explanations of age inequality

Functionalism

Functionalists consider age to be more important than in the past (see, e.g. Parsons, 1977). At one time, age did not really matter because family determined one's place in society. However, since industrialisation, people have been more socially and geographically mobile and age groups have become more important. They provide **role sets** (Parsons, 1977) which create a link between the kinship group and the wider society. Age is therefore important as a mechanism of social integration, allowing people to evolve simply from one age group to the next.

 Identify two other possible effects of increased social and geographical mobility.

Functionalists tend to focus on youth rather than old age and critics point out that it is difficult to see how age has an integrating function for the elderly. Some writers argue that the elderly disengage with society to some extent, to make room for the younger age groups – thus maintaining social cohesion and integration. Critics of this **disengagement theory** point out that this is often not voluntary and that in any case many old people continue to be active participants in society.

Weberians argue that each age cohort can be considered as an **age stratum**, i.e. with its own market position and relative status. Why older groups tend to have a worse market position and status relative to other groups is, however, not explained.

According to functionalists, which other social institutions encourage social cohesion? How?

The Marxist view

Marxists have suggested that the elderly are ignored as they no longer have the disposable income to be attractive to capitalists. Early retirement and increasing life expectancy mean that the elderly spend a long period of their lives either as self-reliant and relatively invisible or as dependent on others. They are seen to be of low status and possessing little power. Cultural and ideological stereotypes help justify this. However, some old people have more power and status and for them the relationship to capitalism is beneficial. A long period of healthy, planned retirement has meant that they have a significant, uncommitted income which gives them consumer power and consequently positive recognition.

From a Marxist perspective the young provide a cheap pool of flexible labour that can be hired and fired as necessary. They tend not to have dependants and so are willing to work for low wages. In terms of full-time employment, their lack of experience legitimates low pay, and competition for jobs keeps wages low.

What other groups might be considered by Marxists to be a 'cheap pool of flexible labour'. Why?

Postmodernism and age status

Postmodernists point out that increased life expectancy coupled with a planned retirement has given old people an ability to consume as never before. The increasing importance of consumerism as an influence upon identity has led certain old people to develop lifestyles that are relatively conspicuous, hence the new advertising acronym of the GRUMPY (grown-up urban, mature professionals), highlighting both their perceived consumer power and negative social characteristics in one go! This is enhanced by the growing phenomenon of early retirement. Laczko and Phillipson (1991) point out that in 1965, 90% of men between 60 and 65 were working whereas this had fallen to 60% by 1990 – and the trend seems to be continuing. Whilst much of this trend is voluntary, the tendency for companies to downsize has had a greater impact on older (more expensive) employees who have involuntarily, in many cases, used their redundancy money to fund their early retirement, knowing that the odds of getting another job

is against them. Ageism is a common experience for older people, not just in terms of social institutions such as employment but also in terms of attitudes. Consider, for example, the range of negative phrases applied to the elderly ranging from the patronising ('old dears') to the insulting.

Age and popular culture

There is little doubt that **popular culture** has transformed its conception of age. Hollywood films of the 1940s seemed to suggest that the most attractive age to be was over 30. Male stars of the popular films of the day such as Humphrey Bogart often played romantic leads in their 40s and 50s, and women, whilst considerably younger, had a much higher average age than women in the films of today.

Before the 1950s most young people wanted to look at least in their mid-twenties and the domination of popular culture by the young which we see today would have appeared ludicrous. Young people simply could not have had enough to offer in terms of the relatively middle-aged conception adult society had then. As a consequence, it was not uncommon for young men in the 1950s to spray talcum powder in their hair to age themselves!

The last 50 years has seen a revolution in the influence of youth on popular culture such that today we talk of the 'cult of youth'. Music, fashion and the new hi-tech industries are dominated by the young in every way and, if anything, the optimum age to be in cultural terms appears to be getting even lower.

Postmodernists are interested in how popular culture is coming to define identity and this area can be clearly illustrated by the extent to which style and status are affected by age. Ironically, the battle cry of the functionalists of the 1950s that age rather than class was becoming the primary definer of social difference may now be being echoed in the postmodern view of how age ties into consumerism. A growing number of middle-class, elderly consumers may well cause a re-formulation of the ageist stereotypes of the past. All age groups, including the elderly, may eventually come to share more in common as consumer groups than do class subcultures and, if this proves to be the case, age (once again) might be said to be more important than class.

KEY TERMS

Age stratum – an age layer in society experiencing differential status and market situation relative to other age groups or layers.

Consumer society – societies that place an emphasis on lifestyle and purchasing patterns.

Demographic timebomb – a population trend so potentially grave in its consequences that it could literally damage society in an explosive way.

Dependency ratio – the ratio of working to dependent members of society i.e. the proportion of children and

elderly relative to those who support them physically and financially through tax payments.

Disengagement theory – the proposition that society enhances its orderly operation by disengaging people from positions of responsibility once they reach old age.

Gerontocracy – a society ruled by the aged.

Popular culture – widely appreciated cultural forms.

Role set – a group sharing similar characteristics of whom a particular set of roles are expected.

1 Give examples to show how social characteristics may interact to produce inequalities.

2 Give examples which show how some members of both the young and elderly may suffer disadvantages relative to the majority of the population.

3 What evidence is there for the suggestion that age stratification is socially constructed?

4 a Why do some commentators suggest that the increasing numbers of elderly people constitute a 'demographic timebomb'?

 b How can this view be criticised?

5 What evidence is there that young people experience inequality in the workplace?

6 Why according to functionalists is age an important mechanism of social integration?

7 a What is an age stratum?

 b Which age strata would you say enjoy the highest status and market position in the contemporary UK. Why?

8 Why according to Marxists are both the young and old marginalised in capitalist society?

9 What evidence is there of increasing opportunities for consumerism among the elderly?

10 How has age status shifted in popular culture?

WWW Webtask

Visit the 'Age concern' website www.ageconcern.org.uk. Click on 'Facts for you' then 'Statistics'. Take one or more of the headings and present a summary of the key patterns and trends in that area.

Research idea

Ask a sample of your peers to come up with phrases commonly used to describe the elderly (e.g. 'dirty old man', 'little old lady'). Analyse your results and try to formulate a range of ageist terms highlighting the social exclusion of the elderly in society.

EXAM PRACTICE

Extract from AQA-style question

'As society has industrialised the status of the old and the young has changed greatly.'

Examine the evidence for this statement.
(12 marks)

(Topic not in OCR specification)

Item A

retirement who live in a shared household with an occupational pension, there is a reasonably comfortable lifestyle. In the second world, made up of those over 80 who live alone with few savings, people can suffer acute poverty.

Adapted from: N. Abercrombie and A. Warde (2000) *Contemporary British Society* (3rd edition), Cambridge: Polity Press

Item C Third agers

The later years of life, are increasingly being seen as a time of great opportunity and even celebration. It is a time for reflecting on the accomplishments of a full life, but it also allows people to continue growing, learning and exploring. The years when people are free from parenting responsibilities and work are often referred to as the 'Third Age'. (The first age being child-hood, the second working age). During this period, which is now longer than ever before, individuals are free to lead active independent lives – travelling, pursuing further education or developing new skills. The 'fourth age' then refers to the years of life when people's independence and ability to care fully for themselves is more seriously challenged.

Adapted from: A. Giddens (2001) *Sociology* (4th edition), Cambridge: Polity Press

Item B Grey power?

Relatively affluent older people are much sought after by manufacturers in the United States, where the term 'Grey Power' is sometimes used to refer to the consumption habits and patterns of those over 65. Of course, the term cannot be applied to all older people. First, social class differences continue into retirement. Lifestyle and taste differences and the impact of different occupations as well as different forms of housing tenure persist. Second, ill health is also gendered with men more likely to experience it at an earlier age. The jobs people did also affect their income in old age, ex-professional and managerial workers have more income than ex-manual workers. Finally, older men have generally higher incomes than older women.

A recent study of elderly people in Britain (Milne *et al*. 1999) found evidence of two distinct 'worlds'. In one world, composed of people in the early years of

351

1 What might be the consumption and lifestyle differences between the different groups of elderly identified in Item B?

2 With reference to Item B ,why do you think older women have generally lower incomes than older men?

3 What advantages does being a member of the 'third age' bring? (Items A and C)

4 How is the experience of old age affected by social class and gender?

Preparing for the A2 exam

The A2 Sociology course follows on from the AS course. Together, the AS and A2 courses make up a full A-level. Unlike the AS level, A2 does not exist as a separate qualification.

Two organisations, or awarding bodies, offer qualifications in A-level Sociology.

NAME OF AWARDING BODY	INITIALS	A LEVEL COURSE CODE
Assessment and Qualifications Alliance	AQA	6191
Oxford, Cambridge and RSA Examinations	OCR	7878

You will be following one of these two courses. This means that in this unit you only need to read about the specifications that apply to you. Check with your teacher if you are not sure which course you are following.

A table linking the Units in this book to the two specifications can be found at the start of this book.

The AQA Specifications *Pam Law, Examiner, Moderator and Coursework Advisor for a leading exam board*

What will I study?

Aims/rationale of the course

The AQA specification at A2 builds on the knowledge and skills of the AS level and offers you the opportunity to acquire deeper knowledge and understanding of key aspects of sociological thought, a sound introduction to sociological research methods, and the opportunity to study a number of different areas of social life in depth.

The A2 course allows a choice of topic areas within Units 4 and 6 and the choice of a written examination or a coursework project for Unit 5. It also ensures a thorough coverage of sociological perspectives and of the two 'core themes':

- socialisation, culture and identity, and
- social differentiation, power and stratification.

These 'core themes' are required elements of any A2 level sociology specification.

The knowledge and skills acquired in this course should enable you to take a more informed and critical look at many aspects of all societies and how they relate to people's lives, while at the same time enabling you to develop and practise the skills of informed debate and critical analysis. The skills acquired in a sociology course can be of life-long benefit.

Modules of study and units of assessment

The AQA A2 course is divided into three modules of study, which lay out what you should know. When you enter for an examination, the module becomes a unit of assessment. Module 4 contains three topic areas, and each topic area forms the basis of a question in the written examination unit of assessment. Module 5 covers only one area of study, namely: sociological methods, and you are given a choice regarding the assessment of this unit. Module 6 is the synoptic module that will test your knowledge and understanding of the links between all the sections of the course which you have studied. The two topic areas that form the basis of synoptic assessment are:

- crime and deviance, and
- stratification and differentiation,

and there will be a question on each of these in the unit of assessment/exam paper. You will answer a question on one of these topics only. The questions on this paper will require you to show an informed and critical knowledge and understanding of your chosen synoptic topic and its links with sociological theory, sociological methods, and the other topic areas you have studied over the two years of the course.

MODULE OF STUDY	TOPICS	UNIT OF ASSESSMENT	FORM OF ASSESSMENT
4	Power and politics Religion World sociology	4	Written examination of 1.5 hours Short data-response section with two questions, and one essay from a choice of two per topic area.
5	Theory and methods	5	**Either:** Written examination of 1.5 hours with one compulsory data-response section and one essay from a choice of two. **Or:** Coursework project carrying out your own research.
6	Crime and deviance Stratification and differentiation	6	Written examination 1.5 hours One data-response section with two questions and an essay [no choice] per topic area.

How will I be assessed?

Skills

The skills you will acquire and develop in your A2 course are tested in the examination by two assessment objectives: AO1 counts for 40% and AO2 counts for 60% of the available marks.

Assessment objective 1 (AO1): knowledge and understanding

This requires you to demonstrate your knowledge and understanding of the chosen topic area which forms the basis of the assessment. It covers knowledge and understanding of relevant sociological theories and perspectives, concepts, studies and social policies. You should also be able to make reference to relevant issues, events and social policies. Also included in AO1 is the skill of communication. While this is not assessed separately, and therefore does not carry a particular mark weighting, it is an important skill, as poor communication will prevent you from showing the examiner clearly what you mean.

Assessment objective 2 (AO2): identification, analysis, interpretation and evaluation

This range of skills together counts for 60% of the available marks. To demonstrate them successfully, you will need to be able to identify correctly perspectives, reasons, examples, criticisms, etc. as required by the particular question. The skill of interpretation covers your ability to work out and respond to what the question is requiring you to do, and to interpret different types of evidence, (including research studies and statistical data), by discussing what they can tell us. Good

analysis is shown by presenting an informed, detailed and accurate discussion of a particular theory, perspective, study or event, and also by the ability to present your arguments and evidence in a clear and logical manner. Evaluation refers to your ability to recognise and discuss the strengths and weaknesses of theories and perspectives, studies, sociological methods and data presented in a variety of forms.

Units of assessment/exams

The basic structure of the units of assessment is shown in the diagram above, and the question structure is discussed in more detail in the next section. The weighting given to each of the three A2 units is given in the following table, which shows you the percentage of the marks allocated to each unit in terms of the full A-level.

UNIT OF ASSESSMENT	A-LEVEL WEIGHTING
Unit 4	15% of total A-level marks
Unit 5	15% of total A-level marks
Unit 6	20% of total A-level marks

Coursework

The A2 coursework task is offered in Unit 5 as an alternative to the written examination. It takes the form of an actual research project in the second year of the course. Further details of the A2 coursework are given in the *How can I do well in the coursework task? section*.

How can I do well in the written examinations?

Question style and structure

A2 questions vary from paper to paper but all include a data-response section. In Units 4 and 6 this usually consists of one piece of data (an Item) and contains two questions but in Unit 5 it usually consists of two pieces of data and contains four questions. The Items at A2 level are there to prompt your thoughts and point you in the right direction when answering the questions in that section. They may prompt ideas that you can use in the essay but this will be more accidental than designed.

Each question is marked out of 60, and it might be helpful to think of the 60 marks being allocated in two distinct groups, one of 20 marks and one of 40 marks. It follows, therefore, that if you have 90 minutes for the whole exam you should spend about 30 minutes on Section (a) and about 60 minutes on the essay. Don't forget to leave yourself time to read the Item, plan your answers and read it all through at the end.

Exam tips

- Throughout A2 there is more emphasis than in AS on the AO2 skills so the examiner is looking at how you use the knowledge and how you analyse and evaluate it. Whilst some description will be necessary do not spend too long on this as your use of that evidence is more important than demonstrating the detail. You may assume that the examiner has also read the study to which you are referring.

- Read both the Item/s and the whole question very carefully before you begin to answer. The Item/s will contain information that is essential, helpful or both, and reading the whole question will give you an understanding of which aspects of the topic have been covered.

- Keep an eye on the time, it is very important that you allow sufficient time for each section, but do not spend too long on the first part since the essay carries two-thirds of the marks.

- Plan all the sections of your answer before you start to write. While you are answering the first part you will probably remember points to put into your essay.

- In the data-response section the questions will carry either 8 or 12 marks. Both these questions and the essays are likely to include the following words: identify, explain, examine, assess, evaluate.

  - **Identify:** name whatever you have been asked for; e.g 'identify a system of social stratification' could be the caste system or the class system.

  - **Explain:** pick out distinguishing features of a named phenomenon and say why they are important; e.g the role of religious beliefs in the caste system.
  - **Examine:** look at the advantages and disadvantages of a theory or look at the evidence for and against a statement or theory.
  - **Assess:** look at all sides, or all theories that relate to the topic and come to a conclusion.
  - **Evaluate:** this word is similar to 'assess', and means to look at all sides and weigh up the evidence for and against them all before coming to a conclusion.

- In all your answers, refer to appropriate theories, perspectives, studies and evidence to support and inform your response. Where possible, bring in examples of recent or current events or social policies to illustrate the points you are making. Make quite sure that you have given sufficient demonstration of the AO2 skills, particularly analysis and evaluation.

- Finally – make sure that you answer the question that the examiner has set, rather than the one that you wished for! This is actually a serious point – many candidates fail to achieve marks because they have not kept to the focus of the question. No question is likely to ask you simply to 'write everything you know about…', and yet this is what some students do. However, it is better to write something than to sit there doing nothing. Leaving a blank means you cannot score any marks, but if you write something, it could be correct enough or relevant enough to pick up some marks.

How can I do well in the coursework task?

Requirements

You are expected to carry out a piece of sociological research that relates to one of the areas of the specification. Normally you will do this after you have finished your AS level. You may use either primary or secondary data-collection methods to complete your task. There are recommended word limits for each section and an overall word limit of 3,500 words. You may either carry out the proposal you submitted for AS, or you may start afresh – the choice is yours.

The marks are awarded both for AO1 skills, (24 out of the 60 marks), and for AO2 (36 out of the 60 marks), and the coursework should be laid out in the agreed format of:

- rationale/hypothesis or aim
- context
- methodology
- evidence
- evaluation

with a contents page, bibliography and a photocopied page from your research diary.

Coursework tips

Before you start:
- read a copy of the ethical guidelines
- read the mark scheme
- check the areas covered by the specification.

Ethical guidelines
The most important of these concern:

1 the well-being of those who take part in the research
2 people's right to privacy
3 anonymity and confidentiality
4 bringing sociology into disrepute.

You should consider all these issues before even choosing your topic.

Mark scheme
This is not an official secret! You should have a copy and look at what it suggests you need to do to get top marks.

Specification
Make sure that the area you want to look at is covered by the specification. If it isn't, don't do it.

SECTION AND ASSESSMENT OBJECTIVE COVERED	OUTLINE REQUIREMENTS	RECOMMENDED NUMBER OF WORDS	TOTAL NO. OF MARKS FOR THAT SECTION
AO1 Context	An outline of sociological sources, either theoretical or empirical or both, and relevant sociological concepts which form the context and background to your study.	750	12
AO1 Method	**Primary-based research:** an account of the single research method chosen for the collection of data, saying why you think it is appropriate to test/explore your hypothesis or aim, and a recognition of associated problems, practical, theoretical and ethical. **Secondary-based research:** an account of the methodology used by the author(s) of the data, reasons for that choice and a recognition of associated problems, both with the research under discussion and of using secondary methods.	750	12
AO2 Evidence and how you carried out your research	How you did your research and presenting the evidence you found especially relating these findings both to your hypothesis/aim **and** the context pieces you chose to use.	1,150	18
AO2 Rationale	A hypothesis/aim, objectives where appropriate and reasons for choosing this topic.	150	
Evaluation and conclusions	An evaluation of the methods used (either your own or those used by the authors of the secondary data), conclusions about the findings and recommendations for further research.	700	18
Total:		**3,500**	**60**

Doing the research: tips

- Make sure that your research has a clear sociological focus.

- Keep the hypothesis or aim very simple/limited. This will make it easier to carry it out and to keep to the word limit.

- Keep referring back to your hypothesis or aim – all the other sections should show a clear link to this.

- Make sure that you spend time choosing appropriate pieces of context, and show how and why these provide an appropriate context for the proposed research.

- Having chosen your context pieces keep linking them in to the rest of the piece, refer to them when designing your research, and show how they were proved or refuted by your research in your evidence and evaluation sections.

- Choose only one method to collect your data.

- If your method involves asking questions make sure you use all the information you collect. Have a reason for every question you ask. If, for example, you ask for people's ages, use this information to group their answers according to their age to see whether it had an effect on their response. If you don't use the information the moderator will think 'why did they bother to ask the question?'

- Remember to give clear reasons for all your choices/decisions. Include practical, theoretical and ethical aspects for your choice/decision.

- Allow sufficient time to carry out your research – it always takes longer than you expect. Make sure that you are aware of, and meet, the set deadline.

- Stick to the word limit – and good luck with all you choose to do!

What will I study?

Aims/rationale of the course

The OCR A-level specification aims to offer you a sound introduction to sociology.

In particular, it aims to develop in you a sociological knowledge and understanding of social processes, structures and theories that is both contemporary and relevant to your life in the twenty-first century. You are positively encouraged by this specification to reflect on your own social identity and your experience of the social world in which you live and to apply your knowledge and understanding of sociology to everyday life. Your experience of this specification should equip you with the necessary skills to:

- engage in sociological debate
- be able to interpret, apply and evaluate relevant evidence
- construct convincing sociological arguments.

Finally, this specification is designed to offer you choice and flexibility in terms of its content, its varied assessment system and its coursework options.

Themes

The A2 specification has five inter-linked themes.

- First, it aims to build upon knowledge and understanding acquired at AS relating to how and to what extent individuals shape, and are shaped by, social structures.
- Second, the specification aims to explore those agencies that exercise power and control over our daily lives and to examine how such agencies contribute to the construction of our personal identities.
- Third, the specification aims to build on your understanding of the concepts and skills associated with sociological research. In particular, the focus will be on practical application and evaluation of research techniques and concepts in a range of sociological contexts.
- Fourth, it aims to identify and explain the level and pattern of inequality in contemporary Britain and how inequality and difference underpins much of our everyday experience.
- Fifth and most importantly, the specification aims to develop in you a deeper understanding of the connections between the nature of sociological thought, research methods and all the topics that you have covered both at AS and A2 levels. This is known as 'synoptic understanding'.

Modules

There are three modules at A2-level.

- Module 2536 : Power and Control
- Module 2537 : Applied Sociological Research Skills or
- Module 2538 : Personal Study
- Module 2539 : Social Inequality and Difference (the synoptic unit).

Topics

- The *Power and Control module* builds upon your understanding of the social construction of culture, introduces the concepts of conformity and deviation, and further considers issues of power, control and ideology. It includes the options of: crime and deviance; education; health; popular culture; social policy and welfare, and protest and social movements.
- The *Applied Sociological Research Skills module* enables you to build on your understanding of the concepts and skills acquired as part of AS Sociological Research Skills or the Research Report.
- The *Social Inequality and Difference module* is the synoptic unit and will aim to assess your understanding of social inequalities and differences relating to class, gender and ethnic inequalities, and how these relate to research methods, sociological theory and other topics studied throughout AS and A2.

How will I be assessed?

Skills

For A2 Sociology, you will be tested by the following assessment objectives:

Knowledge and understanding: Assessment objective 1 (AO1)

After studying A2, you should be able to demonstrate knowledge and understanding of abstract concepts and, particularly, theory in some depth. It is necessary to have a detailed and wide-ranging knowledge and understanding of empirical evidence and how this links to theory within the context of sociological debate. You will also need a good holistic knowledge and understanding of the connections between the core theme of social inequality and difference and one or more other topic areas, plus links between substantive topics and how these connect to theory/method.

Interpretation and analysis AO2(a)

This skill essentially involves showing the ability to select and analyse a broad and diverse range of data and evidence. In particular, it involves the ability to apply and link sociological evidence to specific sociological arguments in a focused fashion in support of particular debates. It also involves the ability to interpret quantitative and qualitative data, i.e. to work out what it is saying and/or put it into your own words.

Evaluation AO2(b)

It is important to be able to demonstrate a highly developed critical appraisal of theory and sociological debate. This will involve you evaluating the reliability of sociological inquiry and the validity of sociological evidence is the context of key debates.

Exams

UNIT CODE	TITLE	EXAM	% OF OF A2 AND A LEVELS
Unit 2536	Power and Control	You answer one essay question in 1 hour.	It is worth 30% of the A2 level and 15% of the full A-level.
Unit 2537	Applied Sociological Research Skills	You answer one compulsory data-response question in 1.5 hours.	It is worth 30% of the A2 level and 15% of the full A-level.
Unit 2539	Social Inequality and Difference	You do one data-response question in 1.5 hours.	It is worth 40% of the A2 level and 20% of the full A-level.

Coursework

Unit 2538 Personal Study is offered as an alternative to the written examination in Unit 2537 and represents 30% of the A2 level and 15% of the full A-level.
(See later section 'How can I do well in the coursework task?')

How can I do well in the exams?

Timing

It is important that you use your time effectively in examinations.

The Power and Control examination lasts one hour and is worth 60 marks. You have to do 1 essay in that period from a choice of 12, (2 for each topic area). You should aim to spend 10–15 minutes planning this essay and 45–50 minutes on writing it. Aim to write at least three sides of the examination booklet.

The Applied Sociological Research Skills examination lasts 1.5 hours and is worth 60 marks. It comprises one compulsory five-part question. The first three parts (worth 24 marks) pose questions relating to a piece of data (Item A) on a particular sociological problem. The final two parts (worth 36 marks) will require students to outline and evaluate a research design on a given topic. It is recommended that you spend 30 minutes on Parts (a)–(c) and 1 hour on Parts (d)–(e).

The synoptic Social Inequality and Difference examination lasts 1.5 hours and is worth 90 marks. You have to do one five-part data-response question from a choice of two on the themes of workplace inequality, poverty and inequalities and/or differences based on either social class or gender or ethnicity. Questions (a) and (b) are worth 6 marks each, question (c) 12 marks, question (d) 22 marks and question (e) 44 marks. You should spend 5–10 minutes reading both questions and planning your responses to Parts (d) and (e). It is recommended that you spend 20 minutes on Parts (a)–(c), 20 minutes on Part (d) and 40 minutes on Part (e).

Style of questioning

OCR have decided to use the same action or trigger words and phrases for particular questions for every exam session so that you can respond in the most effective fashion to the question set.

2536 Power and Control

This is an essay question which will ask you to 'outline and assess' a particular 'view', i.e. a sociological debate about a particular social or sociological problem. It is highly recommended that you plan your response to this question and that your response should adopt the following format.

- You should construct a brief introduction identifying the theoretical or empirical source of the 'view' contained in the essay title. This introduction should set the scene or context of the debate, i.e. clearly state who the debate is between in terms of theories or sociologists, and/or define any technical or conceptual terms used in the title, e.g. 'hidden curriculum'.
- You should outline the point of view in the essay title in some depth and detail.
- You should elaborate and/or illustrate that point of view with reference to empirical studies and data that support it.
- You should assess the point of view contained in the essay title with specific criticisms backed-up with empirical studies and/or by outlining alternative views or theories. With regard to the latter course of action, don't be content just to outline another theory. Be quite clear in what way alternative theories differ from the original view.
- Construct a brief conclusion based on the content of your essay. Look at the title again. Have you addressed the essential elements of the question? Clearly state which point of view your evidence supports.

2537 Applied Sociological Research Skills

This is a five-part data-response question. Parts (a)–(c) are focused on Item A, i.e. a description of how a piece of sociological research has been carried out and its findings. The latter is likely to be presented in both a textual and statistical form, i.e. in the form of a table, chart, graph, etc.

- Question (a) will use the phrase 'Using only Item A, identify two reasons why… '. This question is worth 6 marks and will always relate to the research methods mentioned in Item A. Do not do more than the question asks. For example, you only have to identify what is in the Item, you do not have to explain it.
- Question (b) will be worded 'Identify and explain two strengths (or weaknesses)' of a particular method. The method may not necessarily be mentioned in the Item but is likely to be strongly related to it. Note that this question requires an explanation of what you have identified. This question is worth 8 marks.
- Question (c) will be worded 'Summarise what the research findings in Item A tell us about… '. This question is worth 10 marks.

Item B will outline a research problem. It is likely to state that an organisation requires either quantitative or qualitative data in order to investigate a specific social or sociological problem. The proposal will state that you have been invited as a sociological researcher to design a proposal that targets a representative sample of whatever research population the problem is focused on. For example:

The British Government requires qualitative data to discover what problems refugees who have been placed on council estates in Hull and Glasgow have experienced in regard to community relations. You have been asked as a sociological researcher to design a research proposal that will target a representative sample of refugees and British-born residents of the council estates.

- Question (d) will be worded '*Outline and explain the research process you would adopt in collecting quantitative or qualitative data on*' whatever the problem is. The question is worth 14 marks.
- Question (e) will always be worded '*Assess the potential weaknesses of your research proposal, briefly explaining how you intend to overcome them*'. The question is worth 22 marks.

2539 Social Inequality and Difference

This five-part data-response will be accompanied by two Items. It is highly likely that one of these will be text-based whilst the other is likely to take the form of a graph, chart, etc.

Question (a) will ask you to '*identify two*' of something from the data, usually in Item A. The following words are likely to be used: ways, trends, changes, reasons, examples, features, characteristics, etc. The question is worth 6 marks.

Question (b) will also ask you to '*identify two*' ways, patterns, changes, trends etc. related to Item B. It is also worth 6 marks.

Note that both questions (a) and (b) are merely asking you to use the data. Neither is asking you to explain what you have identified (although you should make clear your identification by illustrating it with an example).

Question (c) will ask you to '*identify and explain two*' problems, difficulties, advantages, disadvantages, strengths, weaknesses, etc. related to either the methods used to collect the information in the items or more generally to how sociologists go about collecting information on inequality and difference. This is a *synoptic* question because it focuses on the relationship between inequality and the research methods used to research it empirically. It is worth 12 marks. Note the added action word 'explain' – you now have to justify your choice of whatever it is you have identified.

Question (d) will command '*using your wider sociological knowledge, outline the evidence for*' class, gender, ethnic and workplace inequalities or poverty. This, too, is *synoptic* because you are expected to go beyond the Unit of Social Inequality and Difference to gather evidence to answer this question. You should use evidence gleaned from at least *two* other areas of the specifications. It is perfectly legitimate for you to use evidence gained from both AS and A2 components. This question is worth 22 marks.

Question (e) is an essay question and will always ask you to '*outline and assess*' sociological theories/explanations. It is worth 44 marks. It is important that you plan your response to this question and adopt the essay-format style recommended above in the Power and Control section.

How can I do well in the coursework task?

Requirements

The Personal Study requires you to produce an extended piece of work on a sociological topic using a maximum of 2,500 words. You are required to design a sociological investigation using either primary and/or secondary data and to try out this design by assembling a limited but illustrative amount of data. The emphasis of the Personal Study is on the design of the research, on piloting the design and evaluating the research process. Credit is given for the quality of the design of the investigation and its evaluation rather than for the quantity and type of any data collected. You should aim to complete:

1. A Rationale which identifies the central research issue, question or hypothesis to be addressed, includes a clear statement of the sociological reasons for carrying out the study, and a description, explanation and justification of the research design and procedures. It is recommended that this section should be in the range of 500–750 words.
2. The Research section should focus reporting of the testing of the actual research design and procedures, and analysis and presentation of the research findings and conclusions reached. It is recommended that this section should be in the range of 750–1,000 words.
3. The Evaluation section should include an evaluation of the overall research design and methodology used, some assessment of how your research findings relate to your hypothesis and any ideas for the further development of the research. It is recommended that this section should be in the range of 750–1,000 words.

Coursework tips

- Choose an accessible topic that allows you to use straightforward research methods and on which there is plenty of information available in textbooks.

- You must keep to the word limit otherwise, no matter how good your research is, you will not be able to achieve full marks.

- It is strongly recommended that you keep a research diary from the moment you start your coursework because it will provide with you with invaluable information about how the research process progressed or did not progress. This is essential because it will inform your evaluation section.

- Do try and use concepts like 'reliability' and 'validity' throughout the sections.

- The focus is on 'doing sociology' so make sure you dedicate discussion to the operationalisation of concepts in your hypothesis and how you intend to access the population under study via particular sampling techniques.

- Don't overdo the presentation of your findings in regard to graphs, charts, etc. Choose 4–5 key findings and present them in this way. The rest can be presented textually.

- Make sure your teacher has seen anything you design before you go out and do the research.

- Remember that ethics are important so make sure that your proposed respondents have given their consent.

- Your safety is crucial – make sure all plans are discussed with and agreed by your teacher.

References

Abbott, P. and Wallace, C. (1990/1997) *An Introduction to Sociology: Feminist Perspectives*, London: Routledge.

Abercrombie, N. Hill, S. and Turner, B. S. (1980) *The Dominant Ideology Thesis*, London: Allen and Unwin.

Abercrombie, N. and Warde, A. (2000) *Contemporary British Society* (3rd edition), Cambridge: Polity Press.

Adamson, P. (1986) 'The Rich, the Poor, the Pregnant', *New Internationalist* Issue 270.

Ahmed, L. (1992) *Women and Gender in Islam: Historical Roots of a Modern Debate*, New Haven and London: Yale University Press.

Akers, R. L. (1967) 'Problems in the Sociology of Deviance: Social Definitions and Behaviour', *Social Forces* 46 (4).

Allen, T. and Thomas, A. (2001) *Poverty and Development in the 21st Century*, Oxford: Oxford University Press.

Althusser, L. (1971) *Lenin and Philosophy and Other Essays*, London: New Left Books.

Anderson, S., Kinsey, R., Loader, I. and Smith, C. (1994) *Young People, Crime and Policing in Edinburgh*, Aldershot: Avebury.

Arber, A., Dale, S. and Gilbert, N. (1986) *The Limitations of Existing Social Class Classifications of Women* in A. Jacoby (ed.) *The Measurement of Social Class*, Guildford: Social Research Association.

Armstrong, K. (1993) *The End of Silence: Women and the Priesthood*, London: Fourth Estate.

Aron, R. (1967) 'Social Class, Political Class, Ruling Class' in Bendix and Lipset *Main Currents in Sociological Thought*, Vol 1 and 2, Harmondsworth: Penguin.

Atkinson, J. M. (1971) 'Social Reactions to Suicide: The Role of Coroners' Definitions' in S. Cohen (ed.) *Images of Deviance*, Harmondsworth: Penguin.

Aubert, V. (1952) 'Whiter Collar Crime and Social Structure', *American Journal of Sociology* 58.

Bachrach, P. and Baratz, M. S. (1970) *Power and Poverty: Theory and Practice*, Oxford: Oxford University Press.

Badawi, L. (1994) 'Islam' in Holm, J. and Bowker, J. (eds.) (1994) *Women in Religion*, London: Pinter.

Baldwin, J. and Bottoms A. E. (1976) *The Urban Criminal*, London: Tavistock.

Baran, P. (1957) The Political Economy of Growth, New York: Monthly Review Press.

Barber, B. R. and Schulz, A. (eds.) (1995) *Jihad vs McWorld*, New York: Ballantyne Books.

Barker, E. (1984) *The Making of a Moonie*, Oxford: Blackwell.

Barker, P. (1982) *The Other Britain: a New Society Collection* London: Routledge & Kegan Paul.

Barron, R. G. and Norris, G. M. (1976) 'Sexual Divisions and the Dual Labour Market' in D. J. Barker and S. Allen (eds.) (1976) *Dependence and Exploration in Work and Marriage*, London: Longman.

Baudrillard, J. (1998) *Selected Writings*, M. Poster (ed.) Cambridge: Polity Press.

Bauman, Z. (1978) *Hermeutics and Social Sciences: Approaches to Understanding*, London: Hutchinson.

—. (1983) 'Industrialism, Consumerism and Power' in Theory, Culture and Society, 1 (3).

—. (1990) *Thinking Sociologically*, Oxford: Blackwell.

—. (1997) *Postmodernity and Its Discontents*, Cambridge: Polity Press.

Beck, U. (1992) *Risk Society: Towards a New Modernity*, London: Sage.

Becker, H. (1950) Through Values to Social Interpretation: Essays on Social Contexts, Actions, Types and Prospects, California: Duke University Press.

Becker, H. (1963) *The Outsiders*, London: Macmillan.

—. (1967) 'Whose Side are We On?' *Social Problems* 14.

—. (1970) 'Whose Side Are We On?' in H. Becker, *Sociological Work*, New Brunswick: Transaction Books.

Bell, D. (1973) *The Coming of Post-industrial Society*, New York: Basic Books.

Bellah, R. (1970) 'Civil Religion in America' in *Beyond Belief: Essays in Religion in a Post-traditional World*', New York: Harper & Row.

Benston, M. (1972) 'The Political Economy of Women's Liberation' in Glazer-Mahlbin, N. and Wahrer, H. Y. (eds.) (1972) *Women in a Man-made World*, Chicago: Rand MacNally.

Berger , P. (1967) *The Sacred Canopy: Elements of a Sociological Theory of Religion*, New York: Anchor Books.

—. (1973) The Social Reality of Religion, Harmondsworth: Penguin.

Berger, Alan L. (1997) *Children of Job: American Second Generation Witnesses to the Holocaust*, New York: New York State University Press.

Bergesen, A. (1990) 'Turning World-System Theory on its Head' in M. Featherstone (ed.) (1990) *Global Culture: Rationalism, Globalisation and Modernity*, London: Sage.

Bernard, J. (1976) *The Future of Marriage*, Harmondsworth: Penguin.

Beynon, J. (1986) 'Turmoil in the Cities', *Social Studies Review*, January.

Bhaskar, R. (1986) *Scientific Realism and Human Emancipation*, London: Verso.

Bhavani, K. (2000) *Feminism and Race*, Oxford: Oxford University Press.

Bird, J. (1999) *Investigating Religion*, London: Harper Collins.

Bittner, E. (1967) 'The Police on Skid Row: A Study of Peacekeeping' *American Sociology Review* 32 (5).

Blauner, R. (1964) *Alienation and Freedom*, Chicago: University of Chicago Press.

Bocock, B. J. (1986) *Hegemony*, London: Tavistock.

Bonger, W. (1916) *Criminality and Economic Conditions*, Chicago: Little Brown.

Boserup, E. (1970) *Women's Role in Economic Development*, London: Earthscan.

Bourgois, P. (1995) *In Search of Respect*, Cambridge: Cambridge University Press.

Bowling, B. (1999) *Violent Racism: Victimisation, Policing and Social Context* (revised ed.), Oxford: Oxford University Press.

Bowling, B. and Phillips, C. (2002) *Racism, Crime and Justice* Harlow: Pearson.

Box, S. (1981) *Deviance, Reality and Society*, 2nd edition), Eastbourne: Holt Rheinhart Wilson.

—. (1983/1993) *Crime, Power and Mystification*, London.

Bradley, H. (1996) *Fractured Identities*, Cambridge: Polity Press.

—. (1997) *Fractured Identities: Changing Patterns of Inequality*, Cambridge: Polity Press.

Braithwaite, J. (1984) *Corporate Crime in the Pharmaceutical Industry*, London: Routledge.

Brake, M. (1980) *The Sociology of Youth and Youth Subcultures*, London: Routledge.

Brantingham, P. J. and Brantingham, P. L. (1984) *Patterns of Crime*, New York: Macmillan.

—. (1991) *Environmental Criminology*, (revised ed.) Prospect Heights: Waveland Press.

Braverman, H. (1974) *Labour and Monopoly Capitalism*, New York: Monthly Press.

Brierley P. (ed.) (1979) (1989) (1999) *Christian Research Association, UK Christian Handbook*, Religious Trends 1979, 1989, 1999, London: Harper Collins.

—. (2000) *The Tide is Running Out*, London: Christian Research.

British Crime Survey (1992) London: Home Office.

British Crime Survey (1998) Research and Statistics Directorate of the Home Office.

British Social Attitudes Survey (1998), Survey: National Centre for Social Research.

British Youth Lifestyles Survey (2000) Home Office Research Study 209.

Brooks, A. (1997) *Postfeminisms: Feminisms, Cultural Theory and Cultural Forms*, London: Routledge.

Bruce, S. (1995) *Religion in Modern Britain*, Oxford: Oxford University Press.

—. (1996) *Religion in the Modern World: From Cathedrals to Cults*, Oxford: Oxford University Press.

—. (2001) 'The Social Process of Secularisation' in R. K. Fenn *The Blackwell Companion to Sociology of Religion*, Oxford: Blackwell.

Bryman, A. (2001) *Social Research Methods*, Oxford: Oxford University Press.

Burgess, E. W. (1925) 'The Growth of the City' in Park, R.E., Burgess, E. W., McKenzie, R. D. (eds) *The City*, Chicago: University of Chicago.

Burkey, S (1993) *People First*, London: Zed Books. Taken from R. Carmen (1996) p.70.

Butler, C. (1995) 'Religion and Gender: Young Muslim Women in Britain', *Sociology Review*, 4(3), Oxford: Philip Allan.

Butler, D. and Kavanagh, D. (1985) *The British General Election of 1983*, London: Macmillan.

Butler, D. and Rose, R. (1960) *The British General Election of 1959*, London: Frank Cass.

Butler, D. and Stokes, D. (1971) *Political Change in Britain*, London: Macmillan.

Cain, M. (1986) 'Realism, Feminism, Methodology and Law', *International Journal of the Sociology of Law* 14.

Campbell, B. (1985) *Wigan Pier Re-visited*, London: Virago Press Ltd.

—. (1993) *Goliath: Britain's Dangerous Places*, London: Methuen.

—. (1995) 'Old Fogeys And Angry Young Men', *Sounding* No.1 Autumn.

Caplow, T. (1954) *The Sociology of Work*, New York: McGraw-Hill.

Cardoso, F. H. (1972) 'Dependancy and Development in Latin America', *New Left Review* 74, July/Aug.

Carlen, P. (1992) 'Criminal Women and Criminal Justice: The Limits to and Potential of Feminist and Left Realist Perspectives' in R. Mathews and J. Young (eds.) *Issues in Realist Criminology*, London: Sage.

Carlen, P. (1988) *Women, Crime and Poverty*, Milton Keynes: Open University Press.

Carmen, R. (1996) *Autonomous Development: Humanising the Landscape*, London: Zed Books.

Carnell, B. (2001) Article titled 'Paul Ehrlich' dated 17/5/2000 downloaded from www.overpopulation.com

Carson, W. G. (1970) 'White Collar Crime and the Enforcement of Factory Legislation', *British Journal of Criminology* 10.

Cassen, R. (1985) 'Is Aid Really Work?' *New Society* July 26.

Castles, S. and Kosack, G. C. (1973) *Immigrant Workers and Class Structure in Western Europe*, Oxford: OUP.

Centre for Longitudinal Studies (1991) *National Child Development Study*, London: Institute of Education.

Ceplan, L. (1987) *Studies in Religious Fundamentalism*, London: Macmillan

Chambliss, W. J. (1975) 'Towards a Political Economy of Crime', *Theory and Society*, Vol. 2 pp.149–170.

Chase-Dunn, C. (1975) 'The Effects of International Economic Dependence on Development and Inequality: A Cross National Study', *American Sociological Review* 40 December.

Chrispin, J. and Jegede, F. (2000) *Population, Resources and Development*, London: Harper Collins.

Cloward, R. and Ohlin, L. (1960) *Delinquency and Opportunity*, London: Collier Macmillan.

Clark, T. N, & Hoffman-Martinot, V. (eds) (1998), *The New Political Culture*, Boulder CO: Westview.

Clarke, M. (1990) *Business Crime: Its Nature and Control*, Bristol: Policy Press.

Clarke, R. V. G. (1995) 'Situational Crime Prevention' in Tonry, M. and Farrington, D. (eds) *Building a Safer Society*, Chicago: University of Chicago.

Clegg, S. R. (1989) *Frameworks of Power*, London: Sage.

Cloward, R. and Ohlin, L. (1960) *Delinquency and Opportunity*, London: Collier Macmillan.

Cochrane, A. and Pain, K. (2000) 'A Globalising Society' in D. Held (ed.) *A Globalising World: Culture, Economics and Politics*, London: Routledge.

Cohen, A. (1955) *Delinquent Boys*, New York: The Free Press.

Cohen, L. E. and Felson, M. (1979) 'Social Change and Crime Rate Trends: A Routine Activities Approach', *American Sociological Review*, 44.

Cohen, P. (1972) *Knuckle Sandwich: Growing Up in the Working-class City*, Harmondsworth: Penguin.

Cohen, R. (1994) *Frontiers of Identity: The British and the Others*, London: Longman.

Cohen, R. and Kennedy, P. (2000) *Global Sociology*, Basingstoke: Macmillan.

Cohen, S. (1972) *Folk Devils and Moral Panics*, London: Paladin.

—. (1980) *Folk Devils and Moral Panics* (2nd edition), Oxford: Martin Robinson.

—. (1985) *Visions of Social Control*, Cambridge: Polity Press.

Collins, H. and Pinch, T. (1998) *The Golem: What You Should Know About Science* (2nd edition) Cambridge: Cambridge University Press.

Colllinson, M. (1995) *Police, Drugs and Community*, London: Free Association Books.

Colman, A. and Gorman L. (1982) 'Conservatism, Dogmatism and Authoritarianism Amongst British Police Officers', *Sociology* 16: 1.

Conklin, J. E. (1977) *Illegal but not Criminal: Business Crime in America*, Englewood Cliffs, NJ: Prentice Hall.

Connell, R.W. (1995) *Masculinities*, Cambridge: Polity Press.

Coplan, L. (1987) *Studies in Religious Fundamentalism*, London: Macmillan.

Coussins, J. (1976) *The Equality Report*, NCCL Rights for Women Unit: London.

Coxall, B. (1981) *Parties and Pressure Groups*, Harlow: Longman.

Crewe, I. (1984) 'The Electorate: Partisan De-alignment Ten Years On' in H. Berrington, (ed.) *Change in British Politics*, London: Frank Cass.

Cross, M. (1979) *Urbanisation and Urban Growth in the Caribbean*, Cambridge University Press cited in M. O'Donnell (1983) *New Introductory Reader in Sociology*, London: Nelson Harrap.

Dahl, R. (1961) *Who Governs: Democracy and Power in an American City*, New Haven: Yale University Press.

Dalton, K. (1964) *The Pre-menstrual Syndrome and Progesterone Therapy*, London: Heinemann Medical.

Daly, M. (1973) *Beyond God the Father*, Boston, Mass: Beacon Press.

—. (1978) *Gyn/Ecology: The Metaethics of Radical Feminism*, Boston: Beacon Press.

Dane, G. (1985) 'Competing Fundamentalisms', *Sociology review*, 4 (4), Oxford: Philip Allan.

Davie, G. (1994) *Religion in Britain 1945–1990, Believing Without Belonging* Oxford: Blackwell.

—. (1995) 'Competing Fundamentalisms', *Sociology Review* 4 (4), Oxford: Philip Allan.

Davies, C. A. (1999) *Reflexive Ethnography: A Guide to Researching Selves and Others*, London: Routledge.

Davis, K. and Moore, W. E., (1955) 'Some principles of Stratification', in Bendix, R. and Lipset, S. M. (eds.) *Class, Status and Power*, (2nd edition, 1967), London: Routledge and Kegan Paul London.

Davis, M. (1990) *City of Quartz*, London: Verso.

de Beauvoir, S. (1953) *The Second Sex,* London: Jonathan Cape.

Dennis, N. (1993) *Rising Crime and the Dismembered Family,* London: IEA Health And Welfare Unit.

—. and Erdos, G. (1993) *Families without Fatherhood,* London: IEA.

Denscombe, M. (2001) 'Uncertain Identities and Health-risking Behaviour: the Case of Young People and Smoking in Late Modernity', *British Journal of Sociology* Vol. 52 March.

Denver, D. (1989) *Elections and Voting Behaviour in Britain,* Oxford: Philip Allan.

Department of Health (1992) *The Health of the Nation,* London: HMSO.

Devine, F. (1992) *Affluent Workers Revisited,* Edinburgh University Press: Edinburgh.

—. and Heath, S. (1999) *Sociological Research Methods in Context,* Basingstoke: Macmillan.

Differences in Religiosity', *Journal for the Scientific Study of Religion,* 34 63–75.

Ditton, J. (1977) *Part-time Crime: An Ethnography of Fiddling and Pilferage,* London: Macmillan.

Douglas, J. D. (1967) *The Social Meaning of Suicide,* Princeton, N. J: Princeton University Press.

Downes, D. (1966) *The Delinquent Solution,* London: Routledge.

Drury, B. (1991) 'Sikh Girls and the Maintenance of an Ethnic Culture', *New Community,* 17(3): 387–399.

Durkheim, E. (1897/1952) *Suicide: A Study in Sociology,* London: Routledge.

— (1912/1961) *The Elementary Forms of Religious Life,* London: Allen and Unwin.

—. (1938) *The Rules of Sociological Method,* New York: The Free Press.

—. (1960) *The Division of Labour in Society,* Glencoe: Free Press.

—. (1982) *The Rules of Sociological Method,* S. Lukes (ed.) London: Macmillan.

Duverger, M. (1972) *Party Politics and Pressure Groups,* London: Nelson.

Economic and Social Research Council (1997) *Twenty Something in the 90s: Getting on, Getting by, Getting Nowhere,* Research Briefing, Swindon: ESRC.

Edwards, C. (1992) 'Industrialisation in South Korea' in T. Hewitt, H. Johnson and D. Wield (eds.) Industrialisation and Development, Oxford: Oxford University Press.

Ehrlich, P. (1968) *The Population Bomb,* New York. Ballantyne.

El Sadawi, N. (1980) *The Hidden Face of Eve: Women in the Arab World,* London: Zed Books.

Elliot, D. R. and Harvey, J. T. (2000) 'Jamaica: An Institutionalist Perspective', *Journal of Economic Issues,* June.

Elson, D. and Pearson, R. (1981) 'The Subordination of Women and the Internationalisation of Factory Production in K. Young *et al.* (eds.) *Of Marriage and the Market: Women's Subordination in International Perspective,* London: CSE Books.

EOC (1996) *Facts about Women and Men in Great Britain,* Manchester: EOC.

EOC (1999) *Women and Men in Britain: At the Millennium,* Manchester: EOC.

Esteva, G. (1992) 'Development' in W. Sachs (ed.) *The Development Dictionary: A Guide for Knowledge and Power,* London: Zed Books.

Esteva, G. and Auston, J.E. (1987) *Food Policy in Mexico: the Search for Self-Sufficiency,* Ithaca: Cornell University Press.

Etzionoi, A. (1993) *The Spirrt of Community,* New York: Crown Publishers.

Evans, P. (1979) *Dependant Development: The Alliance of Multinational, State and Local Capital in Brazil,* Princeton: Princeton University Press.

Faludi, S. (1992) *The Undeclarted War against Women,* London: Chatto and Windus.

Family Spending Survey (1996–7) London: ONS HMSO.

Farrington, D. P. and West, D. J. (1990) *The Cambridge Study in Delinquent Development: a Long term Follow-up of 411 London Males';* in H. J. Kerner and G. Kaiser (eds.) *Criminality; Personality, Behaviour and Life history,* Berlin: Springer-Verlag.

Feeley, M. and Simon, J. (1992) 'The New Penology', *Criminology* 30: 4.

Fielding (1995) 'Migration and Middle-class Formation in England and Wales' in: T. Butler and M. Savage (eds.) (1995) *Social Change and the Middle Class,* London: UCL.

Finch, J. and Mason, J. (1993) *Negotiating Family Responsibilities,* London: Routledge.

Forrest, R. and Murie, A. (1990) *Home Ownership,* London: Unwin Hyman.

Foster, J. (1995) 'Informal Social Control and Community Crime Prevention, *British Journal of Criminology,* 35.

Foucault, M. (1963/1975) *The Birth of the Clinic,* New York: Vintage Books.

—. (1977) *Discipline and Punish,* London: Allen Lane.

— (1980) Power/Knowledge: Selected Interviews and Other Writings 1972–77, (ed.) C. Gordon, Brighton: Harvester Press.

Frank, A. (1971) *The Sociology and Development and the Underdevelopment of Sociology*, London: Pluto Press.

Frobel, F., Heinrichs, J. and Kreye, O. (1980) *The New International Division of Labour*, Cambridge: Cambridge University Press.

Fulcher, J. & Scott, J. (1999) *Sociology*, Oxford: Oxford University Press.

Galeano, E. (1992) *Open Veins of Latin America*, New York: Monthly Press Review.

Gallie, D. (1994) 'Are the Unemployed an Underclass: Some Evidence from the Social Change and Economic Life Initiative', *Sociology* 28.

Geis, G. (1967) 'The Heavy Electrical Equipment Anti-Trust Cases of 1961' in M.B. Clinard and R. Quinney (eds) *Criminal Behaviour Systems*, New York: Holt, Rhinehart and Winston.

Gellner, E. (1985) *Postmodernism, Reason and Religion*, London: Routledge.

General Household Survey (2000), London: ONS, HMSO.

Gereffi, G. (1994) 'Rethinking Development Theory: Insights from East Asia and Latin America' in A. Douglas-Kincaid and A. Portes (eds) *Comparative National Development: Society and Economy in the New Global Order*, North Carolina: University of North Carolina Press.

Giddens, A. (2001), *Sociology*, 4th edition Cambridge: Polity Press.

Giddens, A. (1984) *The Constitution of Society*, Cambridge: Polity Press.

—. (1968) "'Power' in the Recent Writings of Talcott Parsons", *Sociology* 2 (3).

—. (1984) *The Constitution of Society*, Cambridge: Polity Press.

—. (1991) *Modernity and Self Identity*, Cambridge: Polity Press.

—. (1999) *A Runaway World?* The BBC Reith Lectures, London, BBC Radio 4, BBC Education.

Gill, O. (1977) *Luke Street: Housing Policy, Conflict and the Creation of the Delinquency Area*, London: Macmillan.

Gill, R. (1999) *Churchgoing and Church Ethics*, Cambridge: Cambridge University Press.

Gilroy, P. (1982 a) 'Steppin' out of Babylon: Race, Class and Autonomy, in *The Empire Strikes Back: Race and Racism in Britain*, London: CCCS/Hutchinson.

— (1982 b) 'Police and Thieves' in *The Empire Strikes Back: Race and Racism in 70s Britain*, London: CCCS/Hutchinson.

Ginn, J. *et al.* (1996) 'Feminist Fallacies: A Reply to Hakim on Women's Employment', *BJS*, 47.

Glaser, B. G. and Strauss, A. L. (1967) *The Discovery of Grounded Theory: Strategies for Qualitative Research*, Chicago: Aldine.

Glasgow University Media Group (1985) *War and Peace News*, Milton Keynes: Open University Press.

Glock, C. Y. and Stark, R. (1969) 'Dimensions in Religious Commitment' in R. Robertson (ed.) (1969) *The Sociology of Religion*, Harmondsworth: Penguin.

Goldthorpe, J. (1980 a) *Social Mobility and the Class Structure in Modern Britain*, Oxford: Clarendon Press.

—. (1980 b) 'Women and Class Analysis: In Defence of the Conventional View', *Sociology* 17 (4).

—. (1997) 'The "Goldthorpe" Class Schema: Some Observations on Conceptual and Operational Issues in Relation to ESRC Review of Government Social Classifications' in D. Rose and K. O'Reilly (eds.) *Constructing Classes: Towards a New Social Classification for the UK*, Swindon: ESRC/ONS.

—. and Lockwood, D. (1969a) *The Affluent Worker: Political Attitudes and Behaviour*, Cambridge: Cambridge University Press.

—. and Lockwood, D. (1969b) *The Affluent Worker in the Class Structure*. (3 vols) Cambridge: Cambridge University Press.

Goldthorpe, J. E. (1975) *The Sociology of the Third World*, Cambridge: Cambridge University Press.

Gordon, P. (1988) Black People and the Criminal Law: Rhetoric and Reality, *International Journal of the Sociology of Law*, 16.

Gouldner, A. W. (1968 b) 'The Sociologist as Partisan: Sociology and the Welfare State', *The American Sociologist*, May.

Graef, R. (1989) *Talking Blues: The Police in Their Own Words* London: Collins Harvill.

Graham, J. and Bowling, B. (1995) *Young People and Crime*, Home Office Research Study 145, London: Home Office.

Gramsci, A. (1971) *Selections from the Prison Notebooks*, London: Lawrence and Wishart.

Greeley, A. (1972) *Unsecular Man*, New York: Schocken Books, Inc.

Greely, A. (1992) *Sociology and Religion: A Collection of Readings*, New York: Harper Collins College Publishers.

Greer, G. (1999) *The Whole Woman*, London: Doubleday.

Gross, E. (1978) 'Organisations as Criminal Actors' in J. Braithwaite and P. Wilson (eds) *Two Faces of Deviance: Crimes of the Powerless and the Powerful*, Brisbane: University of Queensland Press.

Gross, R. M. (1994) 'Buddhism' in Holm, J. and Bowker, J. (eds.) (1994) *Women in Religion*, London: Pinter.

Habermas, J. (1979) *Communication and the Evolution of Society*, London: Heinemann.

Haddon, J. K. and Long, T. E. (eds) (1993) *Religion and Religiosity in America*, US: Crossroad Publishing Company.

Hakim, C. (1996) *Key Issues in Women's Work: Female Heterogeneity and the Polarisation of Women's Employment*, London: Athlone Press.

Halevy, E. (1927) *A History of the English People in 1815*, London: Unwin.

Hall, S. (1985) 'Religious Ideologies and Social Movements in Jamaica' in R. Bocock and K. Thompson *Religion and Ideology*, Manchester: Manchester University Press.

Hall, S. and Jacques, M. (1983) *The Politics of Thatcherism*, London: Lawrence and Wishart.

Hall, S. and Jefferson, T. (1976) *Resistance through Rituals*, London: Hutchinson.

Hall, S., Critcher, C., Jefferson ,T., Clarke, J. and Roberts, B. (1978) *Policing the Crisis: The State and Law and Order*, London: Macmillan.

Hallsworth, S. (1994) 'Understanding New Social Movements', *Sociology Review* vol. 4 no.1, Oxford: Philip Allen.

Hamilton, M. (1995) *The Sociology of Religion*, London: Routledge.

—. (2001) *The Sociology of Religion*, (2nd edition) London: Routledge.

Hammersley, M. (1992) 'By What Criteria should Ethnographic Research be Judged?' in M. Hammersley, *What's Wrong with Ethnography*, London: Routledge.

Hanson, E. (1997) *Decadence and Catholicism*, Cambridge, Mass: Harvard University Press.

Haralambos, M. (ed.) (1985) 'The Sociology of Development', *Sociology: New Directions*. Ormskirk: Causeway Press, p.96.

Harris, G. (1989) *The Sociology of Development*, London: Longman.

Harrison, P. (1990) *Inside the Third World: The Anatomy of Poverty*, (2nd edition), Harmondsworth: Penguin.

Hart, J. T. (1971) 'The Inverse Care Law', *The Lancet* i: 405–12.

Hartnett, O. (1990) 'The Sex Role System, in P. Mayes *Gender*, Longman: London.

Hayter, T. (1981) *The Creation of World Poverty* (2nd edition), London: Pluto Press.

Heath, A. (1992) 'Social Class and Voting in Britain', *Sociology Review*.

Heelas, P. (1996) *The New Age Movement*, Cambridge: Polity Press.

Heidensohn, F. (1989) *Women and Crime*, London: Macmillan.

Held, D. (ed.) (2000) *A Globalising World; Culture, Economics, Politics*, London: Routledge.

Hervieu Leger, D. (1993) *The Religion of Memory*, Paris: Stag.

Hetherington, K. (1998) *Expressions of Identity: Space, Performance, Politics*, London: Sage.

Hirschi, T. (1969) *Causes of Delinquency*, Berkeley, Calif: University of California Press.

Hirst, P. Q. (1975) 'Radical Deviancy Theory and Marxism: A Reply to Taylor, Walton and Young' in E. Taylor, P. Walton and J. Young (eds) *Critical criminology*, London: Routledge.

Hobbs, D. (1988) *Doing the Business, Entrepreneurship, the Working Class and Detectives in the East End of London*, Oxford: Oxford University Press.

—. (1998) *Bad Business: Professional Crime in Britain*, Oxford: Oxford University Press.

—. and Bowker, J. (eds.) (1994) *Women in Religion*. London: Pinter.

—. and Lister. (2000) 'Receiving Shadows: Violence in the Night Time Economy', *British Journal of Sociology*.

Holdaway, S. (1983) *Inside the British Police*, Oxford: Blackwell.

Holm, J. and Bowker, J. (eds) (1994) *Women in Religion*, London: Pinter

Hoogvelt, A. (2001) *Globalisation and the Post Colonial World*, (2nd edition), Basingstoke: Palgrave.

Hook, S. (1990) *Convictions*, New York: Prometheus Books.

Hoselitz, B. (1964) *Sociological Aspects of Economic Growth*, Chicago: Chicago Free Press.

Hunter, J. D. (1987) *Evangelism: The Coming Generation*, Chicago, University of Chicago Press.

Huntington, S. P. (1993) 'The Clash of Civilisations', *Foreign Affairs* 72.

Hutton, W. (1996) *The State We're In*, London: Vantage.

Inglehart, R. and Baker, W. (2000) 'Modernisation, Cultural Change and the Persistence of Traditional Values', *American Sociological Review*, (65) Feb.

Inkeles, A. (1993) 'Industrialisation, Modernisation and the Quality of Life' *International Journal of Comparative Sociology* Vol. 34, No.1.

—. (1969) 'Making Modern Men: On the Causes and Consequences of Individual Change in Six Developing Countries', *American Journal of Sociology* 75.

Islington Crime Surveys, Harper, P., Pollak, M., Mooney, J., Whelan, E. and Young, J. (1986) *The Islington Crime Survey*, London Borough of Islington.

Islington Crime Surveys, Jones, T., Maclean, B. and Young, J. (1995) *The Second Islington Crime Survey*, London Borough of Islington.

Johal S. (1998) 'Brimful of Brasia', *Sociology Review*, 8(1), Oxford: Philip Allan.

Katz, J. (1988) *Seductions of Crime: Moral and Sensual Attractions in Doing Evil*, New York: Basic Books.

Kaur-Singh, K. (1994) 'Sikhism' in Holm, J. and Bowker, J. (eds.) (1994) *Women in Religion*, London: Pinter.

Kautsky, K. (1953) *Foundations of Christianity*, New York: Russell.

Kay, T. (1996) 'Women's Work and Women's Work': Implications of Women's Changing Employment Patterns', *Leisure Studies* 15 49–64.

Kenyatta, M. L. and Tai, R. H. (1999) *Critical Ethnicity: Countering the Waves of Identity Politics*, Oxford: Rowman and Littlefield.

Kitching, G. (1982) *Development and Underdevelopment in Historical Perspective*, London: Routledge.

Kitsuse, J. (1962) 'Societal Reaction to Deviant Behaviour', *Social Problems* (9) Winter.

Klein, N. (2001) *No Logo*, London: Flamingo.

Korten, D. (1995) 'Steps towards People-centered Development: Vision and Strategies' in Heyzer, N., Ricker, J. V., and Quizon, A. B. (eds) *Government-NGO Relations in Asia: Prospects and Challenges for People-centred development*, Basingstoke: Palgrave.

Kuhn, T. S. (1962/1970) *The Structure of Scientific Revolutions*, (2nd ed.) Chicago: University of Chicago Press.

Kumar (1978) *Prophecy and Progress*, Harmondsworth: Penguin.

Kundnani, A. (2002) *From Oldham to Bradford; The Violence of the Violated*, from www.irr.org.uk.

Laczko, F. and Phillipson, C. (1991) *Changing Work and Retirement: Social Policy and the Older Worker*, Open University Press: Milton Keynes.

Lakatos, I. (1970) 'Falsification and the Methodology of Scientific Research Programmes' in I. Lakatos and A. Musgrave (eds) *Criticism and the Growth of Knowledge*, Cambridge: Cambridge University Press.

Landes, D. (1998) *The Wealth and Poverty of Nations*, London: Little Brown and Company.

Lappe, F. and Collins, J. (1977) *Food First*, Boston: Houghton Miflin.

Lasch, C. (1980) *The Culture of Narcissism: American Life in an Age of Diminishing Expectations*, New York: WW Norton & Co.

Laurance, J. (1994) 'Bedroom Survey "Can't be Trusted"', [in which P. Tatchell interviewed] *The Times*, January 24.

Lea, J. and Young, J. (1984) *What is to be Done about Law and Order*, Harmondsworth: Penguin.

— (1993) *What is to be Done about Law and Order?* (revised edition) London: Pluto Press.

Leach, E. (1988) *Culture and Communication*, Cambridge: Cambridge University Press.

Lemert, E. (1972) *Human Deviance, Social Problems and Social Control*, Englewood, Cliffs, NJ: Prentice-Hall.

Leonard, M. (1992) 'Women and Development', *Sociology Review*, September.

Lerner, D. (1958) *The Passing of Traditional Society*, Glencoe: Free Press.

Levi, M. (1987) *Regulating Fraud*, London: Tavistock.

Liazos, A. (1972) 'The Poverty of the Sociology of Deviance: Nuts, Sluts and Perverts' *Social Problems* 20.

Lockwood, D. (1966) 'Sources of Variation in Working-class Images of Society', *Sociological Review* 14.

Low Pay Unit (2000) press release on October 26.

Lukes, S. (1974) *Power: A Radical View*, London: Macmillan.

—. (1986) 'Domination by Economic Power and Authority' in *Power*, Oxford: Blackwell.

Lyng, S. and Franks, D. (2002) *Sociology and the Real World*, USA: Rowman and Littlefield.

Lyotard, J-F. (1984) *The Post-Modern Condition: A Report on Knowledge*, Manchester: University of Manchester Press.

Mac An Ghaill, M. (1994) *The Making of Men*, Buckingham: Open University Press.

Mac An Ghaill, M. (ed.) (1996) *Understanding Masculinities: Social Relations and Cultural Arenas*, Buckingham: Open University Press.

MacGuire, M. B. (1981) *Religion: The Social Context*, California: Wadsworth Publishing.

Mack, J. and Lansley, S. (1985) *Poor Britain*, London: George Allen and Unwin.

Maguire, M., Morgan, R. and Reiner, R. (1997) *The Oxford Handbook of Criminology*, Oxford: Oxford University Press, p. 325.

Malinowski, B. (1954) 'Magic, Science and Religion and Other Essays', New York: Anchor Books.

—. (1982) 'Magic, Science and Religion and Other Essays', London: Souvenir Press.

Mamdani, M. (1996) *Citizen and Subject: Contemporary Africa and the Legacy of Late Colonialism*, Princeton: Princeton University Press.

Mann, M, (1993) *The Sources of Social Power*, Cambridge: Cambridge University Press.

Mannheim, K. (1960) *Ideology and Utopia*, London: Routledge.

Marcuse, H. (1964) *One Dimensional Man*, London: Sphere Books.

Mars, G. (1982) *Cheats at Work, an Anthropology of Workplace Crime*, London: George Allen and Unwin.

Marshall, G. (1982) *In Search of the Spirit of Capitalism: Max Weber and the Protestant Ethic Thesis*, London: Hutchison.

—. (1987) 'What is Happening to the Working Class'? *Social Studies Review*, Jan.

—, Newby, H. Rose D. and Vogler, C. (1988) *Social Class in Modern Britian*, London: Hutchinson.

—. Rose, D., Newby, II. and Vogler, C. (1989) *Social Class in Modern Britain*, London: Unwin Hyman.

Martin, D. (1978) *A General Theory of Secularisation*, Blackwell: Oxford.

Marx, K. (1976) *Capital*, Harmondsworth: Penguin.

—. and Engels, F. (1957) *On Religion*, Moscow: Progress Publishers.

—. and Engels, F., (1970) *The German Ideology*, (first pub. 1948), New York: International Publishers.

Mason, D. (2000) *Race and Ethnicity in Modern Britain*, Oxford: Oxford University Press.

Matthews, R. and Young, J. (1992) *Issues in Realist Criminology*, London: Sage.

Matza, D. (1964) *Delinquency and Drift*, New York: Wiley.

—. and Sykes, G. (1961) 'Juvenile Delinquency and Subterranean Values', *American Sociological Review* 26.

Mayhew, H. (1851) *London Labour and the London Poor*, (republished 1985) Harmondsworth: Penguin.

Mayhew, P., Aye Maung, N. and Mirrlees-Black, (1993) *The 1992 British Crime Survey*, Home Office Research Study 111, London: Home Office.

McDowell, L. (1992) 'Gender Divisions in a Post-Fordist Era', in L. McDowell and R. Pringle (eds.) *Defining Women*, Cambridge: Polity Press.

McKay, H. (2000) *'The Globalisation of Culture'* in D. Held (2000) *A Globalising World? Culture, Economics, Politics*, London: Routledge.

McKenzie, R. T. and Silver, A. (1968) 'The Working Class Tory in England' in P. Worsley *Angels in Marble*, London: Heinemann.

McPherson Report (1999) London: HMSO.

McRobbie, A. and Thornton, S. (1995) 'Rethinking: "Moral Panic" for Multi-Mediated Social Worlds', *British Journal of Sociology* 46 (4).

Melucci, A. (1989) *Nomads of the Present*, London: Hutchinson.

Merton, R. K. (1938) 'Social Structure and Anomie', *American Sociological Review* 3.

—. (1993; first published 1938) 'Social Structure and Anomie' in C. Lemert(ed.) *Social Theory: The Multicultural Readings*, Boulder, Colo: Westview Press.

Messerschmidt, J. (1993) *Masculinities and Crime*, Lanham, MD: Rowman and Littlefield.

Metcalf, H., Modood, T., Virdee, S. (1996) *Asian Self-Employment*, London: Policy Studies Institute.

Mies, M. (1993) 'Towards a Methodology for Feminist Research' in M. Hammersley (ed.) *Social Research: Philosophy, Politics and Practice*, London: Sage.

Miles, R. (1989) *Racism*, London: Routledge.

Miliband, R. (1970) *The State in Capitalist Society*, London: Quartet.

Miller, A. S. and Hoffman, J. P. (1995), 'Risk and Religion: An Explanation of Gender Differences in Religiosity', *Journal for the Scientific Study of Religion* 34 63–75.

Miller, W. B. (1962) 'Lower Class Culture as a Generating Milieu of Gang Delinquency' in M. E. Wolfgang, L. Savitz and N. Johnston (eds). *The Sociology of Crime and Delinquency*, New York: Wiley.

Modood, T. (1992) *Not easy Being British: Colour, Culture and Citizenship*, Runnymede Trust and Trentham Books.

—., Beishon, S., and Virdee, S. (1994) *Changing Ethnic Identities*, London: Policy Studies Institute.

Molyneux, M. (1981) 'Women in Socialist Societies: Problems of Theory and Practice', in K. Young *et al.* (eds.) *Of Marriage and the Market. Women's Subordination in International Perspective*, London: CSE Books.

Morgan, I. (1999) *Power and Politics*, London: Hodder and Stoughton.

Morris, L. (1993) *Dangerous Classes: The Underclass and Social Citizenship*, London: Routledge.

Morris, T. P. (1957) *The Criminal Area: A Study in Social Ecology*, London: Routledge.

Mosca, G. (1939) *The Ruling Class*, New York: McGraw Hill.

Murie, A. (1983) *Housing Policy and the Inner City*, Bristol: University of Bristol.

Murray, C. (1990) *The Emerging British Underclass*, London: Institute of Economic Affairs, Health and Welfare Unit.

Murray, C. (1994) *The Crisis Deepens*, London: IEA.

Myrdal, G. (1968) *Asian Drama: An enquiry into the Poverty of Nations*, New York: The Twentieth Century Fund.

Need, N. and Evans, G. (2001) 'Analysing Patterns of Religious Participation in Post-communist Eastern Europe', *British Journal of Sociology*, Vol. 52 No.2.

Nelkin, D. (1997) 'White Collar Crime' in Maguire, M. Morgan, R. and Reiner, R. *The Oxford Handbook of Criminology* (2nd edition), Oxford: Claredon Press.

Nelson, G. K. (1986) 'Religion' in M. Haralambos (ed.) *Developments in Sociology* Vol. 2, Ormskirk: Causeway Press.

New Earnings Survey (2000) London: HMSO.

New Internationalist (1986) 'Fly Me to the Moon' Issue 169.

Newton, K. (1969) 'A Critique of the Pluralist Model', *Acta Sociologica* 12.

Niebuhr, H. R. (1929) *The Social Sources of Denominationalism*, New York: The World Publishing Company.

Nightingale, C. (1993) *On the Edge*, New York: Basic Books.

O'Connell Davidson, J. and Layder, D. (1994) *Methods, Sex and Madness*, London: Routledge.

Oakley, A. (1974) *Housewife*, London: Allen Lane.

Offe, C. (1984) *The Contradictions of the Welfare State*, London: Hutchinson.

Oppenheim, C., Harker, L. (1996) *Poverty: the Facts* (3rd edition), London: CPAG.

Owen, D. W. and Green, A. E. (1992) 'Labour Market Experience and Occupational Change amongst Ethnic Groups in Great Britain', *New Community*, 19, 7–29.

Paglia, C. (1992) *Sex, Art and American Culture*, New York, NY: Vintage Books.

Painter, K. (1988) 'Different Worlds: The Spacial, Temporal and Social Dimensions of Female Victimisation' (1992) in D. J. Evans, N. R. Fyfe and D. T. Herbert (eds) *Crime and Policing: Essays in Environmental Criminology*, London: Routledge.

Pakulski, J. and Waters, M. (1996) *The Death of Class*, London: Sage.

Pareto, V. (1935) *The Mind and Society*, New York: Dover.

Parker, H. (1974) *View from the Boys*, Newton Abbott: David and Charles.

Parkin, F. (1972) *Class Inequality and Political Order*, St. Albans: Paladin.

Parsons, T. (1937) *The Structure of Social Action*, New York: McGraw-Hill.

—. (1963) 'On the Concept of Political Power', *Proceedings of the American Philosophical Society*, 107.

—. (1964) 'Evolutionary Universals in Society' *American Sociological Review*, June 29.

—. (1965) 'Religious Perspectives in Sociology and Social Psychology' in Lessa, W. A. and Vogt, E. Z. (1965) *Reader in Comparative Religion: An Anthropological Approach* (2nd edn), New York: Harper & Row.

—. (1977) *The Evolution of Societies* edited by J. Toby, Englewood Cliffs, NJ.: Prentice-Hall.

Patrick, J. (1973) *A Glasgow Gang Observed*, London: Eyre-Methuen.

Patterson, S. (1965) *Dark Strangers*, Harmondsworth: Penguin.

Payne, G. (1987) *Economy and Opportunity*, Basingstoke: Macmillan.

Pearce, F. (1976) *Crimes of the Powerful*, London: Pluto Press.

Pearson, R. (2001) 'Rethinking gender Matters in Development' in T. Allen and A. Thomas (2001) *Poverty and Development in the 21st Century*, Oxford: Oxford University Press.

Phillips, C. and Brown, D. (1998) *Entry into the Criminal Justice System: A Survey of Police Arrests and their Outcomes*, Home Office Research Study 185, London: Home Office.

Philo, G. and Miller, D. (2000) *Market Killing: What the Free Market Does and What Social Scientists Can Do About It*, Harlow: Longman.

Platt, T. and Takagi, P. (1977) 'Intellectuals for Law and Order; a Critique of the New Realists', *Crime and Social Justice*, No 8, pp.1–16.

Popper, K. (1959) *The Logic of Scientific Discovery*, London: Hutchinson.

Porrit, J. (1985) *Seeing Green: The Politics of Ecology*, Oxford: Blackwell.

Poulantzas, N. (1973) *Political Power and Social Classes*, London: New Left Books.

Pryce K. (1979) *Endless Pressure*, Harmondsworth: Penguin.

Punch, K. F. (1998) *Introduction to Social Research*, London: Sage.

Punch, M. (1994) 'Politics and Ethics in Qualitative Research' in N.K. Denzin and Y. S. Lincoln (eds.) *Handbook of Qualitative Research*, Thousand Oaks, Calif: Sage.

Ransom, D. (1996) 'The Poverty of Aid', *New Internationalist* Issue 285.

Redheed, S. (ed.) (1993) *Rave off: Politics and Deviance in Contemporary Youth Culture*, Aldershot: Avebury.

Reiner, R. (1992) *The Politics of the Police*, Hemel Hempstead: Wheatsheaf.

Reiss A.J. (1961) *Occupations and Social Status*, USA: Free Press of Glencoe.

Rex, J. and Tomlinson, S. *Colonial Immigrants in a British City*, London: Routledge & Kegan Paul.

Ritzer, G. (1993) *The McDonaldisation of Society*, Thousand Oaks, California: Pine Forge Press.

Robbins, T. and Palmer, S. (eds.) (1997) *Millennium, Messiahs and Mayhem*, New York: Routledge Press.

Roberts, K. (1977) *The Fragmentary Class Structure*, London: Heinemann.

Roberts, K. (2001) *Class in Modern Britain*, Hampshire: Palgrave.

Robertson, R. (1992) *Globalisation: Social Theory and Global Culture*, London: Sage.

Robinson, P. (2001) 'Choosing Justice' in *New Economy*, The journal of the Institute of Public Policy Research.

Rock, P. (1988) 'The Present State of British Criminology' in *The British Journal of Criminology*, 28(2).

Rorty, R. (1980) *Philosophy and the Mirror of Nature*, Oxford: Blackwell.

Rosenhahn, D. L. (1973/1982) 'On Being Sane in Insane Places' in M. Bulmer (ed.) *Social Research Ethics* Holmes and Meir

Rosenhahn, D. L. (1973) 'On Being Sane in Insane Places', *Science*, 179: 350–358.

Rostow, W. W. (1971) *The Stages of Economic Growth*, Cambridge: Cambridge University Press.

Rowntree, B. S. (1901) *Poverty: A Study of Town Life*, London: Macmillan.

Runciman, W. (1966) *Relative Deprivation and Social Justice*, London: Routledge.

Runcimann, W. G. (1990) 'How many Classes are there in Contemporary British Society?', *Sociological Review* (4) 3, Oxford: Philip Allan.

Rusche, G. and Kircheimer, O. (1939) *Punishment and Social Structure*, New York: Columbia University Press.

Sachs, W. (1992) 'Where all the World's a Stooge', the *Guardian*, May 29.

Sahlins, M. (1997) 'The original affluent society' in Rahnema, M. and Bawtree, V. (eds) (1997) *The Post Development Reader*, London: Zed Books.

Saunders, P. (1990 a) *A Nation of Homeowners*, London: Unwin Hyman.

Saunders, P. (1990 b), *Social Class and Stratification*, Routledge: London.

—. (1995) *Capitalism – A Social Audit*, Buckingham: Open University Press.

—. et al (1979) *Urban Politics*, Harmondsworth: Penguin.

Savage, M. (1995) 'The Middle Classes in Modern Britain', *Sociology Review*, 5 (2) Oxford: Philip Allan.

—. and Egerton, M. (1997) 'Social Mobility, Individual Ability and the Inheritance of Class Inequality', *Sociology* 31 (4).

—, Barlow, J., Dickens, P. and Fielding, I. (1992) *Prosperity Bureaucracy and Culture: Middle-class Formation in Contemporary Britain*, London: Routledge.

Sayer, A. (1992) *Method in Social Science: A Realist Approach* (2nd edition) London: Routledge.

Scarman, Lord (1981) *The Scarman Report*, Harmondsworth: Penguin.

Scott, A. (1990) *Ideology and The New Social Movements*, London: Unwin Hyman.

Scott, J. (1982) *The Upper Classes: Poverty and Privilege in Britain*, London: Macmillan.

—. (1991) *Who Rules Britain?* Cambridge: Polity Press.

Scraton, P. (1985) *The State of the Police*, London: Pluto.

Scraton, P. (1987) *Law, Order and the Authoritarian State: Readings in Critical Criminology*, Milton Keynes: Open University Press.

Scraton, P. and Chadwick, K. 'The Theoretical and Political Priorities of Mars, G. (1982) *Cheats at Work, an Anthropology of Workplace Crime*, London: George Allen and Unwin.

—. (1991) 'The Theoretical and Political Priorities of Critical Criminology' in K. Stenson and D. Cowell (eds.) (1991) *The Politics of Crime*, London: Sage.

Select Committee on Home Affairs (1999) *Examination of Witnesses*, (Questions 1060–1079) Wednesday, March 10 1999, Sir Paul Condon QPM, Mr Denis O'Connor QPM and Commander Richard Cullen.

Sen, A. (1987) *Hunger and Entitlements*, Helsinki: World Institute for Development Economics Research.

Sharpe, S. (1994) '*Just Like a Girl: How Girls Learn to be Women – From the Seventies to the Nineties*', Harmondsworth: Penguin

Shaw, C. R. and McKay, H. D. (1942) *Juvenile Delinquency and Urban Areas*, Chicago: University of Chicago Press.

—. (1931) Social Factors in Juvenile Delinquency, Washington, DC. Government Printing Office.

Shearing, C. and Stenning, P. (1983) 'Private Security: Implications for Social Control', *Social Problems* 30(5), pp. 493–506.

Shiva, V. (1989) *Staying Alive: Women, Ecology and Development*, London: Zed Books.

Sim, J. Scraton, P. and Gordon, P. (1987) 'Introduction' in *Crime, the State and Critical Analysis*, Milton Keynes: Open University Press.

Skogan, W. G. (1990) *Disorder and Decline: Crime and the Spiral of Decay in American Neighbourhoods*, New York: Free Press.

Skolnick, J. (1966) *Justice without Trial*, New York: Wiley.

Smart, C. (1990) 'Feminist Approaches to Criminology; or Postmodern Woman meets Atavistic Man' in L. Gelsthorpe and A. Morris (eds.) *Feminist Perspectives in Criminology*, Milton Keynes: Open University Press.

Smith, D. J. and Gray, J. (1985) *People and Police in London*, London: Gower.

Solomos, J. (1993) *Race and Racism In Britain*, Basingstoke: Macmillan.

Spender, D. (1985) *Man Made Language*, London: Routledge.

Spybey, T. (1998) 'Globalisation or Imperialism', *Sociology Review* Feb.

Stark, R. and Bainbridge, W. (1985) *The Future of Religion: Secularisation, Revival and Cult Formation*, Berkeley: California University Press.

Stern, P. M. (1988) *The Best Congress Money Can Buy*, New York: Pantheon.

Stinchcombe (1963) 'Institutions of Privacy in Determination of Police Administration,' *American Journal of Sociology* 69.

Sutherland, E. H. (1940) 'White-Collar Criminality', *American Sociological Review*, 5; 1–12.

Sutherland, E. M. and Cressey, D. (1966) *Principles of Criminology* (revised ed.) Chicago: University of Chicago Press.

Swartz, J. (1975) 'Silent Killers at Work', *Crime and Social Justice* 3: 15–20.

Tarling, R. (1988) *Police Work and Manpower Allocation*, Paper 47, London: Home Office.

Taylor, J., Walton, P. and Young, J. (1973) *The New Criminology* London: Routledge.

Taylor, S. (1990) 'Beyond Durkheim: Sociology and Suicide': For a Social Theory of Deviance, *Social Studies Review*.

Taylor-Gooby, P. (with Vic George) (1996) *Welfare Policy: Squaring the Welfare Circle*, Basingstoke: Macmillan.

The Centre for Longitudinal Studies (1991) *National Child Development Study*, London: Institute of Education.

Thompson, D. (1996) *The End of Time: Faith and Fear in the Shadow of the Millennium*, London: Sinclair Stevenson.

Thompson, G. F. (2000) 'Where do MNCs Conduct their Business Activity and what are the Consequences for National Systems' in S. Quack, G. Morgan and R. Whitely (eds.) *National Capitalisms, Global Competition and Economic Performance*, Amsterdam: John Benjamins.

Thompson, H. (2001) *Culture and Economic Development: Modernisation to Globalisation, Theory and Science*, downloaded from http://www.icaap.org.

Thrasher, F. (1927) *The Gang*, Chicago: University of Chicago Press.

Timmons Roberts, J. and Hite, A. (2000) from *Modernisation to Globalization*, Oxford: Blackwell.

Touraine, A. (1982) *The Voice and The Eye*, Cambridge: Cambridge University Press.

Townsend, P. (1979) *Poverty in the United Kingdom*, Harmondsworth: Penguin.

Troeltsch, E. (1931/1976) *The Social Teachings of the Christian Churches*, Chicago: University of Chicago Press.

Turner B. (1983) *Religion and Social Theory*, London: Sage.

Urry, J. (1990) *The Tourist Gaze*, London: Sage.

Valier, C. (2001) *Theories of Crime and Delinquency*, Harlow: Longman.

Vincent, J. (1995) *Inequality and Old Age*, London: UCL Press.

Walby, S. (1990) *Theorising Patriarchy*, Oxford: Blackwell.

—. (1997) *Gender Transformations*, London: Routledge.

Wallerstein, E. (1979) *The Rise and Future Demise of the World Capitalist System: Concepts for Comparative Analysis from the Capitalist World-economy*, Cambridge: Cambridge University Press.

Wallis, R. (1984) *The Elementary Forms of New Religious Life*, London: Routledge.

Walter, N. (1998) *The New Feminism*, London: Little, Brown and Company.

Warde, A. (1997) *Consumption, Food and Taste: Culinary Antimonies and Commodity Culture*, London: Sage.

Weber, M. (1958) *The Protestant Ethic and the Spirit of Capitalism*, London: Unwin.

—. (1920/1963) *The Sociology of Religion*, Boston, Mass: Beacon Press.

—. (1947) *The Theory of Social and Economic Organisation*, New York: Free Press.

Wedderburn, D. (1974) *Poverty, Inequality and Class Structure*, Cambridge: Cambridge University Press.

Wellings, K., Field, J., Wadsworth, J. (1994) *Sexual Behaviour in Britain: The National Survey of Sexual Attitudes and Lifestyles*, Harmondsworth: Penguin.

West, C. & Zimmerman, D. H. (1991) 'Doing Gender' in J. Larber & S. A. Farrell (eds.) *The Social Construction of Gender*, London: Sage, pp.13–37.

Westergaard, J. (1996) 'Class in Britain since 1979; Facts, Theories and Ideologies', in D. Lee and B. Turner (eds.) *Conflicts about Class: Debating Inequality in Later Industrialisation*, Harlow: Longman.

Westwood, S. (1999) 'Representing Gender', *Sociology Review* September.

—. (2002) *Power and the Social*, London: Routledge.

Whyte, W. F. *Street Corner Society*: The Social Structure of an Italian Slum, Chicago: University of Chicago Press.

Wilkins, L. (1964) *Social Deviance: Social Policy, Action and Research*, London: Tavistock.

Wilkstrom, P. H. (1991) *Urban Crime, Criminals and Victims: the Swedish Experience in an Anglo-American Comparative Perspective*, New York: Springer-Verlag.

Willis, P. (1977) *Learning to Labour*: How Working-class Kids get Working-class Jobs, Farnborough: Saxon House.

Willott, S. A. & Griffin, C. E. (1996) 'Men, Masculinity and the Challenge of Long-term Unemployment', in M. Mac An Ghaill (ed.) (1996) *Understanding Masculinities: Social*

Relations and Cultural Arenas, Buckingham: Open University Press.

Wilson J. Q. and Kelling G. (1982) 'Broken Windows', *Atlantic Monthly*, March.

Wilson, B. R. (1966) *Religion in a Secular Society*, London: B. A. Watts.

Wilson, B. (1982) *Religion in Sociological Perspective*, Oxford: Oxford University Press.

Wilson, J.Q. (1975) *Thinking about Crime*, New York: Vintage.

—. and Herrnstein, R. (1985) *Crime and Human Nature*, New York: Simon and Schuster.

Woodhead, L. and Heelas, P. (2000) *Religion in Modern Times: An Interpretive Anthology*, Oxford: Blackwell.

Wright Mills, C. (1956) *The Power Elite*, Oxford: Oxford University Press.

Wright, E. O. (1978) *Class Crisis and the State*, London: New Left Books.

Young, J. (1971) *The Drug Takers*, London: Paladin.

Young, J. (1999) *The Exclusive Society: Social Exclusion, Crime and Difference in Late Modernity*, London: Sage.

Zweig, E. (1961) *The Worker in an Affluent Society*, London: Heinemann.

Index